Reader Testimonials for *Homeschc*

"Denise's book gave me the confidence to homeschool my ~~son through high school because of his aca~~demic focus and skills, I wasn't sure I could prepare him adequately for those first-tier colleges and universities. But after reading her book when he was in ninth grade, I was able to plan out a challenging and exciting high school course of study that would meet his needs as an individual, and yet convince college admissions officers that our schooling would indeed produce a successful and prepared college student. We saw the results in multiple admissions offers with handsome scholarships. Thank you, Denise, for the expertise and encouragement I received from your thoughtful and meticulous research."

– Michelle B.

"This book was such a relief to me! I needed information about the homeschooled student who was striving for, and had the capacity for, attending an upper-level university. The topics in the book are so well-laid-out and well-written. I'm grateful to have had this book at such an important time in our lives. As of this printing, our older daughter has earned her B.A. in Sociology/Anthropology from Lewis and Clark College, while our youngest is pursuing acting and attending classes in Los Angeles. *Homeschooled & Headed for College* definitely helped reduce our anxiety level and gave us many things to consider so that we could plan our path."

– Sharron W.

"Almost ten years after I used it with my own daughters, *Homeschooled & Headed for College* is still relevant —even with the ease of today's internet searches. With a plethora of information available, having it all in one place is so convenient. As a private school administrator serving homeschooled students, I keep several copies handy and refer anyone I counsel to it. It is an excellent one-stop resource, a trustworthy reference book, and—for those wondering if the college prep journey is even possible—an inspiration. Denise's clear and concise instructions will help you step by step on your journey."

– Angela A.

"The prospect of homeschooling from middle school through high school seemed like an overwhelming responsibility, especially when homeschooling was practically unheard-of to me back then. Moreover, the thought that the courses my children would be taking from then on would impact their college application process was quite nerve-racking. This book is a godsend to me and served as my resource and reference guide for many years. I have used it so much and highlighted so many pages throughout my homeschool journey that I can say it's one of the reasons why I was able to successfully homeschool my children. They are now doing extremely well in top-tier engineering schools. *Homeschooled & Headed for College* is a must-have!"

– Billie N.

"The college application process is more complex than it was thirty years ago. Traditionally schooled students have access to professional college counselors to hold their hands through the process—and yet most of these professionals are not familiar with the unique aspects of the application process for homeschoolers. This book helped me, a homeschool mom, become my students' college counselor. Denise's detailed advice helped us prepare and present a challenging college prep course load and guided us through the details of preparing their transcripts, college applications, and resumes. I highly recommend this resource for homeschooled students who plan to apply to a four-year college."

– Kathy Y.

"As a homeschool mom of a high school sophomore, I was overwhelmed when my son indicated that he was interested in going to medical school after undergrad. Mrs. Boiko's book helped immensely in information on AP classes, selective schools, and extracurricular activities. I have recommended this guide to all my friends, even those with children in seventh grade, because her book speaks to planning in middle school. I am so thankful to have gleaned so much from Mrs. Boiko's wisdom and research."

– Christie H.

"*Homeschooled & Headed for College* was my trusted, go-to guide, as I nervously treaded and navigated the unknown waters of homeschooling my first child through high school. Not only did it serve as a ready reference for the nuts and bolts, but it was also a treasure trove of creative ideas for courses, extracurriculars, and leadership/service opportunities. Whenever I felt uncertain, I looked to it for encouragement and reassurance that I was on the right track. Homeschooling high school is an adventure of faith, and Denise's advice was one of God's provisions for me at just the right time."

– Grace K.

"After being introduced to Denise's book, I was relieved to find that homeschooling my high schoolers and sending them to college was no longer an impossible mission, but a feasible, exciting, and rewarding quest. *Homeschooled & Headed for College* helped guide our family step by step, from the middle school years through the transition to life as a college freshman. Though we were already emphasizing a rigorous academic course of study, the book expanded our family's focus to include a variety of meaningful and creative extracurricular activities, internships, and even part-time jobs, as this is what truly highlights the passion and uniqueness of a college bound student. Words of inspiration, encouragement, and pro tips fill every chapter. I highly recommend having this book handy as soon as your students enter middle school. Armed with this resource, we were able to send both of our sons to their first-choice universities after garnering acceptances and scholarships from many schools, both private and public. Thanks to Denise's exceptional work, we finished our homeschool journey strong!"

– Cindy P.

"Using Denise's advice, tips, and clear, step-by-step guidance, our family was thrilled to see our son be accepted into his first-choice, top-level university. Though he was definitely a strong student, the application and admission process for homeschoolers seemed daunting and at times mysterious, with numerous unexpected twists and turns. With its organized curriculum suggestions and practical, detailed four-year plans, Denise's book helped us navigate the path with confidence, and we are delighted with the results!"

– Sophie H.

"Got the college-planning jitters? This book is *very* comprehensive and will answer most, if not all, of your questions when it comes to preparing for college. Go directly to the table of contents and then start reading up on the topics that interest you the most. If you are ambitious, get together with moms from your support group and talk about a chapter once a month. Don't forget to enjoy this journey with your young adult!"

– Jere & Crissi A.

Homeschooled
&
Headed for College

Your Road Map
for a Successful Journey

Homeschooled

&

Headed for College

Your Road Map
for a Successful Journey

Denise Boiko • 2nd Edition

Homeschooled & Headed for College: Your Road Map for a Successful Journey.
Second Edition.
Copyright © 2019 by Denise Boiko
ISBN-13: 978-1-08-275294-0

First edition copyright © 2010 by Denise Boiko
ISBN-13: 978-1-61623-607-6

Requests for information should be addressed to:
Denise Boiko
contact@homeschoolroadmap.com
Author's website: https://HomeschoolRoadMap.com

Front cover photo © iStockphoto. Used by permission.
Photo credit: © iStockphoto/Vasyl Dolmatov
Background pattern: © iStockphoto/fourleaflover

Printed in the United States of America.

TRADEMARKS

CONTENTS

SECTION III: MASTERING THE COLLEGE ADMISSIONS PROCESS

SECTION IV: THRIVING, NOT JUST SURVIVING— AND EQUIPPING YOUR STUDENTS FOR THE REAL WORLD

SECTION I

TAKING THE MYSTERY OUT OF COLLEGE PREPARATION

Chapter 1

Daunting But Do-Able:

Homeschooling the College Bound Student

When our daughter, Julie, was three years old, she loved to shop. Accompanying us on shopping trips, whether for groceries, clothing, or common household items, was a big delight, and she enjoyed exploring each new store. One day, my husband and I mentioned the word *college* in our conversation. Julie perked up right away and exclaimed, "College? That's my favorite store!"

Though we have no idea why she was already fascinated by the concept of college at age three, her statement proved prophetic. From about seventh grade on, Julie became increasingly interested in researching colleges to discover how she, as a homeschooler, could maximize her chances of being accepted at a selective college. Her research paid off admirably and became the subject of this book.

MEET THE BOIKO FAMILY

To back up a bit, I'd like to introduce my family. My husband, Ron, and I took the plunge into the homeschooling adventure when our daughter was a kindergartner and our son was two years old. Since then, we've navigated the college application process not once, but twice. During our active years of schooling, our house was a typical homeschooling house, with piles of books and papers adorning our tables and other surfaces. Science projects often lurked in our kitchen, competing with hungry teenagers —Julie once accidentally ate her brother's science experiment relating to growing mold on bread!

Our family was originally drawn to homeschooling because it allowed us to teach godly values and to spend time with our children. We also appreciated teaching them according to their own learning styles and at their most appropriate pace. Although at first we planned to homeschool for only three or four years, those years swiftly grew to nine, and suddenly our homeschooling had naturally progressed into the high school years.

Little did we realize at the outset of this adventure that, though daunting, even high school at home could be a rewarding and "do-able" endeavor. Yet that progression from grade school to high school raised dozens of major questions and hundreds of smaller ones that needed answers. The most insistent of those questions was "What about college?"

We are now on the other side of that question, with a successful conclusion. Having been accepted by five universities, Julie chose to attend Stanford University for her undergraduate education, earning both a B.S. and an M.S. in biology. From there, she went on to complete medical school and is now a pediatrician. Her journey prepared us well for the second round of college applications with our son. After receiving acceptances from six public and private universities, he chose to attend the University of Southern California in Los Angeles (USC), where he earned an engineering degree. He is now putting that degree to good use in the technology industry.

As for me, over the past thirteen-plus years I have taught homeschool group classes in biology, literature, and composition. Additionally, I have provided personal college application help and advice to more than 150 students and have presented numerous workshops and seminars on college prep topics.

SEARCHING AND RESEARCHING

As Julie entered her high school years, she began to search out information about the college admissions process. In a traditional school, much of this information is doled out to students by their teachers and guidance counselors. Homeschoolers, however, need to do more digging to seek it out. What types of courses should a student take? How can a homeschooler take honors or Advanced Placement® (AP®) courses? Is community college an option? How does a student prepare for the SAT® and ACT® exams? How can a home educated student show leadership ability without being elected class president?

Julie's high school journey and her intense desire *not* to be left out of the running for the more selective colleges fueled her search for answers, and I, the persevering but frequently perplexed mom, followed along in her wake.

In the process, we read nearly twenty books and perused countless websites. Some of these dealt with the subject of high school for homeschoolers. Others covered college admissions for students in traditional schools. While the books for homeschoolers did an excellent job of describing how to do high school at home, they did not provide enough detail on the college entrance process—especially for selective colleges. And although the college admissions books presented helpful tips about applications, essays, and academic planning, they did not address the specific needs of homeschoolers. The story was incomplete. Though we picked up a wealth of information from both types of books, we did not find an exhaustive resource specifically for homeschoolers seeking advice about the often-competitive area of college admissions. Nor did we come across a book that addressed in great detail some of the key issues (such as Advanced Placement courses) for students who wish to apply to selective universities.

Additionally, we recognized that the task of teaching high school still seems daunting to many homeschoolers. Foreign languages, higher math, and lab science require some specific planning and strategizing. Extracurricular activities, particularly the pursuit of leadership roles, take some ingenuity. Yet parents still desire to provide a home-directed education for their children. As we delved more deeply into our research, Julie and I were gratified to discover that college prep homeschooling was quite possible. In fact, it could be extremely rewarding.

Recognizing a Growing Trend

Homeschooling is a rapidly growing form of education in America. Estimates are that as of 2016, about 2.3 million students were being homeschooled in the U.S., and that number is increasing by 2 to 8% every year.[1] As a result, more students continue to homeschool through high school. Colleges have witnessed a surge in homeschooled applicants and have, for the most part, opened their doors to them and made the process more straightforward than it once was. Many colleges have created policies specifically designed to evaluate homeschooled applicants. To thrive in this environment, homeschooling families need practical information about high school courses, record keeping, and, of course, college admissions.

Sharing Our Findings

Eventually, Julie and I decided that *we* should write the book we would have found so useful in the college preparation process. We wanted to show that high school at home can be accomplished successfully and that parents should not give up just when their efforts are beginning to bear fruit. In particular, we wanted to help students aiming to apply as freshmen to four-year colleges, where admissions staffs might be looking for Advanced Placement or honors courses, strong recommendations, and evidence of leadership ability. However, we wanted the book to be helpful to *all* homeschooled students, regardless of the level of competition they would face in college admissions.

So, beginning in Julie's freshman year of high school, we tackled this project. Though Julie did much of the research and drafted some of the initial chapters, her busy high school (and later, college) schedule prevented more involvement. The task became mine to finish, but because I would never have launched this project without her, I am indebted to Julie's enthusiastic "digging" early on.

PROMOTING VISIBILITY AND CREDIBILITY

A key focus of this book is helping homeschoolers gain *visibility* and *credibility* as they apply to college. By *visibility*, we mean that colleges, particularly selective colleges, are seeing homeschooled applicants in greater and greater numbers. But beyond this, they need to recognize the achievements and unique educational experiences homeschoolers can bring to their campuses. We want colleges to know that homeschoolers are not confined to the home but are out in the community learning, contributing, and innovating with passion and commitment. Visibility is crucial.

Credibility of homeschoolers is also essential. Though it is natural to dislike the extra scrutiny that homeschoolers' applications receive from certain colleges, it is not difficult to understand why some colleges hesitate to admit homeschoolers without the extra requirements. A home-directed education is stimulating and innovative, but it is also nonstandard and difficult to compare to that of other applicants. Without some standard benchmarks such as detailed curriculum descriptions or college entrance exam scores, colleges would be taking a guess as to the potential success of a particular homeschooled applicant. Valid or not, this additional scrutiny has been a factor in many colleges' treatment of homeschooled applicants.

Consequently, one major goal of this book is to help families learn how to make their students' applications comparable to—though certainly not identical to—those of their traditionally-schooled peers. By taking advantage of community college courses, AP courses, techniques to improve SAT or ACT scores, and other strategies, homeschoolers can pursue their individualized style of education while still presenting themselves favorably before admissions committees. Our method of education is credible, but we need to *demonstrate* it, not just *defend* it.

Reporting Some Good News

Fortunately, most colleges have put in the effort to understand homeschooling and to welcome homeschoolers through their front gates. These changes include adding homeschool-specific instructions to their websites, allowing student portfolios in place of or in addition to transcripts, accepting parental evaluations in place of a guidance counselor's letter, or simply expressing enthusiasm for the diversity that homeschooled applicants bring. Revamping application policies to view the applicant more holistically, instead of "statistically" as a collection of GPAs and test scores, even a few of the large state university systems are now more welcoming to homeschoolers and other nontraditional applicants.

Even top-tier universities such as Harvard, Yale, and Stanford have become more homeschool-friendly as they have seen homeschoolers excel. Jon Reider, a former senior associate director of admissions at Stanford University and a recognized college admissions expert, commented some years ago, "Home-schoolers bring certain skills—motivation, curiosity, the capacity to be responsible for their education—that high schools don't induce very well."[2] Similarly, Katie Fretwell, Amherst College Dean of Admission and Financial Aid, told NBC News in 2016 that homeschoolers have "thicker folders, in a good way" and that they are often "innovative thinkers with a lot to bring to the table."[3]

In the 1990s and 2000s, the first college bound homeschoolers blazed the trail for other homeschoolers. With their excellence in academics, their love of learning, and their passions and involvement, they set a shining example for those who would follow them. Many were admitted to top colleges—primarily because of their abilities, of course, but perhaps partially because of the innovative, fascinating features of their education. Even today, homeschoolers frequently retain an edge because of the uniqueness of their education. However, in some cases they still meet difficulties at colleges that are not homeschool-friendly or that insist on adhering to traditional methods of evaluating applicants. And of course, homeschoolers now face competition from fellow homeschoolers for limited spots in selective colleges.

OUR PURPOSES

Recognizing this competitive atmosphere and wanting to help homeschoolers shine, we outlined four main purposes as we planned this book.

To offer encouragement for all college bound students

Because homeschoolers pursue all kinds of educational paths, we want to encourage and advise homeschoolers aspiring to attend a college of any type—two-year or four-year, highly competitive or less competitive. And despite the disgusting presence of cheating and fraud in the college admissions world—as evidenced by the massive scandal uncovered early in 2019—we want to encourage homeschoolers with legal, ethical, common sense advice. "Connections" and falsified credentials have no rightful place in the application process; hard work, motivation, and genuine pursuit of passions all have a prime place.

To provide insight into selective college admissions

We want to describe the traits that colleges, especially the selective ones with unbelievably low acceptance rates, are looking for in a student. More importantly, we want to present ideas for providing these elements in a home-directed environment. For example, we include detailed discussions of Advanced Placement courses and community college courses as stepping stones to four-year colleges. And if you were intrigued by the reference on this book's back cover to the "number one secret" for college admissions, we won't leave you in suspense. It is *passion*. Students who can show dedication, a love of learning, and most importantly, a proven track record of pursuing their skills and interests to the deepest level possible will stand out from the crowd of applicants. Homeschoolers, with their flexible time schedules and with their course designs often guided by strong interests, are in a perfect position to display passion in one or several areas at application time. Keep this in mind as you read through this book and plan your student's high school courses and activities.

To inspire excellence in academics and character

Through this book, we want to encourage families as they seek excellence in academics as well as in character. Homeschooling parents have rightly placed a strong emphasis on character development and personal integrity. As a result, their students are some of the most responsible, mature, and hardworking young people to be found anywhere. Even more, their compassion and service are exemplary traits. "Character first" is a fitting motto, and we wholeheartedly promote the development of strong, godly character.

In addition, we seek to equip homeschoolers with the tools they need to pursue excellence in academics. In this way, these students' commendable character traits may be put to use in fields that require rigorous, disciplined study. Homeschoolers, with their emphasis on a life of character and integrity, can positively influence the world. Why *shouldn't* they be represented in medicine, law, scientific research, the arts, journalism, and other fields frequently populated by individuals who are sharp and intelligent but who sometimes lack basic human and godly values? In order to be represented here, our students need to have the robust academic background to compete in these fields. Granted, these highly competitive goals are not for everyone, but for these aspirations to be attainable in the first place, families must understand how to provide strong preparation for all colleges, including those with the stiffest competition.

To provide support in nonacademic areas

Furthermore, we want to assist parents with a few of the nonacademic issues that come up during high school. These include extracurricular activities, leadership, and career planning, including finding internships in the field of interest. Homeschooling a high schooler is a holistic undertaking, and your student is a multifaceted jewel with academic, social, physical, spiritual, and practical natures. In your homeschooling, you can intermingle school lessons with life lessons. As a bonus, a chapter on preparing for the big send-off to college is included.

WHO CAN BENEFIT FROM THIS BOOK?

Though we focus on giving homeschoolers the "inside scoop" on what selective colleges want to see in students, this book can be used successfully by several different groups of readers:

Families deciding whether to continue or start homeschooling a high schooler

If you arrive at the middle school years, or even at that crucial summer between eighth and ninth grades, and are still unsure about whether homeschooling through high school is right for your family, this decision time may be quite stressful. Some families in this category are new homeschoolers who may come with a history of unfortunate experiences in previous schools. They may even feel a sense of desperation about how to provide the best educational and social environment for their students. Other families may already be homeschooling but are wondering about taking the plunge into the high school years. This book, along with similar resources, can help solidify your decision for homeschooling. Discovering that others have thought through all the areas that are causing you anxiety—and have found solutions for them—is a tremendous comfort. If you have a middle schooler, these years are the ideal time to warm up to the idea of college prep homeschooling. We hope that this book will alleviate most of your fears and make the task look manageable—and perhaps even exciting.

Families committed to homeschooling through high school

Families who approach the high school years with a commitment to continue homeschooling may not need convincing, but they do need information and help. This book seeks to encourage families who see high school as the next step in the progression of teaching these children God has entrusted to them. We desire to provide you with the information you need to do a great job.

Concerned relatives and friends of homeschooling families

Though homeschooling is growing in popularity, grandparents or other relatives and friends may continue to harbor concerns about homeschooling and its success rate. These concerns may escalate as your child approaches high school. They may have tolerated seeing your children homeschooled during the earlier years, but they may express serious doubts about whether homeschooling through high school will work. The questions may begin in earnest now. Will your student have a valid diploma? Will he or she be admitted to college—and do well there? Reading about others' experiences and successes can be a tremendous help in easing familial anxieties and bringing peace to family gatherings.

Families of students with special needs

Families whose students intend to apply to college but who are home educated because of health issues, physical challenges, or learning differences may find advice in this book to help their students present themselves in the best light to college admissions committees. Knowing what a university is looking for and then understanding how to communicate the student's strengths and skills is vital information for any family. However, it is especially important for families who need to plan ahead and work harder to help their students achieve their life goals.

Homeschooled high school students

Not only parents, but also high school students, may appreciate reading this book to receive advice for their journey. Motivated students who want to take ownership of their studies and maximize their options for college should read this book to understand the college preparation process.

HOW TO USE THIS BOOK

The subtitle "Your Road Map for a Successful Journey" provides an apt word picture for the homeschooling adventure. Journeying from the late middle school years to the desired destination—college admission—can appear to be a long road fraught with bumps and surprises. But, as with any journey, a proper map or GPS helps tremendously. And rarely do maps show only one way to reach the destination. More commonly, the traveler can choose a combination of roads, depending on the goals of this particular trip (timing, scenery, or opportunities for side trips along the way).

As you traverse the sometimes-smooth, sometimes-bumpy road of homeschooling a college bound high schooler, use this book as your map to show you your options. Certain stops along the journey will be required for nearly every student, but many others will be entirely up to you. During the middle school years, read through this book quickly to get "the lay of the land." Enjoy the panoramic overview of high school and begin to set expectations for what is to come. You can do a more focused reading later, setting your intended itinerary as plans firm up and the high school course of study takes shape. Do leave time for plenty of side trips, though!

While planning your trip through high school, read with the goal of seeking out the topics most pertinent to your family. You will also want to explore the roads that seem most mysterious to you at the outset of the high school journey. If you already have a good idea of how to accomplish the academics, you might appreciate the tips on extracurriculars and leadership. If you need advice on constructing Advanced Placement or honors courses, you can turn to these sections for guidance. If the college application is a complete puzzle, schedule a sightseeing trip through those pages. Follow up the ideas presented in this book by searching out the websites and other resources recommended in the chapters. Also check with local school districts to see what is required of or recommended for students in your area, and check with community colleges to find out how enrollment of high schoolers is handled. These policies vary from community to community and also change rapidly over time.

Seeking out what is uniquely important to you and your family is part of the beauty and joy of homeschooling. Remember that no single "itinerary" exists for the journey of successful homeschooling through high school. The map will show you the options, and even a suggested route, but your family will decide on the details.

THE "TWO-PATH" CONCEPT FOR HOMESCHOOLED HIGH SCHOOLERS

As you read this book, realize that homeschooled high schoolers follow one of at least two typical paths. Like two roads that eventually converge at the same destination, these two approaches to college admissions will appeal to different types of students coming from different points of origin.

One path is for students who need an extremely strong college prep program so that they may apply to selective colleges. The other is a more mainstream (and perhaps more sane) college prep program for those who may start at a community college or at a less selective to moderately selective public or private college. While students on the two paths will use the information in this book differently, both groups of students possess valuable skill sets, gifts, and abilities. In fact, students pursuing the second path are frequently just as capable academically as those on the first path. They may simply have different goals, or their family finances may dictate the choice of a less expensive route to a good education.

If your student is on the ambitious, competitive path, he or she will want to ponder all the concepts in this book and use them to assemble an attractive college application. Learning about honors and AP courses, strategic extracurriculars, internships in the field of interest, strong leadership activities, and focused attention on college essays and recommendations will all be worthwhile at application time.

If your student is interested in a somewhat less competitive path to college, find out which elements of a high school program are non-negotiable with his or her favorite colleges. This student may not need to display quite as many outstanding characteristics as the students on the competitive path must demonstrate, but since more students are competing for admission to all colleges today, it makes sense to present oneself in the best possible light when applying. Thus, a certain number of key extracurriculars and advanced courses may very well be in order.

For the most part, the advice in this book will address students on the competitive path, since the task is more complex for these students and requires more instruction and insight. Families of students on the less competitive path can still use this information by adjusting it to their students' needs. Thankfully, their students will not need to jump through so many hoops.

Parents, remember that at the outset of high school, you cannot always predict what your student's interests, ambitions, and abilities will be by the time his or her senior year rolls around. Keep the options open for as long as possible by planning and pursuing a reasonably rigorous program that matches your student's capabilities and interests. However, pay attention to the natural bent of your child and don't force him or her into the wrong academic mold. After all, homeschooling is designed to eliminate the molds and stereotypes of traditional schooling.

A FEW IMPORTANT MESSAGES

First, realize that, inevitably, some of the information in this book will change over time and may even go entirely out of date. Examples include online resources, details about college entrance exams, college admissions procedures, or Advanced Placement course and exam guidelines. Do be proactive as parents, recognizing that you will need to double check some facts when you and your student begin the college preparation process. Fortunately, it takes only a few minutes to visit a website and confirm pertinent information.

Next, even though parts of this book have a Christian focus, please know that if you are homeschooling a high schooler and do not happen to be a Christian, this book is still for you. The vast majority of the book, providing academic information and college application advice, is directed to all homeschoolers. Feel free to skim or skip over the sections that address Bible curriculum or prayer. In this adventure of homeschooling our high schoolers, we parents have a great deal of common ground, and we all want the best for our children. Seek out the information that speaks to you the most.

Additionally, understand that the ideas in this book are based on our research and experiences—which, though extensive and encompassing more than sixteen years, are not exhaustive. *Moreover, this book and its implied or stated content should in no way be considered legal advice*, nor a guarantee that if you follow all these suggestions, your student will be admitted to the college of his or her choice. Continue to abide by your state's homeschooling or private school regulations, as applicable. If you are a member of Home School Legal Defense Association (HSLDA), check with this organization for assistance with details specific to your state or to your situation. HSLDA is an extremely helpful organization, open to all homeschoolers regardless of religious affiliation. All homeschoolers would be wise to join this organization for protection of their homeschooling and parental rights.

For college admissions information, start your own research by going to the College Board® website and the sites of your student's favorite colleges. You will always want to have the most up-to-date information. Keep in touch with these colleges throughout the high school years so that you and your student fully understand what will be required for a successful application as a homeschooler.

Above all, please do not let this book cause more anxiety than it alleviates. We did not even come close to doing everything we suggest or describe—and even so, we faced our share of stress and fatigue along the way. You will likely have better ideas or wiser perspectives in some areas, so use only the advice that helps you, and ignore that which is not for you. Tap into your creativity, follow your instincts, pray for wisdom, and use our suggestions as guidelines as you design your student's education in this last and most significant phase before he or she goes out into the world. While the journey is not exactly easy, the rewards are tremendous.

Spending these last four years with our high schoolers is a joy. Since the teen years are such a busy time, we parents know that if our students were in a traditional school, we would rarely see them. Remember to thank God for this opportunity and aim to enjoy these *last and best* four years with your students, with a minimum of anxiety and a maximum of excitement for the next phase of the journey.

One more piece of advice: don't keep your eyes on the map the whole time. Be sure to look out the window and enjoy the pretty scenery!

1. Ray, Brian D., Ph.D., "General Facts, Statistics, and Trends," *Research Facts on Homeschooling*, National Home Education Research Institute, January 13, 2018. Accessed August 15, 2018. https://www.nheri.org/research-facts-on-homeschooling/.
2. Golden, Daniel, "Home-Schooled Kids Defy Stereotypes, Ace SAT Test," *The Wall Street Journal*, February 11, 2000. Accessed August 15, 2018. https://www.wsj.com/articles/SB950223885404935034.
3. Tate, Allison Slater, "Colleges Welcome Growing Number of Homeschooled Students," *NBCNews.com*, February 17, 2016. Accessed September 11, 2018. https://www.nbcnews.com/feature/college-game-plan/colleges-welcome-growing-number-homeschooled-students-n520126.

Chapter 2

Warm-Up Time:

Designing a Personalized Middle School Program

During the middle school years, parents who enthusiastically plunged into homeschooling when their children were five or six may begin to worry a bit. High school is just around the corner. It is one thing to teach a first grader, or even a fifth grader, the "three R's," with some creative science and history projects thrown in. It is quite another thing to tackle algebra, trigonometry, advanced writing, lab science, *and* a foreign language.

But "pre-high school jitters" in and of themselves are not a reason to abandon homeschooling. Don't let the looming lineup of courses tempt you to discard a type of learning that has worked for you so far. You won't need to be an expert in all high school subjects; many sources of help are available.

During your student's sixth through eighth grade years, you will "warm up" to the idea of high school. As you review your reasons for homeschooling and recognize your many options, you will be equipped to enjoy these prime years with your students.

REVIEW YOUR REASONS

If you are standing at the middle school/high school crossroads, you are at the perfect vantage point to review your reasons for homeschooling. These reasons, which you may have articulated when you began homeschooling, include some combination of the following:

- Freedom to work at the student's pace and according to the student's optimum learning style in order to remedy weaknesses while intensifying strengths.
- Flexibility of the school schedule, allowing time for hobbies, sports, jobs, travel, or volunteer work.
- Increased time and bonding with family members, as well as opportunities to reinforce the rich heritage of your family's beliefs and traditions.
- Lower likelihood of peer-dependent behaviors, since the student does not need to seek approval from agemates.
- Opportunities to delve deeply into areas of strong interest and to design projects that integrate several school subjects.
- Option of starting college courses during high school, possibly shortening the time to a degree.

- Benefit of parental advice and insight when the student encounters controversial or "mature" concepts in textbooks or literature reading. Because they are learning together, parent and student can discuss these issues and put them into perspective according to the family's values and beliefs.
- Ability to practice an independent, responsible style of learning that will serve the student well in his or her future education. Home education is a great preparation for college.
- Freedom to choose books, media, real-life experiences, and other curricular elements to create a customized course of study.
- Most importantly, the privilege of learning, discussing, and practicing the family's spiritual values without daily resistance from a peer or school culture that might tend to erode these values during the critical teen years. Parents and other adults, not peers, can be the role models for teenage students.

Homeschooling your middle schooler or high schooler can continue under the tenets of your highest priority philosophies. While not easy, homeschooling a teenager can be even more rewarding than homeschooling a younger student. The middle school years allow you to gear up for the task by seeking out information and thinking about the courses your student will tackle during high school. And, of course, they are opportune years for *you* to enjoy your middle schooler rather than allowing someone else the privilege of teaching this unique and lovable person!

RECOGNIZE THE ADVANTAGES OF FORESIGHT

Parents who look ahead proactively to the high school years gain certain advantages over those who "wing it." The following are some of these advantages:

Solid Preparation of the Student

Planning ahead eliminates the dismay of discovering that an essential course has been overlooked.

Relief of Parental Anxieties and Ability to Counsel Others

The earlier you begin investigating the idea of high school at home, the less daunting it seems. You can spend time gathering resources and ideas at a more leisurely pace, allowing you to "warm up" to the idea of high school. Additionally, families who approach the high school years but cannot do extensive planning and research on their own will be grateful for the advice of those who have blazed the trail for them. You will be a valued mentor in your homeschool support group if you have diligently investigated the options for homeschooling the high schooler and are willing to help other families.

Discovery of What Type of Student You Have

You may have a student who is still growing and maturing in the area of study skills, perhaps needing extra help in one or more areas. This scenario is *very* normal and is nothing to worry about. Or, you may have a student who is exactly at grade level and right on track for upcoming high school studies. For this student, middle school will be a time of enriching the current knowledge and laying the groundwork for high school courses. Finally, you may have a middle schooler who is already a high schooler at heart, at least in a few subjects. This student will be ready for more advanced work right away, and you may, in fact, have your first clue as to which college admissions path to pursue.

REASSESS YOUR STUDENT'S NEEDS

Keep on looking at your *whole* child—academic, physical, spiritual, and emotional—and keep doing this throughout high school. Don't worry if your student is in sixth, seventh, or even eighth grade and does not yet appear ready for more advanced studies. The last thing you want to do is to burn your student out with an unmanageable workload or with stress-producing expectations. Follow your instincts while continuing to investigate courses of study and college/career options. Some students make a leap in maturity and academic abilities during the early high school years, while others do not make this jump until late in high school. A high variability on this timing is entirely normal.

During the middle school years, families begin to reap the harvest of the love of learning they cultivated in the earlier years. Many students begin to go "full speed ahead" during their early teens, while their traditionally-schooled peers are still sitting in classrooms reviewing basic grammar and math.

How can a homeschooling parent best utilize these years from the sixth through eighth grades? Three basic options exist (with variations, of course), depending on the type of student you have.

Reinforce the Basics and Close Up Any Gaps

At the outset of middle school, inventory your student's "reading, 'riting, and 'rithmetic" skills. Now is the time to solidify your student's understanding of these vital areas. Needless to say, reading skills should be addressed so that by the end of eighth grade, your student reads rapidly, fluently, and with good comprehension. Pay attention to the comprehension questions at the end of reading selections, or make up your own to discuss with the student. If you need more help, find a reading comprehension workbook requiring students to read a selection and answer comprehension questions, but do your best to jazz it up and make it more meaningful and fun. Choose one whose selections encompass literature, poetry, science, social studies, and other diverse areas of study. By the time high school starts, students should be able to read both fiction and nonfiction selections with adequate comprehension.

If, despite your best intentions, you have not done much writing practice with your student, now is the time to remedy that. Writing skills are important and should be built year by year. Before entering high school, a student should know how to construct coherent sentences and paragraphs and then should build on these skills to begin to write essays. One foundational book I like is *The Elegant Essay* by Lesha Myers, a resource that walks students (and parents) painlessly through the steps of the essay writing process. You can also use interest-driven activities to practice writing skills. Have your student write business letters to companies, requesting information that will be fun to receive in the mail. For instance, our son wrote letters to professional hockey teams requesting information and photos. He was pleasantly surprised to receive decals, buttons, bumper stickers, and other freebies. Another idea would be to write to a food company asking for specific information and perhaps a sample or a coupon. You could also have your student read factual material such as biographies or articles about science or inventions and then summarize the information in the form of an engaging "magazine article" aimed for younger children.

If math skills are lacking, analyze the problem areas and make a concerted effort to address them during these years. The task will not get any easier as your student moves on to algebra and higher math. This is a good opportunity for timed drill work, using paper-and-pencil resources such as CalcuLadder® Math Drills produced by The Providence Project® or websites such as https://www.math-drills.com/ to speed up and automate basic arithmetic calculations. Or go higher tech with gizmos such as FlashMaster® or math websites (for example, https://www.multiplication.com/ or any fun sites currently recommended by fellow parents). Use interactive activities and games to drill these math facts and prepare your student for more fluency in higher math. By now, students should be old enough and mature enough to handle daily drills without fuss. However, a small incentive system can't hurt.

In short, you should use these years to address any deficiencies while utilizing as many enjoyable modes of learning as possible.

Investigate Special Interests and Spark New Ones

If your student's basic skills are in place, but you sense that he or she is not yet ready for high school studies during middle school, seek to explore current interests and to prompt new ones. This may be the time to investigate hands-on skills and interests that could lead to hobbies, talents, a small business, or even a career path later. Depending on the student's interest, you might try computer projects, robotics, chemistry sets, sewing or needlework, music lessons, cooking, or outdoor skills such as camping, rock climbing, or survival skills. For high-energy, athletically inclined students, you could encourage increased participation in sports. Other ideas include dance, theater, or visual arts.

Some students will be ready to take current interests to the next level. Those with a flair for writing might help with a homeschool newsletter, write stories for children, or enter writing contests. Math whizzes might seek out competitions or enjoy "brainteaser" math problems. Science or history buffs might collect biographies or other nonfiction books in their areas of interest, scope out local museums, or tinker with experiments and in-depth projects.

Don't overlook the talents of students with a strong aptitude for computer skills. Find opportunities to go beyond the basics. Perhaps someone has a computer system that your student can dismantle and reconfigure. Seek out programming courses while also encouraging your student to become completely literate with documents, spreadsheets, photo editing, web design, and other useful programs and apps. With time, this practice may work into a hobby, a ministry, or even a small business. Our son used the middle school and early high school years to teach himself a number of skills, including web design, which provided him with income during high school.

You may find that the middle school years are your "prime time" with your students. They need less direct help from you with their schoolwork and with daily tasks. Additionally, they may not have started the whirlwind schedule of the high school years, when they need Mom or Dad to drive them to numerous events. This is the time to explore interests that may not find their way onto the calendar in later years.

If you don't yet know your student's key interests, browse fun catalogs and websites such as the one produced by the Timberdoodle Company. This company's products span the categories of science and technology, arts and crafts, language arts, and practical skills. Kits, games, and hands-on activities teach these skills in engaging ways and make a great starting point for discovering potential interests.

Dive into High School Studies

If your student is ready to tackle high school level work, go for it! Using the tips in the following chapters, you might choose one or two subjects for advanced work and keep the others at grade level. Or your student might forgo traditional middle school and plunge entirely into high school work. Depending on your goals, this path could result in an early graduation date, transferable community college credits, or deeper study in areas of interest before graduation.

The middle school years are also an opportune time to begin study of a world language, and you may introduce the language more slowly than you would at a high school level. Rather than completing "Spanish 1" all in one year, you could take two years or even the full three years from sixth through eighth grades. In doing so, you would have more time for games, media, field trips, and other non-textbook approaches—and still prepare your student for the next level of study in high school.

You'll be ahead of the game in high school if you have your middle school student begin reading some classic literature. While certain books would be too difficult or sophisticated at this stage, many enjoyable classics would be just right. As soon as your student is able to handle more advanced reading, investigate lists of books commonly known as the Great Books for classics that begin with ancient Greek literature and move through the centuries to survey time-honored Western literature. Two books that parents of middle schoolers might want to read are *The Well-Trained Mind* by Susan Wise Bauer and Jessie Wise and *The Well-Educated Mind* by Susan Wise Bauer. The former is a road map of classical education for homeschoolers; the latter, a guide to a classical education and to the art of reading.

By the way, middle school students are at a prime age for memorization. Take advantage of this developmental stage and have fun at the same time by challenging your student to memorize poetry, Scripture, and even longer speeches and portions of literature.

During the middle school years, begin compiling a list of books you would like your student to read by the end of high school. Then assign the easier ones during middle school or toward the beginning of high school. You can find dozens of "suggested reading" lists online, and no single list will meet every family's needs. One book that might be helpful is *Reading Lists for College-Bound Students* by Doug Estell, Michele L. Satchwell, and Patricia Wright, a compilation of lists from 103 colleges and universities. The book challenges high schoolers to try to read one hundred books from this list before entering college.

If you think your student will be interested in taking Advanced Placement® courses in high school, obtain suggested reading lists for AP English courses. By starting with the lighter and easier works, you can spread the reading list over four to six years (middle school and high school) rather than condensing the reading into a one-year course during a busy high school year. Your student will be truly prepared by the time high school is over. More detail on AP courses can be found in Chapter 12.

If you have a gifted or high-achieving student, check into programs such as the Duke Talent Identification Program and similar regional programs, open to seventh graders who receive high scores on standardized achievement tests such as the SAT or ACT exams. The other programs are Northwestern University Center for Talent Development, Johns Hopkins University Center for Talented Youth, and the Center for Bright Kids Western Academic Talent Search. The Davidson Institute for Talent Development is another key program for highly gifted students. Its Young Scholars program offers summer programs, support services, an online community, and many other resources to help nurture academic giftedness. Additionally, investigate the Jack Kent Cooke Foundation Young Scholars Program, which works with high-achieving, low-income students through the high school years, providing them with individualized educational resources. Students apply as seventh graders and, if chosen, receive scholarships to cover high school educational expenses. In general, if your student is gifted, make a habit of regularly browsing gifted and talented websites and forums to seek out opportunities, classes, tips, and ideas to help your student thrive. (See the Appendix for websites of these programs.)

Some students may be ready for high school level extracurricular activities. For example, many students join a speech or debate team during middle school or take their art or music studies to a more intense level.

RELISH THE MIDDLE SCHOOL YEARS

Besides focusing on strengths and weaknesses, parents can take advantage of this time for other purposes and truly embrace these years of opportunity. Here are a few ideas.

Teach Life Skills

Since your time with your student is plentiful during the middle school years, begin teaching basic life skills, such as meal preparation, laundry, business letters and phone calls, public transportation skills, and the rudiments of money management. In short, teach whatever your student is ready for.

Eighth grade is a good time to have your student try a career aptitude profile. Such a tool might highlight skills and strengths, point your student in the direction of potential careers, and help you plan a high school course of study. To start with, find a career aptitude book or website and have your student complete the various aptitude tests. You may also purchase books and more elaborate career planning programs, such as the Career Direct® Complete Guidance System, from Crown Financial Ministries at https://careerdirect-ge.org/. See Chapter 27 for more career research tips. Obviously, your student will change and grow during the high school years, but some parents like to get an early start on thinking about the future.

Concentrate on Spiritual Training

Parents often, though not always, find that spiritual training can progress rapidly during the early teen years. Spending time with your student conversing about faith-related issues, studying the Bible, and praying together during the ups and downs of adolescence can yield real rewards. If you postpone some of these pursuits until later, you may find that "later" never comes.

Venture Beyond the Birds and the Bees

Assuming that your student already knows the rudiments of reproduction, build on that information and begin communicating your family's views on dating and sexual purity. Before your teen starts dating, you'll want to keep the dialogue open on how to guard his or her heart, mind, and body in the years before marriage. Take the time for a one-on-one weekend away, during which you can provide advice and insights into these issues, answer your young teen's questions, and assure him or her of your willingness to talk more about any concerns in the future. Keep that promise by making time to talk and listen to your student over the next few years in an open and honest context.

Try a "Parents' Warm-Up" for High School Routines

Check Your Laws

If you haven't already done so, thoroughly understand your state's homeschooling laws and identify how you are complying with them—for instance, by filing a private school affidavit or by associating with a private school satellite program. Examine state and local graduation requirements so that you can plan your student's course of study to meet these if required by your state, or if your student may eventually return to traditional schooling. If you aren't already a member, join Home School Legal Defense Association for legal support and a wealth of advice and resources. The HSLDA website at https://hslda.org/ also has a link for families to look up homeschooling regulations in their states.

Build a Support System

To ease some pre-high school anxieties, seek out parents who have already homeschooled high schoolers. Support groups with lots of high schoolers will give you chances to ask questions and glean ideas from other families. Begin reading books and attending seminars about homeschooling the high schooler and applying to college. *And remember that you do not need to be an expert in high school subjects, let alone be a trained teacher, to homeschool during high school.* According to Dr. Brian Ray of the National Home Education Research Institute, "Home educated students score above average on achievement tests regardless of their parents' level of formal education or their family's household income."[1]

Don't let your lack of experience in certain subjects keep you from homeschooling. Many resources are available to help you. Chapter 4, "Beyond the Three R's" and Chapter 5, "Sources for Courses," provide ideas for customizing your student's education. Homeschooling is not easy, and you will have to make a plan for the subjects you will teach and the subjects you will "outsource." However, if you stay in touch with fellow parents and with "live" and online support groups, you'll be in good company.

Gather Parent Resources

One of the most practical books on the topic of homeschooling a high schooler is *The High School Handbook* by Mary Schofield, which highlights the "nuts and bolts" of doing high school at home. It is thorough and yet concise enough to read several times during the middle school and high school years. The Home School Legal Defense Association (HSLDA) website also offers numerous tips and resources that are a vital piece of the puzzle. Definitely visit this site as a way to educate yourself about high school issues and to search for resources and answers to your questions.

As you select books and materials to help you on your journey, choose those that speak to *you* the best and align most closely with your philosophies. For instance, since many students start their college education at the community college, the competitive four-year college admission process with its emphasis on test scores, transcripts, and a slew of extracurricular activities may not be applicable for all students. Resources that cover the basics in a practical, no-nonsense way will be helpful. If, however, your student has the ambition to apply to a selective university, you and your student will want to grasp all the information you can on making a homeschooler's application attractive to such an institution.

Don't make the mistake of buying too many books and then letting them sit on a shelf unread for three or four years. Though the trend is growing rapidly, high school at home is still enough of a "less-traveled" path that you will need to internalize lots of advice at the outset of this adventure. As you plan your student's course of study, you may also want to read about the college admission process from books that *don't* specifically address homeschoolers. Much of the advice in these books is just as relevant for homeschoolers as for traditionally schooled students.

If you feel the need for more personalized attention and advice, you might consider utilizing the services of a college application consultant. An excellent source for this type of guidance is Jeannette Webb of Aiming Higher Consultants. Jeannette specializes in helping homeschoolers walk the path from home to college. Even if you don't sign up for her help, be sure to subscribe to her email list for welcome doses of encouragement and wise perspective. Her website is https://www.aiminghigherconsultants.com/.

Select High School Curriculum

Probably the most enjoyable (albeit overwhelming) part of the parent warm-up is selecting high school curriculum. As experienced homeschoolers know, a wealth of curriculum choices awaits parents and students. Now that your student is in middle school, he or she may be more interested in curriculum choices—in other words, ready to partner with you in creating an appealing lineup of courses. This would be a good time to try out a type of curriculum you've never used before. If you've been heavily textbook-oriented, try an online course, a science course with lots of experiments, or a highly literature-focused course. If you've emphasized hands-on learning or unit studies, select a traditional approach for one subject so that your student becomes accustomed to more reading and objective test-taking.

Tailor your high school curriculum to your student's emerging interests and abilities. Don't be afraid to challenge him or her a little beyond previous experiences: more writing, more accountability in the form of tests and projects, or more reading of longer literary works. Just be patient, especially if you are introducing significant changes, and be sensitive to the amount and type of work your student can realistically handle and enjoy. Enjoying learning is still crucial.

Scope out what classes and activities are typically offered in your local area, and investigate whom to contact. Knowing what is available outside the home may help you plan the remaining courses that will be entirely home-based. Chapter 5 delves into ideas to help you search out options in your local area.

Practice Record Keeping

These years are also a chance for parents to warm up to the idea of teaching a high schooler. Middle school is the time to draft a rough plan for high school. You will fill in the details later, and you will undoubtedly change many of those details as the years go on.

Since record keeping and planning will become more important than ever, use these years to begin "high school-style" course planning. For practice, try to plan one or two of your student's middle school courses as you would if the student were in high school. This involves creating a course description, deciding on the number of credits for the course, and writing a course syllabus or an outline describing what assignments will be used and how grades will be calculated. See Chapter 3, "Course Planning Basics," for instruction on planning courses and calculating credits.

Encourage Growth in Areas of Giftedness

Community College

Some students, even as early as eighth grade, may be ready to try a community college class. If your local colleges allow students this young to take classes, you might consider this option, for a number of reasons. First, chances are that your student will eventually take one or more community college courses during high school. Because the high school years are a little more focused, with less time to dabble or to try a course that's not on the "must do" list, you can use the late middle school years to orient your student to a classroom environment.

Julie took her first community college course as an eighth grader. Since this was her first-ever classroom experience, our goals were for her to be accountable to an outside teacher and to learn the routines of a classroom. We chose a subject she had already taken at home (Algebra 1) so that the material would be familiar and not challenging. The semester was a great success, and in retrospect we are glad we tried the first course during middle school. However, this option is not for everyone (see Chapters 13 and 14 for a full discussion).

Many community colleges offer basic courses in math or in English grammar, which can acquaint students with a school environment while not being academically overwhelming. Even though these might not be eligible for dual enrollment (see Chapter 13) they might be good first courses for a young student to take. P.E. or basic music or art courses could be other useful choices.

One caution before you plunge too wholeheartedly into community college courses relates to your student's future university education. Some universities, in order to discourage the "perpetual student" who takes up space and resources for more than his/her share of the time, set limits on the number of college credits that a student may earn, or set time limits to earn a degree. In some cases, the "credit clock" starts ticking with that first college course, and if your student racks up too many credits or too much time at a college, he or she may reach the limit before finishing up the college degree. This scenario is not universal, and will be discussed more in Chapters 13 and 21 under SAP (Satisfactory Academic Progress).

Online Courses for Gifted Youth

Parents who are not yet comfortable with their middle schoolers taking college courses might look into online courses designed especially for gifted youth. Online courses will be covered again in Chapter 5, but for now, keep in mind that these opportunities may work well for your student.

Competitions

Seek out competitions in your student's area(s) of giftedness, whether this be writing, math, science, history, geography, spelling, music, or any other strong focus. Contests can provide stimulation, fun, skill development, friendships, and enhanced confidence. Some programs, such as the AMC 8 (American Mathematics Competitions® through The Mathematical Association of America® https://www.maa.org/), MOEMS® or Math Olympiads (http://moems.org), and the MATHCOUNTS® math enrichment and competition program (http://mathcounts.org), are designed specifically for middle school students. Others may be open to both middle school and high school students.

Leadership

Students gifted in the social or leadership areas may take this opportunity during the "calm before the high school storm" to develop some leadership roles within ministries or organizations with which they are already involved. If your student is already in 4-H Clubs®, Scouts, children's ministries at church, or sports teams, encourage him or her to seek out any leadership positions available to committed members of the group. This venture will give your student a head start for the high school years, when college bound students are expected to display leadership ability.

Development of Talents and Extracurricular Activities

With a lighter academic load, middle school is also the perfect time for students to develop new skills and talents. Students have time to join a band or orchestra, take more art or music lessons, play on sports teams, or join groups that will stimulate and nurture their interest in drama, computers, science, volunteer work, or numerous other areas. At the conclusion of middle school, these students might be ready to focus on one or two areas that they can pursue with commitment during the high school years.

TO SUM UP

The middle school years are exciting times for both parents and students. At home, students are shielded from some of the issues traditionally schooled students face, such as male/female interactions, pressures to conform to the peer group, or temptations to smoke, drink, take drugs, or defy authority. Instead, students can put their energies toward discovering their greatest interests and developing these without interference. Homeschooled middle schoolers enter these years as children but emerge as young, confident teenagers ready for the challenges of high school.

---

1. Ray, Brian D., Ph.D., "Academic Performance," *Research Facts on Homeschooling*, National Home Education Research Institute, January 13, 2018. Accessed August 15, 2016. https://www.nheri.org/research-facts-on-homeschooling/.

SECTION II

DIVING INTO
THE HIGH SCHOOL
EXPERIENCE

Chapter 3

Course Planning Basics:

Credits and Graduation Requirements

That first day of kindergarten might seem like only yesterday, but now that it's time for high school, the thought of the "official" records you may need can bring up some key questions. How can you document your student's path through high school at home so that it will make sense to colleges at application time? How can you produce the "right" records if and when you are asked to document your student's education? If you're like most parents, you're seeking helpful, concrete details at this early stage of high school. This chapter will show you how to research and set graduation requirements, how to distinguish these from college admission requirements, and how to calculate credits.

Remember that homeschooled high schoolers—even those who are college bound—may be on one of two or three paths: highly rigorous, less rigorous, or something in between. Your main goal is to develop a sound course of study that matches or exceeds your student's post-high school plans, whether these are ambitious or laid-back. As you plan courses, keep these college goals in mind so that your student is prepared for any path you think he or she might reasonably pursue. For some families, starting with more rigor makes sense. Obviously, it is easier to ease up on expectations later than to add requirements midway through high school.

GRADUATION REQUIREMENTS VS. COLLEGE PREPARATORY REQUIREMENTS

Deciding which classes your student will take in high school is both exciting and momentous. First, you need to distinguish your state's or district's high school graduation requirements from various colleges' admission requirements. Some states or districts, for example, require only three years of English, while most colleges expect four years of English. Note that private schools, including home schools, are often not bound by state or district regulations. Still, public school requirements are a convenient starting point and general guideline.

To look up your district or state graduation requirements, simply go to the website of your local school district or of your state's Department of Education. Here is a sample of typical requirements:

4 years of English
3 years of mathematics
3 years of lab science

3½ years of history/social studies, to include a year of U.S. history and a semester each of U.S. government and of economics *(note that some colleges consider economics an elective, not a social studies course)*

2 years of a world language

2 years of visual or performing arts

4½ years of electives

2 years of P.E.

Total of 24 year-length courses

Some states or districts require fewer years of some of the subjects. Additional regulations vary by state but may mandate instruction in health, safety, first aid, or driver education. These are courses you may consider adding to your homeschool graduation requirements.

Students wishing to go on to four-year colleges directly from high school will need to meet more stringent requirements. To get a full picture of the possible requirements you might encounter, browse through several sets of graduation and college entrance requirements. Look at requirements from your state, local school districts, local community colleges, your state university system, and a few of the colleges in which your student is interested. If your student doesn't yet have any college ideas, find both a selective college and a less selective one, as well as a state university and a private university.

You can find admission requirements on the websites of each college your student is considering. The typical recommended college prep course of study may resemble the list of graduation requirements above but may also elaborate on some of the subjects. For instance, mathematics may need to include courses at least to precalculus. Lab science requirements may state that at least one year must be biological and one physical (such as chemistry or physics). Language study may require two to three years of the same language. Additional college prep electives (rather than any elective of choice) may be required. Keep in mind that students who want to be strong candidates for colleges should take *more* than these minimum requirements. To accomplish this goal, the "electives" may go toward additional years of the required subjects, or may be entirely different courses, such as speech and debate or computer science.

SELECTIVE COLLEGE REQUIREMENTS

Because of their large numbers of applicants, highly selective private and public universities have instituted more rigorous requirements. If your student is even remotely interested in a selective university, plan on additional courses in each subject, just to keep these doors open. Extremely selective universities, such as the Ivy League schools, often have minimum requirements similar to the following list.

4 years of English *(some universities are now recommending 5 years)*

4 years of math

3-4 years of laboratory science

3-4 years of history/social studies

3-4 years of the same world language

1-2 years of fine arts

Additional college prep electives

Not only do selective colleges look for these courses, but they also expect to see that your student has completed several of these courses at an advanced level, often through the rigorous Advanced Placement program. Tips for how to incorporate rigor into your student's course of study through honors and AP courses are presented in detail in Chapter 12. Additional requirements at selective institutions may include math through calculus, English courses with extensive writing and literature analysis, history and social studies courses incorporating essay writing, world language courses with strong instruction in reading, writing, speaking, and listening, and lab sciences in biology, chemistry, *and* physics.

SKETCHING OUT YOUR STUDENT'S PERSONALIZED COURSE OF STUDY

As you plan your high schooler's four-year course of study, you probably won't know just what path to college your student will eventually take. So begin by choosing courses according to the most challenging scenario that could materialize. *You do not have to continue with this course of study if it becomes apparent that it is not right for your student.* As you choose courses and curriculum, be flexible. Don't hesitate to change tactics after the first year or two of high school. However, if all goes well, planning the more rigorous course load ensures that you won't have to scramble later to make up for lost time if your student changes from an "I'll never go to college" type to an Ivy League prospect.

That said, even if you are planning a rigorous set of courses, schedule the more basic courses in ninth and tenth grades and the more in-depth courses in eleventh and twelfth grades. As your student grows in maturity and capability over the first two years of high school, he or she will become ready to handle increasingly advanced work. For example, ninth grade English might include a brief review of grammar, a foray into the fundamentals of academic essay writing, and an initial overview of literary types such as short stories, novels, plays, and poems. The junior and senior years would focus on heavier literature reading, literary analysis, and advanced composition techniques. One observation we noted in our homeschooling was that if the student has a solid foundation in literature, writing, and critical thinking skills by the end of freshman year, the sophomore year is ideal for the first Advanced Placement class, as the rest of the course load will not be as heavy as it will be during the junior year.

PLANNING COURSE CONTENT

Chapters 4 and 5 provide ideas for fleshing out your courses and finding sources for curriculum and instruction. Once you have a list of college prep requirements, work with your student to decide what courses will fulfill these areas and what content will be included in these courses. The more involved your student is in planning, the more interested he or she will be when it comes time to study the material.

One rule of thumb for any specialized subject area, such as science or fine arts, is that *if this is your student's passion and potentially the focus for a college major or life's work, consider adding extra years of study, including some outside classes with specialized instructors, sophisticated equipment, or advanced teaching techniques you might not be able to access at home.* A community college class, online AP courses, private lessons, or other specialized instruction might be in order. On the other hand, if the subject does not generate great interest and if this is likely the last time your student will encounter it, you can be more comfortable designing a home-based course with materials and resources you have on hand (though, if your student is aspiring to attend a selective university, you want to make sure that even the "unimportant" courses are taught in a quality manner). This way, students who will go on to study this subject further in college will have a solid foundation of skills and will have used the common equipment and techniques with which their academic peers are familiar. In contrast, students who are seeing this material for the first time (and perhaps the last) can learn in a way that best suits their comfort and their learning styles.

RECORD KEEPING 101 FOR HIGH SCHOOL COURSES

You may already be brimming with ideas for the subjects you want your student to study. This enthusiasm will help carry you into the next step of course planning despite the need to wade through a bit of "educator-ese" terminology. Calculating credits and designing official transcripts does not sound like a simple project. But if you learn a few basic principles and are conscientious about maintaining records once per quarter or so, you will discover that producing a useful set of records is quite do-able.

A neat, complete set of records documenting your student's journey through high school is a necessary tool to "close out" the homeschool years and to serve as a bridge to the college years. Your task as a parent/teacher, especially at college application time, is to translate your student's homeschooling experience into the aforementioned "educator-ese." In other words, you will want to communicate what your student studied and at what level of rigor, using terms the colleges are familiar with. While *you* may know that your student is prepared, the college does not know it—yet. The following pages will show you what types of records you might want to keep so that this task of communication will be as straightforward as possible. Details on assembling a transcript or portfolio will be covered in Chapter 11.

Note that most of the information in this chapter applies to students on the path to selective four-year colleges as well as to those on a less selective path. Students who start at a community college may not need a detailed high school transcript or course descriptions. In some cases, the community college application simply asks students whether they have a high school diploma or are over the age of eighteen. Check with your local community college to discover whether a transcript or other high school records are required for entrance. Regardless of your student's current plan, document your courses carefully so that you can provide details about your student's high school education if requested later.

DOCUMENTING COURSES

When your student was in grade school, a simple label of "Math" or "Science" on the report card would suffice as a course description. But in high school, courses must be given meaningful titles and descriptions. These descriptions become an important part of your student's records and may be needed later. By creating course titles and course descriptions, you can show *equivalency* to the courses that admissions staffs are accustomed to seeing on transcripts. Several college admissions officers repeatedly emphasized to us how important this is.

To fully document high school courses, you will need to do the following tasks, at least briefly:

- Draw up high school graduation requirements
- Calculate credits for your courses
- Prepare a course of study for each school year
- Create titles and descriptions for the courses
- Prepare course syllabi (Sometimes called a course standard, a syllabus is a clear, logical plan describing how the material will be presented and how learning will be evaluated.)

After conducting your courses, you will need to summarize the courses and grades on an official transcript of your student's high school work. This chapter and the next few will walk you through the process.

THE HIGH SCHOOL HANDBOOK: A "MUST-HAVE" RESOURCE

A particularly helpful homeschooling resource, one that complements this book, deserves a special mention here. *The High School Handbook: Junior and Senior High School at Home*, by Mary Schofield, is the classic guidebook for families navigating the journey of doing high school at home. This manual clears up many mysteries for parents and students and shows how the journey can be both manageable and enjoyable. In addition to describing course planning in great detail and with much creativity, Mary provides a treasury of common sense advice. Numerous samples are included so that families can clearly follow the process of course planning and documentation. This book is one of those "must-haves" for homeschooling through high school.

While I did not want to omit the essential topic of course planning and documentation from my own book, neither did I want to risk including too many details that would be similar to what Mary has presented in *The High School Handbook*. Since I learned general course-designing techniques under Mary's tutelage (from her book and her homeschool seminars), I have sought to be extremely conscientious here. In fact, my copy of the book was outside of my home, loaned to a friend, the entire time I drafted the chapters on course documentation. Thus, I have tried to present just the basics and then to provide my own modifications of these basics so that I would not be rehashing Mary's ideas. And yet, her instructions are so sensible and foundational that you will definitely want to read her book yourself.

Throughout the high school process with both of my students, I used Mary's pattern of course documentation—and it worked beautifully. It kept us on track all the way through high school and gave us highly practical documents to use during the college application process. During the four years of high school, the knowledge that those documents were in place provided much order and peace of mind amidst the frequent chaos of homeschooling a high schooler. Mary also clearly describes how to plan, document, and grade courses that are non-traditional, either in their subject matter or in their pacing or "calendaring" within your school year. I strongly recommend that you buy her book and use it side by side with this one as you plan your high school courses. You will be grateful for Mary's practical information.

HIGH SCHOOL GRADUATION REQUIREMENTS: CREDITS AND COURSES

The first document you will prepare is a list of high school graduation requirements. But before you can do that, you will need a brief lesson on credits.

Credits Defined

Calculating credits for high school courses is a mini-mystery that is easy to solve. Credits are simply measurements to indicate the amount of work or time a student has put into a course. You can calculate credits based either on the actual amount of time spent on the course or on the amount of content covered. Two types of credits are commonly used on transcripts. One system, used mostly in California, is based on *10 credits* for a year's worth of study of a subject (5 credits for a semester-length course). A student may need 200 to 250 credits to graduate, depending on local requirements. The total may rise to greater than 250 for a full pre-college lineup of six or seven courses per year.

The other system, used commonly in the rest of the United States, grants *one unit* (a Carnegie unit) for a year of a subject. For high school purposes, a Carnegie unit is equal to a conventional one-hour class taken four or five times per week throughout the school year. The meaning of the Carnegie unit varies; it may represent from 120 to 180 hours of instruction. To add to the confusion, the definition of "hour" varies, and may equate to 40, 50, or 60 minutes in real time. Moreover, the number of weeks per year may range from 36 to 40 weeks[1], though 36 weeks comprises a typical school year. A one-semester course is worth one-half of a Carnegie unit. A student typically needs a minimum of 20 to 25 Carnegie units to graduate, but again, this number varies widely, depending on the state and the school district. College prep students will definitely need more than the minimum number of units to complete all requirements. Always check applicable requirements in your area if homeschoolers are required to abide by them.

While the Carnegie unit system is more widely used, the 10-credit system makes it easier to coordinate community college courses on your student's transcript, as these are generally 3 to 5 units per semester (or 4 or 5 units per quarter), and thus you can call them 5 credits of high school work, or 10 credits if you are considering a semester of college credit to be equivalent to a year of high school credit (see Chapters 13 and 14). For simplicity, this book uses the 10-credit-per-year system for some of its examples. Divide by 10 to convert to Carnegie units.

Not all classes need to be full semester- or year-length courses. For example, P.E., electives, life skills, or fine arts courses may be worth half the normal workload of a semester: 0.25 Carnegie units per semester or 0.5 per year—or 2.5 credits and 5 credits, respectively, for the 10-credit system.

Calculating Credits for Individual Courses

Homeschoolers commonly use one of two methods to calculate how many credits a course should earn: the time-based method or the completion-based method.

Time-Based Calculation of Credits

For some subjects, especially those that use no textbooks or that cover portions of several books or media resources, it is most convenient to calculate the credits using the number of hours spent on the course. The rule of thumb among most homeschoolers (see Mary Schofield's *The High School Handbook*, for instance) is that one year's worth of work is anywhere from 120 to 180 hours of work, with 150 being a happy medium. Thus, one semester represents about 75 hours of work.[2]

This rule of thumb is based on the fact that, with the exception of schools with block scheduling, many traditional school classes are about 50 minutes in length, meeting five days per week for 36 weeks, for a total of about 150 hours per year. (The block schedule mentioned above reallocates course time in a given week by allowing longer class periods—say, 90 minutes—but fewer class periods per day. Daily classes attended may alternate from day to day so that each subject ends up with equal time.) In reality, in our own home school, the most challenging courses consumed far more than the 150-hour minimum, because of the demanding nature of these college prep courses. 120 to 150 hours works well, though, as a baseline for planning most courses.

Two Methods for Documenting Time-Based Courses

If you intend to calculate credits based on time spent, you have another decision to make. You may either estimate hours or actually log hours.

The Estimate System

In short, you will just *estimate* the hours the student will spend on the course. At the beginning of the semester, once you have an idea of the types of assignments you will use for a given subject, make a rough prediction of how many hours per week your student will be working on assignments. Include time spent on reading assignments, essays, speech preparation, discussions, problem sets or homework questions, studying for tests, taking tests, preparing projects, and completing other required tasks. Chances are, the workload for one subject will amount to at least five hours per week (90 hours per 18-week semester), and you will have already exceeded the 75-hour guideline. As long as your student completes all the activities you planned, or substitutes others of approximately the same quality or time commitment, you do not need to laboriously log the hours spent. Over time, you will become very adept at estimating the number of hours in a course, until eventually it will be second nature to just "know" that a certain amount of material meets the time minimum. As your student works through the course, you do not have to keep strict track of time, since you have already accounted for it at the beginning.

The Time Log System

This second method works well for courses in which you will "discover" activities as the year goes along, in order to meet the suggested number of hours.. For instance, a P.E. class for which you log hours of exercise, or an art, music, or life skills class for which you keep track of the hours spent on projects, is suitable for a time log system. At the beginning of the semester, create a simple log with spaces to record the date, amount of time, and description of the activity. As you approach the end of the semester, total the hours spent on the course to see if they meet the number of hours required for the credits you are granting. If not, instruct your student to keep working to achieve the desired number of hours.

Completion-Based Calculation of Credits

Not all courses need to be planned in terms of time. In any subject for which you use a single textbook or a set of packaged curriculum, the completion of the book can be assumed to be one year's worth of study. Math, science, and world language courses are good examples. Using a typical curriculum consisting of lessons and tests, you may assume that a student who completes the whole book—or perhaps all but a few lessons—has completed the course and should be granted a year's worth of credit. In other words, the student will most likely be working at least four or five hours per week on that subject.

Sometimes a student needs a prerequisite course in order to move on to a more advanced one. If a student has already gained knowledge in a subject without actually taking a course in it, you may allow him or her to fly through the elementary course in a compressed period of time. Do this by having the student study the textbook as needed and then "test out" of the course by completing and passing the curriculum tests or by demonstrating mastery in some other way. This scenario should be the exception rather than the rule, however—usually with the goal of having the student enter a higher level of the course, either at home or in an outside setting.

Credits Required for Graduation or College Entrance

While school districts and states vary in their graduation requirements, many high schools require from 20 to 24 Carnegie units for graduation (or 200 to 240 credits for the 10-credit system). This works out to be five or six year-long courses per year. For a strong college prep course of study, at least six full-year courses per year, and sometimes seven, would be a more typical course load, amounting to 24 to total 26 credits (or 240 to 260 for 10-credit-per-year systems). Some of this work could be done during the summer if desired. Always check recommended course requirements for admission to colleges your student is interested in so that you can plan the appropriate course lineup.

Course Requirements

Of course, not only a given number of credits, but also an array of specific courses, must be completed for a solid high school education. At the outset of high school, draw up a list of your own home school's minimum graduation requirements. Collect and browse several sets of graduation requirements as described at the beginning of this chapter. Customize these lists to suit your own home school, and then add courses over and above this minimum in order to build a solid college prep course of study.

Sometimes school districts require a few courses you might not have considered offering, such as vocational education, health and safety, or parenting education. Depending on your state's homeschool laws and whether your home school is considered a private school (and thus not subject to the requirements of public schools), you may or may not choose to include these courses in your own requirements.

The following are some circumstances in which you *might* consider including them:

- If your student might begin high school as a homeschooler but later enter the public school system. In this case, you would want to complete certain requirements to keep him or her on track.
- If these courses are what you want your student to study anyway.
- If even the private schools in your community commonly include these requirements.
- If the colleges to which your student applies will be looking for these courses.
- If you feel the need to demonstrate that you are offering this traditional course lineup.

Since *you* are in charge of your student's education, don't feel tied to a particular course of study. Always listen to what God is saying to you about your student's schooling and future plans.

If at all possible, prepare this rough list of graduation requirements while your student is still in eighth grade, so that you will have a clear idea of your goals before your student even starts high school and before you start buying curriculum and arranging for group and online courses. After preparing the list, leave yourself some time to let your thoughts settle. Because you may change your mind, make this document "fluid" and come back to it to make adjustments as you feel led.

GRADUATION REQUIREMENTS COMPLETION CHART

Once you are satisfied with your list of requirements, prepare a final version and keep it handy as you plan courses every year. Then, create a blank chart or spreadsheet for documenting how the student has satisfied each requirement. If you belong to a PSP (private school satellite program), ISP (independent study program), or other homeschool study program, your administrator may give you a similar document to fill in and have on file. On the left side of the page, list the subject requirements, and across the top, make columns for ninth through twelfth grades. As your student completes courses (or at the beginning of the school year, if you prefer), fill in the course name(s) that satisfy each subject requirement. For instance, under ninth grade math, you might fill in Algebra 1. As you glance at your chart each year, you can quickly tell which subject areas have gaps and are thus the highest priorities for the coming year.

In the chart titled "Sample Graduation Requirements Chart," the student exceeded the number of credits required for graduation and fulfilled all the subject areas over the four years of high school. Notice that courses of any level suitable for the student's abilities could have been filled in; they did not need to be high-level college prep courses. For instance, if the student was not strong in math and was not aiming for admission to a four-year college, the courses could have been Algebra 1, Geometry, and Consumer Math unless Algebra 2 is specifically required by your state or program.

Remember that the document you are creating is simply for *graduation* requirements for your home school, whether or not your student ever goes to college. Set your requirements at a realistic but minimum level that is still in line with local requirements. A college bound student will exceed these minimums and will take additional courses based on personal strengths, interests, and college admissions requirements. However, you might later find yourself in a dilemma if you begin with an overly ambitious set of graduation requirements. If your student turns out not to be interested in a college prep course of study, you will have to revise your graduation requirements late in the game or deny graduation to your student, neither of which leaves a warm, fuzzy feeling.

With your basic graduation requirements as a foundation, take a look at typical college entrance requirements that might apply to your student. Then make some notations in the "subject requirements" area of your chart to show what you will need to add to the basic requirements. For example, under the three years of math, you can note "+1 for college prep." Your student can *graduate* with the lower number of years or credits; he or she will be in the running for colleges with the higher number.

SAMPLE GRADUATION REQUIREMENTS CHART
(DISPLAYING COMPLETED COURSES)

(Carnegie units used: multiply credits by 10 for the 10-credit-per-year system)

REQUIREMENT	GRADE 9	GRADE 10	GRADE 11	GRADE 12
ENGLISH (4 yrs/4 credits)	English 9H 1 credit	English 10H 1 credit	AP® Eng Lang 1 credit	AP® Eng Lit 1 credit
MATH (3 yrs/3 credits) (+1 for college prep)	Algebra 1 1 credit	Geometry 1 credit	Algebra 2 1 credit	Precalculus 1 credit
SOCIAL STUDIES (3.5 yrs/3.5 credits)	World Hist 1 credit	Geography 1 credit	US History 1 credit	US Gov't 0.5 credits
SCIENCE (3 yrs/3 credits)	Biology 1 credit	Chemistry 1 credit	Anat/Physio 1 credit	Physics 1 credit
WORLD LANGUAGE (2 yrs/2 credits) (+1 for college prep)	Spanish 1 1 credit	Spanish 2 1 credit		Spanish 3 1 credit
FINE ARTS (2 yrs/2 credits)			Drawing 1 credit	Drama 1 credit
ELECTIVES* (4.5 yrs/4.5 credits)	Hebrew Scriptures 1 credit	New Testament 1 credit	Spch/Debate 1 credit	Computer Scicnce 0.5 credits Economics 0.5 credits
P.E. (2 yrs/2 credits)	P.E. 9 0.5 credits	P.E. 10 0.5 credits	P.E. 11 0.5 credits	P.E. 12 0.5 credits
CREDITS EARNED TO DATE:	6.5	13.0	19.5	26.5

**CREDITS REQUIRED
FOR GRADUATION: 24**

*In this example, because the student had extra years of math and science, these courses satisfied some "elective" credit, though they have been recorded under their own subject categories.

THE NEXT STEP: DECIDING <u>WHAT</u> TO TEACH

After you have set basic graduation requirements and have thought about what else your student will need for college, you can sketch out the courses you *might* plan for each year of high school (emphasis on *might*). If you do this planning alongside your student, he or she can begin to take ownership of the process. Admittedly, junior and senior years seem far away and hazy at this point, and your grand plans made during the summer before freshman year may change drastically by the end of high school. Ours certainly did, becoming *more* ambitious rather than less. But at least take time to sketch out these plans so that you have some idea of where you are going.

Ponder at length about that very first year, ninth grade. Brainstorm what resources you might choose, using ideas from Chapter 5 as well as suggestions you will find in Chapter 7 on course design. For right now, though, let's assume that you have made some decisions about your first year's courses and have tentatively chosen your curriculum. Using this information, you will create your course titles, course descriptions, and course of study.

COURSE TITLES AND COURSE DESCRIPTIONS

When selecting course titles, seek to come up with a one- to three-word title to be used on the student's transcript. Instead of English or Math or History, your title may be English 9H (H for Honors) or Algebra 2 or World History. Titles should be specific enough to show the focus of the course without being so elaborate as to be impractical, unclear, or too long for the space on the transcript.

Likewise, your course descriptions should cover the salient points of what the course will teach. Your goal is to communicate from your description of, say, tenth grade honors English, that your literature selections, writing assignments, and course objectives were similar to those of other tenth grade honors students. You can create a longer version and a shorter version, depending on the needs of those who will eventually see them. These might include your PSP or ISP administrator or the college admissions staff. A short course description is a one- or two-paragraph overview of what the course will cover, similar to what you would find in a typical college course catalog. A longer course description, sometimes called a syllabus, outlines the content, goals, and main topics of a course and may go into detail about types of assignments and grading policies. Also include titles of textbooks and resources and, optionally, the ISBNs for these resources.

Since you may need this documentation when your student applies to college, keep the information on your computer (backed up securely) as well as printing it and keeping it with your homeschool files. Not all colleges will ask for this information, but it is best to have it ready ahead of time, rather than trying to reconstruct it later when you no longer have the books and materials to refer to.

Chapter 7, which walks you through the course designing process in detail, provides suggestions and concrete examples to help you as you choose course titles and write course descriptions. Also browse high school and homeschool websites, including HSLDA, for course description ideas.

COURSE OF STUDY

Put simply, the course of study is a basic listing of subjects, course names, and textbooks. This document is usually just one page long and covers one year of school. It is a strategic document that should spring from your high school graduation requirements as you decide which of the required courses and electives will be studied in the current school year. The course of study forms the skeleton of the full course syllabus for each subject. Since your PSP or homeschool program, if you belong to one, may require a course of study from you each year, it is good practice to get in the habit of writing them.

The course of study is an easy document to create. Simply list general subject areas such as math or English, one at a time, on the left side of the page, along with the specific name of this year's course. On the right, create and fill in columns for textbook titles, publishers, and grade levels, if appropriate, as well as a brief listing of other resources to be used.

See the sample course of study later in the chapter for one way of presenting this information.

After you have finished writing a course of study, you will write longer course descriptions or syllabi for each course. To help you in planning and record keeping, you may also prepare quarterly and weekly assignment lists. See Chapter 7 for more details on these documents.

FINDING THE HELP YOU NEED

As you plan homeschool courses, you can find a great deal of help online. For example, you can seek out scope and sequence documents, course descriptions, course outlines, and even entire courses used by traditional brick-and-mortar high schools across the nation.

A *scope and sequence* is a curriculum plan displaying a list of instructional objectives and skills, along with the grade level when they are usually taught. Every state has a scope and sequence, sometimes called content standards, for its public schools, and from these you can collect ideas for what to include in your student's courses year by year, especially for courses you are creating from scratch. You may not be required to write up a scope and sequence for your personal homeschool or for your PSP or ISP, but taking the time to do it can help crystallize your thoughts. Don't feel compelled to include everything you see listed, and customize your own scope and sequence to add skills you believe are important.

Course descriptions that you might find online serve as another handy tool to help you in designing your own courses. By searching up a name of a course, you can browse through other schools' course descriptions, reading lists, grading policies, and assignment ideas. For example, try typing "9th grade honors English syllabus" to search for ideas. You can cobble together a winning English course from Mr. Morton's honors course in Dayton, Ohio, merged with Miss Bowers' Studies in Literature course in Anchorage, Alaska *(names are fictitious)*. As a bonus, some teachers' sites link you to educational resources you and your student might enjoy, such as colorful interactive quizzes, videos, or study notes. You may find so much that it's like taking a free online course—minus the grades and accountability.

Don't let the details and the "teacher-ese" of these course syllabi and assignment ideas slow you down. Let them serve their purpose as springboards for your own ideas, but remember that they were designed for classrooms full of students, for which the teacher needs numerous evaluation tools. In your home school, you have many more personal ways to assess your student's learning, and you may not need quite so many assignments.

DOCUMENTING COURSE COMPLETION

Your high school record keeping includes one more important element: a way of tracking finished and unfinished courses. Your student may have one or more incomplete courses at the end of each semester, since the learning does not always fit neatly into eighteen-week blocks. Some of your courses may even be spread over the entire four years of high school.

Consider the following ideas and add them to your record keeping repertoire if they are helpful:

For time-based courses (accumulating a number of hours for course completion) prepare a simple log or spreadsheet with columns for date, activity description, and hours spent. Keep track of the hours completed and total them at the end of each semester and again upon completion of the required hours for the course. This works well for P.E. or for fine arts survey courses in which the student is accumulating activities or experiences toward the final number of hours.

For task-based or proficiency-based courses such as life skills, computer skills, or driver education, prepare a list of all tasks required for course completion. Place a checkoff line next to each task and ask your student to record the date that the task was done and the hours spent on the task. You as the parent might initial the task when you are satisfied with the level of competency.

For traditional academic courses, simply maintain a semester grade record log and continuously enter the student's scores for individual assignments, tests, and projects. When the textbook or all assignments have been completed, the course is finished. A sample of a grade record log is shown in Chapter 8.

Upon completion of a course, record the final score, assign a letter grade, and award credits for completion of the course. File the grade sheet or checkoff sheet, plus any vital supplementary paperwork, with other important student information for that school year. At the end of the semester, issue report cards for your PSP or for your use at home and then enter the grade and credits on the transcript. Construction of a transcript will be covered in detail in Chapter 11.

TO SUM UP

If your head is whirling, don't worry—you are perfectly normal. The terminology, procedures, and ideas introduced in this chapter and reinforced in the next few chapters will become more familiar as you create your own courses. Just remember that you want to show the college admissions staff that your student's courses were academically equivalent to a traditional student's courses. More importantly, you want to create a clear, orderly plan for you and your student to use as you start each school year. The idea is not to generate paperwork for its own sake but to help you conduct your courses smoothly and logically—and then to be able to describe what you did!

(See the sample course of study on the next page.)

---

1. "What Is the Carnegie Unit?" The Carnegie Foundation for the Advancement of Teaching, 2018. Accessed August 15, 2018. https://www.carnegiefoundation.org/faqs/carnegie-unit/.
2. Schofield, Mary, *The High School Handbook: Junior and Senior High School at Home,* 6th ed. (Norwalk, CA: Christian Home Educators Press, 1997), 52.

SAMPLE COURSE OF STUDY

Student: James Roberts   **Birth Date:** 10/10/05   **Grade:** 9   **School Year:** 2019-20

Subject	Book Title	Publisher	Level/Grade
Bible	*Holy Bible*		
(Bible 9)	*Starting Points*	Cornerstone Curriculum	9-10
	Why the Bible Matters	BJU Press	
English	*Starting Points*	Cornerstone Curriculum	9-10
(English 9H)	*Writing & Grammar 9*	BJU Press	9
	Reading Comprehension in Varied Subject Matter	Educators Publishing Service	Book 6
	The Fallacy Detective	Christian Logic	N/A
	Vocabulary	BJU Press	Book A, B
	Student Writing Intensive C	Institute for Excellence in Writing®	9-12
Math	*Algebra 2*	Math-U-See	9-11
(Algebra 2)	*Algebra 2 Honors Book*	Math-U-See	
Social Studies	*Geography*	BJU Press	9
(Geography, Early American History)	*Never Before in History*	Foundation for Thought & Ethics	
Science	*The Physical World*	BJU Press	9
(Physical Science)			
World Language	*Spanish for Mastery I* (with workbook)	D.C. Heath & Co.	9-12
(Spanish 1)	*Easy Spanish Reader*	McGraw Hill	9-12
Physical Ed	None	N/A	9
(P.E. 9)			
Elective	Internet Resources	N/A	9
(Web Design)			
Elective	Internet Resources	N/A	9
(Summer: Photography)			
Elective	*Policy Debate: A Guide For High School and College Debaters*	Southern Illinois University Press	9-12
(Summer: Intro to Debate)			

Chapter 4

Beyond the Three R's:

Subject-by-Subject Suggestions for a

Strong High School Program

So how does a homeschooling parent go from listing courses to knowing what to include in each one? The next few chapters will provide specific, practical ideas for doing just that. Because no two homeschoolers are alike, these guidelines are not meant to dictate but simply to help you construct a reasonably rigorous program. Always customize, enhance, or tone down the courses to fit your family's needs, especially if your student decides on a less competitive path to college. If you are fairly sure that your student will *not* need a rigorous course of study, simply plan a manageable course load to suit your student.

Subject by subject, here are ideas for course content, along with a few suggestions for helpful resources. Note that in this chapter and the next (as well as in other portions of the book) a mention of a particular course, program, website, or author does not necessarily mean that I have thoroughly checked out the resource or that I am endorsing this resource. It only means that the resource has been suggested and enjoyed by one or more homeschoolers I have encountered. As with anything, do your own due diligence in shopping, researching, comparing, and evaluating.

ENGLISH: 4 YEARS

A strong English curriculum for the high school years is not merely a continuation of the reading selections and grammar workbooks that comprised earlier classes. Instead, it should be based on the reading of great literature, with analysis essays and discussions serving as integral elements of the course. Sprinkled into the mix are vocabulary, grammar, research and study skills, and public speaking.

While you may not find a packaged curriculum to meet all your goals, it is not difficult to mix and match materials to assemble your own customized curriculum.

Early High School English Assessment

At the beginning of high school, you'll want to assess your student's English skills. Have him or her read aloud once in a while so that you can evaluate fluency and pronunciation. Take a look at a writing sample to spot the most prevalent problems and to determine whether most of them involve organization, content, or style. Check on spelling, grammar, and punctuation skills to see what needs to be polished up. Then seek out resources that specifically address these needs without wasting time on unnecessary material and without killing your student's enthusiasm for the English language. For example, if your student's only problem is subject-verb and pronoun-antecedent agreement, do not spend an entire year on a tedious grammar workbook. You may need only a ten-minute lesson to clear up the problem.

Typical Areas of Focus in High School English

Writing

Assign simpler writing projects early in high school and then work up to more complex essays. You might consider the following projects:

- Informal letters
- Business letters
- Journal entries
- Blog posts
- Product reviews
- Journalistic news stories or current events
- Interview reports
- Character profiles from fiction or history
- Essays (see types suggested below)
- Précis (a brief, precise summary of an article or essay)
- Literary analysis essays
- Original poetry, short stories, or drama

During the high school years, you will want to cover styles of writing such as descriptive, expository, creative, persuasive, narrative, humorous, comparison/contrast, problem/solution, and cause/effect. A good resource book such as *Writers INC*, produced by the Write Source® educational group, will provide instructions and examples for each of these categories. This handy manual features colorful, user-friendly pages containing examples and instructions for dozens of types of writing. Its supporting website provides even more help.

A foundational writing skill is the ability to write an essay with a clear, arguable thesis, an organized pattern of development, and sufficient and relevant support in the form of quotations or other evidence from sources (assimilated smoothly into the essay). These skills are not developed overnight, but repeated practice will pay off. Teach your student to carefully edit and proofread his or her essays before turning them in. To help with this process, provide a checklist or rubric ahead of time. See Chapter 9 on grading your student's work for an example of an essay rubric.

At least once a year, assign a longer research paper. These assignments develop researching, note-taking, organizing, and synthesizing skills and build the student's attention span for a complex project. Teach your student to avoid the "quick fix" of Wikipedia articles. In fact, ban Wikipedia as a source (though the articles are useful for obtaining a quick overview of the topic). Instead, require your student to explore more tried-and-true sources such as books, magazine and journal articles, and specialized online articles written by experts in the field.

You will also want your student to practice timed essays, since the SAT and ACT exams have timed essay components (the SAT has a rhetorical analysis essay and the ACT has an argumentative essay). The Advanced Placement exams require timed essays as well. Additionally, your student may encounter timed essay exams in community college courses. Thus, it is a wise idea to practice regularly in order to take the mystery out of this particular writing task. Before delving into timed writing, make sure your student's basic essay skills are solid. Then walk through the steps of quickly choosing a position, forming a serviceable thesis, creating an organized but efficient outline of main points, and proceeding to write body paragraphs that are logical, sufficiently supported with evidence, and connected to one another with smooth transitions. Try different types of timed writing: persuasive/argumentative, expository, rhetorical analysis, comparison/contrast, and other structures that may be encountered on exams. Practice the art of budgeting time when every minute counts. You could "warm up" with timed narrative or descriptive writing so that the student gets the feel for a time limit.

For a vast, comprehensive set of writing resources, check out Purdue University's Online Writing Laboratory (Purdue OWL®) at https://owl.purdue.edu/owl/purdue_owl.html. Offering articles, tips, and helpful presentations on literary analysis, creative writing, overcoming writer's block, and much more, this gold mine of information will guide you and your student through high school composition. Full APA and MLA formatting and style guides, required for research papers, are also available on this site.

If grading and evaluating your student's papers is difficult, seek out another homeschooling parent who feels more adept at this. Then suggest something you can do for him or her in return. Alternatively, consider paying a current or former English teacher to grade some essays. You would not need all your student's papers evaluated externally—perhaps just a few per year would do. Writing evaluation services are also available online: one example is Writing Assessment Services℠, provided by Cindy Marsch (https://www.writingassessment.com/). This business also offers several online writing tutorials.

Whether you prefer online or print resources, track down a good thesaurus (my favorite is https://www.thesaurus.com/), a dictionary, and a writer's handbook such as *Writers INC*. Also be sure to pick up a copy of *The Elements of Style* by Strunk and White, a slim but time-honored volume containing invaluable guidance on style and usage. Speaking of slim volumes, another small paperback I have used in writing classes for more than ten years is *The Lively Art of Writing*, by Lucile Vaughan Payne. This book is by no means a full curriculum, but it lays out the goals and objectives of clear, interesting writing, shows students how to brainstorm from idea to thesis to essay, and offers nuts-and-bolts instruction in building sentences, paragraphs, essays, and research papers.

One of my all-time favorite resources, the Institute for Excellence in Writing® (https://iew.com/) offers a wealth of helpful materials in a variety of formats—DVD, audio download, streaming, and print —to guide you and your student down the path to clear, logical writing. In particular, the Student Writing Intensive for middle school and high school can effectively jump-start your writing studies. To cap off the studies later in high school, the *High School Essay Intensive* covers the ACT and SAT essays and college application essays (personal statements), while the *Advanced Communication Series* builds skills for persuasive writing and speaking, advanced note taking, and writing a college-level paper. Yet another set of resources offered by IEW is a selection of literature courses (British Literature, World Literature, American Literature, and guides for teaching classic literature).

Other Resources to Check Out:

Brave Writer, by Julie Bogart (https://bravewriter.com/). One curriculum within this program is *Help for High School*, a self-directed course for high schoolers that teaches academic essays and rhetorical analysis—starting from the thinking phase and continuing to the crafting of a solid, logical argument. Another is *The Writer's Jungle*, designed to teach homeschool parents how to teach writing. The *Brave Writer* program offers both books and online courses.

Literature

Literature Selection

As you choose literature, seek both diversity and quality. Avoid focusing on literature from just one time period, such as the Victorian era, or from one genre, such as the novel. Enjoy a spectrum of time periods and settings—ancient Greece, the Renaissance, or nineteenth century world literature. Explore different genres: novels, poetry, short stories, essays, speeches, historical fiction, biography, autobiography, satire, drama, and other categories that capture your imagination. Try to include eight to ten works of literature per year, encompassing an assortment of full-length books and shorter fiction and nonfiction pieces. Follow up the reading by assigning literary analysis essays for most, if not all, of them. By the end of high school, your student should be comfortable writing three-to five-page essays as well as longer research papers and should show a growing confidence in analyzing literature.

For the backbone of your literature work, choose tried and true authors. Especially for ninth and tenth graders, choose carefully if you venture into more modern works, since your student may not be ready to encounter some of the content, themes, or language in these works. For wholesome yet meaty content, you can't go wrong with Charles Dickens, C.S. Lewis, Shakespeare, and other classic authors whose work has stood the test of time. However, be sure to include plenty of works by female authors and those from diverse ethnic and racial backgrounds, as well as books that tackle issues such as racism, sexism, and other pertinent problems. As suggested in Chapter 2, use a list of classic literary works as your starting point. Take a look at the College Board's list, *101 Great Books Recommended for College Bound Readers* and select the ones most suitable for your goals and your student's level.

The Great Books literary sequence, which should actually be initiated during middle school in order to maximize reading opportunities, would provide an impressive literary education and allow your student to enter "The Great Conversation" with the outstanding authors of our Western tradition. To browse a typical Great Books reading list and curriculum guide, investigate providers such as Escondido Tutorial Service, http://www.gbt.org/, which offers a well-respected Great Books Tutorial. Also be sure to read *The Well-Trained Mind: A Guide to Classical Education at Home* by Susan Wise Bauer and Jessie Wise. Browse the website https://welltrainedmind.com/ for curriculum, informative articles, and a wealth of forums on high school and middle school home education and college preparation. In particular, don't miss the vast high school and college prep forum, packed with questions and insights from other homeschooling parents interested in excellence, empowerment, and encouragement in the journey of home education. I often seek out this forum to gain ideas and perspective on the many questions that come up regarding homeschoolers' college preparation.

As you create a list of classic or modern works you would like your student to read, you may also find the suggested reading lists for AP English Literature helpful. While there is no single "reading list" for this course, numerous lists will come up as you search online. Use such lists to assemble a four-year lineup of literature reading for your high school English courses. As your student reads the literary works you have assigned, encourage active reading to aid comprehension. Highlighting, underlining, marking in the margins of the book, creating informal annotations, or making brief entries in a journal and citing page numbers can be useful ways to note intriguing ideas, quotations, or symbolism that may be used later in discussions or essays. Lesha Myers' *Windows to the World* is an excellent entry-level guide to literature analysis for high schoolers and advanced middle schoolers. (I consider it perfect for many ninth graders, but various ages can definitely benefit from the book.) Myers demonstrates how to annotate literature, how to construct and defend a thesis, how to choose supporting quotations and integrate them smoothly into the essay, and how to come up with intelligent and insightful commentary on these quotations that relates back to your thesis.

Though you are completely free to design literature study in English courses according to what works best for you, one possible sequence is as follows:

9th Grade: Literature Survey

Introduce several genres of literature, designing individual units on poetry, short stories, novels, plays, and nonfiction (either essays or books). Ninth grade is a good year to explore the short story in depth. Themes, character analysis, and plot outlines are easier to extract from a short work than from a novel, and the wealth of quality short stories available—try O. Henry and Saki for starters—makes for an enjoyable time of reading and discussion.

10th Grade: World Literature

You might begin with ancient times and read along chronologically to modern literature. This course dovetails well with a world history course.

11th Grade: American Literature or AP English Language and Composition

Coordinate your literature selections with a study of U.S. history, or plunge into the AP course, which focuses on rhetorical analysis, argumentation, recognizing and using skillful language techniques, and synthesis of multiple sources into a unified thesis. As you study rhetorical analysis, be sure to include the study of speeches (whether historical or modern, text or audio/video). Reviewing a sermon, an informative talk, or a video of Dr. Martin Luther King, Jr. will provide valuable perspectives on how to construct an argument and how to appeal logically and emotionally to an audience.

12th Grade: British Literature or AP English Literature and Composition

Consider a study of Shakespeare and other British authors to cap off the senior year literature study. (Check out Peter Leithart's study guide, *Brightest Heaven of Invention*). Or, instead of British literature, your student might choose to study Advanced Placement English Literature and Composition, which would provide another sweeping survey of great world literature while honing analysis skills.

For more ideas, obtain syllabi from local schools or from high school teachers' websites, to see what students typically study in each grade. Browse online or keep your eyes open at used book sales for literature anthologies containing short stories, poems, and short plays so that you'll have an abundance of literature to choose from. Also, of course, take advantage of the wealth of short stories, poems, and full-length classic works that are available online or free for e-readers.

Discussion Tips

How can a homeschooler enjoy meaningful literature discussions? In a perfect world, you as the parent should read every book along with your student, at least during ninth and tenth grades. In our experience, we found that if both of us had read a certain novel, poem, or essay, we could have a reasonable discussion. Though awkward at first, these discussions gradually became easier and more fruitful. Obviously, since homeschooling parents have intensely busy schedules, it's not always possible to do this reading in tandem.

For classic works of literature, CliffsNotes® or SparkNotes® literature guides (available online for hundreds of literary works) are convenient sources of discussion and essay topics. Despite their "short-cut" reputation, they can be quite helpful for homeschoolers who may not have a seasoned English teacher available to present ideas about theme, character and symbolism. As long as the student is reading the entire work and not just the notes, you need not feel guilty about getting a little help.

For many well-known works, you can also find study guides online that present a plethora of discussion or essay topics. Just search up the title of the literary work, along with the words "study questions" or "essay topics" and browse through the results until you find one or two sites that will best help you and your student. The Glencoe Literature Library and Penguin Classics are two such sources for downloadable study guides for quite a few classic works. Some helpful elements to look for as you browse study guides are background about the author and about the historical context of the book, brief character descriptions, explanatory notes for unfamiliar references, chapter-by-chapter plot descriptions, discussion and/or essay questions relating to a group of chapters or to the work as a whole, discussion of key quotations, analysis of themes and symbolism, and quiz questions you might use, either for a real quiz or for an informal review game.

The best way for your student to participate in literature discussions is to join or form a discussion group. During the early high school years, we joined a group composed of both students and adults, and we have memories of many animated coffee-shop discussions of *The Scarlet Letter, Pilgrim's Progress*, and several modern works. As with most homeschooling ventures, if no group exists, start one!

Literature Analysis

Follow up your literature discussions with writing assignments to help the student synthesize what he or she has learned. Use some of the essay prompts you have found in online study guides. Do not confuse literature analysis essays with the book reports your student wrote during elementary school. Critical essays do not simply recount the events occurring in a book; they explore themes and meaningful ideas of the work by creating a thoughtful thesis and then defending that thesis with textual evidence (quotations) and the student's own commentary and analysis on those quotations. If your student wishes to take the AP English Language and/or AP English Literature exams later in high school, plan ahead by including much early reading and writing practice. Obviously, ninth and tenth graders will construct simpler essays, but it's important to get your student accustomed to writing literary analysis essays.

Other Resources to Check Out:

Reading Lists for College Bound Students by Doug Estell, Michele L. Satchwell, and Patricia Wright. Take a look at this resource to help you get a feel for classics you might include in your students' literature education. You can also look for lists of books recommended for AP English courses, simply by doing a Google® search.

Blackbird & Company Literature Guides, https://www.blackbirdandcompany.com/, give you a pre-packaged tour of a selection of classic books, offering assignments that help the student delve into character, plot, theme, and other key elements through journaling, vocabulary acquisition, reflection, discussion, and essay writing.

Excellence in Literature, https://excellence-in-literature.com/, by Janice Campbell, offers five different one-year English courses for grades eight through twelve (Introduction to Literature, Literature and Composition, American Literature, British Literature, and World Literature) in inexpensive guidebooks.

Sonlight, https://www.sonlight.com/. Numerous homeschooling families appreciate the Sonlight Christian Homeschool Curriculum for its teacher notes, insightful perspectives, and quality readers. The approach of studying history through literature is especially effective.

Project Gutenberg, https://www.gutenberg.org/, an ongoing effort to digitize, proofread, and produce e-books of thousands of books whose copyrights have expired, offers (to date) over 57,000 free e-books for download. Project Gutenberg even offers some audiobooks.

LibriVox, https://librivox.org/. Speaking of audiobooks, be sure to check out *LibriVox*, an entire library of free audiobooks that are in the public domain.

Scholars Online at https://www.scholarsonline.org/ offers online high school literature courses from a classical Christian worldview, as well as offering courses in Latin, math, science, programming, history, philosophy, and other subjects.

They Say, I Say: The Moves That Matter in Academic Writing, by Cathy Birkenstein. This is a book I have only recently discovered but have already fallen in love with. Students will learn how to select, introduce, integrate, and analyze quotes and other textual evidence, not only in literary essays but also in research papers and other academic essays that depend on crafting solid arguments. The book is written for college students, but upper level high schoolers could benefit from it, or you as parent/teacher could select key concepts to use with younger high schoolers.

Public Speaking

Public speaking is an important part of a strong English course, and your student should grow in his or her speaking and presentation skills through every successive year of high school. You might consider forming a group with other homeschoolers for the express purpose of presenting speeches. Another useful resource is the Toastmasters® organization, https://www.toastmasters.org/, a network of groups established to sharpen public speaking skills in business or other public environments. In many locations, this group offers Youth Leadership Programs to acquaint teens with public speaking. Or, your older teen might inquire about joining the adult Toastmasters group for support and encouragement. Although the minimum age for full membership is eighteen, some clubs may welcome younger members.

Consider including some instruction in debate as well. Homeschool speech and debate groups are thriving all over the nation, with students rapidly showing their proficiency in this specialty. NCFCA (National Christian Forensics and Communications Association, website http://www.ncfca.org/), is one source of homeschool speech and debate groups throughout the U.S. Others to check out include Stoa® and National Catholic Forensics League. If you attend a local tournament, you will be impressed by the clear thinking, knowledge, and facility with argument for which these students have been trained. Speech and debate is a tremendous opportunity for students to grow in thinking and communication skills, and it's also a great deal of fun. As students travel together to tournaments, they build teamwork and friendships.

Note that some colleges consider a stand-alone speech and/or debate course an elective instead of a full English course. Check college policies to be sure. However, you can include speech and debate as a component of an English class that is also solid in literature and writing.

Grammar and Miscellanea

If you have covered grammar thoroughly during middle school, your student will need only a brush-up during high school. Focus on proper usage of words and phrases, correction of common errors, and remediation of any lingering punctuation or capitalization difficulties. During high school, grammar study should be highly practical, not busy work. Rather than assigning hundreds of sentences to correct, address the specific problems as they come up and apply the instruction to your student's own writing.

Resources to Check Out:

Fix It! Grammar. This resource, available through the Institute for Excellence in Writing, puts students to the task of hunting for grammar, punctuation, spelling, and capitalization errors in passages that build a storyline. Consider *Fix It!* for a student who needs more intensive practice, rather than just incidental grammar correction from his or her written work.

Winston Grammar. Again, if your student needs another season of nuts-and-bolts grammar instruction before high school is well underway, take a look at the Advanced Level. A pretest is available for appropriate placement.

Vocabulary

You and your student will thank yourselves at SAT or ACT exam time if high school vocabulary study is steady and diligent. Begin some vocabulary exercises during ninth and tenth grades (and even earlier), but place greater emphasis on these skills during the junior year. The current versions of these tests rely mostly on comprehending vocabulary in context, not so much on strict definitions, so offering a wide variety of reading material is, once again, the best preparation. Resources that homeschooling families have mentioned include *Word Up!* by Compass Classroom (fun Latin/Greek roots and English words presented in the form of a TV show) and *WordBuild*.

Logic

The study of logic, and particularly a review of logical fallacies such as "straw man" arguments or circular reasoning, can boost your student's skills in writing and speaking. Learning to draw appropriate conclusions and to construct clear, logical arguments will help your student, both now and during college. If you won't be doing a full-fledged logic course, a helpful and entertaining book called *The Fallacy Detective* by Nathaniel Bluedorn and Hans Bluedorn can guide your student painlessly through fallacies, propaganda techniques, and critical thinking skills.

Research and Study Skills

Research and study skills, including library and internet use and techniques for outlining, organizing, and taking notes for a major research paper, are also a must. The best and most authentic papers will emerge after a time of deep, enjoyable immersion in a subject so that your student is not simply plucking facts out of online articles or paraphrasing another author's thoughts. Your job as a parent/teacher is to help your student experience this "enjoyable immersion" through which even historical characters and events come alive.

After completing the complex task of writing a research paper, your student can then turn the written masterpiece into a visual slideshow presentation. This learning process helps the student to distill the important points of the paper into an outline and then into individual slides for the presentation. The addition of music, artwork, video, fancy fonts, graphics, and special effects makes the process much more enjoyable for the student. Other creative modes of presentation include delivering a "lecture" on the subject, preparing props and displays relating to the project, or presenting a skit, drama or original video.

Another skill that you may want to work into your assignments is the art of note taking. Occasionally, ask your student to take notes while listening to a recorded message such as a sermon or lecture. The notes should be complete enough so that the student can later retell the main points and details of the message, but it should not involve a wild scramble to record every word verbatim. With practice, the student will learn to record legible, usable notes.

The Great Courses® offers a useful set of lectures entitled "How to Become a SuperStar Student," which would be excellent for a freshman to view. Produced to help students enhance and maximize their study skills, these lessons cover note taking, studying for tests, outlining, time management, and many other student survival techniques.

Test Preparation

As a homeschooling family, you can incorporate SAT or ACT test preparation into your yearly plans by selecting a couple of good preparation books or free online practice tests (check Khan Academy®, the College Board® site, and the ACT site) and then regularly assigning small portions for the student to work on, either independently or with you. Pay special attention to the critical reading sections. This skill does not always come naturally but can be improved by practicing the tips and techniques offered in prep books, and of course, by reading loads of good quality literature.

Mini-Units

If either you or your student has a short attention span, try dividing each year up into several unit studies, such as History of the English Language, American Poetry, or Powerful Public Speaking. These mini-courses may have more appeal to your student than a seemingly infinite year of English, and you will still be able to incorporate plenty of literature and writing into each unit.

MATHEMATICS: 3-4 YEARS

Assessment

Math is often the most straightforward, though not always the easiest, subject to teach at home. Maintain a consistent, progressive pace; don't jump ahead unless your student is motivated and fully ready to do so. If your student is progressing at a slower pace, you might try continuing math work during the summer. In addition to the benefits of catching up, your student will maintain the momentum in important concepts over the summer.

Even for students who have no trouble with math, plan to assess fundamental skills at the outset of high school. Check your student's speed on basic arithmetic calculations, using materials such as the CalcuLadder® Math drills or similar products, and then remedy deficiencies before it is too late. For additional course assessment, try using a placement test, available from some math curriculum publishers, to determine which textbook level is most appropriate for your student. As you appraise your student's skills, observe whether he or she is consistently showing the work for each problem, step by step. This discipline becomes increasingly important with advanced levels of math.

Typical Sequence

College prep math sequences follow some variation of the following scheme:
Algebra 1
Geometry
Algebra 2 (may include Trigonometry)
Precalculus (sometimes called Advanced Math; may include Trigonometry if not already taken)
Calculus (standard level or AP Calculus AB or BC and then sometimes more advanced college math)

Students who are not strong in math frequently stop after Algebra 2; the more math-oriented students may have already studied algebra in middle school and can progress through calculus in high school. In general, math courses are a high priority, since the level of mathematics courses completed will drive the science curriculum, keeping doors open for STEM (science, technology, engineering, math) and other mathematical fields.

Students on the competitive paths to college will need to complete Algebra 1 and perhaps geometry during middle school so that they can complete one or more calculus courses by the end of high school. Students aiming for highly selective colleges or for STEM majors often complete two years of calculus before high school graduation. Thus, the first year of calculus is taken during or before the junior year so that the student can take a calculus-based physics course and a more advanced calculus class during the senior year.

Optional Math Courses

Elective math courses might include consumer math or statistics. Consumer math teaches students about budgeting, investing, saving, taxes, insurance, loans, and interest. Statistics may help students who are interested in business, science, or the social sciences. Students who are highly talented at math will want to pursue further courses, either at the community college, online, or through other venues.

Tips for Teaching Math

As your student works through the math curriculum, make sure that each concept is learned thoroughly before progressing. Unless your student grasps concepts rapidly, don't skip around or skimp on practice problems. This shortcut could come back to haunt you later.

Even if you don't feel like a math whiz, your choice of curricula can help. Some are designed to be self-directed, while others require instruction from someone well-acquainted with the material.

Regardless of the claims of the curriculum, students who move into higher math will need help from someone who knows the material. Since math is so important, don't try to "wing it" if your student will go on to take numerous college math courses.

If you want to teach math at home but feel a bit rusty about the fine points, try an audiovisual supplement to boost comprehension, especially for auditory learners. Seeing and hearing the lesson presented on-screen rather than simply reading it may help your student grasp the concepts more firmly. As just one of many examples, take a look at a company called DIVE Interactive Education (Digital Interactive Video Education, https://diveintomath.com/), which supplements the *Saxon® Math* curriculum with video instruction including lectures, demonstrations, and practice problems. Live classes are also available from DIVE.

Another sanity-saving tip is to purchase a solutions manual, rather than just an answer key, if available from the curriculum publisher. Solutions manuals contain complete worked-out solutions for each homework problem in the textbook, providing a tremendous boost in understanding concepts. Some textbook publishers offer solutions online by subscription or via other fee-based arrangements.

If your student has trouble with an independent study format, you might consider homeschool co-op classes or other available group academies. Receiving instruction in a group setting from someone well-acquainted with the material could be a viable solution. Online courses can also be extremely helpful. See Chapter 5 for types of courses you can explore.

As you seek out math courses, pay careful attention to the scope and sequence and the depth of topics so that your student will be ready for the PSAT/NMSQT®, SAT®, and/or ACT® exams.

Other Resources to Check Out:

Art of Problem Solving www.aops.com. Highly recommended online math classes geared for gifted students, with a focus on problem solving and competition-style problems. These problems go far beyond what is normally covered at each math level.

ALEKS® Math (Assessment and LEarning in Knowledge Spaces) https://www.aleks.com/ allows personalized, self-paced learning in math and science via web-based artificial intelligence to assess the student's current level and then to instruct the student on the appropriate next steps and topics.

DerekOwens.com https://derekowens.com/. Derek Owens offers online courses in many levels of math as well as in physics, physical science, and computer science. Courses are not live; students watch video lectures, follow lecture notes, and complete homework and tests that are submitted for grading. Flexibility and customizability of the schedule is also a plus.

Life of Fred https://www.lifeoffred.uniquemath.com/. Entertaining, whimsical, and genuinely unique, this program follows a professor on adventures in which he sees math everywhere and engagingly introduces the student to the concepts. Though it sounds like a children's program (and does have courses even for the youngest mathematicians), *Life of Fred* includes algebra, geometry, trigonometry, statistics, and calculus. If you want something out of the ordinary, check it out.

Community College Courses

Your local community college probably offers courses ranging from pre-algebra through advanced calculus. For both of our students, this option worked well for advanced math classes in the later high school years. Your student will likely receive competent teaching and will not miss out on explanations of key concepts, as sometimes happens with self-instruction.

LABORATORY SCIENCE: 2-4 YEARS

Chemistry in your kitchen? Biology in your backyard? Physics in your family room? While the thought of conducting lab science at home may give you pause, remember that many options are available. A laboratory science course involves regular experiments and activities in addition to the learning accomplished via the textbook. The three most frequently studied lab sciences are biology, chemistry, and physics. If your student has a passion for science, you can delve into it more deeply by conducting additional classes in astronomy, anatomy and physiology, botany, marine biology, environmental science, or biotechnology. However, you may want to draw the line at conducting nuclear physics experiments in your house!

Experiments: A Key Element

Homeschoolers sometimes make the mistake of simply reading the science textbook and skipping the experiments. For a science class to be considered a high school level laboratory science course, it must include regular experiments. No, that doesn't mean you must conduct extensive research on the effects of antibiotics on parakeets. It does, however, mean that your course should include lab investigations related to the material being studied. Though it is impossible to cite nationwide rules or guidelines, traditional schools' science courses frequently spend about one hour per week on lab activities.[1] In a lab science class, students should practice analytical skills by keeping a laboratory notebook containing reports for each experiment. While these need not be elaborate, they must be accurate and organized records of the experiment's purpose, hypothesis, materials, procedures, results, and conclusions. Biology courses should require detailed, labeled drawings of the specimen being observed. Chemistry and physics classes should include some experiments involving quantitative data, and reports need to contain appropriate calculations using significant figures.

It is easy to obtain materials for lab science courses. Science companies catering to homeschoolers or small private schools offer dissecting kits with specimens, chemistry sets with appropriate chemicals, and physics apparatus for the small-scale home science lab. See the Appendix for some sources of science equipment.

Choosing Courses Wisely

If science is your student's passion and potential college major, he or she should consider some outside classes at the community college, where more elaborate equipment and detailed instruction is available. If, on the other hand, science is not a strong interest and this is potentially the last time your student will study it, you can be more comfortable designing a home-based course with materials and resources you can easily gather.

Usually a student's math background will determine the choice of science courses for a given year of high school. Chemistry requires a student to have studied at least Algebra 1, and physics requires Algebra 2 and perhaps some trigonometry (plus calculus if it is a calculus-based physics class). Thus, many high schoolers begin with biology, not so much because it is easier, but because it does not have a math prerequisite. Thus, freshmen often take biology, sophomores take chemistry, and juniors and seniors take physics and/or additional biology and chemistry courses. Students who are strong in the sciences frequently take more than one science course per year.

Sources for Courses

Not surprisingly, you have choices as to how you will conduct science courses at home or through an outside source. Science curricula written specifically for homeschoolers often include student textbooks, teacher's guides, and ready-made tests. Lab experiments use mostly household materials, plus just a few specialized scientific items which can be ordered from companies such as Home Science Tools®.

Once again, community colleges and homeschool group academies can be useful places to take science courses. Our daughter took biology, chemistry, and physics at the community college, and while the classes were fast-paced, she found them enjoyable. Our son took biology, chemistry, and physics in a group academy setting alongside other homeschooled students, before taking more physics at the community college. In a group setting, trained teachers or qualified parents teach the students, and microscopes and other equipment is purchased by the group, using lab fees paid by each family.

Other Resources to Check Out:

Bozeman Science *http://www.bozemanscience.com/*. Be sure to check out this ultra-helpful source of hundreds of engaging, interesting, informative videos by Paul Andersen on science topics ranging from biology to chemistry to physics to environmental science, including AP versions of these subjects. (Yes, that last sentence included many superlatives, but take a look and you'll agree.) His topics within the AP Chemistry, Biology, Physics, and Environmental Science videos are aligned with the AP curriculum. Whether you need a quick video to explain a tough concept, or a whole set of videos as companions to your textbook, this resource certainly fills the bill.

Friendly Chemistry: A Guide to Learning Basic Chemistry *http://www.friendlychemistry.com/*. For students who need a more relatable and, well, *friendly* approach to chemistry, try this text. Utilizing analogies, down-to-earth language, and engaging games and activities, this book by Joey and Lisa Hajda would be ideal for the somewhat reluctant chemistry learner.

DIVE Interactive Education *https://diveintomath.com/*. As mentioned in the mathematics section, this company provides video instruction, animations, digital flash cards, games, and problem solving practice to help students make sense of science and math curricula.

HISTORY AND SOCIAL STUDIES: 2-4 YEARS

Some students can't get enough history, seeing it as a fascinating panorama of human triumphs and struggles from ancient to modern times. By and large, homeschoolers find that history and social studies courses lend themselves to creative teaching methods with which they are already familiar: historical fiction, biographies, timelines, hands-on projects, and other intriguing ways of learning the story of man and his interactions.

Typical Courses

Using your state's social studies requirements as a guideline can help you design a course of study. Typically calling for two or three years' worth of study, most states require U.S. history, U.S. government, and economics. Some states also require world history, state history, or state and local government. Frequently, students start with world history early in high school and then move on to U.S. history in the junior year. They finish their social studies sequence with a semester each of U.S. government and economics in the senior year. Other intriguing courses could be world geography, ancient and medieval history, political science, current events, sociology, ethnic studies, or psychology. Do note that for certain university systems, economics and certain courses such as psychology and sociology count as electives and do not fulfill social studies requirements. Always check with several universities' college prep requirements.

The goal is for students to be literate about their world and their nation. In order to be intelligent conversationalists and to possess a historical frame of reference as they read literature, students should learn about the major events that shaped the nations of the world. As a student-parent team, you can learn together about time periods or cultures that interest you, without being forced into a rigid schedule while covering the material.

If your student finds textbooks dull and uninspiring but loves to read books for fun, consider mixing it up a bit by supplementing the standard lessons with a selection of literature. Choose historical fiction and quality nonfiction (such as biographies or well-written accounts of historical events) matching the time period being studied. Your student will retain more information as he or she receives some of it in the framework of a story. An even deeper non-textbook approach, though significantly more challenging, includes seeking out source documents (documents written at the time of the event or shortly thereafter) to study the issues and the prevailing opinions in their contemporary settings. These documents can include letters, journals, newspaper articles, speeches, essays, proclamations, or any other documents pertinent to the context of the event. Books of source documents are sometimes published as companion volumes to high school or college history textbooks. And of course, source documents can be found online with a little searching.

Creative Variations

Don't feel boxed in by the traditional course titles you might find on a high school transcript. Within the constraints of local or state requirements, you may craft courses that have a creative slant or focus. For instance, you could construct a Contemporary Issues course to examine current events using a theological or philosophical approach.

History courses lend themselves to projects and presentations in addition to or instead of tests and essays. PowerPoint® presentations, games, skits, mock newspapers of the time period, artwork, and debates can all provide both learning and entertainment. For an economics class, an investment project—using real money, if you are bold—makes for an unforgettable lesson. During an election year, delve deeply into a study of U.S. government and political science.

As with science, consider homeschool group classes if teaching history and social studies at home doesn't strike your fancy. If they are taught by a parent or teacher who loves to learn history right along with the students, these classes can provide a way for students to learn and discuss historical happenings in a group larger than that of a typical family. Online courses are another viable option.

Resources to Check Out:

iCivics https://www.icivics.org/. Printable lesson plans and teacher resources on dozens and dozens of civics topics, from the Constitution to citizenship to civil rights.

Visualize World Geography *http://www.visualizeworldgeography.com/*. A clever, effective way to learn and memorize world geography by associating every country with a picture (Italy is a boot, etc.). Additional mnemonic devices and in-depth information help guide students in learning about each country and eventually drawing the world map from memory.

WORLD LANGUAGE: 2-4 YEARS OF THE SAME LANGUAGE

To be considered for admission to most colleges, your student should study a language other than English. Benefits of studying another language are many and include a better grasp on grammar and vocabulary skills, sharpened memorization skills, the ability to communicate during international travel or missions work, opportunities to converse with local speakers of that language, a heightened appreciation of one's own heritage (especially if the student has a chance to converse with relatives in that language), an increased understanding of other cultures, and a head start in learning future languages. That's a lot of bang for your buck!

Questions to Ask

Before you and your student settle on a language, ask yourselves the following questions.

How useful is the language?

The thought of learning Ukrainian might thrill your student, but will it really be of any practical use? Probably not—unless you happen to have Ukrainian-speaking relatives. Some of the most useful languages to learn are Spanish, Chinese, and Latin. Latin is useful because about two-thirds of our English words come from Latin, and thus vocabulary skills will be enhanced after Latin study. It is also the basis for other Romance languages such as Spanish, French, and Italian, so these languages will be easier to learn after learning Latin. As another selling point, higher SAT exam scores in both the language *and* the math sections have been demonstrated among Latin students.

Usefulness of other languages can be determined by geography (is the language spoken in your vicinity?) or heritage (does the language have significance in his or her ancestry?). Your student might also choose a language that would be useful in a future career.

In some states, the study of American Sign Language fulfills the world language requirement for high school graduation. If this is the language your student wants to learn, be sure to check for its acceptability with your student's favored colleges.

Which language is your student motivated to learn?

The more motivated a student is to learn a language, the more diligent he or she will be when it comes time to study.

Who will teach the student?

The thought of teaching your student a second language at home may seem daunting at first, but you have options. You might consider private or group tutoring, or an online course. Even if you decide that you will be your student's primary teacher, you may choose from an assortment of independent study language programs available to homeschoolers. If at all possible, see if you can work with a live teacher for best results in learning proper pronunciation and in correcting mistakes.

What curricula and courses are available?

Language curricula come in a variety of forms, from the traditional book format to online courses. The most popular languages are available in more curricular options. Before settling on a particular curriculum, make sure it will give your student the opportunity to practice *reading, writing, speaking,* and *listening.* Also remember that if you plan to teach the language at home and later send your student to an outside class (such a community college course or an online course), you'll want him or her to be prepared to study the language at a potentially advanced level or at a more rapid pace.

Curricular Options

Many organizations or universities offer online language courses. When choosing these courses, look for the level of support (i.e., is the student able to interact with an instructor?), ease of use (available via mobile apps if desired?), and thoroughness in the various types of language learning tasks: reading, writing, listening, and speaking.

A plethora of online and other computer-based courses is available, but one curricular option we used and enjoyed was the Rosetta Stone® language program (https://www.rosettastone.com/). Originally used by NASA, the U.S. State Department, and the Peace Corps, this program offers a highly convenient self-paced way for the student to study a language independently, from the comfort of a home computer or by using a mobile app. The Rosetta Stone® Homeschool program utilizes an immersion method to present words and concepts solely in the new language, similar to the way a child learns a language. Available in more than 30 languages, the program features interactive speaking and learning activities, built-in proficiency tests, speech recognition, and thousands of photographs to represent objects and concepts. Best of all, the parent does not need to know the language—and the program provides administrative tools to help parents monitor progress. One drawback of the Rosetta Stone® program is that it is weaker in teaching grammar skills than most language learners might prefer. Also, several online reviews indicate technical glitches and trouble with tech support.

If online programs do not suit your student's needs, you may want to explore homeschool group academies or community college classes. Some group classes are taught by a homeschool parent; others by an outside teacher. Thus, you'll want to make sure that the teacher is very comfortable with the language and can teach students proper pronunciation and accent. Native speakers are ideal.

One point to note about community college courses is that a semester of a college-level language class is equivalent to a full year of a high school class. Your student should be prepared to study faithfully to keep up with the weekly expectations.

Course Objectives

For any language course, you'll want to investigate its scope and depth. Is it recreational/conversational, or rigorous? This due diligence is especially important if your student plans to take a standardized exam such as the SAT Subject Test or AP exam. Particularly if your student will take an AP exam in the language, look for a College Board-approved course. For any student, look for courses with built-in reinforcement and sufficient repetition so that your student can build new skills while continually keeping up with past skills.

If your student experiences difficulty, try to identify a friend who speaks the language fluently and who will not mind being consulted from time to time. One homeschooling family we know solved the language dilemma by hiring a tutor to come to their home to teach their sons German.

Immersion programs are especially helpful because they force the student to begin thinking in the target language. Traveling to a country or area where the language is spoken is the ultimate language course. Another excellent way to reinforce language study is to listen to native speakers, whether they are "live" in your local community or are recorded. If possible, try to attend a church service in this language, watch TV, movies, or online programs in the target language, or just eavesdrop on the language being spoken in your community. A fun visual learning technique is to label objects around the house with the word in the target language until the student stops thinking in English and goes directly from seeing the object to saying its name in the new language. Pictures, games, and multisensory activities are other ways of associating the word with the object or action. From time to time, the student might try to read the Bible or memorize a few Scripture verses in the language.

Foreign language study lends itself to enjoyable activities such as food nights, games, outings, and movies in the language—or days when you try to speak mostly in the target language. Children's books (especially those with accompanying audio recordings) are another entertaining resource for hearing and learning the language. For example, try reading a familiar *Berenstain Bears* book in Spanish. The bottom line is for you and your student to *enjoy* your study of a new language.

Other Resources to Check Out:

Homeschool Spanish Academy https://www.spanish.academy/. Online courses taught via Skype by certified native Spanish speakers. Homeschool families will appreciate the flexible, customizable schedule of lessons, as well as the affordability. The program fully covers grammar as well as vocabulary and conversation skills, and meets requirements for high school language courses.

Memoria Press Online Academy https://www.memoriapressacademy.com (Latin, Greek, Hebrew, and French). Also offering courses in history, science, math, English, and other subjects (including AP courses), Memoria Press provides live online courses with evaluation based on discussions, quizzes, tests, writing projects, and other appropriate assignments.

Classical Academic Press https://classicalacademicpress.com/ (Latin, Greek, and Spanish). Presenting live online courses in many classical subjects through its Scholé Academy, Classical Academic Press is also a provider of a variety of curricula for classical education.

FINE ARTS: 1 YEAR

Many colleges require that applicants complete one or more years of fine arts instruction. In fact, some school districts and colleges require two years of study. These courses can involve vocal or instrumental music, visual arts such as drawing, painting or sculpture, drama and theater, architectural design, or photography if taught from an artistic rather than a technical approach. For homeschoolers, extracurricular activities can dovetail nicely with fine arts courses. If your student plays the piano and participates in recitals, design a course around piano performance. Keep track of hours of practice and performance, designating some toward fine arts courses and some toward extracurricular activities. Similarly, drama programs, drawing and painting lessons, or orchestra participation can serve as portions of fine arts courses. You might also consider having your student take an art or music class at the community college.

If your student is not into fine arts and you need a more basic course, consider a fine arts survey, for which you plan a collection of fine arts activities from various disciplines. You could spread this survey over as little as one semester or as much as all four years of high school, still calling it a one-semester or a one-year course according to how many hours your student spends on activities. Suggestions for content could include a short series of drawing lessons, a brief unit each on art and music appreciation, and attendance and evaluation of music concerts, drama performances, museums, or other "artsy" activities. Teaching your student to recognize a few key artists and their representative paintings *before* viewing paintings in museum art galleries can make the gallery time much more interesting and educational.

With that said, bear in mind that some universities have specific stipulations for the content of high school fine arts courses. "Arts and crafts" courses that simply dabble in artsy activities are not considered high school level fine arts courses. As one example, the University of California requires such courses to incorporate artistic perception, creative expression, historical/cultural context, aesthetic valuing, connection relations, applications, intention, and performance/production. If this sounds like quite a mouthful, it is! If the college in which your student is interested has such stipulations and you are hoping that your homeschool work will be accepted, be sure you know what the procedure would be to design such a course, or know where your student could take such a course in order to have it accepted later. Here is where a community college class might come in handy. The ultimate irony would be to have a stellar student rejected from such a university merely because the fine arts credit was not completed in the way the university wanted it to be. However, this scenario would be quite unlikely.

Other Resources to Check Out:

How Great Thou Art http://www.howgreatthouart.com/. Barry Stebbing's well-loved art resources offer books, step-by-step instruction, and DVD courses aligned with classical Christian education. Painting, drawing, and art history are just a few of the adventures introduced through these materials.

ARTistic Pursuits® https://artisticpursuits.com. Covering elements of art, composition, color, and other topics, ARTistic Pursuits emphasizes observation and creativity to nurture joy in artistic expression.

PHYSICAL EDUCATION: VARIABLE REQUIREMENTS

Physical education requirements differ from state to state. Barring any specific content requirements in your area, feel free to have your student choose favorite sports or exercise activities to fulfill P.E. requirements. While some students choose traditional team sports such as basketball or soccer, others swim, play tennis, or participate on crew teams. Still others might enjoy more solitary activities such as running, fitness, or weight training. Some families use dance activities, such as ballet, for P.E. fulfillment. Your student might also enjoy joining a gym to work out individually or with a few friends. Regardless of the activity chosen, make sure that your student has a program in place for health and fitness, for ultimately this is what P.E. is all about. You might also want to include a unit on health and nutrition or to require the student to read some articles on health and fitness. To prepare documentation for your course, log the hours and record the activities in which your student participated.

P.E. has its perks. Personal fitness is a lifelong benefit for overall health, and studies have shown that students who exercise actually get better grades. What's more, this is the perfect opportunity to get the family involved in activities that you can do together for enjoyment and exercise.

BIBLE, THEOLOGY, WORLDVIEW, AND FAITH-BUILDING STUDIES

Certain courses, while not in the typical college prep lineup, are of great interest to Christian families and can help prepare students for college in more ways than one. Surveys reveal that a large percentage of Christian young people walk away from their faith during or after college. Although in some cases this represents a temporary shift rather than a permanent renunciation, it frequently happens because students have not been prepared to defend their faith logically and reasonably.

To help counteract this trend, basic Bible courses can teach the student how to study the Scriptures and, more importantly, how to apply them to life. Going further, Christian worldview courses can help your student compare biblical principles with historical and modern secular philosophies. Additional faith-building studies of your choosing can point your student toward a personalized, mature faith as well as demonstrating ways to respectfully communicate his or her convictions to friends and colleagues.

Bible and Theology

While dozens of different ways exist to interest your student in studying and applying the Bible, some ideas include mini-courses on Bible study techniques, the use of study tools such as a concordance or Bible dictionary, a course on how to share one's faith, or the study of specific books of the Bible. You could also incorporate memorization of key Bible verses or reading and discussing Christian classics such as the works of C.S. Lewis. By assigning essays that apply biblical principles to ideas found in literary works or history textbooks, you can combine Bible assignments with a student's other coursework. Be careful not to assign "Bible homework" that is simply busy work. It should always be meaningful and practical. And discuss, discuss, discuss! Biblical concepts are meant to be applied to real life so that your student can take ownership of them.

If the student serves in church ministries, teaches younger children at Sunday School, or works in a club program such as AWANA® Clubs, these volunteer hours might be counted toward Bible courses. Attendance at classes or seminars (Bible literacy, evangelism, or youth seminars) as well as participation in missions trips, can also count as activities toward your student's courses in Bible and theology.

Worldview Education

A worldview, which is the overall perspective from which one sees and interprets the world, consists of a collection of beliefs about life and the universe used to guide everyday actions and decisions. A few of the common Western world views today are biblical Christianity, Marxism, secular humanism, and New Age philosophy. In our global society, worldviews are commonly communicated through media, politics, education, literature, the arts, and science and technology. Since these views are encountered frequently in classroom discussions and conversations, an educated student should have at least a basic acquaintance with the tenets of these philosophies.

A biblical worldview course will show a student that with logic and reason, he or she can demonstrate that Christianity consistently and comprehensively explains our world. Worldview education also provides tools for analysis, so that students do not blindly believe everything that they hear. Additionally, worldview education can help students learn to discern truth and error and to recognize both solid and faulty arguments. As they examine the tenets of their faith and discover the reasonable basis that undergirds them, they will be able to articulate not only *what* they believe, but *why* they believe it.

Students who exercise both faith and reason will be much more effective in living and communicating God's principles than those who believe only because their parents or pastor taught them to believe. However, without a proactive plan to teach these principles, the best of intentions may result in a weak faith that can't defend itself, or in a strong but "stubborn" faith that cannot effectively relate to and dialogue with other ideas.

Several curricula and resources for Christian worldview studies are described in the Appendix.

Faith-Building Studies

Beyond learning Bible study techniques and understanding Christian doctrines, a college bound student will want to develop deeper skills and knowledge. Some of these concepts include the following:

- *Building on one's faith to make it personal and active.*
- *Interacting with God and finding one's unique style, mission, and strengths.*
- *Articulating the Christian faith reasonably and logically.*
- *Communicating and dialoguing about one's faith in a sensitive, loving way.*

- *Developing an awareness of cults and their recruitment tactics.*
- *Recognizing the difference between essential faith issues and "side issues," to avoid creating strife.*
- *Learning how to speak with highly intellectual individuals about faith-based ideas.*

As your student encounters people from countless different backgrounds, he or she will meet atheists, agnostics, skeptics, born-again Christians, nominal Christians, Catholics, Protestants, and students with Jewish, Muslim, Hindu, or Buddhist backgrounds, to name a few. In the classroom and the residence hall, in apartments and cafes, the age-old questions about God, the universe, right and wrong, and the existence of absolute truth will be repeatedly raised, discussed, and debated.

To make sure that these conversations are fascinating and productive rather than threatening and destructive, your student should spend time—either in person or through books and media—with Christians who have thought about these questions at length and can address them in an understandable way. Christianity holds up excellently to intellectual discussions, and its principles can be followed to their logical conclusions without contradictions or breakdowns in reasoning.

Helpful books that deal with Christianity in a postmodern and increasingly intellectualized world are listed in the Appendix.

ELECTIVES AND VOCATIONAL COURSES: VARIABLE REQUIREMENTS

Here's an opportunity for some fun! Electives are courses that fall outside your student's core academic curriculum. These classes may include character-based or hands-on skills that you want your student to develop for life, such as computer programming skills or basic life skills. On the other hand, they might be based on specific units of study that your student enjoys. For instance, a student who enjoys studying English might like a semester-length course focusing on Shakespeare's work. Another student might prefer the study of philosophy or logic. Speech and debate, constitutional law, accounting, or health and nutrition are other ideas for electives.

College Prep Electives

Some colleges and universities require that a student take a few "college preparatory" electives in order to be considered for admission. This term simply refers to academic classes outside of the core subjects, or to *extra* courses within a subject category whose requirements have already been completed. For instance, a third year of a foreign language if only two are required would qualify as an elective. Other examples of college prep electives include science classes without a lab component, architecture, psychology, and creative writing. Encourage your student to delve into subjects in which he or she has great interest, such as photojournalism, drama, or political science. Computer programming or an introduction to business principles might be other ideas for elective courses. Through careful selection of electives, your student can demonstrate interest in a particular subject and increase his or her college admission chances.

Elective courses need not be a full year or semester in length. Feel free to design mini-units just a few weeks long, enough time to explore the subject but not so much that it encroaches on other academic demands. These courses can be just the thing for keeping learning fresh and interesting.

College prep electives could include the following:

Science-Based Electives:
Botany
Plagues and Epidemics
Environmental Science
Forensic Science
Agricultural Science
Animal Science
Health and Nutrition
Biotechnology
Astronomy
Engineering
The Immune System
Geology

English-Based Electives:
Film and Literature
Shakespeare
Russian Literature
The Short Story
Poetry
Speech and Debate
Utopia and Dystopia in Literature
Bible as Literature
Storytelling
Broadcast Journalism
Publications and Publishing
Modern Media
Creative Writing

Math and Business-Based Electives:
Math Problem Solving
Mathematical Theory
Personal Finance
Economics
Entrepreneurship
Accounting
The Music Business

History and Social Science-Based Electives:
World War II
Cold War
History of Science
History of Medicine
History of Invention and Innovation
Sociology
Anthropology
Women's Studies
Psychology
Child Development
Geography and Missions
Ethnic Studies
Constitutional Law

Arts-Based Electives:
Graphic Arts
Photography
Photojournalism
History of Theater

Technical Electives:
Computer Programming
Robotics
Web Design
Digital Electronics
Game Design
Architecture

Religion and Philosophy-Based Electives:
Hebrew Scriptures
Christian Scriptures
Comparative Religion
World Religions
Philosophy
Logic
Ethics or Bioethics

Nonacademic Electives

Not all electives need to be college prep in nature, although a busy student preparing for college may not have a great deal of time for other pursuits. Still, if your student is interested in gourmet cooking, woodworking, or interior design, go ahead and design a course to enhance this interest. In addition to vocational courses listed in the next section, consider the following ideas: study skills, ornamental horti-culture, or organic gardening. Driver education is another nonacademic course that most high schoolers take. After checking your state's requirements, ask around to determine online and behind-the-wheel courses recommended by other families.

As you plan electives, feel free to combine subject categories to create interdisciplinary courses, such as the study of history through literature, or a philosophy/theology course. Homeschooling provides the perfect setting to teach your students the interrelationships among disciplines—concepts that they might not encounter in a traditional school setting.

Vocational Courses

Traditional schools offer some vocational courses including wood, metal, or auto shop, and other practical, skills-based courses. As you decide whether to include these courses, based on state or local requirements and on your student's interests, you might receive help from friends or relatives who can lend the proper skills or equipment. Other ideas for vocational education include career preparation assessments, first aid courses, or home economics/life skills courses. Students who are not on the highly competitive college prep path will have more flexibility to follow their interests and aspirations in these courses.

Other Resources to Check Out for Electives:

Codeacademy https://www.codecademy.com. Learn coding in at least 12 languages for free, or sign up for a premium "pro" option for intensive courses involving a fee. With a huge active community and a wide knowledge base, Codeacademy is worth checking out for programming instruction.

RayWenderlich https://www.raywenderlich.com. At a quick glance, it appears that hundreds of different programming tutorials and video courses are offered on this fun, colorful site.

TO SUM UP

Before you leave this chapter, be aware that Chapter 5 suggests even more ways to design courses and make use of traditional, community, and online resources. While Chapter 4 has focused on subject-by-subject suggestions, Chapter 5 will give a more global view of how to be creative and to mix and match educational resources to fit your student's learning style, your curricular needs, and your budget.

Don't feel limited by these brief suggestions for high school courses. The beauty of homeschooling lies in the fact that you can custom-fit courses to suit the needs of your student and your family. As you plan your student's course of study, keep his or her post-high school plans in mind, whether they include a community college, a highly selective college, or a particular "dream" career. Having a rough idea of future plans will help you make these decisions. As you plunge into the high school journey, knowledge of the destination is half the battle.

1. Singer, Susan R., Margaret L. Hilton, and Heidi A. Schweingruber, eds., Board on Science Education, Center for Education, Division of Behavioral and Social Sciences and Education, *America's Lab Report: Investigations in High School Science* (Washington: The National Academies Press, 2005). Accessed August 15, 2018. http://books.nap.edu/openbook.php?record_id=11311&page=122.

Chapter 5

Sources for Courses:

Where to Find Your High School Curriculum

*E*ven parents who have sailed through the elementary and middle school years full of creativity and confidence can find themselves puzzling over the prospect of providing an entire high school curriculum for their students. Suddenly all the questions from well-meaning relatives and friends come back to haunt them. "How are you going to do higher math?" "What about foreign language?" "How can you possibly do lab science at your kitchen table?" It is here that some parents are tempted to put their college bound students into a traditional school.

Fortunately, home-directed high school is entirely do-able. Parents can maintain the same creativity, confidence, and courage that upheld them throughout the earlier grades. Moreover, parents are still the best judges of their students' learning styles and educational needs. Use that knowledge as you seek out options for the areas that you find most perplexing.

GENERAL TIPS ON FINDING SOURCES FOR YOUR COURSES

Pray for the Right Opportunities

Address your trepidation by reminding yourself that you don't personally need to know everything in order to provide your student with the right lineup of courses. Your first step is to pray for God's providence in bringing teachers, classes, experts, and opportunities at just the right time for your student. Homeschoolers who have completed this task can look back and point to instance after instance where the right opportunity became available and, in turn, opened the door to other opportunities later.

Start at Home ... And Then Branch Out

If your goal is to keep your schooling mostly home-centered as you gradually transition to outside courses, consider using mostly home-based options in several subjects during the first year or so of high school. Extracurriculars and sports can provide a stimulating addition to the schedule while still allowing you to spend plenty of time with your student.

However, be open to excellent opportunities and venture out to community or homeschool group-based classes as soon as your student is ready. First, assess what kind of student you have. You may have one who thrives on learning at home and is only mildly interested in taking outside courses. For this student, enjoy the fact that learning at home is such a good fit, and ease into the outside courses gradually—perhaps by scheduling a "fun" course or by finding a class your student can take with a couple of friends.

In contrast, you may have a student who is champing at the bit to experience the world, suddenly feeling that the four walls of "home school" are far too confining. This student may be complaining or sluggish about studying at home and may be begging to go to "real school." For this student, a course or two each semester at the community college or at a homeschool group academy can go far in rekindling that initial spark of motivation and love of learning. Accountability to an outside teacher, together with healthy competition in the classroom, can inspire your student to perform well, both in the outside courses and at home.

Perhaps you have a student who is doing well at home but has college or career aspirations that require some outside learning—either because of equipment needs such as for lab science or art, or because you have reached the limit of what you as a parent can teach in this subject. Scope out your options early in high school and plan a selection of outside courses to help your student advance to the next stage of education. For this student, courses outside this area of specialty will probably still work well at home. Remember that in the field of your student's passion and potential life work, you should include as many outside classes as possible with knowledgeable instructors and with the typical equipment and techniques your student will be expected to use.

If you are overseeing and facilitating your student's courses, you are still homeschooling—even if many of these courses take place outside the home.

Choose Options Wisely

Choose options based on your student's comfort level, personality, and learning style. Most homeschoolers deliberately set out to avoid the typical "one size fits all" classroom environment. Your goal is to design an individual approach that will encourage your student to excel and to pursue each subject to his or her greatest abilities. Don't lose sight of this goal during your quest for supplementary courses. As you investigate community college courses or homeschool group courses, find out about the course expectations and assess how you think your student will do. In all cases, know your student and what he or she is capable of handling academically, socially, and emotionally. It's one thing to "stretch" your student in order to encourage growth and increased responsibility. It's another thing to place him or her in an academic environment that is overwhelming, or in a social environment that is intimidating or demoralizing.

Beyond this, consider a few other questions. Does the student learn better in a small group or in a large group? Is he or she motivated enough to take an online course where instruction is received from a remote teacher? Would your student fare better in a discussion-oriented course, or in a course focusing on producing written work or projects? Are you looking for a basic course, a rigorous honors or AP course, or something in between? Certain group classes may favor one extreme or the other. Of course, you won't always have a choice in some of these variables, but asking these questions will help you know how best to assist your student.

Naturally, a homeschooler's very first experience in an outside classroom will create some temporary nervousness. But beyond this, if you get partway through the course and realize that it was a big mistake, don't be afraid to change gears and try something else. Or, depending on the situation, you may use it as a learning opportunity and encourage your student to tough it out as a step of maturity.

Mix and Match to Create the Right Learning "Recipe"

"Recipe" is an apt metaphor here. The beauty of homeschooling a high schooler is that a parent-student team can cook up just the right concoction that will "taste good" to both of them. You do not need to do all the work at home, nor are you obliged to farm out all the work to an assortment of teachers. Mixing and matching is fun and creates variety in the homeschooling experience. In fact, you may find that each year of high school contains a different blend or flavor. Perhaps the ninth and tenth grade years will be more home-focused, with a homeschool group class or two thrown in. Then the eleventh and twelfth grade years might contain an increasing lineup of community college and online AP courses, along with leadership activities that will amaze both you and your student.

The growth that occurs between ninth grade and eleventh or twelfth grade can be phenomenal. You may find yourself marveling at your student's progress over these two or three years. At the end of eleventh grade, Julie commented, "When I first started ninth grade, I never dreamed I'd be doing all these things outside of home." "All these things" included taking numerous community college courses, teaching a Shakespeare course to other homeschoolers, working as a tutor at the community college, and gearing up for a summer of immunology research. In short, don't set all your plans in concrete at the outset of high school, and don't hold back. Your student *can* and *will* grow tremendously throughout high school.

As you contemplate all your choices for educational approaches and individual courses, remember that you have an almost limitless lineup of options. Allow your student some freedom and flexibility in the schedule to encourage personal pursuits and passions. The following are some suggestions from which you can choose as you construct a high school course of study.

HOME-BASED OPTIONS

Standard Packaged Curriculum

Using curriculum purchased directly from the publisher, complete with student books, workbooks, teacher's guides, tests, and answer keys, is a straightforward way to assure that you are covering all the bases in a given subject. Since most of the planning work has been done for you, preparation can be as easy as dividing up the table of contents to set up a schedule for the year. If you are short on preparation time or creativity, this is a no-nonsense method for planning one or more subjects. At the high school level, your student may not even need you to present the material in the teacher's guide but can simply read that day's section for additional notes, tips, and strategies. If you choose, the student can grade his or her work using the answer key, and you can be available to answer questions. Or you may prefer to be more active in the teaching process by presenting the lesson yourself. If it is a subject with which you have no expertise, a well-written textbook with notes and tips can help you learn along with your student.

One disadvantage is that this approach can become tedious for all but the most motivated students. One could successfully argue that most students do *not* learn best by reading textbooks and doing workbooks. Also, some of these courses involve too much busy work, especially if you assign all the activities suggested in the course and all the problems in the problem sets. As you already know, you need to choose the assignments that are most beneficial for your student.

"Customized" Curriculum

Packaged curriculum does not have to be used "as is." Consider customizing your curriculum using a spectrum of additional materials. For instance, you might choose a particular history curriculum because you like the textbook's approach and plan to use it as a foundation for the course—but then you decide that instead of purchasing the accompanying student workbook, you will substitute the reading and discussion of historical novels and biographies, after which your student will write essays based on these discussions. You might still use the publisher's chapter tests to evaluate how well the student internalized the textbook information, or you might decide to base the entire grade on reading, discussion, and essay writing.

Alternatively, you might design an entire course using non-textbook materials. For an English course, you might select a number of novels, essays, poems, and biographies your student will read during the year. For assessment, instead of tests and quizzes, you might design writing topics, speech topics, and other literature-based projects such as a PowerPoint presentation of relevant photos, or an art project that demonstrates an understanding of the literature. Instead of using a grammar textbook, you might plan to go over grammar mistakes that appear in your student's essays, and instead of working through a vocabulary text, you might have your student find and define ten new words per week from the assigned literature reading, making flash cards of definitions, sample sentences, and word origins. As you can imagine, a customized non-textbook curriculum can be an inexpensive way to go, especially if you obtain many of the books from the library.

Classical Education

Sometimes the "oldies" really are the "goodies." The classical approach to education teaches the student how to learn, using the subjects and sequence of the Trivium, a course of study derived from medieval times. The three stages of the Trivium are grammar, logic (dialectic), and rhetoric. The grammar stage encompasses the elementary school phase, during which the student learns basic facts and concepts in all subjects, with a focus on memorization. The dialectic stage is ideal for the middle school years and includes learning formal logic and argumentation as well as developing the art of reasoning, asking questions, and discovering how facts relate to each other. The rhetoric stage, corresponding to the high school years, emphasizes the formal application of the earlier stages of learning. The student now employs abstract thinking to produce personal interpretations, problem solving, and creative thinking. With these, he or she can put facts and ideas together using skills in reasoning, persuasion, and oral and written expression.

The classical approach is highly focused on language. For their world language courses, most students study Latin, commonly beginning in middle school or even earlier. Not surprisingly, history studies start with the ancient world and then cover European, American, and modern history, including a focused study of government. English courses encompass composition, literature (such as American, classical, and British), literary analysis, and rhetoric. The senior year might culminate in the student's preparing and presenting a senior thesis. For Christian families, classical biblical studies focus on interpretation, doctrine, apologetics, and the defense of the Christian worldview. In mathematics, the student completes a fairly traditional sequence from algebra through calculus. Similarly, science courses delve into the traditional subjects of biology, chemistry and physics.

One popular program you might look into is Classical Conversations®. In this classical Christian community, students attend a weekly community day, where parent/tutors facilitate learning seminars in six foundational subjects. Parents are still the primary teachers. Note that this is a structured program with specific curriculum to purchase and keep up with; thus, it would not be for everyone. The website is https://www.classicalconversations.com/.

Unit Studies

Unit studies allow the student to examine a particular topic or theme across many disciplines and from many angles, using detailed research, in-depth investigation, projects, and hands-on study. After selecting a theme of study, parents and students create assignments that encompass disciplines such as English, history, science, and/or fine arts.

Since unit studies utilize a variety of learning activities, they can be a viable alternative for students who are easily bored with the textbook approach and need a more creative method of exploration. A unit study can take anywhere from a few days to a few weeks to complete. Whether you are using a ready-made unit study curriculum or are designing your own, this study can help the subject come alive. An example of a unit study approach covering multiple disciplines could involve the study of the New England states. On the surface, this would be a history or geography topic, but the student could accomplish the following tasks utilizing other subjects:

- Research and discuss the colonial origin of each state. *(History)*
- Write an essay describing the founding of the colony or state with the most interesting background. *(English, History)*
- Investigate factors such as soil composition or climate patterns that led to the rise of industries such as fishing and shipbuilding rather than agriculture in these colonies. *(Geography, Science)*
- Construct a relief map or a political/demographic map of the colonies, using different colors for attributes such as population density and country of origin of its early settlers. *(Geography, Art)*
- Prepare a speech or debate on the topic of religious freedom and its role in the founding of these colonies. *(Bible, English)*
- Analyze population growth over a period of time in the history of these states. *(Math)*
- Find music and lyrics to traditional songs of these areas. Sing them, play them on an instrument, or construct an audiovisual presentation using these songs as background music while displaying artwork and photos depicting these states. *(Music, Technology)*
- Research a typical meal from the colonial days of one of these states, and cook and serve it to the family. *(Life Skills)*

Ideas for unit study assignments are unlimited. The more active and involved a student is in planning a unit study, the more he or she will be motivated to take ownership of the work. High school students should be expected to invest more time and effort than would be expected in middle school, so you want these studies to be appropriately substantial and rigorous. They should not simply scratch the surface of the topic.

With the advantage of *depth* of study comes the disadvantage of a lack of *breadth*. In other words, time does not permit studying all aspects of every school subject in this way. Additionally, you will still need a daily math curriculum, and your lab science will not be adequately covered by unit studies. But this option could work quite well for creatively covering English, social studies, Bible, and fine arts. Remember that you can always insert these creative ideas into your traditional curriculum plans too.

The World Wide Web of Distance Learning

Distance learning, in all of its flavors, is the homeschooler's friend. In the first edition of this book, I mentioned DVD courses, educational CDs, and several genres of online courses. Today, while you can still choose DVD as a format for some materials, the online market has exploded, with live streaming courses, on-demand courses that you can view at any time, and text-based online courses with no audio or video. Add in mobile apps for phones and other devices, and learning can definitely take place on the go. As you browse the nearly limitless offerings, you can take your pick of formats, providers, price ranges, and styles of content. Obviously, online educational possibilities will only continue to change and expand, and just as obviously, this section of the book will be out of date before it is printed. Use the following information—which barely scratches the surface—as a general overview and an idea-sparker. Then do your own research to find the right approach that is customized to your student's needs and makes use of the resources out there right now.

Online Courses

As mentioned above, the internet is a great boon to homeschooling, for students now have access to just about every educational tidbit on the planet. And as we all know, many businesses have jumped into the action by providing online courses for students who want to study from home. Online courses are attractive for various reasons. First, the teacher is educated in the subject being presented and can bring in facts and ideas to which the parent or student may not have access. Additionally, the teachers are skilled at presenting the lesson in an engaging way (of course, this will vary with the course and teacher). Some online courses are live, providing the opportunity to interact with the instructor and the other students. For these, the student needs to be available for class at that particular time. Other courses offer on-demand or download formats, giving the advantage of versatility with respect to time. Your student has the benefit of an hour's worth of teaching at any convenient time of the day.

Typically, these courses involve students receiving assignments from a teacher, turning them in electronically, and logging on at certain times for live class sessions, if applicable. To communicate the lesson material, interactive class sessions may use audio, video, platforms such as Skype, text chat, slide presentations, virtual "whiteboards," or a variety of other technological innovations. Advantages include having access and accountability to an instructor with expertise in the field while still enjoying a flexible time schedule for learning at home—in the proverbial pajamas, if desired. Disadvantages may include falling behind if technical difficulties occur or if the family's schedule does not mesh with the instructor's, in the case of a live class. Also, online teachers, like any other teachers, can be good, bad, or mediocre. Overall, these courses can help the student learn accountability to an outside teacher while still facilitating the learning from the home base.

Note that with some online providers, lab science courses may not have arrangements for "real" wet labs. Instead, they may use virtual experiments or have the student simply view the experiment as the instructor performs it. This may not be enough lab experience for science-minded students and, more importantly, may not be acceptable for lab science credit at college application time. Be sure to check the arrangements for laboratory science and correlate these with requirements for colleges of interest.

A few familiar names in online course providers include the following: Pennsylvania Homeschoolers (http://www.pahomeschoolers.com/), The Potter's School (https://at-tps.org/), Escondido Tutorial (http://www.gbt.org/), Schola Classical Tutorials (http://scholatutorials.org), and Apex Learning® digital curriculum (https://www.apexlearning.com/). Since new online courses and schools are constantly springing up, search online, gather recommendations from fellow homeschoolers, and check providers carefully before signing up, especially if you are contemplating an expensive program or a critical subject or course.

Online High Schools

In addition to stand-alone online courses, entire online high schools are another option—either full-time accredited diploma-granting programs, or part-time course-by-course options. A few of the hundreds of programs available are Laurel Springs School, Northstar Academy, Stanford Online High School, Keystone National High School, and Liberty University Online Academy. Programs vary in the level of course rigor, as well as in the target audience of students. For instance, Stanford Online High School is designed for gifted students, and some of the courses are taught at the university level. The Stanford program, as well as other online high schools, may also offer regional in-person meetups, online and in-person events, summer residential programs, clubs, and other extracurriculars. Do your due diligence as you check into these programs, and be sure to read reviews from other families.

DVD Content

In these days of online content, streaming, and downloads, the humble DVD may seem to be a relic of the past, but families often have good reasons for using DVD-based content for a portion of their studies. DVDs can still be your friend and your faithful teaching assistant. If a lack of time or knowledge is a disadvantage in some of your homeschool subjects, a video course can fill the gap nicely. For example, one popular publisher, Abeka®, offers courses with a choice of DVD or streaming, through its Abeka Academy® (http://www.abeka.com/abekaacademy/). The daily lessons are completed using Abeka's textbooks. Accredited by the Florida Association of Christian Colleges and Schools, Abeka Academy offers report cards, a transcript, and a high school diploma upon graduation from this program. You would need to check with your state educational laws to make sure that this arrangement is valid in your state (if this is important to you or if it is needed for college admission). Students could also choose to take just a few courses from this program or could opt not to use the record keeping and diploma option.

Individual DVD courses are also available through vendors such as The Great Courses (website https://www.thegreatcourses.com/). This company offers courses in literature, history, music and art appreciation, business, economics, religion, philosophy, and other intriguing topics. Students may benefit from a helpful geometry course, delve into the life and writings of C.S. Lewis, or pursue a study of argumentation and reasoning. History and literature courses from this company could easily form the backbone of your own custom-designed course at home. They are not true "courses," in that they do not include tests, quizzes, or other evaluation resources, but many of them do come with a course guidebook including an outline of the topics, a list of suggested readings, and other helps. If you used a resource such as this, you would design your own evaluation methods to assess your student's grasp of the material. For some courses, this company also offers audio-only formats, if this is of interest to you.

Many other curriculum companies offer DVD-based courses, and these can help students who need both visual and auditory input as they learn. For instance, as mentioned in the previous chapter, the Institute for Excellence in Writing, through Andrew Pudewa's courses such as the *Student Writing Intensive*, *High School Essay Intensive*, and *Advanced Communication Series*, provides practical, focused instruction in essay writing at various skill levels. From this same company, a literature analysis course called *Teaching the Classics* by Adam and Missy Andrews is available. This program is an excellent way to acquaint students with the art of literary analysis, including plot, conflict, setting, character, and theme. These might not necessarily serve as stand-alone English courses, but they could be used as supplements or as significant elements of a course you are designing.

OpenCourseWare and MOOCs

Another useful trend, OpenCourseWare (OCW), provides an exciting way to find free university-level course content online. Students can access content from a wide variety of courses and can study at their own pace, though they will not receive credit or certification and will not meet or interact with faculty. One example (and the first OCW in the U.S.) is MIT's OpenCourseWare project, a free and open resource for students, teachers, and anyone interested in accessing the courses taught at MIT. You can browse courses from any department or subject and view or download the course syllabus, lists of readings, lecture notes, quizzes, exams, and, in some cases, solutions. Realizing that these courses are taught at the university level, you can tailor them to your older high schooler and use them as frameworks, supplements, or full courses. Because the material is available as a resource only, no grades, accountability, or college credit is given. Other institutions, such as Carnegie Mellon, University of California Berkeley, Princeton, Stanford, Yale, Harvard, Johns Hopkins, and many other universities, followed MIT's example and also offer OCWs.

Going a step beyond OCWs, you can look into MOOCs: massive open online courses. MIT and Harvard led the way in 2012 by creating the edX™ platform, but many others have sprung up since then. Whereas OCWs offer access to the course materials, MOOCs actually allow open, free (or very low cost)enrollment and may offer credit upon completion, after the student takes supervised exams. Additionally, MOOCs offer student-to-student and student-to-instructor interaction in online forums. MOOCs are more structured than OCWs but less structured than online college courses, and the "on-demand" courses allow flexibility for the student's schedule. Course content is presented via some combination of the following: video lectures, other media, course reading material, forums for discussion and questions, assigned projects, and final exams or projects evaluated on a pass/fail basis. Assignments are usually graded by computerized graders and/or peers in the class, not by professors or faculty. In addition to edX, other top-rated MOOC platforms include Coursera®, Udacity®, FutureLearn™, and iversity®. The opportunity to take a college course and explore a particular subject area and potential major without an investment of cash is extremely attractive, so be sure to check out these options.

Even More Tech-Based Educational Helps

Whether your screen of choice is a laptop, a tablet, a smartphone, a traditional desktop, or another gadget invented five minutes after this book is published, you can find a wide variety of content for your homeschooling. In addition to using the online courses described above and in the previous chapter, families can seek out websites and programs to meet specific homeschool needs, while enjoying much flexibility and customizability. Math programs can act as an entire curriculum or simply as an interactive tool to help the student brush up on necessary skills. Foreign language programs can take the place of a classroom teacher and provide the proper native speaker's accent and pronunciation.

One example is Alpha Omega Publications' computer-based curriculum called Switched-On Schoolhouse® (https://www.aop.com/). This program takes the traditional workbook or LIFEPAC® unit, (the form in which Alpha Omega Publications' main curriculum is sold), and places it in an interactive, colorful form on the computer. Courses are available in all core subjects and in a variety of electives.

The Rosetta Stone language program, introduced in the previous chapter, offers instruction in a huge variety of languages and covers speaking, listening, reading, vocabulary and spelling skills. The option called Rosetta Stone Homeschool provides a convenient way to accomplish two to four years of language instruction and provides parent administrative tools to help in organizing lesson plans, setting goals, and monitoring student progress.

As discussed in Chapter 4, DIVE (Digital Interactive Video Education) can provide help with Saxon Publishers' mathematics curriculum and several other publishers' science curricula. These helpful resources use technology to display math and science lectures on a computer whiteboard that simulates a lecture in a classroom. DIVE lessons are available for Shormann Math, Saxon Math, and Saxon Physics, as well as offering courses for earth science, biology, chemistry, and physics as prep for AP or CLEP® exams.

A Few Pieces of Advice

With a little searching, you can find the digital tools you need to augment your high school program. Because this genre is rapidly growing and constantly changing, any list of resources becomes obsolete almost immediately. So, when you need help, go on a search and ask some experienced friends (either in person or online) which programs or websites they recommend. Always evaluate these providers and courses with respect to your own needs and goals. If your high school courses need to be College Board-approved AP courses or state university-approved college prep courses, perform due diligence and check these attributes. Read reviews of courses before buying them, especially if they will serve as your primary course content for a particular subject. See if you can access a sample lesson and evaluate it alongside your student, gauging how engaging, clear, and informative the course is. Assess the workload (hours per week) the course will entail and make sure this is acceptable to you and to your student. Through reviews or through comments from friends, seek to ascertain how responsive the teachers are to the student: will they promptly answer students' questions, give constructive feedback, and grade work in a timely manner? Also realize that online teachers vary in quality just as face-to-face teachers do. So the fact that your homeschooling friend appreciated a particular online provider in one subject with Teacher A doesn't mean that your student will have the same outstanding experience in a different subject, or with Teacher B. Finally, investigate the level of tech support so that you can be up and running promptly even if you encounter glitches.

The listing of providers, sites, and programs here or elsewhere in this book is not a guarantee or indication of quality, nor is it intended to be an endorsement or approval of the program. These options will also vary widely in course rigor and suitability for higher academic levels. But these ideas will at least get you started.

Providers of online courses in one or several subjects:

PA Homeschoolers® – *http://www.pahomeschoolers.com/* or *http://www.aphomeschoolers.com/*. Offers a full slate of AP courses. PA Homeschoolers' courses receive high reviews from students and received a top mention from PrepScholar, a widely respected source for advice on college prep issues.

The Potter's School – *https://www.pottersschool.org/* or *https://at-tps.org/*. Live online courses, both AP and regular college prep, in all academic subjects. Biblical worldview; teacher feedback on student's performance; high school transcript option available through The Potter's School Online Homeschool Academy.

HSLDA Online Academy – *https://academy.hslda.org/*. Rigorous courses, both AP and non-AP, in a spectrum of subject areas. Courses are taught from a Christian perspective, and teachers provide weekly live online lessons, while course materials such as readings, lectures, and study materials can be accessed 24/7.

Florida Virtual School® – *https://www.flvs.net/online-courses/advanced-placement*. Praised for affordability, comprehensive exam preparation, quality of courses (with a couple of exceptions), and straightforward admissions process with no test scores or prerequisites required. Courses are free to Florida residents.

Scholars Online – *https://www.scholarsonline.org/*. Classical Christian academy offering online courses in a variety of classical subject areas. Committed to providing rigorous college prep courses to homeschoolers; course grades assigned by teachers if these are needed or requested by parents.

The Lukeion Project – *https://www.lukeion.org/*. Online courses offered by a husband/wife team of Christian archaeologists, along with a teaching faculty. Live weekly courses cover classical languages, philosophy, literature, writing, and more.

UC Scout – *https://www.ucscout.org/*. Delivers University of California-approved college prep courses to students around the globe. In the "On Demand" option, students can progress through the courses at their own pace.

Khan Academy – *https://www.khanacademy.org/*. Excellent source of free resources! Provides videos, tutorial articles, practice problems, unit tests, and other helps for numerous levels of math extending to college level, as well as science, humanities, computing, economics, SAT prep, and more (including AP-level study aids for several courses). Self-paced, self-directed online work (not actual College Board-approved AP courses, but a useful source of solid test prep if you are not concerned about listing an AP course on your transcript). Career and college planning articles are also presented on this site.

Blue Tent Online – *https://www.bluetentonline.com/*. English (including AP) and science courses, mostly on asynchronous schedules, allowing students to view classes and complete assignments according to their own timelines.

Virtual Homeschool Group – *http://www.virtualhomeschoolgroup.org/*. Network of homeschooling families offering free courses (volunteer-based and donation-supported). "By homeschoolers, for homeschoolers" – some live courses and some at your own pace.

Study.com® – *https://study.com/*. Thousands of instructional video courses, homework helps, and tutorials, as well as SAT, ACT, AP, and CLEP test prep materials. Plans and pricing include Basic, Premium, and College Accelerator levels of membership, required to access the videos and study materials.

Veritas® – *https://www.veritaspress.com/*. Choice of live online courses or self-paced courses in classical subjects from a Christian perspective.

School Yourself – *https://schoolyourself.org/*. Free online math courses utilizing short videos to review concepts.

AIM Academy – *https://debrabell.com*. Online courses in core academic areas as well as SAT exam prep. Some courses are live; others, self-paced. One highly praised course from a family I know is the "Novel in a Year" course, which guides students in the process of writing a twenty-chapter novel in one year. Students receive detailed feedback and critique from the teacher, a published author. Also take a look at Debra Bell's beautiful and practical homeschool planner, "The Ultimate Homeschool Planner." More than just a calendar, this planner incorporates student and family goal setting, character achievements, prayer reminders, places to record memorable moments and evidences of grace, and other unique features.

Sites with helpful resources and practical "extras" for particular subjects:

DonnaYoung.org – *http://donnayoung.org/*. Printables for a variety of homeschooling applications: science, lesson planning, art, English, and more.

BrainPOP® – *https://www.brainpop.com/*. Colorful, entertaining videos, animations, and quizzes on a huge variety of topics. Though the format appears to be geared to younger students, the content (diffusion, active transport, probability) is applicable to high school subjects.

CurrClick – *http://www.currclick.com/*. Downloadable curriculum and resources in a variety of formats and subjects (not free, but quick!). CurrClick also offers some online courses.

Quizlet® – *https://quizlet.com/*. Free flashcards, quizzes, and learning games on a whole host of topics—or use this site to create your own.

My Audio School – *http://myaudioschool.com/*. A collection of audio recordings of classic books, old-time radio theater, historical radio and TV broadcasts, great speeches, and more.

ClickSchooling® – *http://clickschooling.com/*. Subscribe (free) to get daily emails containing a web-based curriculum or learning idea to put into practice with your students (Monday math, Tuesday science, Wednesday language arts, Thursday social science, Friday virtual field trip, Saturday music, art, and foreign languages). You can also explore the archives of each of these topics to see the learning ideas, such as a virtual tour along the Oregon Trail.

HippoCampus.org® – *https://www.hippocampus.org/*. Free mini-lectures, short videos, animations, and other helpful resources for a variety of subjects: math, science, social science, humanities.

Sites offering blogs, forums, training, or other sources of advice and insights for parents and/or students:

PrepScholar – *https://blog.prepscholar.com*. This is one of my favorite sites for college prep advice (OK, probably *the* favorite). Articles are all well-researched and spot-on, with great advice for SAT, ACT, and AP prep, as well as for many aspects of the college search and the college prep pathway in general. Besides practical, step-by-step advice for studying for the SAT or ACT exams, you'll find sample timed essay prompts, tutorials on how to write the essays, and suggested study schedules. A sampling of articles from blog posts includes "113 Great Research Paper Topics," "Nurse Practitioner School: How Long Is It? What Do You Learn?" and "ACT vs. SAT: 11 Key Differences to Help You Pick the Right Test."

Well-Trained Mind Forums – *https://forums.welltrainedmind.com/*. Many of my searches for college prep homeschool issues land me squarely within posts and discussions in this community. It's helpful, heartening, and "grounding" to read posts from other parents who have asked and received answers to the same questions you are dealing with. Quite a few of these discussions deal with high-achieving or gifted students and how to accommodate advanced academics. In particular, take a look at the High School and Home Education Board.

The HomeScholar – *https://www.homehighschoolhelp.com/*. Veteran homeschooling mom Lee Binz offers a wealth of resources: informative blog posts, lists of freebies to make your day, and items for purchase including her *Total Transcript Solution* to make your high school record keeping both professional-looking *and* a breeze.

Weird Unsocialized Homeschoolers – *https://www.weirdunsocializedhomeschoolers.com*. Despite the cringe-worthy title, you will love the fact that this site is quirky, fun, and very, very real, offering a refreshing mix of comic relief and practical insight on the subjects we all puzzle and ponder about.

Private or Group Tutoring or Lessons

OK, screen time has reached its limit, and now we will get off the computer for a moment! For some subjects, the most sensible approach might be to find an expert in the field to give your student private tutoring or lessons. In the fine arts, for instance, a student could benefit from the constant training and accountability provided by an expert instructor. But for subjects such as math, languages, or writing, personal tutoring can also work well if the family can afford it. After finding an appropriate tutor, select convenient times and locations for the lessons and set objectives you would like to see met. To cut down on the cost, several families might go together to hire a math or foreign language tutor to work with a group of students. Instructors need not be "professional" teachers; they may be homeschool parents with expertise in that subject, or simply with the willingness to dive in and study the subject.

Nationwide Academy Programs

Some families (albeit a minority) desire the convenience and confidence of signing up with a single program that will administer the high school record keeping and issue an accredited high school diploma at the end. A few of these programs are Alpha Omega Academy®, Abeka Academy, Calvert® Education Services, and Lighthouse Christian Academy. The HSLDA website can also help as you search for correspondence schools and distance learning sources. When browsing programs, check for the rigor of the courses, particularly mathematics, languages, and lab science, to assess whether your student will receive adequate preparation for college. Before enrolling in a full high school program, make sure that you will be able to get all the college prep courses your student will need—or if not, that you can out-source a few courses and have them added to the official transcript.

Test Preparation Books

For some subjects, preparation books for standardized tests can serve as a good supplement or even a basic skeleton of a homeschool course. For instance, if your student is studying for an Advanced Placement exam, test prep books can supplement the primary textbook and highlight the most important concepts to know. (See Chapter 12 for specific requirements for College Board-approved AP courses if you wish to list them as such on your transcript.)

Readily available online and in bookstores, prep books such as those for the SAT and ACT exam can be a worthwhile supplement to an English and math program. In addition to reviewing key elements of high school math and providing practice with critical reading and language arts skills, these books can be used to diagnose weaknesses in preparation for further study.

The Public Library

Even with the plethora of resources available online, you don't want to overlook a significant free resource: your local library. In addition to offering novels, poetry, and historical fiction for literature and history courses, or biographies and nonfiction for research papers, the library holds a wealth of other resources. Travel videos will enhance your geography or history courses, while children's books in foreign languages (whether print or audio) will inject some fun into the daily drill of language study. Art books will bring philosophical trends of a historical era to life. If your library has a large collection of DVDs, you can supplement any course with well-chosen films to illustrate historical events or dramatize classic works of literature. Even for materials you will eventually buy, such as test prep books, the library allows you to review several versions of the same subject so that you can select the best book for your needs.

With the convenience of library websites and inter-library loan programs, you can reserve materials with a couple of clicks and do not need to leave the house until it's time to go pick them up. If you are not into visiting the physical library for print books, check out your library system's offerings of e-books. These are delivered automatically to your device, and they conveniently disappear on the due date. (Of course, print books also seem to disappear on the due date, but that's another story.)

Your Own Books ... Or Useful Book Purchases

As we all know, the excellent materials we want to own can usually be purchased "pre-owned" for just a few dollars. Become a frequent browser on Amazon or your favorite used book site—also be on the lookout for educator discounts, either online or at brick-and-mortar bookstores. Keep in mind that you can also look for used textbooks for community college courses. Just be sure to buy the proper book: if the edition is important, be careful about ISBN numbers.

And remember to scour your own bookshelves at home. You may discover just the right collection of books to provide the raw materials for an interesting and useful course.

Encourage your student to become a bibliophile, collecting favorite books for a personal library that may eventually follow him or her across the country to college and career sites. And if packing and dragging boxes of books is not appealing, he or she can become a collector of free classic books (and other inexpensive finds) for the Kindle® e-reader or another e-reader.

Career-Based Continuing Education Courses for Home Study

Parents whose career fields require refresher courses may find a source of curriculum in a most surprising place: career-related continuing education courses. Certain fields may offer online courses that would be basic enough for a motivated and interested high schooler. For example, my background is in the hospital laboratory as a clinical laboratory scientist. From time to time, I receive fliers for courses in basic microbiology, HIV/AIDS, and other topics that would make interesting unit studies within a broader biology or health course. While some of these courses would be beyond a high schooler's level, others are written as a quick "crash course" and would be perfect for a bright, motivated high schooler.

Unschooling

With unschooling, or interest-directed learning, students follow their interests and construct their own learning paths. This approach often uses little formal instruction and can be tricky to document for a college application. Use unschooling with caution, but don't shy away from it if you know it is the best choice for your student and if your student's unique skills, strengths, and creativity can shine strongly through this approach. Do make sure that your student completes foundational instruction in mathematics and that you as a parent/student team can document or describe learning activities in all the required subjects such as sciences, English, and social studies. Approached with creativity and appropriate depth, unschooling can be an attention-getting option.

Combination Approaches

Why force yourself to choose just one educational approach? An effective and popular option for homeschoolers is to combine several of the above ideas into a customized method of learning. For instance, your math course might use traditional textbooks, history might use unit studies, and fine arts might use the unschooling or interest-directed approach. Or you may decide to incorporate a few elements from each approach into a given course. A science course could be primarily textbook-based while incorporating a unit study project as well as a student-led, interest-directed study on a particularly intriguing topic. Have fun with this approach!

HOMESCHOOL GROUP-BASED OPTIONS

Notice that the previous ideas for curriculum were *all* options that could be undertaken entirely at home. Only now do we begin to step outside your front door—but first, into the relatively comfortable zone of proximity to other homeschoolers.

Homeschool Academies, Co-ops, or Group Classes

Simply defined, a homeschool co-op is a group of families who come together to provide one or more courses for their students. Some co-ops are offered for a wide range of ages—preschool through middle school or high school. Others focus on high school students. In informal co-ops, parents agree to teach one or more courses in exchange for their student(s) being taught by other parent/teachers in the co-op. Sometimes outside teachers are brought in to teach a subject. Parent/teachers may be paid by the students' families or may be volunteers. Homeschool academies that operate with more structure use a consistent staff of teachers, and the arrangement likely involves tuition and registration fees, more rigid schedules, and other "bells and whistles."

Academies and co-ops typically meet one to three times per week, and students complete assignments at home before the next meeting date. If a group is large, it will frequently have the benefit of "expert" parents or teachers who can teach within their specialties.

Group classes allow students to learn in a community setting, which can be an excellent venue for discussion, science experiments, and other cooperative forms of learning. The group may also be able to purchase equipment such as microscopes or pricier sets of curriculum and supplies, to be shared among the group. Many students and families find that they become close friends with their classmates, providing a social element to homeschooling. If interest and size allow, these groups may give rise to extracurricular activities such as a student newspaper, field trips, theater productions, or occasional guest speakers teaching in their fields of expertise.

If you don't have a group option already, it may be easy to start one. If you have access to a potential pool of middle school and high school age students, tap into the expertise of the parents—perhaps scheduling some of the classes so that even working parents can do some teaching in their career fields or areas of education. Recruit one parent to teach math, one to teach literature or writing, and one to teach science, with lab fees sufficient to purchase necessary equipment. These group experiences can be the ideal link between home and the "outside world" for high schoolers who need a more advanced course and are interested in cooperative learning. Cooperative arrangements may run for just one year, or they may thrive for many years in your community. For instance, I have taught high school biology, literature, and writing for thirteen years at a large homeschool academy that meets once a week to serve elementary through high school students. On the more temporary side, I have taught seven or eight "stand-alone" courses that met at a church or in a private home and ran for only a year at a time.

Homeschool ISP or PSP Classes

If you belong to a homeschool independent study program (ISP) or private school satellite program (PSP) that offers courses, or if a program near you offers classes to non-members, you have another excellent resource. Again, "strength in numbers" means that the more people your group contains, the greater are your chances that several families are looking for the same type of course. And if your PSP administrator or other designated teacher is willing to organize courses, this effort can result in a good course with a reasonable fee. Lab science, math, and discussion-based English or history classes readily lend themselves to being offered through a PSP, but almost any course will work.

In some communities, full-fledged "schools" oriented for homeschoolers meet two or three days per week and offer a full lineup of courses for all grades. Parents supervise the learning at home on the off days. For families who prefer not to handle the full responsibility of high school, perhaps because of younger children in the family, these arrangements can be an attractive option. Ask around to find out if such a program exists in your locale.

Independent Study Programs Associated with a Private Day School

Some independent study programs are actually satellite programs of "brick-and-mortar" private schools, either Christian or nonsectarian. Here, your student can enjoy a home-based, home-directed education, while also having access to classes, sports, and other activities offered by the day school. It is worth checking around to find out whether any private schools near you open their courses to homeschoolers.

Discussion Groups or Study Groups

Similar to co-ops or group academies, but more loosely organized and potentially more temporary, discussion groups can be formed around a particular focus of study, such as American literature.

Especially where multiple viewpoints are involved, these groups can prepare high schoolers for discussion-oriented courses in college. Hearing the thoughts of others can spark their own ideas and make essay writing easier. Defending these ideas provides experience in exercising valid reasoning.

To start a discussion group, advertise among students who might be studying the same subject and who could take advantage of your group. The group need not be limited to students; a few adults might like to join in. Just be sure that the students, especially those who might be a little more reserved, get plenty of opportunity to speak up without feeling intimidated by the adults.

Competitions and Contests

How about a little healthy competition? Local or nationwide competitions can be a stimulating way for your student to learn, either individually or as part of a team. For example, the MATHCOUNTS competition and MOEMS (Math Olympiads), both for middle schoolers, or the American Mathematics Competitions for middle and high schoolers, are ideal for students strong in math. The Scripps National Spelling Bee®, local robotics contests, science fairs and competitions, and essay and poetry contests, such as those sponsored by HSLDA, may attract a student who wants to take an interest to the next level.

Student-Designed Courses

There's no reason why your student can't create, design, administer, and *teach* a course. An eleventh or twelfth grader with strong interests and abilities to share might be inspired to design a course to simultaneously take and teach. With the flexibility of homeschooling, no rule states that one can't be both a teacher and a student at the same time. And as you might imagine, a course like this would look impressive on your student's college application.

Julie did this successfully with a Shakespeare course. After choosing a study guide, deciding on eight plays to delve into, selecting a set of video lectures from The Great Courses, and finding supplementary material online, she planned a Shakespeare course during her eleventh grade year. The extra element of teaching this material to a group of nine or ten students ranging from eighth through twelfth grade made this an especially beneficial learning experience.

COMMUNITY-BASED OPTIONS

Venturing into your local non-homeschool community, you can find many ideal solutions to your course design dilemmas. Here are a few possibilities:

Community Center Courses

Whether you are looking for a tennis class for P.E., a watercolor class for fine arts, a basic keyboard class for music, or a technology class for computer skills, your local community center may offer just what you are looking for at bargain rates. The YMCA®, in addition to featuring fitness programs, may also offer courses on babysitting skills, health and nutrition, or other practical skills. Each of these could potentially form a mini-course or a portion of a larger course. Since course content will vary from community to community, ask around to discover the quality and availability of these courses. Then determine whether the time spent in the course will be worthwhile and will give you the results you need.

Adult Education Courses

Similarly, your local high school, or some other community organization, may offer night classes. While these are geared for adults rather than for teens, it wouldn't hurt to ask the administrators if your student might enroll. It's possible that as long as space is available and all the interested adults have already signed up, instructors may allow a younger person to enroll or to audit the class, perhaps with a parent present.

Courses Held at Churches

Churches sometimes offer classes—either geared to homeschoolers, or geared to any interested individual—which can be of use in your course lineup. Obviously, the faith-based courses would be helpful for your Bible and elective requirements, but other classes may be offered, such as art, music (church choir or orchestra), book discussions, fitness, sports, or even science. For several years, our church sponsored a weekly homeschool science class for elementary age children, which took place during the women's Bible study. Younger students were enrolled in the course, while older students took an active role in serving as teaching assistants. You might be able to get a similar class going at your church that would specifically benefit older students.

Community Clubs and Groups

Other organizations in your community might present knowledge and information your high schooler can use. For example, perhaps a gardening club is presenting a series of lectures on plants native to your area, or an art store is offering drawing lessons. In many communities, Toastmasters groups meet regularly to teach and encourage members in the art of public speaking and may offer a Youth Leadership Program for teens. Elsewhere in your city, you might find courses in first aid, emergency preparedness, or local history. Consider becoming members of any museums in your area—and hunt up educator discounts while you're at it. Use your creativity and brainstorming abilities to put together courses or portions of courses from community opportunities.

"Circles"

Though these programs may exist for various subjects, I am most familiar with science and math circles: outreach programs sponsored by universities and designed for elementary, middle school, or high school students. Mathematicians or scientists lead the group and introduce creative, challenging, and intriguing topics and problems that would not be encountered in an ordinary curriculum. An admission process is involved, and tuition is charged each term, but these programs can serve as a supplement to your curriculum and as a motivator to a high schooler who is passionate about science or math. Moreover, your student may meet a guest lecturer, facilitator, or other expert involved in the program and make a connection for further study, mentorship, or research opportunities.

TRADITIONAL SCHOOL-BASED OPTIONS

Private or Public High Schools

With the advent of homeschooling, more and more traditional private brick-and-mortar schools—and sometimes even public schools—are offering programs for homeschoolers who want to take a few courses. If this is of interest to you, check with your local high school to see about making arrangements for one or two strategic courses. Whether this be precalculus, AP English, a world language, or a P.E. course, you can choose a subject that would be difficult for you to teach at home. Private school tuition is generally prorated for part-time students. For public schools, inquire with the school district to find out whether homeschoolers are allowed to enroll on a part-time basis.

Most states have seen the development of publicly funded charter schools, which may be operated through live classrooms, online education, or some other flexible arrangement. Though the prospect of home-based charter schools can be tempting, especially when the school covers costs of books and supplies, recognize that these schools are actually another arm of the public school system. As you consider whether to join public school programs or publicly funded charter schools, make sure that you understand all expectations. You might be subject to accountability checks, teacher oversight, mandatory testing, or limitations on your choice of curriculum, especially religiously-based curriculum. With some charter schools, curricular choices are limited with respect to honors and advanced courses, as well.

Community Colleges

Community colleges offer one popular way for homeschoolers to get some courses out of the way and to gain additional credibility for their transcripts. Lab science, math, and world languages are some of the more common courses that high schoolers take at college. While regulations vary from state to state, these "dual enrollment" classes will probably count for both high school and college credit, and thus the student may enter the four-year college with some transfer credit. Though you will need to decide when your student will be mature enough to take courses, you may be pleasantly surprised at how he or she rises to the occasion and, in many cases, rises to the top of the class as well. Taking community college classes is also a good way to gather teacher recommendations that will be needed for college applications. Chapters 13 and 14 provide more information about navigating the community college system.

Summer University Programs

Some universities offer summer programs to gifted high school or middle school students. The Center for Talented Youth (CTY), sponsored by Johns Hopkins University, holds residential summer programs at several universities throughout the nation, as well as offering online courses during the school year. These programs cover a wide variety of subjects and interests, and, while not for everyone's budget, could be an element of your high school course of study. Boston University's Tanglewood Institute provides advanced music education for young, talented performers (singers, instrumentalists, and composers) through its summer programs for high school musicians, similar to what Interlochen Center for the Arts in Michigan does for students interested in music, theater, or visual arts. For budding scientists and engineers, the Research Science Institute (RSI), sponsored by the Center for Excellence in Education® and by MIT, provides research experience for talented high school students. The Duke Talent Identification Program (TIP) and similar regional programs offer a spectrum of programs during the summer and throughout the year for talented youth. Again, since most of these programs are expensive, you will want to seek out courses that fit within your family's budget. Also, qualifying credentials may include taking the SAT or ACT exams earlier than your student may have planned, so if you have high interest in these programs, check into them early.

In addition to these programs catering to gifted students, many colleges offer summer "bridge to college" programs, usually for students who have completed tenth or eleventh grades. Colleges benefit because more students apply to a given college after attending its summer program. Students benefit because they receive a taste of the demands of college-level coursework as well as an idea of what it is like to live on campus. Courses offered in the summer may be mini-courses or full-fledged courses awarding college credit. Others may focus on high school topics such as intensive math review or SAT preparation. Investigate your local colleges and universities to see if any of their programs would be useful additions to your student's course lineup.

"HYBRID" OPTIONS

Some solutions to the course design puzzle are neither fully home-based nor fully school-based. Just as hybrid autos help drivers make the most of limited fuel resources, hybrid school options help families make the most of their educational resources without feeling compelled to put their students in school full time.

Tutorial Businesses

In our community, and undoubtedly in others as well, educational businesses provide individualized tutoring and academic courses. Frequently, but not always, these focus on honors and AP courses. These tutorial businesses cater both to homeschoolers and to traditional students who do not have certain courses available to them, or who may have scheduling difficulties. Classes may be offered one to three days per week, leaving time for homeschoolers to pursue their other studies and activities. As you check into these options, ask lots of questions to assess the background of the teachers and administrators, to investigate how the courses are taught, and to determine if this option is right for your student. Some of these programs offer classes in drama or music, with the goal of putting together a musical production. For students who lack opportunities in these areas, this can be a source of a valuable extracurricular activity.

Retired or Part-Time Teachers

A good teacher enjoys teaching even when he or she is no longer pursuing it full time. Keep your ears open for names of high school teachers who are retired, who have temporarily stepped away from full-time teaching—for instance, to raise young children—or who have dropped to part-time hours either by choice or because of school budget cuts. Any of these might be willing to offer private or group tutoring for a reasonable fee and would probably enjoy the challenge of teaching in a nontraditional setting.

Assistance from a Classroom Teacher

Sometimes all you need to get going with a course is a little advice from a seasoned teacher. If you already have a friend or relative who is a high school teacher, perhaps he or she can put you in touch with a fellow teacher of the appropriate subject. If not, take a deep breath, contact your local public or private school, and ask to leave a message or send an email to a teacher in your particular department of interest. Make your call or email polite, friendly, brief, and to the point. Introduce yourself as a homeschooling parent and ask a specific question. For example, say, "Would you please recommend some good literature resources for a sophomore level honors English course and provide some tips on what types of assignments to give?" As the conversation progresses, you will discern whether this teacher is interested in helping you further. You might find that the teacher is willing to sit down with you and give you more advice —perhaps even letting you borrow some books or study guides. Teachers who are passionate about teaching are often quite excited to meet a homeschooling family who loves to learn. As a result, they may go out of their way to help you. But if not, don't force the issue. Teachers are busy people!

If the teacher seems genuinely willing to help, you might ask to see a copy of his or her syllabus or course outline. This document will list the texts and resources used, outline major units of study for the year, list assignments such as papers, projects, and speeches, and possibly provide a grading scale. The tips and ideas gleaned from teachers' syllabi can jump-start your own planning and customization of the course.

During our homeschool journey, we greatly appreciated the help we received from the local Christian high school. The head of the English department spent about an hour with me and gave me syllabi for all four years of English. The AP European History teacher took such an interest in us that he spent two one-hour sessions with us, shared his syllabus and other useful notes, allowed us to borrow some textbooks, recommended a useful teacher training workshop, and included Julie in several review sessions during the year. We were absolutely amazed—and extremely grateful.

If you do receive significant help from schoolteachers, do not abuse the privilege. Be respectful of their time, be prompt for appointments, and take meticulous care of any resources they lend you. Additionally, be appropriate and respectful in how you share this information with other homeschoolers. If it is fine with the teacher, it is better to share the tips he or she has given you than to refer every homeschooling friend to this teacher to ask the same questions over and over again. Be as professional and considerate as you can, remembering that you represent all homeschoolers.

One note on the tips mentioned above: *always* do your "homework" first by researching your particular subject online, seeking out sample high school course syllabi, and finding lists of commonly used textbooks and resource materials. Obviously, the web is rich with helpful ideas, and there is no need to burden a classroom teacher with questions for which you could easily find answers on your own.

"Phone a Friend"

Often the lifeline the student needs in a tough course is simply the knowledge that a friend, tutor, or other well-educated helper is just around the corner in case of difficulty. Before beginning some of the more complicated high school courses, identify an "expert" relative or friend and ask permission to call on him or her for help with rough spots during the year. If this is not an option, try to identify a tutor who comes well-recommended by other families. Although your student may not need help every week, it's good to know where to turn when difficulties arise and the student has exhausted all the help in your own household.

This "phone a friend" arrangement can be an alternative to a full-fledged co-op arrangement. Your friend or acquaintance might teach your student on a regular basis or just occasionally. You might, in turn, help that family with another subject (if they homeschool) or help them in some other way. This friend might be a current teacher, a retired or former teacher, or simply someone who has studied that subject and is proficient at it.

OTHER TRICKS OF THE TRADE

Especially if you use many home-based options in your curriculum choices, be sure that your choice of materials will help and not hinder your student's progress. Here are a few things to consider.

Math textbooks that come with solutions manuals are worth their weight in gold. This way, you can see the full process of solving a problem, not simply the correct answer.

Additionally, try to collect inexpensive extra textbooks or workbooks for subjects you're studying. You will use only one as the main text, but it can be helpful to see other ways to explain a topic, other methods to solve a problem, or other viewpoints on a historical perspective. Accessing additional resources can enrich your student's experience if he or she can consult them on an occasional basis, such as when working on projects or research assignments. Collect these items at used curriculum sales, at garage sales, from friends, or even from library discards. Of course, there's always the entire internet available for help and resources, but books still have their place for "unplugged" times of study and research.

As you design courses, use your creativity. Don't stop with just locating a textbook or signing your student up for an outside class. Recognize that you can enhance your student's educational experience by mixing and matching to achieve a rich and varied approach to the subject. Find interesting books to supplement the textbook. Seek out fascinating documentaries, detail-rich websites, and pertinent magazine articles. Assign your student to interview an expert, create a movie, build a 3-D model, organize a group activity, or plan and carry out a key lab project relating to the subject. Be on the lookout for interesting field trips and tours, local speakers, and other "real life" applications of the material being studied. The possibilities are endless. As a homeschooler, you have the schedule flexibility to pursue some of these activities that would be logistical challenges for students in traditional schools. If you embrace the opportunity to use diverse teaching methods, both you and your student will benefit.

TO SUM UP

As you ponder high school courses, open your mind to the possibilities that will make your student's education deep and exciting. The pursuit of a variety of educational approaches can turn your student on to one or more interests, and it is these areas of passion that will catch the eye of a college admissions officer. So go ahead and enjoy putting together a nutritious *and* delicious "meal" from the smorgasbord of educational opportunities available to you in your home and your community.

Chapter 6

Putting It All Together:

More Tips and Sample Four-Year Plans

Now that you've taken a tour of the high school subjects you might want to offer and have explored *where* you might find resources, you are ready to actually plan these courses. After the section on course planning tips, you will find some sample four-year course plans presented at three levels: most rigorous, rigorous, and standard college preparatory. Use these as a jumping-off point to develop a personalized course list for your high schooler.

MORE COURSE PLANNING TIPS

Honors and Advanced Placement (AP) Courses

Selective colleges and universities desire students who have taken the most rigorous course of study possible at their schools. Honors and Advanced Placement courses provide this rigor for serious students. Compared to a typical high school course, an honors course presents more advanced concepts and requires the student to spend more time and thought on coursework. These courses place a greater emphasis on critical thinking, analysis, and higher level reasoning skills. Additional reading assignments, writing projects, or research tasks may be required.

As you begin to design honors courses, first construct a standard course and then add extra projects and assignments that will exercise thinking skills and enhance learning. Challenging honors courses can include community college courses, online classes, co-ops taught by a parent specializing in the subject, home-based courses using an advanced textbook, or courses designed with help and input from a local high school teacher. Read Chapter 12 for additional information on honors and AP courses.

Depth Requirements

To be adequately prepared for college, your student will need to have a certain amount of depth in each course rather than just skimming the surface of the subject. This depth comes from analysis, writing, discussion, and/or frequent testing—in other words, interacting with and being accountable for the material presented. College prep courses will require a reasonable amount of work, and at times will seem quite difficult. However, depth and rigor are necessary if the student is to succeed in college.

Homeschooled & Headed for College

Along these lines, be sure that your student's senior year continues the pattern of depth and rigor shown in the earlier years of high school. While students are tempted to take a break or to "play" during the last year of high school, colleges will still be looking for a solid course load. If your student wants to maximize his or her options at college admissions time, a strong senior year course lineup is necessary.

Interdisciplinary Courses

Interdisciplinary courses work well for homeschoolers, because you can minimize duplication of assignments while maximizing your student's learning. If you plan a course whose objectives intersect two or more subjects such as English and history, your student's work on projects or essays can receive some credit for each of these subjects. This technique serves to increase the depth of learning and maintain a higher interest level. For instance, if your student has a fascination for Western Civilization, you could design a course tracing the history of early to modern European civilization. The essays, reading assignments, and speech presentations for which you would award English credit would then mean more to your student than would a generic essay assignment on a topic of little interest. In addition, the student could research the art and music of the Western world to receive fine arts credit.

Ideas for interdisciplinary courses are almost limitless. With almost any interdisciplinary course, you could grant some English credit based on research skills, essays, speeches, or presentations. When your student turns in assignments, you allocate points or hours to each subject studied. If a research paper on the history of Italian music took fifteen hours to complete, you might allocate five hours of historical research toward history credits, five hours of writing and revision toward English credits, and five hours of research directly relating to music toward fine arts credits.

Examples of Interdisciplinary Courses

Be creative in thinking of courses that would work well with an interdisciplinary approach. You might try the following:

History of Science

Your student could trace key discoveries and changing attitudes toward science from ancient times through modern times, focusing on notable scientists, landmark theories, and notable inventions. Typically, this course would not count as a lab science unless you incorporated classic experiments in physics, life science or chemistry to go along with the reading and writing assignments. Actually, this sounds like a fascinating plan! (Beautiful Feet Books has a course of this type.) Always check universities' definitions of lab science courses if you are seeking lab science credit.

History of Government

Your student might enjoy studying governmental forms through the ages: absolute monarchies, constitutional monarchies, empires, constitutional republics, totalitarian governments, and other forms.

Fine Arts Meets Graphic Arts

A student with computer skills could earn fine arts credit by incorporating design elements, color theory, and other visual artistic concepts into technical fields such as website design, creation of logos and banners, layout of books and magazines, or advertisement design. Artistic students and parents could certainly use their imagination to add even more concepts and elements to the list.

Nontraditional Approaches to Courses

Not surprisingly, many families want to design unusual courses for their students, and these courses may also be attractive to a college admissions committee. Some subjects, such as math, generally require the use of a traditional textbook—but even that is changing, with online instruction or certain options for hands-on learning. Other subjects, such as history, lend themselves quite readily to a nontraditional approach. If your family travels extensively or lives abroad, you have the makings of a fascinating history, geography, or language immersion course that will keep both your student *and* the college admissions officer awake far longer than would a typical textbook-based course. Students interested in government or political science could immerse themselves in local, state, or national politics and learn more without ever opening a textbook than the typical high school student learns by the traditional method. Likewise, if your student has a deep interest in a specialized scientific topic and wants to devote extensive time to experimenting, reading, researching, tinkering, creating, inventing, and pondering, do your share as a parent to document, journal, photograph, or otherwise immortalize the fruits of your student's labor so that colleges may appreciate the depth of this study. Use your imagination and have fun designing a one-of-a-kind course. To a certain extent, colleges actually *expect* nontraditional learning methods from homeschooled applicants. It is our job not to disappoint them!

Designing Creative Projects

With the flexibility of homeschooling, creative projects can be an ideal way to learn and assimilate new material, whether it be from literature, history, science, or even math. If your student enjoys learning this way, you may accomplish a large percentage of your teaching by assigning projects.

Here are some tips on the use of projects:

- Give your student a general idea of the goals of the assignment ahead of time.
- Clearly communicate how the project will be evaluated. You might grade on creativity, content, details, accuracy, insight, style of presentation, interesting features, effort, neatness and professionalism, punctuality, or other aspects important to that project.
- If your student tends to procrastinate, establish checkpoints and due dates for the project's components (idea, outline, sketch, draft, finished assignment). This practice also teaches your student how to break down any large project into manageable chunks.
- If it is a visual project, be sure to take a picture of the finished product. Aside from capturing memories, this photo may be used later in a portfolio for college application purposes.

Creative Assignment Ideas

Consider using some of the following ideas to "spice up" your student's school day, especially for subjects that normally provide very little thrill.

Literature or History

Dramatize a literature selection with a skit or recitation of a monologue.
Conduct a real or imaginary interview with a character or key figure.
Present a "radio broadcast" or news program.
Debate two sides of an issue from the story or from a historical situation.
Write your own ending to a story or event.
Make a timeline of important events.

Follow the events in journal form from one character's point of view.

Write and recite a poem based on a literary work or historical event.

Research the author, setting, or other background of a literary piece.

Make a colorful, informative poster.

Design a book cover or advertisement featuring the literary work.

Create a drawing, painting, or 3-D diorama depicting events or settings in the literary work.

Make a model of a building from the story.

Cook a dish or a meal based on the story.

Construct a costume of a character and recite a monologue from the story.

Make a movie based on a scene from the story, or watch and critique a movie based on the literary work.

Create a personalized scrapbook of favorite stories, poems, and readings—all illustrated with the student's own artwork or photographs.

Plan a party involving décor, games, food, and activities based on the literature (for instance, throw a *Great Gatsby* party, or an Ides of March party based on Shakespeare's *Julius Caesar*).

Math or Science

Find or devise a hands-on method of demonstrating a mathematical or scientific principle.

Research and perform extra experiments.

Use online math helps and problem simulations to clarify a confusing concept.

Research and perform multiple ways to solve complex math problems.

Design a long-term science project and follow it through to its results (perhaps enter a science fair).

Create a poster describing or explaining a process.

World Language

Create a board game, guessing game, or card game with vocabulary words.

Cook a meal typical of the country being studied and learn words for all the food and tableware.

Read a children's book in the new language and translate it into English.

Watch TV or a movie, or listen to an online program in the language.

Attend a church service or other public gathering where the language will be spoken.

Learn several songs, such as Christmas carols, in the language.

Any Subject

Create a model or sculpture.

Write and perform a song.

Create a scrapbook or photo album detailing the interesting features of the subject.

Design a game—a board game, a card game, or an active "Jeopardy" game requiring rapid-fire answers.

Assemble a photo essay or journal with captions or paragraph entries alongside the photos.

Draw a cartoon strip or an entire graphic novel.

Create a digital slide show presentation.

A FEW CAUTIONS

"Preapproval" of Courses

Bear in mind that some of the more bureaucratic large universities or public universities may not recognize your homeschool transcript, primarily because they utilize a system of preapproval of high school courses. What this means is that public and private high schools that generate applicants to these universities must submit descriptions of all their college preparatory courses. After approval by the university, these courses are then considered valid courses for students to take toward admission to this university. Courses listed on the applicant's transcript may be matched against the approved list kept on file by the university system for that particular high school. As you might imagine, this streamlines the transcript evaluation process by the university, but it can create complications for homeschoolers or students from small non-accredited schools that have not gone through the preapproval process.

What can a homeschooler do if faced with course preapproval requirements? If possible, check with the university two or three years in advance of application time to discover your options. These might include admitting the student based on high SAT or ACT scores, or allowing the student to take community college courses, AP exams, or approved online courses to validate coursework. Perhaps you will be pleasantly surprised to find that the school has an altogether different path for homeschoolers to gain admission to the university. Check with other homeschoolers, whether local or in online forums, who have applied to these universities, and gather tips from them.

As will be described in Chapter 12, the Advanced Placement program has course audit and preapproval requirements as well. Suggestions about how homeschoolers can navigate these requirements are provided in that chapter.

Balancing Home-Based Courses with Outside Courses

While perusing the course offerings of a nearby homeschool academy or community college, you may be tempted to enroll your student in a full slate of classes outside of your home. Before making a final decision, take inventory of your energy level, your schedule constraints, your academic and social goals for your student, and the quality of these outside courses. Decide whether you prefer to limit outside courses during the first year or two of high school, or whether your student is stimulated and motivated by being around other homeschoolers and is ready to go "full speed ahead."

REALITY CHECK: SOME PRACTICAL EXAMPLES

You may be wondering what all this theoretical information looks like in real life. In particular, how do the previous chapter's suggestions for "sources for courses" dovetail with advice for a strong high school course of study? Obviously, this all depends on the path your student has chosen, whether for a highly competitive college, a moderately competitive college, a less competitive college, or a community college. Although the following four-year plans are only examples, they will show you what a typical lineup of courses *might* look like, depending on your student's goals and college aspirations. In addition, they have been "fleshed out" with a sample suggestion for how you might choose to accomplish those courses.

Remember that these are just samples: your choices may vary greatly. Note also that the information given is not a full course description (a concept which will be explained in the next chapter).

Even though these courses are listed in a full lineup from ninth grade through twelfth grade, you will almost never know at the outset of high school just how you will execute all these courses. The yearly pattern of "nagging mystery" followed by "creative discovery" is a familiar part of the journey of homeschooling. As you actively seek opportunities in your home, in your community, and online, your student's school year will take shape bit by bit. Take heart—your diligence in seeking out opportunities will make your student's final transcript and homeschool experience that much more interesting to college admissions officers.

Note that all Advanced Placement courses mentioned below would need to go through the official course audit process described in Chapter 12 before a college would recognize the AP designation on your transcript. But even without the official designation, your student would be eligible to take the AP exam at the end of the year and potentially earn college credit or advanced standing.

Most Rigorous Course of Study for Highly Selective Colleges

This course lineup incorporates the following number of years of each subject area:

4 years of English (some universities recommend 5 years)
4 years of math
3-4 years of lab science
3-4 years of social studies
3 years of a world language (many highly selective universities recommend 4 years)
1 year of fine arts
3 or more years of college prep electives
2 years of P.E. (1 semester of credit each year, spread out over the entire year)

Though many of the following suggested courses are at AP or honors (H) level, the student does not necessarily have to take all of these at that level. However, English, math, and subjects that reflect the student's strengths and interests should be at honors or AP level if available. Taking courses at the community college is another good way to demonstrate that the student has taken the most rigorous courses possible.

For Christian students, a Bible course would likely be included each year as an elective. You might consider designing and titling some of your Bible courses as "Theology" or "Comparative Religions" courses. In addition to providing course variety, this might help the college better relate to the content of the course, since such courses are offered at some traditional high schools. Also note that for school years with seven or more subjects, one or two courses could be taken during the summer. And remember: your student does not have to study this entire lineup. Customize the list to your student's interests and passions. In particular, the choice of electives is up to you. Your student may be a scientist, an artsy type, a history buff, or a math whiz. These interests will affect his or her lineup of courses.

9th Grade

English 9H (Honors) – Home-designed course based on a ninth grade honors English syllabus found online. General survey of literature genres, primarily using library books. Essay and discussion questions will be gleaned from literature websites. Grammar review will be incorporated into essay revisions, based on errors the student has made. The Institute for Excellence in Writing's *Advanced Communication Series* will be used to enhance writing instruction. SAT preparation will begin by having the student work through an SAT preparation guide for critical reading, and writing/language skills.

Honors Geometry (assuming Algebra 1 was taken during middle school) – Standard textbook course supplemented with a geometry course from The Great Courses.

Honors Biology – Cooperative class taught by another homeschool parent. Class will meet once a week for lab and discussion, with the bulk of the study done at home.

World Geography – Home-based study using a traditional textbook but supplemented with hands-on projects such as map making, presentations, and culture nights complete with food, music, and interesting facts about a particular region.

Spanish 1 – Computer-based instruction using Rosetta Stone language program, supplemented by a workbook such as *Spanish in 10 Minutes a Day®*.

Intro to Drawing and Painting – Group lessons taught by another homeschool parent.

Bible 9 – Home-designed program incorporating Bible study, reading of selected Christian authors, and volunteer work in ministries. A youth Bible study at church will provide a group dynamic.

P.E. – Student will pursue one sport per season (soccer, tennis, and softball) through community leagues.

10ᵗʰ Grade

English 10H – Home-based course similar to the ninth grade course, but with a focus on more advanced literature and on speeches and presentations. Course will focus on a few classic fiction and nonfiction works found on typical AP reading lists. Attention to the European writers from the Renaissance through modern times will dovetail with this year's European history course. A weekly literature group with other homeschoolers will offer a chance to discuss the works and to present short speeches based on essays written. Heavy emphasis will be placed on the prewriting, writing, and revision process, using a solid writing text. Student will work through an SAT prep book and take practice tests.

Algebra 2H – Home-based course using a *Saxon Math* textbook, with help from the DIVE (Digital Interactive Video Education) program and the *Saxon Math* solutions manual. An outside tutor is available if needed.

AP Biology – College Board-approved online course. An AP Biology prep book will be utilized to review all concepts for the exam.

AP European History – Self-study home-based course using an approved AP course syllabus in preparation for the AP European History exam. A typical AP textbook and an AP exam review guide will be used, along with the partnership of a local high school teacher who has offered to share his syllabus, invite the student to review sessions, and be available for questions. Student will meet weekly for discussion and support with two other homeschooled friends who are studying this course.

Spanish 2 – Student will continue with Rosetta Stone language program, supplemented with a basic Spanish grammar book.

Elective: Creative Writing – Home-designed course using a guidebook for creative writing. Student will write original short stories, poetry, or even the beginnings of a novel, and will research publication opportunities.

Bible – Home-designed course similar to the ninth grade course but requiring more in-depth study and reading, as well as discussion of biblical principles in light of the ideas encountered in the history and literature readings. Summer missions trip to a Spanish-speaking location will supplement the Spanish language study and provide spiritual and life experience.

P.E. – Sports or activities of choice. Student will try one new sport this year: swimming on a YMCA team.

11th Grade

AP English Language – Online course with continued focus on rhetorical analysis and essay writing. The course will focus on American authors to complement the study of U.S. History. Will use a prep book to prepare for the AP English Language exam. Course will also include instruction for the SAT essay and college application essays, using the *High School Essay Intensive* from the Institute for Excellence in Writing.

Precalculus H – Community college course.

AP Chemistry – College Board-approved course taken at a local homeschool academy; will also use an AP prep book to finish preparing for the AP exam.

AP U.S. History – College Board-approved online course using a typical AP textbook and occasional help from a local teacher. Student will use one or more AP exam prep books as well as historical novels and nonfiction to aid in understanding of the historical eras.

Spanish 3 – Continuation of Rosetta Stone language program. Will continue supplementing with a grammar workbook and will also assign some translations of Spanish children's books from the library.

Elective: Journalism – Student will start a homeschool newspaper, a literary magazine, or a newsletter for a club or charity and will gain experience in writing, editing, layout, and leadership of a team of students.

Bible (or Comparative Religions) – Home-designed course similar to the ninth and tenth grade courses. Will continue pursuing more advanced concepts and application of these concepts to ministries and everyday life. Focus will be on comparing Christianity with other religions.

P.E. – Sports or activities of choice, focusing on skill development and overall fitness. Student will take a P.E. class at the community college during one of the semesters.

12th Grade

AP English Literature – Homeschool academy course (College Board-approved) including extensive reading of literature from the AP suggested reading list, essay writing to analyze literature, and a unit on poetry analysis. Will use an AP prep book to prepare for the exam.

Calculus – Community college course, followed by taking the AP Calculus AB exam in the spring.

AP or Honors Physics – Online course supplemented by an AP prep book.

AP Government (1 semester) and *AP Macroeconomics or AP Microeconomics (1 semester)* – Courses will be studied in a group format with local homeschoolers but will be based on the online course which they are all taking. Because of the guidance of the online course, the students can moderate their own study group without parental involvement. For Economics, in addition to textbook activities, students will prepare a semester project relating to investments.

Musical Theater – Community-based activity sponsored by a local theater group. *(If the school year schedule is tight, this could be a summer activity.)*

College Prep Elective – Five ideas for options:

Spanish 4 (for world language focus) – Home-designed immersion course in which student listens to Spanish TV and radio, reads simple articles or books written in Spanish, takes one or more short ministry trips to a Spanish-speaking location or volunteers in a local ministry among Spanish speakers, occasionally attends a Spanish-speaking church, and works with a native-speaking friend or tutor who can help with advanced concepts. Student will prepare for the AP Spanish exam if desired.

Statistics (for math/science focus) – Home-designed course using a textbook for a first college course in statistics, utilizing a friend or tutor to help with tough concepts as needed.

Speech and Debate (for English focus) – Course is based on membership in a local speech and debate club involving meetings, speech practice, and participation in tournaments. *(Alternatively, the student could seek out a 4-H Clubs program or a Toastmasters Youth Leadership program for speech practice.)*

Political Science (for social studies focus) – Community college semester-length course, followed by another semester of participating in local or state politics (campaigns, ballot initiatives, or other local issues). The student will try to arrange a formal or informal internship with a local group.

Bible (Theology) – Home-designed course, encouraging student to display leadership in ministries, develop maturity in biblical concepts, and use theological concepts to interpret secular literature. Course will focus on deeper understanding of Christian doctrines and theology.

P.E. – Sports or activities of choice.

Rigorous Course of Study for Moderately Selective Colleges

Students aiming for moderately selective colleges may slightly reduce their number of science, social studies, and/or foreign language courses. Although honors and/or AP designations have not been marked on the courses listed below, the student should seek to take a few honors and/or AP courses in areas of strength and interest. Many students will have a "specialty" which they will favor as they choose their electives and decide how many years of each subject they will take. For instance, a student focusing on math and science will add extra courses in these subjects. Students who enjoy social studies and languages will choose additional courses in these fields. Students talented in the fine arts who intend to continue studying in college will choose electives and extra courses in the fine arts disciplines.

The Bible, world language, and P.E. course ideas will be essentially the same as in the previous example, so these have not been repeated. The student may take fewer years of the world language.

9*th* Grade

English 9H – Home-based course similar to the one described for the most rigorous course of study.

Algebra 1H (or Geometry if Algebra has already been taken) – Home-based course using a standard textbook, with supplementation from online videos or DIVE CDs for the *Saxon Math* book if needed.

Physical Science – Home-based course using a standard textbook but with labs performed weekly with a group of other homeschoolers who are studying the same subject.

Piano Performance – Based on student taking piano lessons and participating in recitals.

World Language, Bible, P.E. – See note above.

10*th* Grade

English 10H – Similar to the course described for most rigorous course of study, studied as a cooperative course with other homeschoolers. Course will strongly emphasize writing skills.

Geometry H or Algebra 2H – As described for most rigorous course of study.

Biology – Community college biology course.

World History – Online course, with parent reading textbook as well and learning alongside student.

Journalism – Similar to course described under most rigorous program.

Speech and Debate – Studied in the homeschool community by joining a homeschool speech and debate club and participating in local and regional tournaments.

World Language, Bible, P.E. – See note above.

11*th* Grade

English 11H or AP English Language – Similar to course described under most rigorous program.

Algebra 2 or Precalculus – Community college course.

Chemistry – Homeschool co-op course using a homeschool-friendly curriculum, with labs utilizing household materials. *Or preferably, if student is ready, this could be a community college course.*

U.S. History – Group course with other homeschoolers, using a typical high school textbook of choice. For honors course, assign an extra research paper.

Biotechnology – Self-designed course using biotechnology education websites as resources to introduce key aspects of biotechnology such as agricultural biosafety, genetic engineering, and bioterrorism. Suitable lesson plans found online will be used; field trips will be taken to local labs using some of these techniques.

World Language, Bible, P.E. – See note above.

12ᵗʰ *Grade*

British Literature or AP English Literature – Similar to course described under most rigorous program.

Precalculus or Calculus – Community college course.

U.S. Government (1 semester) – Online course supplemented by group study with other homeschoolers.

Economics (1 semester) – Community college course.

Bible, P.E. – See note above.

Elective Options:

Spanish 4 (for foreign language focus) – As described for most rigorous program.

Statistics (for math/science focus) – As described for most rigorous program.

Creative Writing or Speech and Debate (for English focus) – As described for most rigorous program.

Political Science (for social studies focus) – As described for most rigorous program.

Theater Arts (for fine arts focus) – A course using a youth community theater program as a resource.

Standard College Prep Course of Study

Less competitive colleges will not be as concerned about seeing honors or AP courses on the student's transcript, but if your student is capable of such courses, these will make his or her application stand out. Likewise, taking extra years of courses beyond the basic requirement is always a good idea if the student wants to be a strong applicant for these schools.

Just as a reminder, a typical "standard college prep" lineup might be as follows:

4 years of English

3 years of mathematics

2-3 years of lab science

2-3 years of social studies, including a year of U.S. history and a semester each of U.S. government and economics

2 years of a world language

1-2 years of visual or performing arts

Electives to fill in additional graduation credit requirements

2 years of P.E.

Courses in this group have not been described in detail. General principles will be the same as for the more rigorous courses of study, but the following differences may apply:

- Your student will not need to prepare for as many standardized exams such as APs or SAT Subject Tests, and each subject area can be less rigorous.
- Mathematics may not reach the calculus level.

- In English courses, writing assignments can be paced to the student's own level rather than to an advanced standard.
- Lab sciences will focus on one year of physical science (chemistry or physics) and one year of life science (biology or physiology).
- Check with colleges to find out which courses will and will not satisfy their requirements.

Because the course load will not be as heavy in this plan as in the more rigorous ones, you and your student will have much more freedom to incorporate innovative elements, fine arts, travel, vocational or business courses, field trips, life skills and practical applications, unit studies utilizing community resources, and other individualized projects. With your use of these special opportunities, your student's record of homeschool experiences will still be attractive and interesting, without the extra rigor of the previous two examples. Of course, for the more rigorous plans, you will want to include as many of these experiences as you can fit in; it just may be a little more difficult in the wake of all the rigorous courses. Whatever you choose to do, be sure to document it so that you can later provide a lively description of your student's path of learning during high school.

Preparation for Community College Entrance

Complete the graduation requirements for your local school district, such as the following:

4 years of English
2-3 years of math
2-3 years of lab science
2-3½ years of history/social studies
2 years of a world language in some states or districts
1-2 years of fine arts or vocational/technical education
½ year of health education in some states or districts
6-8 years of college prep electives
2 years of P.E. (or enough to conform with local graduation requirements)

A course of study for community college entrance will look very similar to the course of study for the standard college prep program described earlier. Notice that some school districts' *graduation* requirements are actually more stringent than some colleges' *entrance* requirements. Plan accordingly!

TO SUM UP

Hopefully, these course lineups have demonstrated that you have a number of choices for arranging your student's four-year high school plan. Every student's course of study will be different, because every student has different goals, college aspirations, abilities, and opportunities for courses. Use these special characteristics of your student, along with help and suggestions from homeschool mentors, to create an individualized plan to meet your student's needs.

Summer is a good time to pause for a few days and really *think* about the upcoming year. Use this time to finalize course content, gather books and materials, and lay out course descriptions and detailed plans for each subject. As you plan each school year, check to make sure that your student is on track with courses needed for college admission. If the course of study needs more rigor, add a few challenging courses. If your student is suffering under a heavy load, back off a bit so that he or she can enjoy the learning process. The option of customizing the educational mix is one of the prime benefits of home education.

Chapter 7

Education by Design:

Creating Customized Courses

When your student was in elementary school, course planning may have been as simple as choosing packaged grade-level curricula or mixing and matching items from different publishers. If you got creative and planned a course from scratch, using a textbook here, a library book there, a sprinkling of field trips, and hands-on activities galore, the process may have seemed more like play than work.

With high school, course design may appear a bit more complicated, because these courses now count on that all-important document, the transcript. Rest assured that designing courses can still be a fun and creative process because of the wealth of curricula and resources available. A thoughtfully planned course that you create from scratch can be just as acceptable to a college as a course from the local high school. Now that you have a working knowledge of credits, graduation requirements, and course selection for a given year, you are ready to examine the planning process in greater detail.

OVERVIEW OF THE COURSE PLANNING PROCESS

Here are the basic steps for designing courses from scratch:

1. *Select the courses your student will take during the coming year. This is called a course of study.*
2. *Select the approach you will use, based on your goals for the year or on what is available to you.*
3. *Select materials and resources.*
4. *Title your courses and write course descriptions.*
5. *Gather assignment ideas.*
6. *Create a course syllabus.*
7. *Design a grading plan.*
8. *As desired, make up yearly, quarterly, and weekly goals or assignment lists to help you and your student stay on track.*
9. *Design grade recording logs in spreadsheet or journal form, or in a form most useful to you.*
10. *List and gather specialized materials needed for the course.*
11. *Conduct the course and record assignment grades.*
12. *Calculate semester grades, record grades and credits, and file the course description and syllabus for future use.*

As you mentally multiply the number of courses your student will take each year by the four years of high school, you may wonder how you will ever have time to plan and document all these courses. But realize that as high school progresses, you will probably design fewer courses each year from scratch, because your student will be taking more pre-designed outside courses. Community college courses, co-op or group academy classes, and online courses will cut down on your workload. You will simply keep the syllabus provided by the instructor and include it in your own records.

Additionally, not all courses will need all the steps of the planning process. Some will be much simpler than others. For example, math and other courses that use traditional textbooks are fairly straightforward to document. Finally, remember that once you have completed a batch of course plans, you may use many of them as templates when you plan similar courses in the future for the same student or for younger siblings. "Copy and paste" is definitely your friend.

Before presenting ideas for course planning, I cannot emphasize enough that *every homeschooling family has a unique style and routine*. Feel free to simplify this process to best suit *your* goals, preferences, and schedule. There is no single correct way of doing it. For instance, you may not be as addicted to paperwork as I tend to be. If you can keep more of it in your mind and less of it on paper, go for it!

Course planning is best done during the summer. If you wait until school has already started, you may find yourself "winging it" by handing out assignments with no rationale for what you want to accomplish. Though course planning can be time-consuming and takes some focused thought, remember that once the course is mapped out, you can launch into the school year with a clear idea of where you are headed. If you are sick, busy, or out of town, you can hand over your course plans to your student and have him or her work from those plans. Additionally, you can save these plans to use for your next student.

Now for an in-depth look at each of the course planning steps. Some were hinted at in previous chapters, but here you will see them again as part of the "big picture." You might think of these steps in five stages: choosing, planning, making lists and logs, learning, and documenting.

PHASE ONE: CHOOSING

1. Select the courses your student will take during the coming year.

Consult your graduation requirements as discussed in Chapter 3 and look at requirements for a few likely colleges. From these, decide which requirements your student will complete this year.

2. Select the approach you will use, based on your goals for the year or on what is available to you.

Even after you have selected a course, you have several choices. How will the course be taught? Will it be a home-based course or an outside course? What are your goals for the course? For instance, will your student be preparing for an SAT Subject Test or an AP exam on the basis of this material? Is group discussion or social interaction an important priority? Can you afford tuition for the "perfect" online or homeschool academy course? After reviewing the many options you have for crafting a customized course, examine your current options for outside courses. For example, consult a list of the courses that will be offered this year in your homeschool community or at the community college.

3. Select materials and resources.

Now you can go shopping! Examine curricula, supplementary books, audio or video materials, online resources, project ideas, group classes, local seminars or mini-courses, and other resources you come across. Then create the ideal mix of resources for your student's learning style as well as for your budget and schedule. Do not limit yourself to typical homeschool curricula or traditional textbooks. Make use of your library, community resources, online courses or study aids, friends with expertise, community courses offered in your area, or dreams you and your student may have for fascinating long-term projects.

PHASE TWO: PLANNING

4. Title your courses and write course descriptions.

Course Titles

Creating titles for your student's courses is necessary for transcript purposes and for clear communication with the colleges to which your student will apply. Course titles should be brief but meaningful. To gather ideas, browse through a high school or college website's course listing, noticing both the titles of the courses and their descriptions. For instance, a high school science course could be Biology or Anatomy and Physiology or Intro to Chemistry. Courses taken every year, according to grade level, could be English 9, English 10, and so forth, using Arabic numerals, or they could be English I or English II, using Roman numerals. You may also choose to name your English classes according to the topic studied. Your student might take Elements of Literature and Composition, followed by World Literature, American Literature, and British Literature.

Courses can also be designated as honors or AP courses—English 9H or AP Biology or Honors Geometry. See Chapter 12 for full details on honors courses; importantly, note that all AP courses must be College Board-approved to be listed on the transcript. Courses taken a semester at a time may be designated with "A" or "B" for the first and second semester, as in Algebra 1B or Spanish 2A, or you could use sequential numbers for each semester, as in Spanish 1 through Spanish 8. You can also use "Advanced" or "Intro" as descriptive words in course titles.

Keep your course titles short and specific. Aim to be clear and fairly traditional rather than fancy and innovative. Remember also that the titles will need to fit your transcript's limited space or be readily abbreviated.

Course Descriptions

Next, write a succinct description of the scope of the course and its major objectives. Admissions staff at both the community college and the university may need to evaluate your courses or may use this information to clear the prerequisites for more advanced courses. Additionally, this description makes your school look organized and well-run.

If you are stumped, consult the preface or table of contents of your textbook, or even a well-written advertisement for the textbook from a catalog or website. And again, looking at examples on college websites will give you ideas for describing your courses. Three or four sentences describing course content, primary methods of instruction, and concepts to be learned will provide a frame of reference for the college.

Creating a shorter version (as described above) and a more detailed version of your course description is wise. The shorter version can be used for colleges that request a brief rundown of your student's course of study. The longer version, which could be a full course syllabus, will be ideal for your own planning purposes as well as for colleges requiring more details.

Sample Course Descriptions

The following examples from our own homeschooling will give you an idea of what you might include in a very brief course description. Later, you will learn how to put more "meat on the bones" by writing a full course syllabus as a planning and documentation tool. Course descriptions that you intend to submit for college applications will be more detailed than these brief samples, but not as detailed as full course syllabi. (See Chapters 20 and 21.) Include titles of textbooks and resources, and perhaps also ISBNs.

Algebra 1

This course covers the standard topics of first year algebra plus introductory geometry, including signed numbers, integer exponents, scientific notation, linear equations, graphs and equations of linear functions, ratio problems, percents, variation problems, unit conversions, perimeter, area, and volume.

Timed drills to review basic computation skills will also be performed using CalcuLadder® Math Drills, Levels 4, 5, and 6, covering advanced division, place values, estimation, decimals, advanced fractions, percents, English and metric units, and geometric concepts. *(Derived from textbook introduction and table of contents, and from a description of the drill program.)*

AP® English Language and Composition

In this College Board-approved course, the student will integrate skills learned in the first two years of high school in preparation for the AP English Language and Composition exam. The student will read a wide variety of literature, examine rhetorical devices, techniques, and strategies, write argumentation and synthesis essays, and analyze texts using both writing and discussion. A study of vocabulary from classical roots will supplement the literature and writing portions of the course. *(Constructed from AP course description plus our own add-ons to the course.)*

Shakespeare

This course will provide an opportunity to read a number of Shakespeare's plays, discuss them in a group, analyze the plays by answering thought questions in writing and in group discussion, and practice literary analysis skills by writing essays based on the plays. Since the student has initiated, designed, and publicized this course herself, it will also provide experience in leading group discussions and assisting others in their understanding of Shakespeare and his plays. *(Written from scratch to describe a student-initiated course.)*

Principles of Cell Biology

This course is a comprehensive course in cell biology, including the principles of cell chemistry and metabolism, structure and function of procaryotic and eucaryotic cells and viruses, molecular genetics, genetic engineering, and hypotheses of the origin of life. *(Derived from a community college course description.)*

Physical Science

This high school science course forms the basis for later study of chemistry and physics. Beginning with the scientific method and a discussion of science for the Christian, the course delves into measurement, properties, and classification of matter, and then into atomic theory and structure, including models of atoms, the periodic table of elements, and forces between atoms. Chemical applications such as reactions, solutions, and acid-base properties, are also covered. A discussion of basic physics includes the study of energy and momentum, mechanics, work and machines, fluid mechanics, heat, temperature, electricity and magnetism, sound waves, and the electromagnetic spectrum. The course includes lab activities and reports as well as mathematical activities. *(Derived from publisher's description of textbook.)*

World Geography

This one-semester study of world geography will acquaint the student with the regions and nations of the world, including their geographical features, industries, cultural characteristics, major cities, people, languages, and other features. Units on North America, Latin America, Western Europe, Central Eurasia, Asia, the Middle East, Africa, and Oceania will give the student a familiarity with our world and its people. *(Derived from publisher's description of textbook.)*

AP® US History

This College Board-approved course, designed to be the equivalent of a freshman college course, is a two-semester survey of American history from the age of exploration and discovery to the present. Solid reading and writing skills, along with a willingness to devote considerable time to homework and study, are necessary to succeed. Emphasis is placed on critical and evaluative thinking skills, essay writing, and interpretation of original documents. The student will accomplish the following objectives:
Master a broad body of historical knowledge.
Demonstrate an understanding of historical chronology.
Use historical data to support an argument or position.
Differentiate between various historical schools of thought.
Interpret and apply data from original documents, including cartoons, graphs, and letters.
Effectively use analytical skills of evaluation, cause and effect, comparison and contrast.
Prepare for and successfully pass the AP exam.
(Derived from AP course objectives and a syllabus from a high school offering the course.)

Bible 11

This course will encourage the student to grow in spiritual maturity and put his or her faith to work in a number of ways: through in-depth Bible study, through examining the biblical Christian worldview, through commitment to service to others, through daily devotions and Bible reading, and through reading of Christian literature. Many discussions will focus on the reading the student is doing for English class and will seek to compare or contrast the author's worldview with biblical Christianity. *(Written from scratch.)*

Spanish 1A/1B

This introductory Spanish course utilizes conversation, oral and written activities, pronunciation practice, and colorful, interesting stories and cultural descriptions to give the student an appreciation for spoken and written Spanish as well as for the culture of Spanish-speaking countries. The student will participate in one-on-one oral activities, learn and memorize basic vocabulary and grammar rules, and translate Spanish stories both orally and in writing. The course will cover nouns, verbs, and other vocabulary relating to greetings, numbers, telling time, social events, classroom, travel, clothing, and other practical words and phrases. *(Derived by flipping through the textbook activities and table of contents.)*

Russian 3A/3B

This online Russian program builds on the foundation laid in Russian 1 and 2, with practice in listening, reading comprehension, speaking, and writing. Each lesson involves previews, exercises, automated tutorials, and tests. Student works exclusively in Russian with the aid of native speakers and several thousand photographs to create a context of meaning. Grammar practice will be continued through a separate textbook. *(Derived from descriptive information about Rosetta Stone language program.)*

Web Design 1

This introductory web design course will acquaint the student with what makes a website useful and attractive and will allow him to put that information into practice by developing and launching at least two fully functioning websites. Student will learn some basic HTML programming and will also learn to use Java applets. Topics will include website style reviews, HTML editor/tutorial selection, HTML editing, making a placeholder web page, keeping order on web pages with tables, adding images to a document, hyperlinks, GIF files, JPG files, practicing with "print screen," tweaking HTML code, web colors and hex codes, making a cascading style sheet, web ethics (copyrights and fair use), and creating a website for a "client." *(Derived from a description of an online course with similar objectives to our home-designed course.)*

Vocal Music

This course will introduce the student to vocal music by providing opportunities for participation in various forms of vocal technique and performance: (1) mixed choir of soprano, alto, tenor, and bass, (2) ensemble singing, and (3) solo or duet singing. The course is designed to increase the vocal skill and performance levels of the student and to develop aesthetic values through critical listening. Student will sing a wide range of music, including church music, patriotic music, and secular music. Student will perform medium to difficult choral literature for performances in concerts and special productions. In addition to participation in choir and ensemble singing, student will take a semester-long introductory voice class at the community college for focused instruction in vocal techniques and for experience with critical evaluation of others' singing. *(Derived from community college voice class description and our own descriptions of student activities toward the goal.)*

Fine Arts Survey

This course will provide an overview of the world of music and art by introducing the student to music and art appreciation studies and by encouraging practical projects. Components of the course include music appreciation, art appreciation, artistic skills (with applications in graphic design and websites), field trips to museums and concerts, and a multimedia project on an artist or composer of the student's choice. *(Written from scratch.)*

P.E. 11

This course will involve regular exercise workouts to develop and maintain physical fitness. Student will be expected to spend at least 45 minutes, three times per week, on fitness workouts. Each semester, the student will also read and discuss at least one article or one chapter of a book on nutrition, fitness, or a specific type of exercise. *(Written from scratch.)*

5. Gather assignment ideas.

As you explore the books and resources you have chosen, think about your goals for the course. What is important to you and your student? What areas of giftedness or interest do you want to address? What skills need development—writing, speech, research, computer, laboratory, or project skills? Spend time brainstorming and then make a list of possible assignments. Traditional assignments could include reading assignments, essays, tests, quizzes, and speeches. If you are using a traditional textbook, *do not feel bound* to assign every problem set, quiz, worksheet, or map activity spelled out in the book. Since you are the teacher, you get to choose the most important assignments for *your* purposes for *your* student.

Instead of or in addition to traditional assignments, you could include projects such as art creations, dramatic interpretations of the material learned, formal debates, science projects, or any of the creative assignment ideas listed in Chapter 6. Keeping your student's learning style in mind, you could use supplementary books, video and audio resources, museums, art galleries, concerts, online resources, or, best of all, human interaction to communicate the material to your student. Assignments could include time spent doing volunteer or paid work in the field of study, with a journal or final project to sum up the learning. The student could also tutor someone else in the subject or could interview an expert in the field.

When you are finished listing possible assignments, choose the most suitable ones—hopefully a balanced mix of traditional and creative—and decide approximately *when* you will have your student complete them. In other words, place them in the fall or spring semester and in their approximate sequence. Also divide up the chapters or concepts in the textbook to allocate them into their sequence in the school year. If you prefer, divide each semester into two quarters and allocate assignments to each. For instance, if the textbook has sixteen chapters and you hope to complete the whole book, you would plan to cover four chapters per quarter, or eight per semester. Along with this, jot down assignments that would logically accompany the topics studied in these chapters. Strive to create a fairly even workload throughout the year so that the student's workload is balanced and predictable. If you are assigning a ten-page research paper, reduce the number of shorter essays and other assignments during that semester.

6. Create a course syllabus.

Because colleges may possibly ask for more information than your brief course description provides, another document, called a *course syllabus*, is helpful to have on hand. More importantly, creating this document gives *you* a useful "road map" for where you are going with this course.

The syllabus, which is longer and more detailed than the course description, presents the scope and objectives of the course, the textbooks and curriculum, the main assignments you will use, and the grading criteria. College students and many high school students receive syllabi from their instructors at the beginning of the school year. In your syllabus, you will start with your brief course description but will then go on to list textbooks and other resources as well as the number and types of tests, essays, and projects. Other elements you might include are specific course objectives, prerequisites (courses that must be taken before the current course), and the method of instruction.

Syllabi for courses such as math, using a single textbook organized by lessons or chapters with a test after each chapter, will be fairly simple to write. Syllabi for multi-book courses, or courses involving many different modes of learning and evaluation, will be more complicated. However, taking the time to write them out will serve you well. This exercise compels you to thoroughly think through your goals and methods. Be sure to allow yourself enough time to work on these plans and make adjustments. Make sure that the assignments adequately address your goals and provide a realistic workload—not too much and not too little. Obviously, you want to minimize busy work and maximize true learning activities.

Sometimes you may decide to write the course syllabus *after* the course is completed. This may sound backwards. However, for some courses, especially the less academic ones, you might continuously record activities and experiences that pertain to your goals for the course, keeping track of the approximate hours spent. When your student has logged enough hours for you to grant credit for this course, write up the syllabus based on what activities were used and how you evaluated your student.

For example, you may plan a life skills course requiring the student to accumulate hours in categories such as cooking, home repairs, auto maintenance, emergency preparedness, and hospitality. At the outset of the course, you may not know exactly which activities your student will use to fulfill the time requirements. After the hours have all been accumulated, write up a description of the skills the student learned and the tasks he or she accomplished. Courses such as a fine arts survey also work well for writing a descriptive syllabus after the fact: you'll log activities in the visual, musical, and theater arts. It is wise, however, to initially create a skeleton plan of what you will require your student to do and to learn.

For outside classes such as community college courses, your student will probably receive a syllabus at the beginning of the course. File these with the syllabi you write from scratch, and keep them for a few years into your student's college education. Syllabi from community college courses may be needed when transferring courses to a four-year college or university or when challenging a prerequisite.

To get a feel for the look of a typical high school course syllabus, simply do a quick web search on "High School English Syllabus" or another appropriate phrase and then examine a few of the syllabi that come up. And since an example is much more useful than a vague description, I have included an example of a syllabus in Chapter 8, "The Life Cycle of a Typical Course."

7. Design a grading plan.

As part of your syllabus, or as a separate document called a *course standard*, include a section describing your grading plan. Here is where you will outline the types of assignments and how they will be graded. You will also describe the relative weights that various assignments will carry toward the calculation of the final grade. A well-thought-out evaluation plan will save you time and energy later when you need to record scores and calculate a semester grade. It will also prevent you from being influenced, midway through the semester, to change your grading policy based on your student's performance on certain assignments.

One key aspect of constructing a grading plan is the *weighting* of multiple assignments when calculating a final grade. This is entirely up to you as the teacher. In some courses you'll want to emphasize performance on tests as the final authority on how well the student learned the information. In this case, tests could make up 75% or more of the grade. If your student has difficulty with tests but works hard on homework, daily work may be your favored benchmark. A student who successfully assimilates material via discussions, writing assignments, and creative projects may benefit from having these assignments weighted heavily. Do think seriously about this choice, since different weightings will result in different letter grades. The important point is that you need to set up your grading standard ahead of time, deciding what percentage of the total grade each type of assignment will comprise. Don't change these figures mid-semester unless it becomes apparent that you were totally off in your earlier planning and projection.

Creating a Grading Plan

Here's one way you might approach this task:

a. Divide the year into two semesters and write a syllabus for each semester. Though they are usually almost identical, they may differ slightly based on the number or types of assignments planned.

b. Prepare a rough count of assignments: books to read, long or short essays to write, speeches, tests, quizzes, homework assignments, and other projects. Be realistic, not overzealous, so as not to overburden your student. Estimate the amount of time each assignment will take and then total up the number of hours per week to see if your plan sounds reasonable. If you're coming up with five or more hours per week for each major school subject, that is about right. Five hours would be a standard course, while rigorous honors or AP courses could take up to ten hours per week. These figures all include instructional time as well as independent homework and study time.

c. List the types of assignments (tests, essays, projects) in order of importance toward the semester grade. This ranking reflects what you believe the most significant assignments are in terms of student time and effort. For instance, a ten-point quiz and a 200-point final exam should not count equally toward the semester grade. Exams might be at the top of your priority list and quizzes might be near the bottom.

d. Now assign percentage values to the weight of each type of assignment. As long as the total of all the weightings is 100%, you are free to choose any percentages that sound reasonable. For example, if a math course is graded equally on tests and homework, the tests are weighted 50% and the homework 50%. For a lab science class, an example might be as follows:

> Tests: 40%
> Lab reports: 20%
> Research paper: 15%
> Homework questions: 15%
> Quizzes: 10%

e. At the end of the semester, you will *average* all the grades for each type of assignment (coming up with a percentage score for each category), and then *multiply* that percentage by the weight factor you decided upon at the beginning of the semester. It sounds complicated but is really quite simple. Suppose a student received the following *average* grades on each type of assignment throughout the semester:

> Tests: 88%   (average of 5 tests)
> Lab reports: 92%   (average of 6 reports)
> Research paper: 95%   (score on one paper)
> Homework: 89%   (average of 12 assignments)
> Quizzes: 84%   (average of 5 quizzes)

To calculate the final grade, multiply the *average percentage* earned in each assignment category by the *weight* you assigned at the beginning of the year. (Change the % weight to a decimal first.) By themselves, these intermediate figures will be meaningless, but when you add them up, the total will be the final percentage in the course:

> Tests (worth 40% of grade) $88\% \times 0.40 = \textbf{35.2\%}$
> Lab reports (worth 20%) $92\% \times 0.20 = \textbf{18.4\%}$
> Research paper (worth 15%) $95\% \times 0.15 = \textbf{14.25\%}$
> Homework (worth 15%) $89\% \times 0.15 = \textbf{13.35\%}$
> Quizzes (worth 10%) $84\% \times 0.10 = \textbf{8.4\%}$
> **Total: 89.6%**

Now round this to 90%, and the student squeaks by with a very low A if you are using a 90% to 100% scale for an A.

f. When the semester ends, calculate and record the grade and file the course description and syllabus, together with your other official records for that year as an explanation of how you arrived at the grade.

PHASE THREE: MAKING LISTS AND LOGS

8. As desired, make up yearly, quarterly, and weekly goals or assignment lists to help you and your student stay on track.

If you have survived the instructions for creating a syllabus and a grading plan, you are doing well and may now move on to actually *scheduling* the work. Before you tackle this step, decide on the beginning and ending dates of your school year, the number of weeks you will hold school, and the timing of holidays and breaks. Divide your year into two semesters and your semesters into two quarters each. If you homeschool year round, or if you use a system such as three weeks on, one week off throughout the year, you will still want to divide your year into smaller divisions for planning purposes.

Yearly Assignment Goals, Broken Down by Quarter

Working from the big picture—your entire year's plan sketched out on the syllabus—divide the assignments by semester and then again by quarter. Although grading is done by semester, planning is more conveniently done by quarter. A nine-week quarter is a manageable chunk of time for which to schedule individual assignments, and the end of the quarter is a logical checkpoint to see if the schedule is actually holding up. Usually it won't be, but having this goal is important.

Without great detail, briefly list the assignments you would like your student to accomplish in each of the four quarters of the school year and record these in a document of your choice. As you do this, refer to your calendar and note key dates that might affect your plans. These might include due dates for grades or semester evaluations, dates of AP, SAT, or ACT exams, holidays, vacations, or educational opportunities such as seminars being held in your community.

For example, the following yearly assignment list for a ninth grader, broken down by quarter, covers algebra, a *Starting Points* worldview curriculum, writing and grammar skills, science, geography (a one-semester course), and a Spanish course. Similarly, you would also divide up any other courses your student would be studying. Remember, these are *goals* and may be too ambitious. You will probably not achieve 100% of them, so don't be discouraged if your assignments "slip" as the weeks go on. Just do your best to keep up with them. Also, if possible, give yourself a cushion of time by scheduling a week's worth of catch-up for each subject at the end of each quarter.

Sample Yearly Assignment Goals for 9th Grade, Broken Down by Quarter

Algebra 2

The *Math-U-See* textbook includes 30 lessons, each with four worksheets and a test. Lessons are designed to take about a week to accomplish. Unit tests are provided after every eight lessons. An optional Honors book is also available for honors or extra credit work. CalcuLadder drills 80 through 96 will be used weekly to keep up on calculation skills.

Quarter 1   Lessons 1-8, Tests 1-8, Unit I Test
                     CalcuLadder 80 through 87: 1 drill per week

Quarter 2   Lessons 9-16, Tests 9-16, Unit II Test
                     CalcuLadder 88 through 96: 1 drill per week

Quarter 3   Lessons 17-24, Tests 17-24, Unit III Test
                     CalcuLadder 80 through 87 reinforcement: 1 drill per week

Quarter 4   Lessons 25-30, Tests 25-30, Unit IV Test
                     CalcuLadder 88 through 96 reinforcement: 1 drill per week

Geography
       Using the Bob Jones University Press textbook *Geography,* focus on chapters 11-29 for a one-semester survey of world geography.

Quarter 1
Read chapters 11-19
Do one or two "fun" activities per chapter
Do chapter test for each chapter
Turn in one country profile

Quarter 2
Read chapters 20-29
Do one or two "fun" activities per chapter
Do chapter test for each chapter
Turn in one country profile

Physical Science
       The Physical World textbook contains 20 chapters. Do five per quarter.

Quarter 1
Chapters 1-5 and corresponding lab experiments

Quarter 2
Chapters 6-10 and corresponding lab experiments

Quarter 3
Chapters 11-15 and corresponding lab experiments

Quarter 4
Chapters 16-21 and corresponding lab experiments

Spanish I

In the *Spanish For Mastery I* textbook with accompanying workbook, cover 8 of the 10 units during the year. Use workbook for written homework assignments and use textbook for oral lessons.

Quarter 1
Units 1 and 2, pp 1-79
Workbook pp 1-36 (including unit tests 1 and 2)
Aim to do one fun or interesting activity per week (ideas: cook a typical Spanish dinner, try to speak in Spanish during dinner; label items in the house with Spanish words; watch Spanish TV programs; translate a children's story)

Quarter 2
Units 3 and 4, pp 80-165
Workbook pp 37-68 (including unit tests 3 and 4)
Aim to do one fun or interesting activity per week

Quarter 3
Units 5 and 6, pp 166-251
Workbook pp 69-100 (including unit tests 5 and 6)
Aim to do one fun or interesting activity per week

Quarter 4
Units 7 and 8, pp 252-337
Workbook pp 101-136 (including unit tests 7 and 8)
Aim to do one fun or interesting activity per week

Starting Points World View Primer

Curriculum includes syllabus with 36 weekly lessons. Reading, note taking, and answering key questions in writing or through discussion are incorporated into each week's lesson.

Quarter 1   Weeks 1-8 syllabus
Answers for Difficult Days by David Quine
Know What You Believe by Paul Little
How to Read Slowly by James Sire

Quarter 2   Weeks 9-17 syllabus
The Magician's Nephew by C.S. Lewis
The Lion, the Witch, and the Wardrobe by C.S. Lewis
The Horse and His Boy by C.S. Lewis
It's a Wonderful Life (film)
The Wizard of Oz (film)
Frankenstein by Mary Shelley
Dr. Jekyll and Mr. Hyde by Robert Louis Stevenson
The Deadliest Monster by Jeff Baldwin

Quarter 3   *Weeks 18-26 syllabus*
Know Why You Believe by Paul Little
Mere Christianity by C.S. Lewis
Assumptions That Affect Our Lives by Christian Overman

Quarter 4   *Weeks 27-36 syllabus*
Never Before in History by Gary Amos

Writing and Speech

  Writing assignments will be based on assignments from the *Starting Points* worldview curriculum. In addition, the student will practice a variety of essay types and will develop essay techniques learned from the Institute for Excellence in Writing *Student Writing Intensive C* course. Bob Jones University Press *Writing & Grammar 9* will be used as a supplement for some writing instruction as well as for grammar review. Student will do only selected exercises, not the whole book.

Quarter 1
Institute for Excellence in Writing *Student Writing Intensive Level C* course
Example essay
Classification essay
Definition essay
Creative essay
Personal worldview essay *(Starting Points)*
Two speeches based on previously written essays

Quarter 2
Concepts from BJU *Writing & Grammar 9*, pp 386-395
Starting Points essays:
The World of Narnia essay
The Land of Oz essay
It's a Wonderful Life essay
Mary Shelley's Worldview essay
Stevenson's Worldview essay
Three speeches based on previously written essays

Quarter 3
Process essay
Analogy essay
Cause and effect essay
Precís writing assignments
Comparison essay
Briefly cover Chapter 13 in *Writing and Grammar* book on Library Skills
Start SAT prep books on topics of reading comprehension
Three speeches based on previously written essays

<u>*Quarter 4*</u>
Starting Points essays:
5-paragraph American history essay
English Common Law essay
Colonial Education essay
Family Life and Nomenclature essay
American Revolution essay
Two Founding Documents essay
Separation of Church and State essay
Three speeches based on previously written essays

Grammar and Mechanics Skills

From *BJU Writing & Grammar 9* book, use worksheet quizzes at end of book as a diagnostic pretest for chapter material. Assign homework in weak areas and then give chapter test. Assign more homework if more than 10% of questions are missed on chapter tests. Cover one chapter every two to three weeks.

<u>*Quarter 1*</u>
Chapters 1 3

<u>*Quarter 2*</u>
Chapters 4-6

<u>*Quarter 3*</u>
Chapters 7-9

<u>*Quarter 4*</u>
Chapters 10-12

Quarterly Assignment List Broken Down by Week

Now that you have listed the basic assignments that will comprise each quarter of the school year for each subject, you will create a document laying out tentative assignments for *each week of the quarter* with dates and days of the week noted. Allow yourself a couple of hours to create this document, and fortify yourself with coffee, tea, or chocolate, as needed. (Maybe all three!)

Working with only one quarter at a time, place the assignments into the appropriate weeks or days, spreading them out to account for how long each assignment should take. It helps to prepare a separate page for each subject or group of two or three related subjects, with dates in the left column and textbooks or subject categories along the top. Individual daily assignments, such as lesson numbers, page numbers, or writing assignments, are filled in for each week. The example later in this chapter shows the assignments from the algebra, geography, science, and Spanish courses for the ninth grader described above. To be complete, the spreadsheet would also need to include the English assignments and any other subjects being planned. In short, your goal is to list each subject's specific assignments for each week and day during the quarter. As a rule of thumb, aim for about one hour of schoolwork per subject per day, five days per week. More work will be required for honors and AP courses and for extensive projects such as research papers or science projects. For these, the student will likely have to spend extra time in the evenings or on the weekends.

Making a quarterly assignment sheet can be tedious and can generate discouragement if you are not able to keep up with the proposed schedule. Consequently, you might be tempted to skip this step. However, I have actually found this document to be a sanity saver. From it, I can quickly prepare assignment lists to give to the student for each week of school without consulting every textbook again from scratch. If—or should I say, *when*—we begin to get off schedule a few weeks into the quarter, I simply make adjustments in my computer file as we go along, and I try to make up for it in some other way. This might mean dropping some less important assignments, doubling up on assignments until you are caught up (easier said than done), assigning weekend homework, or rethinking an assignment to come up with one that takes less time but still accomplishes your objectives. If your quarterly plans get seriously out of order and the subject is a critical one, you may just decide to keep working during the summer until you finish.

When your first quarter of school is almost over and it is time to make up another quarterly assignment list, look back on the first quarter's list for any unfinished assignments or projects. These will either become first priority assignments for the new quarter or be waived or modified by you, the teacher-in-charge, depending on how important you think they are.

Needless to say, you would not want to make up a whole year's worth of quarterly assignment lists at one time. For most homeschoolers, the school year is just too changeable and unpredictable. However, it is wise and practical to "force yourself" to think through this structure nine weeks at a time, especially if you and your student want to keep up with your goals for college preparation. In the meantime, your list of yearly goals, broken down by quarter, will suffice to keep you looking ahead toward completion of each subject.

Weekly Assignment List

Theoretically, a motivated student could work directly from the quarterly assignment list, although for some assignments you will still need to provide more detail and direction than what fits in your spreadsheet columns. For instance, your quarterly list might say "descriptive essay." In reality, you will need to provide your student with details on the subject, length, and other criteria for the essay. But for math assignments that simply indicate a lesson number or page numbers, the student could easily work from the spreadsheet.

Typically, though, your student will need a weekly list of assignments. This list springs directly from your quarterly list. When we were homeschooling, I usually sat down on Sunday evenings and prepared the list for the coming week, but if you prefer to keep Sunday free, you might do it on a Friday night or on Saturday to prepare for the coming week. Like most of your documents, this one is best done on the computer, rather than handwriting it, as it is much faster and allows changes to be made with little effort. From week to week, you can even copy and paste last week's list onto a blank page and simply change the pertinent page numbers. After all, some of last week's assignments are probably still unfinished!

As you think about the weekly assignment list, find out how your student prefers to see this list. Does he or she like to view the subjects one by one, with the days of the week for various assignments noted? Or does your student want to see the day of the week first, with *all* the subjects listed underneath? (This is how I did my students' lists.) Does your student prefer separate lists of tasks you will do together and tasks he or she will do independently, or could you get by with showing the "together" work in bold print? Would it be helpful if you also listed outside activities and commitments to make it easier to plan each day's work? For instance, you could list park days, field trips, dental appointments, and other activities that would take up time during the day.

Once you have planned the general format and presentation of the week's assignments, updating it each week will be easy. An example of a weekly list for the first week of school as planned in the sample quarterly assignment list is provided later in the chapter.

9. Design grade recording logs in spreadsheet or journal form, or in a form useful to you.

Take heart—you are almost done creating forms. The next forms you create will allow you to record scores for assignments in a quick, streamlined way. A full discussion of grading, including how to design recording sheets, will appear in Chapter 9. In brief, though, take a look at your list of assignments for each subject and ask yourself what kind of recording sheet—simple or detailed—will best suit your needs. In the long run, your goal is to design a form that will make it easy for you to calculate grades at the end of the semester. If possible, take the time to create a log that is customized for that particular subject and includes groups of similar assignments listed together.

If that statement sounds confusing, here are some suggestions:

Grading Suggestions for Specific Subjects

Math
- Separate the test scores from the homework scores.
- Allow plenty of lines to record the score for each homework assignment or test, and include a space at the end for the average score.
- Allow a few lines to record extra credit points to be added to test scores or to homework scores.

English or Social Studies
- Create separate sections to record scores for types of assignments such as essays, reading assignments, tests or quizzes, speeches, practice SAT exams, grammar workbook pages, or major research projects.
- For each type of assignment, allow enough space to briefly describe the assignment, record the score, and record an average score at the end of each group.
- You may list the specific assignments at the outset of the semester if you are confident that you will stay with this list (*Macbeth* essay, Grammar Quiz Chapters 1-5, Persuasive Speech, etc.), or you may keep your log more generic and leave room for spontaneity by leaving space for Essay #1, Grammar Quiz #1, Speech #1, etc.

Science
- Create a list with space for each chapter, including the title or concept if desired.
- For each chapter, create a column for tests, quizzes, homework, reports, and lab experiments, as appropriate.
- Create a space for longer-term science projects, if applicable.

World Language
- If you are using a textbook, set up a sheet to record homework, quizzes, translations, and tests from each chapter.
- If you are using a computer-based curriculum and need to record the hours your student spends, set up a log with space for hours spent, lesson completed, concept studied, and score on tests or quizzes.

<u>*Physical Education, Life Skills, or Fine Arts*</u>
A simple time log may be all you need. Construct a log in which the student can record the time spent and activity accomplished.

A sample grading log for an English class using a variety of assignment types is displayed in Chapter 8. For all subjects, create a space at the bottom of the recording log to fill in the *average score* for each type of assignment, the *weight percent* for each type of assignment, and the *final percentage* value for each type of assignment and for the course as a whole.
For example:
Algebra 2
Average test score: 89% x weighting (50%) =   44.5
Average homework score: 82% x weighting (50%) =   41.0
Total score in course: **85.5%**   **B**

10. List and gather specialized materials needed for the course.

Lab science courses will need supplies; courses heavy in research or outside reading will need trips to the library or online book orders; art courses will need appropriate materials. Making a master list of what you will need all year, and then breaking it down roughly according to the month of school when it will be needed, will keep your course moving smoothly without interruption.

PHASE FOUR: LEARNING

11. Conduct the course and record assignment grades.

Obviously, the bulk of your time will be spent not in grading and recording, but in teaching, learning, and enjoying the subjects you have chosen. Having user-friendly forms ready to go will help you as you homeschool. Keep them in a 3-ring binder that you can grab and carry around with you as needed.

Do your best to grade or evaluate assignments quickly so that your student will have feedback on what he or she is doing right or wrong before moving on to the next assignment. Assuming that you are giving your student verbal or written feedback, you can be a bit more relaxed about writing these scores down in your own logs. Preferably weekly, but at least monthly, record recent assignment scores on your record keeping sheets. At the end of the quarter (midway through the semester), take inventory and inform the student of any missing assignments. If you like, give an approximate overall grade thus far.

DATE	GEOG TEXT	GEOG ACTIVITY	SPANISH TEXT PGS	SPANISH ACTIVITY	ALGEBRA 2	MATH DRILL	SCIENCE READ/DO	SCIENCE ACTIVITY
MON SEPT 1	246-252	GEOG GAME		LISTEN TO	LESSON 1A			
TUES SEPT 2	253-258		2-5	PRONUNCIATION	B		2-11	
WED SEPT 3	258-264			TAPE	C		11-18	
THURS SEPT 4	264-269		6-9	WORKBOOK PP 1-4	D			LAB 1A/1B
FRI SEPT 5	CHAP 11 TEST				TEST	80	LAB REPORT	
MON SEPT 8	271-277	COUNTRY	10-12	LEARN 2 SPANISH	LESSON 2A		CH 1 TEST	LABS DUE
TUES SEPT 9	277-281	POSTER		SONGS	B		20-29	
WED SEPT 10	281-289		13-16		C		30-36	
THURS SEPT 11	289-296			WB PP 5-6	D			LAB 2A/2B
FRI SEPT 12	CHAP 12 TEST			MEMORY GAME	TEST	81	LAB REPORT	
MON SEPT 15	300-306	MUSIC	20-23		LESSON 3A		CH 2 TEST	LABS DUE
TUES SEPT 16	306-310	ACTIVITY		WB PP 7-10	B		CATCH UP	
WED SEPT 17	310-316		24-27		C		40-46	
THURS SEPT 18	316-322			SPANISH BINGO	D		46-51	
FRI SEPT 19	CHAP 13 TEST		28-30	VOCAB QUIZ	TEST	82	51-57	
MON SEPT 22	324-331	GEOG GAME	31-33		LESSON 4A		58-61	
TUES SEPT 23	331-335			WB PP 11-12	B		62-65	
WED SEPT 24	336-342		34-36		C		APPLICATIONS 3A 3B	
THURS SEPT 25	342-346		37-42	CHILD'S BOOK &	D			LAB 3C
FRI SEPT 26	CHAP 14 TEST		STUDY	AUDIO	TEST	83	LAB REPORT	
MON SEPT 29	348-355	ETHNIC	TEST 1		LESSON 5A		CHAP REVIEW	
TUES SEPT 30	356-360	MEAL	43-47	WB PP 13-16	B		CH 3 TEST,	LABS DUE
WED OCT 1	360-366		50-51		C		68-74	
THURS OCT 2			52-54		D		75-79	
FRI OCT 3	CHAP 15 TEST				TEST	84	80-85	
MON OCT 6	370-377		55-57	LABEL ITEMS	LESSON 6A		85-88	
TUES OCT 7	377-384	COUNTRY		IN SPANISH	B		CHAP REVIEW	
WED OCT 8	384-391	PROFILE	58-59		C		CATCH UP	
THURS OCT 9			60-61	WB PP 17-20	D			LABS 4A/4B
FRI OCT 10	CHAP 16 TEST				TEST	85	REVIEW	
MON OCT 13	393-396	ART PROJECT	62-63	WATCH SPANISH	LESSON 7A		STUDY	
TUES OCT 14	396-401			TV	B		CH 4 TEST	LABS DUE
WED OCT 15	402-408		64-65		C		90-93	
THURS OCT 16	408-412		66-67	WB PP 21-24	D		94-97	
FRI OCT 17	CHAP 17 TEST				TEST	86	98-101	
MON OCT 20	414-418	GEOG GAME	68-69	TRANSLATE	LESSON 8A		CHAP REVIEW	
TUES OCT 21	418-421			CHILDREN'S BOOK	B		CATCH UP	
WED OCT 22	422-424		70-71	WB PP 25-28	C		ORAL REVIEW	
THURS OCT 23	CHAP 18 TEST		72-73		D			LABS 5B,5C
FRI OCT 24					TEST	87	STUDY	
MON OCT 27	428-434	ETHNIC	74-75	WB PP 29-32	LESSON 9A		CH 5 TEST	LABS DUE
TUES OCT 28	434-439	MEAL			B		106-112	
WED OCT 29	439-440		76-77	WB PP 33-36	C&D		112-116	
THURS OCT 30	441-445		78-79	COOK SPANISH	TEST		116-123	
FRI OCT 31	CHAP 19 TEST		TEST 2	MEAL	QTR TEST I	88	124-129	

Sample Weekly Assignment List

Monday
Algebra	View lesson video and do Lesson 1A together
Starting Points Curriculum	No assignment
Writing, Grammar	View IEW Student Writing Intensive w/ me and do activities
Science	No assignment
Geography	Read pp 246-252 from Chap 11
Spanish	Listen to pronunciation tape
Bible	Devotions together
P.E.	Optional
Other Activities	FIRST DAY OF SCHOOL MYSTERY OUTING!

Tuesday
Algebra	Lesson 1B
Starting Points Curriculum	Read and discuss Syllabus Introduction
Writing, Grammar	View IEW Student Writing Intensive w/ me and do activities
Science	Read pp 2-11
Geography	Read pp 253-258. Play Geography Game.
Spanish	Do pp 2-5 together
Bible	Devotions together
P.E.	Soccer practice

Wednesday
Algebra	Lesson 1C
Starting Points Curriculum	*Answers for Difficult Days*, first section
Writing, Grammar	View IEW Student Writing Intensive w/ me and do activities
Science	Read pp 11-18
Geography	Read pp 258-264
Spanish	No assignment
Bible	Devotions together
P.E.	Work out at gym 30-45 minutes

Thursday
Algebra	Lesson 1D
Starting Points Curriculum	*Answers for Difficult Days*, second section
Writing, Grammar	No assignment if IEW lessons are finished
Science	Do Experiments 1A and 1B together
Geography	Read pp 264-269
Spanish	Do pp 6-9 together and do workbook pages 1-4
Bible	(Together) Read Ch 1 of *Why the Bible Matters*
P.E.	Work out at gym 30-45 minutes

Friday
Algebra	Lesson 1 Test, CalcuLadder Drill 80
Starting Points Curriculum	Continue with Week 1 Syllabus assignment and reading
Writing, Grammar	Writing and Grammar Pretest for Chapter 1
Science	Write up lab report and study Chapter 1 for test Monday
Geography	Chap 11 Test
Spanish	No assignment
Bible	Study verses for AWANA handbook
P.E.	Soccer game (Saturday)

PHASE FIVE: DOCUMENTING

12. Calculate semester grades, record grades and credits, and file course descriptions and syllabi for future use.

At the end of the semester, average each subject's scores for the entire semester, put these scores into their weight formula calculation, add in any extra credit points your student may have earned, and calculate a final overall percentage and course grade for your student. This final letter grade will be submitted to your homeschool study program if you belong to one. If you are constructing your own transcript, enter the title, credits, and grade for each course your student completed this semester. Some of your courses, such as Life Skills or Fine Arts, may take more than one year to complete because your student is accumulating hours or checking off a long list of tasks. Keep tabs on the progress, and from time to time you will be ready to enter grades and credits for these courses as well, placing them into the most appropriate semester(s) on the transcript. Chapter 11 will explain the creation of a transcript.

The documents you worked so hard to create have one more destination—no, not the wastebasket! After the course is completed and you have recorded the grade and credits, file the course description and syllabus in a file folder labeled for that student and that year of school. In another file, to be called the "portfolio" file, you may choose to keep the grade recording sheets, yearly and quarterly assignment sheets, and perhaps even the weekly assignment sheets. The most important pieces of documentation to have available, though, are the course description and course syllabus. You will probably need to refer to these when describing your homeschooling on college applications, and you may also need them to clear prerequisites for community college courses.

ONLINE PLANNING TOOLS

Since we are comfortably settled in the 21st century, you may very well be asking if there are online tools that can accomplish these same tasks and help you stay organized. Yes, there are! Though you can find many excellent planners and organizers out there, one I've recently become aware of from a homeschooling mom who absolutely loves it is called Homeschool Planet®. With this nifty subscription-based organizing system, you can plan out your whole year (down to each day's assignments) and then change it all up to reschedule effortlessly if "life" gets in the way and things don't get done. Lesson plans, reports, grading, scheduling of family tasks and appointments, color coding, student logins, reminders, customizable views and formats…it's all there! Check out https://homeschoolplanet.com/ for more information.

TO SUM UP

Whew! You have just completed a field trip to the Course Planning Factory and have lived to tell about it. As you read the next chapter, you will take the tour again, but this time with one sample course in mind. While the process sounds complicated, the more you do it, the more accustomed you will become to the routine. Ultimately, you will be able to recycle many of the documents you create. Knowing that your course plans and grade recording worksheets are at your fingertips any time they are needed is a satisfying feeling. Having the confidence that your homeschool high school is well-documented is, as they say, *priceless.*

Chapter 8

A Real Example:

The Life Cycle of a Typical Course

*B*ecause it may take a while for all this information to sink in, a concrete example is now in order. Here is a review of what happens in the creation and follow-through of a typical course. We will follow an English class through all the steps from creation to the recording of a grade and credits.

PHASE ONE: CHOOSING

1. Select the courses.

The course will be a junior year English class, designed to prepare your student for the AP English Language and Composition exam as well as for the Evidence-Based Reading and Writing portions of the SAT exam.

Important Note: As you will discover in Chapter 12, the Advanced Placement program has a procedure for course design and preapproval. If you are seeking college recognition of your AP course, as opposed to simply preparing your student for the exam, you must understand and abide by the guidelines described on the College Board AP Central® website at https://apcentral.collegeboard.org/ to get your course syllabus approved. The following course is not necessarily designed to meet these guidelines.

2. Select the approach.

Rather than using a single textbook, you will combine library books, AP and SAT prep books, a vocabulary study workbook, and online resources to meet the objectives of the course.

3. Select materials and resources.

After perusing syllabi online for several high school AP English Language and Composition courses, you have come up with a list of possible literature readings. You decide to use mostly American authors and poets, to tie in with your student's U.S. History course. To your delight, you discover two other homeschooling families interested in a similar course. After conferring about which literary works to select, you agree to meet every two weeks for a "Discussion and Dessert" evening, which will also serve as a forum for the students to present speeches from time to time. To augment your student's vocabulary study, you will use a vocabulary workbook, *Vocabulary from Classical Roots.*

PHASE TWO: PLANNING

4. Title your course and write a course description.

You model your brief description on the AP English Language and Composition course objectives available online, as well as on several sample syllabi. (This sample course has not been titled "AP" but is simply called "English Language and Composition" because it is not a College Board-approved course. However, you might choose to seek approval through the AP Course Audit process. See Chapter 12.)

English Language and Composition

In this English course, the student will integrate skills learned in the first two years of high school to prepare for the AP English Language and Composition exam. The student will read a wide variety of literature, examine rhetorical devices, techniques, and strategies, and analyze texts using writing, discussion, and oral presentation. A study of vocabulary from classical roots will supplement the literature and writing portions of the course.

5. Gather assignment ideas.

As you browse high school English teachers' websites, you discover a few common themes for AP English Language and Composition assignments. These, in combination with your goals for SAT exam preparation, form the backbone of your assignment list for the year.

Assignments (placed in order of importance and given percentage weight toward grade):
Essays: 45%
One essay written on each literary work, plus timed essays to practice for the SAT exam
Reading and discussion: 15%
5 novels, 2 plays, 2 autobiographies, and selected short nonfiction and poetry
Speeches: 15%
Four speeches based on the literary works
Tests: 15%
Multiple choice practice tests for the SAT Evidence-Based Reading and Writing section, using SAT prep books, and AP practice tests using an AP prep book
Vocabulary quizzes: 10%
Based on sections of the vocabulary workbook. Sixteen quizzes will be given throughout the year, plus a longer final exam at the end of each semester.

6. Create a course syllabus.

After much thinking, rewriting, crossing out, tossing drafts into the recycling bin, and consuming chocolate, you come up with your masterpiece: a syllabus combining the course description, the major books, resources, and assignments, and a general grading plan. Moreover, you have even backed up the file in case your computer crashes. You have every right to be proud of this accomplishment!

Remember that you may pattern your syllabus on community college course descriptions and syllabi, as well as on those for high school courses you find online. The following is my conglomeration drawn from high school and college course syllabi. Many syllabi contain additional details, describing numbers and topics of tests, essays, and other assignments to be completed each quarter or semester. I normally use a separate document for this purpose (the quarterly and weekly assignment goals).

English Language and Composition
Syllabus for 2019-20

Instructor: *(list any outside instructors, including their credentials if possible)*
Grade Level: 11   **Prerequisite:** English 10
Credits: 1.0 per year, 0.5 per semester *(using Carnegie unit system)*

Course Description

In this English course, the student will integrate skills learned in the first two years of high school to prepare for the AP English Language and Composition exam. The student will read a wide variety of literature, examine rhetorical devices, techniques, and strategies, and analyze texts using both writing and discussion. A study of vocabulary from classical roots will supplement the literature and writing portions of the course.

Evaluation Criteria

Writing Assignments **45% of grade**
Literary analysis essays and timed essays will display student's understanding of themes, meanings, structures, and literary devices used by the authors.

Reading and group discussion of literature **15% of grade**
Selections or entire works in the genres of autobiography, fiction, essays, drama, and poetry will be read and discussed, with student required to participate actively and contribute thoughtful insights.

Speeches **15% of grade**
Student will present short speeches based on four of the literary works.

Tests **15% of grade**
Student will take multiple choice practice tests for the SAT Evidence-Based Reading and Writing sections, using prep books, as well as preparing for and taking AP practice tests using an AP English Language and Composition prep book. Essay sections will be scored using the AP rubric.

Vocabulary Quizzes **10% of grade**
Student will take weekly quizzes from a vocabulary workbook, plus a final exam each semester.

Extra Credit   Additional essays or reading/discussion of additional literature may earn extra credit points.

Grading Scale

90-100% =   A
80-89% =   B
70-79% =   C
60-69% =   D

(continued)

English Language and Composition
Syllabus for 2019-20
(continued)

Curriculum and Resources

How to Read a Book by Mortimer J. Adler and Charles Van Doren, Touchstone, 1972.

The Lively Art of Writing by Lucile Vaughan Payne, Penguin Group, 1969.

Vocabulary from Classical Roots, Book E by Norma Fifer and Nancy Flowers, Educators Publishing Service, 2004.

5 Steps to a 5: AP English Language, 7th edition, by Barbara Murphy and Estelle Rankin, McGraw-Hill Education, 2015.

The Official SAT Study Guide™, 2016 edition, College Board, 2015.

Reading selections from the genres of autobiography, fiction, essays, drama, and poetry as listed below.

Reading List for English Language and Composition

Autobiography
The Autobiography of Benjamin Franklin
Narrative of the Life of Frederick Douglass, an American Slave

Fiction
The Scarlet Letter by Nathaniel Hawthorne
The Red Badge of Courage by Stephen Crane
O Pioneers! by Willa Cather
The Great Gatsby by F. Scott Fitzgerald
To Kill a Mockingbird by Harper Lee

Essays
Walden by Henry David Thoreau
Selected Essays by Ralph Waldo Emerson

Plays
The Crucible by Arthur Miller
Death of a Salesman by Arthur Miller

Politics & History
The Souls of Black Folk by W.E.B. DuBois
"A Testament of Hope," an essay by Martin Luther King, Jr.

Poetry
Selected poetry from *The Norton Anthology of Poetry, 6th edition* by Margaret Ferguson, Tim Kendall, and Mary Jo Salter, W.W. Norton & Co. 2018.

7. Design a grading plan.

You have already determined the percentage weight that each type of assignment contributes toward the grade. Now, for each assignment category, you need to decide and record how you will construct these assignments and evaluate your student's learning. You come up with the following criteria.

Essays

You plan to use literature-based essay prompts gleaned from teacher websites or from literature websites. As you select these, you will assign several essay structures, including descriptive, narrative, comparison and contrast, cause and effect, and persuasive. You will grade the essays using a rubric (see Chapter 9) covering content, organization, style, and mechanics. AP and SAT essays will be scored according to rubrics described in the preparation books, but for your purposes they will be graded largely on improvement from one practice test to the next.

Reading and Discussion

You intend to search for discussion questions from literature websites. You want to encourage your student to keep brief annotations or journal notes during reading, and you have found a useful article that describes journaling as a preparation for essay writing. As you discuss the literary works together and also in the biweekly discussion group, you will give a subjective grade for discussion on a scale of 1 to 10, based on preparation for discussion, insightful comments, interest and alertness, and respect for others' comments.

Speeches

You have made up a simple rubric covering speech content, organization, delivery, and use of props and visuals. On your discussion nights, you will have the students informally evaluate each other's speeches, communicating what they liked about the speech as well as what improvements are needed.

Vocabulary

Vocabulary quizzes from the workbook will be graded based on the percentage of correct answers.

SAT and AP practice tests

For the first practice test, you will give your student credit simply for doing the tests. After he or she is more accustomed to them, the grade will be based on *improvement* compared to the previous tests, not on the absolute percentage correct. You will grade the tests according to the answer key in the prep book and will then convert these scores into an approximate percentage grade (just for the sake of recording the scores toward the semester grade).

PHASE THREE: MAKING LISTS AND LOGS

8. Make up yearly, quarterly, and weekly goals or assignment lists.

The goals you set for the school year will be divided in half for each semester. Then half of this (half of the literature, essays, speeches, vocabulary, and SAT or AP prep) would comprise a typical quarter. (*Skip down to the samples referenced in the section on designing recording logs to see what a typical semester's assignments might be.*) After dividing the semester work in half, simply lay out the quarterly list of assignments, week by week, fitting the assignments into the individual weeks based on their logical order and on how long the assignments will take. A sample quarterly assignment list, broken down by week, for the English Language and Composition course is shown at the end of the chapter, as is a list of the assignments you might give for one typical week of this nine-week plan.

9. Design grade recording logs.

See the samples of grade recording logs provided at the end of the chapter. Logs are shown for both fall and spring semesters, since the spring will have a different literature lineup. For the fall semester, hypothetical scores have been filled in. You could also use an online grade book tool or purchase a traditional teacher's grade book and label the pages and columns to suit each subject you are teaching.

10. List and gather specialized materials needed for the course.

Since you have decided to purchase some, but not all of the reading materials for this course, you make a library list of the books you will borrow and pencil in the approximate dates you will have to check out these books. Any that you cannot find in the library or that you want in your possession for the whole year, you search out for purchase, either in print format or for an e-reader.

PHASE FOUR: LEARNING

11. Conduct the course and record assignment grades.

You launch into the school year with your student. For the most part you keep up with your plans, but you adjust here and there. Due to time constraints, you drop one of the essay assignments and one of the chapters of vocabulary. After the first semester, you have recorded grades as shown on the chart at the end of the chapter.

PHASE FIVE: DOCUMENTING

12. Calculate semester grades, record grades and credits, and file the course description and syllabus for future use.

Update your student's transcript and record 1.0 units of credit earned, with a letter grade of A.

TO SUM UP

Hopefully, this second field trip to the Course Planning Factory has revealed a bit more about designing a course that is specific to the needs of your student. Again, take heart that you won't have to do this for each and every course. "Outside courses" will be designed for you already; other courses may be closely modeled after a course you have already designed; still others may be much simpler to design than this advanced English course was. And of course, your personal homeschooling style may not require all these steps and documents. Use what makes sense to you and is helpful to you; discard the rest as you develop customized courses for your own student.

ENGLISH LANGUAGE AND COMPOSITION
QUARTERLY ASSIGNMENT SHEET BY WEEK
11TH GRADE, QUARTER 1

WEEK		LITERATURE	WRITING	SPEECHES	AP TESTS	SAT TESTS	VOCAB
1	MON	*THE CRUCIBLE*	DESCRIPTIVE	READ	GO OVER	GO OVER	STUDY
	TUES	READ & DISCUSS	ESSAY	CHAPTERS	FORMAT OF	FORMAT	LESSON 1
	WED	FIRST HALF		IN SPEECH	EXAM	OF EXAM	
	THURS	& RESEARCH		BOOK -			
	FRI	*BACKGROUND*		INTRO			
2	MON	*THE CRUCIBLE*	NARRATIVE			STUDY	QUIZ 1
	TUES	READ & DISCUSS	ESSAY	ORGANIZATION		PREP BOOK	
	WED	SECOND HALF	REVISE DESCRIP			PAGES: __	
	THURS		ESSAY				
	FRI	*DISCUSSION/DESSERT NIGHT*					
3	MON	*SCARLET LETTER*	CAUSE/EFFECT	DELIVERY	PRACTICE	STUDY	
	TUES	CH 1-8 READ,	ESSAY	TECHNIQUES	ESSAY	PREP BOOK	
	WED	DISCUSS			TOGETHER	PAGES:___	
	THURS		REVISE NARR				
	FRI		ESSAY				
4	MON	*SCARLET LETTER*	REVISE	GESTURES		SAT RDG	STUDY
	TUES	CH 9-16	CAUSE/EFFECT			TEST 1	LESSON 2
	WED	READ, DISCUSS	ESSAY				
	THURS						
	FRI	*DISCUSSION/DESSERT NIGHT*					
5	MON	*SCARLET LETTER*		PREPARE	PRACTICE	GO OVER	QUIZ 2
	TUES	CH 17-24 READ,		SPEECH ON	ESSAY	SAT RDG	
	WED	DISCUSS		*SCARLET*	TOGETHER	TEST	
	THURS			*LETTER*			
	FRI						
6	MON	*AUTOBIOGRAPHY*	CHARACTER			DISCUSS	STUDY
	TUES	*OF BEN*	ANALYSIS	PRESENT		TECHNIQUE	LESSON 3
	WED	*FRANKLIN*		SPEECH ON		FOR SAT	
	THURS	PART I READ, DISCUSS		*SCARLET*		WRIT/LANG	
	FRI	*DISCUSSION/DESSERT NIGHT*		*LETTER*			
7	MON	*AUTOBIOGRAPHY*	REVISE			SAT	QUIZ 3
	TUES	*OF BEN*	CHARACTER			WRIT/LANG	
	WED	*FRANKLIN*	ANALYSIS			TEST 1	
	THURS	PART II READ,					
	FRI	DISCUSS					
8	MON	*AUTOBIOGRAPHY*			AP PRACTICE	GO OVER	STUDY
	TUES	*OF BEN*		CRITIQUE	TEST #1	WRIT/LANG	LESSON 4
	WED	*FRANKLIN*		ANOTHER		TEST	
	THURS	PART III & IV		STUDENT'S			
	FRI	*DISCUSSION/DESSERT NIGHT*		SPEECH			
9	MON	REVIEW &	COMPARE/		GO OVER		QUIZ 4
	TUES	CATCH UP	CONTRAST		AP PRACTICE		
	WED		ESSAY		TEST #1		
	THURS						
	FRI						

Sample Weekly Assignment List
ENGLISH LANGUAGE AND COMPOSITION

Monday, September 1
Research background of the play *The Crucible*
Read first half of *The Crucible*
Read first section of SAT prep book describing the exam
Discuss SAT exam with me

Tuesday, September 2
Discuss first half of *The Crucible*
Read first section of AP prep book describing the exam
Discuss AP exam format with me

Wednesday, September 3
Start a 2-3 page descriptive essay based on the historical setting of *The Crucible*
Study Vocabulary Lesson 1

Thursday, September 4
Study Vocabulary Lesson 1
Work on descriptive essay

Friday, September 5
Study Vocabulary Lesson 1 for quiz on Monday
Finish descriptive essay
Read intro chapter in speech book

Grading Log - English Language and Composition — Fall Semester

Literature	Writing Assignments		Reading & Discussion
	Descriptive	88%	
	Narrative	86%	
The Crucible	Cause/effect	92%	90%
The Scarlet Letter	Character analysis	90%	100%
Autobiography of Benjamin Franklin	Comparison/contrast	99%	95%
Narrative of the Life of Frederick Douglass	Persuasive	88%	85%
The Red Badge of Courage	Character analysis	(waived)	90%
O Pioneers!	Theme analysis	92%	100%
	Average essay score	91%	
	Average reading/discussion score		93%

Speeches
The Scarlet Letter	85%
The Red Badge of Courage	90%
Average speech score	87.5%

Tests
AP English Language Practice Tests Grading Scale:

0% improvement = 85%	5-10% improvement = 95%
1-4% improvement = 90%	10% or higher improvement = 100%

Note that this is a very subjective set of scores and is simply a suggestion. Even the percentages you assign here will be approximate, based on number of correct multiple choice questions and your best estimate of a score on the essay portion of the test.

AP English Language Practice Test 1   85%
AP English Language Practice Test 2   88% Improvement 3% Grade recorded as 90%

SAT Practice Tests:

0 pt improvement = 80%	15-20 pt improvement = 95%
5-10 pt improvement = 90%	25 pt or higher improvement = 100%

SAT Practice Test 1   Score 575
SAT Practice Test 2   Score 590 Improvement 15 pts   Grade recorded as 95%

Average test score (not counting first SAT or AP practice test)   92%

Vocabulary Quizzes

1	89%	5	91%	
2	92%	6	95%	
3	84%	7	assignment waived	
4	80%	8	96%	

Final exam (counts as 4 quiz scores)   93% x 4
Average vocabulary score   91%

Semester Grade Calculation Using Weighting of Subject Areas:

Writing Assignments	91% x 0.45 =	41.0
Reading/Discussion	93% x 0.15 =	14.0
Speeches	87.5% x 0.15 =	13.1
Tests	92% x 0.15 =	13.8
Vocabulary	91% x 0.10 =	9.1
Total:		91% Letter Grade: A

Grading Log - English Language and Composition   _Spring Semester_

Literature	_Writing Assignments_		_Reading & Discussion_
Walden	Descriptive	_____	_____
Emerson, selected essays	Process	_____	_____
The Great Gatsby	Cause/effect	_____	_____
Poetry unit	Creative writing	_____	_____
The Souls of Black Folk	Theme analysis	_____	_____
To Kill a Mockingbird	Character analysis	_____	_____
A Testament of Hope	Problem/solution	_____	_____
	Average essay score	_____	
	Average reading/discussion score		_____

Speeches

Walden	_____
The Great Gatsby	_____
Average speech score	_____

Tests

AP English Language Practice Tests Grading Scale:

0% improvement = 85%	5-10% improvement = 95%
1-4% improvement = 90%	10% or higher improvement = 100%

AP English Language Practice Test 3	_____
AP English Language Practice Test 4	_____
AP English Language Practice Test 5	_____

SAT Practice Tests:

0 pt improvement = 80%	15-20 pt improvement = 95%
5-10 pt improvement = 90%	25 pt or higher improvement = 100%

SAT Practice Test 3	_____
SAT Practice Test 4	_____
SAT Practice Test 5	_____

Average test score	_____

Vocabulary Quizzes

9	_____	13	_____
10	_____	14	_____
11	_____	15	_____
12	_____	16	_____
Final exam (counts as 4 quiz scores)			_____
Average vocabulary score			_____

Semester Grade Calculation Using Weighting of Subject Areas:

Writing Assignments	_____ x 0.45 =	_____
Reading/Discussion	_____ x 0.15 =	_____
Speeches	_____ x 0.15 =	_____
Tests	_____ x 0.15 =	_____
Vocabulary	_____ x 0.10 =	_____
Total:	_____	**Letter Grade:** _____

Chapter 9

The Dreaded Red Pen:

Grading Your Student's Work

The thought of grading your own student's work can bring up yet another raft of questions. How will you come up with a fair grade that you can justify? Will colleges accept these grades (sometimes referred to as "Mommy grades")? For that matter, will your *student* accept them?

Actually, if you understand the previous few chapters' instructions on creating an overall grading plan, with types of assignments weighted appropriately toward the final grade, you are halfway there. Now you will deal with the day-to-day grading tasks. First, you will learn to create grading logs, since before you can record a single grade, you need a useful form on which to write it. Next, frequent questions about grading will be raised and addressed to help you become more familiar with the process.

One note before this chapter proceeds much further. Many homeschoolers choose not to give grades, especially during the elementary and middle school years. Some even forgo grades during the high school years and instead provide narrative evaluations of the student's progress and achievements. While your own homeschooling philosophy and goals will guide your grading and evaluation methods, I believe that giving grades during the high school years is largely beneficial. The homeschooling parent is encouraged to set specific performance criteria; the student has something "solid" to aim for and to be accountable for; the student is better prepared for "mandatory" grading environments such as community college classes; and the list of courses and grades (i.e., the transcript) will be fully understandable to the college at application time.

SEMESTER GRADING LOG

To begin with, you will need a place to record the scores your student earns on individual assignments, which will later be averaged to come up with a semester grade.

The Chronological Method

Often the forms that are simplest to make are the most tedious to use, and vice versa. For instance, you could simply take a blank sheet of paper, title it "English Grades," and record each assignment in the order it was completed:

Romeo and Juliet essay	93%
Vocabulary quiz	100%
Discussion of *Hamlet*	95%
Grammar test	85%
… and so on	

However, these assignments may carry different weights toward the semester grade. If you use this method, you will eventually need to sort the assignments into categories so that you can average all the test scores, all the essay scores, and all the discussion scores.

The Category Method

The category method takes more thinking at the outset but is a lifesaver at semester's end when you're rushed and overloaded. Create a worksheet listing the basic assignments *already in their categories*. Or purchase a teacher's grade book and label the columns with these categories. Here is an example:

Essays (50% of grade)

1. Narrative: _____
2. Descriptive: _____
3. Autobiographical: _____
4. Literary analysis (*Hamlet*): _____
5. Research paper (worth 3 grades): _____
    _____
    _____

Average essay score: _____

Literature Reading and Discussion (20% of grade)

1. *Romeo and Juliet*: _____
2. *Hamlet*: _____
3. *Julius Caesar*: _____

Average reading and discussion score: _____

Grammar Tests (10% of grade)

1. _____
2. _____
3. _____

Average grammar score: _____

Vocabulary Quizzes (10% of grade)

1. _____
2. _____
3. _____
4. _____

Average vocabulary score: _____

Speeches (10% of grade)

1. *Hamlet* character analysis: _____
2. Autobiography: _____
3. Persuasive: _____
4. Humorous: _____
Average speech score: _____

This worksheet prepares you for a quick summary of scores at the end of the semester. Use the suggestions from the previous chapter to convert these category scores into a final grade.

If you prefer to be more free-spirited, you can leave a few blank lines for extra assignments you may add. Or, simply create category headings such as Essays or Speeches, place a few blanks under each, and wait to fill in the specific assignments when they are finished. For example, you would list *Speeches: #1, #2, #3, #4*. You would fill in the speech topic when you record the grade.

A customized grading form or log takes more thinking at the beginning of the semester but is easier to use at the end. Remember that this form is just a *guide* to get your semester going—you may delete assignments and add others as the semester gets underway.

Grading forms for math-based courses with only homework assignments and tests are even easier to construct. List the test numbers (Chapter 1, Chapter 2, etc.) in one part of the worksheet and the daily homework lesson numbers in another part, and record the student's grades in each.

At the end of the semester, file these grading logs in a designated folder (paper and electronic) so that you have a record of your rationale for grading. Remember also that you can re-use the templates of these logs for future courses—thus cutting down on your work for the upcoming school years.

GRADING FAQS

Parents want the answer to the burning question: *How do I grade a high schooler's work fairly?* It used to be so easy. A quick glance at your child's math worksheet or written paragraph would tell you how he or she was doing, and grading was more informal. But for high school work, you need to determine ahead of time how those grades will be figured. Below are some common questions about grades.

Where Do I Begin?

Grades can be based on *achievement* (such as a percentage of total points earned), on *basic completion* of the required tasks, or on some *combination* of these factors. Not all courses are easily gradable on a numeric scale. Some require more subjective observations of the efforts or outcome. If the student is learning an entirely new skill, such as drawing, the grade may be based on the student's effort, on completion of projects, and on applying new skills in each project, rather than on outstanding results. P.E. grades, especially for the non-athlete, should be based on cooperation, participation, and effort, not on innate athleticism.

Achievement-Based Grading

In many subjects, grading is based simply on achievement. For most math problems, some science questions, and objective questions on history or grammar tests, an answer is *usually* either right or wrong. However, it's not always as simple as it looks. Many complex math problems have multiple parts or require the student to show work for full credit. Thus, on tests and homework, you may want to assign multiple points to most problems. If the student succeeds in a portion of the problem, he or she receives partial credit. Sometimes, even if the right answer is given, you may want to deduct points if the student does not show all work properly. Similarly, thought questions and essay questions in history and science may earn partial credit for partially correct responses.

A commonly used grading scale for determining letter grades from percentages is as follows:

A   90-100%
B   80-89%
C   70-79%
D   60-69%
F   59% and lower

You may also use a scale that includes "+" and "–" grades, such as A- or B+. As you set the percentages you will use, it can be helpful to ask around and find out what grading scale most high schools are using, since you want the grades on your student's transcript to be comparable to the grades other high schoolers who scored similar percentages would have received. You don't want to be guilty of grade inflation, but you also don't want to do your student a disservice by using an overly strict standard.

Completion- or Effort-Based Grading

For some subjects, grades may be based on completion of assignments or progress toward a list of skills, without regard to talent or achievement. Art, music, P.E., and life skills are good examples, as are project-based courses such as woodworking or graphic design. You might use a point scale to evaluate criteria such as neatness, overall design and planning, project completion, creativity, and technique.

Combined Achievement and Effort-Based Grading

Writing assignments, speeches, and projects are quite subjective to grade because the student is demonstrating a combination of achievement in past skills and effort in learning new skills. Prior to the assignment, give your student a brief description of what you will be looking for. What components will be graded, and what will be expected of the student? For instance, a writing assignment might require an arguable thesis statement, three body paragraphs with three subpoints and examples in each, an attention-getting introduction, and a thoughtful conclusion. If you provide these expectations as a checkoff sheet—preferably with point values included—the student can refer to it while working on the assignment. Because you are combining achievement-based grading with effort-based grading, you will be looking for increased competency on "older" skills as well as initial effort on unfamiliar skills.

What Options Do I Have?

Monitoring your student's progress can be done in a number of ways, from formal to informal, simple to complex, traditional to newfangled. Choose what best suits the subject, the assignment, and the student.

Tests and Quizzes

During high school many homeschoolers continue to emphasize hands-on projects and other creative methods of learning. But acquainting your student with the inevitability of tests is also a wise idea.

Many curricula include tests and quizzes that are already written for you. If you use these, glance over them and advise your student how to study. In other words, the student may need to read and study maps, diagrams, and side notes in the text if these commonly appear on the tests. Sometimes the curriculum comes with too many tests to fit into your school schedule. Feel free to test less frequently, while still testing on the most important content. Perhaps portions of several chapter tests may be combined into one larger test, given less frequently.

You may need to write your own tests or quizzes. Very short, frequent quizzes allow you to break up the material into bite-sized chunks, keeping students on their toes day by day. You might focus these quizzes on new vocabulary appearing in the reading material, or on new types of math problems being introduced. Or, you might make up a few multiple choice questions on material *you* consider vital.

You do not need to dream up quizzes or tests out of the blue. Always look for ready-made sources first. For instance, you may borrow from comprehension questions at the end of the chapter, or from math problems that were not assigned as homework. Math, chemistry, or physics books may also contain sections with extra practice problems, many of which have answers available. And be sure to check online, where you may find a goldmine of raw material for quizzes on any subject imaginable, simply by searching up a few key words such as "algebra quizzes" or "American history quizzes."

Quizzes do not need to be in written form. Oral quizzes allow both of you to interact with the material. Some quizzes can be given without the student even knowing he or she is being quizzed. As you discuss the material, ask a few pertinent questions and see if the student can answer.

Whatever you do, don't give so many tests and assignments that you can't keep up with grading them. If the teacher is overloaded, the student is probably overwhelmed as well. Besides, the real value of a test is in allowing students to see their mistakes early on, so that they can make corrections for next time. Thus, you want to give your student feedback as soon as possible. Be encouraging as you evaluate progress and review tests and quizzes, and use these as positive learning experiences.

Writing Assignments

Because writing skills are so critical for college preparation, almost all high school courses except math should have a few essay or research paper requirements. Instead of parroting information in factual form, the student needs to absorb, assimilate, and analyze the information. Crafting an essay expressing one's own ideas, backed up by facts and illustrations, is an excellent way to organize new information. As you evaluate these papers, you will get a glimpse of how well the student understands the concepts.

Discussions

Through discussions, you can simultaneously teach, learn, and evaluate. Valuable discussions can take place between you and your students alone, or perhaps at the dinner table with the rest of the family. Whenever possible, seek out other students who are studying the same subject. Because hearing other viewpoints is stimulating, discussions are always richer when more people are present.

Generally, you will find no lack of available discussion questions. If you are using a packaged curriculum, the teacher's guide and student text usually include thought questions that require more than just a simple answer. Use a few of these to get the ball rolling. And of course, you'll find an infinite supply online as well. After "priming the pump" with some of these questions, you may soon find that your discussion takes off on its own.

Projects

Projects call upon the student's creativity to summarize or demonstrate the lesson in an innovative way. Assignments such as skits, posters, dioramas, radio interviews, videos, science experiments, and mock newspapers help your student assimilate facts and concepts and present them in a way that both of you will find enjoyable. Projects may end up being one of your and your student's favorite types of assignments. Refer to the list of project ideas in Chapter 6. Always clarify your expectations and guidelines ahead of time so that the student will have some direction.

How Can a Parent Possibly Be Fair and Objective?

This may be the number one question parents ask as their students enter high school. Understandably, it is also a big question in the minds of college admissions officers. Can a parent actually come up with objective, credible grades? Wouldn't parents be tempted to give their children all A's to help them get into college? For this reason, colleges place less emphasis on homeschooled students' grades than they do on those of traditional students. Unfortunately, this often means that they emphasize test scores more.

In my own experience as a homeschool parent, I tend to grade more rigorously than a traditional schoolteacher would—perhaps as a subconscious reaction to the fear of being too lenient. At any rate, you *can* find ways to make your grading objective and fair.

The first, of course, is to prepare a sensible grading plan and to make sure your student reads it. If you have communicated ahead of time exactly what is required to get an A, and your student accomplishes that, then it stands to reason that you have given a fair grade. Both student and teacher will understand the expectations before the course ever starts.

Of course, another prerequisite to fairness is making sure that the requirements you list on your grading plan are neither too easy nor too difficult. Looking at a syllabus or grading policies from a traditional school (for each subject, if possible) can be extremely helpful. You can examine the numbers and types of assignments given and use these as rough guidelines for your course. Honors or AP courses will involve more rigorous requirements than will typical grade-level courses. Remember, you do not have to duplicate what is being done in your local school, since you as the parent know which types of assignments best suit your student's learning style. Using the school syllabus as a starting point, add some assignments, delete or modify others, and integrate some assignments with other subjects.

Hopefully, your student's grade record will correlate roughly with the scores he or she receives on the SAT or ACT exam. In other words, a straight-A student should also score reasonably well on the college entrance exams. There are exceptions, of course, since some students are not good test-takers but are adept at other types of learning. But a few eyebrows may be raised in the admissions office if homeschoolers with 4.0 GPAs consistently receive low scores on the SAT or ACT exams.

What Is a Rubric, and How Is It Used?

For many subjects, a well-planned *rubric*, or scoring guide, is a necessity. A rubric defines the expectations for an assignment and assigns point values so that a *subjective* assignment can be scored on a more *objective* basis. For example, when grading writing assignments, which are typically quite subjective, you want to grade your student as objectively as possible. You also want to communicate the grading criteria to the student ahead of time. For these assignments, you might divide the total points possible into four categories: content, organization, style, and mechanics. Within each category, you list criteria that are important to the assignment. One assignment may focus on style; another, on content. Point values could be adjusted accordingly, or you may choose to use the same rubric for all writing assignments.

During the writing process, the student should use the rubric page as a guide and then should turn it in with the paper so that you can record points earned and give a final grade. This helps both student and parent. For instance, if a student knows that a history essay will be graded on strength of thesis, organization of content, quality and quantity of facts, and well-thought-out arguments, he or she will (hopefully) strive to include these points. You as teacher will specifically look for them in the paper. With a well-written rubric, the grading process will be fair and will contain no surprises. It will also help grading go much more quickly.

A sample rubric for essays is shown later in the chapter. Over our years of homeschooling, this checklist has served as a useful tool to assess content, organization, style, and mechanics skills. Some of the items in this rubric have been modified from Susan Bradrick's *Understanding Writing* curriculum, which utilizes a P.E.T. Sheet (Planning, Evaluation, and Teaching) as a checklist for essay content, style, and mechanics. Other components, including the specific style elements, sentence variety guidelines, and "special elements," are loosely derived from concepts taught by the Institute for Excellence in Writing by Andrew Pudewa. As the rubric has "evolved" over the years, I have added or modified a few other items. The authors of both of these curricula have given their permission for the rubric to be published in this book.

In short, you want to create a rubric that helps you give grades that are fair, objective, and consistent from assignment to assignment. Some simple rubrics might resemble the following samples:

Biology Lab Report

Format (Title, Name, Date)	_____	(10 pts)
Neatness	_____	(15 pts)
Labeling of Drawings	_____	(15 pts)
Accuracy	_____	(15 pts)
Completeness	_____	(15 pts)
Analysis of Outcome	_____	(15 pts)
Reasoning and Thought	_____	(15 pts)
Total	_____	**(100 pts)**

History Research Project

Originality	_____	(25 pts)
Historical Accuracy	_____	(50 pts)
Neatness	_____	(25 pts)
Quality of Presentation	_____	(25 pts)
Thoroughness	_____	(30 pts)
Creative Features/Elements	_____	(20 pts)
Total	_____	**(175 pts)**

HIGH SCHOOL ESSAY RUBRIC

Date _____   **Essay Type and Title** _____

I. Content Checklist (2.5 pts each)   *Total Content* _____ 25 pts

    Main idea clearly identified and defended throughout essay _____
    Main topic and secondary ideas suitable for essay format _____
    Content properly reflects type of assignment or essay prompt used _____
    Logical sequence followed _____
    Sufficient depth of topic demonstrated _____
    Material and facts used well _____
    Ideas interpreted appropriately with respect to context _____ *(Literature essays)*
    Examples, quotations, citings, and details used to fill out "skeleton" _____
    Sufficient detail included to communicate effectively to reader _____
    Significant thoughts and interesting content keep reader's attention _____

II. Organization Checklist   *Total Organization* _____ 25 pts

Introduction   _____ 5 pts
    Intriguing statement used for opener   _____
    General to specific transitions included   _____
    Arguable thesis (purpose) stated clearly   _____
    Body paragraph topics alluded to, hinted, or previewed in thesis statement _____

Body Paragraph #1   _____ 5 pts
    Transition from introduction included   _____
    Topic sentence #1 stated clearly   _____
    Supporting ideas and evidence presented   _____

Body Paragraph #2   _____ 5 pts
    Transition from paragraph #1 included   _____
    Topic sentence #2 stated clearly   _____
    Supporting ideas and evidence presented   _____

Body Paragraph #3   _____ 5 pts
    Transition from paragraph #2 included   _____
    Topic sentence #3 stated clearly   _____
    Supporting ideas and evidence presented   _____

Conclusion   _____ 5 pts
    Transition from paragraph #3 included   _____
    Thesis restated   _____
    Body paragraph concepts summarized   _____
    Effective appeal to reader included in closing   _____

(CONTINUED)

HIGH SCHOOL ESSAY RUBRIC *(Page 2)*

III. Style Checklist   *Total Style* _____ *30 pts*

General use of style: variety of style elements used   _____ *9 pts*
    Adverbial clauses used to create complex sentences   _____
    Adverbs, strong verbs, quality adjectives, and concrete nouns included   _____
    Sentences flow together well   _____
    Individual sentences worded well   _____
    Balance in presentation displayed (sentence length/ideas roughly equal)   _____
    Variety of vocabulary used, including some more sophisticated words   _____

Sentence variety   _____ *9 pts*
    At least half of sentences begin with non-subject-verb pattern   _____
    Overall variety in sentence length and use of compound, complex,
    and simple sentences   _____

Concreteness *Vivid nouns and verbs used instead of excess adjectives*   _____ *6 pts*

Conciseness *Redundant words and ideas removed*   _____ *6 pts*

Special elements included (extra credit):   _____ *pts*
Original, vivid similes or metaphors (no clichés), quotations, questions, repetition of words, phrases, or clauses for emphasis, alliteration, attention-getting statistics, startling statements

IV. Mechanics Checklist   *Total Mechanics* _____ *20 pts*

(Points given on overall composition.)
    Formatting: Double spaced, name and title, page numbers   _____ *2 pts*
    Spelling and Typos   _____ *6 pts*
    Punctuation and Capitalization   _____ *6 pts*
    Grammar and Usage   _____ *6 pts*
    Promptness (Points deducted for late papers)   _____ *pts (-)*

Outline (if required by assignment) Outline turned in with essay. Written in proper outline form, including thesis/topic sentence, logical division of ideas. Content of essay follows outline. _____ *10 pts*

Total points (100 possible, 110 with outline) _____   _____%

Letter grade _____

Score on revision _____   _____%

Comments:

Some elements of this rubric were modified from Susan Bradrick's *Understanding Writing* curriculum (Bradrick Family Enterprises, 1991); others from Institute for Excellence in Writing curriculum and its evaluation checklists by Andrew Pudewa (Institute for Excellence in Writing, various publication dates). Used by permission.

Do I Grade Based on "Perfection" or on an Imaginary Curve?

The short answer is "on an imaginary curve." In a traditional school, many assignments are graded on a curve, either explicitly or implicitly. With an *explicit* curve, a teacher decides not to use the traditional grading scale for which 90% is an A, 80% is a B, and so on. Rather, the grading scale is modified according to the difficulty of the test or assignment *for this particular group of students*. Usually, the mean (average) student's score is set to be the middle C grade, with those scoring higher than that getting A's and B's, and those scoring lower getting D's and F's. Another way to use a curve is to decide that the highest grade in the class, say, 90%, will set the standard as if it were 100%. Other grades will follow from there as a percentage of the highest grade.

With an *implicit* use of a curve in more subjective courses such as English or history, the instructor will not announce a curved grading scale but may tend to look at the top student's paper as the one that sets the standard for the way the others will be graded. In other words, for "A" quality work, the instructor is not necessarily looking for perfection, but rather, seeking evidence of a strong grasp of the concepts.

As homeschoolers, we have no opportunities for grading on the curve, nor even for knowing how other students of the same grade level would do on a given assignment. As a result, in our effort to give a meaningful grade, we sometimes slip into using *perfection* as the standard for 100% or for an A. In reality, if we had a pile of thirty tests or essays, we would be able to group them more realistically, assigning them A through F grades based not on how close they were to perfection, but on the students' relative grasp of the material in comparison with their peers. Because of the lack of opportunities for true comparison, I try to use an "imaginary curve" and often give the student the benefit of the doubt when the score falls between two letter grades.

Most important is knowing whether the student has done his or her best and has grasped the required concepts. If not, a re-do might be in order.

Must I Grade Every Piece of Work?

In a word, no. Classroom teachers come up with their own strategies for dealing with the mass of homework that comes their way. Here are some options:

- *Grade tests and essays only, and don't even count daily homework in the semester grade calculation.*
- *Grade daily homework with a check mark if completed, or a zero if incomplete (or award ten points or so for completed homework), but then do no further grading.* The homework grade will be based solely on the number of assignments completed and turned in.
- *Have the student correct his or her own homework, tests, and quizzes from the answer key and redo the missed problems, or at least understand the mistakes.*
- *Grade all the tests, quizzes, and homework with a percentage grade* (this is very tedious).
- *Grade routine homework using a plus sign, a check mark, or a minus sign, based on the number of problems missed.* For instance, on a thirty-problem math lesson, zero to four problems missed could earn a plus, five to eight missed, a check mark, and more than eight missed, a minus. This system works well for difficult subjects such as math or physics, where problems are commonly missed during the learning phase. At the end of the semester, use the homework grade to enhance, rather than to lower, the test grade percentage. For instance, earning mostly "plus" scores could raise the average test score by 4 or 5%, while check marks would raise it by 2 or 3%, and minuses not at all.
- *Grade only every few homework assignments.* The student will not know which ones will be graded and must be diligent to keep up with homework.

- *Provide a carefully planned rubric and ask the student to come up with his or her own grade on essays, speeches, and projects.* Initially, compare this with the grades you would have given. If the grades consistently match up, have the student do the evaluation from then on. Interestingly, students often grade themselves lower than a parent or teacher would.

- *Regardless of the options you might choose, do consider downgrading late or incomplete work.* Unless there is good reason for changing the due date and you and your student have discussed it, this policy helps accustom your student to putting effort into meeting deadlines and turning in finished assignments that represent his or her best work, not a halfhearted effort.

How Can I Award Partial Credit?

In high school work, the middle ground between a right and a wrong answer can cause confusion for both the student and the teacher.

The issue of partial credit often comes up in math-related courses. However, it can appear anywhere—in a vocabulary definition that is partially but not entirely right, in a short essay question on a history exam for which the student covered *some* of the important points but left others out, or on a Spanish quiz on which the student used the proper verb root but added the wrong ending. You will want to reward your student for what is correct while demonstrating that the answer left something to be desired.

For any course, decide before you grade the test or homework how many points each problem should be worth. Obviously, more complicated problems will be worth more points—possibly ten points or more. Simple, straightforward problems may earn only one or two points. In math and science courses, examine the answer as well as the process of getting to the answer. Did the student write down the appropriate formula? Did he or she show enough work and attach the correct units to the answer? Did the student use proper mathematics to arrive at the answer—but then a small arithmetic error caused the final answer to be incorrect? Each of these criteria can justify awarding or withholding some points. You may choose to subtract points for answers that are correct but have no formulas or intermediate work shown. Make sure your student understands how you will grade complex problems and also understands how to properly work out an answer.

Is it "Legal" to Drop the Lowest Test Score at the End of the Semester?

Yes, this practice is common in both high school and college. Not every teacher does it, but it is a way to insert some breathing room into a heavy course load. With a student's busy schedule, an occasional test or essay may fall due during a chaotic week and thus receive a low score. Or a particular topic may have been difficult to grasp. This method allows for a bit of grace along the way and works especially well when more than seven or eight tests and essays are assigned per semester. With even larger numbers of assignments, you may justify dropping the *two* lowest tests or essays, or allow students to skip one.

May I Give Credit/No Credit or Pass/Fail Grades to My Student?

Always give letter grades if your student is going on to college. Credit/No Credit or Pass/Fail grades cannot adequately be figured into the grade point average and thus will be detrimental to your student. Colleges may not include these courses in the GPA, or perhaps a "Pass" will be calculated as a C grade even though your student may have performed far better than that.

What About Extra Credit?

Your mental image of extra credit may involve a desperate student begging the teacher for additional work in an attempt to salvage a low grade. But extra credit need not carry this "last ditch" reputation. It can mean projects the student has done above and beyond the course requirements, either by his or her own initiative or at the recommendation of the parent.

Create a couple of lines for extra credit assignments on your grade sheet. Here is where you can record the fact that the student read extra books, wrote extra essays, or utilized outside learning opportunities. Anything extra that your student did that was related to the subject but was not anticipated at the beginning of the year can be credited. You can use *appropriate* extra credit, not busy work, to help students boost grades from a C to a B or from a B to an A. The work should enhance the student's understanding of the subject and help justify that grade increase.

Extra credit can also help "even the score" if you originally weighted the assignments unrealistically. For example, if you weighted homework heavily in a math class, but it took several lessons for a concept to sink in, the student might have low homework scores but higher test scores. Some extra credit, such as working with an online math program or doing extra practice with the most troublesome types of problems, could help boost the grade.

Other ideas for worthwhile extra credit include the following:
- Producing a creative project based on literature.
- Writing a speech or research paper on the topic being studied.
- Teaching the topic to someone else.
- Preparing a detailed outline of the textbook chapters—a great help in studying for tests.
- Writing a multiple choice or true/false quiz based on the material.
- Developing a board game or quiz show on the material.
- Writing up a "current event" related to the subject, based on a recent news item.
- Researching and summarizing one focused aspect of the subject.

TO SUM UP

Grading your own student's work can be much more straightforward than it might initially sound. As long as you clearly communicate your expectations ahead of time, you simply need to judge whether your student met or exceeded those expectations. Then assign scores or grades accordingly. Be creative and flexible as you come up with grading sheets, extra credit opportunities, and other ways to make your task as effective and streamlined as possible for *you*.

Chapter 10

Keeping Tabs on the Paperwork:

Record Keeping and GPAs

*I*f you have concluded that the course-planning adventure generates a fair amount of paperwork, you're right! However, before your desk grows too cluttered, think about how you will hang onto these records and quickly retrieve what you need. By addressing your record keeping needs early in the high school journey and then making a commitment to maintain those records regularly, you will avoid any last-minute scrambles when college applications are due. More importantly, you will free up both your mind and your time for your main focus: enjoying the learning process with your student.

KEEPING ORDERLY RECORDS: WHO DOES WHAT?

Record Keeping by Independent Study Programs or Private School Satellite Programs

If you belong to an independent study program (ISP) or Private School Satellite Program (PSP), your administrator will probably create a high school transcript from the "raw materials" (course titles, descriptions, and grades) you provide each year. Depending on the agreement you have, the program may also issue your student a diploma upon completion of high school and provide other administrative services.

Even though your ISP or PSP is maintaining the records, always keep an extra copy of everything you submit to it, and be sure to proofread the high school transcript before it is officially submitted. Because mistakes and misunderstandings can occur and items can be misplaced, it is ultimately up to you to take ownership of your student's records. Stay in close contact with your program administrator, especially in the later high school years, and keep him or her apprised of your student's goals and accomplishments. Be timely in providing grades and other documents when they are due so that your administrator will not be rushed when preparing the transcript for you.

Record Keeping by Parents

If you are keeping your own records, come up with a workable organization system. One useful way to organize them is to keep three file folders for each student, plus a planning binder for day-to-day teaching. Note that these folders work equally well as paper folders or as electronic folders containing documents, scans, and photos—you choose the format. The first folder is the cumulative (cum) file which you may already have from earlier years. The other two, generated anew each school year, are an *Official* folder and a *Portfolio* folder. The *Official* folder holds academic information such as course descriptions, grades, standardized test scores, and attendance records. The *Portfolio* folder stores samples of the student's work as well as keepsakes from the year's events or projects.

Now for a tour through the three folders.

Folder #1: Cum (Cumulative) File

This file begins with your child's kindergarten year, or the year you started homeschooling, and documents vital statistics all the way through high school. It is an individual student record; thus, you will create one for each of your students. The list of essential records varies by state, so check your state homeschooling organization for specifics. In general, the file may contain some or all of the following information[1]:

- *Student's legal name, address, gender, and parents' names and address(es); guardian/custody information if applicable*
- *Teacher/faculty (home teacher) qualifications*
- *Date and place of birth; also birth certificate number or photocopy of birth certificate*
- *School attendance records for each year with notation of all days absent*
- *Dates of first and last days of each school year*
- *Copy of your private school affidavit if applicable in your state, or ISP/PSP membership information*
- *Health examination and immunization records*
- *Other official forms specific to your state's rules*
- *Final grade reports including course titles, grades, and credits earned for each year or term*
- *Test scores for standardized tests, or for high school equivalency tests if your student has taken any*
- *High school transcript to date*
- *Date of high school graduation (projected, and eventually the actual date)*

Many people also enjoy attaching a photo of the child for each school year. In a traditional school, the cum file follows the student from year to year and from school to school. Even if your state requires only a minimal number of records, it is wise to keep more than you think you'll need, in case your state laws change or you move to a different state.

As the high school years begin, use this folder to store a copy of the graduation requirements for your school, as well as an updated transcript and a record of each year's progress toward graduation (i.e., the course of study for each year). In your planning binder (described later), keep a duplicate copy of the graduation requirements and your plans for meeting them year by year. Also keep HSLDA membership information and important school-related correspondence.

At the beginning or end of each school year, update your cum folder by filing recent documents and making sure nothing has gone missing during the year. If your student ever transfers into a public or private school, you may be asked to provide this file or the required information contained in the file. Likewise, if your student started in a traditional school but is now homeschooling, you will want to ask the school for previous records.

Folder #2 — Official Records: One Per Student Per Year

This file, containing teaching records specific to one school year, could include the following items:

- *Course of study for the school year*
- *Course descriptions*
- *Course syllabi for both home-based courses and outside courses*
- *Community college grades or transcripts, class schedule printouts, and financial statements*
- *Documents showing the student's performance in outside courses*
- *Report cards generated by you or by your ISP/PSP*
- *Standardized test scores if they are not in the cum file*
- *Documents relating to academic performance, such as notification of Dean's List status at the community college, or letters of recommendation written that year*
- *Quarterly or weekly goals or assignment schedules (if desired)*
- *Lists of books or literature read (if desired)*

Folder #3 — Portfolio Records: One Per Student Per Year

This third collection, which may need to be stored in a box or which may be an electronic collection of photos and scanned documents, will produce a more detailed "3-D" view of your student's year. Here you may store the following items:

- *Essays*
- *A sampling of math lessons or tests*
- *Science project reports*
- *Art work or projects of any type*
- *Programs from dramatic or musical productions the student performed in or attended*
- *Brochures from field trips and tours*
- *Photos from extracurricular activities*
- *Certificates or letters of commendation*
- *Awards*
- *Quarterly or weekly goals or assignment schedules if not included in the "Official Records" file folder*
- *Copies of textbook title pages and/or table of contents to document the content of your courses*
- *Practice or rehearsal schedules for sports, music, or theater activities*
- *Other documentation about your student's extracurricular activities*
- *Newspaper clippings or web page printouts of articles or photos involving your student*
- *Any other mementos you'd like to include*

From these treasures, you may one day assemble a formal portfolio of your student's high school years if this would be helpful to a college (see Chapter 11). And if not, these files are great fun to browse through later, and they provide raw materials for a one-of-a-kind scrapbook.

Planning and Record Keeping Binder

In addition to the records stored in these three folders, you will need a portable, dynamic system for day-to-day and future planning. To avoid the dreaded "binder shuffling," if binder size permits, use a single binder to hold materials for all of your homeschooled students, not just one student. You might set up this binder with the following section titles:

- *Attendance*—Include an attendance chart and a copy of the school year calendar.
- *Weekly Plans*—If you plan your student's schoolwork by the week, keep a copy here for your own reference.
- *Quarterly Plans*—Store a copy of your overall quarterly goals for each subject.
- *Graduation Requirements*—Include both graduation and college entrance requirements. Refer to this list each spring and summer as you plan the next year's courses. In this section of the binder, also place a chart summarizing the student's progress toward graduation requirements.
- *Grades*—Place your grade recording sheets for each subject into this section.
- *Subjects*—Create a section for each school subject, and in addition to storing your course descriptions and syllabi, insert a pocket folder into each of these sections. Here you can store your grading rubrics, notes, newspaper or magazine clippings, reading lists, curriculum ideas, notes on possible field trips and projects, and ideas for course content—for the current year or for future courses.
- *Extra Paper*—Tuck in a few sheets of notebook paper to keep you from having to get up and hunt for paper when you are immersed in planning.

MORE RECORD KEEPING TIPS

Deal with the Day's Books and Papers

Designate a shelf, storage crate, or decorative basket for each student's books, as well as a single place where each day's papers go. This "catch-all" doesn't even have to be ultra-neat, as long as you can whisk it aside when tidying up.

Keep Track of Important Papers

As the school year gets underway, a steady stream of papers will travel from your student's desk to yours. Designate a brightly colored file folder labeled "TURN IN" for work your students are turning in to you. You can easily grab it on your way to your next "grading pit stop." Use another folder, or one per student, for work you have already graded and discussed with the student and which you are now ready to file. Since filing one piece of paper at a time is inefficient, continue to collect up to one quarter's worth of work in this folder. At the end of the quarter, toss the unimportant papers and file the important ones in the folder designated for that student's current school year—or electronically scan and save selected items. Having this "holding tank" nearby makes it easy to retrieve a recent assignment and just as easy to park it back in its temporary, but categorized, location.

Location, Location, Location!

To ensure that new paperwork is easy to put away and won't accumulate in piles, keep all your current files where you usually do your grading and recording. Because you may need to refer back to information from previous school years, also keep one or two previous years' folders near your work area rather than packed in a dusty box in a closet. But rejoice—your elementary school records can now be packed away, or even tossed out after you have saved enough keepsakes to make that graduation scrapbook!

Keep Your Computer Files Orderly

Designate separate folders in your computer to hold documents you've created for each student (lesson plans, grading sheets, quizzes, and assignment instructions). Further subdivide these folders by making one folder for every school year. At the end of the year, decide which files might be reused as templates for next year's files. Then make an extra copy for this purpose, storing it in a folder for the upcoming school year. Meanwhile, keep the original file intact and store it in the folder for the school year just completed. This way, old files don't clutter up your current year's folder, but you have all the reusable information ready and waiting for the next student.

Always make backup copies of any computer files relevant to your homeschooling. Computer crashes are never fun, but you would especially hate to lose your homeschooling files.

Copy, Copy, Copy!

Keep duplicate copies of your most important records. Even if you submit records to a homeschool program on a regular basis, keep a copy (preferably electronic) of those records. You might even consider keeping a copy of the most vital records (attendance, grades, or brief course descriptions) at the home of a nearby relative, in case of fire, flood, or other calamity.

Strive for Simplicity and Efficiency

Beware of keeping too many or too few records. If you save everything, you will soon be overtaken by a sea of paper. But if your records are too sketchy, you will not have the depth or detail you need when preparing college applications, and you will need to take the time to go back and resurrect more of the information.

In general, it's easy to keep almost everything for one school year, such as essays, math tests, or art work. At the end of the year, discard what is unnecessary and then sort and categorize the rest. Place the "keepers" in that year's portfolio folder (or scan or photograph them) and put them away with the other years' folders. Keep just enough to put together a rich, detailed portfolio of your student's accomplishments. Remember that even if you do not plan to put a particular item in the final portfolio, it may help trigger memories of what was studied that year.

Be Legal

During the high school years, be especially certain that you are following your state's provisions for homeschooling and that you can retrieve records quickly in case you need documentation. By all means, keep up your membership with HSLDA (Home School Legal Defense Association). It is well worth it even though your student is now on the home stretch.

With the everyday paperwork under control, you can think about some of the longer-term records, such as the grade point average and (in the next chapter) the high school transcript.

CALCULATING GPAs: A MYSTERY SOLVED

Like transcripts and credits, the GPA calculation may seem a bit mysterious early in the game. Fortunately, the GPA can be calculated in just a few minutes, using a calculator and one sheet of paper.

Assigning Grade Points

The grade point average is a measure of the average grade received in relation to the number of credits the student has earned. In most high schools and colleges, letter grades receive the following *grade point value* per credit earned:

A = 4 grade points
B = 3 grade points
C = 2 grade points
D = 1 grade point
F = 0 grade points

Courses that earn more credits also earn more total grade points. For each course the student takes, you will need to multiply the *number of credits* for the course by the *grade point value* for the letter grade earned.

For example, if you are using Carnegie units, which award one credit for a year-length course, an A in a 0.5 credit semester course earns 0.5 credits times 4 grade points, or 2.0. A grade of C earns 0.5 times 2, or 1.0.

For the 10 credit per year system (5 credits per semester), the calculation would just be offset by one decimal place. In other words, an A in a 5-credit semester course earns 5 times 4 grade points, or 20. A C grade in the same course earns 5 times 2, or 10. If the course is worth only 2.5 credits, multiply 2.5 by 4 for an A (10 total points), or by 2 for a C (5 total points).

A *weighted GPA* typically awards AP courses and sometimes honors courses with an extra grade point. A's are worth 5, B's 4, and so on, to compensate for the difficulty of the course. Some school systems use 5 points for an A in an AP course and 4.5 points for an A in an honors course. Thus, a student with many advanced courses can easily exceed the 4.0 "straight-A" GPA. If you use a weighting system, explain it briefly but clearly on the transcript. Also note whether colleges want you to report a weighted or an unweighted GPA, and calculate accordingly.

If you plan to give your student grades such as A- or B+, as some school districts do, your GPA calculation will use some intermediate grade point values. One example is as follows:

A+	4.0
A	4.0
A-	3.7
B+	3.3
B	3.0
B-	2.7
C+	2.3
C	2.0
C-	1.7
D+	1.3
D	1.0

Note that A+ and A receive the same grade points, since this scale cannot go any higher than 4.0. Some institutions break this convention and award 4.3 grade points for an A+. Honors or AP courses could, however, count for extra grade points (5 for an A) and boost the GPA above 4.0.

Calculating Grade Point Average

To calculate a semester GPA, add up *total grade points earned*, and then divide by *total credits earned*.

Example of homeschooler Molly Mason's semester GPA calculation (using Carnegie units):

Course	Credits	Grade	Grade Points	Calculation
Biology I	0.5	A	4	0.5 credits x 4 = 2.0 grade points
English 9	0.5	B	3	0.5 credits x 3 = 1.5 grade points
Spanish I	0.5	A	4	0.5 credits x 4 = 2.0 grade points
Algebra IH	0.5	A	5 (Honors)	0.5 credits x 5 = 2.5 grade points
P.E.	0.25	B	3	0.25 credits x 3 = 0.75 grade points
Bible	0.5	A	4	0.5 credits x 4 = 2.0 grade points
Life Skills	0.25	C	2	0.25 credits x 2 = 0.5 grade points
Total credits: 3.0				**Total grade points: 11.25**

Semester grade point average: 11.25 grade points divided by 3.0 credits = **3.75**

Here is the same GPA calculation using the 10 credit per year system:

Course	Credits	Grade	Grade Points	Calculation
Biology I	5	A	4	5 credits x 4 = 20 grade points
English 9	5	B	3	5 credits x 3 = 15 grade points
Spanish I	5	A	4	5 credits x 4 = 20 grade points
Algebra IH	5	A	5 (Honors)	5 credits x 5 = 25 grade points
P.E.	2.5	B	3	2.5 credits x 3 = 7.5 grade points
Bible	5	A	4	5 credits x 4 = 20 grade points
Life Skills	2.5	C	2	2.5 credits x 2 = 5 grade points
Total credits: 30				**Total grade points: 112.5**

Semester grade point average: 112.5 grade points divided by 30 credits = **3.75**

Semester GPA vs. Cumulative GPA

The calculation described above yields the *semester* GPA. This can be recorded on the transcript directly below the courses for that semester. However, you will also want to record a running total of the credits and grade points in order to calculate the cumulative GPA as of each completed semester. Colleges usually ask for the *cumulative* GPA through the junior year or the first semester of the senior year for college application purposes.

To calculate cumulative GPA, you *do not* simply average the GPAs of the previous semesters. The differences in numbers of credits earned each semester will make this figure inaccurate. Instead, you need to go back to the *total grade points* for each individual semester of high school—the letter grade value times the credits—and then add them up for a grand total of all semesters. Then divide by the *total credits* earned to date.

For example, let us return to Molly Mason and add another semester's worth of grades. Suppose that for the second semester, Molly's grades looked like this:

Carnegie unit system:

Course	Credits	Grade	Grade Points	Calculation
Biology I	0.5	A	4	0.5 credits x 4 = 2.0 grade points
English 9	0.5	A	4	0.5 credits x 4 = 2.0 grade points
Spanish I	0.5	A	4	0.5 credits x 4 = 2.0 grade points
Algebra IH	0.5	B	4 (Honors)	0.5 credits x 4 = 2.0 grade points
P.E.	0.25	A	4	0.25 credits x 4 = 1.0 grade points
Bible	0.5	A	4	0.5 credits x 4 = 2.0 grade points
Life Skills	0.25	B	3	0.25 credits x 3 = 0.75 grade points
AP Macroeconomics	0.5	A	5 (AP)	0.5 credits x 5 = 2.5 grade points
Vocal Music	0.5	A	4	0.5 credits x 4 = 2.0 grade points
Total credits:	**4.0**			**Total grade points: 16.25**

Semester grade point average: 16.25 divided by 4.0 credits = **4.06**

Remember that for the first semester, Molly had a total of 3.0 credits and 11.25 grade points, or a GPA of 3.75 after the division step. Now to get a *cumulative GPA for the entire year*, add up the two semesters' worth of grade points (totaling 27.5) and the two semesters' worth of credits (totaling 7.0) and divide the grade points by the credits. The cumulative GPA is **3.93.**

10 credit per year system:

Course	Credits	Grade	Grade Points	Calculation
Biology I	5	A	4	5 credits x 4 = 20 grade points
English 9	5	A	4	5 credits x 4 = 20 grade points
Spanish I	5	A	4	5 credits x 4 = 20 grade points
Algebra IH	5	B	4 (Honors)	5 credits x 4 = 20 grade points
P.E.	2.5	A	4	2.5 credits x 4 = 10 grade points
Bible	5	A	4	5 credits x 4 = 20 grade points
Life Skills	2.5	B	3	2.5 credits x 3 = 7.5 grade points
AP Macroeconomics	5	A	5 (AP)	5 credits x 5 = 25 grade points
Vocal Music	5	A	4	5 credits x 4 = 20 grade points
Total credits:	**40**			**Total grade points: 162.5**

Semester grade point average: 162.5 divided by 40 credits = **4.06**

For the first semester, Molly had 30 credits and 112.5 grade points, or a GPA of 3.75 after the division step. To get a *cumulative GPA for the entire year*, add up the two semesters' worth of grade points (totaling 275) and the two semesters' worth of credits (totaling 70) and divide these two totals. The cumulative GPA is **3.93.**

This same calculation can be used for all future semesters. To streamline the process, keep a running total of all grade points to date and a running total of all credits to date, and do the division calculation after each semester's grades are in, to come up with the new cumulative GPA.

Other GPA Terminology

Academic GPA

Colleges may ask for the *academic GPA*, which is calculated after including only academic courses. To calculate it, go back to the transcript and omit courses such as P.E., life skills, vocational education, and other nonacademic courses. Check with the college for its definition of *academic*. After removing these courses, with their credits and grade points, add up the rest as usual and complete the calculation.

Weighted or Unweighted GPA

Remember how you learned to account for honors and AP courses in the GPA by giving them an extra point in the GPA calculation? This is a *weighted* GPA. The *unweighted* GPA, often requested on college applications, reverses this calculation and assumes that all courses are equal. The course titles on the transcript, though, will demonstrate the level of rigor. Note that many high schools and colleges now look primarily at AP courses (not necessarily honors courses) for the extra grade point. But whatever you decide to do in your own home school, note it on an explanatory legend on your transcript.

To calculate an unweighted GPA, simply give all courses equal grade points (no "5" scores for A grades in honors courses). Then calculate the GPA as usual.

Cumulative GPA for Specific School Years

Sometimes colleges ignore the ninth grade year and request the GPA calculation for tenth through twelfth grades only, or perhaps just tenth and eleventh grades if senior year grades are not available at application time. To calculate a more limited GPA, examine only the years of interest, add up the total grade points earned in those years only, and divide by the total credits earned in those years only.

TO SUM UP

To many of us, the task of record keeping is like the task of ironing clothes. Viewing it as a distasteful chore, we put it off until a good batch has accumulated. Then, with a sigh, we settle in to catch up on several weeks' worth. However, record keeping does not need to be a burdensome chore. Whether you prefer to do your record keeping a little at a time or in large batches, your goal is to build a set of credible records that will help your student at college application time. Being able to look back at course content, objectives, scores, and final grades can be a handy memory-jogger. Find the style of record keeping that works best for you, whether detailed or simplified, and use it faithfully to produce a clean, understandable record of what your high schooler has studied. You'll be glad you did!

---

1. Some cum file content recommendations were drawn from the following article:
Woodfin, Karen Middleton and Susan Beatty, "Recordkeeping: Reviewing and Planning for Next School Year," adapted from *An Introduction to Home Education*, Christian Home Educators Press, article published in *The California Parent Educator*, Spring 2006, 37.

Chapter 11

Your Official Documents:

The Transcript, Portfolio, and Diploma

For parents who are just embarking on the high school adventure, the idea of creating a transcript can seem a bit daunting. After all, this document has such an *official* air about it. A transcript, however, is simply a listing of your student's courses, credits, and grades accumulated throughout the four years of high school.

In this chapter, you will learn how to assemble a neat, complete, and professional-looking transcript and how to design a portfolio if your student's accomplishments would be better displayed this way. The chapter will conclude with a discussion of how to issue a high school diploma to your student.

THE HIGH SCHOOL TRANSCRIPT

If your student will apply to college as a homeschooler rather than as a student from a small private school, your home-designed transcript need not masquerade as a transcript from a traditional school. Most colleges are accustomed to receiving applications from homeschoolers. Realize, though, that colleges will view homeschool transcripts a bit differently from the way they view traditional schools' transcripts, since a homeschooler's grades are generally less useful as a measurement of performance or of comparison with peers. Consequently, the other elements of the application (test scores, leadership, and extracurriculars) may carry more weight to make up for the nontraditional transcript. Nevertheless, the rigor of your student's course of study will convey useful information and should be carefully documented.

The transcript is also useful for obtaining "good student" auto insurance discounts, for admission into specialized programs or internships, and for scholarship applications. Keep the high school transcript readily accessible even after your student starts college. In addition, keep a sealed official transcript from the community college if your student has taken courses. Early on in the university years, before your student has taken many courses, he or she may discover scholarship or internship opportunities requiring transcripts and may not have time to request a community college transcript without paying rush fees.

WHEN TO START CREATING A TRANSCRIPT

You will thank yourself over and over again if you construct at least a rough draft of the transcript during or just after the ninth grade year. As you experiment with formatting, try varying the layout, spacing, columns, and font size to optimize readability, maximize space for information, and create an attractive page layout. Limit your transcript to one page. At the conclusion of each semester, fill in the course titles, credits, and grades from that semester, update the GPA, and make improvements to the formatting of the transcript. *Do not* wait until your student's senior year to start a transcript. You will be far too busy, and it may be harder to lay your hands on all the course titles, credits, and grades. Besides, you will likely need an official transcript before this time.

DISSECTING THE TRANSCRIPT

To take the mystery out of the high school transcript, this next section will walk you through the elements of a typical transcript. As you read the descriptive information, take a look at the samples later in the chapter. You can also go to the HSLDA website and search up sample transcripts to help you get started. Or, if you would rather not create your own transcript from scratch, check out Lee Binz's *Total Transcript Solution*, an excellent set of resources providing several different transcript templates as well as full instructions and tips for grading, calculating GPAs, assigning credits, and portraying your student's education in a clear and professional format. Lee Binz's website, called The Home Scholar, is https://www.homehighschoolhelp.com/.

The following information should be included on your transcript:

School Name and Title of Transcript

- Along with the term "High School Transcript," use the name of your own home school or your home school program (PSP or ISP). You may also use wording such as "Independent Study High School Transcript," if desired.

Student Information

- Student's full name, address, phone number and email address.
- Student's date of birth and gender. Transcripts once included the student's Social Security number; however, it is best to omit this from the transcript for privacy reasons.
- Actual or projected graduation date.

School Information

- School name, with optional designation of "Home School" or "Independent Study."
- School address and contact information for parents or home school program administrator, as appropriate.
- Previous high schools attended, with dates and location. Note that these would be actual brick-and-mortar schools or official school programs in which your student was enrolled—not simply homeschool support organizations or co-ops where your student took a few classes. If your student attended for more than a semester, include separate transcripts from these schools when you submit official transcripts to colleges.
- A legend of institutions or organizations providing courses, such as community colleges, online providers, or homeschool academies. Within the main part of the transcript, use a symbol or abbreviation referring to the site or location of the course; down below, create a legend that explains these symbols.

Course Information

- List of courses taken, including levels such as I, II, H, or AP, with credits and letter grades earned for each class. These should be organized neatly and logically by year and semester. For each semester, you may want to list core subjects first and electives and P.E. last. For AP courses, use a registered trademark sign (e.g., AP® Biology).
- *(Optional)* A column for the weighting of grades for each course. For instance, an A receives 4 points for standard courses, 5 for honors and AP courses. (See Chapter 10 for explanation). Instead, you could simply add this as a legend item.
- *(Optional)* A column for weight points (weighting of the letter grade times the number of credits for the course), used in the GPA calculation.
- Semester and/or cumulative total of credits and semester and/or cumulative GPA.
- List of courses in progress for the first semester of senior year and list of proposed courses for second semester. You will probably not have first semester grades available at the time of college application unless the application isn't due until January or February. Thus, you will enter IP for "In Progress" and PR for "Proposed" in place of grades. Do indicate the number of credits the courses will be worth.

Explanatory and Supplementary Information

- Brief explanation of grading system (such as "A = 90 to 100%"), definition of credits (such as "1.0 credit = 180 hours"), number of credits required for graduation, explanation of weighting for honors courses, and explanation of special symbols used, such as asterisks for community college courses, bold type for honors or AP® courses, IP for "In Progress," or PR for "Proposed."

Test Scores (optional, since you will also send official scores from the testing organization)

- PSAT/NMSQT, SAT, ACT, and AP scores, neatly arranged and dated.
- *(Optional)* Standardized grade-level achievement test scores: core or total battery percentiles. Use the National Percentile Rank and/or Stanine scores.

Validating Information

- Signature of the person validating the transcript, with degree or title as applicable, such as John Smith, Parent/Teacher.
- Date of signature.
- *(Optional)* The words "Official Transcript" or an official school seal, logo, or graphic if you have one.
- If you are sending the transcript electronically, which is usually the case, you may sign, date, and scan a copy of a transcript with the above information.

UPDATING THE TRANSCRIPT

The transcript will need "maintenance" each semester, but once you have set up the basic format, this maintenance is very straightforward. At the end of each semester, add in the recently completed courses and grades. You may need to abbreviate course titles here and there to make them fit into a small space. Indicate the level of the course, such as Spanish 1 or 2, or English 9 or 10. Also indicate AP, honors (H) or community college courses that will receive extra weight toward the GPA by using asterisks, special symbols, or bold or italic type. Important: AP (Advanced Placement) designations may be used only for College Board-approved courses. See Chapter 12. Decipher all of this information with an explanatory legend at the bottom of the page. In your legend, also show where the courses were taken if they were not home-based. For instance, abbreviate South City College as SCC and use this designation next to the course title, spelling out the whole phrase in the legend.

Make sure that all the course titles, credits, and grades appear exactly as you want them. Update the credit totals and GPA calculations, and check your math for accuracy. This task should take less than an hour each semester. Also update the section containing test scores each time your student receives new scores. Of course, these scores must eventually be reported officially to the college by requesting them from the testing agency such as the College Board or ACT, Inc.; the transcript is simply a way to display unofficial scores all in one place if desired.

OFFICIAL AND UNOFFICIAL TRANSCRIPTS

College or scholarship applications usually require official transcripts, but occasionally an unofficial transcript will suffice.

An official transcript is a sealed document or official electronic document sent directly from the school issuing it. If sent by mail, it typically has a seal, stamp, or signature across the flap of the sealed envelope to show that it has not been opened. For traditional schools, the document itself also has an official school seal or signature. Some schools even use tamper-proof paper.

An unofficial transcript may look identical to an official transcript, minus the special seal, signature, or envelope. It may also be a simple grade report printout of all the courses taken at the school.

As a homeschooler, your official and unofficial transcripts will often be virtually identical, and if the recipients know your student is a homeschooler, they will not be expecting a hermetically sealed official transcript. You may, if desired, write "official" on your transcript or design a school seal, stamp, or logo to print or emboss a seal onto your transcript if it will be mailed (this is irrelevant if it is being sent electronically), but it actually does not make a difference. At any rate, you as the parent/homeschool administrator should sign and date the official transcript on each copy you send out by mail or electronically.

For many college applications, you as the school administrator will be asked to upload an official transcript into the electronic application. After your transcript is formatted to your liking, simply prepare (and proofread) an electronic file specifically for these purposes. The Common Application®, for example, requests that the school administrator submit a transcript online along with the counselor recommendation portion of the application.

If your homeschool program administrator prepares your transcripts, she or he will have a procedure in place for producing official transcripts. Your job as the parent will be to provide course titles, grades, and credits in a timely manner each semester and then to proofread the finished transcript before it is sent out. When requesting transcripts, give your administrator sufficient time to prepare them. Be proactive, not reactive, in assessing your needs for transcripts.

TRANSCRIPT DOS AND DON'TS

Do:

- Decide whether your student will portray himself or herself as a homeschooler or as a student from a small private school. Your choice of school name on the transcript will follow from this decision. Most homeschoolers use the former option ("homeschooler") with great success.

- Carefully note when an official as opposed to an unofficial transcript is needed.
- Keep the transcript to one page if possible, two at the most if there is a compelling reason for this.
- Before sending out a transcript, recheck all credit and GPA calculations.
- Explain codes, abbreviations, and course providers with a clear legend at the bottom of the page.
- Make sure your transcript has a professional appearance and is neat, clean, and sharp.
- If you are mailing the transcript, print it using good quality paper and dark ink or toner.
- Sign and date the transcript before mailing or scanning.
- Always have a "bug-free" electronic version of your transcript ready for use with the Common Application or any other circumstance requiring electronic submission.

Don't:

- Include any misspellings, punctuation/capitalization errors, or inconsistencies.
- Use pass/fail grades for courses, as they adversely affect the GPA calculation. Always use letter grades.
- Use cute logos, gimmicks, or slogans such as "There's No Place Like Home."
- Include crooked columns, inconsistent fonts, inconsistent line justification, or odd spacing.
- Submit a transcript that is difficult to read because of font size, font style, or odd formatting.
- Submit a handwritten transcript. This is an absolute NEVER!
- List extracurriculars, leadership, or awards on the transcript. It will make the transcript look too crowded, and you will have opportunities to describe these elsewhere on the college application. The transcript is intended to be an academic summary.

SAMPLE TRANSCRIPTS

The following pages show three examples of high school transcripts. The first one uses a formula of ten credits per year-long course, or five credits per semester. The second uses Carnegie units (one credit per year, or half a credit per semester). While the first two transcripts list courses chronologically, grade by grade, the third is a *subject transcript* that groups courses by subject instead of by grade. This format is especially useful when your student has completed several high school courses before ninth grade (in this case, you could leave off the "year" designations on the sample). By looking at these examples and reviewing typical transcripts from other homeschooling families or from schools in your area, you can evaluate the pros and cons of various credit calculations and formatting choices and then customize them for your own purposes.

Each transcript is a bit different, and this slight variation is deliberate. The format, appearance, and items presented differ in order to demonstrate that there is no single "right" way to construct a transcript. In short, you will want to include all courses, grades, and credits, as well as including an appropriate legend to explain abbreviations or other informational "nuggets."

Homeschooled & Headed for College

INDEPENDENT STUDY HIGH SCHOOL TRANSCRIPT

STUDENT:
NAME:
ADDRESS:
PHONE:
EMAIL:

GENDER:
DOB:
GRADUATION DATE: JUNE 2, 2020
(PROJECTED)

SCHOOL ADDRESS:
(STUDENT IS HOMESCHOOLED)
ADDRESS:
PHONE:
EMAIL:
CONTACT: (PARENT NAME)

	SUBJECT	GRADE	CREDIT	WT	WT PTS	SUBJECT	GRADE	CREDIT	WT	WT PTS
	1ST SEMESTER – COMPLETED JANUARY 2017					**2ND SEMESTER – COMPLETED JUNE 2017**				
SCHOOL YEAR 2016/2017	INTRO BIOLOGY*	A*	5.0	5	25	INTRO CHEM*	A*	5.0	5	25
	HONORS GEOM*	A*	5.0	5	25	HONORS GEOM*	A*	5.0	5	25
GRADE 9	ENGLISH 9H*	A*	5.0	5	25	ENGLISH 9H*	A*	5.0	5	25
	WORLD GEOG	A	5.0	4	20	WORLD GEOG	A	5.0	4	20
	SPANISH 1A	A	5.0	4	20	SPANISH 1B	A	5.0	4	20
	PE 9	A	2.5	4	10	RUSSIAN 1A	A	5.0	4	20
	BIBLE 9	A	2.5	4	10	PE 9	A	2.5	4	10
						BIBLE 9	A	2.5	4	10
	SEMESTER CREDITS		30.00	WT PTS	135	SEMESTER CREDITS		35.00	WT PTS	155
	CUM CREDITS		30.00	CUM WT	135	CUM CREDITS		65.00	CUM WT	290
				CUM GPA	4.50				CUM GPA	4.46
	1ST SEMESTER – COMPLETED JANUARY 2018					**2ND SEMESTER – COMPLETED JUNE 2018**				
SUMMER 2017:	RUSSIAN 1B	A	5.0	4	20					
SCHOOL YEAR 2017/2018	GENERAL CHEM 1A*	A*	5.0	5	25	GENERAL CHEM 1B*	A*	5.0	5	25
	PHYSICS	A	5.0	4	20	PHYSICS	A	5.0	4	20
GRADE 10	TRIG/ PRECALC H*	A*	5.0	5	25	TRIG/ PRECALC H*	A*	5.0	5	25
	ENGLISH 10H*	A*	5.0	5	25	ENGLISH 10H*	A*	5.0	5	25
	AP® EURO HISTORY*	A*	5.0	5	25	AP® EURO HISTORY*	A*	5.0	5	25
	RUSSIAN 2A	A	5.0	4	20	RUSSIAN 2B	A	5.0	4	20
	BIBLE 10	A	2.5	4	10	BIBLE 10	A	2.5	4	10
	PE 10	A	2.5	4	10	PE 10	A	2.5	4	10
	SEMESTER CREDITS		40.00	WT PTS	180	SEMESTER CREDITS		35.00	WT PTS	160
	CUM CREDITS		105.00	CUM WT	470	CUM CREDITS		140.00	CUM WT	630
				CUM GPA	4.48				CUM GPA	4.50
	1ST SEMESTER – COMPLETED JANUARY 2019					**2ND SEMESTER – COMPLETED JUNE 2019**				
SCHOOL YEAR 2018/2019	CELL BIOLOGY*	A*	5.0	5	25	HUMAN ANATOMY*	A	5.0	5	25
	GENETICS*	A*	5.0	5	25	CALC/ANALY GEOM*	A	5.0	5	25
	CALC/ANALY GEOM*	A*	5.0	5	25	AP® ENG LANG*	A	5.0	5	25
GRADE 11	AP® ENG LANG*	A*	5.0	5	25	AP® US HIST*	A	5.0	5	25
	AP® US HIST*	A*	5.0	5	25	SHAKESPEARE	A	5.0	4	20
	SHAKESPEARE	A	5.0	4	20	VOCAL MUSIC	A	5.0	4	20
	VOCAL MUSIC	A	5.0	4	20	BIBLE 11	A	5.0	4	20
	BIBLE 11	A	5.0	4	20	PE 11	A	2.5	4	10
	PE 11	A	2.5	4	10					
	SEMESTER CREDITS		42.50	WT PTS	195	SEMESTER CREDITS		37.50	WT PTS	170
	CUM CREDITS		182.50	CUM WT	825	CUM CREDITS		220.00	CUM WT	995
				CUM GPA	4.52				CUM GPA	4.52
	1ST SEMESTER – TO BE COMPLETED JANUARY 2020					**2ND SEMESTER – TO BE COMPLETED JUNE 2020**				
SCHOOL YEAR 2019/2020	HUMAN PHYSIO*	IP	5.0	IP	IP	MICROBIOLOGY*	PR	5.0	PR	PR
	ENGNR PHYSICS 4A*	IP	5.0	IP	IP	ENGNR PHYSICS 4B*	PR	5.0	PR	PR
GRADE 12	DIFF EQUATIONS*	IP	5.0	IP	IP	STATISTICS*	PR	5.0	PR	PR
	AP® ENG LIT*	IP	5.0	IP	IP	AP® ENG LIT*	PR	5.0	PR	PR
	AP® US GOVT*	IP	5.0	IP	IP	ECONOMICS	PR	5.0	PR	PR
	RUSSIAN 3A	IP	5.0	IP	IP	BIBLE 12	PR	5.0	PR	PR
	BIBLE 12	IP	5.0	IP	IP	PE 12	PR	2.5	PR	PR
	PE 12	IP	2.5	IP	IP					
	SEMESTER CREDITS		37.50	WT PTS		SEMESTER CREDITS		32.50	WT PTS	
	CUM CREDITS		257.50	CUM WT		CUM CREDITS		290.00	CUM WT	
				CUM GPA					CUM GPA	

TEST SCORES

SAT®	SAT SUBJECT TESTS™	PSAT/NMSQT®	ADVANCED PLACEMENT® (AP)	
(3/17): 700 RDG, 780 M	CHEMISTRY (5/18): 750	(10/18)	CHEMISTRY (5/18): 5	BIOLOGY (5/19): 5
(11/18): 690 RDG, 790 M	LITERATURE (5/18) 770	RDG 680	EURO HIST (5/18): 5	CALC BC (5/19): 4
(3/19): 690 RDG, 790M	MATH 2 (10/18): 760	M 750	ENG LANG (5/19): 5	CALC AB SUBSCORE (5/19): 5
	BIOLOGY-M (5/19): 740		US HIST (5/19): 4	
	US HIST (5/19): 710			

CREDITS & GRADING (*) DESIGNATES HONORS OR AP COURSES; BOLDFACE DESIGNATES COMMUNITY COLLEGE COURSES

A* = 5 (HONORS, AP, COLLEGE COURSES), A=4, B=3, C=2, D=1, F=0   IP= IN PROGRESS   PR = PROPOSED
GRADING SCALE: A=90-100%, B=80-89%, C=70-79%, D=60-69%, F=59% OR BELOW
5 CREDITS = 1 SEMESTER COURSE   10 CREDITS = 1 YEAR COURSE (150 HOURS OR MORE)
60 CREDITS = REQUIRED TO PASS TO NEXT GRADE LEVEL   240 CREDITS = HIGH SCHOOL GRADUATION
GPA'S CALCULATED ABOVE (WEIGHTED) ARE FOR ALL COURSES, ACADEMIC AND NONACADEMIC
To calculate academic GPA, remove PE, Bible, and Vocal Music courses

SIGNED: _____   DATE: _____

Evergreen Academy - Official Transcript

James B. Woods
6857 Example St.,
St. Louis, MO 63107
(314) 222-2222
DOB 8/21/02, Gender: M

School Contact: Martha C. Woods (314) 222-2222
School Address: 6857 Example St., St. Louis, MO 63107
Email: contact@homeschoolroadmap.com
Student Graduation Date: 5/30/20 (Projected)

9th grade (2016-17)

Semester 1	Credits	Grade	Semester 2	Credits	Grade
Algebra 1	½	A	Algebra 1	½	A
English Lit/Gram*	½	B	English Lit/Gram*	½	B
Spanish 1	½	A	Spanish 1	½	A
Biology	½	A	Biology	½	A
Art History	½	B	Music Apprec.	½	B
P.E.	¼	A	P.E.	¼	A
Bible	¼	A	Bible	¼	A
Cum. Credits 3	Cum. GPA	3.83	Cum. Credits 6	Cum. GPA	3.83

10th grade (2017-18)

Semester 1	Credits	Grade	Semester 2	Credits	Grade
Geometry	½	A	Geometry	½	A
English Composition*	½	B	English Composition*	½	B
Spanish 2	½	A	Spanish 2	½	A
Chemistry 2A*	½	**A**	**Chemistry 2B***	½	**A**
World History	½	B	World History	½	B
P.E.	¼	A	P.E.	¼	A
Bible	¼	A	Bible	¼	A
Cum. Credits 9	Cum. GPA	3.89	Cum. Credits 12	Cum. GPA	3.92

11th grade (2018-19)

Semester 1	Credits	Grade	Semester 2	Credits	Grade
Algebra 2	½	A	Algebra 2	½	A
American Lit*	½	B	American Lit*	½	B
Spanish 3	½	A	Spanish 3	½	A
Adv. Biology 2A*	½	**A**	**Adv. Biology 2B***	½	**A**
U.S. History	½	B	U.S. History	½	B
P.E.	¼	A	P.E.	¼	A
Bible	¼	A	Bible	¼	A
Cum. Credits 15	Cum. GPA	3.93	Cum. Credits 18	Cum. GPA	3.94

12th grade (2019-20)

Semester 1	Credits	Grade	Semester 2	Credits	Grade
Trigonometry 3A*	½	**A**	**Precalculus 3B***	½	**A**
World Lit*	½	B	British Lit*	½	B
Spanish 4	½	A	Spanish 4	½	A
Physics 1A*	½	**A**	**Physics 1B***	½	**A**
Economics 20*	½	**B**	U.S. Gov.	½	B
P.E.	¼	A	P.E.	¼	A
Bible	¼	A	Bible	¼	A
Cum. Credits 21	Cum. GPA	4.0	Cum. Credits 24	Cum. GPA	4.02

*Honors course. **Bold type:** Community college course. Honors and college courses receive an additional grade point toward weighted GPA. Credits required for graduation: 24.

Signed _____   Date _____

OFFICIAL TRANSCRIPT

STUDENT: Kathryn H. Robinson	**SCHOOL:** Logos Academy (Home School)
ADDRESS: 348 Greentree Pl.	**ADDRESS:** 348 Greentree Pl.
Orange, CA 92861	Orange, CA 92861
PARENTS: Tyler and Mary Robinson	**CONTACT:** Mary Robinson
PHONE: (555)555-5555	**PHONE:** (555)555-5555
BIRTH DATE: 8/25/02	**EMAIL:** contact@homeschoolroadmap.com
GENDER: F	**GRADUATION DATE:** 5/25/20

STUDENT ACADEMIC RECORD (BY SUBJECT)

MATHEMATICS
SUBJECT	PROVIDER	YEAR	GRADE	CREDIT	WEIGHT	WT PTS
GEOMETRY		2015-16	A	1.0	4.0	4.0
ALGEBRA 2	KA	2016-17	A	1.0	4.0	4.0
PRECALCULUS	CCC	2017-18	A	1.0	4.0	4.0
AP® CALC AB	PAH	2018-19	A	1.0	5.0	5.0
DIFFERENTIAL EQUATIONS 5A	CCC	2019-20	IP	1.0	IP	IP
ACADEMIC CREDITS			TOTAL	5.0	WT PTS	17.0
			TO DATE	4.0	UWT PTS	16.0

ENGLISH
SUBJECT	PROVIDER	YEAR	GRADE	CREDIT	WEIGHT	WT PTS
AMERICAN LIT/COMP		2016-17	B	1.0	3.0	3.0
SHAKESPEARE		2017-18	A	1.0	4.0	4.0
BRITISH LIT/COMP	KA	2017-18	A	1.0	4.0	4.0
AP® ENG LANG	PAH	2018-19	B	1.0	4.0	4.0
AP® ENG LIT	PAH	2019-20	IP	1.0	IP	IP
ACADEMIC CREDITS			TOTAL	5.0	WT PTS	15.0
			TO DATE	4.0	UWT PTS	14.0

SOCIAL SCIENCE
SUBJECT	PROVIDER	YEAR	GRADE	CREDIT	WEIGHT	WT PTS
WORLD GEOG		2016-17	A	1.0	4.0	4.0
AP® EURO HIST	KA	2017-18	B	1.0	4.0	4.0
AP® US HIST	KA	2018-19	A	1.0	5.0	5.0
AP® US GOV	PAH	2019-20	IP	0.5	IP	IP
ACADEMIC CREDITS			TOTAL	3.5	WT PTS	13.0
			TO DATE	3.0	UWT PTS	12.0

LAB SCIENCE
SUBJECT	PROVIDER	YEAR	GRADE	CREDIT	WEIGHT	WT PTS
BIOLOGY	KA	2016-17	A	1.0	4.0	4.0
CHEM 20	CCC	2017-18	A	1.0	5.0	5.0
AP® CHEMISTRY	PAH	2018-19	B	1.0	4.0	4.0
AP® PHYSICS	PAH	2019-20	IP	1.0	IP	IP
ACADEMIC CREDITS			TOTAL	4.0	WT PTS	13.0
			TO DATE	3.0	UWT PTS	12.0

FOREIGN LANGUAGE
SUBJECT	PROVIDER	YEAR	GRADE	CREDIT	WEIGHT	WT PTS
LATIN 1	KA	2015-16	A	1.0	4.0	4.0
LATIN 2	KA	2016-17	A	1.0	4.0	4.0
LATIN 3	KA	2017-18	A	1.0	4.0	4.0
AP® LATIN	PAH	2018-19	A	1.0	5.0	5.0
ACADEMIC CREDITS			TOTAL	4.0	WT PTS	17.0
			TO DATE	4.0	UWT PTS	16.0

ELECTIVES
SUBJECT	PROVIDER	YEAR	GRADE	CREDIT	WEIGHT	WT PTS
C++ PROGRAMMING 20	CCC	2016-17	A	1.0	5.0	5.0
SPEECH/DEBATE	KA	2016-17	A	1.0	4.0	4.0
ACADEMIC CREDITS			TOTAL	2.0	WT PTS	9.0
			TO DATE	2.0	UWT PTS	8.0

FINE ARTS
SUBJECT	PROVIDER	YEAR	GRADE	CREDIT	WEIGHT	WT PTS
AP® MUSIC THEORY	PAH	2017-18	A	1.0	5.0	5.0
ACADEMIC CREDITS			TOTAL	1.0	WT PTS	5.0
			TO DATE	1.0	UWT PTS	4.0

PHYSICAL EDUCATION
SUBJECT	PROVIDER	YEAR	GRADE	CREDIT	WEIGHT	WT PTS
PE 9		2016-17	A	0.5	NA	NA
PE 10		2017-18	B	0.5	NA	NA
PE 11		2018-19	A	0.5	NA	NA
SWIM TEAM		2019-20	IP	0.5	NA	NA
ACADEMIC CREDITS			TOTAL	2.0	WT PTS	
PE NOT COUNTED IN ACADEMIC GPA			TO DATE	1.5	UWT PTS	
ACADEMIC GPA TO DATE	4.24 WEIGHTED	3.91 UNWEIGHTED				

PROVIDER LEGEND
KA	KAIROS ACADEMY
CCC	CENTRAL COMMUNITY COLLEGE, ANAHEIM, CA
PAH	PENNSYLVANIA HOMESCHOOLERS® (ONLINE)

ALL ADVANCED PLACEMENT® COURSES ARE COLLEGE BOARD-APPROVED

COURSE/GRADE LEGEND
WT	WEIGHTED	0.5 CREDIT = 1 SEMESTER COURSE
UWT	UNWEIGHTED	1.0 CREDIT = 1 YEAR COURSE (150 HRS OR MORE)
IP	IN PROGRESS	24 CREDITS REQUIRED FOR HIGH SCHOOL GRADUATION
PR	PROPOSED	GPA CALCULATION: A=4, B=3, C=2
P	PASS	AP® AND COLLEGE COURSES RECEIVE AN EXTRA GRADE POINT TOWARD WEIGHTED GPA

THIS TRANSCRIPT IS A TRUE AND OFFICIAL RECORD OF THE STUDENT'S HIGH SCHOOL STUDIES.

SIGNATURE _____   DATE _____

SPECIAL CIRCUMSTANCES

AP and Honors Courses

If your student has taken AP or honors courses and you are calculating a weighted GPA, use this extra grade point calculation as you construct the transcript and record the student's GPA. An A will earn five grade points instead of four; a B, four instead of three, and so on. Establish a clear method of designating honors and AP courses on the student's transcript. Some schools give only half of an extra grade point for honors courses and a full extra point for AP courses, but decide on your own system and then explain this information in the legend of your transcript.

Community College Courses

Academic community college courses are generally considered to be honors courses for the high school student. Because of the large amount of course content covered in a semester-length course, they can also optionally be treated as year-long high school courses. For your transcript purposes, choose to treat them as semester-length honors courses, year-length standard courses, or year-length honors courses. The decision depends partly on how many courses your student takes and whether it would look excessive to grant year-length honors credit for numerous courses. For instance, if he or she ends up taking six semester-length science courses, are you comfortable equating this to six years of high school science at the honors level? Use your common sense in deciding what is best, but do give your student ample credit for his or her accomplishments. To be more competitive, students aiming for the most selective colleges should still try to take three or four complete *years* of a subject such as science, or whatever is recommended by the college, even though technically only three or four *semesters* of community college credit would fulfill the requirement. This would especially be true of students planning to major in that discipline. For colleges that are not so selective, the equivalence of a semester-length college course to a year-length high school course is generally applicable.

Supplementary Transcripts

If your student has been enrolled at another high school, a correspondence school, or an online school as a regular student (i.e., not just taking a few classes a la carte) you may need to submit these transcripts as well. Generally, it is best to include all outside courses on your main transcript, with a note or legend about where they were taken. Then, if needed, include the supplementary transcripts along with your own transcript. As of this writing, the Common Application has four transcript upload buttons available. One will be used for your main transcript; the other three can be used for a course description document (see Chapter 20) and any other transcripts the colleges may want to see.

Likewise, a transcript of community college courses and grades should be submitted in addition to your own transcript, even though you will have recorded these college grades on your transcript. I recommend uploading an unofficial transcript into the Common Application, and then requesting that an official transcript be sent from the community college to the colleges to which your student is applying. For community colleges, *unofficial* transcripts may be provided free or at a minimal charge from the community college because they are simply printouts of the student's history at that school. The student can probably access his or her unofficial transcript at any time from the online student portal. *Official* transcripts, however, must be requested ahead of time. They may take from one to four weeks to process and cost a few dollars each, with an extra fee for rush service. Ask the university if an official community college transcript should be mailed or sent electronically directly from the community college to the university. Alternatively, the community college could mail *you* the official transcripts, with each one in its own sealed envelope, and you could send them out from your home—without opening them, of course.

In some circumstances, you'll want to specify which community college courses were taken for high school credit and which for college credit. This notation might be useful if the college or university limits the number of units a student may take at another college and still be considered a freshman. See Chapters 13 and 14 for more details. You could communicate this information by scanning or photocopying a transcript and making your own notations next to the course names. Students who do want to transfer some courses can take care of this with the registrar at the university when it is time for enrollment.

Incomplete Courses

One of the beauties of homeschooling is its flexibility and personalized pacing. Either by design or as a result of circumstances, your student may start a course in one school year and complete it the next, or perhaps not complete it until twelfth grade. At the outset of the course, you would write up the course description and syllabus, but you would wait until after the student actually *finishes* all the requirements to record the grade and credits on the transcript. You may then record this course in the semester where it makes the most sense.

Summer School

Many homeschoolers work year round; some keep their summers entirely free; still others use this time for catch-up or for focusing on just one or two courses. Use time-based or completion-based calculations to plan how many hours per day, days per week, and weeks per summer your student will need to work in order to complete a semester's worth of a subject. Then record it with courses from the previous spring or (more commonly) the upcoming fall. Or note it on a separate line as a summer course.

High School-Level Courses Taken During Middle School

With the flexibility of homeschooling, many students work ahead of their chronological age. If your student has taken high school math, world languages, computer science, or any other high school-level courses during the middle school years, you may put these on the transcript as well. To include only a couple of courses, you may insert them in a separate small section prior to the ninth grade courses, or simply list them in the ninth grade lineup. If he or she took a significant number of courses, you may want to use a subject-based transcript format rather than a chronological transcript. In this case, the courses would be grouped by general subject area, such as mathematics, and you would list all mathematics courses that were high school level.

THE PORTFOLIO

Some students' high school careers can be portrayed impressively with a traditional transcript. Others are better served by a more personalized medium that portrays them as three-dimensional human beings, not simply a collection of grades, credits, and test scores. A portfolio is a logically and attractively organized portrait of a student's accomplishments and characteristics, using such concrete elements as work samples, photos, media, or detailed descriptions to highlight the student's achievements. For some homeschoolers, and particularly for the smaller, more personal colleges, a portfolio makes much more sense than a transcript.

A portfolio can take the form of an elegant, professional-looking folder, a website, a video presenlation, a printed book, or any other medium strategically designed to communicate the student's accomplishments. As you prepare the portfolio, keep in mind convenience of mailing, if applicable. A slim folder will travel more easily than will a bulky binder. And a web link will travel effortlessly!

When to Use a Portfolio

For a student whose high school experience has been largely arts-based, sports-based, activity-based, or otherwise different from the typical academic profile, a portfolio can display these skills and accomplishments advantageously. Other groups of homeschoolers may also benefit from this method.

Students Who Pursue Unschooling

Families who have pursued an unschooling educational approach, in which the student's learning is loosely structured and largely self-directed, will want to clearly communicate to college admissions committees what this has entailed. A portfolio will help gather the highlights of each school year and show the productive accomplishments that grew out of this student-directed learning environment. Particularly if you do not have formal grades, the portfolio will be essential.

Students with Distinctive Talents or Achievements

Some homeschoolers use large blocks of their time to hone special talents. Examples include athletes who have taken a sport to national or Olympic level, or skilled musicians who travel to national and international competitions. These students may or may not have a traditional lineup of high school courses alongside their stellar accomplishments. Whether they have placed less emphasis on academics or simply want to emphasize their talents, these students can showcase their education via a personalized portfolio.

Certain students, even if their education is fairly traditional, have several unusual achievements best displayed by means of a portfolio. Examples might include publications, national recognition for community service, exceptional internships or work experience, or technology-related accomplishments such as inventions, competitions, or website development. Excerpts, descriptions, photos, online articles, newspaper clippings, website links, or other means of describing the student's achievements can be readily displayed in a portfolio.

Students Whose Grades Don't Reflect Their Talents

Perhaps your student's grades are not impressive, but his or her experiences and talents *are*. If a traditional transcript would not do justice to your student, or if supplementation of the transcript would give your student an edge, consider putting together a portfolio. Portfolios show, in living color, how homeschooling has allowed your student to broaden, deepen, and enrich his or her learning. If a portfolio is the best way to demonstrate your student's passion, definitely use it. Consider utilizing a transcript and a portfolio together to display your student's accomplishments to their best advantage.

Some universities, including many large state university systems, do not accept portfolio submissions. However, be sure to check—you might be surprised. In general, private colleges and universities, especially the smaller ones, tend to be intrigued by homeschooling and might welcome a portfolio or a creative supplement to the transcript.

What to Include in a Portfolio

Because you will not know which items are destined to become the treasures for a distinctive portfolio, find an easy but organized way to save potential "keepers" as they accumulate during the high school years. Your collection container might be a large folder or a box for each school year. For digital files, accumulate those you'd like to keep in a specially labeled folder. Later, you will carefully select the best and most representative items to include in a college application portfolio. The selection process will be challenging but enjoyable as you revisit the homeschool journey. Your goal is to choose the items that best represent your student's skills, goals, passions, and achievements. Be prepared to describe each item briefly so that the admissions officer understands its significance. Of course, you will not use every item "as is" or physically send it to the college, but each one will remind you of accomplishments and provide supporting details for your written descriptions.

Here are some ideas.[1] While you won't include all of these, choose the items that will provide an accurate and appealing portrait of your student. Keep in mind that the admissions committee does not have a great deal of time to peruse page upon page of "goodies," so select your items carefully for maximum impact.

- *Schoolwork samples from a variety of subjects, showing excellence, ingenuity, or an innovative approach.*
- *Lists of textbooks or resources used for each course.*
- *Lists of books read each year for school assignments or for pleasure.*
- *Selected essays, especially those demonstrating creative or critical thought or insightful research.*
- *Copies of published stories, articles, or poems.*
- *News clippings, web page printouts, or electronic links describing the student's achievements.*
- *Certificates relevant to academic or extracurricular awards or given for special training such as Red Cross certification.*
- *Letters of commendation from others with whom the student has studied or worked.*
- *Brochures or photos from unique field trips.*
- *Travel-related photos or journals, especially for missions projects or humanitarian work.*
- *Photos of art projects, science projects, and other 3-D items, including awards.*
- *Photos or videos of the student participating in sports, dance, music, debate, science, or other pursuits.*
- *Descriptions of extracurricular activities, research, or educational experiences.*
- *Descriptions or photos of any student-created innovations or inventions.*
- *Research abstracts from pending or published articles.*
- *Descriptions of paid or volunteer work experience.*
- *Samples of course exams.*
- *Syllabi and course descriptions.*
- *Items demonstrating the student's leadership of groups or projects.*

A web-based portfolio could include photos of activities and projects, audio/video clips, descriptive paragraphs about the student's education, and links to other pertinent websites detailing awards or programs involving the student.

In short, a portfolio is a thoughtful, strategic compilation selected from all the items that parents save anyway. Even if you plan to send a transcript rather than a full portfolio, a few of the items listed above, *very* selectively chosen, could form an attention-getting supplement to a transcript. Always make sure that the college is open to receiving such items, either by mail or electronically.

THE HIGH SCHOOL DIPLOMA

Issued by Parents

The high school diploma is one more document that can bring up many questions in the minds of homeschoolers. Parents wonder, "Can we create our own diploma?" "Will it be accepted by a college?" For most families' circumstances, the answer to these questions is "Yes." A diploma is always issued and signed by those who supervised the high school education and can attest to the fact that it was completed. This person or entity may be a traditional school, a correspondence program, a private school satellite program, or the parent. The fact that your school is not an accredited school is beside the point. In reality, chances are that no one will ever ask to see the diploma. Instead, the college application will simply ask if the student will *earn* a diploma, or when it will be granted. No one has ever asked to see our kids' diplomas, which is a shame, because they look quite attractive! Furthermore, the homeschool diploma was never an issue with any of the dozen-plus universities to which our students were accepted.

If your student plans to start at the community college, note that some community colleges may ask to see a copy of the high school diploma at the time of application. This request will vary according to the particular college's policies. In our area, some of the colleges do not ask for a diploma at all; others ask to see it only if the student is under eighteen years old. Obviously, a student who is pursuing dual enrollment is not expected to have a high school diploma; this rule would potentially apply if your student enrolls at the community college to begin his or her college education after high school graduation.

When your student completes the graduation requirements you originally set, you will issue a diploma and have the transcript and supporting documentation (such as course descriptions) ready in case anyone ever asks for more details. The diploma itself should be signed and dated by the parent(s) and should include the student's name and the date of completion of secondary school (high school) with the school's name and perhaps the city and state. It should definitely include wording, (simple or elaborate), to the effect that the student is being awarded a high school diploma. You may want to look at several samples if you are making your own, or you may order a personalized printed diploma from sources such as https://www.homeschooldiploma.com/. You may also order a diploma from HSLDA, personalized and inscribed with your student's name and the school name. The HSLDA website contains tips on how to word your diploma and on what to do if a college claims that you need an "accredited" diploma.[2]

Issued by a Homeschool Program

Your PSP or ISP, if you belong to one, may issue a diploma when your student graduates. While this document might seem more "official," it is not essentially different from issuing your own—especially since you provided the grades and course information to the program in the first place.

Issued by a Correspondence or Online School

If it is important to you, you can use an accredited correspondence or online school as the source of your student's diploma. You will need to exercise due diligence as you research these programs and seek out a quality program that offers the rigor and variety of courses your student needs. In reality, however, you will be pleasantly surprised at the acceptability among colleges and the military of homeschool diplomas issued by parents. If you have any misgivings or issues with regard to homeschooling laws in your state, be sure you are thoroughly familiar with these laws. HSLDA is a good place to start this research, since you will receive accurate, homeschool-pertinent answers.

Diploma Tips

Since a few states do have requirements about the wording or issuing of diplomas, check the HSLDA website for the latest state-specific information. Also examine college applications to see how they inquire about high school diplomas. Chances are, all that happens is that your student marks a box with the answer "Yes" or "No" to "Do you or will you have a high school diploma?" and then fills in the date of issue. Don't feel compelled to contact the college about diploma issues unless its website (or other source of information you find) implies that the diploma *must* be from an accredited high school—but even so, confirm it with the college. It is extremely rare these days that colleges insist on accredited diplomas, but it is somewhat common that they are confused about the legitimacy of homeschool diplomas (especially with respect to financial aid rules). Again, look to HSLDA for advice and help.

If, based on other homeschoolers' experiences, you anticipate a problem with one of the colleges to which your student will apply, community college courses can help. By taking a few courses—perhaps a semester in each core college prep subject—your student can "validate" the homeschool diploma. Find out how many units or courses the college or university would like to see. Keep the community college transcripts, course descriptions, and syllabi as a backup until your student is safely settled in college. In fact, keep this documentation for a few years, since your student may need to provide descriptive information in order to transfer these courses to the university.

That said, it is now rare for colleges to take issue with homeschool diplomas, so don't worry.

Military- and Law Enforcement-Related Diploma Issues

If your student plans to join the armed forces after high school, monitor the process closely to make sure that you will not hit a snag over the issue of the diploma. According to HSLDA (and as a result of their strategic work over the years), the armed forces now recognize parent-issued diplomas awarded upon completion of high school at home.[3] Carefully read all articles on the HSLDA site relating to enlisting in the military, and be sure to have a professional-looking, up-to-date transcript to document the student's courses, credits, and grades.

One remaining issue with homeschool diplomas is in the area of law enforcement careers. Depending on the state or local community, police and fire departments may require a high school diploma from an accredited school. If your student has a strong interest in law enforcement, check out your options early on so that you can reduce the likelihood of unpleasant surprises.

TO SUM UP

Transcripts, portfolios, and diplomas—these documents bring you closer to launching a home educated student into the world. As you prepare these items, do your most careful work so that your student's accomplishments will be clearly communicated to colleges, scholarship committees, the military, or employers. Hopefully this chapter has removed the mystery and inspired you to find the best way to sum up your last and finest years of homeschooling.

1. Cannon, Ronald, and Inge Cannon, "Alternative Ways to Earn College Credit," *The Teaching Home*, January/February 2000. (A few ideas for portfolio contents were gathered from this article.)
2. Home School Legal Defense Association, "High School Diploma." Accessed August 17, 2018. https://www.hslda.org/highschool/faq.asp#D8
3. Estrada, William A., Home School Legal Defense Association, "Armed Forces Finally Accept Homeschool Enlistees on Equal Terms," March 18, 2014. Accessed August 17, 2018. https://hslda.org/content/docs/news/2014/201403180.asp

Chapter 12

Jumping Ahead:

Honors and Advanced Placement® Courses

Whether homeschooled or traditionally schooled, serious students will want to tackle the most rigorous courses available. Honors and Advanced Placement (AP) courses provide excellent opportunities to dig deeply into a subject and to prepare for college-level work. Though they require extra effort, honors and AP courses provide a strategic stepping stone to college.

HONORS COURSES

Not surprisingly, honors courses are more demanding than typical college prep courses and involve advanced coursework, a greater time commitment, and the use of more rigorous textbooks. Honors courses emphasize critical and analytical thinking rather than rote memorization, and they promote research skills, reasoning, and independent work.

Reasons to Consider Honors Courses

Students should undertake honors courses for reasons that make sense to them in their individual circumstances. These reasons might include the following:

To Take on a Challenge

Honors courses take the high school education "up a notch." Quite simply, students who invest extra work and extra hours to pursue more complex ideas will grow in their academic abilities. The inclusion of honors courses communicates the desire for broader and deeper learning. To stretch their learning far beyond the minimum, students who are capable of these more demanding courses should take them.

To Add Rigor to the Transcript and to Enhance the GPA

Colleges look for students who have taken the most rigorous courses of which they are capable. A transcript showing several honors courses will be more impressive than one showing only the more basic courses. In addition, honors and Advanced Placement courses, by virtue of their difficulty, deserve more weight on the transcript. When calculating a weighted GPA, honors and AP courses receive extra grade points (often one point for AP and one point or one-half point for honors, depending on the system used), so students who have earned A's in honors courses can potentially earn GPAs higher than 4.0.

To Prepare a Student for Difficult College Courses

In addition to helping students earn admission to college, honors courses help them do better once they get to college. Students who can practice faster-paced learning, deeper understanding, and sharper critical thinking skills before college will reap rewards during college.

How Can Homeschooled Students Take Honors Courses?

In a traditional high school, students may choose from standard, honors, or AP courses. Obviously, homeschoolers must either search out honors courses or design them from scratch. Technically, to offer an honors course, your school should also "offer" a standard course in this subject, although your student does not actually need to take it. Each honors course should have a formal or informal prerequisite which the student has met. Prerequisites may include a previous course in the same subject, high standardized test scores, or other demonstrated skills such as writing ability.

Examples of honors courses include academic community college courses or online, co-op, or independent study courses specifically labeled as honors courses.

You can also design your own honors courses by augmenting a standard course. Increase both the quantity and the quality of assignments to add complexity, enrichment, and acceleration. Incorporate a variety of problem-solving and research activities. OpenCourseWare programs such as those from MIT, Yale, Carnegie Mellon, Tufts, Notre Dame, University of Michigan, and many other institutions can be useful resources for free course outlines, objectives, and supplementary material.

Math

For math courses, accelerate the pace of study and include challenging problems. Some textbooks present problems grouped by degree of difficulty. For honors courses you would deliberately select a large sampling of these tougher problems. For example, honors geometry should include formal proofs and geometric constructions, not just basic geometric principles. For any math course, be sure to include proofs, multi-step problems, and word problems—don't have your student skip these. If your textbook publisher offers an honors supplement, use it with your student to provide extra challenge.

English

An honors English course is a writing-intensive course. Both the number and the quality of the literature reading and writing assignments should exceed the requirements of a standard course and should focus on critical analysis. Require the student to revise papers and to strive for excellence in content, organization, mechanics, and style. To encourage in-depth learning, assign research papers, presentations, or projects. As you choose literature for reading and discussion, favor the reading of classic literature and complex nonfiction at or approaching college level instead of popular literature. Essays and discussions should address themes, literary and rhetorical techniques, symbolism, and character development.

Overall, honors work in an English course should encourage students to become actively involved in the literature and its content, to express and defend their ideas, and to use creativity and critical analysis to enhance their learning.

Science

Honors science courses should require frequent experiments, with lab writeups prepared according to the scientific method. Compared to standard courses, they should involve activities that are more exploratory and experimental, to deepen the thought process, but they should follow these explorations with full calculations and conclusions. During the high school years, the student should become familiar with handling data, reading and creating tables and graphs, and reasoning from data. Exams should be comprehensive and should include some essay questions. You might also require your student to read a few scientific journal articles, to conduct online research, and to follow up this investigation with research papers or projects on the topics studied.

Social Studies

In social studies courses, students should learn to research, think, and respond to historical or contemporary topics, and not simply to answer factual questions. Assign research projects, debates, and presentations. Use essay questions on homework and exams, and encourage more involved discussions of the material. Provide increased breadth and depth by seeking well-researched historical novels, commentaries on current or historical issues, and source documents.

In general, honors courses begin with the concepts presented in a standard course but then add depth and critical thinking by means of extra reading, additional research and projects, more challenging problems, and enhanced accountability for complex ideas. If you need specific ideas for designing honors courses, search for sample high school honors course syllabi online or obtain them from teachers at your local public or private high school.

THE ADVANCED PLACEMENT® PROGRAM

The Advanced Placement program was created by the College Board in 1955 to increase student achievement and to form a bridge between high school and college. Accordingly, courses are designed to be taught at college level but to be taken by high schoolers. AP courses and exams are available in numerous subject areas, including English, mathematics, sciences, social studies, world languages, art, computer science, and several others. Currently, 38 different courses and exams are administered. In May, immediately following the course, students take a rigorous exam scored from 1 to 5. Scores of 3 or more are considered passing, and colleges award credit or exemption from prerequisites or lower level classes on the basis of these scores. Policies differ widely from college to college and also by department within the college.

The program takes honors courses to a higher, more challenging level and provides important preparation for college courses. The AP program is so popular among college prep students that in 2018, more than 5 million AP exams were administered worldwide to more than 2.8 million students.[1]

While the AP program is one of the key components for competitive college admissions and, to some extent, for less competitive colleges, some homeschoolers underutilize it, and others know very little about the program. Advanced Placement courses have become a major benchmark for high-achieving students. No longer are selective colleges content to see strong SAT scores and stellar GPAs—they see these all day long. In addition, they are looking for a lineup of Advanced Placement courses on applicants' transcripts, demonstrating that these students took the most rigorous courses of which they were capable. Therefore, understanding and taking advantage of the AP program is a wise move for some homeschoolers (it is not for everyone, though) and will provide another opportunity to compete on equal footing with traditionally schooled counterparts.

Note that a student need not take an AP course in order to sit for an AP exam. Students can prepare independently and will receive credit or advanced standing from the college if they pass with an appropriate score. Taking year-long AP courses, however, demonstrates the student's commitment to a challenging course of study.

As you investigate the Advanced Placement program, realize that this is yet another area of education that changes rapidly, so plan to keep up with recent developments by checking the College Board website for updates and confirmation of the following information.

ADVANTAGES OF AP COURSES

Though rigorous, AP courses offer advantages over typical high school courses. Designed to resemble college courses, they actually mirror the self-directed, in-depth study that is characteristic of motivated homeschoolers. AP courses provide the following benefits:

College Credit or Exemption from Introductory Courses

With the high costs of college tuition, every opportunity to save money is welcome. Students who pass the AP exam in a given subject may receive credit toward college graduation or may be placed into a higher level course rather than having to take an introductory course. This privilege enables them to progress more quickly through their college education. At some institutions, a qualifying score may fulfill a world language or English composition requirement. Some colleges require a score of 4 or 5 before granting credit or advanced standing; others require only a 3. Score requirements also vary by department at the college. AP credit may not be as widely accepted in the student's major as it is in other departments.

Although each institution sets its own AP credit policies, it is easy to check on these policies for hundreds of colleges by consulting the College Board website. Importantly, follow this up later with updated information from the admissions office of the institutions your student is considering. Some schools limit the number of AP courses and college credits a student can transfer in, so be sure to check.

Enhanced High School Transcript

Tackling AP courses shows the college admissions staff that a student is serious, motivated, and mature. Because these courses are not easy, a student who is willing to attempt them is a student who is not afraid of an academic challenge. Most selective colleges review applications to determine how many AP courses students have taken. Students applying to less selective schools need not worry about presenting an impressive lineup of APs; they can simply take these courses as their interests and abilities guide them—or forgo them if that makes more sense.

Generally, colleges do not penalize students whose schools do not offer AP courses, but they want students to take full advantage of the opportunities their schools do offer. Homeschoolers have a somewhat reduced opportunity to take AP courses compared to their traditionally schooled counterparts. However, with the availability of online courses and the chance to design AP courses at home and submit syllabi, homeschoolers *do* have access to advanced level courses. A homeschooler applying to a competitive college would be wise to have at least a few AP courses on the transcript. All in all, college admissions officers expect that top students will make every effort to include some AP courses.

Improved Study Skills and Preparation for College Courses

Another benefit of the AP program is the improved study skills that students develop during a rigorous year-long course. Knowing that a three-hour exam is coming up in May motivates the student to budget time during the school year and to select and study the most important concepts. Because of the large quantities of material that must be read and assimilated, students will need to "work smart" and not just "work hard." Additionally, many courses teach problem-solving strategies that will be invaluable later on. Because these courses are indeed at college level, students who take several AP courses find themselves well prepared for college.

Increased Depth of Study

One strong characteristic of home education dovetails nicely with another benefit of AP courses. Students who study AP subjects cover them in great depth. A superficial treatment of U.S. history, for instance, will not be enough to pass the exam. In AP courses, students not only learn facts and names (lots of them) but also delve into political and diplomatic concepts, social trends, cultural and intellectual developments, and economic issues that contributed to events in history. Working through an AP English or history curriculum together as a parent-student team can be gratifying and stimulating, albeit exhausting at times. Both student and parent will definitely expand their knowledge.

Enhanced Writing and Organizing Skills

Because many of the AP exams contain significant essay portions, students will grow in their writing skills during the year. A thirty- or forty-minute time limit has a way of prompting a student to be organized and "to the point." The skills learned during a year of AP prep will carry over into writing for the student's non-AP courses. Generally, students discover that they are capable of writing better, more organized essays in a fraction of the time it once took.

Potential for Receiving AP Awards

One more advantage of AP courses is the chance to receive recognition for high achievement. A student can earn commendations such as AP Scholar, AP Scholar with Honor, or AP Scholar with Distinction based on exam scores and number of exams taken. Homeschoolers should take advantage of any opportunity to earn academic honors to list on college applications, as it can be a little more difficult to find these opportunities in a nontraditional setting.

EXAM SCHEDULING AND FORMAT

Exams are given only once a year, during the first two weeks of May. Most exams last for about three hours and consist of a multiple choice section and one or more "free response" sections, whose format varies depending on the subject. Free response sections may require the student to write essays, solve mathematical or chemical problems in detail, design a biological experiment, or analyze a piece of literature. Since the exams are administered at high schools, homeschoolers need to identify a testing location and to communicate with that school's administration well in advance (tests are ordered the previous fall). Each year's schedule of test dates is posted on the College Board website. To receive helpful, practical assistance with AP courses, access both the section for students *and* the section for educators, which is called AP Central. The website also has an information page for homeschoolers signing up for exams.

WHAT MAKES AN AP COURSE AN AP COURSE?

While classroom teachers and homeschooling parents have a certain amount of freedom in designing most of their courses, AP courses must follow a more regimented plan for coverage of topics. This structure serves not only to prepare students for the exam, but also to assure equivalency from school to school. Consequently, when a college admissions officer sees "AP English Literature and Composition" on the transcript, he or she will know something about the rigor and depth of the course. AP is also a registered trademark of the College Board, and therefore teachers and parents should not use the AP designation without adhering to the required content of the course. Because AP courses address a specific set of content goals, teachers must be familiar with official course descriptions before planning the year's study.

AP Course Audit

A policy that affects homeschoolers seeking to design AP courses is the College Board's AP Course Audit procedure. In short, schools that use the AP designation in their course titles must complete an AP Course Audit form for each subject and submit a course syllabus demonstrating how the course will be taught and how it will meet the required course objectives. A more detailed discussion of this process and its ramifications for homeschoolers is included later in this chapter.

Thus, one key characteristic of AP courses is that they provide standardized depth of coverage of the material. Whether it be chemistry, calculus, or computer science, each course will cover the topics and depth that one would expect of a freshman level college course in that subject.

International Baccalaureate® (IB): A Similar Program

The International Baccalaureate program is similar in rigor and esteem to the AP program. More focused than the AP program, IB is offered at selected high schools, mostly overseas. Students typically take six or seven IB courses during their junior and senior years. Because the program is school-based, most homeschoolers do not have access to it. We include this information just so that parents and students will be aware of the terminology if they encounter it in their research or on college applications.

HOW TO CHOOSE AP COURSES

Believe it or not, some of the most "driven" students in traditional schools take as many as thirteen AP courses over their years of high school, generally from tenth grade on. This is arguably an excessive number, and the time invested could be spent on leadership and on pursuing passions. Your student, if interested and motivated, might aim for two or three courses in the junior year and two or three in the senior year, with perhaps one more in the sophomore year, depending on readiness. This would be a total of five to seven courses; some students might be able to handle even more. As a general rule, students hoping for admission to the most selective colleges should try to complete as many AP courses as they can without torturing themselves—but should keep life in balance as well. Choice of courses depends on some or all of the following factors.

Areas of Strength

A student who is particularly strong in a subject such as calculus or English literature may want to try AP courses in these areas. Likewise, studio art, social studies, and other AP courses appeal to students already primed for a challenge in these subjects. Tackling AP courses shows that a student is ready to stretch his or her abilities to the next level of learning and performance.

Availability of Courses and Resources

In some areas of the country, it is easy to find a local homeschool academy that offers College Board-approved AP courses. In other areas, this is more challenging, but you may find an online provider that offers the course(s) you are interested in. If neither of these options is available for a particular school year, consider forming a group with other interested homeschoolers and inviting a qualified parent or teacher to design and submit a syllabus for College Board approval. The previous three options (local live class, online class, and local group with an approved syllabus) would all offer the chance to title the course as AP on the student's transcript.

Two more options are available if you do not have your heart set on an approved AP course but simply want your student to prepare for and take the exam in May. First, the student could self-study, using appropriate textbooks and an AP test prep book. Alternatively, if the student has access to community college courses, or to academy classes that are rigorous but not AP-approved, he or she could use these courses as a basis for exam preparation. For example, the student could take a community college chemistry course and then take the AP Chemistry exam.

For AP science subjects with lab requirements (biology, environmental science, chemistry, and physics), some of the experiments may use equipment not found in basic "home labs." Well in advance of the course, become familiar with the recommended or required lab experiments and decide where the student can acquire appropriate materials (such as buying a prepackaged lab kit designed for the course). Once these have been identified, the student can complete the labs at home or in a group environment. Virtual labs or simulations found online may give the student some additional exposure, knowledge, and familiarity with the concepts. Just don't assume that virtual labs will suffice for approval of a course through College Board and/or through colleges and universities at application time. When shopping for online AP science courses, carefully check on how they handle laboratory work. Many of them have the family purchase lab kits with materials to perform experiments at home. In addition to the College Board not approving AP science courses without a physical or "live" lab, some universities' credit procedures state that they will only give credit for courses with hands-on labs.

Realize also that community college courses do not always cover topics with the same depth or breadth that the AP program recommends. The student may need to supplement the community college class with some extra study in order to cover all the concepts that will appear on the exam. Even when taking a full community college course in the subject, a student should have an AP prep book handy for reinforcement of weaknesses and for completing practice exams.

Desire to Enhance a Required Subject

Since students must take subjects such as English and U.S. history anyway, why not enhance the required course by tackling an AP course? Although it will mean extra reading, discussion, analysis, and writing, these efforts will result in extra learning as well. College prep students should take at least one of the AP English courses (English Language and Composition or English Literature and Composition), as this provides a great boost to writing and analysis techniques that will be used in college.

Consideration of Student's Grade Level and Abilities

AP courses work well for juniors and seniors. However, motivated and capable sophomores, and even some gifted freshmen, can certainly handle a class or two. We had great success with AP European History, our daughter's first AP course as a sophomore. During that school year, she was not yet so overloaded that she couldn't do justice to the course. In fact, the sense of unfamiliarity about the exam looming in May kept her on her toes, prompting her to faithfully dig into the material all year long.

A motivated high school junior or senior can handle two or more AP courses each year. A more intense student might load up with four or five per year, but be prepared to go in and dig your child out from under piles of books every few days!

Completion of Courses the Student Prefers Not to Take in College

The AP program allows a student to get one or more courses out of the way for good. For example, a potential science major might fulfill a college history requirement, or a humanities major might knock out a science requirement. Successful AP exam scores allow students to test out of a first-level lower division course so that they can move on more quickly. Remember that each college sets its own AP policy regarding which exams will or will not satisfy the college's degree or major requirements. Be familiar with these policies before you and your student get your hearts set on a certain scenario.

Strategic Planning

Students who will be applying for special programs such as internships, tutoring jobs, advanced community college classes, or scholarships may choose to take courses that will pave their way toward acceptance into these programs. For instance, a science-oriented student applying for a research internship may decide to complete AP Chemistry, Physics, or Biology prior to applying, in order to show seriousness of intent and to enhance skills.

HOW TO PLAN AN AP COURSE

Understand the AP Course Audit Process

All schools that list AP courses on the high school transcript must participate in the AP Course Audit. This includes traditional schools, online schools, and home schools. The reason for the audit is to clarify and standardize the requirements for all AP courses and to prevent schools from using the AP trademark for courses that do not include appropriate content and rigor. Colleges and universities can more readily compare student transcripts when they know that courses marked "AP" have been audited for a proper level of rigor. For each AP course they offer, schools must submit a course syllabus containing all requested details. If the courses are approved and validated, the school may then use the AP designation on student transcripts. Colleges and universities will receive an AP Course Ledger, which is a listing of authorized AP courses at all schools that have submitted audit materials and have had courses approved.

Students are still free to register for and take AP exams even if their school has not participated in the audit. Thus, they can still receive college credit or advanced placement, based on university policy, if they pass the exams with the appropriate scores. However, they may not use the AP designation on the transcript if the course has not successfully passed the audit process.

If you desire to conduct your own AP courses as a homeschooler or to take AP courses online or in the community, consider the following advice.

Keep Current with AP Central

If you will be planning your own course(s), start by visiting the AP Central portion of the College Board website at https://apcentral.collegeboard.org/ and thoroughly reading the instructions for AP course planning and AP Course Audits. Skim through pages marked "For Educators" and specifically search for information directed to homeschoolers, as well as understanding deadlines for submitting course syllabi and registering for exams. (Note that registration happens in the fall.) Fortunately, as of this writing, the audit guidelines do not require certification of AP instructors, and the audit process is free of charge. To create an AP course for your home school and have it approved by the College Board, start by creating an account on the AP Course Audit homepage, indicating that you are a "Home School Provider." From there, follow the directions to submit your syllabus (see more ideas and tips below). During and after the AP planning process, continue to keep tabs on instructions for homeschoolers.

Look for Preapproved Courses

As you look for AP courses, seek out providers that have already participated in the audit process, including local academy programs, independent study programs, online schools, or public or private schools if they are open to homeschoolers. For instance, a prominent online provider, PA Homeschoolers, only offers courses that have passed the audit. Your student may also be able to take AP courses at a local public or private high school. If you are considering any outside sources of AP courses, confirm that these courses are College Board-approved. Note that as of this writing, the edX platform offers free online AP courses. Go to https://www.edx.org/.

Gather Information on the Course(s)

To get acquainted with your AP subject, you will first want to visit AP Central and read the official detailed course description. You will definitely want to keep coming back to this site to gather teacher tips and a plethora of course information. This site offers subject-specific teaching strategies, practical resource guides, sample syllabi for each course, exam preparation tips, course overview videos, reviews of teaching resources, an online community where you can chat with other teachers, and helpful FAQs. Teachers whose courses have passed the AP Course Audit can download free practice exams and may also sign up for e-newsletters containing program updates and course-specific changes. Syllabus development guides and checklists, information on teacher training courses, demonstration ideas for complex science topics, and many more resources are available on this site.

While the official course description provides general information about the course, including sample multiple choice questions and sample essay questions, you will also want to see how other high school teachers plan year-long AP courses. Even if you are not taking part in the AP Course Audit but simply plan to have your student self-study for the exam, take advantage of the many course design resources on the AP Central site. View the sample syllabi and customize them for your course. In fact, the easiest way to have your homeschool course approved is to simply adopt one of the sample syllabi as is, submit it for approval, and follow this instructional plan during the year.

You will also want to become familiar with course goals and recommended textbooks. In addition to the syllabi on the AP Central site, browse sample syllabi from websites of high schools around the nation simply by searching up a few key words: for example, "AP U.S. History syllabus." After examining a few syllabi, you will get a feel for the textbooks commonly used, the pacing of the course, the types of assignments given, and enrichment activities you might use for your student. Many teachers have also designed fun and flashy websites, featuring lots of valuable resources such as quiz games, colorful presentations and animations, and links to other helpful sites.

Research the Course Design Process

If you cannot find an approved AP course online or in your area, or if you prefer to design your own AP course, go ahead and plan it. First, see if your homeschool program has a school code with the College Board and can submit audit materials for your course. If not, you may submit your own course plans as a homeschooler according to the instructions on the AP Central site. Create a home school account on the AP Course Audit sign-in page and then follow the directions for submitting your syllabus.

If you choose to plan and conduct an AP course without obtaining College Board approval, or if you submit a syllabus but it is not approved, plan to explain the situation to the university later, when your student completes college applications. Particularly if your student takes and passes the AP exam, you may indicate via a legend on the transcript and/or an explanation in your course description document that the student self-studied and passed the AP exam. Private universities, in particular, may offer flexibility and a case-by-case evaluation. In all likelihood, they will look favorably upon the efforts of a homeschooler who has pursued challenging courses.

For a more straightforward experience, consider patterning your course after one of the sample syllabi on the AP Central site. Use one of the recommended textbooks, assign similar essays, exams, labs, and projects, and, in general, make your course as rigorous as the courses described in the samples. One homeschooling parent I knew did this for 13 AP courses, and it was actually quite simple.

Realize that the course audit is an annual procedure, and previously approved courses need to be renewed each year.

Assess Sources for Instruction and Guidance

With proper research and planning, a home-designed AP course can be the most cost-effective method for covering the material. Armed with the knowledge of topics to be covered, a parent and student together can seek out recommendations for the best textbooks, AP prep or review books, open source courses, and websites for practice quizzes and review materials. Here are some resources to get you started:

Teacher Training Courses

One way to connect with other AP teachers is to attend a College Board-endorsed AP Summer Institute. Most are week-long courses held during the summer, but weekend courses are also offered during the school year. These are designed to train AP teachers, and homeschooling parents certainly fall into this category. You can search for these courses in the Professional Development and/or Institutes and Workshops section of the AP Central site

Summer institutes can be expensive: $800 to $1,000 or more for a week-long course or $200 to $300 for a Saturday course during the school year. However, if you are interested in a course, particularly if it is held locally, use your negotiating skills. Contact the director of the program and ask if you can attend just one or two days of the course for a prorated fee. I have successfully done this for two of these seminars. By choosing to attend the most strategic day of the training, I gleaned dozens of useful teaching ideas, received free textbooks, and gained contacts with other teachers. The instructors at summer institutes are generally AP readers—the "chosen few" who travel to the exam grading sites every summer to read and grade hundreds of essays or written problem sets. In my experience, these instructors have been extremely impressed by the idea of homeschoolers tackling AP courses. Consequently, they have been accessible and supportive during the school year. One local instructor I met also invited Julie to attend Saturday review sessions at the high school where he taught. My contribution was to bring baked goods for the hungry teens. Since the course was European History, we had fun labeling the goodies "Bonaparte Banana Bread," "Metternich Muffins," and so forth.

A complete list of College Board-approved teacher training courses can be found at AP Central under the Professional Development section for educators. For brief teaching tips, also search for YouTube® videos posted by teachers in your subject area.

As you gather resources and investigate how to teach an AP course at home, realize that this knowledge can be put to work for other students besides your own. Consider recruiting a group of motivated students to study alongside your student. Enhanced group dynamics, insights from multiple students, additional enjoyment of the subject, and the building of friendships are some of the benefits of this arrangement.

Local Schools

You might also seek help from a local school, whether private or public. If you can meet the teacher of your chosen AP subject, ask for his or her recommendations of textbooks, useful websites, and other resources. Often these teachers will take an interest in helping your student and may even lend you books and materials. Some may allow you to use their exams (consider this hitting the jackpot!) and, as we experienced, may invite your student to attend their review sessions in the weeks leading up to the exam. All you have to do is ask.

Online Courses

If home-designed courses are not practical, consider online courses from providers offering approved AP courses. For instance, PA Homeschoolers (Pennsylvania Homeschoolers) offers AP courses for about $650 to $800, plus books and lab kits. Laboratory exercises for lab-based courses utilize either virtual labs or labs done at home with materials from purchased lab kits. PA Homeschoolers is an extremely well-respected provider for online AP courses.

Many other online course providers, such as HSLDA Online Academy, Apex Learning Florida Virtual School, Johns Hopkins University Center for Talented Youth, Scholars Online, and scores of others, are available. Carefully evaluate each provider to determine whether it will meet your student's needs. Wherever possible, check with other families who have used these resources and ask about problems or pitfalls they have encountered. Criteria to check, besides College Board accreditation, are quality of teachers, user-friendliness of the tech interface, scheduling of live lectures, track record for passing the AP exam, and workload. With some programs, certain courses or teachers are excellent while others are not so good—just as is true with any school or educational program. Online forums such as the Well-Trained Mind forum, mentioned in Chapter 4, can be a valuable environment for checking in with other home-schooling families and getting their opinions.

Community Colleges

First, remember that AP courses are for high schoolers. Community colleges do not offer AP courses—they offer college courses. That said, some AP exams, especially those for lab sciences, are well-suited for preparation via community college-based instruction. By gaining familiarity with the AP course description and comparing it with the syllabus and textbook from a community college course, you will know whether a certain course might prepare your student for the AP exam. For instance, if the community college biology course covers all the AP course objectives except anatomy and physiology, your student may read that material in an additional textbook and do practice exams from test prep books. This would not be an approved AP course, but simply a variation on self-study.

Remember also that community college courses are only a semester or a quarter long. Your student may be able to take two courses that will together provide all the material for the exam, or take one course and use the remaining semester or quarter to study independently. Also note that AP exams may take place a few weeks before the college's spring term is over. Your student may have to "self teach" the last portion of the textbook to finish preparing for the exam.

One question that might arise is, "Why take the community college course *and* the AP exam? Can't the student just transfer the college credits and accomplish the same result?" This is an excellent question, and the short answer is that yes, the community college course is sufficient. The final and more complicated answer for each individual family depends on the transfer policy of the college the student will eventually attend. Early in the game, you may not know which college this will be. However, some universities, especially selective ones, do *not* accept transfer credits from a community college, or they accept only a limited number. Moreover, out-of-state colleges do not have articulation agreements with your state's community colleges, and thus, transferring will be more complex or even impossible. In these cases, passing the AP exam will be an advantage to your student, because he or she may be able to gain credit from that exam. Additionally, taking as many AP courses and/or exams as possible, even if some of the material was completed at the community college, is a good asset for the transcript and is helpful for admissions. Finally, preparing for a comprehensive exam such as the AP is a worthwhile educational experience in and of itself and will prepare your student for similar exams at the university level.

Tutorial Businesses

In some communities, private "schools," which are actually more like businesses, cater to students desiring extra tutoring, enrichment, or preparation for SAT, ACT, or AP exams. By investigating these options, you may find a suitable AP course to take.

The College Board (AP Central)

Home-based AP courses would not be quite so do-able were it not for the plethora of online resources. An almost infinite amount of information is available with just a few clicks. On the AP Central website, each AP subject has a home page with subject-specific resources. Some, such as course descriptions, syllabi, and articles on teaching strategies, are free of charge; others are for purchase. The *Released Exam* is one resource you'll definitely want to purchase. It is an actual AP exam that your student should take as practice shortly before the exam date. The *Released Exam* also provides sample graded student essay answers and commentary about scoring.

Free of charge on the AP website, students and teachers can download previous free response questions for all AP subjects, as well as some actual student responses and how they were scored. The site also contains suggested course calendars, study tips, links to individual colleges' AP credit policies, and many more resources. To gain a full understanding of the AP Program and its nuances, cruise through the entire AP site, both the educator-specific and the student-specific portions. Also sign up for your subject-specific site at AP Central to gain access to forums allowing teachers nationwide to share advice and tips.

Other Useful Websites and Resources

Individual AP teachers at local high schools can also provide useful information for students and for fellow teachers. Get acquainted with one or two teachers and ask them to recommend their favorite websites. Your student can explore colorful interactive quizzes, read handy summaries of important concepts, see art work pertinent to a historical period, and benefit in many other ways.

OpenCourseWare sites such as MIT OpenCourseWare (https://ocw.mit.edu/index.htm), edX (https://www.edx.org/), and Coursera (https://www.coursera.org/) can help by providing free AP content, support for students who are self-studying, and/or course outlines through open courses.

Test Prep Books

Numerous publishers—Barron's®, The Princeton Review®, REA®, Kaplan®, Peterson's®, Cliffs AP®, and others—offer books to prepare students for the AP exam. While these review guides are no sub-stitute for a full year course, they can be lifesavers when it comes to homing in on what is important for the exam. With sample exams, sections of review and reinforcement, and sample essay questions, these books are well worth the investment of $10 to $20. You can scour your local library system and borrow various books first to evaluate which publisher you like best, or read online reviews and then decide.

Draw Up a Syllabus and Schedule

Whether you will submit your home-designed plans for an official AP Course Audit or will have your student self-study for the exam, the next step is to put together a syllabus. The syllabus will contain a description of assignments and a schedule of when each chapter will be studied and when tests, papers, and projects will be due. If you are planning to submit the course for an AP Course Audit, the audit opens in March (always check AP Central for updates) and continues through the next several months. It is wise to complete your syllabus sooner rather than later so that you will have time for revisions, if required.

At any rate, aim to finish your plans in time for your student to begin the course in the late sum-mer. This also gives you time to gather your books, your materials, and your thoughts. Most AP courses will need to start by the second or third week of August in order to complete the entire course with time to review before the May exam.

Using an approved syllabus as a guide, divide up the textbook and assign chapters at a pace such that the student will finish by mid-April if possible. This schedule will allow a couple of weeks devoted to reviewing for the exam. Your student may need to do some work during Christmas vacation or spring break to finish by April and to allow for that important review time. Plan rigorous learning activities such as writing assignments, debates, research projects, or, for science and math courses, laboratory and prob-lem-solving activities. In addition to regular assignments, schedule in practice exams and timed practice essays so that the student becomes familiar with the format of the exam.

Work Diligently All Year

The planning of an AP course, though at times tedious, can be intriguing and even exhilarating. But the hard work of keeping up the momentum during the school year will be the true test of the perse-verance and diligence required to do well on the exam.

Work Together if Possible

If the course lends itself to a team approach to study, by all means work with your student so that both of you are in this together. For example, for English and history courses you can schedule discus-sions, mini-debates, and sessions of orally quizzing your student on multiple choice questions. At times, you may want to read portions of the textbook aloud to your student or have him or her read it to you so that you can both benefit from the material.

Design Tests

Finding sample essay questions is not difficult, but finding enough multiple choice questions to use in assembling chapter tests can be challenging. Your textbook publisher's website may post sample quizzes, and these can work well as chapter exams. Also, study guides for the textbook may be available for purchase. AP prep books often contain practice questions. And again, the AP Central site offers free practice exams to those who have participated in the audit process.

Hang in There!

Don't be discouraged if you and your student sometimes feel exhausted, inadequate, and ready to give up. Unfortunately, tears and frustration frequently come with the territory of rigorous courses, but if you persevere and seek creative ways of getting the work done, you will both be rewarded in the end. Use these times of frustration to examine your syllabus. Perhaps it is overzealous. Try to eliminate some assignments or streamline others to make the best use of your student's time.

Seek Help and Advice During the Year

As the course progresses, seek tips and encouragement from local teachers or from websites, forums, and message boards designed for AP teachers and students. As previously mentioned, try to develop a relationship with a local teacher who may invite your student to review sessions in the spring.

Register Your Student for the Exam

Begin by deciding where your student will take the exam. If a teacher at a particular high school is helping you with the course, he or she may offer to let the student sit for the exam at this school. If not, contact your local public or private high school well in advance and explain that your homeschooled student has prepared for the AP exam(s) and would like to register for these tests.

Since schools need to order their exams by November, they typically post a cutoff deadline early in the fall for students to register and pay for exams. Thus, as a homeschooler, you need to be proactive and contact the potential school *during the summer or even at the end of the previous school year* to confirm signup deadlines. If you miss the deadline, you are out of luck at that particular school, as most schools submit one and only one order for AP exams—but you may be able to sign up late and pay a higher fee.

Registering for exams generally means appearing at the school in person, paying exam and administration fees, providing the student's name and list of planned tests, and leaving your contact information. The school will order the tests and inform your student when and where to arrive on exam day. Be sure to record the name and contact information of the AP coordinator; also ask for a receipt showing that you paid for AP exams. If you do not hear from the school in a timely manner, especially as exam dates approach, contact the coordinator to make sure your student is on the list of test takers. Once tests are over, send your contact person a kind thank you note to pave the way for future homeschoolers!

Receive Scores and Report Them to Colleges

AP exam scores are sent out at the beginning of July. Depending on the college, a score of 3, 4, or 5 is a "pass" and may earn various levels of credit or advanced placement.

During the senior year AP exams, your student should fill out the information designating the name of the college that should receive the scores. At this time in the spring of senior year, your student should know where he or she will be going to college. This request for reporting can be made on the day of the exam at no charge, or requested later online for a fee. During the summer, as freshman year approaches, check to make sure the report was received by the college. The college registrar's office will notify the student of any credits awarded or advanced standing earned.

TIPS AND CAUTIONS

Sanity

Try not to go crazy on AP courses. Many students love learning so much that they are like "kids in a candy store" when selecting a lineup of courses for the year. Still others show a competitive streak and a desire to "out-AP" the next college applicant. Keep a hearty dose of sanity as you plan courses year by year and for the high school career as a whole. AP courses are tough and time-consuming, and scheduling too many in a given year is simply not wise. Your student needs time to pursue extracurriculars, socialize, sleep, and enjoy life. High school is much more than just a slate of APs, and homeschoolers, of all students, should keep the awareness that a love of learning and a pursuit of passions should take precedence over an insane number of highly advanced courses. Be wise and be moderate in order to avoid burnout.

Pacing

Since AP courses must finish by early May, including pre-exam review time, the only way to finish in time is to start by mid-August. Try to keep up a steady pace during the school year. While falling behind is inevitable, aim to get back on track as soon as possible. The pacing will be rapid and heavy, with little room for delays. Your student will begin to live, eat, breathe, and dream about this subject.

Credit

Be sure to check with colleges your student is interested in to confirm their AP credit policies. Additionally, students who intend to apply later to medical, law, or graduate school should check with some of these potential schools to understand their restrictions regarding AP credit. Some institutions will not accept AP credit to fulfill course prerequisites for graduate work; instead, the course(s) must actually be taken at a college or university. Sites such as AAMC (Association of American Medical Colleges) and databases such as Medical School Admission Requirements®, or similar banks of information for law schools, can help clarify these policies early in the game. Online discussion boards can also be helpful in gaining a general understanding of the issues, but always follow up by searching out specific information from the graduate programs themselves.

Credibility

If you, or any course provider, designate a course as "AP" on the transcript, you must adhere to the content and curriculum goals as described in the AP course description and must participate in the AP Course Audit. Use of "AP" without the associated content is an infringement of the College Board's registered trademark. AP courses are expected to be high quality and rigorous.

By the same token, it is not usually recommended that you list an AP course on your student's transcript without also having him or her take the exam. While this is not a hard and fast rule, you will maximize credibility with colleges by having your student take an AP exam for every AP course undertaken. Many colleges do not attach value to AP courses, especially for students in tenth grade or younger, without an accompanying AP exam grade.

TO SUM UP

In conclusion, the AP program is rigorous but rewarding. Likely the most difficult academic venture you will ever begin with your student, it may at times feel like a roller coaster ride. Yet the learning and sense of accomplishment that it yields, as well as the validation of your homeschool program by colleges, offer their own rewards. If you have a capable student, don't hesitate to give AP courses a try.

---

1. The College Board, "AP Program Size and Increments (By Year)," *CollegeBoard.org*. The College Board, 2018. Accessed October 13, 2018. https://secure-media.collegeboard.org/digitalServices/pdf/research/2018/2018-Size-and-Increment.pdf.

Chapter 13

New Kid on Campus:

Community College During High School

Can young high schoolers really succeed in college classes? They certainly can and do—however, your mixed feelings about sending your student directly from home to a college classroom are understandable. In this chapter, you'll receive a rundown of the advantages and disadvantages of sending your student to a community college, as well as tips on how to evaluate your student's readiness.

THE CONCEPT

Called *dual enrollment* or *concurrent enrollment*, the option for high schoolers to take classes at the community college allows students who need a greater academic challenge to take courses that will count for both high school and college credit. In fact, high-achieving students from traditional schools flock to community colleges to rack up advanced courses in math, science, and other fields. Sometimes these courses are taken during the summer, but frequently students arrange their school schedules to fit in courses at the community college. Thus, homeschooling parents need not feel that their students are too young to attend a community college. However, do check the procedures at your local college to find out how dual enrollment is handled.

WHICH COLLEGE PREP PATHS BENEFIT FROM COMMUNITY COLLEGE COURSES?

Students who are not aspiring to attend Harvard or Princeton but simply want to get started with some college courses can benefit from advanced courses and acclimation to a classroom environment. Additionally, students who wish to start their education at the community college and then transfer to a university will gain a head start by taking courses while still in high school.

If, however, your student wants to be competitive for those limited seats in the freshman class of the Ivy League and other selective universities, community college courses may be an expected, not optional, ingredient on the high school transcript. As mentioned, high school students commonly supplement their school course offerings this way. For instance, we often hear about public school students who "max out" their schools' math departments and continue their study at the community college.

ADVANTAGES OF COMMUNITY COLLEGES

It wasn't until our own students started taking community college classes that we realized how useful they can be. A transition from home to college, enhancement of the high school transcript, and the opportunity to make use of labs and key resources are just a few of the perks of this educational choice.

Opportunity to Ease into the Classroom Environment

Community colleges provide a way for your student to ease into a classroom environment, making the eventual college experience less stressful. Though going from home to college may not sound like "easing," the option to take just one class helps tremendously. For Julie, the transition from eighth grade to community college was smooth, partly because she took a course with which she was already familiar. Skills such as note taking, test taking, group projects, and classroom discussion can all be introduced at the community college. Your student will also face deadlines and learn effective time management.

Assistance with Difficult Courses

Aside from the classroom experience, community colleges provide classes that your student may not have the opportunity to take at home. Perhaps you feel inadequate when it comes to teaching advanced courses in lab science or French, or you can't find a homeschool-friendly curriculum with which to teach them. Maybe you and your student need a break from homeschooling when it comes to trigonometry. Depending on what you're looking for, a community college may be your solution. In Julie's case, the college met her needs for rigorous lab sciences and higher math, as well as a voice class for fun.

Additional Credibility for the High School Transcript

Community colleges provide a valuable element for a homeschooler's college application: credibility. If your student has successfully completed a few community college courses, college admissions committees will see that he or she has the academic abilities needed for success in a college environment. Even better, your student can take classes in several disciplines to demonstrate capability for advanced work in more than one subject. Particularly if your student is thinking about applying to a selective university, community college classes can make a tremendous difference. Admissions officers at these universities have specifically recommended this path to homeschoolers, since it shows that the student has challenged himself or herself by taking more rigorous courses.

Option of Taking Advanced Placement Exams

A side benefit of taking community college courses is that upon completion of certain courses, usually with a bit of further study, a student may take an AP exam in that subject. The Advanced Placement program is *in no way* associated with community colleges—it's just that these courses represent one method by which to learn the material that may appear on the exams. This path allows homeschoolers to prepare for AP exams without having to seek out approved courses or to design every course from scratch. In our case, chemistry, biology, and calculus courses at the community college provided successful preparation for AP exams in these subjects. As you make your plans, however, carefully read Chapter 12, which fully describes the AP program. If it is important to you to have *officially approved* AP courses on your student's transcript, note the important caveats about the AP Course Audit process. A community college course will likely not suffice to pass the audit process, and, prior to actually taking the course, you may have trouble accessing the full course syllabus you need to submit.

Source of Variety for the Student's Course of Study

During the late middle school or early high school years, the homeschooling routine may start to drag a bit. The student may become bored, demotivated, or just tired of the routine. Community college courses can provide interest, variety, and challenge. No longer reporting only to Mom and Dad, the student may take more ownership of his or her education. The prospect of keeping up with college students may be just the motivation your student needs to work hard and enjoy a new dimension of learning.

Inexpensive Way to Receive College-Level Instruction

Though tuition rates vary, community colleges are usually quite inexpensive. A high schooler may accumulate credits that can later be put toward a degree. However, don't send your student to a community college for the sole purpose of getting a head start on a college degree. Your student may, in fact, finish college a year or two early, but don't count on it without investigating the policies of the four-year college. Colleges *may or may not* accept community college credits, or they may rule that the student must apply as a transfer student and meet all transfer requirements. Thoroughly check out the scenario before making any firm plans.

Still, your student will be in relatively small classes and in a supportive environment, compared with what is the norm at the larger universities. He or she will have opportunities to learn, to ask questions, to receive extra help if needed, and to benefit from instructors who are committed to teaching. Taking these courses is a great way to get started on college-style learning. If all goes according to plan, many of the credits will be transferable, resulting in an early bachelor's degree and money in the bank.

Availability of Campus Resources

Community colleges provide campus resources that would be otherwise unavailable to homeschoolers. For instance, the library may contain materials not available in your local public library: more extensive works of literature, historical material, and other useful sources for study.

Obviously, laboratory equipment in science classes is a major benefit as well. Although homeschool science curricula offer experiments using common household materials, plus a few esoteric items for purchase, they are limited when it comes to exposing your student to typical high school or college science equipment. Science-minded students should take at least one or two courses at the community college so that they will be familiar with a standard laboratory before they attend the four-year university.

Tutorial services and academic counseling represent another valuable resource your student may seek out if needed. Tutoring may even be offered free of charge for students who have difficulties with coursework. Career or educational counselors can help your student think about a major or choose courses to transfer to the university. Nonacademic benefits include fitness, music, drama, and technology classes. Your community college may also have departmental clubs, interest-based clubs, or Christian clubs where your student can meet other students with similar career goals or life values.

Source of Recommendation Letters

Community college instructors may be willing to write college recommendation letters for your student. These letters will provide the "third party" objectivity colleges are looking for. If a student takes quite a few classes, he or she will have a choice of several teachers from whom to request letters.

Possibility for Academic Honors and Scholarships

Your student may do so well that he or she is placed on the Dean's List because of a high GPA or is accepted into the college's honors program. These honors will help to augment the student's record at college application time. Two homeschoolers we know graduated as the community college valedictorians. Additionally, your student may be eligible for departmental awards or scholarships.

Chance to Meet a Wide Variety of People

At the community college, students can meet people from all possible backgrounds, learn from others' mistakes and struggles, and be encouraged by others' ambitions and efforts. Your student may find it inspiring to see a forty-year-old mother go back to school to get a degree in physical therapy. On the other hand, he or she may learn an eye-opening lesson by observing a nineteen-year-old wasting time and money by failing to take his studies seriously. Additionally, your student can be an "ambassador" for homeschooling among both instructors and fellow students.

PRECAUTIONS REGARDING COMMUNITY COLLEGES

Since community colleges also have their disadvantages, keep these precautions in mind.

Determine Academic Readiness

Before your student starts at the community college, even for just a class or two, carefully consider whether he or she is academically prepared. Here are some signs that your student may benefit from, or even thrive in, a community college class (your student does not need to present all these characteristics).

Your student:
- *Is asking to take a community college course.*
- *Is completing all of his or her schoolwork and then asking for more.*
- *Seems capable of handling and even enjoying additional hours of study.*
- *Is inquisitive and intellectually curious, asking questions you can't answer without an encyclopedia.*
- *Expresses interest in specialized subjects that do not lend themselves easily to home study.*
- *Knows the difference between homework and studying; takes the initiative to learn material before a test.*
- *Enjoys an intellectual challenge.*
- *Is amenable to having a more rigid schedule imposed on his or her life.*
- *Is a good student who was once strongly motivated but is now lacking in motivation, especially for the homeschooling routine.*
- *Has a homeschooled friend ready to take a class with him or her and is otherwise ready to take the class.*

If, on the other hand, your student is not yet willing to spend several hours per day on serious study, you may be better off waiting a year or more. This interval will give your student a chance to work on study skills and time management. Community college courses do consume quite a bit of time, and assessments may amount to only three or four tests or essays per semester. Students will have to be mature enough to keep up on studying between exams, since daily homework may not boost the grade much. Remember that the grades for these courses will appear on the student's official college transcript unless they can be taken for high school credit only.

Realize, too, that the homeschool subjects may take a back seat to community college work. Frequently, the outside accountability drives the priorities, and the student will choose to do the necessary tasks to avoid embarrassment in class. You may have to come to an agreement as to how best to prioritize the semester's slate of classes, and when to finish the home-based assignments.

Prepare for Administrative Issues

After assessing academic readiness, you may face some administrative hurdles. Because community colleges are accustomed to working mostly with adults over age eighteen, the prospect of a young high school student or even a middle school student can raise some barriers. These barriers can come in the form of extra paperwork, delays, or even the dreaded "No." The college may also limit the number of courses a high schooler may take.

To prepare for or prevent some of these roadblocks, thoroughly understand your college's dual enrollment policies, especially for younger students. Since many traditionally-schooled students take a class or two at the community college, the precedent should already be in place. Do your homework before you even begin talking to an advisor. Realize also that the clerks in the admissions office may dole out misinformation. We have learned this from personal experience.

Talk to other homeschoolers who have attended this college and find out how they have solved any problems that have come up. For instance, if the college has a rule that students under age sixteen may not take classes, don't give up. You may discover exceptions to this rule, such as having the student fill out a petition form or take some placement tests. When you are armed with the information, visit the admissions office and find someone who is knowledgeable about what can and can't be done. Then determine how to enroll your student. Start gathering your information a few weeks or even months before your student wants to start classes. Colleges are always extra busy at the beginning of the semester, and even if your student hasn't missed any deadlines, it can be difficult to talk to the right person about your situation. You don't want to be at a disadvantage before you even get started.

Prepare Your Paperwork

Understand what forms you will be required to fill out, and be ready with your homeschool records. For instance, you may need to submit an unofficial transcript or grade report from your student's recent semester. You may be asked to fill out a separate form in addition to the normal application to authorize your teen to concurrently enroll in both high school and college. Since it must be signed by the school principal or counselor, decide who will sign, whether this be a parent or a homeschool program administrator. Also make sure that you know what documentation the college requires in order to clear any prerequisites for the course. Test scores, report cards, course descriptions, or other information about the rigor of the previous course may be required. If your student needs to take placement exams, find out when and where these will be held. By understanding all the items required and turning them in well ahead of time, you can avoid delays in your student's registration.

Choose Classes and Leap the Registration Hurdles

If at all possible, try to sit in on the class or meet the instructor during the semester before your student will actually take the course. In our experience, most instructors were positively disposed toward enthusiastic homeschooled students.

Often, high school students will not be allowed to register early for courses but will need to wait until a couple of weeks before classes start. Of course, many of the course sections will be full by then. Here is where persistence pays off and where meeting the instructor ahead of time can come in handy.

Homeschooled & Headed for College

The student should go ahead and attend class for the first couple of days and find out what the prospects are for adding the class. Sometimes the instructor will allow students to attend an already-full class for a few more days in hopes that enough students will drop the class to make room for those who want to add. At any rate, your student should communicate continued interest and then hope for the best.

Investigate Prerequisites and Placement Tests

Placement or assessment tests may be required if your student plans to take a class in the English or math department. These tests determine whether a student is eligible to register for the class, or whether a more basic course should be taken first. Take note of when these tests will be administered.

Course prerequisites, too, should be viewed realistically and without false optimism. For example, if algebra is a prerequisite for chemistry, make sure your student has learned the algebra well. Granted, some prerequisites may be unnecessary, but in most cases, students need a firm foundation in a prior subject before venturing to learn another. If your student has completed the prerequisite with home study, be ready to provide documentation showing completion. Usually this will be a report card showing a grade of C or better, but if you happen to have some pertinent standardized test scores, they may help your student's case. If you have questions about the prerequisites, talk to the instructor, who can look through your textbook and tell you if the homeschool course was an adequate preparation for his or her course. In some cases, you may be able to clear a prerequisite during this short chat with the instructor. In other cases, it must be done through the administrative offices.

Determine Social Readiness

A common stereotype of homeschoolers is that they do not have the social skills necessary to succeed in the "real world." Though this is not universally true, you need to assess your student's ability to function in a group setting before he or she begins community college classes. In a few cases, homeschooled students may be pulling the top A's but may also lack the maturity to get along in a classroom full of older adults.

The student should be ready to handle social situations with the appropriate level of wisdom, caution, and good manners. For instance, he or she will need to learn classroom etiquette, such as refraining from asking too many questions and from asking for too much individual help. Additionally, your student should be able to pick up on social cues and use discernment with regard to appropriate and inappropriate friendships and to dangerous situations.

Many homeschooling families ask, "Why would homeschooling parents send a student to a community college when they have made the conscious decision *not* to send him or her to a public or private high school?" This is a good question!

At a community college, the student can take just one class at a time and then increase or decrease the next semester's enrollment, depending on how it goes. Even if the student takes more courses, the amount of social mingling will be far less than it would be at a high school, and this mingling takes place with a wide variety of adults rather than with the peer group. Cliques, peer pressure, and teen culture are far less prevalent at community colleges than at high schools. Of course, the influences that *are* encountered are more adult-oriented. For example, many college students are of legal drinking age (not to mention underage drinking), so if your student socializes with them, even for a restaurant dinner, some of them may be consuming alcohol.

Be Aware of the Community College Environment

In a similar vein, another issue to consider is the moral environment at the community college. Your student will be attending school with older, but not necessarily wiser students. If your student isn't entirely sure of his or her stance on key moral issues or is so innocent as to be naïve and vulnerable, you might carefully consider your decision. Issues you might have to deal with could include objectionable language or "mature" subject matter in conversations, class discussions, or assigned reading. Your student will likely also encounter other students' experiences with drinking, drugs, sex, and attitudes toward God, their families, and authority.

Although our students' experiences at the community college were fairly smooth and positive, some families have had other experiences. Even in classrooms or libraries, students may overhear conversations or be exposed to situations for which they are not ready. Parents should assess what their students can handle.

If you think socializing with college students might present some difficulties, limit your student's time spent on campus. You can also help by maintaining open communication. Talking about these experiences and putting them into a proper perspective can be more valuable than trying to avoid them or pretending that they do not exist.

But don't let these cautions scare your student away from an enriching experience. He or she is likely to find a comfortable niche and to gravitate toward friendships with people of similar values—at least academically, but often socially and spiritually as well. The community college campus is filled with students and faculty who can encourage your student in educational and life pursuits. Julie treasures the impact that dozens of friends and teachers made on her life during her years at the community college.

Prepare for the Teaching of Different World Views

English, history, and other humanities classes often present ideas that clash with the views and beliefs of the student and family. Christianity, and faith in general, may be subtly or blatantly put down; morality may be questioned or ridiculed; other philosophies may be promoted. If your student plans to take classes in the humanities, go to the bookstore to get a feel for the reading material used by various instructors. Flipping through these books may help you decide which class or instructor to choose.

You may decide to have your student wait until the junior or senior year before taking any English or humanities courses, since younger students may have difficulty processing and filtering new ideas in these subjective areas. On the positive side, if your student takes these courses while still in high school, you are available to walk him or her through this phase of learning and to discuss any controversial topics in light of your family's beliefs and according to Scripture.

Investigate Transferability of Credits

Many students plan to use their community college credits (also called units or semester hours) toward bachelor's degrees. Be aware that some of the accumulated units may not apply toward the chosen major when the student officially starts college, and some may not transfer at all. Suppose a home-schooled student who has accumulated 65 semester units enters a four-year college where 130 semester units are required for a bachelor's degree. As far as the number of units is concerned, the student is a junior and has two years' worth of work left to finish the bachelor's degree. However, suppose that upon closer examination, this college allows only 40 of the credits to apply toward the degree, necessitating additional time spent working on the degree. (Note that degree requirements and transferability of credits vary from school to school, and schools on the semester system will require a different number of units than will schools on the quarter system.) A document called the articulation agreement for a given university and a given community college spells out the transferability relationship among courses at the two institutions. Search up this term on the university website to understand course transferability and course-to-course equivalency between a university and a community college.

Some Ivy League universities and other selective colleges do not accept community college credits for transfer at all. Other universities do not take community college credits from out-of-state schools. Still others limit the number of credits transferred in, or do not count those taken before high school graduation. (However, these units may be used by the student's major department to grant him or her placement into more advanced classes, thus shortening the time to the degree.) Check the policies ahead of time to avoid both disappointment and the waste of time and money. Note that taking AP exams after completing certain community college courses can be one way of gaining credit. Colleges clearly spell out their AP policies and explain how they grant credit or advanced standing to students who score well on the exams. Refer to Chapter 12 for more information. Additionally, students who hope to attend graduate, medical, or law school will want to find out whether prerequisite courses completed at a community college will count toward admission to graduate school, or will in any way reflect negatively upon the student's application. Sometimes key prerequisites must be taken at a university.

In spite of these cautions, don't avoid the community college. Even if the course units do not transfer to a selective university, they are extremely beneficial educational experiences and can be instrumental in getting admitted to the university. Also, if the student ends up taking a similar course at the university because the community college course did not transfer, he or she will be ahead of the game, having already studied the material at the college level. In our daughter's case, even though we had been told by the four-year university office that community college units would not transfer, she was able to transfer a few of her courses after all. We were glad we had kept the course syllabi, since this paperwork was required by the registrar's office. Likewise, our son chose to transfer a couple of his community college courses and retake a couple of the courses at the university for further reinforcement and preparation for higher-level courses.

Determine Whether Your Student Will Accumulate Too Many College or AP Credits

The flip side of investigating whether credits will transfer is that your student may have *too many* college credits to enter the four-year university as a freshman. This depends entirely on the university's policies and should be a consideration before you delve too deeply into community college courses.

Freshman vs. Transfer Status Considerations

Reasons that your student might want to maintain status as a freshman applicant include the intent to retain eligibility for generous merit scholarships offered to freshmen, or the desire to have a full four years of the university "experience." Aside from these reasons, "transfer status" does not necessarily mean that a student can slide right in to the university. More likely, he or she will have a whole slate of university transfer requirements to meet besides the lineup of college courses already completed. Furthermore, at some universities the acceptance rate for transfer students is lower than that for freshmen.

Note that some universities clarify that it is fine for a student to accumulate college credits while in high school, but only the credits earned *after high school graduation* will affect freshman or transfer status. In this case, your student would not have a problem if the courses were taken prior to graduation.

A couple of strategies might help if you find yourself in the college credits dilemma. First, consider whether a high number of credits will hinder opportunities for financial aid. For example, at a certain school, freshman merit scholarships may be offered only to students with fewer than 27 semester credits of college courses. If your student plans to enter the university as a transfer student, this may be a non-issue. If, however, your student plans to enter as a freshman after having taken a number of community college classes, you may be affected by the university's policies. In reality, the forfeiture of a scholarship may be offset by the money saved by taking these courses at low cost at a community college (*if they transfer*) rather than at an expensive university. In our own students' cases, we wondered about this issue early on, since some of the universities placed limitations on college credits for freshman status. However, since the highly selective universities encouraged homeschoolers to take as many college courses as possible to be competitive for admission, we decided not to worry about the accumulation of units.

At some universities, freshman scholarships are not the only issue for incoming students with many units. Sometimes a student with more than 27 or 28 units must apply as a transfer, not as a freshman. As a transfer applicant, your student would have to comply with all transfer requirements, including completing general education and other applicable courses. Some universities do not accept many transfer students, especially as sophomores, while others do. If transferring as a junior is not your student's intent, work with the admissions office and explain the situation. You may be able to communicate that a certain number of units were taken for high school credit or for your homeschool high school course of study and that your student does not intend to transfer these particular courses.

Many times, understanding that the student is homeschooled changes the rules in the eyes of the university. So, when inquiring about these details, first be sure to explain that your student is a homeschooler who took these courses to fulfill high school requirements. As a bonus, your student may still be able to transfer some community college credits when he or she enrolls at the university.

For some universities, you need to help the admissions office understand why these courses were taken and what the student's intent is. You will have the most success with smaller colleges and universities, which tend to be more flexible than larger ones. Prepare an annotated version of the community college transcript, labeling some of the courses "taken for high school credit" and others "taken for college transfer" so that you reduce the total number of "college" units to below the number allowed. For instance, if your student took a biology class at the community college and used it as part of the high school lab science requirement, you could explain that as a homeschooler, your student took the course at the college simply to fulfill a requirement for a biology course. The same reasoning could be used for some of your student's math, fine arts, or other courses. By labeling these courses as *high school* courses, you may be able to negotiate with the college and agree that the student does not have to count these units in the incoming college credit total if there is a credit limit for freshman status. The interpretation, of course, is ultimately up to the college registrar's office, but it is worth a try. If your student passes any AP exams, he or she may still receive college credit or advanced placement as a result, depending on the institution's policies. Certain colleges place a limit on AP credit as well as on actual college credits transferred in; others do not limit AP credit.

Student Athletes and Community College Units

Students who intend to play collegiate sports have yet another consideration. They should stay up to date with NCAA® (National Collegiate Athletic Association) rules as to when the college "clock" starts ticking and whether taking community college courses during high school will compromise their years of eligibility for playing sports in college. If your student has athletic aspirations, become familiar with the NCAA website and its rules for high schoolers, with respect to college courses taken before high school graduation.

University-Mandated Unit Ceilings (Satisfactory Academic Progress Policies)

Finally, one additional issue involves the concept of a "unit ceiling." Many universities—for example, the University of California—in an effort to discourage "professional students" who spend several years at a campus racking up units and taking up valuable space that other students could occupy, set limits on the number of units and semesters or quarters a student may accumulate. For example, a university may limit a student to eight semesters if he or she enters as a freshman, or four semesters as a transfer. Additional time may be allowed if the student is double majoring. The limit may also be expressed in terms of the number of units allowed: for instance, 130 semester units. Students who exceed these limits may find it difficult or impossible to enroll for a succeeding term. Financial aid packages may also be affected if students extend their "stay" beyond the allowed period or exceed a stated number of units. These policies are often referred to as SAP (Satisfactory Academic Progress) regulations. At universities with these policies (often crowded state universities), the student must graduate or withdraw from the university after a stipulated number of credits have been earned.

Because these excess community college units can be a disadvantage as the student progresses through the university years, be knowledgeable, aware, and wise as you plan. You may want to browse the *articulation agreements* between your local community college and the in-state four-year colleges your student is interested in, as well as searching for *SAP or Satisfactory Academic Progress* policies for the colleges and universities of interest. Articulation agreements, also called transfer agreements or transfer pathways, take the guesswork out of the transfer process by stipulating which community college courses transfer directly to the university or satisfy general education or major course prerequisite requirements. In general, it makes most sense to take courses that will count towards general ed or prerequisites, rather than choosing interesting but less useful courses that simply rack up the total count of college units.

It is wise to investigate whether your "favored" universities have unit ceiling rules and importantly, *whether these include courses taken during the high school years.* The key question might be to define "When was high school graduation?" particularly if your student passed a high school proficiency exam (see Chapter 19) and then began taking college courses. If you suspect your student might be affected by unit ceiling rules, make sure the courses taken at the community college are "worth their weight" in helping him or her progress toward a degree. Avoid "fluff" courses that count against the unit total without shortening the path to the degree.

Despite the previous cautions, it often makes sense for students to stretch their wings and challenge themselves with community college courses. These courses demonstrate a desire for enhanced learning, provide classroom experience before college, and open your student's world to a source of teachers, mentors, and valuable educational resources. And they may shorten the path to a college degree.

TO SUM UP

After thinking about the advantages and disadvantages of community college, you may have a sense of whether your student is ready to try this option. Not all students need or want this educational option, but if your student is willing to take the plunge, go for it! The next chapter will provide you with more tips to make your high schooler's road to college as smooth as possible.

Chapter 14

More Tips:

Making the Most of Your

Community College Experience

The community college offers valuable opportunities for taking advanced courses, meeting people, and adjusting to classroom routines. But this option is not necessarily right for every high schooler. Families should weigh the pros and cons that specifically affect them. If your student is ready to try the community college, this chapter will help maximize positive experiences and minimize negative ones.

DECIDING HOW TO USE COMMUNITY COLLEGE COURSES

As you consider issues such as freshman and transfer status, you and your student will want to decide how to count the community college courses on your high school transcript. Will you consider them to be high school courses, college courses, or both, depending on which is more beneficial?

In general, you have at least three options for how to treat your student's community college experience. First, you may use it to supplement the high school program. Second, your student may take a few strategic courses to transfer to a four-year university. Third, he or she may actually start college while still high school age. With all of these choices, make sure you understand the transfer policies relevant to the community college and the four-year university. In particular, be aware of exceeding the limits of courses allowed for freshman status or for the unit ceiling, if applicable. (See Chapter 13.)

Supplementing the High School Program

Some students take just a few courses to round out their homeschool curriculum. For instance, a student may decide, "I just want to get my high school lab science requirement out of the way at the community college." Without planning to transfer these courses, he or she may focus on one subject area such as science, or might take one course from each general subject area. These courses can be recorded on the high school transcript and used to meet high school requirements. However, your student may also have the option of transferring them to the university later if desired.

Taking Strategic Courses to Transfer to a University

Many homeschoolers use these courses to strategically fulfill a few requirements before attending a university. In this case, they definitely plan to transfer the courses. For instance, your student might take college-level chemistry or physics at the community college to avoid the stiffer competition at a four-year school. Or, he or she might get some general education courses out of the way. Offering smaller classes and a more supportive environment, the community college is a good place to tackle these courses.

Since some selective or out-of-state colleges may not accept these courses for transfer, *always check first*. When applying to colleges that claim that they do not accept community college course transfers—though you might be pleasantly surprised when you run the paperwork through the registrar's office—your student could strategically use Advanced Placement exams as a tactic to gain credit for that subject. For instance, if the student took a chemistry course at the community college and then took and passed the AP Chemistry exam, the college would probably grant AP credit for the chemistry course even if it did not allow the community college credits to transfer.

Remember, too, that the previous chapter described another scenario that arises with some colleges. Students may lose their freshman status if they have taken *too many* college units prior to applying—often about 28 units, but sometimes fewer. Use the strategies described in Chapter 13 to explain to the college that your student is a homeschooler and has taken these community college courses *prior to high school graduation* (that's the magic phrase) to supplement his or her high school work at home. A simple explanation may be enough, or you may have to show the college an unofficial copy of the community college transcript on which you've marked just which courses were "high school" and which your student would like to transfer to college, up to the limit allowed to retain freshman status.

Starting College a Year or Two Early

Some high schoolers choose to start college early, taking community college courses with the goal of transferring to a four-year college as a junior. General education and prerequisite courses for the major may be taken at the community college, and some students are even ready to transfer as juniors by the time they graduate from high school. This commonly chosen path saves quite a bit of money. It is easy to see how the line between high school and college quickly becomes blurred for homeschoolers.

Local requirements will determine what your student needs to do to in order to enroll at the community college, since he or she has not yet graduated from high school. Since policies differ, carefully check the rules at your local community college and confer with other homeschoolers about any tips they may have for navigating the system.

Transfer programs to universities are usually well defined, but make sure you speak to the right person and receive the correct information. Always check with potential four-year colleges for their requirements—this information is most typically found in a document called the *articulation agreement*, specific to a particular community college and a particular university. If policies are unclear, keep asking questions until you understand what will be required.

Some community colleges have honors programs that facilitate acceptance into certain state universities. In addition to giving the student this advantage, participation in an honors program may provide other perks such as priority registration dates. If your student is eligible to join such a program, by all means take advantage of it.

No matter what your student plans to do with the community college units, *always save the course description and syllabus* for each course taken. These documents may be needed by the registrar's office at the four-year university when your student applies for transfer of these units.

FOR STUDENTS: OPTIMIZING YOUR COMMUNITY COLLEGE EXPERIENCE

Since the quality of a student's education is due largely to what he or she makes of it, here is some specific advice addressed directly to the high school student:

Applying and Registering for Classes

Apply in a Professional Manner

Find out exactly what the application process entails and gather all paperwork needed. Sometimes high school students must fill out petitions or appeal forms before being admitted to the college. Do a thorough job of expressing yourself and describing your reasons for wanting to take courses.

Keep copies of all documents submitted in case they get lost. Be sure to follow up if time passes and you have not heard from the college. In phone calls, be businesslike and professional, take notes, and record names of people you speak to. In the earlier years, your parents may make phone or personal contacts with the admissions office on your behalf, but as time passes, you can transition to doing this yourself. In your contacts with the college, keep your communication pleasant, even if you must begin going "up the ladder" to talk to someone who will understand your situation.

Plan Your Courses Wisely

Before even looking at a class schedule, decide with your parents which college classes you might want to take during the years of high school. For example, you might take some chemistry, biology, and calculus classes spread out over three years of high school. Or you might take an entire foreign language series of two to four semesters. If you have an idea of your future college major, try to take a class as close to university level as possible, after first working up to it with appropriate prerequisite courses. Also investigate transferability to the university if this is your goal.

See if you can sit in on a class session the semester before you will take the course, preferably with the same instructor. To arrange this, contact the instructor ahead of time to receive permission and to find out when would be a good day to visit. You would not want to visit on a test day, for instance. Other ways to prepare for the course are to obtain a course syllabus and to look at the textbooks in the bookstore.

Choose courses carefully to avoid having to drop them after the semester starts. Especially for courses that fill up rapidly, dropping courses is extremely inconsiderate to other students who could have had your seat in the class. It also conveys the idea that homeschoolers are not realistic about what they can handle. Of course, once in a while, dropping a course is the right decision.

Choose Familiar Classes First

Attending a community college can be a bit unnerving at first, especially if you have never been in a classroom setting. If you have time in your schedule, you may want to take a course you're already familiar with so that you can devote your time and energy toward getting a feel for the community college environment and classroom routines. Of course, most students do not have the luxury of spare semesters in order to arrange this, and it is not really necessary.

Take Advantage of "Study Skills" Classes

In Julie's first semester at the community college, she took a one-unit biology study skills class with a teacher from whom she eventually took more classes. This informal course helped her tremendously in getting to know the professors, the department, and the type of lab and lecture work she would be doing later. As a rule, classes held in a more personal setting can open many doors later.

Search Out Excellent Teachers

Starting out in a new environment can be perplexing, and not knowing who the best teachers are makes it even more so. As much as possible, confer with other students who can recommend instructors who teach clearly and grade fairly. A site called Rate My Professors (http://www.ratemyprofessors.com/) can be helpful, as well as amusing, in sorting out the good from the bad. Take the student-generated advice with a grain of salt—especially since much of it is contradictory.

Economize on Textbooks

The cost of college textbooks is astronomical. Moreover, multiple books may be required or recommended for courses, but only one or two end up being used. If possible, visit the bookstore or its website a few weeks before the start of class and record the titles and ISBN numbers of books you'll need. You may be able to find these books online, used or even new, at lower prices and you may also determine just how necessary the "optional" books are. Understand the bookstore's refund policies, which often involve returning the book in mint condition by the first week of classes.

Attending Classes

Know What You're In For

As a rule of thumb, a one-semester community college class is equivalent to a year-long high school class. Be prepared for a fast and furious pace—you may finish an entire textbook in 15 weeks. Whatever you do, don't allow yourself to fall behind. Get help or tutoring if necessary, and schedule your time so that you're prepared for labs, tests, and papers. On the plus side, you may find that your independent, self-directed method of learning at home will serve you well at the community college.

Be a Responsible Student

While it may be a cliché, it is also generally true that students who sit near the front of the class get better grades. Whether they are more interested in the subject matter and thus *choose* these seats, or whether the teacher gets to know them better and gives them the benefit of the doubt when grade time comes, it is still a good suggestion for being an active learner. In the front row, you'll be less tempted to doze off or zone out, and you can stay engaged. Resolve to ask good questions, too—teachers enjoy interested students. However, do not ask "dumb," obvious, or excessive questions.

Get the "Halo Effect" Going

If you make a favorable impression on an instructor early in the term, he or she may continue to think well of you all semester. Try your best to get this "halo effect" going early in the semester by scoring well on the first test, using office hours for valid questions, and demonstrating interest in the subject. It must all be genuine, though! This halo may earn you some grace later if your scores drop a bit.

The first exam of the term is particularly important, not only for the halo, but also for a strong standing in the class so that you won't need to scramble throughout the semester to make up for a poor showing on the first test. *Overstudy* at first to make sure that the material is sinking in. You can ease up later as you discover how much studying is actually required. It's much harder to go the other direction.

Another way to be a strong student and a credit to homeschooling is to be prepared for each class. If you take the time to read the textbook or lab manual and to finish assignments with a bit of breathing room before they are due, you will place yourself at an advantage and thank yourself many times over during the course of the semester.

Get to Know Your Teachers

Let's face it: some teachers are better than others. In fact, a good teacher can make a boring subject interesting, while a bad teacher can make an interesting subject boring.

For both types, getting to know your professors brings many rewards. Office hours are an ideal time to reinforce fuzzy concepts or to converse with the instructors and help them learn about you and your goals. Topics you do not understand in lecture can often be cleared up in a few minutes. If you have the opportunity for a short chat, your professors will get to know you and may be happy to write recommendation letters later when you apply to four-year colleges. Other perks may include being recommended for tutoring jobs at the college or even for departmental scholarships.

Because instructors are not babysitters, students should enter the class with maturity and without expecting to have their "hands held." By displaying responsibility and interest in learning, homeschoolers can build a good reputation for homeschooling.

Avoid Advertising Your Age

When you first begin taking college courses, avoid advertising your young age. Obviously, teachers and fellow students will realize that you are young, but they do not have to know *how* young. After you've established your reputation as a good student and have shown maturity and perhaps even leadership in this environment, you may choose to reveal your age. Be prepared for shocked looks.

Be Available to Help Other Students

You may be surprised (or not!) to learn that a reasonably intelligent high schooler can be a significant help to college students who are struggling to understand the material. Maintain a helpful attitude inside and outside of classes. Within the context of a "safe" location such as a library or a well-populated study room, you may be able to provide assistance or even formal tutoring for fellow students. For safety's sake, never agree to meet in an isolated or off-campus location.

Request Unofficial Transcripts

From time to time, request an unofficial transcript from the college office to file with your homeschooling records. You may be able to download this document yourself by accessing your college record online. You may need an unofficial transcript if you are applying for another academic program, an internship, a scholarship, or even auto insurance. Besides, you will want to check the document and make sure that the information is correct and complete.

Additionally, learn how to request official transcripts. Understand costs, lead times, and who may request them. Generally, the parent may *not* request this document without written permission from the student.

FOR PARENTS: A FEW TRICKS OF THE TRADE

Work Out Transportation and Schedules

Taking courses at the community college requires some juggling of the schedule, both for the high schooler and for other siblings. Think through the whole process to figure out how each week will look in terms of transportation and waiting times. Knowing, at least approximately, how you will structure your days and weeks will help you retain *some* of your sanity.

Transportation may not be an issue if your student can drive and has the use of a car. If not, perhaps you can work out a carpool with another family whose student wants to take classes. If your student is taking only one class, you might be able to drive him or her to class and wait on campus until the class is over. You may even get some schoolwork done with younger siblings while you wait. Public transportation may be an option if your student is ready to navigate the system.

Your student should be equipped with phone numbers of trusted friends and relatives, in case a need arises and you are not available to help.

Address Safety Issues

If the student will be spending a significant amount of time at the college, think about safety issues. For one thing, make sure that the student emergency form, often required by the admissions office for students under age eighteen, is on file and is updated with current contact information.

Go over safety rules with your student. Unlike a high school, which has a fairly tight peer and teacher network, a community college is more of a "fend for yourself" environment. Caution your student about safety concerns such as walking in deserted hallways after dark, taking medicines (even ibuprofen) from other people, and leaving valuables unsupervised.

Stop by the student health office and meet the nurse, familiarizing yourself with the procedures used for injuries or illnesses. If you do not want your student given medication, contraception advice, or other specific interventions, write a note, sign it, and attach it to the student emergency form and health form. Ask the office to contact you for anything more than minor first aid.

Our students' only experiences with the college health office were for a badly skinned knee and a TB test for a campus job. Hopefully, your student will not need anything more than a small bandage during his or her time at the community college.

Consider Joining In

If your schedule and family situation permit, consider taking a class while your student is in class. Some parents choose to take a class *with* their student; others take a totally different course. One year, our son and I enjoyed a tennis class; another year, I took a fitness class, as this was a good way to get an exercise workout using the college's equipment and instruction.

TO SUM UP

No matter how you decide to use the community college—and sometimes you'll decide as you go along—this experience can be a great way for homeschoolers to transition to both a classroom environment and a college environment. Being the "new kid on campus" can expand your student's horizons in ways you never imagined possible.

Chapter 15

Extra! Extra!

Extracurricular Activities and Employment

Collage admissions committees evaluate not only what an applicant does *during school hours* (the academic record), but also what he or she does *outside of school hours* (the extracurricular activities). In this chapter, you'll learn about the benefits of extracurriculars, as well as what colleges are seeking.

BENEFITS OF EXTRACURRICULAR ACTIVITIES

Simply put, anything that your student does outside of the school curriculum qualifies as extracurriculars. For homeschoolers, the line between schoolwork and everyday life is blurred, and students often merge school subjects with leisure time activities. Dance doubles as P.E.; flute lessons fulfill fine arts requirements; creative writing serves not only as a hobby, but also as part of the English curriculum. Even so, extracurricular activities bring several benefits independent from their role in enhancing school courses.

Extracurricular Activities Encourage Involvement in Nonacademic Areas

If school were nothing but an endless parade of academics, life could quickly grow boring. Extracurriculars give the student a respite from schoolwork and a chance to develop some specialized interests. While all students have interests that extend beyond the classroom (or the kitchen table, as the case may be), they may need organized activities to help them develop these interests and talents. Students who enjoy practical skills and leadership can sharpen these affinities through clubs such as 4-H. Budding musicians will have much more fun playing their music when they are part of a band or orchestra. Students skilled at sports will naturally want to play on a team, perhaps on progressively more competitive teams as the years go by. Spending time with people of similar interests challenges students to take their skills to the next level.

Extracurricular Activities Allow the Student to Meet a Variety of People

While you have no need to worry that your high school student is being undersocialized, participating in extracurricular activities is a fun-filled and valuable way to encourage contact with more people. Whether the student is taking music lessons, acting with a drama group, playing sports, volunteering at a hospital, or participating in Scouts or 4-H, these social encounters will enhance his or her education, life, and character. On the college application, extracurriculars demonstrate that the student is socially involved, can work as part of a team, and enjoys being around people.

Extracurricular Activities Develop Leadership Skills

One of the most valuable benefits of extracurriculars is the opportunity to exercise leadership. Traditionally schooled students have ready-made opportunities to be leaders, since each one of the many campus clubs needs officers. Although homeschoolers do not have this same selection of campus groups, they still have plenty of community opportunities, and they may also show leadership and initiative by starting an activity completely of their own volition. See Chapter 16 for a discussion of leadership skills.

Extracurricular Activities Build Responsibility and Commitment

Certain extracurricular activities, especially employment and volunteer work, can train the student in positive character traits such as initiative, dependability, perseverance, and creativity—all of which are important for future work. If a student makes a commitment to a job or volunteer work, he or she must arrive on time each day and stay for the entire shift. For some students, such responsibility is a developing concept, but it is vital for future success. Similarly, leadership positions such as serving as an officer in a club develop the student's skills in planning, public speaking, teamwork, diplomacy, organization, and perhaps budgeting and public relations as well.

WHAT COLLEGES LOOK FOR IN EXTRACURRICULARS

On a college application extracurriculars are "showcased" in two main places: the application itself and the essays or personal statements. In the main part of the application, the student lists extracurricular activities, along with the school year(s) of participation, the number of hours per week and weeks per year invested, and any honors won or leadership positions held. Although the student does not need to hold leadership positions for every activity, having a few will demonstrate a higher level of commitment for this activity.

Extracurriculars can also be highlighted in the application essays. An essay prompt may specifically ask the student to describe a meaningful extracurricular activity, or your student may choose to work these descriptions and reflections into some of the other prompts. If your student has excelled in one or more extracurriculars or has an unusual, interesting, or in-depth activity, by all means encourage him or her to write about some aspect of this activity. A full-length essay, rather than only one or two lines on the application, will give the admissions committee a much better picture of your student.

Though no "magic formula" exists for choosing a winning lineup of extracurriculars, here are a few basic characteristics that colleges value.

Consistency of Participation

While middle school may have been a time to dabble, high school is a time to begin devoting more consistent energy toward a few favorite activities. Obviously, if your student simply cannot tolerate another year of orchestra or has other valid reasons for dropping an activity, do not force him or her to continue. But if the desire to quit is merely a whim, or is a result of temporary discouragement or poor time management, you might remind your student about the consistency principle. Besides, the way to excel in any activity is to keep at it. Sometimes students become discouraged with their progress (or lack thereof) and stop just before they would have begun to see definite improvement.

Passion

Colleges want to see evidence that the student has invested time, energy, and effort into one or two key activities. They can tell which pursuits students are most passionate about by noticing the time spent on these activities and by reading the student's application essays highlighting them.

Passion, however, does not manifest itself solely through time, leadership positions, and consistency. Students show impressive passion when they take the initiative to organize activities that would not exist were it not for their ideas and impetus. Fortunately, a homeschooler's schedule offers flexibility for these self-directed pursuits. One example might be to start a program of free tutoring for disadvantaged students in the community. If your student organizes and expands the program by recruiting others to help, he or she has shown tremendous leadership.

Focused Extracurricular Interests

In some senses, a high schooler will want to appear "well-rounded" by displaying a variety of interests and skills. However, your student should not look so well-rounded that his or her outstanding traits are no longer prominent. Because the proverbial "well-rounded" profile has become commonplace, and because so many applicants are involved in a spectrum of activities, colleges now tend to look for "angular" students. Angular students shine with definite skills and interests in specialized areas (sometimes called a "spike"), while still displaying involvement in a few other categories. Spotting these talents helps the admissions committee "shop" for students to fill certain needs. For example, the music department may be looking for a bassoon player because it is losing two graduating seniors. A skilled writer or two for the campus publications, or a star volleyball player for the athletics department, may be in demand. If your student has a field of expertise in an area for which the school is seeking applicants, the decision may swing in his or her favor. And even if not, investing dedicated time and effort into a couple of primary activities will help build your student's character, add depth to these life experiences, and make him or her an engaging young person with highly developed pursuits—all of which is attractive to the college as well.

So, how critical is an impressive slate of extracurricular activities in helping your student get into college? Remember that first of all, your student needs to present a transcript of rigorous courses, with a solid GPA in these courses. Beyond the academic foundation, strong extracurricular activities are important, but not necessarily a "must," for all but the most selective universities. Also keep in mind that the foremost rule is that your student should *enjoy* all of his or her extracurricular activities. They should be fun and meaningful. Never contrive a list of activities just to look impressive to the admissions committee.

That said, students who are on the path to more selective colleges must thoughtfully select their extracurriculars so that they display leadership, passion, and commitment. As they participate in extracurriculars, students should also consider which aspects of their activities could be described well in their essays. Again, these should always be activities they enjoy and have a heartfelt interest in.

For students who are applying to less selective colleges, notable extracurriculars will not be quite as important as they are for the other schools. Students can afford to dabble and explore a bit more. Additionally, they may not need to display leadership ability to such an impressive extent.

GENERAL CATEGORIES OF EXTRACURRICULAR ACTIVITIES

Extracurricular activities come in many shapes and sizes. Here are a number of activity categories your student could consider.

Clubs and Youth Organizations

Parents, do you remember all the clubs from your high school days? They're still going strong in high schools across the country. Being a homeschooler can make participation slightly more challenging, but by no means difficult or impossible. Whether your student wants to start a new club or join one that already exists, clubs can provide fun, teamwork, friendships, and settings for a student to "shine" as a leader. A student who initiates projects, makes and carries out plans, rallies the support of others, delegates tasks, encourages the involvement of students who are quieter or less experienced, and practices organizational skills is developing key leadership abilities. Besides social and leadership opportunities, *purpose* is another key attribute of clubs. Club members will generally be doing something worthwhile— and having fun at the same time.

A few existing community groups that your student can join include Scouts, 4-H, and Civil Air Patrol®, the volunteer auxiliary of the U.S. Air Force. Regardless of the activity, the key is showing passion and interest by faithful attendance, involvement, and, where possible, service as a leader.

Athletics

Colleges like to see that a student has pursued activities that are entirely nonacademic, and the most notable nonacademic activity is athletics. Though it may be a bit harder to find opportunities in the homeschool arena than in a traditional school, the benefits are worth your persistent effort. The three main options for organized leagues are *community leagues, school teams*, and *homeschool teams*.

Community Leagues

Community sports leagues are available in most cities. While some of these organizations focus on fun, fitness, and recreation, others are more intense, offering elite levels of the sport with the chance to develop higher skill levels and to participate in local and more distant tournaments. Soccer, basketball, swimming, gymnastics, baseball, lacrosse, and numerous other sports are offered through these community or club teams. Look for sports league opportunities through recreation centers, local churches, YMCA branches, and health clubs.

School Teams

Another way to participate in organized sports is through a school team. In some districts, homeschooled students are allowed to participate on their local public school teams, and you can also check out the policy for private high school teams. Sometimes the student must be enrolled in one or more classes at the school while participating on the team, so in the case of public schools this could involve some decisions about whether your student is eligible. As an attractive benefit to students with strong skills, the school team option allows the student to be scouted by university coaches and to potentially be offered scholarships.

Homeschool Teams

Some homeschooling communities offer organized homeschool sports teams or leagues. These may be rather informal and noncompetitive, or they may involve significant levels of competition. The National Christian School Athletic Association (NCSAA) invites homeschool groups to join as member schools of NCSAA with the goal of providing opportunities for these students to participate in athletics. This group aims to become a liaison between Christian school leagues and homeschoolers looking for opportunities to play in sports leagues. Check the NCSAA website at http://www.ncsaa.org/ to keep up on details of programs, tournaments, skills camps, and other scheduled events.

Recreational Sports

A less competitive way to enjoy sports is to plan sports and game days for homeschoolers to get together for organized soccer games. Or you might organize hikes, bowling days, or roller or ice skating days. If these are scheduled regularly, and especially if the student is involved in planning and organizing them and recruiting participants, they can count as an extracurricular activity with leadership roles.

Individual Sports

Of course, students need not participate in team athletics to have a viable sport on their lineup of extracurriculars. Many sports can be played on an individual basis or with a handful of others. Sports such as swimming can be practiced at a local YMCA or community facility; a student who loves running can seek out opportunities for competitions or races, such as 10Ks or half marathons. Sports that require only one or a few other players, such as tennis or golf, are further options. Another idea for a student desiring individual experience with a particular sport is to take a series of lessons or classes, either at the introductory level or with a private coach for more advanced work.

Obviously, individual sports will not provide benefits such as team leadership, and your student will find fewer opportunities to receive awards. If your student wishes to compete, look for competitions in which anyone can participate without a team. For example, you may find a triathlon club that sponsors an annual triathlon for kids and teenagers.

Opportunities for Talented Athletes

If your student is extremely skilled at a sport, you will want to pursue opportunities for him or her to play the sport as much as possible. In addition, you will need to find venues allowing the student to play alongside athletes of similar skill, for only in this way can players sharpen their abilities and take them to the next level. As previously mentioned, joining a local high school team may be an option—do thoroughly investigate the policies and whether the student will be required to take some classes at the school. Additionally, if your student is particularly talented and is possibly Olympic material, check out opportunities for the most elite levels of play possible. For example, if you have a swimmer, become familiar with national swim programs and seek out local teams.

After searching out all your options, you may find that the appropriate league is expensive or that practices are held at quite a distance from your home. However, if your student has exceptional potential for awards and athletic scholarships and desires to play the sport in college, it may be worthwhile to sign up for such a team. Look into Junior Olympics teams, community or regional teams with competitive levels, and opportunities such as the National Christian Homeschool Basketball Championship and the Homeschool World Series for baseball. Additionally, arrange for your student to develop athletic skills through summer sports camps or skill clinics. You might also look into hiring a private coach to work specifically with your student.

Students who show significant promise and hope to play collegiate sports must register with the

NCAA Eligibility Center (found on the NCAA website at http://www.ncaa.org/) and comply with all regulations, including academic specifications for core courses. The NCAA Eligibility Center has specific requirements for homeschoolers. Be sure to check these out earlier rather than later so that your student will not miss out on recruitment by colleges. In addition to the recruiting done by traditional universities, military academies such as West Point, the Naval Academy, and the Air Force Academy recruit athletes.

Matching your student's sport to a college that needs such athletes is a wise strategy. Resources such as *Peterson's® Sports Scholarships and Athletic Programs,* or similar books and websites, can provide a start in identifying suitable colleges. Your student may want to contact college athletic departments and individual coaches to briefly sum up his or her accomplishments and express interest in playing for a particular college and coach. A personal visit to the college would be the logical next step in this process.

Fine Arts

Fine arts, a collective term for music, dance, visual arts, and theater arts, is one popular extracurricular category that homeschoolers may avidly pursue in their flexible time. They can incorporate the arts into their course of study as well as into their lineup of extracurriculars.

Virtually anyone can find a niche in the field of music. If a student plays a musical instrument, he or she can join a community band or orchestra, perhaps even pursuing individual competitions. State and nationwide music teachers' organizations have curriculum contests and exams equivalent to first-year college music classes. These are an ideal objective tool for evaluation and can lead to high-level competitions, awards, and recognition.

Alternatively, a student whose talent is singing could opt to sing in a choir, ensemble, or other vocal group—perhaps even forming a singing group or band. Worship teams, special events, and solos at sports games are other viable ways to develop musical abilities and visibility. Songwriting is another musical skill that intrigues many students; this creative outlet can be an excellent way for students to express their ideas.

Fine arts also encompasses visual arts such as painting, drawing, sculpture, and photography. Start with your homeschool community and investigate whether an artistic parent or an outside teacher is offering classes. Other resources include community centers, private studios, and the community college.

Of course, if your student has unusual talent and is so inclined, he or she may want to teach others to draw, paint, or sculpt. This activity would clearly fall under the category of leadership and perhaps also paid employment.

Competitions, large or small, can be exciting and encouraging for a young artist. For example, some greeting card companies run contests for children and teenagers, with the winners having their works published on greeting cards. Local clubs and community groups may sponsor art shows or contests for logos and designs. Larger groups, too, often run art contests. HSLDA sponsors an annual art contest and photography contest for homeschoolers. In any case, let your student pursue the possibilities, and remember the principle of taking the interest to higher levels by honing skills and using them out in the community.

The field of fine arts is not limited to music and visual arts. Dance is considered a fine art as well as a fitness activity. If your student is a beginner, taking some classes or joining a community dance team at his or her level is the first step. If your student has been involved with dance for a number of years, the next step might be to move on to full-scale musical productions—perhaps even choreographing these productions. Teaching younger children basic skills in dance or taking charge of choreography for a children's recital is another excellent outlet for talent. And again, local and regional competitions can be rewarding events for your ambitious dancer.

Theater may be the perfect niche for the student who enjoys the creative expression of putting on a new identity. As with dance, if your student is brand-new to acting, a class at a community theater program may be the first option. Some of these classes focus on developing specific acting skills, while others perform a full-scale production of a play or musical. Many local theater companies offer summer intensive courses culminating in a production. This schedule might work well for a student who wants to try theater but whose schedule is filled up during the academic year.

A student who has learned the basics of acting and gained confidence and experience can proceed to audition for other community plays and productions. Also, don't overlook programs that may be available through churches and other local organizations. Your student may even consider organizing kids and teens to perform an end-of-summer play for the neighborhood.

Regardless of which types of fine arts your student favors, seek out opportunities for skill development, competition, service, or ministry—preferably all of the above. As your student shows passion and commitment in the arts, brainstorm ways to take this skill to the next level and develop leadership.

Volunteer Work/Community Service

Volunteer work can be one of the most fulfilling activities on your student's slate of extracurriculars. Besides enhancing the community and helping others, he or she can build relationships with potential employers or gain career skills even without being formally hired. While paid work is naturally desirable among teenagers, volunteer work can serve as a bridge to future work and can place the student's focus on others rather than on himself or herself. Because many high schools require students to perform community service, a *lack* of community service might jeopardize your student's chances of being accepted into a selective college. Thankfully, most homeschoolers are not even close to having this problem.

As you ponder volunteer options, remind your student to choose an area of genuine interest. With some searching, you'll find many suitable opportunities. Julie studied Russian and enjoyed volunteering at a day camp for Russian orphans seeking adoption—and gained language practice at the same time.

Field trips can be one way to spark a student's interest in a volunteer project. For example, suppose your student is considering helping out at the food bank but can't quite visualize what the work would be like. Arrange a field trip to the food bank to see firsthand what a teen volunteer might do there.

Sometimes busy homeschooling families can't picture adding one more activity to the schedule. In this case, try having your student participate in a volunteer activity with which a family member is already involved: anything from helping at a soup kitchen to participating in a church ministry. You can promote family unity while cutting down on driving.

If you are short on ideas, examine the list below, which covers some common venues for volunteer opportunities and may spark ideas of your own.

- Hospitals or nursing homes
- Public libraries, including story time or summer reading programs
- Veterinary clinics
- Child care centers, preschools, or day camps
- Food banks
- Special Olympics and similar programs
- Camps
- Tutoring centers—or organize your own program
- Ministries and church-related activities
- Soup kitchens, homeless shelters, or children's shelters

- Fundraising for charitable causes, through creative means such as holding walkathons, selling homemade goods, or offering "Parents' night out" babysitting
- Trips to other countries to help build shelters or conduct schools or camps
- Organizations that work with youth, such as YMCA®, Big Brothers Big Sisters®, Scouts, or youth sports teams
- Wildlife preserves or parks
- Community centers with programs for children, teens, or seniors

In addition to investigating these ideas, try a website called Idealist (http://idealist.org). This site catalogs volunteer opportunities by geographical location, type of work needed, and age or other requirements for volunteers. Also, you can simply search "Volunteer opportunities for high school students" and begin narrowing down the choices to what is available in your area.

Paid Employment

Learning responsible job skills and practicing a strong work ethic can take place during the teen years if your student works as a paid employee. Before your student applies for a job, consider these pros and cons of students holding down jobs during high school.

Pros:

Income

Obviously, employment will provide a constant supply of income for your student, which theoretically means less spending for parents. Your teen will now have an incentive to work hard for extras and entertainment expenses, and will learn about budgeting.

Responsibility

Though there are exceptions, part-time jobs can help students to become increasingly responsible with their time, money, and abilities. Time management skills must be acquired sooner or later, and students with jobs often learn to budget their time even better than those without jobs do, in order to fit in all their responsibilities. Additionally, hard-earned money may be more carefully budgeted.

Skills and Employment Contacts

The skills acquired on the job will give your student abilities that may be used later, not to mention providing potential contacts for a full-time job several years down the road.

Enhancement of the College Application

A part-time job can enhance your student's college application, provided that he or she spends a considerable amount of time per week working. Colleges like to see applicants who have conscientiously pursued an activity. Commitment to a part-time job is one way to portray discipline and consistency.

Cons:

Time Constraints

Probably the number one disadvantage of a part-time job is that it ties up hours that could be spent on schoolwork or other extracurriculars. If your student hasn't even begun to master the art of time management with existing responsibilities, it is unlikely that adding another responsibility will improve the situation. It will probably worsen it.

Transportation and Safety Issues

Another potential disadvantage is the issue of transportation, especially if your student does not have a driver's license or access to a car. Will the student need rides from a parent, or will he or she walk, bike, or take public transportation? Safety is another issue to consider when choosing a job. If your student is working late nights in a questionable part of town, his or her safety may be endangered.

Possible Negative Influences

Unfortunately, the influences from the student's coworkers may not all be positive. You will want to assess the social scene at the workplace to determine whether your student is being negatively impacted. Sometimes it is not so much the workplace itself as it is the after-hours get-togethers that you might need to monitor.

Restrictions

Students under age eighteen will be subject to child labor laws, and the younger the student, the more restrictions he or she will need to comply with. These laws limit the number of hours your student can work during the months when local public schools are in session, and they disallow working for pay during school hours or late at night. Look into the regulations in your state and have your student apply for a work permit. This can often be done through your local school district even if your student does not attend the public school. For a rundown of youth labor laws from the Department of Labor, nationally and by state, go to http://youthrules.dol.gov.

Job Ideas

While the following list is by no means exhaustive, it may spark ideas for possible jobs.
- Stores (grocery, clothing, drug, hardware, sporting goods, or gift stores)
- Restaurants, fast food establishments, or cafes
- Local businesses – try starting with family and friends' businesses
- Libraries, community centers, gyms, or churches
- Child care centers or private homes for child care or nanny work (make sure you "vet" the family to make sure it is a safe situation for your student)

Your student could also get started as an entrepreneur: hosting children's parties, teaching classes, running a lawn care service or a house cleaning service, providing tutoring, or performing computer-related jobs such as data entry, programming, or website development. Also check the list of volunteer work ideas earlier in this chapter, as some of them could yield paid work as well.

Use your imagination to come up with ideas for interesting and fruitful job opportunities.

Church Activities

Besides providing spiritual growth, your church can also be a source of extracurricular activities, especially those related to community service. For example, a student can help with children's ministries, music ministries, ushering, or greeting. Special events such as camps or Vacation Bible School always need helpers as well.

Being active in the church youth group may also be a viable activity. Encourage your student to volunteer for a position of leadership if this is an option, whether it be leading programs to help under-privileged children or leading music and worship during meetings. If your church, or a nearby church, offers the AWANA Clubs program, this provides a great opportunity for students to memorize God's word and to serve as volunteer leaders for the younger children.

Academic Activities

Homeschoolers can also seek out clubs and organizations that feed their academic interests. One example is the Eta Sigma Alpha National Home School Honor Society, an organization with local chapters throughout the United States. If your region has no chapter, it is easy to establish one. See the website for details: http://www.etasigmaalpha.com/.

Other ideas for academic extracurriculars include starting a research club, a foreign language club, a science club, a math club, or any club relating to a particular interest. Students can also seek out how to participate in competitions such as Quiz Bowl.

Journalism and Writing

Not attending a traditional school is no excuse for "writing off" school publications. If your student is truly interested in writing, editing, and newsletter production, the opportunities are numerous. Many students put their talents to use in creating printed or electronic newsletters or blogs for their homeschool support groups. The publication might include columns for field trips and events, helpful hints, featured student or family of the month, sports, and editorials. Artistic graphics, literary creations, or feature articles submitted by students could round out the publication.

A homeschool yearbook would be another intriguing project. After collecting photos of students, local homeschool events, and other memories of the school year, students could assemble them into page layouts, add text, and have the whole book printed and bound for families to enjoy. Budgeting, ad sales, and fundraising would be an integral part of the project.

Similarly, a team of students could plan and produce a literary magazine to be published monthly or just once or twice a year. Your student might also help with a newsletter produced by your church, a local ministry, or a community group such as the recreation department or the YMCA. Volunteers may be needed to write articles, design the layout, sell ads, or perform any number of journalistic tasks.

Students with excellent writing skills and creative ideas might even look into publishing their short stories, articles, or children's stories in print magazines or online. Although writing and marketing are two very different ventures and require different skill sets, any good writer who would like to be published needs to learn how to study the market and write up attractive proposals or queries for publishers. You could definitely incorporate these efforts into an English class. Self-publishing of student work would also be a worthwhile option, as the process involves valuable skills of writing, editing, proofreading, layout, design, and final distribution and sales.

Writing contests, such as the essay contest and poetry contest sponsored annually by HSLDA, present another outlet for homeschooled students' literary talents. Your student need not stop here but can also search online for other essay, poetry, or short story contests. And of course, journalism includes media such as radio, TV, and the internet. Exploring any of these venues that are open to your student could allow him or her to express creativity and gain journalistic skills.

Political Action

Particularly for students interested in public policy, law, or politics, involvement in the political process can be worthwhile. At the city, county, or state level, a politically inclined student could work on campaigns, bring information on initiatives and propositions to the public, or participate in youth government programs.

One resource for Christian youth between the ages of eleven and nineteen is the Generation Joshua® program (see website at https://hsldaaction.org/GenJ/). This program offers civics courses, voter registration programs, awards, clubs, and leadership camps. Most significantly, Generation Joshua offers Student Action Teams, which allow students to volunteer in political races. In many aspects, this program could be equivalent to the Boys State® and Girls State® civics and leadership programs for traditionally schooled students. Note that some states do allow homeschooled students to participate in Boys State and Girls State. Check the programs in your own state for details.

Speech and Debate

Through debate and public speaking, students gain skills in clear thinking and solid presentation of arguments. While polishing their techniques in writing and speaking, students also sharpen organizational and research skills. Since debate helps students analyze issues effectively and present clear, well-organized arguments, it is an excellent preparation for college.

Homeschoolers have a tremendous opportunity to get involved in debate through NCFCA, the National Christian Forensics and Communications Association (website http://www.ncfca.org/). Another organization is Stoa Christian Homeschool Speech and Debate Program https://stoausa.org/. Local clubs hone their debating skills, and student teams then enter regional and national speech or debate tournaments. Numerous competitive events are available for middle school and high school students.

Scientific Activities

Just as in other areas, students interested in science can seek out extracurriculars that suit their interests. Science fairs and science competitions, many of which feed into regional, state, and national fairs, are frequently open to homeschoolers as well as to traditional students. One respected competition is the Regeneron Science Talent Search, formerly Intel® Science Talent Search, website https://student.societyforscience.org/regeneron-sts). Students need to conduct a well-designed research project (with help and support from an institution as needed), write up their results in the form of a scientific paper, and enter it in the competition.

If your student has a passion for STEM, seek out other programs and competitions, such as the Google Science Fair, the Zero Robotics Tournaments, the Imagine Cup™ (sponsored by Microsoft®), the Intel® International Science & Engineering Fair, and CS-STEM Network competitions. These are just a few of many. Keep searching!

Another activity Julie enjoyed was conducting her own original neighborhood science clubs for children. These week-long summer clubs, featuring hands-on experiments and science-related crafts, snacks, and games, were an excellent way to bring science out of the laboratory and into the back yard.

Competitions

Young scientists are not the only ones who can enjoy the thrill of competition. Contests in math, robotics, the arts, history, geography, spelling, and writing can serve as worthwhile extracurricular activities. For some of these competitions, students work in teams and gain experience in group problem-solving techniques. Although some contests are limited to students from traditional schools, others might allow any groups of interested students to form teams. If you need information about competitions or competitive clubs in your student's field of interest, search online using key words relating to this interest, and also seek out information from your local high school and from like-minded friends.

Community Health and Safety

The practical pursuit of health and safety can be a great asset to a student interested in medicine, nursing, or public health. Some ideas include American Red Cross® training and volunteer service, first aid, disaster preparedness, lifeguarding, hospital volunteering, the Make-A-Wish® Foundation, and community health programs. Excellent opportunities for leadership and initiative exist here as well. For instance, a student could start a program to teach basic health and safety in a club for younger kids. Creative thinking, combined with your student's interests and skills, can yield productive and rewarding project ideas.

TIPS AND CAUTIONS

As you and your student choose extracurricular activities, keep the following tips and cautions in mind. Not only will they save many headaches, but they may also increase your student's chances of being accepted to college.

Don't Focus Exclusively on One Activity

It's easy to get carried away by one type of extracurricular activity. For example, if homeschooled student Molly Mason is a natural athlete, she may want to participate in lacrosse, water polo, field hockey, and swimming but may neglect any involvement with volunteer work or fine arts. Since showing diverse interests is important, a student should achieve a bit more balance in extracurricular activities while still developing that angularity mentioned earlier.

Don't Be the Proverbial Jack-of-All-Trades

Conversely, it is rarely sensible to dabble in *every* extracurricular activity imaginable. Suppose Molly's neighbor, Dexter Louis, attends French club meetings sporadically, plays soccer eight weeks per year, played the violin for one year and then quit, volunteers once per quarter at the hospital, worked at the grocery store for three months before quitting, and occasionally attends his church's youth group. While Dexter has experience in virtually every category of extracurricular activities, he doesn't appear to be showing focus or commitment. Moreover, he has not demonstrated any leadership experience. To some extent, colleges look for well-rounded students, but they are most attracted to students who have strong talents or unusual experiences that have led them to deep involvement and leadership roles.

Show Passion in One or Two Areas

One of the most popular buzzwords flying around college admissions offices is *passion*. As discussed in Dexter's case, colleges want students who are well-rounded—but that's not enough. They also want to see that the student deeply loves a particular activity. This passion should display itself beyond a few courses on the transcript or an infrequent extracurricular activity. The student might enter competitions, teach or tutor other students, or seek out a related job or volunteer position. Students who focus on and develop what they love will automatically display passion. Remember that summers are an excellent time to "go deep" with your areas of passion. In particular, look for ways to show initiative by designing and running a program, a backyard club, a fundraiser, or another activity in an area you care about.

Display Commitment to Your Extracurriculars

Commitment is also important when it comes to extracurricular activities. While a student may be well-rounded and display a passion for a certain area, these activities have much less impact if he or she spends very little time participating in them. Let's take a look again at Dexter's extracurricular activities. If Dexter had volunteered several hours per week at the hospital instead of just two hours per quarter, he would stand out more to college admissions committees and would be using his talents more effectively. Likewise, if Dexter had continued with violin for more than one year, he would display more commitment.

Develop Leadership

As mentioned earlier, colleges look for leadership in extracurriculars. Chapter 16 provides a more extensive discussion of leadership, but as you and your student seek out quality extracurriculars, choose activities in which your student will likely be able to rise to positions of leadership.

Observe Legalities

If your student designs an activity working with children (without the oversight of an established organization such as a church or community group) be cautious of health and safety concerns or potential areas of risk or legal vulnerability. Be sure to require a medical release form from parents, and obtain emergency phone numbers of parents, physicians, and dentists in case of any mishaps. Check into whether your homeowner's insurance covers such activities, and make sure you have sufficient adult oversight as you conduct activities in your home, yard, or other locations. Minimize (and preferably remove) all possible hazards that could result in injury of children or volunteers.

Embrace the Overlap

Frequently, homeschoolers' extracurriculars mingle and overlap with the curriculum. Use this feature of homeschooling to its fullest advantage. Obviously, activities such as music and sports can be used for fine arts and P.E. credit, respectively, using some of the hours for school credit and others for the extracurricular activity. However, other interest-related activities, even clubs, can serve as projects to enhance science, history, and civics study. Many homeschoolers use Scouts and merit badge work to serve as curriculum or to augment a course. For example, the unit "Citizenship in the Nation" could be used during a course on American history or government. Feel free to use travel and missions trips as significant extracurriculars, as well as curricular bonuses in the pertinent subjects. This is homeschooling at its finest!

Find Ways to Fit It All in Without Losing Your Mind

Though a dozen activities may intrigue your student, the schedule may permit "passionate" or "committed" participation in only four or five at the most. On top of that, time with friends and family and time for academics must be scheduled. You need to find a way to *prioritize* the most appropriate outside activities and choose which should be pursued. Some of the criteria to consider include the following, in no particular order:

- Potential for leadership roles.
- Involvement with key interests and passions.
- Convenience with respect to location and time slots available in the family schedule.
- Opportunity for other members of the family or for a group of friends to get involved (thus saving car trips).
- Opportunity to create variety or provide depth in the student's lineup of extracurriculars.
- Opportunity to help others or to connect socially with others.
- Opportunity to explore a future career and/or to earn needed funds.
- True enjoyment (activities that are relaxing, invigorating, or stress-reducing).

While some of these criteria are more compelling than others, each can be a good reason for choosing a given activity. Before each school year begins, look at the lineup of school courses and then think about how many extracurricular activities will fit into the schedule without your student becoming overextended. If certain activities simply won't fit into a particular school year, but your student is intent upon trying them, you can use a summer or the following school year to get started. Realize that your student may have to drop one or two activities to accommodate a new one. It's always a balancing act. But by consciously adjusting the schedule, you and your student will be better able to manage your time, enjoy the extracurriculars you've chosen, and focus on the favorite activities.

If your family calendar is getting too full, try some of these solutions:

- Drop activities that do not add anything of significance to the student's life.
- Look for carpool arrangements to help with transportation scheduling.
- Arrange for some activities to meet at your own home, so that other students come to you rather than your student going out to other locations.
- For ongoing weekly activities, let your student know that it's acceptable to skip once in a while.
- During extremely busy weeks, adjust the academic expectations so that the student can make it through the "push" of the extracurricular demands (such as back-to-back theater performances). Then make up for lost time the next week.
- Make some activities do double duty as coursework and extracurriculars. Aside from team sports for P.E. and orchestra for fine arts credit, try having your student assist with a political action group for part of a civics course, teach a Sunday School class for a Bible course requirement, or edit a homeschool literary magazine while gaining English credit.

TO SUM UP

Extracurricular activities allow students to show their commitment, leadership, responsibility, and passion to the college admissions staff. As your student selects activities, encourage him or her to be strategic in these choices, but above all, to have fun and enjoy every one of the activities chosen!

Chapter 16

Being a Leader When There's No Student Body:

Leadership Skills

Duning a conversation with an admissions officer from a highly selective college, I was asking questions about academics—how a homeschooled student could best prepare for college. After answering my questions, the admissions officer gave this advice: "Be sure that your student doesn't neglect the social and leadership aspects of high school." This concept was echoed by an admissions officer at MIT in a message to homeschooled applicants: "One quality that we are looking for in all of our applicants is evidence of having taken initiative, showing an entrepreneurial spirit, taking full advantage of opportunities."[1] In other words, while academics are important, leadership is another essential piece of the puzzle.

For high school students, the word "leadership" conjures up images of student government or club presidents, and so at first glance, it may seem out of reach for homeschoolers. But homeschoolers are fully capable of displaying genuine leadership in numerous arenas. The challenge is to identify these opportunities, to develop leadership skills by diving into worthwhile activities, and then to communicate these accomplishments in a meaningful way to college admissions departments.

WHAT IS LEADERSHIP?

First of all, what is leadership and why is it important? While specific definitions could be discussed endlessly, one simple description is that "leaders lead." Students who can rally the support of others for a cause or organization will generally continue to be leaders when they are active in the adult world. Good leaders will promote the well-being of society, innovate useful products and technology, organize the workplace so that it runs smoothly, and inspire people to think of others and not only of themselves.

From our own high school years, many of us remember that leadership "looked good" on the college application. As a result, ambitious students joined several clubs and sought to be elected president, vice president, or secretary. It didn't matter whether one actually *did* anything in that position. The title was the important part, and the most prestigious titles of all were schoolwide roles such as student body president or class president. While some of these positions provided meaningful leadership experience, many served merely to pad the resume—and the ego.

Genuine leadership, however, involves distinct character qualities that can be practiced in a number of creative ways in real life, not just in campus politics. As you read the following descriptions of key aspects of leadership, be thinking about strengths your student already has, as well as ways he or she can develop weaker areas by entering less comfortable environments filled with unaccustomed challenges.

Administration and Management

A leader must make sure that the organization runs smoothly and has all it needs to function on a daily basis. Communicating with group members, keeping up with administrative tasks, delegating action items, and planning events are all administrative and management tasks. To perform well, a leader needs to be attentive to detail—in short, he or she must be a good list maker and task prioritizer. Look for opportunities, including nontraditional ones, for your student to practice these skills and work up to managing a small project or a larger undertaking. Coordinating special events is one good example. Ideas might encompass anything from a child's birthday party to a week-long day camp. Homeschool outings, fundraisers, graduation ceremonies, conferences, and other such events can be venues for students to develop their administration and management skills. Perhaps your student can oversee one small piece of a project before eventually taking on additional responsibility.

Authority and Influence

A leader who holds the top position in an organization, such as president or chairman, clearly has authority over the rest of the group. Being elected or appointed to this position means that the leader has been deemed worthy to hold this authority and has been trusted to use it wisely. A good leader does not use authority in a dictatorial way. Nor does he or she act hesitantly, afraid to make a decision or to enforce a rule. For high school students, one position requiring authority and influence is that of club president. If your student has the opportunity to preside over a homeschool or community group, he or she will need to learn how to wield authority in a sensitive, diplomatic, and decisive way. A leader needs to think before speaking and to consider all aspects of a problem before recommending a solution. Encourage your student to accept advice and input from others but not to become paralyzed by indecision when considering multiple viewpoints.

Direction and Foresight

Proactive, forward-looking leaders can see potential problems looming and then take steps to prevent them. An astute leader also spots opportunities beyond the horizon and can position the organization to take advantage of them. Inspiring the rest of the group with this vision is yet another leadership skill. Looking beyond *today* to see what lies ahead *tomorrow*—and then taking steps to do something about it—is critical to the group's success.

For example, your student might notice that litter is building up along a favorite biking trail. Having the foresight to see that this problem will only grow worse if left unattended, the student might rally others to raise money for more garbage cans along the trail, as well as for city services to empty them. He or she might organize monthly hikes for the purpose of picking up litter. Or, through posters, emails, petitions to the city, letters to the newspaper editor, and maybe even local radio spots, this enterprising student might publicize the message about keeping the trail clean and beautiful. All of these activities show foresight, in that the student sees a problem developing and does something about it, rather than waiting for someone else to act.

Initiative and Creativity

Some of the most effective leadership takes place even before there is a group of people to lead. Similar to the example of the student concerned about trail litter, a natural leader can see a need and think of ways to solve it. By turning thoughts into actions, the leader has taken the initiative to use his or her talents to make a difference in the world. Leaders also notice opportunities—for a business, for a ministry, for a way to reach out to others—and turn them into reality.

For instance, your student could start a service group that visits elderly people in nursing homes. By recruiting students to be involved and by organizing and delegating the tasks that need to be done, the student takes the initiative to help others and to start something where nothing previously existed.

Service and Compassion

One of the oldest and most basic definitions of leadership comes from the words of Jesus Christ: "Whoever wants to become great among you must be your servant."[2] And in fact, this definition is still valid today, for service is one of the most far-reaching forms of leadership. A servant leader is involved in the day-to-day duties of a group, faithfully working alongside the other members without being afraid to "get his or her hands dirty." A genuine leader is not one who sits at a mahogany desk and gives orders, but one who sets an inspiring example, leading others to share the vision and to participate in the goals of the group.

For example, if your student is appointed leader of a group of teens helping in a children's club program, he or she has the chance to lead by example. The leader should be the first person to arrive and the last to leave. Displaying servant leadership, the student should leave the room orderly and clean and should be just as willing to do the more menial tasks as to participate in the enjoyable or high-profile parts of the job. By pitching in alongside the others and by displaying an enthusiastic and willing attitude, your student can inspire other young people to serve.

CHALLENGES FOR HOMESCHOOLERS

On the surface, developing and displaying leadership abilities appears to be a bit of a challenge for homeschoolers. Because they cannot typically run for student government, serve as captain of a varsity sports team, or preside over a campus club, homeschoolers must work a little harder to find these opportunities. However, when you keep the previous definitions of leadership in mind, many activities become ideal opportunities for the development and demonstration of leadership skills. Make every effort to pursue these options as you map out your student's high school years.

Even from the earliest years of the homeschooling movement, homeschoolers were not daunted by the apparent challenges but were reliably exercising leadership skills. A study conducted by Dr. L. R. Montgomery back in the 1980s—before the days of large support groups and homeschool academies—found that homeschoolers were in no way deficient in leadership potential. Compared to students in private schools, the homeschooled students she studied were just as involved as traditional students in extracurricular activities predicting leadership in adulthood, and they were actually more involved than a sampling of publicly schooled students.[3] Today, homeschooled students continue to show strong evidence of leadership, initiative, and concern for their communities.

Just how concerned about leadership should students be as they plan their high school years? Again, this depends on the student's educational goals. Applicants to selective colleges will receive extra scrutiny by admissions committees to see if they led, initiated, set good examples, used administrative talents, and inspired others to follow them. If your student wants to attend a selective college, think strategically about leadership long before your student applies.

On the other hand, students applying to less selective colleges need not go out of their way to seek outstanding leadership roles. They may simply use leadership abilities for life experience and enrichment —not as a "must" on a college application.

Regardless of a student's college aspirations, a quest for leadership positions should never be undertaken simply to "look good" to the college admissions staff. Remember those students of our own school days who joined or started a club, got themselves elected to an office, and then did very little in that position? These students are not the ones to emulate. The student should be truly interested in the activity and willing to put effort into serving, administering, influencing, and directing a group whose purposes mean a great deal to him or her. The experience should be life-changing and character-building —not simply a line item on a college application.

LEADERSHIP IN CURRENT EXTRACURRICULARS

As they search for leadership opportunities, homeschoolers should first look at their current activities. Here are some questions to ask yourselves early in the high school years as you seek to develop your student's repertoire of leadership experiences. For some of these, leadership positions already exist. If so, find out what your student needs to do to earn a chance at these positions. Generally, a history of faithful work and the ability to get along with others will give your student the best chances. For activities with no built-in leadership opportunities, use that vital quality of initiative to *create* a leadership position to fit the student's interests and skills.

Sports

Could the student earn the position of captain or co-captain on a homeschool or community sports team? Would the coach appreciate assistance with record keeping, drills, or communications? Could the student coach a team of younger players or perhaps serve as an administrative assistant—ordering awards, organizing events, communicating with parents, or assisting players who need extra help?

Clubs and Youth Organizations

If the student is in a community club such as 4-H, what traditional or nontraditional leadership positions are available? Could your student seek out positions in areas of his or her genuine interests and work up to a more responsible position in the organization? Does your student have creative ideas or suggested improvements that he or she could implement?

Ministries

Does the student participate in ministries at church such as child care, children's ministries, AWANA Clubs or other club programs, ushering, sports ministries, midweek ministries, or youth groups? These groups may already have leadership positions defined, or they may welcome someone to step up to a newly created position. Generally, church is one place where committed volunteer leaders are always in short supply. Under the supervision of an adult in the ministry, could your student use his or her gifts and abilities to bless others, far beyond the scope of an ordinary volunteer position? Could your student take charge of teaching, training, leading, or organizing groups of younger children? Chances are, the adults in charge of the ministry would be delighted to have help from someone who could take ownership of a small or larger part of the program. Encourage your student to speak to those in charge and to brainstorm for ways he or she could "go beyond" and help the ministry in an exciting and valuable way.

Likewise, does the student assist one or both parents in some of their ministries? Could you create a leadership position to suit the student's abilities and meet particular needs of the ministry? For instance, if you are editor of a newsletter, assign your student to be assistant editor. Provide training with the goal that he or she will eventually work into the role of editor. If you create and maintain websites for ministries or organizations, have your student serve as the assistant webmaster. If you help out at a food pantry or organize charitable donations, create a leadership role for your teen. Working alongside you will give your teen valuable experience, and having your assistant live in the same house with you certainly facilitates communication and project completion.

Scouts and Community Organizations

Is your student active in Girl Scouts® or Scouts BSA™? Both of these groups offer opportunities for growth in leadership skills. Encourage your student to use his or her original ideas and initiative to make the group even better. In Scouts BSA, the rank of Eagle Scout is greatly respected because of the level of responsibility and leadership required to attain it. Similarly, Girl Scouts offers bronze, silver, and gold awards based on achievement and leadership. The Gold Award, the highest award in Girl Scouts, is also project-based and focuses on leadership skills, career explorations, self-improvement, and service.

By the way, even for students who are not in Scouts, the websites of these organizations, or related sites such as http://usscouts.org, which list requirements for merit badges, are a great source of ideas for leadership or service projects your student could perform in the community. Additionally, they provide a handy list of practical life skills to develop in your student. Don't overlook this useful resource.

Another organization that promotes leadership skills is Civil Air Patrol. With its emphasis on project management, team leadership, volunteer service, and advancement through demonstration of responsibility, this program can be beneficial to a teen seeking leadership opportunities. Your local YMCA may also be a resource for leadership training or practice. For instance, many branches in 38 states offer a program called Youth and Government, giving high schoolers an opportunity for hands-on civics experience with the YMCA Model Legislature and Court Program. Statewide conferences, an opportunity to spend a week in the state capital, and a chance to learn about government make this and similar programs good choices for leadership skill development.

Your civic-minded student can also find leadership opportunities through political activism, assistance with elections or voter registration, or volunteering with local, state, or national political campaigns.

Publications

Does your homeschool support group need someone to handle the monthly newsletter? Would your student like to start a literary publication for homeschoolers who love to write? Could he or she assist with the local community newspaper, perhaps serving as the teen editor? Investigating these options might yield the perfect opportunity to develop and use writing and editing skills.

Music and Drama

Does your student sing or play an instrument well? Could he or she try out for musical productions, orchestras, bands, or choruses and eventually develop a leadership position? Could your student teach music or drama to younger children?

Visual Arts

Is your student skilled at drawing, painting, or photography? Could he or she conduct classes for beginners, or organize a special event such as an art show featuring works by young people—perhaps even donating the proceeds to charity?

Employment or Volunteer Work

Does your student have a part-time job with possibilities for supervisory positions? In his or her volunteer work, is there an opportunity to lead groups of other teens, or of younger children? Students who work diligently and dependably at paid or unpaid jobs may be rewarded with leadership or management opportunities.

LEADERSHIP BY INITIATIVE

As mentioned earlier, one of the most worthwhile ways your student can show leadership is by *creating* the leadership position—or even the organization itself. This type of leadership uses every possible aspect: administration, authority, influence, direction, and service. The student sees a need or an opportunity and, by careful planning, seeks to fill this need. The opportunity could be a service club, a much-needed community project, or a special interest club among youth. The student needs the right set of skills to generate the vision for a group, organize it, bring it into existence, inspire others to participate, and keep it running smoothly. Since this process shows initiative and innovation, colleges would clearly see it as a noteworthy endeavor. Note that summers can be excellent times to plunge in and to brainstorm, plan, design, execute, and lead a special program or event in the areas of the student's deepest passions. At the outset of high school, you might even consider sitting down and sketching out a few ideas for each summer. As time goes on, see if you can make some of these come to fruition.

Over the years, I have watched with excitement and pride as homeschooled students have taken the initiative to design, launch, and run programs that provide benefits both in the local community and around the globe. One student created a week-long backyard science club, "The Backyard Exploratorium," where kids ran fizzy, messy, colorful experiments and learned the principles behind them. The proceeds of the club were donated to an organization that dug fresh-water wells for underprivileged people in villages in Asia. This student's younger brother created a similar camp a couple of years later—with charitable donations to provide wheelchairs for those in need. In this camp, each student built a fully functioning 3D printer from a kit and learned how to use it. Another student (with her younger sisters following suit after she went off to college) established a Young Musicians Workshop in her home, featuring private lessons, ensemble sessions, a performance on the last day, stories of composers, and music-themed games, crafts, and snacks. She donated the proceeds to a charity that helped children in China receive lifesaving heart surgeries, and to a project involving building houses for impoverished families in Vietnam. Over the course of five years, $8800 was raised, funding six houses and one heart surgery. Yet another student's heart was touched with sympathy for victims of devastating California wildfires. Within days of hearing the news, he had initiated, planned, and publicized a benefit concert that ultimately raised $3500, donated to the American Red Cross to help with disaster relief for fire victims.

I could name project after project, with the point being that a motivated student with a great idea and the willingness to devote time and energy to such a pursuit can bring joy and benefits near and far, while definitively demonstrating an essential type of leadership: that of creating something good where nothing existed before.

How to Start Your Own Organization

For a motivated, creative student, starting an organization does not have to be complicated. All it takes is a good idea and a source of members. Here is some guidance for those in-between steps.

Create the Concept

First, the student needs to decide what type of organization to create. Envisioning whether this group will be for homeschoolers or will be open to any interested youth, the student should think through the types of clubs that would appeal to these students and would fill a gap in your community's existing opportunities. Ideas might include literary clubs, foreign language clubs, drama groups, bowling leagues, or hiking clubs. Math, gourmet cooking, science, robotics, public speaking, chess, or even board games could be other interests around which to form clubs.

Or, your student could start a group specifically organized for community service—with a little fun thrown in, of course. Students could provide tutoring or after-school clubs for disadvantaged youth, volunteer in a hospital, paint dilapidated park benches around the city, or do yard work or household services for elderly neighbors. Offering special interest classes, either for peers or for younger students, might be another option. These might encompass art, science, drama, literature, or sports.

Starting a business is yet another way to demonstrate leadership. Aside from the traditional lawn mowing, car washing, and babysitting jobs, your student could produce items for sale (crafts, baked goods, or handmade greeting cards), start a service to help people with their computer problems, or plan and supervise birthday parties for young children. Getting other students involved in the business would demonstrate additional leadership skills, and doing the legwork of checking into the appropriate municipal regulations and tax considerations would further enhance your student's skills.

Think It Through and Write It Down

Once the concept has begun to take shape, the student should articulate these ideas in writing. From where will group members be recruited? What is the best way to publicize the group? How often, and when, should the group meet, and what is the best way to communicate among the group members? What exactly will take place during meetings? How many adults should be involved? Who will plan activities or service projects? Asking these questions *before* starting an organization can prevent many headaches.

Find a Friend or Two

These questions will naturally lead to a phase of brainstorming possible answers and then researching the best ways to carry out these plans. A session with two or three interested people is a good idea at this point, for the others can help generate questions, answers, potential pitfalls, and ideas your student may not have considered.

Publicize and Plunge In

When the concept has been firmed up and most of the questions have been answered, the student now has a direction in mind and can publicize the group to other students. If you live in a community with many homeschoolers, placing an announcement in a regional homeschool newsletter or distributing fliers at a highly-attended event may yield many interested students. Email, social media, websites, word of mouth, neighborhood newsletters, or community newspapers are other ways to publicize the group.

When a number of young people have expressed interest, your student can hold a meeting to determine future direction, to set goals, and to plan activities. At this point it may be helpful to select other leaders or officers to firm up the next steps.

Consider Starting New Chapters of Existing Organizations

Occasionally, the opportunity will arise to start a local chapter of a national or regional organization. Because some of the legwork has already been done, your student simply needs to publicize the idea and gather interested members. Together, they can flesh out the plans for this particular group based on the guidelines already in existence.

One example is the Eta Sigma Alpha National Homeschool Honor Society mentioned in the previous chapter. When Julie was a freshman in high school, she read about this organization in a homeschool newsletter. After discovering that there were no chapters in California, she established a local chapter of ESA. Although our chapter chose to keep our activities low-key because of our members' busy schedules, the group could just as well have become a highly active club, meeting a couple of times a month and participating heavily in community service projects. If your geographical area does not have a chapter of Eta Sigma Alpha, you may want to contact the national headquarters to see about starting a club.

OPPORTUNITIES FOR NATIONAL LEADERSHIP RECOGNITION

Leadership also goes beyond the local area. If your student successfully achieves national recognition, colleges will take notice. One such opportunity, well-suited to homeschooling, is The Congressional Award. Established in 1979, this program encourages youth achievement in voluntary public service, physical fitness, personal development, and expedition/exploration. Young people between the ages of 13½ and 23 can earn gold, silver or bronze medals, or gold, silver, or bronze certificates by participating in the four required categories of activity. Students set their own goals, based on guidelines set by the program. Upon completion of these goals, the students are awarded their medals or certificates; gold medalists attend an awards ceremony in Washington, D.C. The sheer number of hours it takes to earn the medals demonstrates diligence and perseverance. Website is http://congressionalaward.org/.

A similar program is the President's Volunteer Service Award, https://www.presidentialserviceawards.gov/, which recognizes students, adults, and families based on hours of community service performed. For homeschoolers, working toward this award might coordinate well with what they are already doing for volunteer community service.

Other opportunities for national recognition that could loosely be considered leadership—some more than others—involve excellence in activities such as sports or music on a national level, or participating in programs such as the Regeneron Science Talent Search, the National History Day Contest, or the Scripps National Spelling Bee. There are many others – search the keywords that describe your student's interests and passions, and ask his or her mentors and coaches for more ideas.

TRANSLATING LEADERSHIP INTO "ADMISSIONS COMMITTEE-ESE"

If your student's leadership accomplishments do not resemble those of the traditional student, he or she may need to help the admissions committee understand these leadership experiences. This is not difficult. In essence, it is like writing a resume for a job opening. The student should use active words and phrases (*organized, initiated, led, supervised*) as well as details that will help explain what the project entailed. For instance, instead of saying, "Was a student leader at AWANA," your student might explain, "Organized games, projects, and awards for twenty elementary school children in a community club program and supervised two younger teen helpers. Planned and prepared weekly activities and was chosen to lead the entire group on several occasions when an adult helper was absent."

Since this description would probably not fit on the small line on the college application, your student would find some other way to detail this project. Perhaps a vivid description could be worked into an application essay. Perhaps a succinct depiction would be perfect for a paragraph-length prompt that asks the applicant to elaborate on a favorite extracurricular. Or perhaps the activity could be described in the parent/counselor's explanatory document outlining the homeschooling process. This is why you as a homeschool parent should *rejoice* when you are asked to submit extra material.

In describing leadership experiences, seek to use specific or numerical information to help clarify your student's position. Examples might include numbers of people the student led or supervised, hours and weeks spent in the activity, dollars raised, number of students tutored, hours of community service volunteered, or number of badges earned. If your student's project received community or statewide recognition, such as being written up in a newspaper or on a website, be sure to mention that fact or, if appropriate, even submit a copy of the article. Positive quotations or complimentary comments from other adults who work with your student should be included or mentioned, because this is important "outside" input on your student.

TO SUM UP

Leadership, if defined as being able to organize, guide, and inspire others, is by no means limited to traditional school settings. In fact, homeschoolers, who display dedication in their daily work, independence in their ideas, perseverance in pursuing their passions, and respectfulness in their relationships with people of all ages are ideally positioned to discover and take full advantage of leadership opportunities. Encourage your student to be creative and to find the best "niches" in which to shine and lead.

1. McGann, Matt, "Homeschooled Applicants: Helpful Tips," MIT Admissions, *McGann's Factors*, September 5, 2006. Accessed August 17, 2018. http://mitadmissions.org/blogs/entry/homeschooled_applicants.
2. Matthew 20:26 (*Holy Bible: New International Version*).
3. Montgomery, Linda R., "The Effect of Home Schooling on the Leadership Skills of Home Schooled Students," *Home School Researcher* 5, no. 1 (1989).

Chapter 17

Staying on Track:

Timetables for a Smooth Journey

Old-fashioned railroad stations, modern urban subways, and commuter train lines—all of these feature that all-important set of posted timetables. In bygone days, these may have been printed paper sheets or blackboards; today, they are high-tech electronic boards. Either way, timetables and schedules are essential to passengers who have places to go and schedules to keep. Without them, travelers can only guess at the departure or arrival time of the next train. By paying close attention to the timetables, travelers can reduce the odds of the train pulling out of the station without them.

When the planned journey involves college preparation, paying attention to the timetables of the high school experience can keep your family on the right "track" and prevent the "train" of college admissions from pulling away without your student on board.

This chapter will help you and your student understand the long-term and short-term college prep tasks from seventh through twelfth grades so that you can map out a realistic itinerary for your journey.

GETTING YOUR BEARINGS

For the college bound homeschooler, the timetable starts, not in the junior or senior year, but much earlier. Without the convenient prodding of a traditional high school guidance counselor to steer students toward the right courses and exams, a homeschool family must constantly be thinking ahead. Don't worry —a student is definitely *not* out of the running for college if the planning process starts later. However, it makes for a smoother transition from middle school to the day of college acceptance if the family knows the destination *and* arrival time of the train that's hurtling down the tracks.

College prep timetables come in many forms. Most of the task lists found online are designed for traditionally schooled students, and they vary somewhat with regard to just when students should meet certain checkpoints.

The timelines suggested in this chapter consider the unique needs of homeschoolers and are designed to help families understand what is involved in preparing a student for college. After reading through these generic timetables, you'll definitely want to check with individual colleges and specialized programs to make sure your student is on target for college-specific requirements.

This timetable is a year-by-year view of suggested tasks as the student prepares for college applications. The timetable for each year contains a statement of purpose and vision for that year as well as comments on several categories: academics, testing, record keeping, extracurriculars, college hunting, recommendations, application essays, spirituality, life skills, and finances. Because the senior year is so critical, the twelfth grade timetable includes a month-by-month view of the tasks.

Please do not let these timetables overwhelm you, and do not be ruled by them. You may not need to complete all the tasks on the list, especially if your student is not applying to a selective college. In fact, in this case, the list should be pared down significantly and can be slowed down as well. If your student is on this "saner," less stressful set of railroad tracks, follow these instructions in a more leisurely manner. Your student will travel more lightly and arrive at the destination with energy to spare.

Select only the information you can use, and customize it according to your family's needs and plans. These timelines are simply general guidelines. No two families will choose the same list of tasks, the same itinerary, or the same travel time for the journey.

7TH AND 8TH GRADES – YEARS OF ACCLIMATION AND EXPLORATION

As discussed in Chapter 2, the middle school years are the perfect time for parents and students to begin acclimating to the demands that will eventually be placed on them during high school. Doing some preparation during these years will make the high school years easier because the transition has been more gradual. That said, do not feel that seventh and eighth grades need to be years of heavy academics. This is simply a time of adaptation and acclimation—a transition from the more informal ways of schooling in the elementary school years, to some of the types of work that will be required in the higher grades. Let your student *explore* special interests and new ways of learning. Don't overdo the workload, or your student may burn out early in the journey and forget to look out the window to enjoy the picturesque scenery!

Academics

A seventh or eighth grader's academics should be reasonable, but not overwhelming. This is a time in a young person's life when much is changing—his or her body, and perhaps also friends and outside activities. Too much change and too many unaccustomed demands will be stressful. An overzealous parent or even an overambitious student may set lofty goals during these pre-high school years, only to wonder why things are not getting completed as planned, and why student and parent are *both* getting grouchy. In short, the mind, the body, and the will have not yet matured. In the next year or two, you will begin to notice great improvements in the student's ability to concentrate and finish more tasks, but in all likelihood, these traits have not yet appeared. Some students may be ready for high school level work in math, English, or other subjects. Other students should spend this year cementing their basic skills. Encourage organization, time management, and solid study skills, which will be needed as the workload increases. But inject a good dose of fun, humor, and creativity wherever possible.

Testing

No special testing is required yet. If your state or PSP requires standardized testing, or if you want a confirmation of the student's strengths and weaknesses, by all means have the student sit for the typical grade-level standardized tests available to you.

If your student is extremely gifted, he or she might try taking the College Board SAT exam or the ACT exam early. A high score opens doors to talent search programs offering enrichment in summer programs, weekend programs, or online courses. Depending on your region, a different program will be applicable: the Duke Talent Identification Program, the Johns Hopkins University Center for Talented

Homeschooled & Headed for College

Youth, the Center for Bright Kids Western Academic Talent Search, or the Northwestern University Center for Talent Development. These are just a few of the programs available to gifted students, and eligibility involves testing with one or more nationally available tests.

Record Keeping

For now, you can get by with fairly informal record keeping. Read up on record keeping techniques that might work for you in high school. Also be thinking about the best PSP (private school satellite program) arrangement for your high school record keeping preferences, and if you are not already a member, be prepared to join by the time your student is in eighth grade, or certainly by ninth grade. You may want to practice "high school" style record keeping for one or two of the eighth grade courses. Additionally, create and use an organized electronic and paper filing system for student records.

Extracurriculars

Seventh and eighth grades are a time for exploring a variety of extracurricular activities to determine the student's interests, talents, strengths, and leadership abilities. Encourage your student to try these new activities while balancing time commitments among school and outside activities.

College Hunting

While it is too early for formal college hunting, encourage your student to think about what fields of study *might* be interesting and to rule out those which are definitely "out." This guided daydreaming can help later in choosing colleges that are strong in certain majors. Don't close any doors yet, for much can change. For example, as a seventh grader Julie aspired to be an executive for a music recording company. By her junior year, her ambition was to be a biomedical researcher, and before long, that ambition expanded to becoming a physician. Consider some informal visits to nearby universities, as well as to the local community college. The goal now is simply to expose your student to the many options for the college environment.

Recommendations

Although it will be years yet before letters of recommendation will be needed, you can help your student build relationships with adult leaders involved in ministries and volunteer work.

Application Essays

College essays are four to five years away, but start to build solid writing instruction into your curriculum so that your student develops the skills that will be essential later.

Spirituality

Incorporate basic biblical skills into your school day so that your student can navigate through the Bible to find timeless truths for everyday living. Encourage Scripture memory, Bible study techniques, and practical application. In addition, welcome your student's questions about faith-related subjects and investigate the answers together, using the Bible and solid, user-friendly resources.

Life Skills

Draw up a list of skills you would like your student to learn by the end of high school. Begin working on the skills that are now age-appropriate. While some of these can be addressed at home, others may be covered in Scouts, 4-H Clubs, or other clubs and groups. Middle school is an excellent time to work on these skills, before the demands of high school set in.

Finances

Practice wise earning, spending, saving, and investing policies in your home in order to maximize the funds available later for college. Consult financial professionals if needed, and look into college savings plans if they are appropriate for your family.

7TH AND 8TH GRADE TIMETABLE

Parents

1. Begin to research and plan a strong high school program that the student can handle. As eighth grade approaches, check your state guidelines or local school district requirements for high school graduation, to give you ideas for common courses of study. Choose a couple of prospective colleges as well, noting their entrance requirements so that you can plan your student's courses accordingly.

2. Attend seminars and meetings about homeschooling through high school, bookmark useful websites, collect books and articles on the subject, and become familiar with what's involved.

3. Investigate outside courses in your area, such as community college and homeschool academy courses. Even if you're not ready to enroll your student, scope out what is available and make a list of "possibilities."

4. Begin to assess your student's strengths and weaknesses. With the student taking some of the responsibility, plan to reinforce strengths and remedy weaknesses before the student enters high school.

5. Develop a reading plan for high school and consider starting it in eighth grade so that your student has time to read a wide variety of classic and modern literature.

6. Think about nonacademic areas you want to cover in high school: character and spiritual development, extracurriculars, and life skills. Begin to lay the groundwork for these goals.

7. For at least some of your eighth grade courses, practice writing up course descriptions, assigning credits, and using a preplanned grading system, as you would in high school. This will allow bugs to be worked out of your system before the start of high school. Some of these documents may come in handy if your student needs to meet a prerequisite for an outside course.

8. Plan a *tentative* lineup of courses for the four years of high school. Work on fitting all the required courses into the appropriate years. Realize that this lineup will flex and change.

9. If you and your student are interested, look into special opportunities for gifted students, such as those mentioned earlier. This involves taking the SAT or ACT exam early, so gauge your student's readiness at this point. Scores do not need to be stellar.

10. Begin to set the student's expectations with regard to colleges you can afford, but at this point, do not exclude any schools purely on the basis of cost. Discuss career options and consider trying some career aptitude tests, either now or later.

Student

1. Become serious about school if you haven't already.
2. View middle school as an exciting time of transition between elementary school and high school.
3. Investigate extracurricular activities. Find out what you like to do and do more of it. Be sure to have fun doing it! You may find an activity you will be passionate about through high school.
4. Begin thinking about possible fields of study and career fields that interest you. Find ways to research, explore, or even try some interesting career fields firsthand.

9TH GRADE – YEAR OF FOUNDATION

Academics

Ninth grade, or freshman year, is a strategic year in many ways, for the student will be introduced to college prep work. But fortunately, it is not an "end-all" year. Some colleges do not even count ninth grade courses in the final GPA, recognizing that students are still acclimating to high school level work. Thus, this might be the year to boost some of those skills that are still underdeveloped. Make sure your student is reading good literature, learning to write well-organized paragraphs and essays, making steady progress in high school level math, and delving deeper into history and lab science concepts. Look for opportunities for your student to take honors courses.

Testing

Students who have had two years of algebra, one year of geometry, a bit of trigonometry and advanced math, and a solid English, writing, and critical reading background may be ready to try the SAT or ACT exam at the end of the freshman year. Otherwise, no standardized testing is needed this year unless you choose to continue grade level testing or unless your homeschool arrangement requires it. Begin to incorporate test preparation into your curriculum, and perhaps informally try a couple of practice tests at home to detect deficiencies.

Record Keeping

Ninth grade is also a key year for the parent in the task of record keeping. While many of the records you are keeping will never be seen by anyone but you, they form the basis for important records you will need later. With them, you will create a transcript, prepare course descriptions for colleges that want to see them, and perhaps most important of all, keep your sanity as you realize that this year now counts toward your student's future educational plans. Create a rough high school plan that will cover college requirements and still leave opportunities for electives and delight-directed learning.

Extracurriculars

The student should become more involved in a few extracurriculars he or she would like to pursue all the way through high school—especially those with leadership potential. Begin to investigate The Congressional Award (see Chapter 16) if the student would like to make this a goal, as the award can take a few years to complete. Use high school summers wisely to investigate out-of-the-ordinary pursuits.

College Hunting

Have the student start a tentative list of colleges he or she might be interested in attending. This year, make it a point to visit one or two schools a bit more distant from your home—perhaps those near relatives or friends you are visiting. If the school is on your student's preferred list, plan an official visit. Take a tour, meet with an admissions officer, and sit in on a class. If it is not practical to make an appointment, take a self-guided tour after learning all you can about the school from its website.

Recommendations

If appropriate, begin to collect non-confidential letters or short signed statements from the adults with whom your student works. This is completely optional, as your student will ask teachers or other adults for more formal recommendation letters during senior year. However, these early insights, which comment on character, work habits, and accomplishments, may possibly be used later in a portfolio or in a counselor letter written by the parent.

Application Essays

Continue with frequent writing assignments that focus on content, organization, style, and mechanics. Although writing assignments can be painful, and you may be tempted to skip them, don't succumb to the temptation. Your student needs to become more proficient so that writing will eventually come naturally.

Spirituality

Encourage your student to be involved in a group Bible study. These are the years for students to solidify their beliefs and transform their childhood faith into a faith that takes them through the experiences and questions of the teen years. Throughout the year, pray with and for your student about his or her life plans and future education.

Life Skills

Ninth grade is another prime year to work on basic life skills. You may even want to design a whole course around them. Most ninth graders are not as busy as they will be later in high school, so feel free to have fun with some "survival skills"—cooking, navigating public transportation, tackling basic home repairs, making business phone calls, and writing business letters and emails.

Finances

Keep on saving for college expenses and encourage your student to open an account and start saving too. Begin to search out private scholarships for which your student may be eligible. If some of these require membership in a group or organization and the group is something you would be willing to be a part of, consider joining so that your student is eligible. Also investigate scholarships or contests that require applicants to complete a project, conduct research, or perform significant community service. Your student may need to get started a couple of years early.

9ᵀᴴ *GRADE TIMETABLE*

Parents

1. Keep track of credits, GPA, and course details using an organized plan for record keeping.
2. Use your own system or that of your homeschool program for transcripts and accountability. Create a transcript document even if your PSP also creates one, and update it each semester. This is handy for occasions when you are asked for an unofficial transcript or grade report at short notice.
3. Begin saving materials that could be used for a portfolio: certificates, letters, documents, photos, well-written essays, reading lists, project descriptions, awards, and similar items.
4. Assess and address the student's weaknesses.
5. Consider whether your student is ready for a community college course this year (if allowed by local rules).
6. Look ahead to AP courses, if applicable, and seek out sources. Think about which courses your student might take in tenth, eleventh, and twelfth grades.
7. Begin foreign language instruction. Many selective colleges want the student to have at least three years of the same language; the most elite recommend four.
8. Begin integrating SAT or ACT exam preparation into the school curriculum. The student will not necessarily take the test yet, but fitting in all that critical reading practice can take a couple of years. Stay strong in math, too.
9. Encourage your student to remain involved in extracurricular activities and community service, transitioning naturally into leadership roles.
10. Come up with an information tracking system for the college search, and designate a place to keep college mailings, testing information, and financial aid information. Additionally, in this "guidance counselor's office," collect creative and practical ideas for future course planning, subject by subject.
11. During family vacations, arrange informal visits to a couple of colleges, if convenient. Also visit one or two local colleges sometime during the year.
12. Keep family finances in order, file records in an organized way, and save and spend wisely.
13. If your student might be in the running (no pun intended) for an athletic scholarship, contact the athletics department at the prospective colleges to find out the procedures and how to become eligible. Also be sure to study the NCAA website for other rules and important information, particularly for homeschoolers.

Student

1. Think about your academic strengths and possible career interests.
2. Get on the mailing lists (both print and electronic) of a few favorite colleges and browse websites, printed information, the *U.S. News and World Report* annual college profiles, and other literature. Draw up lists of questions you need to ask each college, especially those pertaining to how homeschoolers should apply. Make a long, flexible list of potential colleges.
3. "Own" your high school plan as it comes together, and commit to managing your assignments more independently.
4. Maintain good grades and challenge yourself with some honors level courses. Get into the routine of working "smart" (efficiently), not just "hard."
5. Read a lot!
6. Work on writing skills – you'll be needing them in many different subjects.

7. Begin initial study for the SAT or ACT exam by diagnosing your weaknesses and deciding how best to address them.

8. Take community college courses if you are ready, or investigate options such as online courses or home-school academies.

9. Develop extracurricular activities and leadership skills, keeping a log or resume of your experiences. Participate in some community service work and keep track of the number of hours you have contributed. Take advantage of opportunities for unusual experiences such as missions trips or major service projects.

10. Begin discussing college financial arrangements with your parents. Who will be paying? Which colleges are in the realm of possibility? Which are out of the question?

11. Use your summer strategically to develop a current skill, explore new interests, or volunteer for an interesting charity or ministry.

10ᵀᴴ GRADE – YEAR OF DEVELOPMENT

Academics

Academics start to undergo a transformation during the sophomore year. Hopefully, the basics should all be nailed down by now, and the student's developing intellect can handle some more advanced concepts. Some students may be ready for their first AP or community college courses. Support your student in "learning how to learn" in these higher level courses. Although you will continue to assist and advise, let the student take more responsibility and ownership of his or her schoolwork, even to the point of taking the consequences for missed deadlines or insufficient studying. On these occasions, help your student rearrange the schedule and find a better mix of recreation and study time.

If finances permit, begin thinking about summer programs your student might apply for, either the summer after sophomore year or the summer after junior year. These might be intensive academic camps, leadership or research-based programs, or anything that will develop your student's existing interests or spark new ones. If finances are tight, be creative and assemble your own unique experiences.

Testing

Decide whether your student will be taking the SAT exam, the ACT exam, or both, and work on test preparation at home or through an alternate resource. If your student has already studied geometry, second-year algebra, and a bit of trigonometry, he or she may be ready to try the SAT or ACT exam after taking some practice tests at home. For the critical reading and the writing/grammar portions, a steady diet of nonfiction and fiction literature reading and quality writing assignments will steadily prepare your student.

Some students may want to take the PSAT/NMSQT exam for practice this October; however, to be in the running for the National Merit® Scholarship, they will need to take it again in October of the junior year. If your student does take the PSAT/NMSQT exam, review the results when they are returned to you and make a plan to remedy deficiencies.

If the student has taken an AP course, springtime will herald the arrival of the first crop of AP exams. SAT Subject Tests may also be appropriate if the student has just finished an applicable subject. SAT Subject Tests are usually taken at the end of the school year, as soon as the student has finished that particular course.

Record Keeping

Keep up with documenting the student's courses via course descriptions, syllabi, and a home-generated transcript updated each semester. Also update other records such as reading lists and portfolio items that may later be of interest to the college.

Extracurriculars

Extracurricular activities should be going strong this year. If the opportunity arises, the student should take initiative to serve in leadership roles. Colleges would rather see a few activities performed with consistency and passion than a longer list of short-term activities pursued halfheartedly.

College Hunting

As appropriate, pursue one or two more college visits and much more web research. Also take your student to college fairs or information sessions offered locally. Make a list of desirable characteristics and begin to identify colleges that fit these characteristics. Sign up for electronic and paper mailing lists of colleges the student is interested in, request additional information from the top few, and talk to families whose students have attended these colleges. Begin to find out from colleges if they will need any different documentation from homeschoolers.

Recommendations

Encourage your student to continue developing relationships with key adults. If the student is taking classes outside the home, consider signing up with teachers for the junior year who might be excellent recommenders during the senior year. Most colleges ask for recommendation letters in two or more subjects from teachers who taught the student in the junior or senior year.

Application Essays

In English class, over the course of the year, assign two or three essays modeled on college application essay prompts. Have your student revise them carefully until they communicate *who* the student is and *what* he or she would like to do. Though these will be mostly for practice, some of these essays may be quite good and may need only slight revisions when the student eventually applies to college. Begin looking at https://www.essayhell.com/ , an excellent website guiding students through the process of writing college application essays.

Spirituality

Continue the progress begun in ninth grade, encouraging your student to be actively involved in living out his or her faith through church groups, ministry projects, missions trips, and other real-life opportunities. Seek out thought-provoking books that grapple with modern issues and show how to apply one's faith in a practical way. Gradually, your role will shift from teacher of biblical concepts to fellow learner and fellow believer. Continue to pray for your student's future.

Life Skills

Work on chipping away at your list of life skills, especially the more time-consuming ones. Many students pursue driver education in tenth or eleventh grade, so if your student is ready, check into approved online training courses and behind-the-wheel training in accordance with your state's regulations. Whether you are teaching your student cooking, woodworking, auto maintenance, or navigation of the public transportation system, enjoy working together on these skills. Some skills, such as sewing or auto maintenance, might best be taught in a group format with other homeschoolers.

Finances

Some families might want to preview their approximate eligibility for financial aid. The College Board website, the FAFSA site at https://studentaid.ed.gov/sa/fafsa (under "FAFSA4caster"), and other sites have financial need calculators to give you a rough idea of how much the family will need to contribute, assuming that the numbers do not change much by the senior year. And again, if your student will be eligible for athletic, service-based, or project-based scholarships, find out all the pertinent information early, in preparation for applying during the senior year.

10TH GRADE TIMETABLE

Parents

1. Assess curriculum progress and address any gaps. Review your four-year plan and make sure the student is on track to complete all requirements for graduation and for college admissions.
2. Integrate test preparation into the curriculum rather than tacking it on as an "extra." Have your student practice the SAT or ACT exam at home, including the timed essay, and, if ready, have him or her sign up to take it officially.
3. Try assigning one or two essays for English class that could later be the basis for a college application essay. As mentioned above, explore the site https://www.essayhell.com/ to get a feel for the topics and styles of writing that work best for application essays.
4. Continue to talk, plan, and set goals with your student for choices of colleges and for a possible major.
5. Visit more colleges. Discuss family preferences on whether to focus on private, public, Christian, secular, local, or distant colleges. Together, browse websites of potential colleges.
6. Encourage the student to develop and commit to special talents, ministries, and activities, including leadership opportunities.
7. Investigate driver education and other life skills for which your student is ready.
8. Become familiar with https://www.collegeboard.org/ a site you will be visiting frequently over the next two years.
9. Check into athletic scholarships or other specialized scholarships for which your student may be eligible. Remain informed and connected with the appropriate organizations.
10. Look into possible summer programs. Note that application deadlines are often around January.

Student

1. Take one or two community college courses and/or AP courses if appropriate.
2. For practice, consider taking the PSAT/NMSQT exam, *or* take the actual SAT or ACT exam if you are ready. First, find out how "your" colleges use multiple sets of test scores. If they select your best score rather than averaging all your scores (most colleges do), you have nothing to lose by taking the test early. If their policy is less favorable, consider waiting a year.
3. If you're ready, take SAT Subject Tests in the spring for courses you have just completed.
4. Take AP exams for any AP courses completed.

5. Work on your college preference list. Continue to browse websites in general, but also examine course lists from your favorite colleges to see what courses are offered in your major department, and what the general education and major requirements are. As time and geography permit, attend college fairs and information sessions.

6. Keep track of your extracurricular activities, especially the hours of community service you have performed. Move into leadership roles wherever possible. As you coordinate these activities with your interests and passions, be creative, proactive, and leadership-minded.

7. Begin developing quality relationships with teachers, coaches, ministry leaders, and other adults who could later write letters of recommendation for you.

8. Consider a summer job or an interesting volunteer position.

11ᵀᴴ GRADE – YEAR OF PERSEVERANCE

Academics

The junior year is generally the year when the academics are the heaviest *and* when they count the most. Encourage your student to persevere through a full load of college prep courses, which may include some AP and community college courses. Help him or her strike the proper balance: taking the most challenging courses appropriate for his or her abilities.

As mentioned in the previous year's suggestions, consider summer programs in a particular academic subject or specialized extracurricular area. Be aware that application deadlines are often in January.

Testing

SAT or ACT preparation should continue in earnest, as most students who haven't yet taken these exams will do so by the end of the junior year. High school juniors also take the PSAT/NMSQT exam in October to practice for the SAT and to qualify for the National Merit Scholarship competition. Go over the results and target the skills needing the most work. Consider a formal preparation course if your student would benefit; otherwise, plan to work on test prep at home.

If your student is taking AP courses, these exams will occur in the spring. And again, SAT Subject Tests should be taken in the spring for subjects completed this year.

Record Keeping

Eleventh grade is another important year of record keeping. Nothing needs to be officially turned in yet, unless your student applies for a summer internship program or other program requiring transcripts and test scores. However, make sure all your "ducks are in a row" for the fast-approaching senior year. Update the transcript and organize all test scores, grades, community college paperwork, and the like. Obtain and save an unofficial copy of the community college transcript. Keep supporting documentation about your classes, and save certificates, awards, and other information that might be suitable for a portfolio if you decide to create one.

Extracurriculars

Encourage your student to participate in extracurriculars with passion, commitment, and leadership. Extracurriculars should always be chosen for true enjoyment—not simply because they look good.

College Hunting

Interspersed among the heavy academics, your student should be putting together a list of favorite colleges. Emails and snail mail should now be coming in almost daily from colleges, and the student should examine the most interesting brochures and emails. Schedule college visits as they work into your family's travel schedule, or plan a deliberate college exploration trip. Of course, you may not be able to visit every college your student is interested in; you may wait until after the student is admitted to visit one or two key colleges. As much as possible, talk to the admissions departments, especially about special procedures for homeschoolers.

By the end of the junior year, your student should have a well-thought-out list with at least two to four *target* schools, two or three *safety* schools, and two or three *reach* schools. See Chapter 18 for a description of these terms. For these six to nine schools, gather as much information as possible: informative brochures, web information, application essay prompts if the college is not a Common Application member, cost figures, and specific instructions for homeschoolers.

Recommendations

If your student applies for a special program such as a summer internship, he or she may need recommendation letters. Follow well-organized practices as described in Chapter 23 to make sure the letter gets to the right place on time. If the writer allows the student to see the letter(s), this is a good way to discern which of these significant adults can write the best college recommendation letters next year.

Application Essays

Assign two or three more college essays as English assignments. Use the most commonly occurring prompts from the Common Application and/or from your student's prospective schools. By year-end, your student should have a collection of drafts to choose from. Polishing them up, with appropriate style, diction, mechanics, and a suitable organizational method, is excellent writing and editing practice and gives your student a running start on college applications. One highly practical resource I've discovered is EssayHell.com (https://www.essayhell.com/), offering a useful step-by-step guide, *Escape Essay Hell*, and an inspiring collection of sample essays, *Heavenly Essays*. Take the time to read these books; they provide a quick boost up the steep learning curve of college essay writing.

Spirituality

You may very well find that this is an exciting and gratifying year spiritually. Greater mental capabilities, combined with more experience and a fresh outlook on the world, often bring forth spiritual, theological, and philosophical discussions. Use your driving time, in-between activities time, and other opportune times, even late at night, to take advantage of these irreplaceable moments—or is that *hours?* Your student may feel more equipped this year to reach out to others and to put his or her faith into action. Again, keep praying for your student. Your prayers are needed more than you might imagine.

Life Skills

Depending on your family's focus, don't be surprised if this subject takes a back seat from now until graduation. You may be able to work on a few skills, such as driving practice, but by and large, your student will be busy with academics and extracurriculars. If some of your student's extracurriculars, such as Scouts or 4-H, include practical skills, so much the better.

Finances

Both parents and students should educate themselves about the federal, state, and college-specific financial aid forms that will need to be filled out. To expedite this process, make sure that your family financial records are in order. Note that the FAFSA application opens October 1 of your student's senior year. To seek out private scholarships, after signing up for Fastweb® scholarship search service or a similar free search (see Chapter 25), make a list or construct a spreadsheet of the private scholarships your student might qualify for. Include their requirements, deadlines, and other pertinent information. Attend financial aid workshops and seminars, but never pay for advice on filling out the FAFSA or CSS/Financial Aid PROFILE®. It is all available at no charge on their websites.

11TH GRADE TIMETABLE

Parents

1. Review your four-year course plans and adjust as necessary to meet requirements by the end of twelfth grade.
2. Plan for two or three AP courses if possible this year, and/or have your student take a couple of community college courses each term.
3. Register your student for the PSAT/NMSQT very early in the fall at a local high school. It may take a few emails, phone calls, or personal visits to get it all arranged. Some school districts order their tests so early that you should contact them during the summer to make sure your student will be included.
4. Encourage your student to keep up with deadlines, test signups, and test preparation. Continue SAT or ACT prep in earnest, since junior year is the year when most students take their exams for the first time.
5. Think through a workable system to track deadlines so that none of them are missed once the busy senior year starts. Also fine-tune your filing systems for the barrage of print and electronic college materials that may have already begun invading your home and inbox.
6. Update the transcript at home and/or at the PSP. Also obtain and keep an unofficial copy of the community college transcript if your student is taking college classes.
7. Assist the student in choosing and scheduling colleges to visit, beginning with local schools and working up to more distant ones if this is your plan.
8. Get a good book on college essay tips, such as the *Essay Hell* resources mentioned above. Collect potential essay prompts from the Common Application and from applications of your student's favored colleges and assign these topics several times during the year for writing practice. Keep the best of these essays to revise later for potential submission.
9. Begin to investigate financial aid. Some private scholarships require essays, projects, or membership in a particular organization. Consider having your student apply for some of these, and plan accordingly. Also mark your calendar for October 1, when the FAFSA opens for submissions.
10. If your student is eligible for athletic, scientific, or arts-based scholarships, gather pertinent information, contact the appropriate people, and make sure your student complies with all rules and procedures.
11. Look into summer programs if this is of interest. Investigate costs, application procedures, and deadlines, which are often around January. Or brainstorm together to come up with a creative and valuable activity the student can initiate, design, and lead.

Student

All year

1. Work especially hard on junior year grades—they are the most critical grades on the transcript.
2. Continue to develop relationships with teachers or other adults for potential recommendations. Community college teachers and co-op teachers may be good choices.
3. Prioritize your interests, talents, and goals and decide how they fit in with various colleges. Make lists of colleges you are interested in and focus your attention on investigating these.

Fall

1. Take the PSAT/NMSQT exam to practice for the SAT exam and to qualify for the National Merit Scholarship program. When scores come in, review them and address deficiencies to prepare for future exams.
2. Consider taking the SAT or ACT exam now or in the spring; address deficiencies when results come in. Take a prep course or design a home-based preparation schedule.
3. Begin researching private scholarships. Sign up for Fastweb scholarship searches or other free searches.

Winter/Spring

1. Prepare, register for, and take the SAT or ACT exam if not taken earlier. Register no later than one month ahead for these tests. Also take SAT Subject Tests and AP exams for any applicable courses completed this year.
2. Consider creating your student account on the Common Application website. Your account will roll over to an active high school senior account the summer before your senior year; in the meantime, you can explore the application and all its features.
3. If possible, visit a couple of colleges on a school day during the spring or summer term. Make plans for a tour, an information session, meeting a professor in your department, visiting important campus offices, talking to students, and sitting in on one or two classes. With prior arrangement, you might also be able to spend a night in a residence hall.
4. Begin working on rough drafts of application essays, using essay prompts from the Common Application or from colleges of interest.
5. Request financial aid information from colleges. Attend financial aid workshops if possible.
6. Arrange for an interesting summer job, a major community service project, a summer internship, or another out-of-the-ordinary experience.

12TH GRADE – YEAR OF DECISIONS

Academics

If your student survived the grueling junior year, only one more tough semester remains: the first semester of twelfth grade. Here's a warning—it may be the most grueling of all. The student will still want to take the most challenging courses (as appropriate) and to continue working hard, as these grades will count for college admissions. Even for students admitted via Early Action (this process will be discussed later), the college reserves the right to require satisfactory senior year performance as a condition of admission. Some students even have their offers rescinded because of drastic drops in performance.

In addition to tackling the academic load, your student will have the task of completing college applications—a time commitment roughly equivalent to taking an additional class. However, if essays have been drafted during the summer and the college list has been properly pared down, you can minimize some of the stress.

Testing

If your student took the SAT and/or ACT exams in the junior year and is happy with the results, and if all SAT Subject Tests are taken care of, you're home free! Some students, however, will retake the main exam or finish up one or two SAT Subject Tests. Be sure to register for them early in the fall.

Do not forget to officially request that SAT and ACT scores be sent to all the colleges to which your student will apply. This can be done on the test day or completed later on the College Board website.

Other than these, the only exams that will rear their ugly heads are any remaining AP exams in the spring. Some students may consider taking a state high school equivalency exam if this is required by their state or by the university. Certain students may also be interested in CLEP exams (College-Level Examination Program) to gain college credit by examination. See Chapter 19 for issues to consider.

Record Keeping

In addition to continuing with your normal record keeping, you will have a few other tasks this year. You will need to make sure your student's transcript is complete through the junior year and to finalize it and polish it to a professional appearance. If your student is taking community college classes, an unofficial copy of the college transcript thus far is also a useful tool in preparing college applications (an official transcript will be submitted as well). As mentioned above, you will likely be asked to provide documentation of your homeschooling: descriptions of courses, methods of evaluation, key projects, and perhaps names of textbooks and other resources. If you have been maintaining this information all along, you will have no trouble with this project. Go back to your "raw" information from previous years and pull it all together into as concise a format as possible—perhaps about ten or fifteen pages. You may also want to write a few paragraphs describing how homeschooling benefited your student. Additionally, you will probably be writing the School Report and Counselor Letter ("guidance counselor's" documents) for the Common Application, which give information on your school and on your student's performance and characteristics. See Chapters 20 and 23 for more information.

Instead of, or in addition to a transcript, you may prepare a portfolio to highlight your student's accomplishments and talents. Thus, you will need to pull this project together early in the senior year.

Your record keeping tasks are not quite done when the applications have been submitted. For the Common Application, you will also be submitting a Mid Year Report to the colleges, with semester grades and commentary on the student's recent performance, as well as a Final Report at the end of the year, with a final transcript.

Extracurriculars

Again, your student should continue participating with commitment and passion and should now be taking leadership roles. Projects initiated by your student will be an especially valuable way to showcase leadership, so encourage your student to brainstorm and come up with some ideas for launching a project, program, or fundraiser to meet some needs in the community.

College Hunting

The student should have pared the college list down to six to nine schools—though some students have reasons for applying to more. Of these, two to four should be *target* schools for which the student's qualifications exactly match the college's requirements. Two or three should be *reach* schools—the selective "dream" schools to which the student would love to be admitted and for which he or she may actually have a chance. Finally, the student needs a couple of *safety* schools in case the unthinkable happens and even the target schools send rejections, or if finances or other issues preclude attendance at these schools. All of these, even the safety schools, should be schools which your student would be happy to attend and where he or she will receive an excellent education in the major field chosen. If you did not visit all of these schools over the past three years, consider scheduling a visit this fall before applications are due. Alternatively, you might wait until the acceptances come in before planning a visit.

College Applications

The time has come. You and your student will need to devote up to a few hours per week to making sense of all the applications, supplements, letters of recommendation, essays, test score submissions, and interviews. Remember that some colleges will want a detailed document describing your home-schooling—usually from the parent, but sometimes in the student's words. This is where your course descriptions, prepared ahead of time, as well as your insights on extracurriculars and leadership, will come in very handy.

Recommendations

For Early Action or Early Decision applications, typically due around November 1, your student should gather all the instructions together in September to send to teachers and other adults who will write recommendations. Otherwise, he or she can wait a couple of months, depending on the application deadline. If at all possible, the student should initially request recommendations four to six weeks before the deadline and then remind teachers shortly before the deadline.

Application Essays

Your student will need to decide which prompts to choose and will need to finish up, revise, and customize these essays for the colleges. Thankfully, some prompts are similar enough that the same essay can be revised and "tweaked" for two or more colleges. During the revision process, your student should save several versions of the various essays, as some colleges will call for a longer essay and others for a shorter version. Note that all member colleges on the Common Application system will receive the same main essay; different colleges will require their own supplementary essays, though.

Spirituality

During the senior year, pray as never before for your student. Encourage him or her to stay active in ministry opportunities. Also encourage adult-level spiritual discussions, sometimes with room to disagree and sometimes with a promise to do further digging before resolving a deep question. This is the year when you hope to see your student truly "owning" his or her faith, in preparation for experiencing a new environment during college.

Life Skills

Parents, if your student is overloaded with courses and applications, don't make a big deal of ambitiously adding life skills lessons this year, but try to tackle one or two strategic skills, especially those that come up naturally during the course of the year. Fortunately, as your student rapidly grows in maturity and ability, many of these skills will be a cinch to learn.

If your student has not yet completed driver education and training, work out a plan for this project. The more time and practice your student can fit in while he or she is still at home with you, the better, as time constraints will become even more intense once the college years start.

Finances

Check and re-check all your opportunities at the federal, state, college, and private scholarship level. The FAFSA may be submitted beginning on October 1. If your student is applying Early Action or Early Decision, you may also need to fill out the CSS/Financial Aid PROFILE in the fall so that the college can estimate your financial aid at the time of acceptance. The CSS/Financial Aid PROFILE is a financial aid application form that some colleges use in addition to the FAFSA. It is submitted online within the College Board website. Be sure to allow several weeks to gather the information for these financial aid applications, as you will be asked detailed questions about parent and student income, assets, expenses, taxes, and estimated income for the next year.

Keep up with all deadlines and make sure you know where all your financial records are and what information will be needed. The FAFSA will ask you for information based on the previous tax year, so have this information handy.

Senior Year Strategy

As the senior year gets underway, you may be surprised (read: *shocked*) by the sheer volume of paperwork, essays, and interactions with colleges and recommenders—and by how much time this all consumes. The more colleges to which your student applies, the more this phenomenon is magnified. Adjust the following timetable to create the most "sane" arrangement of senior year tasks for you and your family. Remember that your student will still want to do well in academic classes while also enjoying extracurriculars and having fun being a senior. Make your personalized timetable realistic in order to fit in school, work, and unexpected contingencies and still submit applications on time. This, of course, is easier said than done.

12ᵀᴴ GRADE TIMETABLE

Summer Before 12ᵗʰ Grade

Student

1. Participate in an interesting job, volunteer position, or internship—either pre-existing or based on your own initiative, ideas, and leadership.
2. Once and for all, narrow down your final list of colleges: two to four *target* schools, two or three *reach* schools, and two or three *safety* schools. Beyond these, you may add more colleges for strategic reasons if you have the time for applications and the funds for application fees.
3. Visit colleges that interest you. Talk to admissions officers and professors. See Chapter 18 for tips.
4. Prepare a resume of your accomplishments, activities, leadership positions, community service, honors, awards, goals, ambitions, and other useful information about yourself. You may send this handy document to some of your colleges if they allow extra documents (not all do), as well as giving a copy to those

writing recommendations for you. Finally, you can use it as a guide as you fill out applications.

5. Access pertinent college applications and begin completing as many sections as possible. The Common Application goes live in early August; many state university systems open around this same time.

6. Compile a list of homeschool-specific questions to ask admissions staff at your prospective colleges. Summer is a good time to call or email admissions offices with your questions, as they are not as busy as they will be in the fall. Try to get all your questions answered by the end of September.

7. If you will apply Early Action or Early Decision to one of your top schools, note the deadlines.

8. Draft your college application essays.

9. Decide which teachers and other adults you will ask for recommendations.

10. Register for any final SAT or ACT exams you will take in the late summer or the fall. Study in a focused and efficient manner if you need to raise your scores.

11. If (and only if) you have concluded that you need state high school equivalency test to fulfill any administrative requirements, plan for fall or spring administration, depending on the date that works for your situation. For most colleges and universities, a homeschool diploma is acceptable.

12. If you plan to create a portfolio in addition to or instead of a transcript, begin to assemble a portfolio of your accomplishments, with sample essays, projects, and other items. If you are a fine arts student, assemble your materials for portfolio or audition, according to what the college has requested in the pertinent section of the admissions or department website. Note any early deadlines. (See Chapter 11 for tips on portfolios.)

13. Make a list of scholarships to apply for. Gather information about these scholarships, either through the college or through private sources. Make use of Fastweb or other search sites to search up applications if they are available now, and make a list of deadlines.

Parents

1. Check your student's course of study one last time to make sure all requirements will be met for college admissions and for high school graduation. Schedule any remaining courses right away.

2. Make decisions about college choice parameters (distance, cost, or type of college) and communicate these thoughts as a family.

3. If your student is still undecided about schools, attend college information nights or help him or her gather information in other ways.

4. As desired, visit colleges during summer vacation, or plan a visit in the fall when classes are in session.

5. Begin gathering and/or polishing up materials that describe and document your homeschool courses. Scrutinize the applications and college websites for special instructions for homeschoolers, or for requirements that do not seem applicable to homeschoolers. Find out how to address them by calling or emailing the admissions office to clear up any confusion.

6. "Clean up" the student's transcript if you are preparing one from home. Make sure it is correct and complete through the junior year. Enter courses in progress for fall of the senior year as "IP" and courses proposed for the spring as "PR." If your PSP prepares your transcript, ask for an unofficial copy and review it carefully for errors. Also obtain a current unofficial community college transcript if your student is taking courses. Official copies will be ordered during the application process.

7. As soon as the Common Application posts the new season's application (approximately August 1), go through it together to make sure you both *thoroughly* understand what is needed for each college. Similarly, put other colleges' updated applications "on your radar" to check out earlier rather than later. You may discover a few details that need attention before your student can begin filling out the applications.

8. Become at least generally familiar with financial aid application requirements and deadlines. The federal financial aid form (the FAFSA) may be filled out beginning October 1, and it is wise to file as early as reasonably possible. In particular, Early Action or Early Decision applications will need to have this information submitted during the fall. Know state aid deadlines and procedures as well.

September (Some Items Apply Primarily to Early Action Applicants)

1. Register for the SAT or ACT exams to be administered in October, November, or December, if needed, as well as for any remaining SAT Subject Tests.
2. Submit previous or current test scores to colleges.
3. Organize all paperwork and digital communication from your "favorite" colleges, such as catalogs, viewbooks, and homeschool-specific instructions. Keep the paperwork for each college in its own folder. Discard the piles of other viewbooks and mailings that are now causing chaos and confusion.
4. Make a master list of deadlines and post it on the refrigerator or in another central location. Give yourself "soft" deadlines that allow a few days' breathing room for you to finish each task before it is actually due.
5. Put finishing touches on essays, especially if you are applying Early Decision or Early Action.
6. Request official transcripts from your community college courses or from other high schools you have attended (schools that were your "school of record" for that particular year).
7. Request official transcripts from your PSP, or prepare your own official transcripts from home.
8. Visit colleges; try to arrange to sit in on some classes.
9. Register for AP exams for the upcoming spring.

October

1. Parents: Finish the explanatory documents regarding your home school, in accordance with what the college is requesting from you. Generally, the parent completes the School Report and Counselor Letter for the Common Application. In a few cases, another teacher or an adult who knows the student well might complete it.
2. Parents: Complete the FAFSA as soon as possible, as well as the CSS/Financial Aid PROFILE for colleges that request it and for which your student will apply Early Action or Early Decision. When you receive the Student Aid Report (SAR) check it carefully and correct any errors.
3. For early applications, contact the people from whom you are requesting recommendations. You can do this later if you are not applying early, but try to give them four to six weeks' notice. Communicate how to access the college-specific forms and include a resume of your accomplishments. If any letters must be mailed, include an addressed, stamped mailing envelope.
4. Take the SAT or ACT exams if you registered, and request that scores be sent to your colleges of choice.
5. Put the final touches on your essays, especially for Early Action/Early Decision.
6. Submit Early Decision or Early Action applications.
7. Check that your recommendations have been submitted.
8. Keep up with your courses so that the fall grades will be strong. These will be requested by the college as part of the admissions process.
9. Begin thinking about the more enjoyable senior year activities, such as graduation ceremony planning and senior portraits.

November

1. Submit any regular admission applications that are due in November. Most Regular Decision applications will be due in late December or early January.
2. Schedule interviews as needed.
3. Keep orderly records of when and where you've applied, including electronic copies of completed applications or postal receipts from mailed items. Also take note of responses or requests for additional information. Provide this in a timely manner.
4. Continue to research scholarships and seek out applications.
5. Parents, if you have not yet submitted it, look at the FAFSA online and start gathering information.

December

1. Receive responses from early applications. Revise your game plan based on acceptances or rejections.
2. If you are accepted under a binding Early Decision admission, withdraw all other applications.
3. Work on any applications due in December or January, including requesting teacher recommendations.
4. Continue working on the FAFSA forms as needed.
5. As deadlines approach, check that all your teacher recommendations have been submitted.
6. If you are a young man approaching age eighteen, register for the Selective Service within thirty days of your eighteenth birthday. In addition to being required by law, this registration is a requirement for receiving federal financial aid. Register online, by mail, at a post office, or within the FAFSA application.

January

1. Submit Regular Decision applications if due in early January.
2. Complete the FAFSA and CSS/Financial Aid PROFILE (if required), if you have not already done so. Check and comply with all deadlines and forms for financial aid from your state *and* from the college.
3. Send mid-year transcripts and/or Mid Year Reports (Common Application) to colleges.
4. Check whether colleges have received all of your materials. Some of them send emails or links to a web portal to apprise you of the status of your file.
5. Continue with plans for your homeschool graduation.

February

1. If you have not yet done so, complete the FAFSA and file it by the recommended deadline. Some colleges allow until early March; others prefer it by early February. Regardless, earlier is always better.
2. Apply for private scholarships, whether local, regional, or national.
3. Begin to line up a summer job – the best ones go to the early birds.

March

1. As you receive your Student Aid Report, based on FAFSA information, review it for errors.
2. If requested for verification, send a copy of the parents' income tax form to the college. Note any other financial aid-related deadlines, and send information appropriately.
3. Begin to receive decision letters from colleges.
4. If you are placed on a waiting list for your first choice college, write a well-worded letter to the college, communicating your continued interest and providing updates about your accomplishments.
5. Consider visiting campuses to which you have been admitted.

April

1. Receive the last few decision letters from colleges.
2. Plan to attend Admitted Students Weekend or similar events to help you make your final decision.
3. Evaluate financial aid offers. Appeal or discuss any that are not adequate if you have new information that affects your financial eligibility.
4. Prepare to reply to your first choice college by May 1 or by the date set by the college. Send your reply along with your deposit to your first choice school. Notify other colleges that you will not be attending.
5. Study for the last round of AP exams.
6. Continue to keep up your grades.
7. If you haven't already done so, send thank-you notes to those who wrote your recommendation letters.
8. Relax—the decision making will soon be over!

May

1. Respond to postal mail and emails from your college regarding financial aid, residence hall arrangements, and other details.
2. Take AP exams and request that your scores be submitted to the college you have chosen.
3. Prepare and register for CLEP exams if you intend to take them.
4. Enjoy your last month of high school and prepare to celebrate your graduation with family and friends!

June

1. Parents: Issue a high school diploma.
2. Submit the Final Report through the Common Application, providing the spring semester transcript and any other requested information. For colleges not on the Common Application, send a final transcript to the college when the spring semester grades are in.
3. Celebrate your homeschool graduation, if you haven't already.

Summer Before College (See also Chapter 30, "Ready, Set, Go!")

1. Participate in an interesting job, internship, or volunteer activity.
2. Prepare mentally, spiritually, and financially for college experiences.
3. Communicate with the school regarding housing information, roommate surveys, and financial aid business. Also complete paperwork for health insurance, immunizations, and pre-college physicals.
4. Send in tuition and room and board deposits.
5. Attend orientation as offered by the school.
6. Take a deep breath. You made it through homeschool high school and are off to college!

TO SUM UP

Once again, remember that not every item on this tremendous list of tasks will apply to every family. Depending on your student's goals, you will refine and personalize this list until it reflects your student's own "quest" for college admission and, more importantly, his or her personal style for pursuing this quest. Nevertheless, knowing what to consider and *when* to consider it is useful information for every homeschooling family. So browse through these timetables. Choose what is important for you and adjust the timing as necessary to lead you and your student to the right destination at the right time.

SECTION III

MASTERING THE COLLEGE ADMISSIONS PROCESS

Chapter 18

Decisions, Decisions:

The College Search

*B*ecause choosing a college is one of the most important decisions you and your student will ever make together, this chapter is designed to give you a "heads up" about what to consider when the time comes. Of course, not every student will need to launch a detailed college search. For many families, finances dictate choosing the state university system. Others may want the student to stay close to home —narrowing the choices down to only one or two campuses. Some students will start at the local community college and then transfer to a four-year university. Still other students are pursuing specialized fields of interest and thus find their choices automatically narrowed down to a few universities that offer their specific major.

However, students who can broaden their horizons will want to know what criteria to consider as they search for colleges. Enjoy this exhilarating, eye-opening time of exploring your student's interests and preparing for the next phase of this adventurous academic journey.

PHASE ONE: DOING YOUR HOMEWORK

Before even beginning The Search, ask your student what he or she wants in a college. You as parents should also bring up your preferences, especially if price tag or proximity is a major issue. Then, begin searching and see what both student *and* parents end up liking.

Listing Your Criteria

Private vs. Public

Since public schools educate the majority of the undergraduates in the nation, students who choose these schools have lots of company. Public schools are typically less expensive than private schools, since they receive funds from the state or local government. In-state residents pay the lowest tuition rates, while out-of-state students may pay tuition approaching that of private schools.

Designed to serve thousands of students in the state, most public universities are larger than private universities. As a result, students generally receive more personal attention at private colleges, beginning with the application process and continuing with the attention received as an undergraduate.

University vs. Liberal Arts College

What's the difference between a university and a liberal arts college, other than the names? Universities are educational institutions offering graduate degrees, such as master's or doctoral degrees. So in addition to the typical population of undergraduate students, a university also includes graduate students. These students frequently serve as TAs (teaching assistants) for undergraduate courses, with some universities utilizing TAs more than others. In contrast, liberal arts colleges are almost always small (under about two thousand students) and consist mostly or entirely of undergraduate students. Consequently, liberal arts colleges don't routinely use TAs for teaching. While universities offer more classes and research opportunities, liberal arts colleges tend to be more focused on the student. The faculty at universities, being research-oriented, are often less teaching-oriented compared to those at liberal arts colleges. However, students can still receive excellent teaching at large universities.

Some students want a more teaching-oriented school offering personal interaction with professors, including access to them outside of class hours. Others are content with less interaction in lectures as long as they can do research with the faculty. As a team, you and your student can discuss whether a university or a liberal arts college is the best choice.

Location

Before beginning a full-fledged college search, confer with your student on *where* to focus the search. While you may want your student to stay within your home state, he or she may envision going to school across the country. Conversely, you may have dreamed that your offspring would attend your alma mater two thousand miles from home, but your student may prefer to stay close to your hometown. Discussing these expectations ahead of time can prevent misunderstandings later on.

Homesickness can be a significant factor for some students, but fortunately, the worst of it is usually over after the first few weeks. If your student is intent on attending college hundreds of miles away, prepare yourselves as a family for how you will *all* handle homesickness if it hits. Perhaps you can put away a little extra money for an "emergency" flight home, or you can locate friends or relatives living near the college who can develop supportive relationships with your student.

Realize that your student may settle permanently near the college after graduation. Jobs, internships, and marriage may all redefine "home" for your student sooner than you might expect. Additionally, after the first year or two of college, many students find summer jobs near the college and announce that they will not be coming home for the summer. Be prepared for this as you initially discuss locations of prospective colleges.

Religious Affiliation

For some families, a college with a strong, vibrant faith-based philosophy lived out in the classrooms, residence halls, and campus life is a high priority and can be instrumental in affirming and enhancing the student's faith. Some colleges are Christian or Catholic in name or origin only, and the atmosphere may not be much different from that of a secular school. Definitely seek more information and pay a visit to the college so that you'll know what to expect.

If you are not necessarily looking for a religiously-affiliated college, but you do want a college that supports values, ethics, and character, you might be interested in the book *The Templeton Guide: Colleges That Encourage Character Development* by the John Templeton Foundation. This book examines more than 400 colleges in light of how they teach lifelong values such as service, honesty, respect, and personal responsibility.

Regardless of whether the college is Christian or Catholic in name and nature, you will also want to find out about nearby churches or campus chapel services. Spiritual growth can also thrive through interdenominational parachurch organizations such as InterVarsity Christian Fellowship® or Cru®, so check into which organizations meet on campus. Investigate social media pages for the pertinent groups at this university to get a feel for the dynamics of these fellowships. Your student may even consider contacting the leaders of these groups to seek out more information. For students at secular colleges who want a strong Christian fellowship on campus, the presence of these groups can be a key faith builder during the college years.

Size

Size—referring both to the number of students and to the physical size of the campus—can make all the difference in a student's college experience. One student might feel claustrophobic at a small school but might enjoy the sense of freedom at a large, bustling university. A second student might feel lost and lonely on a large campus but might enjoy the personal attention available at a small college. At a small school, friendships might come more easily, since students run into the same people over and over again. However, this need not be the case, since a large school breaks down into smaller groups by residence halls, classes, and extracurriculars. Another consideration is that academic competition is frequently less intense at a small school, whereas it might be a significant issue at a large university.

Another size-related factor is the *average class size*, usually indicated by the student-to-faculty ratio. Ratios of 20:1 or lower are desirable, but these advertised figures can be deceiving. For instance, at some universities, freshman lectures may have 300 students, but advanced upper division courses may have only ten or twelve students. Thus, the statistical "average class size" of thirty students is lower than what you would find in reality. What you actually want to know is the typical class sizes your first-year student will encounter. Some students will not feel comfortable in huge lecture environments and will seek out schools with freshman class sizes of thirty to sixty students. The largest lecture classes I have personally heard of have more than 1200 students, and the award for the smallest class hearkens back to my own college days: a Medical Mycology course with only two students. Note that even at schools with large lecture environments, electronic access to videos and lecture notes provide ways for the material to be accessible and understandable; also, these large lectures are only part of the picture. Smaller discussion, lab, and quiz sections offer the chance for more personalized learning. Alongside examining the raw numbers and student/faculty ratios, you also want to get an idea of how accessible the professors are to students who need help.

Regardless of the size, look for a school where your student has opportunities to be involved in campus activities and to feel at home. Fortunately, this can be accomplished at both large schools and small schools.

Major Areas of Study and Course Offerings

Certain schools are known for excellence in particular fields of study—computer science, pre-law, classical studies—a factor that may help your student advance to graduate school. Find out how each college stacks up against other schools with regard to your student's academic interests or strengths. Also investigate the typical course requirements, both for general education and for coursework in the major or minor. Find out when students need to declare their majors and whether certain majors are routinely "impacted," meaning that more applications are received than can be accommodated. Schools with many impacted majors may require students to declare a major at application time. Admission to the university may then be based on space available in that major field.

If your student is completely undecided about possible majors, peruse websites of colleges with abundant course offerings. Navigate to the web pages of the specific academic departments and begin browsing. This is time well spent, for these searches may spark some interest and give your student an idea of what he or she would—or at least would *not*—like to study. Required and elective course lists for each major will reveal not only the course titles, but also the types of courses offered. Are they mostly lecture courses, or would your student have ample opportunities for seminar, discussion-based, or project-based courses? Read the brief course descriptions to get an even better idea of the scope and content of the courses.

Likewise, using these same tools, students who know what they want to study can ask themselves if this college offers classes they would need for their career or for graduate school. And is a minor or double major possible in their chosen field? Related questions include how many students drop out of certain programs and how many successfully graduate (these statistics can hint at the level of intentional student support vs. the more heartless "weed-out" processes). Additionally, check on how easy it is for freshmen and sophomores to register for the classes they want, and what percentage of the students graduate in four years. If classes are consistently full at freshman/sophomore registration times, the graduation date may eventually be impacted.

If your student will be going on to graduate school, find out the percentage of students who are accepted to the graduate program of interest or to medical or law school. Also ask what kind of alumni networking is available. Is career preparation advice offered? Do companies recruit or hire actively from this college? What are recent graduates doing—working in their fields, or hunting for jobs?

Academic Rigor and Overall Reputation

Some schools are known as party schools; others are politically active. Some are liberal; others, conservative. Some are extremely tough academically; others are an easy ride. Some are down-to-earth; others have the reputation for being a bit snobbish. Some schools specialize in science and technology at the expense of the liberal arts; others are strong in the humanities but light in the sciences. Some schools are strong across course offerings in all majors. Some focus on their graduate students and pay less attention to the undergraduates; others strongly support and nurture their undergraduates. Some schools are well-known for research; others have talented teaching professors.

Depending on your student's needs and preferences, certain colleges will be a perfect fit, and others may be disastrous. By visiting colleges, you will get a feel for some of the intangibles about each school and can discover what is distinctive about each one.

Selectivity

You and your student will certainly want to know how selective a particular college is—that is, how difficult it is to be admitted. While some selective colleges have acceptance rates below 5%, other colleges admit nearly 100% of the students who apply. One indication of the selectivity of a college is the minimum SAT or ACT score required. Some schools express their selectivity in terms of the *average* score of admitted students or the *middle range* (25th to 75th percentile) of scores. For the latter figure, if the school's reported 25th to 75th SAT score percentile was 1300 to 1460, you can conclude that only 25% of accepted students had a score less than 1300, 50% of students had scores in the posted range, and 25% of students had scores above 1460.

Remember that the 25th to 75th percentile does not mean that your student *cannot* be admitted with scores under this value, since 25% of the admitted students have these lower scores. Nor does it mean that your student is guaranteed admission with a score that is higher than the 75th percentile. However, the likelihood of acceptance rises in proportion to the scores earned. Some colleges post breakdowns of the percentage of accepted students with various score ranges.

The number of standardized tests required can also indicate selectivity. Some colleges require two or three SAT Subject Tests in addition to the primary SAT exam. Others do not require these additional tests or may request them only from students with nontraditional backgrounds, such as homeschoolers.

Other clues to the competition a student will face at admission time include GPA requirements and the recommended lineup of high school courses. As you compare admissions guidelines, discuss realistically how your student measures up to these standards. Schools with competitive admissions criteria are, of course, the schools where competition and academic rigor continue throughout the degree program. Thus, if your student is on the low side of admissions standards, he or she might face significant stress at this college if admitted.

Knowing the percentage acceptance rates for each school can give a ballpark idea of a student's chances of admission to a particular college. Your student would not want to apply *only* to highly selective schools, because with 5 to 10% acceptance rates, admission to these "reach" schools is very unlikely. In addition to "reach" schools with 30% or lower acceptance rates (assuming your student's GPA and test scores fall within the college's posted range), make sure your student includes a few "target" schools with a 30 to 80% acceptance rate. Additionally, he or she should apply to two or three "safety" schools with a higher acceptance rate. Of course, all of these must be schools he or she would enjoy attending.

Cost and Financial Aid

While you shouldn't initially rule out a college purely on the basis of cost, you shouldn't be oblivious to the price tag, either. One important figure to track down is the *total cost* of attending the college: tuition, room and board or off-campus living expenses, fees, books, transportation, and other costs. Remember, though, that many colleges offer grants and scholarships that modestly or drastically reduce the true cost of attending the school.

Core Curriculum

The core curriculum or general education program consists of the courses the college requires of all students. Your student should examine these course lists carefully to see how extensive the requirements are and then should decide how happy he or she will be taking these courses.

Living Arrangements

While most colleges have residence halls, not all have room for every student who needs housing. Find out whether housing is guaranteed for all four years, for the first year only, or not at all. If housing on campus is tight, investigate the off-campus housing arrangements. In particular, find out how difficult it is to find a rental, how expensive it is, and what the driving, biking, walking, or public transit distance is to campus.

While checking out the dorms is usually best done during a campus visit, use your "prescreening" web research time to make notes of what you want to find out for each college. Your questions may involve options for campus living arrangements, available meal plans, and number of students who share a room and bathroom.

Setting

Academics aren't everything. The way a student feels about the college's setting—whether urban, suburban, or rural—can influence his or her view of campus life. To some students, the beauty of the campus grounds, landscaping, and architecture, as well as the atmosphere of the campus and the surrounding community (quiet or bustling) is important. Find out what opportunities are available on and off campus: shopping, dining, employment, research, places of worship, and lodging for visiting family members. And, while it is not a deal breaker, the climate of the area is worth considering. If your student wilts in humid heat or cannot handle snow and ice, steer your college search to more temperate climates. Many of the nonacademic factors mentioned above will also come into play if and when the student permanently settles in this location after graduation.

Graduate Programs

A student with a graduate degree in mind may enjoy attending a university with a graduate program in that field on the same campus. While no one can guarantee that he or she will be accepted into that program, benefits include getting to know graduate students and professors as well as the possibility of doing research with some of them during both the undergraduate and graduate years. Some universities offer undergraduate students the option of taking a few graduate courses, thus shortening the length of time toward a master's degree.

Admissions Process

In addition to assessing school characteristics, begin to gather information on the application process—deadlines, forms and recommendations needed, essays and tests required (including whether the optional essay portions of the SAT or ACT exams are required), Early Action or Early Decision policies (defined and discussed in Chapter 20), interviews, and the like. This will help you and your student to mentally prepare yourselves for what it will take to apply.

Calendar

Colleges run on various calendars. Some are on the semester system, with the first semester starting in August or September and running through December, and the second semester starting in January and running until May. One variation is the 4-1-4 calendar, in which the first and second semesters are separated by a one-month interim term during which students focus on only one intensive class—perhaps an innovative, experience-based class.

The quarter system involves three ten- to twelve-week quarters: a fall quarter running from September through December, a winter quarter from January through late March, and a spring quarter from March or April through mid-June. A summer quarter may also be offered from June through August.

While your student will be unlikely to choose a school based purely on its academic calendar, his or her preferences can be a factor when choosing between two extremely similar schools.

Other Factors

Every student's quest for the "perfect" college will be different, but here are a few other features that might be important: opportunities for international study, cross-registration privileges with nearby colleges, opportunities for research, internships, independent study, or student-designed courses, availability of intriguing interdisciplinary courses, and acceptance of AP or CLEP exam credit.

Prioritizing Your Criteria

As your student thinks carefully about criteria for the perfect school, he or she should list these characteristics in order of importance. For instance, this list might read:

1. Small college
2. Strong business program
3. In our home state
4. Urban or near a large city
5. Guaranteed on-campus housing for freshman and sophomore years
6. Internship opportunities available nearby

By keeping the list in a prioritized order, your student can search for schools that meet his or her most important criteria. Note that the list may morph as you go along.

Gathering Information

Once you and your student have listed the desired college criteria, you can begin the search in earnest. The goal is for the student to assemble a list of up to fifteen or twenty schools of interest (the list will be pared down later) and to request additional information from the admissions office.

College Websites and Online Searches

Using college search websites, your student can prescreen the nation's colleges after entering his or her preferences. Colleges can then be accessed through their own websites.

For instance, the College Board website has a search feature called Big Future™ (https://bigfuture.-collegeboard.org/college-search) through which your student can browse information on more than 3,800 colleges and universities. Search filters include location, test scores and selectivity, majors offered, size, type, and affiliation of school, and more. A favorite college can be compared side by side with several similar colleges. The site also contains useful articles on the college selection and application process, choosing a career, time management, and dozens of other pertinent topics. Also on the College Board site, students can explore numerous college majors and career fields—a helpful bonus to the undecided.

The following sites also offer college search features:
http://nces.ed.gov/ipeds/cool — Provides a quick national college search.
http://princetonreview.com — "Explore Colleges" section contains articles, tips, and college search tools.
http://colleges.usnews.rankingsandreviews.com/best-colleges *U.S. News & World Report* College Rankings — Contains helpful college search materials and relative rankings of the nation's colleges and universities.
http://ecampustours.com —Offers virtual tours of college campuses.

And of course, if you want videos, check out YouTube or college websites for official and unofficial views of the college.

Current Students and Alumni

In addition to searching for information online, your student should seek out past or present students as a valuable source of "inside" information. Especially useful is information about colleges where homeschoolers have fared well in admissions policies.

College Fairs and Information Sessions

Colleges regularly send admissions staff to high schools, convention centers, and hotels for college fairs at which multiple colleges offer information to prospective students. If your student is on the mailing list of a particular college, he or she should automatically receive emails and/or paper mail about upcoming events; the information will be posted on the college website as well. Local Christian high schools will have schedules for Christian college fairs held at their campuses, so try to stay in touch or regularly check the websites of nearby Christian schools.

PHASE TWO: REFINING YOUR INFORMATION

Gathering Homeschool-Pertinent Information

As you gather information, you need to find out what a homeschooler should do differently in the admissions process and perhaps even in the lineup of high school coursework. Fortunately, many universities have formed positive opinions about homeschoolers and are quite "homeschool-friendly." Their websites may present useful information for homeschoolers seeking to apply. For other schools, you may have to pry the information out of them. Keep good records of the answers you receive to your questions. You might designate a notebook for information gleaned from phone calls, with a page or two dedicated to each college. Or keep a file in your computer or mobile device. Record the date of your inquiry as well as the name, title, and phone number of the person providing the information.

While the vast majority of homeschoolers choose to specifically portray themselves as homeschoolers during the admissions process, some opt to apply as students from a "small private school." In this case, you would simply submit the transcript and letters of recommendation as originating from a school office rather than from home. However, "marketing" your student as a homeschooler generally provides an intriguing edge. If the student has taken the initiative to accomplish an array of strong courses and extracurriculars, the fact that this was all done independently will add to the strength of the application.

Questions to Ask

The following are some homeschool-specific questions for a parent or student to ask.

- Do you accept homeschool transcripts? Do you consider them equally with those of traditional students?
- Are any additional tests required for homeschoolers, such as SAT Subject Tests?
- Who should fill out the counselor recommendation forms, including the Common Application School Report and Counselor Letter—a parent, or a non-relative? (Note that teacher recommendations are always from a non-relative who has taught your student.)
- Are any additional recommendation letters required or recommended? Are extra letters allowed, in order to give a fuller picture of the homeschooled student?
- How do you view community college credits homeschoolers earn during high school? Will they transfer as college credits? If so, will accruing a certain number of credits disqualify the student for freshman status or freshman scholarships? In this case, may some of them be designated on the transcript as being for high school credit only? (Typically, credits taken before high school graduation do not disqualify students for freshman status, but make sure to check).

- May a homeschooler send extra information such as a portfolio, resume, or additional essays?
- Do you want detailed high school course descriptions from the parent? Is any additional documentation required? How much detail would you like to see?

Visiting a couple of college admissions offices or information sessions, or making appropriate phone calls early in the game (ninth grade or so) will help you and your student firm up the four-year high school course of study and remedy any weak points in your plan. Much of this information will also be found on the college website.

Organizing Your Information

After receiving information from all of the above sources, your student will want to refine that initial list of fifteen or so possible schools.

Your student's list of schools will fluctuate over the next couple of years, with some dropping off the list and others being added, but in this information-gathering stage, don't be too quick to reject schools. As information comes in, read through it to see how the schools stack up against your list of criteria. Gradually, begin to rank the schools in order of desirability and continue to seek more information. Begin to determine which of the schools appear to be a *perfect fit*, which are *very desirable but difficult to get into*, which are *desirable but not perfect*, and which are *acceptable* but do not generate much excitement.

Set up a "guidance counselor's office" in your home. This might be a small filing cabinet or file crate in which you store college information in individual folders (as well as keeping electronic copies of important information). In addition to college-specific information, store SAT or ACT prep items and score reports, copies of completed applications, and other documents you want to have at your fingertips. Aside from the electronic barrage of emails, video links, and social media posts, be prepared for lots of letters, booklets, and postcards to arrive, especially after your student takes the PSAT/NMSQT exam. If your experiences are anything like our family's, your massive collection of viewbooks and other mail will easily fill a large box or an entire designated shelf.

PHASE THREE: VISITING COLLEGES

Tips for an Effective College Visit

Start Early

The earlier your family begins to visit colleges, the more unhurried the college search process will be. Early in high school might be the time for an informal visit to a nearby college, and perhaps your homeschool group can arrange a group tour.

To help narrow down the list, your student will want to visit as many colleges as possible—within reason, of course. A visit should be made only if the student is seriously considering the college—or if it's nearby and easy to visit early in the college search. Often a visit will either immediately confirm an interest or prompt the student to decisively cross this school off "The List." Make a grid or chart of key criteria to compare schools side by side and see how they stack up to your student's "wish list."

Make the Most of Your Campus Visit

A visit to a college campus should give your family an idea of a school's academic environment and also of its social scene. During the junior year, some families like to plan a college visit vacation focused on visiting a few campuses in a certain geographical area. If you do this, limit your visits to one campus per day—perhaps two if they are geographically very close. Taking your time allows you to acquire a feel for the campus without being rushed. Of course, it will still be challenging to gather enough information in one day to make a decision that will impact four years and beyond.

If at all possible, try to visit when school is in session and the campus is in full swing. For local colleges, a flexible homeschooling schedule makes it possible to spend a day exploring a college. For more distant schools, taking a few days off from school might also work. But if you are on a family vacation during the summer and find yourself reasonably near a college on the list, go ahead and visit the campus to get a feel for it.

Visit a few schools during your student's sophomore through senior years, and include at least the favorite schools, in addition to those that are not at the top of the list but happen to be geographically close to you. Seeing additional colleges will provide reference points for the schools your student is truly interested in.

Before your visit, contact the admissions office or check the college website to schedule tours, information sessions, class visits, or meetings with admissions staff. Before arriving, make sure you know where to park and how to get to the visitor center or admissions office. If you have a specific timed appointment, allow plenty of time in case you get lost or have trouble parking. During your campus visit, budget your time carefully. Rank order the items you most want to accomplish, leaving other items optional if time permits. Wear comfortable shoes, for you will be doing a lot of walking!

Seek Out the Admissions Office

Homeschoolers have a vested interest in scheduling a meeting with an admissions counselor or attending an information session during which you can ask homeschool-specific questions. To avoid embarrassing yourselves by asking obvious questions, do your homework first, finding answers to most of your questions on the college website. Prioritize your remaining questions and have them readily available. Listen closely to the presentation at the information session or during your tour or personal session with the admissions officer. *Then* ask any of your questions that were not covered. In personal sessions with an admissions officer, let the student take the lead and do most of the talking; the parent should not dominate the discussion.

Your first encounters with the admissions office will indicate how easy it is to work with this college. If your student does have the opportunity to meet privately with the admissions staff, he or she should send a follow-up thank-you note.

Take a Campus Tour – Official or Unofficial

Absolutely essential to the campus visit is the campus tour. Usually student-led, this tour will show you the highlights of the college. Student-led tours are good opportunities to ask about student life, residence halls, interaction with faculty, and availability of help that students might need, especially during the freshman year. After the tour, venture around the campus so that your student can gauge whether he or she would be comfortable attending here. Try to get a good sense of how adequate the facilities will be for what the student would like to do. Are labs, classrooms, art studios, sports and fitness facilities, and technology centers attractive and practical? If the residence halls are distant from the classrooms and labs, are there other convenient sources of food on campus? Will the student be self-sufficient on this campus, or will frequent trips off campus be needed to supplement study, entertainment, or other needs?

Visit Some Classes

If possible, your student should arrange ahead of time to sit in on a class or two that might pertain to his or her major, or a general education class such as freshman writing. While it's unfair to judge a college's academic quality by the teaching style of one or two professors, visits to classes can give your student a general idea of the college's learning environment.

Investigate the Bookstore and Libraries

You can get a quick view of the school's academic environment by taking a look at the course materials in the campus bookstore. Also check out the libraries to see how useful they might be to your student's field of study. If they do not appear adequate, consider whether the student may visit the libraries of nearby colleges for occasional research projects involving specialized materials.

Inquire about Residence Halls and Student Life

After investigating the academic offerings of a college, take a look at the residence halls, on-campus and off-campus apartments, dining halls, and other centers of student life. If your tour includes a look at the residence halls, ask about the noise level, cleanliness, meal plans, and number of students who share a room or bathroom. One key question to ask, if this is important to you and your student, is how the dorms are set up with respect to male and female students. Some schools have separate buildings for men and women. Others have separate floors or wings for men and women in the same building. Still others are entirely co-ed, with rooms for males and females interspersed along the same hallways. Related to this, find out how the showering and restroom facilities are set up, and what the rules and level of enforcement are for having members of the opposite sex in dorm rooms after a certain time at night. Other features of the residence halls, such as location of study, social, and technology areas, method of roommate selection, or choice of all-freshman dorms or mixed-class dorms, may be important to you.

Check into Student Support and Safety

Find out how the school offers support and services to help first-year students become acclimated to the college environment. Freshman orientation can provide useful information, fun activities, and a chance for students to get to know the college and each other before classes start. Academic advising and personal counseling can help students choose the right classes and deal with problems they may encounter. Residence staff should provide support to the students under their "wing" in the residence halls. Other useful types of support include local transportation, student health services, aid and accessibility to students with disabilities, tech assistance, and tutoring. Ask about the dropout rate after freshman year; this can be an indication of the school's freshman-friendliness or lack thereof.

Safety on campus and off campus can be gauged by asking about crime rates. Though this is a disagreeable question to ask, it is an important one. Also ask how entrances to residence halls are accessed (keys, IDs, etc.), how common theft is on campus, and whether safety escorts are available after dark.

Scope Out Social Life and Extracurricular Activities

Look into the availability of clubs, cultural activities, student government, political action, leadership opportunities, volunteer work, fitness facilities, or club and intramural sports. Also ask about campus ministries, publications, school traditions, and other activities that bond students together during their college years. Consider attending a special event or club meeting in an area of interest. Inquire about the weekend climate of the school. Is it a ghost town, with students fleeing for home or friends' homes, or is there vitality and life even on the weekends? Or, at the opposite extreme, is it a nonstop party? How important is Greek life on this campus? Is there pressure to join sororities and fraternities, and how expensive are they?

In addition to checking out the website, look at the college newspaper or the bulletin boards to gather clues to the political and social climate of the school. Find out about the positives and negatives of social life on campus. Are sororities and fraternities a negative influence on this campus? What are the rules about drugs and alcohol, and how easy is it for students to avoid contact with these substances?

Gather Student Opinions

Talking to students provides critical information available nowhere else. Current students are a source of candid perspectives regarding campus life, class size, and relative academic rigor. You can speak to your campus tour guide or to students that you see in the dining halls or out on campus. Ask them if they would choose this school again and what they would consider its pluses and minuses.

Encounter Some Faculty

While on campus, see if any of the faculty in your student's field of interest are holding office hours. A short chat with one or two of them can clear up subject-related questions and provide an idea of the faculty's accessibility and friendliness. If your student will be applying through a special program such as athletics or fine arts, try to make an appointment ahead of time with a coach or professor in the appropriate department. You can also begin inquiring about the process of academic advising in the student's major—is the student assigned to one advisor for the entire four years, or do different advisors work with students of different levels? For your student's proposed major, is there a grid of required and suggested courses and electives to take throughout the four years?

Explore the College Town

Look also at the surrounding community. Find out what public transportation is available for students without cars. Discover whether the community is quiet or bustling, large or small, safe or unsafe, clean or grimy, historic or modern. What cultural activities, churches, shopping, or other points of interest are available? Since the student may eventually live, work, or even settle permanently in this community, liking it would be a big plus.

Arrange for an Overnight Visit

Arranging an overnight visit is often done in the weeks after college acceptance, but these visits can sometimes be set up during the search process. If you know a current student at this college, find out whether your student might arrange to be a guest in the friend's room and also sit in on some classes.

During this stay, the student will discover what really goes on at night in terms of studying, socializing, drinking, and enforcement of rules. He or she should evaluate the noise level and ask where students tend to study (in their rooms, in residence hall lounges, or in the library because the residence halls are too noisy). This visit is also a good opportunity for in-depth conversations with students, or for attending club meetings and college events.

Plan a Debriefing Time

Soon after the campus visit, your student should make a list of pros, cons, and personal likes and dislikes about the school. Though he or she shouldn't make a hasty or emotional decision about whether this is "the" college, college visits are immensely useful in giving your student a sense of whether the college "feels" right. Frequently these intangibles are accurate predictors about how happy a student would be at this institution.

If you are not able to visit the school, you can get a limited—albeit highly edited—look at the campus through a virtual tour online. View these tours with the realization that the college is highlighting its best points.

Your student should write a personal thank-you note to any admissions officer who spent focused time with him or her or who helped arrange the logistics of the day. Writing a thank-you note to the tour guide is an optional but gracious touch.

PHASE FOUR: NARROWING THE SEARCH

Whether or not you have visited many colleges, you have collected a great deal of information. Once you and your student have spent time examining your "long list" of colleges and going over the information you have collected, you are ready to organize this information and narrow down the list of schools to about nine or ten. Your student will want to do this before senior year begins. Many students will not have a long list to begin with, and others will naturally whittle down their lists without any trouble. A few students, however, will have quite a number of colleges still on their list of favorites. The process of refining the list is difficult for some, and simpler for others. Go back through all the characteristics of colleges described earlier in this chapter and analyze each college as to how it fits in with your "must have" and "nice to have" criteria.

Note that you certainly need not visit all of the schools on the list by the time applications are submitted. Your student may choose to wait until after acceptances are received, and then plan a couple of college visits. This option still provides vital information for making that final decision while saving travel time and money earlier in the process.

Work as a Team

A parent-student team is a powerful element in the college search process. Parents, continue to listen closely to your student and dialogue together openly as you discuss the pros and cons of each school. If your student has worked hard to research various colleges, listen thoughtfully to the conclusions he or she has reached based on this information.

Students, don't close your minds to your parents' comments about the merits of one school over another, or about why certain schools may not be right for you. Your parents will be speaking from life experience and years of observations (as well as from practical considerations such as finances); you may be speaking from emotions or from what you have heard your peers say. Still, if you have information your parents may not have considered, bring it up so that you may have a fruitful dialogue.

In case you need help closing in on the favorite schools, here are some additional criteria:

Explore How Each College Addresses the Major Field

At the beginning of the college search, you were looking for schools that offered your student's major. Now, as you whittle down the list, the goal is to look more closely at the excellence of these majors at each school. Your student should closely peruse the list of classes offered or required for the major. Some course lineups may offer more depth, breadth, sparks of interest, or practicality in order to better prepare your student for his or her desired specialty or eventual career. For instance, if your student is planning for a biology major with an eye toward medicine, he or she will be more interested in a college where biology majors take more human physiology, cell biology, anatomy, and microbiology and are not required to take zoology or botany courses. Availability of undergraduate research opportunities, internships, honors programs, combined undergraduate/graduate tracks, or other special programs will also be important points to consider.

Gauge the Student's Sense of Belonging

Unscientific as it may seem, the "gut feeling" the student receives during the first five or ten minutes on campus can be a strong clue as to how he or she fits into the campus atmosphere. Additionally, now is the time to face any negative issues about the school—and to solve the issues or remove the school from the favored list. For example, if the campus is rather far from stores, off-campus jobs, or entertainment venues, are there adequate transportation systems available? If an urban campus is in a high-crime area, does the school have security measures in place for its students in the form of gates, security guards, campus safety escorts, and emergency alert phones? Assess how important the issue is and decide whether the school's positive factors offset the negative.

If the student visited one or more classes, he or she should think about the class environment. Even though the material may have been advanced, the student can assess whether this college appears to offer enough help and personal instruction to students. Do students ask questions in class, and are these questions welcomed and addressed? Do the professors seem genuinely interested in teaching, and are they receptive to students who need help understanding a particular point?

Evaluate Financial Issues

Chances are, some of the schools on your list will be quite expensive while others will be more reasonable. You may also have discovered that some of these institutions have generous scholarship programs or merit aid available. After making some assumptions about merit scholarships and need-based aid (check out the FAFSA4caster feature at https://fafsa.ed.gov/), lay out these differences in a formal or informal spreadsheet to find out how much you would end up paying for each school. This exercise will help your family compare "apples to apples" when acceptances arrive and when financial aid either comes in or fails to come in. The decision between two very similar colleges often comes down to a financial decision.

Discuss the Desirability of the Community

Similarly, reevaluate the school's surroundings for its environment, atmosphere, weather, safety, or other qualities that are important to your student. Remember that your student may search for jobs, internships, churches, and social and cultural activities in this community and may even permanently settle here. Thus, it should be an enjoyable or at least acceptable area.

Come up with "The List"

As mentioned earlier, your student should assemble a list of six to nine favorite colleges by the summer before senior year. Two to three of these will be "reach" schools (dream schools that may have admissions rates of 30% or lower). Two to four will be "target" schools, where your student closely matches the profile of the typical admitted student and where 30 to 80% of students are admitted. Two or three will be "safety" schools that accept at least 60% of all applicants. Even the safety schools should be schools the student would enjoy attending.

Some families deliberately keep a longer list in place, as long as the student is willing to invest the time to complete all the applications and the parent is willing to pay for all the application fees. However, if your student *is* trying to narrow the list down to a reasonable number and is having trouble, he or she should take a closer look at the selection criteria and ask the crucial question about each college on the list: "Would I be happy here, and would it fulfill my academic, social, and spiritual needs?" Chances are that one or two colleges will drop off the list after this question is asked.

On the other hand, your student may have trouble lengthening the list beyond one or two favorite colleges. Work to select three or four more colleges, just in case the hoped-for acceptances do not come in. After your student has applied or been accepted to a number of colleges, consider visiting them again if needed. Then, *finally,* choose one and send in that enrollment commitment and tuition deposit.

TO SUM UP

Depending on your student's goals, the college search process can be long or short, exciting or grueling, inspiring or perplexing. Additionally, it can be an emotionally charged time as both parents and student contemplate a time of major transitions. Navigate the process with patience, teamwork, and a vision for the student's goals and well-being. In addition, travel this road with sensitivity, flexibility, prayer, and a good sense of humor. With time, certain colleges will begin to emerge as ideal places for your student to apply, and the only remaining task will be to gain acceptance!

Chapter 19

Sharpen Those #2 Pencils:

SAT® and ACT® Exams ... and the Rest of the Tests

Homeschooled or traditionally schooled, most high school students have one thing in common: their dislike—even dread—of the college entrance exams. While strong test-takers may consider these exams only an inevitable annoyance, some students wonder whether their scores will permanently define their higher education path or perhaps even their future careers. Thankfully, the situation is rarely so extreme.

In comparison to traditional students, homeschoolers have a somewhat different relationship to the SAT and ACT exams. For one thing, in the earlier grades, homeschoolers generally take fewer standardized tests than do their counterparts in traditional schools, and thus they may be less familiar with formal testing. Additionally, college admissions staff often place more emphasis on tests and less on the transcript when evaluating a homeschooler's application. Homeschoolers may feel that they need solid test scores to "prove" themselves and their educational methods to colleges. Regardless of where you stand on the issue, this chapter will help you understand the tests used for college admission and will guide you as you develop a strategy for test preparation.

HOW IMPORTANT ARE THE SAT AND ACT EXAMS?

Opinions about how much weight should be given to college entrance exams vary greatly, not only among parents, but also among educators, college admissions committees, and, of course, students. Many believe that a student's record of courses, experiences, leadership, and extracurriculars should carry far more weight than a score on a morning's exam.

Though more and more colleges allow or even welcome nontraditional application formats, and though many colleges and universities—including the University of Chicago, Wake Forest, Bowdoin, Bryn Mawr, and Wesleyan—offer holistic "test-optional" admission policies, standardized tests are still a typical aspect of the admissions process. And, justifiably or not, these tests take on magnified significance in the eyes of an admissions officer reviewing a homeschooler's application. Most of the "test-optional" colleges still require homeschoolers to submit SAT or ACT scores, and often ask even traditional students to submit these scores after admission (during the summer before matriculation), for placement into appropriate college classes. Admissions committees need to have a way to compare all their applicants, regardless of the type of high school attended. The upside of jumping through the "hoops" of testing is that students earning high scores may be in the running for merit scholarships.

The SAT exam (produced by the College Board) and the ACT test (produced by ACT, Inc.) are the two primary exams your student will encounter along the path to college (but see the note later in this chapter regarding the Classic Learning Test). Most students will take one test or the other; some choose to take both tests. While the SAT was once more popular with students and colleges on the East and West coasts, and the ACT with those in the Midwest, South, and Mountain regions, these geographic differences have long been erased. Both tests are accepted by all of the nation's colleges and universities, and both are now equally popular with students across the U.S.

Currently, both the SAT and the ACT exams are administered on paper, using a test booklet and an answer sheet on which the student bubbles answer choices. Essay portions are handwritten, using officially ruled paper. The day is coming, though, when students may put away their #2 pencils for good. Both the College Board and ACT, Inc. have begun testing digital versions of their exams in selected high schools and testing facilities. Though it is unlikely that students will ever be able to test from home, computer-based tests would be a welcome change from the years of answer sheet bubbling.

HOW DO THESE EXAMS FIT IN WITH DIVERSE PATHS TO COLLEGE?

Some homeschoolers seek admission to highly selective colleges; others, to less selective colleges. In addition to these two variations, some students plan to begin their college education at the community college. The importance of college entrance exams varies depending upon the student's chosen pathway to college.

Nearly always, students who aspire to attend the nation's most selective colleges must do well on these exams. High scores and GPAs, strong extracurriculars, impressive leadership skills, well-written essays, and insightful recommendations are the norm at these institutions. Occasionally, a student who is extremely strong in all categories except the test scores will still be admitted, but this scenario is the exception rather than the rule and depends on the student's other outstanding attributes.

For moderately selective or less selective universities, students do not need the stellar scores that they would need for the most selective schools, but they should still try to obtain as high a score as possible to maximize their chances of acceptance and merit scholarships.

Students who plan to begin at a community college and then transfer to a university for their junior year will generally not need SAT or ACT scores to enter the community college, though this practice may vary by state. However, the four-year university *may* require scores at the time of transfer. This requirement is relatively uncommon, but it's always a good idea to check. Generally, the longer it has been since high school graduation, the less important SAT or ACT scores are, and the more important college grades are. Check the websites of potential universities to understand what is required for a transfer application.

Early on, you may not know what your student's eventual path to college will be. Thus, preparing well for these exams is a wise idea and will help keep several options open.

THE SAT EXAM

The SAT exam, offered by the College Board, is a three-to four-hour test, depending on whether the student writes the optional essay. Although the SAT can be taken at any time during high school, junior year is the most common time to take the test. It is administered on approximately seven Saturdays during a typical school year, with Sunday administrations available for students who cannot test on Saturdays due to religious observances. The addition of the August testing date in 2017 was a popular move, as many students choose to take advantage of summer prep time.

The test has changed format several times over the years, morphing from a two-section test with a perfect score of 1600, to a three-section test with a perfect score of 2400. The current version, launched in 2016, has returned to a total achievable score of 1600, with an optional timed essay section. The two main sections are now Math and Evidence-Based Reading and Writing. Evidence-Based Reading and Writing is divided into two subsections: a Reading section and a Writing/Language section. The Reading section contains passages several paragraphs long representing content areas such as literature, humanities, history, science, U.S. "founding documents," and career information. Some of the passages contain charts, graphs, and tables. Students are asked to interpret, analyze, and use evidence to answer multiple-choice questions on these passages as well as on the data sources presented. Vocabulary is tested within the context of reading passages rather than with the standalone multiple choice questions used in former versions of the SAT. Additionally, the vocabulary words tested are words encountered in the "real world," rather than obscure, esoteric words. The Writing/Language section asks students to read a passage containing various errors embedded in some of the sentences and to perform an editing task, as well as understanding the meanings of words in context. Logically sequencing sentences and paragraphs, interpreting information from graphs and tables, and editing a portion of the passage to make it consistent with graph information comprise several of the tasks in this section.

The Math section of the SAT includes algebra, problem solving and data analysis, advanced math (involving more complex equations and functions), and college- and career-relevant geometry and trigonometry. On some portions of the SAT, calculators are permitted; other portions are calculator-free. Additionally, most of the problems are multiple choice with four answers to choose from, but several are "grid-ins" where students must supply answers.

In the 50-minute timed essay section, students are asked to read a passage and then analyze the techniques the author uses to persuade the reader of his or her point. The student is not asked to agree or disagree with the author's position, but rather to carefully examine strategies such as use of evidence, skillful diction, logical reasoning, appeals to emotion, and other rhetorical elements that help the author build and express his or her argument. The student must use specific evidence from the passage to illustrate his or her response. The essay score is separate from the rest of the SAT exam score, and is arrived at by two readers, each of whom assign a score of 1 to 4 in each of three areas: reading, analysis, and writing. These scores from the two readers are combined for a total possible score of 8 in each of the three areas. Thus, a perfect score is reported as 8/8/8. As previously mentioned, this section of the SAT exam is optional, but it is a good idea for students to take it, because some colleges and scholarship programs require or recommend it. The College Board website maintains a list of colleges' policies regarding this section.

SAT Subject Tests™

The SAT Subject Tests are one-hour tests offered in approximately twenty subjects such as English, mathematics, world languages, science, and history. Colleges vary in the ways they use SAT Subject Tests. While some colleges require them for admission, others simply recommend that students take them to strengthen the overall application, or consider the scores in the admissions decision if the student submits them. In fact, colleges have been dropping their requirements in recent years: currently, less than a dozen schools (primarily elite universities) expressly require them of applicants. Others require them of homeschoolers or applicants to special programs.

Subject Test scores can also be used as a guide for course selection or placement once the student enters college. Colleges requiring the Subject Tests typically ask students to take two or three different tests and may specify one or two tests in particular, leaving the other(s) to the student's own choosing. For instance, a college may require one test in the math or science area and one in the humanities area. Check the websites of a few potential colleges during the student's freshman or sophomore year so that you can plan which subjects should receive heavier study in order to prepare for these tests.

For homeschooled applicants, colleges often have stricter requirements regarding how many tests and which specific tests should be taken. Some colleges require more Subject Tests of homeschoolers than they require of other students. While this may seem unfair, the reasoning is that colleges desire to gain a clearer picture of the student's capabilities by asking for additional test scores. Subject Tests may also help homeschooled students clear requirements for specific subject areas on their applications to certain universities (the University of California is one such example).

If the colleges your student is considering require Subject Tests but do not stipulate specific tests, the student should choose tests in his or her areas of strength. However, try to include at least one in math or science and at least one in English, history, or a world language to show that the education was balanced. Two different mathematics exams, Level 1 and Level 2, are offered. The Level 1 exam is geared toward students who have taken two years of algebra and one year of geometry. The Level 2 exam is designed for students who have taken these courses plus precalculus and/or trigonometry. Be sure that your student takes the proper exam to fulfill the requirements of the college or university.

Subject Tests are usually taken at the end of the sophomore and/or junior year so that scores will be available for college applications in the fall of the senior year. However, freshmen may take these tests, too, and seniors often take them in the fall, as long as the score reporting dates coordinate with college application deadlines. Students should take the exams as soon as possible after completing applicable courses so that the material is fresh in their minds. Thus, one option is to take a Subject Test in May or June after finishing the course, and another is to take it after a summer of additional study. World language tests should be taken after at least two years of language study. One, two, or three Subject Tests may be taken on a given test day, but the Subject Tests may not be taken on the same day as the full-length SAT exam.

Scoring of Subject Tests is similar to that of a single section of the main SAT exam, with a perfect score being 800. Preparatory books are useful as students study for Subject Tests. *The Official Study Guide for All SAT Subject Tests*™, published by the College Board, is one such book, but others are available from publishers such as Kaplan® and The Princeton Review®.

SAT Exam Registration

While traditionally schooled students receive SAT exam information from their guidance counselors, homeschoolers must be more proactive. However, it is easy to sign up for these tests online. Just be sure to register on the College Board website at least four or five weeks before the test date. Late registration is also available, at a higher fee. Registration involves choosing the appropriate test and date, selecting a test center at a local high school, and entering the student's high school code number. If you belong to a homeschool program with its own code number, you may use this code to identify your student as a privately educated student. If not, use the universal homeschool code which the College Board includes among its listing of high schools. At the time of this writing, the code is 970000, but check the website to confirm.

Registration steps also include uploading a photo of the student to assure proper identification on test day (the student will need to bring a photo ID on the day of the test). An optional step during registration involves answering questions about the student's college and career goals. This will prompt colleges and scholarship programs to send informational material to the student. Additionally, students who have been preapproved by the College Board for special accommodations on test day due to learning differences or other factors will enter information they have previously received from the College Board. If your student needs accommodations, check into these arrangements well before the test registration deadline; approval takes about seven weeks. Types of accommodations offered include extended test time, use of a computer for the essay, extra breaks, small group or private room setting, multiple day testing, and several other options, depending on the student's needs.

After paying for the test registration, your student will receive an admission ticket that must be printed and brought to the test center on examination day. Be sure you know how to get to the test center, where to park, and how much time to allow for the whole trip. In addition to bringing the admission ticket, your student should bring the items listed on the ticket: photo ID (absolutely essential), #2 pencils, an approved calculator, and any other items noted.

Score Reports

Scores are posted on the College Board website two or three weeks after the test date. Additionally, students may designate several colleges to which the College Board will send the scores. If this designation is done at the time of registration or on the day of the test (or soon after, within about a week after the test), reports are free of charge for the first four colleges, and they will arrive at the college around the time you receive your scores online. If it is done at any subsequent time, or for more than four colleges, you will pay a reporting fee for each college. Eventually, the scores must be sent to all the colleges to which the student applies, but it is fine to wait until the student has settled firmly on a "preferred" list of colleges. When it comes time to report scores for college applications, realize that it takes one or two weeks (assuming that the test is already scored) for colleges to receive them and process them into the student's file. Rush reporting is available for an additional fee. If desired, the student may use Score Choice™ to select scores from particular testing dates to send to colleges, thus omitting from the report any test dates that yielded lower scores.

The score report provided by the College Board offers several useful features to help students who plan to take the test again. Students can find out how many questions they answered correctly, answered incorrectly, or left blank for each test section and discover whether the questions were classified as easy, medium, or difficult. Subscores in specific task areas are also reported; these can be helpful in understanding which areas need more study and preparation. Students may also view a copy of the essay they wrote for the timed essay section.

THE PSAT/NMSQT® EXAM

The PSAT/NMSQT, administered each October, is an optional test that can be taken by high school sophomores or juniors to prepare for the actual SAT exam. Officially, the test is called the Preliminary SAT/National Merit Scholarship Qualifying Test when it is taken during the junior year. The College Board and the National Merit® Scholarship Corporation cosponsor the test to provide practice for the SAT exam and to establish eligibility for the National Merit Scholarship program.

Like the SAT exam, the PSAT/NMSQT measures reading, math, and writing/language skills (however, there is no essay). Students who take the test can discover where their strengths and weaknesses lie as they continue to prepare for the SAT exam. With the 2016 revision of the SAT, the PSAT/NMSQT also changed, including rolling out a separate version for tenth graders, called PSAT 10 to distinguish it from the PSAT/NMSQT for juniors. A PSAT 8/9 is also available for even younger students.

The PSAT/NMSQT exam is only one of many tools for preparing for the SAT exam, since a student can also take practice SAT exams before tackling the real exam. The most pertinent feature of this exam for high-achieving students is its role as the qualifier for the National Merit Scholarship. Although the test may be taken during any year of high school, only the junior year (eleventh grade) scores will qualify the student for the National Merit Scholarship program. See https://www.nationalmerit.org/ for details.

If students advance to Semifinalist status in the National Merit competition, they will be notified in September of their senior year. Finalists are notified in February, and winners are notified in March and April. Scholarships are sponsored by corporations, colleges, and the National Merit organization itself. See Chapter 26 for more information on the National Merit Scholarship program.

Registration

Unlike the SAT exam, for which online registration is simple, the PSAT/NMSQT exam has a school-based registration process. Instructions for homeschoolers are available on the College Board website and involve contacting a local high school well in advance of the registration deadline to find out how, when, and where to sign up. Since the test is administered in October, contact the school's principal or guidance counselor no later than June (at least four months before the test) to make sure that administrators will accommodate your student in the fall. Then check back, sign up, and pay the test fee before the deadline. A public or private homeschool independent study program or PSP in your community may also offer the PSAT/NMSQT exam, providing an easier option for some families.

When registering for the PSAT/NMSQT exam and when filling out the test booklet on the day of the test, you will need to clearly indicate that you are a homeschooler, not a student of the school serving as the testing site. If the student advances in the National Merit Scholarship competition, a packet of Semifinalist information will be sent to the high school principal—in this case, the homeschool parent. For this reason, you should *not* use the code number of the brick and mortar high school where your student takes the test, since the Semifinalist information may not find its way to you when it arrives at the high school office.

Score Report

The total achievable score for the PSAT/NMSQT is 1520, based on a maximum of 760 in each of the two sections, Math and Evidence-Based Reading and Writing. Score reports contain overall section scores as well as subscores and "cross-test scores" to demonstrate analysis skills in history/social studies and in science (even though there is no specific science section). The PSAT/NMSQT scoring is structured to roughly predict the student's SAT score. Since the SAT is more difficult, the PSAT/NMSQT scoring has a maximum of 1520 rather than the SAT's top score of 1600. Theoretically, then, a score of 1400 on the PSAT/NMSQT approximates a score of 1400 on the SAT if the SAT had been taken that day. Presumably, by the time a student actually takes the SAT, he or she will score even higher, since several months of additional learning will have taken place.

Another feature of the score report is information on how the student is doing on "benchmarks" that indicate strength of various academic skills, as well as projection of these skills onto future performance on the SAT and suggestions of which AP courses might be a good fit for the student.

The PSAT/NMSQT score report includes a "Selection Index," used as a qualification for the National Merit Scholarship competition. Cutoffs for Semifinalist status vary by state. For full information, check out both the College Board website (https://www.collegeboard.org/) and the National Merit Scholarship Corporation website (https://www.nationalmerit.org/) for information on eligibility, awards, and definitions of Commended Students, Semifinalists, Finalists, and Merit Scholars.

PSAT/NMSQT signups trigger a plethora of mailings (both postal and email) for students who opt in to the Student Search Service® to receive information from colleges and scholarship programs. So if your mail carrier is developing a bad back and your student's inbox is full, this is the reason. Taking the exam also provides access to a helpful profile that suggests appropriate college majors and careers.

THE ACT TEST

The ACT test, offered by ACT, Inc. (https://www.act.org/), is another widely used college entrance exam. For all practical purposes, the nationwide ratio of students taking the SAT exam to those taking the ACT test is currently about 50/50. Though the SAT was the overall leader for decades, the ACT overtook the SAT for a few years, beginning in 2012. Currently, the SAT once again has a slight edge; still, the rising popularity of the ACT is well established.[1]

The ACT test contains multiple-choice sections covering English, mathematics, reading, and science. In the English section, students are asked to recognize errors in grammar and usage and to choose answer responses that provide the clearest and most correct sentences. Some questions also involve understanding the main idea of a passage and assessing whether the author has made his or her idea clear.

The mathematics section presents questions in pre-algebra, elementary and intermediate algebra, coordinate, plane, and three-dimensional geometry, and trigonometry. All questions are multiple choice, and a calculator may be used on all questions.

The ACT reading section asks students to read four passages in various genres (fiction, humanities, social sciences, and natural sciences) and to answer questions relating to main ideas, vocabulary in context, details about the text, and inferences drawn from the material.

Unlike the SAT exam, the ACT includes a separate science component. In this section, rather than recalling rote scientific facts, students are asked to use reasoning skills to interpret the results of experiments described in the form of text, charts, and graphs, and also to project or predict further experimental results by interpolating or extrapolating from the charts and graphs. One section asks students to answer questions based on "conflicting viewpoints" (two or more scientists' hypotheses on a given concept or situation).

Finally, an optional 40-minute timed writing test measures students' essay writing skills by raising a controversial issue, providing brief statements illustrating three perspectives on the issue, and asking the student to choose a position and defend it with logical reasoning.

Scores are provided on the exam as a whole (composite) and also on each of the four skill sections and the optional writing section. Test scores for the four multiple-choice sections range from 1 to 36, with a national mean score of about 21.[2] For the optional essay section, scores range from 2 to 12. In addition to the basic scores, the ACT score report provides useful information such as how the student's performance aligns with ACT College Readiness Standards[TM], as well as presenting data in other reporting categories.

The ACT test is offered on seven testing dates per school year (including a July testing date) and takes a little over three hours to administer, including breaks, plus another 40 minutes for the optional writing test. As with the SAT, ACT scores are accepted by all colleges and universities in the U.S.

Like the SAT exam, the ACT offers online registration, a special high school code for homeschoolers (969999 as of this writing), test preparation guides, college planning advice, test tips, and free practice questions. *The Official ACT Prep Guide* is the official prep book published by the makers of the ACT, and a host of test prep companies mentioned later in this chapter also offer ACT preparation courses and materials. A PreACT® exam is also available for tenth graders and is offered in certain school districts.

Differences Between ACT and SAT Exams

While both the SAT and ACT exams are widely used for college admission, a few differences set them apart. As previously noted, the ACT includes a science section that tests scientific critical thinking, while the SAT does not. In lieu of this separate science section, several groups of questions in the reading and the writing/language sections of the SAT (and, of course, in the math section) include charts, graphs, and tables, and some reading passages deal with scientific topics, so the differences between the two exams are not as marked as one might think.

With both exams, the essay writing component is optional but should be taken if a particular college requires it. Early on, a student will probably not know which colleges he or she will apply to, so it is wise to plan on taking this optional essay section. The 50-minute writing task on the SAT will appeal to students strong in rhetorical analysis of an author's techniques in nonfiction, while the 40-minute ACT essay will appeal to those skilled at analyzing a complex topic and arguing for one perspective while acknowledging other valid views on the issue.

The mathematics section of the SAT includes a data analysis component, while the ACT does not. Thus, the SAT is heavier on algebra and data analysis and lighter on geometry and trigonometry when compared with the ACT. For the ACT, math questions require memorization of common formulas, while the SAT provides formulas at the beginning of the section. The SAT has "calculator" and "no-calculator" sections, while the ACT allows calculator use on all math questions. The SAT asks a number of questions known as "grid-ins" requiring students to fill in an answer; the ACT math section is 100% multiple choice.

Overall, the SAT presents fewer questions than does the ACT, and the total test time is longer, resulting in more time per question (approximately twenty seconds more) compared to the ACT. With the 2016 elimination of the SAT's quarter-point penalty for wrong answers, the SAT and ACT are on an equal playing field in this area.

After investing sufficient study and practice, your student might consider trying a full practice test for both exams, since some students score significantly higher on one compared to the other. Results of this practice test will guide the decision of which test to focus on. Additionally, as your student applies for scholarships, note whether SAT and/or ACT scores are required. If you are aware of this ahead of time, you can plan accordingly and have the scores available.

SAT AND ACT TEST PREPARATION OPTIONS

Not surprisingly, parents and students can find a plethora of ways to prepare for these exams, and the main task becomes settling on appropriate preparation methods and study techniques. Test preparation classes and seminars are offered by companies such as Kaplan® and The Princeton Review®—everything from half-day sessions to summer residential programs. Students may also choose test preparation books or online prep courses so that they can work independently.

Home-Based Preparation (Including Prep Books and Online Preparation)

Families can choose to spend much or little money preparing their students for college entrance exams. Test prep is a big business, and test coaching companies charge anywhere from a few hundred dollars to thousands of dollars for preparation courses or private tutoring sessions—which, depending on the student's motivation and follow-through, sometimes yield only modest score increases. Unless you know for certain that your student needs interaction and accountability from an outside coach, the money you spend on classes could probably be saved for more interesting pursuits such as extracurricular activities in his or her area of passion. Instead, begin with as many *free* test preparation options as possible.

First, look on the websites of ACT, Inc. and the College Board for sample questions and tips, or check out test preparation books from the library (make sure these are for the current edition of the test). ACT and SAT preparation books by The Princeton Review®, Kaplan®, Peterson's®, Barron's®, and other popular publishers are easy to locate. Another excellent free option for SAT prep is Khan Academy®. On this website, which partners with the College Board to provide test prep materials free of charge, students may take practice tests, view videos explaining strategies for answering questions, take diagnostic quizzes to identify strengths and weaknesses, and find other tips for the SAT. For other free or inexpensive ways to study for the college entrance exams, check out the blog posts at PrepScholar® (https://prepscholar.com) or The Perfect Score Project (https://perfectscoreproject.com/category/blog/). If your student is having trouble with the critical reading sections, consider an intense dive into *The Critical Reader: The Complete Guide to SAT Reading, 3rd edition,* by Erica Meltzer. Meltzer has analyzed every possible type of question on the SAT critical reading section and has organized questions into categories, providing tips and plenty of practice. Meltzer also has a book for the Writing section: *The Ultimate Guide to SAT Grammar,* as well as books that provide the same helpful information for the ACT exam. Be sure to purchase the book appropriate for the most current SAT or ACT version.

Not surprisingly, videos on SAT and ACT advice, tactics, and techniques light up YouTube channels, providing yet another source of free test prep. Reviewing high school math textbooks, perhaps by reworking the last couple of exams in Algebra 2 and geometry, is also a worthwhile venture.

After giving the free options a try, you and your student can proceed to *inexpensive* options: buying a couple of the more promising test prep books or signing up for a modestly priced online course. For instance, ACT, Inc. offers a prep course called ACT Online Prep™, which includes personalized study plans based on an initial diagnostic test and utilizes various methods of study including games, quizzes, and study questions. The cost of this course is about $40. ACT, Inc. also publishes a study guide titled *The Official ACT Prep Guide* and offers free sample questions on its website, https://www.act.org/.

Numerous providers offer online test prep courses, and you will need to invest due diligence into sorting through the promised features, the prices, and the content delivery methods. Whether self-paced or rigorously scheduled, these methods may include live, interactive online courses, additional recorded content available online, user-friendly animations, online whiteboards, and other bells and whistles designed to motivate students. Be aware that some online courses (certainly not all) are little more than a higher-priced version of a test preparation book. If your student has enough self-discipline and motivation to study from a book, this type of online course will add little value to that method. Investigate the delivery methods of various online courses to find one that works with your student's motivation level, learning style, and current preparation status for the SAT or ACT exam. Features to look for include access to full-length tests (including an initial diagnostic test to spot weaknesses), scoring of these tests (the more detailed the better), short quizzes on a subset of material, personalized prep that focuses on the student's weakest skills, and *solutions and explanations* (not just answers) to test questions. Additionally, look for short videos that explain concepts and strategies, a large bank of practice questions, quizzes, and flash cards. For your convenience and peace of mind, investigate the availability of the instructor by email, chat, or phone, the accessibility of the course on mobile devices, logical and intuitive navigation of the course platform, and money-back guarantees.

Classroom-Based Test Preparation

Depending on your student's bent, you may never need to use more expensive test preparation modes such as classes or tutoring. Moreover, classes often do not present anything "magical" that a motivated student cannot do at home with the right materials. However, if your student needs the discipline of working with an outside teacher or enjoys the boost of a more social atmosphere, you might try a commercial course. Working with a live mentor can help identify weaknesses and boost confidence as the student prepares for the next test date.

Kaplan, The Princeton Review, and TestMasters® are a few familiar names in test preparation courses. However, new test prep companies, courses, and content delivery methods are cropping up all the time, both in brick and mortar formats and in online courses. Shorter courses tend to focus on test-taking skills and practicing with potential test questions. Longer courses work on teaching the actual content in which the student may be deficient. Since these courses can be expensive, shop carefully by asking for recommendations from friends and by reading customer reviews of courses you are considering. Look for features that can help customize the test preparation to your student's specific needs. For instance, if you are spending a great deal of money, avoid courses that are "one size fits all" and that do not customize the review material to your student's abilities, needs, and timetable. A personalized analysis of your student's strengths and weaknesses will maximize his or her efforts and make study time more efficient than it would be if the student had simply plodded through a prep book without much of a plan.

Private Tutoring

Some families opt to hire a private tutor to work with the student, keying in on his or her specific weaknesses and providing moment-by-moment accountability for the strengthening of skills. Obviously, tutors are paid by the hour or by an overall "package" agreement, and the cost of this option can be quite high unless your student needs only a few focused hours. But for some students, this learning environment can be just what they need to take their test prep seriously. Ask for recommendations from friends who have used tutors, and take the time at the outset to gauge the tutor's rapport with your student.

In short, discern your student's optimum learning style as you decide on a test preparation method. As you consider the costs, the time involved, your student's inherent motivation and self-discipline, the need for accountability, and his or her preferred mode of learning (visual, auditory, or kinesthetic), you can begin to decide whether home-based preparation, commercial courses, or private tutoring will be most suitable for your student.

Test Preparation Strategies

As much as possible, try to weave SAT or ACT preparation into the high school curriculum. The best overall strategy for test preparation is to start early, even in ninth grade, using the following pattern:
- *Take diagnostic tests to detect weak areas*
- *Review the material, especially in weak areas*
- *Take practice tests*
- *Score tests and remediate any deficiencies*
- *Take more practice tests*

Take Diagnostic Tests

Test preparation books generally begin with a diagnostic practice test used to pinpoint weaknesses. After your student takes the diagnostic test, go through the results to discern which skills need the most help. Observe general trends as well as more specific deficiencies. Perhaps math is weak while reading comprehension is strong; moreover, geometry needs the most review, while algebra skills are respectable. Knowing what to focus on will help you design strategies to raise the ACT or SAT score.

Review the Material

Following the diagnostic test, most preparation books present a large section of review material. Your student can review the entire section or simply focus on the most troublesome types of problems. You might also dig out your math, vocabulary, and grammar textbooks for a little brushing up. Whatever you do, don't ignore deficiencies that the diagnostic test has revealed—particularly if your student has completed more than one practice test with similar results. While it is tempting to dive into more practice tests without much analysis, the student will not receive the full benefit of the diagnostic test without devoting focused review to problem areas.

Take Practice Tests

After your student has addressed the most obvious deficiencies, he or she should continue working practice exams—perhaps one every few weeks, depending on how quickly the test date is approaching. Aim to have your student take five to ten full, timed practice tests altogether before sitting for the actual test.

Score Tests and Remediate Any Deficiencies

At the conclusion of each practice test, score the test and then, together, analyze the answers to understand *what types* of questions were missed, and *why*. This thorough review of the practice test is an essential step and should include returning to the instruction portion of the prep book or to appropriate textbooks to brush up on the topics that are problematic. Encourage your student not to shortchange his or her efforts by skipping this step. Without this remediation step, the same mistakes will recur on future tests. By diligently practicing the problems and understanding the errors, your student will avoid repeating these mistakes and should see a gradual increase in scores.

Take More Practice Tests

As your student addresses these weaknesses and takes more practice tests, the full picture should begin to emerge. Perhaps he or she is gaining ground in all of the test sections. Perhaps one section is showing great progress while another is still in need of review and reinforcement. In this case, the scores will lead you in the direction of future review work. Tabulating the scores of each new practice test can be motivating for some students, but if it is demoralizing, downplay the actual scores and just continue to practice the test questions. In general, scores should rise; however, it is not unusual to see some lower ones as well. Certain practice exams seem harder than others.

Other Strategies

Tackle Vocabulary Words

Vocabulary study is one task you should tackle with your student during the entire high school career, and not just for test prep purposes. Vocabulary is such a key part of strong reading comprehension that it should be spread evenly throughout the first three years of high school. In this way, your student will have a large repertoire of words by the end of the junior year. While the most recent SAT revisions have eliminated "esoteric" words, and while the ACT has long been strong on context clues as an aid for deciphering vocabulary, your student should still work to gain a grasp of words used in upper high school and college-level reading assignments. Some prep books contain lists of words and definitions that your student can study. If you obtain a vocabulary guide at the beginning of the freshman year, you can systematically assign a few words each week for the first three years of high school. Your student will learn much more after 100 weeks of consistent vocabulary study than he or she would while trying to "cram" during the five or six weeks before the exam. It goes without saying, however, that the best and most natural way to increase vocabulary is to read quality literature (both fiction and nonfiction), as well as contemporary material such as news magazines, throughout middle school and high school.

Brush up on Grammar and Usage

For the language sections requiring the student to recognize and fix errors in sentences and paragraphs, your consistent work on organizing paragraphs, writing clear sentences, using proper grammar, and recognizing usage errors will develop useful skills. Again, these skills cannot be taught in a few weeks but must spring from a steady program of high school level writing.

Practice Essay Writing Skills

For the ACT or SAT essay section, the best preparation is a strong writing program teaching the student how to express organized thoughts and well-supported positions (think thesis, topic sentences, transitions, evidence, and commentary). Since the essays are timed, your student will need skills in rapid thinking, outlining, writing, and proofreading. In addition, a good background in literature analysis and rhetorical strategies will give the student material to use for the SAT essay when discussing how the author has utilized specific techniques to persuade the reader. Since these essays are handwritten, some students may need to practice rapid handwriting skills, including legibility—until the day comes when these exams are given via computer.

Consider Other Helpful Preparation Techniques

Several other excellent academic activities prepare students well for the SAT and ACT exams. Latin study helps students learn English vocabulary. Experience in debate emphasizes reasoning and critical thinking. Reading and discussion of classic literature provides exposure to critical analysis and advanced vocabulary. Mathematical reasoning problems and word problems prepare the student for problems that might appear on these exams. In general, a challenging academic program is the best preparation for the ACT or SAT.

When to Take the SAT or ACT

How often should your student take these exams? And when should that first sitting take place? This very individual decision depends on your student's skills, background, and attitude toward tests.

If your student has taken geometry, two years of algebra, and a bit of precalculus and trigonometry, and if he or she displays advanced skills in the categories tested on the SAT or ACT and views test taking as an invigorating challenge, you might have him or her take the test in ninth or tenth grade. After a few practice tests at home to get ready for the big one, your student may tackle this test head-on and come out with an excellent score. The remainder of high school can be devoted to trying to raise this score (only if this is important to the student's college ambitions). Students who view this endeavor positively, as a challenge, are less likely to become discouraged than are students who dread the whole ordeal.

If, however, your student has not covered enough subject matter to take the college entrance exams early or would be significantly discouraged by a less-than-successful experience, feel free to wait as long as possible before testing. Although it is preferable to have the first set of scores by the end of the junior year, some students do not take the exam until late summer or fall of the senior year. Be sure to coordinate this date with college application deadlines, though. Also realize that waiting until senior year can mean missing out on opportunities to retake the exam if the student needs to raise his or her scores. You could potentially squeeze in two test dates during the fall, but this plan will not leave much time for prep in between; additionally, the student may be scheduling Subject Tests in the fall.

Although both the SAT and ACT exams can be taken repeatedly, these exams differ in how score reports are sent to colleges for multiple test dates. For the SAT, the default is that all scores will show up on the official score report unless the student opts for Score Choice™ through the College Board. This feature allows students to choose which testing date(s) to use when reporting scores to colleges and is helpful to students who have some lower scores that they would prefer not to reveal. For the ACT, the student chooses which test dates to report and pays for the score report for each test date. Thus, the student can pick and choose among multiple test dates when submitting scores to colleges.

For the SAT, most colleges select the highest score ever attained in each section of the test (even from different testing dates) and record this as the official score. This is called superscoring. For example, suppose a student took the SAT in March and achieved a math score of 700, along with an Evidence-Based Reading and Writing score of 680. Then in May, the student scored 720 in Math but only 660 in Evidence-Based Reading and Writing. The superscored result would be 1400, the sum of the highest math and highest reading/writing sections, gleaned from the two different dates. Some colleges superscore only by selecting scores from the same testing date (i.e., choosing the "highest sitting"), but most colleges use the highest individual scores, regardless of what dates they come from.

For the ACT, since the student selects which test dates to report, superscoring will come into play *if* the college practices ACT superscoring and *if* the student submits scores from multiple test dates. If your student is taking the SAT or ACT exam early, be sure you know the potential colleges' policies about multiple sets of scores. Fewer colleges superscore ACT scores as compared to SAT scores.

Some students can raise their scores quite admirably by strategic, focused study between test administrations. Others, however, find that their scores rise only insignificantly or even drop a bit on subsequent testing. A student should not take the official SAT or ACT exam more than about three times, especially if these test dates are close together. The scores will not improve much, and the student may become burned out and discouraged. If your student takes several practice tests at home and studies diligently in between, you will have a reasonable idea of whether his or her scores are on the rise.

What Is a Good Score?

The $64,000 question about these exams is "Just what is a good score?" The answer depends on the type of college your student is aspiring to attend. A useful benchmark is the middle 50% SAT or ACT score ranges (the 25th to 75th percentile of admitted students), which colleges publicize on their websites and which can also be found in *U.S. News & World Report*'s annual rankings, called *Best Colleges* (https://www.usnews.com/best-colleges), as well as on the College Board website in its College Search section. This range indicates the SAT or ACT scores of the 25th percentile of admitted students, all the way up to the scores of the 75th percentile. In other words, it includes the "midrange" of students—all but the lowest 25% and the top 25% of admitted students. For example, if a college's middle 50% range for the SAT is 1300 to 1460 and your student's score is 1240, the likelihood of being admitted to this college is a bit on the low side, but not impossible, because the student falls into the lowest 25% of admitted students. Likewise, a score of 1520 would put a student in good shape to be admitted. Similar information is available regarding ACT scores for the nation's colleges and universities. Of course, test scores are only one of many factors used in admission.

As a *very* general statement, scores of about 1000 on the SAT (both sections combined, not including the essay) are average scores and could be adequate for the least selective colleges. A score of 1100 to 1200 would put a student in the running for the next level of schools. The 1300 to 1400 range begins to open up possibilities for selective schools, and with a 1500 or so, a student would be eligible for the most selective schools, including the Ivy League universities. Of course, the higher the better, especially for the top schools and for many academic scholarships. For ACT scores, these approximate score levels would be 21 (average), 22 to 25 (somewhat more selective colleges), 26 to 31 (even more selective), and 32 to 36 (most selective). Again, these are only rough approximations and vary widely from college to college.

Many state university systems admit students based on a formula involving GPA and test scores. The higher the GPA, the lower the test scores need to be, and vice versa. Realize, though, that because some of these institutions do not officially recognize homeschool transcripts, validating the GPA may present some difficulties. Fortunately, most of these institutions have developed admissions pathways for homeschoolers and for other students without traditional transcripts.

THE CLASSIC LEARNING TEST

A quick mention should be made of a newer college entrance exam that may be of interest to homeschoolers. Called the Classic Learning Test, this two-hour exam offered five times per year measures Verbal Reasoning, Grammar/Writing, and Quantitative Reasoning (including math through trigonometry). Students register on the CLT website, choosing a local testing site; a practice test is also available on the site, https://www.cltexam.com/. The test is taken online, and results are available the same day. A CLT-10 and a CLT-8 assessment is also available for tenth graders and eighth graders, respectively.

The test was developed as a response to the SAT exam's redesign and alignment with nationwide Common Core standards, with the goal of providing a test that more accurately measures skills and aptitudes generated by the "principles and values which come from the rich heritage of the Western academic and theological tradition"[3] that many homeschoolers pursue. Students do not need to be pursuing a classical-based education to do well on the CLT.

A growing number of colleges and universities—about 140 at this point—accept the CLT. They are largely Catholic and Christian colleges (such as Wheaton, Thomas Aquinas, and Patrick Henry) that are naturally attractive to homeschoolers. The number will continue to grow, and in the meantime, students whose education has emphasized the Great Books and traditional areas of focus will welcome the chance to demonstrate their knowledge with this alternative test.

ADVANCED PLACEMENT® EXAMS

The topic of AP® courses and exams was covered fully in Chapter 12, but just as a review, these exams are based on year-long advanced courses designed to be equivalent to a first-year college course in a given subject. The AP program has become another frequently used tool among college admissions officers to evaluate students' aptitudes for college work.

These exams are given only once a year, in early May. They are administered at local high schools, and in order not to miss out on registration in the fall, homeschoolers need to begin inquiring during the summer, or even at the end of the previous school year. Contact the appropriate counselor at a local high school to find out deadlines and procedures for signing up. You may also be able to register for AP exams at homeschool academy programs that offer AP exams.

With our daughter's experiences in taking her AP exams at both a public and a private high school, we did not encounter any difficulties at all; however, these procedures are district-dependent and you may have to be persistent and resourceful if you encounter resistance. If needed, seek help from AP Central® through College Board to find a testing site for your student. Stay on top of the process and make sure you know when and where to register, pay, and show up for the exams. Since school officials have so many students to deal with at their own schools, you as a homeschooler may fall through the cracks unless you keep up on deadlines and communication.

CLEP® EXAMS

The College-Level Examination Program® (CLEP) allows students of any age to demonstrate college-level achievement by testing out of undergraduate college courses. Nearly 3,000 colleges nationwide grant credit and/or advanced standing for CLEP exams. Homeschoolers can benefit from the CLEP program by taking exams in their strong subjects, thus saving time and money that would have been spent taking college courses.

With the cost of each 90- to 120-minute exam under $100, CLEP is an attractive alternative to expensive college courses. Students who pass CLEP exams in basic college courses can move on to advanced courses, satisfy prerequisites or proficiency requirements, or use CLEP exams to help them graduate college on time if they are having difficulty registering for classes they need. CLEP exams are offered in more than 30 subjects, such as literature, freshman composition, algebra, calculus, world languages, history, government, biology, chemistry, accounting, management, and business law.

Though created by the College Board, CLEP exams are not college entrance exams. They are simply another way—similar to AP exams but not as rigorous—to earn college credit for knowledge the student has gained. As with the SAT or ACT exams, prep books are available for CLEP exams. The College Board publishes the *CLEP Official Study Guide* as well as guides for each individual test. See the College Board website for full details.

Not all colleges grant credit for CLEP exams. Before taking CLEP exams, your student should check websites of potential colleges to discover their policies about credits and the minimum passing score on the exam. Most colleges limit how many credits students can earn through CLEP, AP, or other exams, and some do not allow CLEP credit in a subject already studied in a college course. (Obviously, in that case, your student would likely seek to transfer the credits from the college course rather than take a CLEP exam.) *Another important warning is that students who later intend to apply to medical, law, or graduate school should check with potential graduate schools to find out their restrictions regarding CLEP exams. Some institutions will not accept CLEP credit to fulfill course prerequisites for graduate work; instead, the course(s) must actually be taken at a college, and perhaps even at a university rather than at a community college.* One additional note is that some colleges have rules and restrictions about how many science courses can be completed with CLEP, since CLEP does not have a lab component. Some of the science work may need to be completed at the college or university.

THE GED® TEST AND HIGH SCHOOL EQUIVALENCY EXAMS

The GED test (General Educational Development) is a set of tests comprising a high school equivalency exam, generally taken by older teens or adults who did not finish high school but who want the equivalent of a high school diploma. Information on the GED test can be found at the website for the GED Testing Service® at https://ged.com/. Administered via computer, the test measures knowledge and skills against those of traditional high school graduates and contains multiple choice, short answer, essay-based, and other question types in the areas of reading comprehension, writing, language conventions and usage, social studies, science, and mathematics through algebra and geometry. The test is aligned with high school standards and college- and career-readiness expectations.

To take the GED test, students need to meet their state's age requirements. In some states, the minimum age is 16; in many states, it is 18. Additionally, they cannot be enrolled in high school and cannot be high school graduates. Specific rules vary from state to state, and many homeschoolers find the test to be irrelevant for reasons of age restriction or other parameters, such as the stigma of being considered a high school dropout.

With respect to the use of the GED test, much has changed for homeschoolers over the years. Colleges and universities once required homeschoolers to take the GED test to make up for the absence of an accredited high school diploma. In fact, without passing this exam, students were not considered eligible for federal financial aid. As a result of hard work by Home School Legal Defense Association (HSLDA), this all changed. In 1998, HSLDA drafted an amendment to the Higher Education Act, which was subsequently approved by Congress, eliminating the GED test requirement as a prerequisite for federal financial aid.[4] During this same time period, homeschooled military recruits were also having trouble because of the requirement to pass this exam before enlisting in any branch of the service. Another amendment removed this requirement, and a 2006 federal law eliminated future unequal treatment of homeschoolers. Thanks to HSLDA, homeschool graduates are now designated "preferred enlistees" in all four branches of the Armed Services and are viewed equivalently with traditional high school graduates.[5]

High School Equivalency Exams

Some states offer exams that, like the GED test, are designed to certify equivalency to a high school diploma. Two of these tests are the TASC Test Assessing Secondary Completion™, developed by ETS, and the HiSET® exam, developed by McGraw-Hill. While they still cover the basics of reading, mathematics, social studies, science, and writing, these tests are less expensive and more widely available than the GED test. Students who pass these tests receive a high school equivalency certificate issued by their state. Similarly, students in California may take the CHSPE (California High School Proficiency Exam), a test that assesses proficiency in language arts, writing, and mathematical skills at the high school level. States that offer these tests may provide them instead of or in addition to the GED test, so be sure you understand which tests are being used in your state. Also check on age and residency requirements. As with the GED test, preparation materials for these exams are widely available in the form of books, online courses, and other online help.

If your state offers such an exam, and if students are allowed to take it at a younger age (16 or 17 instead of 18), homeschoolers may use the test in a variety of ways. Some homeschool academy programs may require students to pass this test before graduation. Other families use it to demonstrate that their students have met the state educational requirements. Still others utilize it as an aid to enrolling in community college classes, especially when limitations would normally apply because of the student's age. If the student has passed the exam offering equivalency to a high school diploma, the community college must accept him or her as a college student. Of course, your homeschooler may choose to continue high school studies even after passing the exam.

Prior to your student taking and passing a high school equivalency exam or the GED test, think carefully about how you will use this information. Will you consider your student a high school graduate, completely finished with homeschooling and ready to move on to college? Or will your student continue to take high school courses as if he or she had never passed the exam? Is there a chance that your student will lose motivation for further high school studies after receiving this certificate? Will the fact that your student has passed this exam impact any important aspects of courses, college applications, or extracurricular activities? For instance, will a four-year university consider your student a transfer applicant rather than a freshman applicant if community college courses were taken after passing the equivalency exam? Or will your student be disqualified from participation in certain competitive extracurriculars? Mathematics competitions, elite sports competitions, or national homeschool speech and debate associations may stipulate that participants must be high school students, and passing an equivalency exam may impact this qualification. It is wise to check on these matters ahead of time.

STATE STANDARDIZED TESTS

Some homeschooling parents regularly have their students take grade-level standardized tests such as the Stanford Achievement Test, the Iowa Assessments™, the TerraNova® Tests and Assessments, state-specific standardized tests, or other tests used in their region. Certain states require this testing, and some homeschooling parents appreciate the chance to assess their students' progress. Many homeschoolers, on the other hand, enjoy exercising their freedom *from* standardized tests. If you regularly opt for such tests, you may wonder whether your student should continue taking them throughout high school. Your decision depends on your reasons for doing the testing.

If your student is not yet ready for the SAT or ACT exams, but you would like an annual benchmark of progress and exposure to a formal standardized test environment, feel free to have your student continue to take these tests. Scores may also come in handy as supplementary data if you need to clear prerequisites for community college courses. For instance, if your student wants to take a math class and you can provide the community college with high math test scores and a grade report from the prerequisite course, these items may be all the college needs to approve your student's enrollment.

If your student is ready to try the PSAT/NMSQT, the SAT, or the ACT early in high school, you may choose to let your student prioritize test preparation for these exams rather than continuing the grade level tests. An exception, of course, would be if your state or homeschool program requires homeschoolers to take yearly standardized tests.

COLLEGE-BASED TESTS

Some universities require admitted students to take writing proficiency exams or placement exams in math or in languages other than English (sometimes called assessments) prior to registration. These exams assess the student's skills in order to place him or her into the appropriate course at the college. During the application process, be aware of what exams will be required so that your student can decide whether he or she will need to invest any prep time for them. It is possible that some of these tests can be taken ahead of time if they are available locally or online. They may also be part of the freshman orientation your student will attend during the summer or just before beginning classes. Once your student has committed to attend the university, check out the requirements and dates for these exams.

More pertinent to the day-to-day life of a homeschooler are placement or assessment exams at the community college. For certain courses (often math and English, sometimes science), students need to take a placement exam before being allowed to register for a particular course. Schedules of placement exams are posted on the college website in the weeks before each new term begins, and students usually have several different dates and times to choose from. Rules will vary as to whether retakes are allowed and whether other methods (such as scores on Advanced Placement exams) can be used to challenge the assessment process. The community college website or admissions office will likely offer suggestions for preparation books or online review material.

TEST-TAKING STRATEGIES

Entire books have been written about test-taking strategies or "how to crack" the SAT or ACT exams. Without duplicating information you can find elsewhere, here are a few thoughts and tips to get you going in the right direction. Because the student, not the parent, will be taking the exam, this section is addressed to the student.

General Tips for All Tests

Before the test:

- As you complete practice tests, always learn from your mistakes by consulting the answer key and understanding *why* you missed what you missed.
- Become accustomed to the time limits on the various sections of the test and follow them to the minute when practicing. During practice tests, if you run out of time, mark the point at which the time was up and use only those answers to calculate your score. Then continue answering the rest of the questions, so that you can benefit from all available practice questions.
- Be sure you understand the general test directions before the test day. Preview the latest instructions from the College Board or ACT website, not necessarily from your prep book.
- Before registering, make sure you have a proper photo ID. If you don't have a driver's license or government-issued ID, find out *ahead of time* what is an acceptable form of ID.
- Understand which calculator types are allowed and which are prohibited. If your calculator is prohibited, borrow one from a friend or family member before the test, and practice using it.
- Pay *serious* attention to lists of prohibited items (phones, cameras, tablets, etc.) as explained on the College Board or ACT website. For instance, the use of a cell phone, even during breaks, can result in cancellation of your scores.
- Be aware that the directions for some of the SAT Subject Tests vary, depending on the subject. Language tests have a listening segment with specific types of audio equipment required.
- Prepare all your materials the night before: pencils, eraser, admission ticket, photo ID, approved calculator, snack, and other required or acceptable materials.
- Get a good night's sleep before the test, and eat a nutritious but not overly heavy breakfast. Bring a healthy snack and a drink to revive you during your break.
- Arrive at the testing center early, allowing a margin of time for traffic problems. Remember that parking the car, locating the proper room, and checking in will all take time.

During the test:

- Become familiar with the answer sheet. Answer your questions in the proper section and column of the answer sheet. Mark the answer bubbles clearly, make no stray marks on the sheet, and completely erase any answers you change. Usually you may do scratch work in the test book and transfer your final answer to the answer sheet, but understand the rules on this.
- Don't panic if you encounter difficult questions. You are not expected to know all the answers in order to get a good score. Keep going!
- If you are stumped on certain questions, try to reason out the answer using common sense. Often you can figure them out, even with limited information.
- Watch your time. Answer the easiest questions first, coming back to the more difficult ones as time permits. To save time later, mark the questions you want to come back to and cross off the answer choices you have already eliminated.

Homeschooled & Headed for College

- Especially if you are skipping questions, pay attention to where you are on the answer sheet and avoid getting off track in marking the answers. After every few problems, compare the question number to the number on the answer sheet.
- Don't spend too much time on any one passage or question, since all questions are of equal value.
- After reading a question, anticipate the possible answer before looking at the choices.
- Be sure you are answering the question that is actually being asked. Don't be tricked into providing a partial or preliminary answer.
- Utilize every ounce of your focus, confidence and effort. Put 100% into taking the test, and don't slack off or become discouraged, even though the session is long and grueling.
- Check your work if you finish before time is called. In particular, make certain you have marked answers in the proper place.

Tips for Reading Sections

- As you read the passages, mark words or phrases that may be important and look for main ideas, author's tone, comparisons, contrasts, symbols, and author techniques. This alertness will help you focus on the passage so you don't have to reread it.
- Beware of words such as "always" or "never," which are often a red flag that this particular multiple choice answer may be invalid.
- Look for shades of meaning among vocabulary words, to distinguish between a good answer and the best answer.

Tips for Mathematics Sections

- Do your work on scratch paper (usually the test booklet itself). It is a mistake to try to keep all the calculations in your head as you work the problem.
- Read the questions carefully. Don't rashly assume that you know what the question is asking for. Some questions are worded very specifically to elicit the correct answer, which may *not* be the answer you choose after only a superficial reading.
- Check to see that your numerical answer sounds reasonable in the context of the question. If it appears that you are off by a factor of ten or one hundred, go back and look again.
- Use good judgment on when to use a calculator. Some problems can be solved more quickly with common sense solutions than with elaborate calculations.
- Make use of the list of formulas given at the beginning of the SAT mathematics section. (The ACT exam does not provide formulas.)
- Don't hesitate to draw a diagram of the problem to help you visualize it.
- Avoid solving problems by working backward from the multiple-choice answers given. This is time consuming. Instead, try to solve the problem and then check to see what answers are given.

Tips for ACT Science Sections

- As with other sections, do plenty of practice tests so that you are comfortable with the format of the section and the types of information and questions you will encounter.
- Bear in mind that you do not need a tremendous amount of specific science knowledge; in particular, you do not need to memorize formulas and facts. Nearly all the information you need is provided in the description of the experiment and in the graphs and tables accompanying it. You may need knowledge of a couple of general scientific principles to go along with this information.

- Keep track of the units and scales being used on the graphs; these will figure into the answer.
- Stay calm, stay on your toes, and use your skills of careful reading, critical reasoning, and observation of trends in charts, graphs, and tables.
- Sometimes the answers are easier and more obvious than you might expect. Avoid overthinking.
- One section of the science test asks you to consider two or more viewpoints or hypotheses on a certain observation or experiment. As you read these viewpoints, mark key ideas and terminology so that you can quickly come back and compare these without rereading the entire description.

Tips for Timed Essays

- Practice as many essays as you have time for. Make sure you go into the test having written at least seven or eight of these timed essays.
- Find a teacher or mentor to evaluate your essays and give them approximate scores.
- Understand the writing task objectives and guidelines ahead of time so that you don't waste precious time reading the directions. The instructions are standardized; only the topics change.
- Read the prompt and/or passage carefully and then quickly outline your essay, noting the stand you will take on the issue, the main points you will make, and the evidence you will use.
- Planning the essay is the hardest but most important task. If you can increase your skills and speed here, you will have an easier time with the actual writing.
- *Always* support your main point with specific examples and strong reasoning, not generalities.
- Try to write as much as you can. Studies show that higher scores correlate well with longer essays.
- Write legibly. If your handwriting is normally very difficult to read, devote some focused practice to rapid, legible cursive or printing.
- Save at least two minutes at the end to revise and proofread your essay.

TO SUM UP

SAT, ACT, CLEP, AP, GED, CLT, PSAT/NMSQT—the alphabet soup of standardized tests can appear shrouded in stress-producing mystery. By visiting the websites of these test makers early and often, college bound students can become familiar with what they will be up against during the last half of high school. From there, they can gather useful information that will translate to a fruitful season of test preparation.

1. Strauss, Valerie, "Why ACT Overtook SAT as Top College Entrance Exam," *Washington Post,* The Washington Post, September 2012. Accessed September 3, 2018. https://www.washingtonpost.com/blogs/answer-sheet/post/how-act-overtook-sat-as-the-top-college-entrance-exam/2012/09/24/d56df11c-0674-11e2-afff-d6c7f20a83bf_blog.html?utm_term=.7ca7a074218a.
2. ACT, Inc., "National Distributions of Cumulative Percents for ACT Test Scores: ACT-Tested High School Graduates from 2015, 2016 and 2017," *ACT.org.*, ACT, Inc., 2018. Accessed September 3, 2018.
https://www.act.org/content/dam/act/unsecured/documents/MultipleChoiceStemComposite2017-18.pdf.
3. The Classic Learning Test, "FAQ," Classic Learning Test, 2018. Accessed September 3, 2018. https://www.cltexam.com/faq.
4. Home School Legal Defense Association, "Victory Over College Discrimination," *HSLDA News,* HSLDA.org, June 17, 2002. Accessed September 3, 2018. https://hslda.org/content/docs/news/hslda/200206170.asp
5. Estrada, William A., Esq., "Armed Forces Finally Accept Homeschool Enlistees on Equal Terms," HSLDA.org, March 18, 2014. Accessed September 3, 2018. https://hslda.org/content/docs/news/2014/201403180.asp.

Chapter 20

Information, Please:

A Tour of a Typical College Application

The time has come. Your student is ready to sit down, log on, and type away at that very first college application. Three-plus years of high school must now be summed up succinctly on a few screens and must be intriguing enough to catch the attention of the admissions staff. Although the maze of application options, deadlines, forms, and instructions can be mind-boggling, this chapter will guide you and your student as you seek to communicate the best possible information to the colleges.

APPROACHING THE APPLICATION: A FEW PIECES OF ADVICE

"Work Smart" When Applying to Multiple Colleges

Many students have a single favorite college in mind, which they would love to attend. However, applying to only one college, especially if it's a selective one, is not a wise idea. Instead, students should wrap up their college-searching adventures by grouping their preferred colleges into three categories: target schools, safety schools, and reach schools.

Target schools are colleges for which the student's background and achievements (GPA, test scores, rigor of courses, and extracurricular resume) closely match the profile of students the college typically accepts. In a perfect world, these would be the colleges to which the student should confidently expect to receive acceptances; however, a "target" school for one student may be a "safety" school for students who are in the running for elite Ivy League schools. Thus, students may receive a few rejections even from these schools to which their backgrounds are perfectly matched.

Safety schools are colleges for which the student is, in a sense, "overqualified." Your student's GPA and test scores are comfortably or even greatly above the middle 50% SAT or ACT score ranges posted on college websites. Again, in an ideal world, your student should receive acceptances from 100% of his or her safety schools, but in today's highly competitive college admissions environment, this rate might not hit 100%.

Reach schools are "dream schools." The admission requirements are high—perhaps a nudge higher than where your student stacks up, but not so stratospheric that there is no hope of admission. These are colleges and universities that your student has researched, has fallen in love with, and has at least a reasonable shot at attending. A dose of realism is important even when dreaming about reach schools. Students with GPAs of 2.0 and SAT scores of 1100 need to understand that Harvard is not a feasible goal.

Most students apply to at least half a dozen schools; many apply to ten or fifteen. Each college or university added to the list should be added for a reason, and, importantly, each one should be a college which the student would be happy to attend and where his or her chosen major is offered with a high-quality course lineup. Refrain from frivolously adding extra colleges to the list—such whims can add many hours to the application process and many dollars to the tally of application fees and test score submission fees.

If you and your student have carefully and thoughtfully assembled a strategic list of colleges, this foresight will be rewarded later when admission decisions begin to come in. You can then compare colleges on the basis of their important variables: location, strength of the major program, financial aid, and the academic, social, and spiritual atmosphere of the campus. Your student may even be in the enviable position of having several colleges "recruiting" him or her.

As fall of senior year approaches, keep the lines of communication open as you and your student do that last bit of discussion and soul-searching. Listen to your student's impressions of the various colleges, and pick up on spoken or unspoken messages he or she might be sending about readiness and college preferences. Encourage your student to articulate what he or she would like in a college. Then prepare to tackle those application websites.

Help the Student Take Ownership of the Process

So far, homeschooling has been a team-oriented but parent-driven effort. But as college applications get seriously underway, the student must take true ownership of the process. Parents can help and support, and it is still a team effort, but the student's motivation must drive the process. If the application is completed mostly by the parents, this "hovering" does not speak well of the student's maturity and ability to handle the rigors of college life.

Like it or not, the college application is an exercise in marketing. The student is trying to convince the admissions staff that he or she will be an asset to the school, and the admissions staff is trying to promote the college while discerning which students to accept—all based on a few data points and a couple of essays. The college is asking questions such as "What are your strengths?" and "How are you different from, and superior to, the other applicants, both academically and socially?" Clearly, the college application is not a time for false modesty. Students must use this opportunity to distinctly communicate their talents, strengths, and gifts.

Decide How to Apply

Online Applications

Though paper applications do exist for students without computer access, the online application is the norm. Check prospective colleges' websites, even a couple of years in advance, to get a sneak preview of their application formats. Some colleges have a printable version of their application available on their sites to allow you to view it in its entirety. However, for many schools, you will need to log in to the application site in order to see all of its sections. If you want to take a look before your student is actually ready to apply, set up a fictitious student account, using an alternate email address and a different name so that this information will not be confused with your "real" information later (though the Common Application® allows a practice account to be set up ahead of time and then to "roll over" just before senior year).

The Common Application®

The Common Application (https://www.commonapp.org/) is a time-saving tool for students who plan to apply to several colleges, saving them from entering the same information over and over again. Originally launched in 1975 with a group of 15 colleges, this service now includes almost 900 member colleges for freshman applications and provides a standard online application form that can be submitted to multiple colleges. In addition to answering the garden-variety questions relating to personal and family information, extracurricular activities, and test scores, the student writes and submits one main application essay. Teachers and counselors, including homeschool parents, provide their recommendations online, "once and done." Transcripts are uploaded along with the counselor evaluation.

The Common Application processes several million online applications every year from approximately one million student applicants. However, not all colleges use the Common Application, so find out if your student's favored schools accept it. While some colleges utilize the Common Application exclusively, others accept both this application and their own. In the latter scenario, it doesn't matter which application your student uses—all of the Common Application member colleges have signed an agreement stating their intent to treat the Common Application as if it were school-specific.

Within the Common Application, students may need to submit several college-specific supplements in addition to the basic application. These supplements, ranging from simple to complex, may ask a few short questions about the student's intended major or may request personal information such as whether any relatives have attended the college. Additionally, they may require several short or full-length essays.

In addition to applications for first-year students, the Common Application offers a transfer application, with about 650 institutions currently participating.

GETTING ACQUAINTED

Until you get the hang of the Common Application, you may encounter a few rough spots as you navigate through it, or you may get stuck on the best way to answer certain questions. Help is readily available all over the web. In addition to utilizing the Common Application's on-screen Help features and its Applicant Solutions Center available 24/7/365, you can submit specific help requests. Also take a look at helpful YouTube videos (just search "Common Application" and your topic). Additionally, Khan Academy® has a section for homeschoolers, outlining the differences homeschooled students will encounter in the college application process and showing a sample School Report and transcript as they might be completed by a homeschooler. And finally, you can follow #commonapp on social media.

Before tackling your student's actual college application, both you and your student can set up practice accounts: your student would set up an account as a student applicant, and you as the parent/counselor can set up an account as an education professional. A student who is setting up an account several months before he or she is actually ready to work on applications will "roll over" the account into the next school year and thus should be sure to use an email that he or she will check regularly.

Other College Application Scenarios

The Common Application is not the only application allowing students to submit to multiple colleges. More recent players that have arrived on the scene are the Universal College Application℠, the Coalition for College, and QuestBridge®.

The Universal College Application (UCA), https://www.universalcollegeapp.com/, established in

2007, is used by about 16 institutions as of this writing. These include several elite universities such as Harvard, Cornell, and Princeton, as well as a spectrum of other colleges and universities. Featuring an online student application with a fairly open-ended personal statement prompt, recommender forms, a school report for counselors, supplementary forms for arts and athletics, and a separate application for transfer students, this application accomplishes the same goals as the Common Application by streamlining the application process for students and recommenders. Most of the schools on the UCA also accept the Common Application.

The Coalition for College, http://www.coalitionforcollegeaccess.org/, has over 140 member institutions, including all the Ivy League universities, and its goal is to foster more of the values that epitomize true learning and engagement. To this end, the Coalition seeks to downplay the current trend of students loading up on excessive numbers of AP® courses and stockpiling impressive line items on their resumes, frequently at the expense of showing true passion for life and learning. Instead, the Coalition desires to promote a portfolio approach to college preparation and applications, whereby students are encouraged to explore, experiment, develop, and sharpen their talents and skills from ninth grade on. Another objective of the CAAS is to increase accessibility to college for all students, especially across demographic and economic lines. Member colleges are committed to keeping tuition affordable and/or meeting students' financial needs. The CAAS includes a handy feature called "The Locker" where students can "store" items they create and assemble earlier in the high school years: essays, artwork, projects, awards, videos, or similar creations. Later, they may utilize these personalized items during a portfolio-centered college application process.

QuestBridge, https://www.questbridge.org/, is a nonprofit organization that offers low-income students the chance to be matched into colleges and universities that will offer them full four-year scholarships. Many of the member colleges are highly selective institutions that are actively seeking high-achieving students who, for financial reasons, might not otherwise consider applying. The program actually begins during the junior year with the College Prep Scholars program. Starting in February of the junior year, students may apply for the program by submitting an application, essay, transcript, SAT®, PSAT/NMSQT®, or ACT® scores, a letter of recommendation, and financial information. Based on this information, some students will be chosen as Finalists in the National College Match program; other perks include the possibility of paid campus visits, scholarships to summer programs, and other awards. The National College Match has its own application that opens the summer before the senior year. Deadlines are in late September, significantly earlier than typical college deadlines. Students fill out the application and submit two letters of recommendation, a transcript, test scores, and a Secondary School Report from the counselor. If chosen as Finalists, students rank up to twelve colleges in order of preference, and commit to attending any school that might accept them. The matching process involves being admitted to the college that appears highest on a student's list and that also wants to admit that student. For full details, visit the QuestBridge website.

State university systems usually utilize less complicated applications; still, these may come with their own quirks. For instance, personal essays, teacher recommendations, and lists of extracurricular activities may not be required on some public university applications, but students may be asked to enter their high school courses one by one to make it easier for the admissions office to evaluate whether requirements have been met. Check out your state's public university system early in the game to understand what will be required and to find out if there are any differences or difficulties for homeschooled students.

Decide When to Apply

When it comes to the timing of submitting college applications, students have a number of options. Knowing the terminology, as well as the pros and cons of each option, can help students and parents as they plan the senior year.

Regular Decision

Regular Decision is the admissions schedule used by most applicants. Application deadlines range from late November to February—most commonly around January 1—and admissions decisions are announced in March or April, possibly even earlier. No limitations are placed on the number of colleges to which the student may apply. Note that even with Regular Decision, some students—such as those submitting an arts portfolio or those applying for college-sponsored merit scholarships—may need to meet earlier deadlines. Always read the college websites thoroughly and carefully with respect to deadlines.

Rolling Admissions

Colleges that use Rolling Admissions evaluate applications as they receive them and then respond to the applicant within a few weeks, rather than collecting all applications in one batch and notifying students all at once, as in Regular Decision. Applications are often processed within four to six weeks following submission. While some colleges still maintain application deadlines or "priority deadlines," certain Rolling Admissions schools don't have hard and fast deadlines. In fact, for some colleges, a student can even apply in July for the upcoming fall term. Nevertheless, it is always to a student's advantage to apply as early as possible. Housing and financial aid priority dates may come and go if students wait too long to apply. As a general rule, colleges with Rolling Admissions procedures are less selective than others, but this is not a hard and fast rule—as of this writing, Purdue and University of Pittsburgh, both well-respected universities, have Rolling Admissions policies. Colleges that are not extremely selective or that do not receive an abundance of applicants use a Rolling Admissions policy to continue to fill the freshman class well into the spring season.

Early Decision

Some colleges offer Early Decision admission plans, under which students apply by mid-October to mid-November and make a *binding* agreement to attend the school if accepted. Students are permitted to apply Early Decision to only one college; all other applications must be nonbinding agreements such as Regular Decision, or in some cases, Early Action. In fact, the student must sign a statement agreeing to abide by these stipulations about Early Decision. Admissions decisions are made within several weeks after the application deadline—generally by mid-December. Upon acceptance, students must notify all other colleges to which they have applied and ask that their applications be withdrawn, and they must sign a commitment to enroll in the college to which they have been accepted.

The previous description applies to traditional Early Decision plans, sometimes called Early Decision I. A newer development, Early Decision II, is offered by some colleges. In Early Decision II, the application deadline is later (commonly January 1), and students receive their acceptances or rejections by mid-February. It is still a binding admission plan: if accepted to the university, the student must commit to attending and must withdraw all other applications. Early Decision II can benefit students who want to commit to a particular college but need senior year grades or test scores to strengthen their applications—or who applied to a college under Early Decision I and were rejected in December. In this case, it might be strategic to apply ED II to the second favorite institution.

Early Action

Like Early Decision, Early Action allows students to apply early and receive admissions decisions long before the Regular Decision crowd hears the news in the spring. Unlike Early Decision, Early Action is nonbinding, giving students the option of choosing *not* to attend the school if accepted. Some Early Action programs permit students to apply Early Action to other schools as well. However, some colleges have switched from binding Early Decision programs to Single-Choice Early Action (SCEA) or Restrictive Early Action (REA) plans. These plans are similar to regular Early Action in that they allow students to apply early without having to make binding decisions, but they are similar to Early Decision in that students may apply to only *one* school under an early application plan. Again, read the rules carefully.

Interim Decision

For some schools, an Interim Decision option (terminology may vary) allows students to receive a decision earlier than they would with Regular Decision. Applications are generally submitted in early to mid-November, and the college notifies the student in January or February. This decision plan generally carries no restrictions and should not interfere with Early Decision or Early Action applications, but *be sure to check the rules at each college if your student is submitting any early applications.*

Pros and Cons of Early Applications

Early application plans offer some worthwhile benefits. In many cases, students will know by Christmas whether they have been accepted by their first-choice college. Moreover, admit rates for students applying under early application programs are statistically higher than they are for regular admission—sometimes even double. Presumably, this is because students applying to these schools as their first choice are a self-selecting group. They have researched and planned for admission to these particular colleges, they demonstrate seriousness of intent, and they are much more likely than the average student to meet the admission requirements.

Nonbinding Early Action plans have no disadvantages other than the rush of meeting the early deadline. Students are free to choose whether or not to attend their Early Action college, and they have until May 1ˢᵗ to do so. Receiving an early acceptance can eliminate one big question mark regarding your student's favorite college and shine light on the future college path. If the student is 100% sold on the Early Action college, he or she can save the time and money that would have been spent on submitting more applications. Even if your student is rejected, this information allows him or her to adjust the slate of potential colleges and regroup for the Regular Decision season. Additionally, knowledge of the financial aid being offered at the Early Action school can be a useful piece of data for comparison when other schools begin to report in. A student will still be poised to take the "best offer," so to speak.

In contrast, when students apply through a binding Early Decision arrangement, some special considerations come into play. Students and their families should be absolutely positive that a certain school and its financial aid package (or lack thereof) is right for them. The disadvantage of Early Decision is that holding a student to a decision made in early fall of the senior year can be quite unrealistic. Since a great deal of growth and shifting of priorities can occur between fall of the senior year of high school and fall of the freshman year of college, your student may one day second-guess his or her decision to commit to that college. Additionally, Early Decision forces the student to make a firm commitment to one college without the opportunity to compare financial aid packages from other colleges. Families can only be released from Early Decision agreements for reasons of definite financial difficulties. Information on Early Decision acceptance (and consequently, on reneging on agreements) is sometimes shared with other colleges and could impact admissions decisions to these colleges. Students thinking about breaking their Early Decision agreement for reasons other than finances should consider these factors in light of their future undergraduate and graduate school prospects.

Early Decision and Early Action news can make students very happy—or very disappointed—at Christmas time. Students who previously had their hearts set on one particular school are forced to start from scratch psychologically if they are not accepted in December. Consequently, these plans work more smoothly for students who would be just as happy attending their second or third choice school if they are not accepted at their first choice.

Obviously, options that provide nonbinding early notification of acceptance or rejection give your student more time to consider all options. Moreover, early acceptance at one or two institutions will provide a huge boost in confidence as well as the side benefit of stress relief going into the second semester of the senior year. This option also offers more time to visit these specific colleges before committing to one.

However, students who need that first semester of senior year to pull up an ailing GPA or test scores, or to boost achievements on the extracurriculars list, should wait for Regular Decision or should apply Early Decision II if offered by the university. Early Action and Early Decision plans are for strong students who know where they want to go.

Many colleges are eliminating their early application procedures in order to level the playing field. However, if the college of your choice does offer an early application option, consider the pros and cons thoroughly and make a thoughtful decision as to which box to mark on the application.

Start Early!

As you and your student face the task of completing college applications, *do not wait until the last minute*. Give yourselves plenty of time. The summer before senior year is an excellent time to refine the college list, polish up the transcript, draft some essays, scour the application websites and all chosen college websites, and make a list of tasks and deadlines. You'll find that this process is a team effort among parents and student. You'll also find that it's simply not possible to whip out an application, let alone three, six, or eight, in one evening. A significant time commitment is involved, due to all the attachments and addenda required for a typical application.

Items to Gather

You will want to assemble a few items (whether paper or electronic) as you prepare to complete the college application:

1. The Application Itself

Ideally, you should begin examining the application when it first comes out for the upcoming season. Sometimes this is as early as June of your student's junior year, but it is usually closer to summer's end. If you are really on the ball, you will take a look at the previous year's application during the fall or winter of your student's junior year. From the "old" application, your student can prepare for the most likely essay prompts and for the general format of the application. Chances are, it won't change much. Note that the Common Application is available year round (except for a few days in midsummer), and it, too, does not change much from year to year. Each year's new essay prompts are announced several months ahead of time. As previously mentioned, parents can set up practice accounts to become familiar with the application, and the student's practice account will roll over to a "real" account just before senior year.

2. Homeschool-Specific Instructions

The colleges to which your student applies may have special instructions for homeschoolers. Sometimes these are posted on the website, and sometimes on the application itself. For certain schools, you might have to ferret out the information by calling, emailing, or visiting the admissions office well ahead of application time to inquire about special procedures, requirements, or forms for homeschoolers. These extras may involve additional SAT Subject Tests™ or additional essays. *Don't leave this inquiry to the last minute.* It is a job for the sophomore or, at the latest, the junior year.

3. Your Student's Official Transcript

Whether it comes from your homeschool program administrator or from your home computer, the high school transcript is a key item to have ready. If you belong to a PSP, give your administrator plenty of time to produce an official transcript for your student. Also account for time it might take to fix mistakes on the document (ask to see a draft ahead of time). If you prepare your own transcript, you will thank yourself over and over again if you spend time during the summer updating it with junior year grades and adjusting its appearance until it looks exactly the way you want it. Then, if you will be mailing any transcripts, print out a few copies on good quality resume paper and store them safely in a labeled envelope or folder. More likely, you will create a PDF or other requested file format, since most college applications, including the Common Application, ask you to upload an electronic copy of the transcript. Make sure that the transcripts you upload are professional-looking, easy to understand, and of appropriate file size.

If applicable to your student, you will also need to order transcripts from community colleges and from additional high school programs (only if they served as your student's "school of record" for one or more years—not for programs where the student simply took a few courses). These documents may take three or four weeks to arrive unless you pay extra for rush service. Some universities will want these transcripts to be mailed or sent electronically directly from the school to their admissions office. Others will allow you to enclose a sealed, official transcript within a larger outer envelope and mail it to the university yourself. In this case, you may order several transcripts from the community college and have them sent to your home address, ready to send out as needed. The university may also allow you to scan the community college transcript and submit it electronically. Check with the individual universities to find out their preferences.

4. Your Student's Official Test Scores

If your student requested score reports for colleges on the day he or she took the SAT or ACT test, the colleges should automatically receive them within a few weeks. Otherwise, request scores by going to the College Board or ACT website and ordering score reports. To be official, the scores must be sent directly from the testing agency to the college. Even though your request will be made online, it can sometimes take up to two weeks before the college has the scores. If you are up against a critical deadline, the scores might lag behind unless you have ordered them early or paid extra for rush reporting.

5. A Resume of the Student's Activities and Experiences

Like a job hunter's resume, a student's resume is useful during the application process. A resume for this purpose includes your student's name, address, and other identifying information, as well as sections describing or listing extracurricular activities, academic honors and awards, leadership positions, summer programs, employment, volunteer work, a short goal statement, and perhaps a listing of honors,

AP, or college courses taken. Additionally, the student should highlight any unusual educational or travel experiences, particularly if they involve educational pursuits or volunteer work.

A well-written resume of the high school experience can help in a number of ways. First, your student can give it to teachers who are writing recommendations so that they may gain a better idea of him or her as a person. Note, however, that these recommendation letters should not simply rephrase the resume. Ideally, persons writing recommendations should comment on what they already know about the student, with the resume serving simply as a supplement and a memory jogger. (See Chapter 23 for a full discussion of recommendation letters.)

Second, the student may be permitted to include a resume in the college application to highlight key interests and achievements. About one-third of Common Application member colleges allow resume uploads, as do many other colleges.

Third, the student can use the resume as a "cheat sheet" while filling out college and scholarship applications. Describing an extracurricular activity in just the right words is important. For example, instead of saying "worked at a preschool," a student can say, if it's true, "taught prekindergarten skills to 12 four-year-olds." Taking the time to come up with strong, precise phrasing for each activity or award and then recording these within a well-edited resume eliminates the struggle to recreate this ideal wording each time another application is due.

To make the best use of time, your student may draft the resume over the summer, or even earlier in high school, and simply update it as needed.

6. CSS/Financial Aid PROFILE® and FAFSA (Financial Aid Forms)

Though financial aid applications are not technically part of college applications, you will need to start this task in parallel with college applications. The FAFSA (covered more thoroughly in Chapter 25) is the application for federal, state, and college-based aid and can be filled out beginning in October of the senior year. Some colleges and universities will also require the CSS/Financial Aid PROFILE, an application form available on the College Board website and used by about 180 colleges and scholarship programs. Be forewarned that the CSS/Financial Aid PROFILE form takes some serious time to fill out. Allow several hours of concentrated effort, possibly spread out over a couple of weeks, to gather parent and student income and asset figures. You are almost certain to have questions, which will need to be submitted electronically or by phone. Allow time to deal with these as well. Check the priority deadlines of the colleges and scholarship programs to make sure you know when to file this form.

For Early Decision and Early Action students, the FAFSA and the CSS/Financial Aid PROFILE, if required, are due at about the same time as the application (mid-fall), so work on these concurrently with the application. For Regular Decision students, the forms are usually due in February, but check your specific colleges to be sure. The CSS/Financial Aid PROFILE currently costs about $25 for the first college and $16 for each additional college submission, and it does not take the place of the FAFSA (Free Application for Federal Student Aid), which must also be completed to be eligible for any financial aid. Fee waivers are available for low-income families. See Chapter 25 for additional information on the CSS/Financial Aid PROFILE and the FAFSA.

7. Letters of Recommendation

Obviously, your student will request letters of recommendation ahead of time—nearly always online—but as the application deadline draws near, it is a good idea to politely check with these teachers to assure that the letters will be submitted on time. The student portion of the Common Application will show a green check mark when a teacher has submitted an evaluation, so if your student doesn't see this check mark, he or she should follow up with the teacher. Most colleges ask that the teachers submit the letters electronically directly to the college. See the Teacher Recommendations section later in this chapter for details.

8. Parents' Detailed Description of the Homeschool Course of Study, if Required

This "optional but smart" document will be described in full later, but for now, just note that it may take you several days of intense work to put together a summary of all the high school courses. Another summertime task!

9. Mailing and Printing Supplies and Key Email Addresses

You may not have anything to mail, since the vast majority of the tasks will be completed online, but do stock up on a few common mailing supplies: stamps, 10x13 envelopes, regular business size envelopes, and possibly 6x9 envelopes, as well as fresh ink or toner cartridges for your printer. This reminder might seem trivial, but when time is short and you have just enough time to dash to the post office to meet a postmark deadline, you may not have time for an additional dash to the store for 10 x 13 envelopes. Additionally, if you are in a time crunch and are printing an important document, it is stressful and disheartening to discover that the ink or toner is printing too light for a professional-looking copy.

If you are mailing a paper application or supplementary materials, the college may require that materials be mailed *flat* in a large manila envelope, rather than being folded and crammed into a business size envelope or a smaller manila. Additionally, you will want to have each college's mailing address at your fingertips, including the *exact* department or mail stop.

Likewise, be sure you have appropriate email addresses and contact phone numbers for the admissions departments of the colleges your student is interested in. Of course, this information is found on the college websites, but from time to time you may need to communicate with a particular person in charge of homeschool applications, or in charge of a specific program, department, or scholarship opportunity. Having this contact information organized in your phone and ready to go will save "searching time" when you are in a time crunch.

10. Filing System – Paper and Electronic

Even when completing online applications, you will accumulate a certain amount of paper: printouts of completed applications and miscellaneous forms, college brochures that have come in the mail or that you pick up at college fairs or campus visits, or business cards of key admissions office contacts. Gather a few file folders to keep each college's applications, information, and components separate from one another. Keep these in one place in your house so that you and your student can quickly lay hands on the items. You will frequently "cannibalize" one application to aid in preparing another, and you will also want to double check what you have sent and when you sent it. The last thing you want is an all-out scavenger hunt every time you need one of these documents.

Similarly, make sure you and your student create an organized method for keeping track of documents on your computer. Whether these are application essays (which can be revised slightly to suit each application's specific requirements), course descriptions, or PDF files of completed applications, you will be returning to these basic documents over and over again. Always draft and revise application essays in a separate document, not within the college's online application form. Keep at least one backup of your files, as well as a printed copy of anything important. Maintain good parent-student communication so that during those infamous time crunches, each of you can find the other's documents with just a few clicks. Sharing documents with each other is especially handy when both parent and student are constantly on the run, or when documents are generated in the wee hours.

FILLING OUT THE APPLICATION

It's time for a tour of the typical college application. This overview is based largely on the 2018-19 Common Application, and college-specific applications for institutions not on the Common Application will differ with regard to certain sections. Please remember that forms and instructions, both for the Common Application and for individual college applications, are constantly and rapidly changing. *Always* check to make sure that you have an up-to-date set of instructions, and use the help features available from the Common Application or from the college itself.

One useful tool provided by the Common Application is *Common App Ready,* a portion of the site where students, parents, and recommenders can create an account and log into the application months or even a couple of years before they are ready to apply (https://www.commonapp.org/ready). With this feature, you can preview various parts of the application and understand the way questions will be asked. Additionally, Common App Ready provides a series of lessons in the form of visual slides with accompanying explanations designed to clarify how to fill out each section of the application.

Additional help is found through video segments produced by the Common Application, which are available in its Training Resources Library within the Help Center. Short videos are also embedded here and there within the application itself. These are extremely helpful in providing an overview and demonstrating step-by-step instructions, so be sure to watch them if you have any questions. Finally, be sure to read all the tips found in the right-hand sidebars of the application. These define key terms and provide specific help and guidance.

Getting Set Up

For the Common Application and most other online applications, the first step is to set up a student account, tied to an email address and entered via a password. Basic information such as name, date of birth, and contact information will be entered, and it is important to use a "stable" email address that the student checks regularly. Upon successfully registering an account, the student will be assigned a Common Application ID number, which will be required if he or she needs to contact Common Application's technical support to resolve issues. It is also a good idea to include this number on any application-related correspondence with potential Common Application member colleges.

Student Applicant Information

Profile

The Profile section is quite straightforward, asking for the student's name, gender, date of birth, address, phone number, and similar information. Several sections that follow request demographic information such as religious preference and ethnic background, birthplace and citizenship, residency and language proficiency. Some questions in this section are optional. Students are also asked whether they might qualify for fee waivers due to low family income, and are then asked several qualifying questions.

Family

Family information, such as parents' educational background and employment information, country of birth, and marital status, as well as names and educational status of the student's siblings, should be an easy section to complete.

Education

Within the Education section, the student describes several facets of his or her past and current education. The first task is to enter information on the current high school, including its name, address, CEEB code, date of entry, anticipated date of graduation, and counselor's name and contact information. Note that in the searchable list of schools, you will find a choice for "Home Schooled" along with the appropriate CEEB code to use. For the counselor name, a homeschooler will use the name of the home-school parent or homeschool program administrator, depending on who has been chosen to complete the School Report. This section of the application also asks for names of other high schools at which the student has been enrolled and colleges at which he or she has taken courses for credit. For these other high schools, do not enter programs where a student simply took a few courses. The intention behind the question is that these are schools at which the student was enrolled, and from which he or she transferred to attend the current school (Home School). In other words, do not enter a school or program name unless it was actually your student's "school of record" and took care of all record keeping for your state's educational requirements. A student has only one "school of record" at any given time. The vast majority of homeschoolers will simply list "Home Schooled" as their school for all four years of high school, even if they changed PSPs over the years, and will add details about alternate course venues within their other descriptions and documents.

If you do have other high schools to report in this section, you will be asked for dates of attendance and the reason why the student left the school. In case you are wondering where you enter programs and schools that provided course venues for your home school, you may note these on your transcript and in your course descriptions.

Before your student fills out these sections, decide whether to consider him or her a homeschooler or a student from a small private (independent) school. Generally, if your student has a solid record of academic and extracurricular accomplishments, and/or the chosen colleges are reasonably "friendly" to homeschoolers—most private colleges and many public universities are, these days—it is to your student's advantage to be known as a homeschooler. The nontraditional educational method, together with the self-motivation your student has displayed, will attract the interest of the admissions staff. You and your student will want to make your decision based on your specific circumstances, however. When homeschooling was far less common, many families portrayed their home schools as small private schools. Today, it is much more common for homeschoolers to embrace their identity as homeschoolers.

Within the Education section, students will also enter information on factors that affected their progression through secondary school (high school). Examples include graduating early or late, changing schools, taking time off, or taking a gap year. If there are any items to report, the student is asked to provide an explanation of the "change in progression." These explanations may be very brief and do not need to read like an essay.

Colleges and Universities

Another subsection of the Education section asks students to report college courses taken from ninth grade on, whether online or on a college campus. The student will also provide the name and location of the college, dates attended, how credit was awarded (dual enrollment, summer program, or credit awarded directly from the college), and whether the student received a degree. Typically, homeschoolers who have taken community college courses receive college credit and must send an official transcript from the community college as part of the college application (as well as including these courses on their high school transcripts). Generally, the college or university to which you are applying will prefer to receive the official transcript directly from the community college. Even so, you might also consider uploading an unofficial copy when you upload your own high school transcript, just to make sure all the information is visible in one place. This will be done as part of the School Report completed by the parent. A full explanation of this report follows later in this chapter.

Grades

Another portion of the Education section asks the student to self-report high school GPA, class rank, and graduating class size. Interestingly, the only required item is graduating class size which, for a homeschooler, would be "1." Class rank is irrelevant for homeschoolers, so you can leave this one blank. If you are filling in the other items, you will see that in the section for reporting grade point average, the student fills in the GPA, the GPA scale, and whether it is weighted or unweighted. GPA scale means "What is a perfect GPA at your school?" For most school systems, the GPA is based on a 4.0 scale, since an A receives 4 points, and a 4.0 GPA is a straight-A average. This is true even if an A in an honors course receives 5 points. See Chapter 10 for how to calculate the GPA. As for the term "weighted," a weighted GPA is calculated when AP courses and sometimes honors courses are awarded an extra grade point (so an A receives 5 points instead of 4). (Note: In many school systems, honors courses receive only an extra half grade point, so an A receives 4.5.) An unweighted GPA is the GPA reported when no extra points have been assigned for honors or AP courses. You may report either a weighted or an unweighted GPA, depending on what your transcript shows. Note, however, that weighted GPAs are sometimes used for scholarship purposes, so you may want to display a weighted GPA.

Current or Most Recent Year Courses

Following the Grades section, the student will enter the names and levels of the current year's courses. Choices include standard, accelerated, honors, AP, IB® (International Baccalaureate®), dual enrollment (a college course taken while in high school), and several others that do not apply to most students. In addition, the student will enter the schedule of the course. In other words, is it being taken for the full year, first semester only, or second semester only?

Honors

Another section asks the student to list his or her academic awards and honors, which are defined as scholastic distinctions the student has won since the ninth grade. This could include National Merit® Semifinalist status, private scholarships awarded, publication of articles or creative writing, independent scientific research, membership in a recognized honor society or program for academically gifted students, or other awards. Dean's List or departmental awards at the community college would also be excellent honors to list. Be sure that the awards and honors recorded here are not word-for-word repeats of the extracurricular activities section of the application. On the Common Application, this section is for academic awards only; other college applications may allow students to list a variety of awards, including those for sports or volunteer work. In this section, the student will also fill in the level of recognition for each award (school, state, regional, national, or international).

Community-Based Organizations

Students are asked to list programs that have provided free assistance in the application process (QuestBridge and the Jack Kent Cooke Foundation are two examples).

Future Plans

To finish up the Education section, students quickly answer two questions from drop-down menus, relating to future career plans and the highest degree they intend to earn (such as BS, MS, MD, etc.).

Testing

In the Testing section, students self-report their scores on SAT, ACT, and other tests. These scores are considered unofficial, and reporting them here is optional. In fact, not all colleges require test scores. The "My Colleges" page will display the test policy for a given school.

When self-reporting, the student may provide scores and test dates from any of the following tests: ACT, SAT, SAT Subject Tests, AP, IB, and several others relating to international or immigrant students. The student is asked to report the highest composite (total) and highest individual scores he or she has achieved for a given test, even if the individual tests are from different testing dates. Regardless of whether the student self-reports, colleges also require students to request an official score report from the College Board, ACT, Inc., or other testing agency so that the scores will be sent directly to the college.

Many colleges require or recommend that students take two or three SAT Subject Tests and submit these scores. Even if your student's prospective schools do not require SAT Subject Test scores, it is often to a homeschooler's advantage to submit them anyway (especially if they are good scores), since they provide additional objective information about the student's abilities.

For Advanced Placement® test scores, the student will self-report any available scores on the application but does not need to send an official score report to colleges during the application process. Instead, the student will wait until he or she has been accepted by and has committed to a college. At that point, he or she will need to officially submit the scores in order to receive college credit or placement into a more advanced level of a course.

Activities

In this section, the student lists his or her most important extracurricular, volunteer, and work activities. If you and your student have planned well, this should be a well-rounded list that also indicates passion for a particular area. The Common Application currently has space for up to ten activities and includes choices to indicate when the student participated in the activity. The student can choose from quite a large array of categories, including the standard ones (athletics, academic clubs, volunteer work, debate, music), as well as categories such as religious or cultural groups and family responsibilities. Note that these activities do not need to involve traditional organizations but should be a list of significant productive ways the student has spent his or her time. Students should list their most important activities first. Approximate time spent (hours per week and weeks per year), a brief description of the activity, leadership positions held, honors won, and whether the student plans to participate in this activity during college are other pieces of information to record.

Some college applications have separate sections for work experience and volunteer work; others, such as the Common Application, include volunteer and paid work in the extracurricular activities section. Work experience includes summer jobs or jobs during the school year that were performed on a regular basis or for an extended period of time. In other words, occasional gardening jobs for neighbors should be excluded, but if the student has his or her own gardening business, this venture should definitely be reported. Approximate dates and hours per week, as well as the nature of the work, are recorded in this section.

When describing these extracurriculars, be honest and realistic. For instance, make sure that the hours per week and weeks per year do not add up to more hours than are humanly possible. Before leaving this section, preview the final screen to catch any truncated words or phrases, and condense appropriately so that the wording is complete and sensible.

Entering a List of Colleges

At any time during the application process, a student can navigate away from the sections described above and work on another portion of the Common Application. Sections do not need to be completed in order. However, at some point early in the process, the student needs to set up a list of the colleges he or she plans to apply to. This is done in the "My Colleges" tab, where the student may enter up to twenty colleges or universities. After searching up the college's name, the student will click to add the college to the master list. Then, for each individual college on the list, he or she can click on the name of the college and view the status of the application elements (the main Common Application, "Questions," and "Recommenders and FERPA."

Under "Questions" the student will answer a bank of questions specific to that college: items such as entry term (fall or spring), decision plan (Regular, Early Decision, etc.), and academic and career interests. A few other college-pertinent questions regarding housing plans, desire for financial aid, full-time vs. part-time plans, family members who have attended the college, and similar matters are also asked here. For many colleges, these shorter questions will be followed by some longer statements (mini-essays) of 50 to 250 words. See "Supplementary Questions and Essays" later in this chapter.

"Recommenders and FERPA" indicates the section for each college where the student will choose from his or her list of teachers or other recommenders and "assign" one or more to this particular college. First the student will tackle the FERPA (Family Educational Rights and Privacy Act) section. Here, the student will mark a box indicating his or her permission to release student records, such as grades and test scores, to the colleges. In addition, the student will indicate whether he or she is waiving FERPA rights (the rights to see this portion of his or her educational records—the recommendation letters—after he or she has been accepted to and has enrolled in the college. It is generally recommended that students waive these rights, thus giving up the right to read these recommendations in the future. The student's waiving of FERPA rights will allow recommenders to write more candidly and confidentially about the student. Such letters will carry more weight with the colleges and will convey more trust in the recommender as well.

Inviting Recommenders

After the student has entered his or her Profile information, filled out high school information in the Education section, added some colleges to the My College section, and completed the FERPA release authorization, he or she can begin inviting and assigning recommenders. Having identified the school as a home school, the student will generally invite the parent as the counselor (see detailed instructions for parent/counselors later in this chapter). For teacher recommendations, the student should contact instructors several weeks before applications are due and ask them if they would be willing to complete a teacher recommendation. For certain colleges, students also have the option of inviting another person (pastor, coach, employer, volunteer supervisor, or other adult) as an "Other Recommender."

Managing the list of recommenders is done within the individual colleges under "My Colleges"; each of the student's colleges offers an option to add the appropriate number of recommenders. Some colleges require one teacher recommendation; others two; others require none at all but may still allow recommendations. To invite recommenders and then assign them to submit their recommendations to particular colleges, the student enters the name, title, and email address of the individual chosen and then uses the "Invite Teacher" link to initiate the process of bringing the recommender into the application environment. However, the recommender will not be notified until one more step is completed. The student must use the "Assign" button on each individual college page under My Colleges to assign a particular recommender to a specific college's application. Completion of the "Assign" function will trigger an email being sent to the recommender, instructing him or her how to log in and begin the recommendation process. Once a recommender has been added and invited, his or her name and title cannot be changed. Additionally, a recommender can only be removed from the application if he or she has not yet submitted the recommendation. (It is courteous and wise to notify instructors if you are removing them from a specific school or removing them as a recommender altogether. This way, they will not waste time starting a recommendation letter for you.) The student's "Recommendations and FERPA" page under the My Colleges tab shows the status of each evaluation: not started, started, submitted, or downloaded by the college.

Students may also select and assign up to three persons to be "Advisors" to assist with the application process. Advisors can view the entire student portion of the application and give feedback but do not submit any forms or recommendations on behalf of the student. Note that when an advisor views the student's application, the Social Security number will be masked for security purposes.

Writing

Back in the main part of the Common Application, the Writing section contains an array of deeper questions for which students will need to do some soul-searching before responding. In addition to the main essay (personal statement), this section includes space for disciplinary history and additional information that may not have been covered elsewhere on the application.

The personal essay allows students to communicate their thoughts, interests, and experiences—in other words, to reveal what they would like the admissions office to know about them beyond their grades and test scores. This is an extremely important part of the application, primarily because of its very personal glimpse into the student's background, talents, and dreams for the future. Some non-Common Application colleges require only one essay of about 500 to 600 words. Others ask for additional shorter or longer essays, while a few don't request an essay at all. To make the best use of time and to craft the most effective essays, your student should begin working on essays during the summer after the junior year.

Currently, the Common Application provides seven suggested topics, including one "Topic of Choice," and stipulates a minimum of 250 and a maximum of 650 words. Students should always draft and polish the essay in a separate document before copying and pasting it into the text box provided on the application. This will prevent the unfortunate occurrence of essays being lost within the application screen because they were not saved; additionally, the student is likely more comfortable writing in the programs he or she uses most. The text box on the Common Application will cut off any words beyond the 650-word maximum, so students should carefully read the end of their essays to make sure that nothing has been truncated.

In general, students should not customize the essay for a particular college but should keep it generic enough to show their strengths to the entire spectrum of member college on their lists. With that said, however, students will be allowed to submit an unlimited number of edits or "versions" of the entire

Common Application, so modifications may be made for additional submissions. Thus, if a student is motivated to write a unique essay for every college, he or she would be allowed to do that. The unlimited edit feature will help students update application information (not just the essays) and correct mistakes previously made. However, no edits can be made to applications already submitted to specific colleges. For detailed tips on essay writing, see Chapter 22.

Within the Writing section is a portion called Disciplinary History. Hopefully, your student will have no academic or behavioral misconduct, felonies, or misdemeanors to 'fess up to in this section. Explanations must be provided if applicable.

The Additional Information section is a useful place to explain special circumstances, whether positive or negative. Any relevant information not provided elsewhere may be added here, with a word limit of 650 words. For instance, if a semester of poor grades was due to a severe illness or a family crisis, explain it here. If the student has unusual credentials or qualifications that were not addressed elsewhere in the application, this section is the place to make these notations. In short, Additional Information is for applicants who, in the words of the Common Application, "wish to provide details of circumstances or qualifications not reflected in the application." It shouldn't be construed to be an additional "brag box" except to note qualifications that truly do not fit elsewhere on the application. By no means should it repeat information that is already presented elsewhere.

Supplementary Questions and Essays

As mentioned, many colleges require answers to supplementary questions in order to gather information specific to that college. These shorter applications vary from school to school but may ask questions such as "Why do you want to attend this university?" or "Do you have any relatives who have attended the university?"

It is important, yet often tricky, to search out all these supplementary questions. These are sometimes hidden or nested within other questions and may not appear until the student has responded to a previous question. On the Dashboard the student should be sure to look at each individual college's Writing Requirements tab to see what the college wants—the personal essay (main Common Application essay), member questions (generally shorter questions), and/or a writing supplement (additional essays). Make sure you are aware of these early in the game. In addition to looking at the Dashboard, the student should meticulously click through *each* section of *each* college's requirements page to find anything labeled "Questions" or "Writing." Even seemingly straightforward questions should be answered with at least several days remaining before the deadline, because sometimes a particular answer prompts another short essay. In an already stressful application season, your student does not need the added stress of discovering yet another 250-word essay just a few hours before he or she is ready to submit the application.

Examples of shorter items a college may ask—anywhere from a few words to 100 words in length—are "Describe yourself in three words," "Name your favorite food, fictional character, movie, and dream job." Others include "What does your browser history say about you?" "What is the most significant challenge that society faces today?" "How did you spend the last two summers?" "How did you find out about our university?" or "What historical moment or event do you wish you could have witnessed?"

When additional essays of 250 or more words are requested, the goal is to show that the student's abilities, ambitions, and accomplishments match the college's strengths and features. For instance, if the college is known for community involvement and social action, the student could write an essay about his or her volunteer projects that benefited the community or the underprivileged. Typical essay prompts for supplements include "Write a letter to your future roommate," "Reflect on an idea that has been important to your intellectual development," or "How does our university satisfy your desire for a particular kind of learning?" The University of Chicago's supplementary writing questions are actually authored or inspired by current or past students and cover quirky thoughts along the lines of "Orange is the new black, fifty's the new thirty, comedy is the new rock 'n' roll, _____ is the new _____. What's in, what's out, and why is it being replaced?"

Certain supplementary essay prompts are not unearthed until you express your interest in a particular department or school of a given university. For instance, at the University of Southern California, only those students declaring their intention to apply to the School of Engineering will see the prompt asking them to comment on one of the National Academy of Engineering's fourteen Grand Challenges.

Christian colleges and universities frequently ask one or more supplementary questions or short essays relating to the student's faith journey: describing how they came to faith, how the Lord has worked through challenging situations in their lives, how they live out their faith in their community, or how they see themselves contributing to the mission of the college. Once again, college application time is definitely a time of soul-searching.

Some colleges, but not all, may allow uploaded documents such as resumes or research papers within the section of supplementary items.

Most supplements can be completed online within the Common Application, but some universities may have additional forms that you will access through their own websites. Think of it as a grand scavenger hunt. As you and your student complete college applications, be sure to locate, obtain, and complete *all* forms and questions required. For example, some colleges have financial aid applications specific to the school (but not contained within the Common Application) that must be filed at approximately the same time as the application is filed. These forms will be found on the financial aid pages of the college website.

Portfolios and Arts Supplements

Students applying as fine arts majors, as well as students interested in certain other majors, may need to or opt to complete an additional set of requirements to find their place within their respective departments. Currently, the Common Application uses a platform called SlideRoom® through which students can upload portfolio items in all media formats: images, audio, video, and documents, as well as interactive media. SlideRoom can accommodate a diverse range of projects—science experiments, presentations, robots, artwork, music, video blogs, and other creative ventures for virtually any discipline. For example, MIT (not a Common Application member) accepts portfolios for all disciplines. Students should carefully read the appropriate portions of the university websites and contact the art, music, theater, film, or other specific departments to understand the requirements for applying. Often the deadlines for these portions of the application are earlier than for the regular application. For instance, students may need to have materials prepared by mid-October.

Student Athletes

Student athletes should check with the university's athletic department to understand the steps for applying for admission and athletic scholarships. It is wise to understand these requirements well ahead of time (early in high school) in order to initiate dialogues with the appropriate coaches. In addition, students should become very familiar with the NCAA program regarding the topics of recruiting, scholarships, and eligibility. Registration with the NCAA Eligibility Center by the beginning of the junior year is required for students interested in playing for Division I or Division II schools. In particular, students should check out the NCAA's information pages for homeschoolers. As with many aspects of college admission, rules and guidelines change frequently; check the website early and often to make sure you have the most up-to-date information.

Courses and Grades

A relatively new section of the Common Application, one that is not applicable to all member colleges, is Courses and Grades. Here, students will self-report their entire academic record: course titles, grades, and credits earned. Since not all students will need to complete this section, they will not even see these screens unless one or more of their chosen colleges requests this information. Thus, it is wise to fill out the list of colleges early. If you do need to fill out Courses and Grades, have a copy of the transcript on hand and select the school name from the drop-down menu (most likely Homeschooled). Then, year by year for ninth through twelfth grades, enter the course title, letter grade, and credits earned, exactly as they appear on the transcript. Thus, parents, you will need to have the homeschool transcript finalized in order for this section to be completed accurately.

Other Required Forms:

Early Decision Agreement

The Early Decision Agreement comes into play only if a student is applying with a binding Early Decision plan to his or her first-choice institution. The student, parent, and counselor (which for most homeschoolers *is* the parent) all need to electronically sign that they understand that the Early Decision plan means a definite commitment to attend this school. Students accepted under an Early Decision plan must withdraw applications submitted to other colleges and universities and make no additional applications to any other university. Note, however, that an Early Decision candidate who is seeking financial aid may wait to withdraw these other applications until the Early Decision college has notified him or her about financial aid. The student also acknowledges that he or she understands that with an Early Decision offer of admission, the college may share his or her name and commitment with other institutions.

Submission and Payment

Once all the sections of the application are complete, the remainder of the student section of the application involves previewing and checking the whole application for accuracy, electronically signing it, and paying the application fee for each college. The submission process is done separately for each college. The student will preview a PDF of the entries he or she has provided, and then edit as necessary before confirming that all is OK. Credit card or e-check information is collected unless the student is eligible for fee waivers because of low family income. And at last, this section contains the chance to click the oh-so-final "Submit" button. The Common Application recently added a spray of confetti to this page!

THE SCHOOL REPORT AND COUNSELOR RECOMMENDATION

For homeschooling parents, perhaps the most challenging part of the application is the completion of the School Report and the Counselor Recommendation, along with uploading the transcript. The School Report form asks for background information on the school environment and academic program, while the Counselor Recommendation asks for specific assessment of the student. Together these will give the colleges a picture of your homeschooling philosophy, style, and curriculum, but wading through some of the "school-ese" can slow the process down a bit.

Who Should Complete These Forms?

When deciding who will complete the School Report, think through your application strategies. If you want to portray your student as attending a "small private school" and do not plan to mention your homeschooling, you will probably have your homeschool program administrator write this evaluation. If you are openly describing your student as a homeschooler, as most homeschooling families do, you have a choice. If your administrator knows your student extremely well, he or she could complete this evaluation. Other choices might be a teacher your student has had for several outside courses, or some other adult who knows the student academically. However, if your homeschooling is facilitated largely on your own, even if your student takes many classes outside the home, you as the primary educator are the best person to complete this form, highlighting the accomplishments your student has achieved as a homeschooler. Check with the admissions staff of a few key colleges to see what they prefer, but in our experience and in the experiences of numerous other homeschoolers, nearly all of the colleges and universities have requested that a parent complete this evaluation, since the parent knows the student best.

Even if someone else fills out the School Report, several of the colleges will likely want you, the parent, to provide a description of your homeschooling. Thus, you will still have an opportunity to highlight your student's homeschool-related accomplishments and opportunities.

After logging in to the Recommender portal of the Common Application (not the Student portal) recommenders fill out basic profile information on themselves as "school counselors" (school name and address and other contact information), as well as specific information about the school, before they can get started on the student information, which is found in the "Students" tab of the Recommender page. (For "School Name" there is an option for "Homeschooled.") Here, a dashboard shows the name(s) of the student(s) who have requested recommendations, displays a list of the forms that need to be completed, and provides information on each student's next application deadline.

School Report

The School Report is, of course, tailored to the needs of traditional schools, and some sections are clearly not applicable to homeschoolers.

School Profile/Home School Information

The School Profile section of the School Report first asks some short questions, of which the only required ones relate to graduating class size (mark "1" for homeschoolers), whether classes are taken on a block schedule (generally "no" for homeschoolers), graduation date, whether the school is outside the U.S., whether you are the person who will complete the applicant's academic ratings (generally yes, though you are allowed to opt out of rating your student), and whether your school requires students to complete volunteer work. Optional questions refer to the student body's ethnic makeup, U.S. citizenship status, and what percentage of students go on to two-year or four-year colleges. Also, you are asked about the setting of your school (urban, rural, suburban) and whether you offer AP, IB, or honors courses. For the latter, you would answer "yes" if any of your students have ever taken a course at AP or honors level (not necessarily within your own home; it can be an outside class). A section on GPA allows you to describe your GPA scale (mark "4" if an A receives a 4.0 GPA), as well as indicating whether the GPA is weighted or unweighted, what the school's passing grade is, and what the highest GPA in the class is. Fill out whatever makes sense for your school.

At the end of this section you are asked to attach your school profile. Traditional schools submit this document to give colleges a snapshot of the school: the size and demographic makeup of the student body, the percentage of graduates who attend college, and the environment of the surrounding community. Additionally, this report describes the traditional school's accreditation and educational philosophies, the range of courses offered (including a list of AP and honors courses), the grading scale, average standardized test results, awards and distinctions students have earned, and other descriptors.

The request for School Profile information within the School Report may present a puzzle to homeschoolers. However, a wealth of key information about your home school can be captured in such a document. The "Home School" section of questions that you will later encounter as part of the School Report, which appears in your Students tab, asks about your homeschooling philosophy and setting, your student's participation in online, traditional, or college classes, and your grading scale and methods of evaluation. One approach is to write up a School Profile first (drawing inspiration from the questions in the Home School section) and then copy/paste the appropriate sections into the Home School text boxes. Another approach is to fill out the Home School section first, addressing the requested categories of information. Then if you have additional information, you may add it to the Home School information, write it up in a separate School Profile document, and upload it. See details on the Home School section a little later in this chapter.

So what are these items that may be included in a School Profile for a home school? They include, first of all, a description of your homeschooling philosophy. Here, you might briefly outline the "history" of your homeschooling, pointing out your desire to teach your student according to his or her learning style; to communicate values, citizenship, and character qualities; to provide the student with a flexible school schedule and plenty of opportunities for pursuing passions and interests; or to promote independent learning and intellectual curiosity. You might also describe the "modes" of education you use: traditional textbooks, group classes, classical education approaches, community college classes, online courses, private tutors and lessons, hands-on or project-based work, travel, community volunteer projects, or student-designed courses. If you mention "outside" courses, you may give the particulars and credentials of these teachers or programs here, or refer them to your course description document that will be uploaded with your transcript. A summary of your graduation requirements would also fit into this section.

As previously mentioned, traditional schools are asked to describe their grading scale and methods of evaluation. Here, you want to help the college understand that your student is prepared to enter a college environment fraught with competition for grades. If applicable, communicate that the students in your school have experience in being evaluated by an outside teacher, being compared to other students, and being accountable for meeting performance standards. For the courses that were graded by you as the parent, indicate the percentage scale translatable to letter grades (for instance, A = 90 to 100%) and include a couple of sentences about how grades were assigned (i.e., what rationale was used in giving grades). Also indicate whether honors and AP courses receive an extra point in the weighted GPA, and report how many credits are required for graduation.

Use a section of your School Profile or the Home School section to explain how many courses (and which courses) were taken outside the home. These would include distance learning, traditional high school courses, group homeschool courses, or college courses. If desired, and if you have had previous students graduate from your home school, you may mention which colleges accepted them and where they are attending. Likewise, if your current or previous student achieved national recognition such as National Merit Semifinalist or Finalist, AP Scholar with Distinction, or similar recognition, you may opt to mention this. (Other than this mention of a recognized national distinction, this is not the place to review your previous student's resume.) To see a sample School Profile for a traditional school, go to the College Board website under Education Professionals and search "Sample High School Profile."

Student-Specific Section of School Report

Once you have completed the portion of the School Report that provides a background on your school, you may move on to the student-pertinent questions. In general, you should answer as much as you reasonably can, and leave the rest blank or enter "Not Applicable." This section of the School Report relates to class rank, GPA, curriculum, ratings of the student in several areas, disciplinary history, and transcripts. There is also a Home School section which comes up because the student has entered that he or she is homeschooled. In the Class Rank section, you first answer how you report class rank. It is best to mark "None," because otherwise, the next required questions will ask for the student's rank and other pertinent details. For the GPA section, you are first asked whether you report GPA. It is up to you as to whether you say "Yes" or "No," but if you are giving your student letter grades, you would likely mark "Yes." From here, you will be asked what the student's GPA is, and on what scale (e.g., a scale of 4 if an A receives 4 points). Start and end dates that pertain to the terms involved in this GPA are requested, as well as whether the GPA is weighted or unweighted. "School's passing mark" is either C or D, depending on your standards, and "highest GPA in class" will be your student's GPA.

The Curriculum section asks you to compare your student's selection of courses with that of other college preparatory students "at your school" and to respond with anything from "less demanding" to "most demanding." You may, as a homeschooler, choose to compare your student with other homeschoolers you know, or you may choose "prefer not to respond." You are also asked whether the student is an International Baccalaureate, Advanced Cambridge Diploma, or AP Capstone candidate. This will apply to only a small percentage of students, and you will know whether your answer is "Yes."

Under "Ratings," unless you opted out, you are asked to rate the student's academic and extracurricular achievements, personal qualities and character, and overall quality using categories ranging from "Below Average" to "Outstanding (Top 5%)" or "One of the top few encountered in my career." This comparison is to be based on your student with respect to other students in his or her graduating class. Again, think about other students you have known, and try to come up with an objective rating—not inflated, but not overly demanding, either. You also have the option to mark "No basis," but this would be for evaluators who do not know anything about the student's accomplishments in that particular category. You as the parent know your student better than anyone else knows him or her.

In Disciplinary History, you will comment on whether the student has been guilty of a disciplinary violation at your school that resulted in probation, suspension, removal, dismissal, or expulsion. You will also communicate whether the student has been convicted of any crime.

Transcripts

The official transcript is submitted with the School Report. For the Common Application, it is uploaded from your own computer file into the counselor's portion of the application and should contain all courses and grades to date—generally through the end of junior year, plus summer, if applicable. Since most college applications are submitted in the fall of senior year, fall semester senior courses may still be in progress unless you are completing the application in late December or early January. Thus, list them and mark "IP" for "In Progress." Projected courses for the second term of senior year should be listed in the appropriate location on the transcript, indicating that they are proposed classes. As with the rest of the application materials, make sure that the transcript is neat, professional-looking, and easy to interpret.

In responding to questions on the School Report, you will be asked *how many* transcripts you will be uploading, and at this writing, the maximum is four. How should you reply to this question? The more the merrier, so choose three or four. In addition to your main transcript, take this opportunity to use the remaining upload buttons to upload a *course description document* (see below), an unofficial copy of the *community college transcript*, (if applicable), and any other key documents you may have. You will be asked whether current courses and college entrance examination scores are listed on the transcript, so mark "Yes" if this is true. You are then asked to mark whether you recommend this student "With reservation," "Fairly strongly," "Strongly," or "Enthusiastically."

Home School

In the Home School section, parents/counselors are asked to respond to several open-ended questions relating to the homeschooling environment. These are asked in the context of text boxes that can contain quite a few words (at this writing, 1000 words each). Respond to these clearly, succinctly, and professionally, also recognizing that this is a prime opportunity to display the unique qualities of your home school and to demonstrate how your student was able to take advantage of these qualities. Note that these are all required questions, and that they make good fodder for a School Profile.

The first question asks you to comment on aspects of the homeschool experience such as educational philosophy, reasons for homeschooling, and your instructional setting. In the second box, you will explain your grading scale or other methods of evaluation. Here, in addition to explaining the rationale for giving grades and describing your weighting policies, you may also want to include remarks about outside evaluators who gave descriptive evaluations of your student. The third box asks you to list and describe courses your student has taken from distance learning programs, traditional schools, or institutions of higher learning (i.e., colleges), as well as describing content of the course, schedule, and interactions with instructors and students. If you have quite a few of these courses to list and describe, you may refer to your attached course description document. Additional standardized testing scores (if applicable) would also be entered in this section.

To close this section, you are asked whether you are a member of a homeschoolers' association. This could include HSLDA, your local or regional homeschooling association, or your PSP.

Early Decision Agreement

As the student's counselor, you also play a role in the Early Decision agreement, if applicable. You will be asked to affirm that you have advised the applicant to abide by the Early Decision commitment. To complete this section you will check the appropriate box, electronically sign, and date your affirmation.

Counselor Recommendation

The Counselor Recommendation is a form that contains more student-specific (rather than school-specific) information compared to the School Report, and it is a much more personal document relating to your student's characteristics, accomplishments, and potential. Member colleges can choose whether or not to require this recommendation form, but whether required or not, you may opt to submit it. In fact, you will definitely want to submit it. Essentially a letter of recommendation for your student, this form is completed in a separate section of the School Report.

One portion of the Counselor Recommendation form asks you how long you have known your student (*parents snicker*) and in what context, and you are asked to provide the first words that come to your mind to describe your student. A three- to six-word list is a good response.

The meat of the Counselor Recommendation is the letter or document you will write on behalf of your student, assessing his or her academic characteristics, personality and character, performance in academics, and involvement in extracurriculars and the community. If your student has any marked problems or weaknesses, you should also discuss these situations. You may upload a document or use the 1000-word text box.

Since all parents are naturally proud of their children, you may find it difficult to write an objective evaluation of your student's abilities. Take plenty of time and make many revisions. Consider quoting or paraphrasing comments other adults have made about your student, and make the student come alive in the admissions officer's mind. Seek to *show*, don't just *tell*. See Chapter 23, "The Sealed Envelope," for more detailed advice and for some tips and caveats on writing a letter about your own offspring.

Once the School Report and Counselor Recommendation have been submitted, they cannot be modified or retracted, so check and double check your work to make sure there are no errors or omissions. Upon submission, they will be available to all the colleges to which the student has submitted his or her application.

Mid Year, Final, and Optional Reports

Two updates to the School Report (the Mid Year Report and the Final Report) are submitted in the middle and at the end of the senior year, respectively, to provide updated information on academics and personal characteristics. Primarily, they are a mechanism for reporting senior year grades for fall and spring semesters, but they also provide a way to add any new honors or awards or to indicate a change in academic courses after the original Common Application was submitted. The Optional Report is indeed optional and is intended as a mechanism to update colleges on information that becomes available after the School Report is submitted but before the Mid Year Report is due. However, for homeschoolers, it can be used if you have some information on your school or your student that simply doesn't fit anywhere else, or in case of "emergency"—you have submitted the School Report and Counselor Letter but have inadvertently left some information off. The Optional Report, Mid Year Report, and Final Report can only be accessed after the School Report has been submitted.

Course Descriptions and Additional Information Requested

As you might suspect, colleges may need more than a brief student evaluation from you as you fill out the homeschooler's application and its attachments. Because colleges do not have descriptive information on file for your school, as they do for traditional schools, they may request, or at least appreciate, a detailed description of your homeschooling. This request may be publicized on their websites in a specific section for homeschooled applicants, or you may learn about it as you communicate with the admissions office by phone, personal visit, or email. The admissions staff may also contact you after you have already submitted the application, asking for additional description or documentation. Having an organized, complete set of course descriptions all ready ahead of time—one or two paragraphs for each and every course, along with textbook titles and perhaps the credentials of any outside instructors—makes this request for extra information a "non-issue." Supplying a professional-looking set of course descriptions automatically makes you look as if you know what you are doing educationally—which of course, you do.

As you provide this information, remain calm and professional, even if you feel that the college is being unreasonable by asking you for extra documentation. In fact, it is best to be proactive and professional and have it ready. Avoid feeling resentful of what you might interpret as their apparent distrust of your home education. At the other extreme, never feel that you have to downplay your student's nontraditional experiences or apologize for your homeschooling.

When we filled out both of our students' college applications, most of the colleges specifically requested detailed course information. They asked us to provide *as much information as possible* (their words) about our homeschooling. We ended up sending most of the schools five to fifteen pages of descriptions of our home school and of all the individual courses. Because evaluating homeschoolers' applications is very time-consuming, be considerate of these overworked evaluators by being as succinct and yet as informative as possible. As mentioned previously, one convenient method of sending this information is to upload the document using one of the transcript upload buttons on the Common Application in the Counselor section. Alternatively, find out if it can be mailed and consider assembling a small but strategic packet of information. If colleges do not want to receive mailed items, perhaps you can create a PDF of scanned items (again, be selective) to upload using one of the transcript upload buttons.

What should be included in this detailed description or expanded "packet," whether electronic or paper? (Remember that it's optional.) The materials we chose to send seemed to satisfy all the colleges, and no additional follow-up information was ever requested. For example, our daughter's packet included the following items, but you can use your ingenuity to adapt this list to your own student's achievements:

- Brief course descriptions of all the high school courses—course title, level, credits, type of course (AP, honors, community college), a paragraph or two of description for each course as you wrote them based on Chapter 7's instructions, and textbook titles or reading lists. Some colleges also request the credentials of the outside instructors, so it's good to have this information assembled.
- A document that we jokingly called the marketing piece, highlighting the way homeschooling had allowed Julie to pursue four or five major accomplishments, each of which we described in brief detail.
- The activity schedule of a science club that Julie conducted for neighborhood children.
- The introductory summary of her scientific research project.
- A web page describing an award Julie received at the end of her summer research internship.
- A page from the magazine of a local university medical center, containing an article about Julie and her research program.
- Two short letters from students who had been in a homeschool Shakespeare class that she had taught, expressing their appreciation for what they had learned from her.

Any family could seize this opportunity to highlight aspects of homeschooling that are not fully covered in other sections of the application. Choose your own customized mix of items to provide a "3-D" view of your student and to display how he or she pursued activities with passion—but don't overdo it.

Some colleges ask that any descriptive documents be written in the student's "voice." In other words, they would like the student to describe what homeschooling was like, why he or she chose to pursue it, and what benefits and downsides he or she experienced. You might choose to submit a description in the student's words as well as a set of more detailed course descriptions written by the parent.

Similarly, some colleges ask for a writing sample from the student. Since the personal essay required on the college application is also a writing sample, it seems redundant to request a second sample. Nevertheless, if your student's favorite colleges are asking for writing samples, find out the length required (e.g., short essay or longer research paper). Then look through the English assignments you have saved and find an essay that is thought-provoking and demonstrates your student's best skills in content, style, organization, and mechanics. In general, it's also a good idea to save a few representative and excellent assignments from your high school years (one or two per subject area) in case a college ever asks for work samples.

Some homeschoolers consider it burdensome to be asked to send this additional information.

However, for most families, this request is actually a benefit. Instead of being limited to presenting a brief, cut-and-dried view of your student, you have the opportunity to send a rich, well-rounded portrait of your homeschooling and of the passions the student pursued because of the flexible schedule. This is your chance to showcase your student's accomplishments. Being *invited* to send extra materials or descriptions is one advantage of being a homeschooler. Traditional students typically do not get this invitation...and they would love to have it.

As a side benefit, reviewing your student's high school career in detail will give you a deep sense of satisfaction and thankfulness at what you were able to accomplish together. This trip down Memory Lane is a welcome perk in the midst of the hectic college application season.

TEACHER RECOMMENDATIONS

Another important section of the application, to be completed by a third party, is the Teacher Recommendation. Depending on the college, the number of recommendation letters can range from one to three. The teacher chosen must have taught the student in an academic subject, generally during the junior or senior year. Homeschoolers frequently choose community college professors, co-op or group academy instructors, or others who have directly taught or supervised them. Parents should not write teacher recommendations, as they are already writing the Common Application counselor letter. For non-Common Application colleges, check to see if the admissions department wants a letter from the parent.

These teachers provide background information on the courses they have taught the student and on how long they have known him or her, and then mention words that come to mind when describing the student. The recommendation form provides an area for rating the student on academic characteristics, as well as the opportunity to upload a recommendation letter. As with the School Report, these forms are completed online (only rarely on paper) and sent directly and confidentially to the college. Some teachers, however, may give your student a copy of the letter to keep. Chapter 23 lists and describes the characteristics teachers are asked to rate and explains how to select teachers to write these recommendations.

In addition to seeking academic evaluators, many students ask a pastor, employer, volunteer supervisor, coach, or other adult who knows them well to write a letter of recommendation. Some colleges allow these optional non-academic recommendations (the Common Application calls this the "Other Rec ommender"), and this option clearly opens up a possibility for more holistic evaluations of students' gifts and abilities. Chapter 23, "The Sealed Envelope," provides more detail on teacher evaluations.

Online Evaluations

As previously mentioned, the Common Application's online evaluation function allows the student to "invite" a counselor and several teachers to write evaluations. This is done by entering their names and email addresses when prompted in the indicated section, and clicking "Invite Teacher." From there, the student must also "assign" each recommender to a particular college or university's application. For instance, if the student has invited two teachers, and College A requests two recommendations while College B requests only one, the student will "assign" both teachers to College A and only one of the teachers to College B. These individuals, including the parent/counselor, if applicable, then receive an email with a user name, a password, and a link taking them to a page of the Common Application where they can fill out the recommendation, upload a letter, and submit this information when it is finished.

Within "My Colleges," the student can view the names of the recommenders and see whether they have submitted the forms, but they cannot read these forms. Instructions, FAQs, video tutorials, and the opportunity to submit questions to the Common Application Help Desk are available to walk the student and parent through this 21st century method of doing college applications.

TO SUM UP

You may feel that you are drowning in forms, but try to hold steady as you click your way through applications for a few more weeks. Both student and parents will be busy during the first half of the senior year gathering the essentials of the application and working hard to summarize the high school years. The next chapter will suggest some ways to maximize the results of all the hard work you are putting in!

Chapter 21

Working Smart, Not Hard:

Tips and Precautions about College Applications

*A*fter "touring" the typical college application, you may understand more about what colleges ask students, but you may still wonder how students can best portray themselves in just a few short screens of data. Keep the following tips and strategies in mind during the application process.

TIPS FOR A COMPELLING APPLICATION

One More Time ... Start Early!

At the risk of being annoyingly repetitive, I repeat that starting early is *the* cardinal rule for college applications. Summer is not too soon to start working on them, and students can even begin collecting and pondering essay prompts during the junior year. With their busy workload, most seniors have precious little time to work heavily on applications during the fall. If essays are drafted and recommenders have been identified, the student can handle filling out the rest of the forms before the deadlines. But if too much of this work must still be done from scratch, prepare for some stressful days and sleepless nights.

Make a Master Checklist

If your student is applying to six to ten colleges and three or four scholarship programs, keeping track of deadlines for all the individual pieces of the application will become challenging. Early in your student's senior year, sit down and make a master list of *everything* you can possibly think of that needs to be done. Include applications to complete, transcripts and test scores to submit, recommendations to coordinate—everything. Record all deadlines and assign each one a "goal deadline" of a week or more ahead of the actual due date. Next, arrange all the tasks in chronological order, making a note of who will take care of this task (Dad, Mom, or student). Most tasks must be done by the student, but perhaps the parent can go online and submit SAT or ACT scores to all the colleges or set up digital and/or paper filing systems for all items submitted. And of course, homeschool transcripts, course descriptions, and the counselor materials will be generated by the parents.

Keep this master list in front of your collective faces. Incorporate it into your digital calendars, and post a copy on the fridge to help you keep up with deadlines. You'll receive tremendous satisfaction as you cross off the finished items and see yourselves that much closer to the end of this process.

Work from a Resume

As described in the previous chapter, your student should prepare an organized, well-worded summary of extracurricular activities, leadership positions, honors and awards, employment, volunteer work, career ambitions, and other outstanding experiences. Once the descriptive phrasing of each activity is just right, your student can reuse it each time he or she fills out another application.

Get Those Recommendations Going

As your student fills out the student-specific sections of the application, he or she should initiate the process for teacher references and submit the requests to teachers, allowing plenty of time for them to complete their evaluations before the deadlines. The student resume mentioned above will also be handy for teachers who are writing recommendations. Chapter 23 has more tips on gathering recommendations.

Become Familiar with the Application and Any Specialized Forms

Since the application takes the student to multiple screens of questions, and since different student circumstances may yield new batches of questions, become familiar with the application as soon as your student is able to sign up and create an account. Short-answer questions, and even essay prompts, may differ according to the major or department the student is interested in. They may also vary depending on whether the student is homeschooled or traditionally schooled. Scroll through the application with the goal of ferreting out all the questions and essay prompts that must be completed. For example, an engineering major may be asked to describe a time when he or she had to innovate a solution to a problem. If in doubt about a college-specific question, contact the admissions office, but first make sure that your question is an important one that cannot be answered from the college website or other reliable sources.

Realize That the First Pass Is a Draft

Naturally, the first pass through the online application will generate a few mistakes and a number of questions. Essays may not fit the allotted spaces; ambiguities may arise and require phone calls or emails to clear up the problem; the student may accidentally enter information in the wrong place. Unexpected short-answer or essay-length questions may pop up, and the student will want sufficient time to answer these with care and thoughtfulness. You can avoid a certain amount of stress simply by realizing that it will take several passes through the application until your student feels "done." In the meantime, keep an organized list of the questions or problems you encounter, perhaps by saving screenshots or printouts of the pages where these questions or glitches occur. Follow up on these with the college, with the Common Application Help Center, or with another appropriate resource until all questions have been answered.

Concentrate!

Filling out a typical application can take several hours, not including application essays. Whether or not you are actively helping, set aside a time when your student can focus on the task without interruptions or distractions from the phone, TV, or social media.

Don't Equate "Online" with "Informal"

When filling out online applications, your student should use the same care and completeness that would be appropriate for a paper application. It should not read like a text message, social media post, or quick email; it should be free of punctuation lapses, slang, informal usage, and abbreviated words, except for standard abbreviations used when fitting activity descriptions into a limited space.

Be Honest

One question on the college application asks about any crimes, misdemeanors, academic suspensions, or expulsions the student may have in his or her past. If your student has experienced any of these difficulties, honesty is vital here. The student should explain the situation as clearly as possible and seek to show the growth, learning, and change that has taken place since that time.

Answer All Questions, Even if the Answer Is "Not Applicable"

To prevent misunderstandings over incomplete applications, answer all required questions on the application. Required questions on the Common Application are marked with a red asterisk; there are also optional questions. If the question obviously doesn't apply to homeschoolers, your student should enter "Not Applicable" in the space provided, if possible. For example, if the student is asked to provide his/her rank in the senior class, enter "Not Applicable," since this is irrelevant for a homeschooler.

Be Careful with Extras

Be cautious about submitting additional materials beyond the application and main essay(s), such as extra essays, recordings of the student playing the harp, or packets of artwork. Because the average college application is evaluated in twenty minutes or less—sometimes far less—extra clutter could potentially annoy admissions officers. However, at least two exceptions to this rule exist. Some colleges, as mentioned earlier, will actually *ask* for additional materials from homeschooled applicants in order to gain a more complete view of the student's achievements, curriculum, and academic rigor. Find out ahead of time, via the website, campus information session, phone call, or email, what the admissions office would like to see. Materials could range from a brief description of your homeschool courses to a full portfolio containing samples of work, extra essays, or photos and descriptions of long-term projects or unit studies. As a general rule, smaller schools are more welcoming of extra materials than are larger schools. Colleges may also allow extra recommendation letters from homeschooled students—ask!

A second case in which extra materials will be allowed is if your student is particularly talented in an area of the fine arts (such as visual art, design, music, theater, or architecture) and is seeking a degree in this field of study. Your student should study the college website and contact the admissions office to learn procedures for fine arts submissions and the need for auditions, screening, or portfolio review. Deadlines are often considerably earlier than they are for the typical college application, to allow time for specialized appointments or auditions. Abide by all guidelines set forth by the specific department or by the admissions office. Sometimes an additional Fine Arts application must be completed, or portfolios must be submitted through an evaluation platform such as SlideRoom.

Avoid Gimmicks

Students who are desperate to stand out from the crowd resort to attention-getting tactics: sending baked goodies, delivering singing telegrams, or submitting essays in verse form. The word from virtually all college admissions offices is *Don't*. These tricks will not help your student's application, and they may actually hurt it. Homeschoolers, especially, will want to appear professional, sensible, and bright—not desperate for attention. Instead of dreaming up gimmicks, your student should focus more energy on writing a standout essay or finding the ideal teachers to write letters of recommendation.

Parents – Assist and Advise, But Don't Take Over

The parent's role in the student portion of the college application process is that of a helpful administrative assistant and advisor, rather than that of a master of ceremonies running the entire show. In fact, the student's maturity in taking ownership of the process is an excellent indicator of readiness to start college. So, rather than micromanaging, simply help your student stay on track. Your job is to become familiar with the whole process, help proofread applications, draw up a deadline list with your student, provide your credit card for fee payments, and have mailing supplies ready for a few items that may need to be mailed. You can also make phone calls to the colleges to ask specific clarification questions. The student, however, should make some of these calls. What you should *not* do is to call and ask for special favors or special consideration.

Above all, parents can pray the student through the process. Discuss goals and priorities, troubleshoot questions and problems, and help your student discover the right "fit" for the college years.

Be Timely and Proactive About Submission

When all the pieces of the application have been assembled and your student is ready to submit it, just a few more decisions remain. Make sure your student proofreads and reviews the entire application —every single item on every single screen—before clicking "Submit." Also check to see if anything needs to be mailed in. And even though online applications are convenient, waiting until the last minute is not advisable. Because many students access application websites on the night that applications are due, the servers may become overloaded with hundreds of submissions per minute. Consequently, pages may take extra time to load, delaying the completion of the application. Plan to file a few days early.

If you are completing any paper applications or paper-based elements of the application, take note of whether mailing deadlines are *postmark* deadlines or *arrival* deadlines. If they are arrival deadlines, carefully plan the mailing date to allow enough time for the item to arrive. Consider obtaining a mailing receipt at the post office as proof that the item was mailed on a certain day. Some students even resort to using or overnight delivery services. Check to make sure that this delivery system is acceptable to the college. Also check and recheck the email and/or physical mail addresses for items to be sent.

Be Ready to Deal with Missing Information

Keep both a digital and a printed copy of the completed application in an easily retrievable place. Find out how the college will communicate with your student if pieces of the application are missing. Most electronically acknowledge your online submission; some colleges later send an email stating that the application is complete; others communicate only if something is missing (such as teacher recommendations). Colleges may also send applicants an ID number to log in and check the status of their applications. Often, this site is also used to announce admission decisions when the big day arrives. Today, high school seniors wait anxiously by their smartphones, not by their mailboxes, for that all-important news.

Keep in Contact with the College

Visiting the college for tours, attending campus open houses and regional receptions, and making telephone, social media, and email contacts are all ways to show continued interest in the college. During in-person meetings with the admissions staff, your student should ask good questions and offer positive, specific comments about the college. Later, if a college must decide between your student and another with less demonstrated interest, your student may receive a favorable decision. In fact, "demonstrated interest" is one factor that many colleges deliberately track. Not only are students competing with each other to try to gain acceptance to selective colleges; these selective colleges are also in competition with each other to admit the students who will actually attend. Thus, colleges (particularly elite colleges) try to predict the likelihood of a student matriculating at their institution by examining the clues gleaned from the demonstrated interest. Not surprisingly, the ultimate "demonstrated interest" is an Early Decision application, but the other factors mentioned above all come into play as well. However, students should never contact the college about frivolous matters, such as calling to ask about information that is readily available on the website. In contrast, contacting the college to ask about homeschool-related requirements or to request information that is unclear or absent from the website would be an appropriate contact.

HOW TO SHINE DURING INTERVIEWS

Surprisingly few colleges still *require* admissions interviews. Others *recommend* them, while still others simply offer them as options. Many schools do not offer interviews at all. For students who live far from the college, the admissions department arranges off-campus interviews, either with local alumni or with admissions officers during their regional visits. Most interviews take place in public locations such as coffee shops. Interviews can also take place via phone, Skype, or other convenient medium.

If the interview is optional, interpret this as *required* for students who want to enhance their chances for admission. Especially for homeschoolers, an interview provides an ideal opportunity to describe the educational background, express goals, and explain why this college is an ideal fit. Homeschoolers will want to make the most of this chance to highlight their strengths and interests. Chances are, your interactions with the interviewers will be interesting and pleasant, rather than being awkward or stressful. One major goal is to answer *your* questions about the college in a relaxed, friendly environment. However, I have also heard about students having "tougher" interviews.

Interviewing Tips

Your student should always follow standard interviewing practices. Here are some tips, directed specifically to the student, for making a positive impression.
- Dress neatly. You don't have to wear a suit or a dress, but don't be sloppy.
- Arrive early.
- Smile, make eye contact, and shake hands with the interviewer.
- Seek to make a confident, friendly impression with your manners, voice, and composure.
- Avoid one- or two-word answers. Always seek to share additional insights and details.
- Show genuine enthusiasm and passion about your interests, your goals, your extracurricular experiences, and your view of how this college can help you on your educational journey.
- Prior to the interview, research the college thoroughly so that you don't ask "obvious" questions.
- Be ready to share one or two specific comments about the college and why its programs, courses, and overall philosophy fit well with your own goals and plans.
- Ask specific questions that show that you've done your homework, as well as answering questions about yourself and your goals. For instance, research a couple of special programs the college offers (internships, research opportunities, interdisciplinary studies) and inquire about these.

What Will They Ask?

Here is a rundown of common interview questions. Each college will, of course, customize these.

- What extracurriculars, work experiences, and summer activities have meant the most to you?
- What are your favorite subjects?
- Why do you wish to attend this college?
- What is your proposed major? Why does this interest you?
- What courses at the college interest you most?
- What are some highlights of your high school years?
- What distinguishes you from other applicants to this college?
- How do you hope to contribute to this college's academic, extracurricular, or community life?
- Describe your strengths and weaknesses. How have you addressed your weaknesses?
- What are some of your favorite literature selections, movies, music, or websites?
- Describe an inspiring teacher or mentor.
- What are your goals and ambitions?
- What are some meaningful experiences or leadership activities you have participated in?
- Describe some challenges or obstacles you have faced and explain how you resolved them.

Especially for homeschoolers:

- How was your homeschooling conducted?
- How did you like this form of learning?
- What were its advantages and disadvantages?
- How did homeschooling prepare you for college and the "real world"?
- How did you develop diverse socialization?
- What accountability did you have to outside teachers?

Students who fear becoming nervous or tongue-tied during interviews might want to do some role playing ahead of time so that they can answer questions clearly and pleasantly. Students should simply practice being themselves and explaining their goals and interests.

In our experience, interviewers were fascinated with the idea of homeschooling and asked numerous questions about this nontraditional educational pathway. In fact, it was sometimes difficult to get the interviewer off the subject of homeschooling and onto the college-pertinent topics. If your interview follows this pattern, remember that it is a prime opportunity to make you as an applicant—and homeschooling in general—sound attractive and innovative.

One awkward question that sometimes comes up is "Where else are you applying?" Technically, this is an unfair question, especially if one of the other colleges has a "bigger name" than the one conducting the interview. Admissions officers know that students accepted to a more prestigious university will probably choose to attend that school over a "lesser" school. This principle can sometimes harm a student's chances of admission to the less selective school.

If your student is asked this question, he or she may politely say, "I would prefer not to answer that question," or may respond, "My list is not finalized yet." Even better, the student could name one or two colleges with similar characteristics and selectivity to the one conducting the interview.

Upon completion of the interview, your student should ask for a business card from the interviewer and use this contact information to send a thank-you note or email after the interview.

REMEMBER THAT A FEW FINAL STEPS ARE COMING

When your student has completed the full round of applications, whether this be in the fall or in the winter of senior year, remember that a few more documents must be submitted. Immediately after the end of the first semester (January or early February), send in the Mid Year Report, documenting the fall semester grades. The Mid Year Report is one of the forms included in the Common Application, and an updated transcript will be required at this time too. Schools not on the Common Application will have their own systems for requesting midyear grades and updates.

Later in the spring, following all the excitement of receiving acceptances and officially committing to one college, the last step is to send the final senior transcript and any other documents requested by the college. The Common Application has a form called the Final Report, which is to be submitted at the end of the school year if your student's chosen college is a Common Application member (and again, non-Common Application colleges will have their own protocols). Take note of the deadlines for both the Mid Year Report and the final transcripts and forms. They are easy to forget as the busy senior year proceeds. Also, be sure to submit all financial aid forms on time (see Chapter 25 for details). During the summer, once AP scores come out, submit all AP scores to receive credit according to the college's policy.

TRANSFER STUDENTS—AND INADVERTENT TRANSFER STATUS

While it is beyond the scope of this book to provide full instructions for transfer applications, a few homeschool-specific tips might be helpful. Colleges vary widely in their requirements for transfer students. Many take only junior transfers; some take sophomores or even seniors. Some have a rigid list of required courses that must be taken before transferring; others evaluate students on a case-by-case basis.

The Pros and Cons of Transfer Status

Some colleges are adamant about labeling students as transfer students if they have completed a certain number of college units—anywhere from just one course to 27 units or so. They may or may not stipulate that this refers to courses taken *after* high school graduation. Thus, if your student plans to take any community college classes at all, you will want to check with prospective colleges early in the game and ask whether a given number of units taken *before high school graduation* (the magic phrase) will change the status from freshman to transfer applicant. See Chapters 13 and 14 for a discussion of this and other considerations if your student takes community college courses.

Being considered a transfer student can be favorable or unfavorable, depending on your student's goals. Community college units can speed the path to a bachelor's degree for students who transfer all or most of their courses. But in some cases, these units may be in courses that will not count toward the major field or toward general education, or will not even transfer in the first place. Additionally, having too many college units may disqualify the student for freshman scholarships (which are often quite lucrative).

As mentioned in Chapter 13 on community college tips, you may want to browse *articulation agreements* between your local community college and the in-state four-year colleges your student is interested in, as well as searching for *SAP (Satisfactory Academic Progress)* policies for any colleges and universities of interest. Articulation agreements (also called transfer agreements or transfer pathways) take the guesswork out of the transfer process by stipulating which community college courses transfer directly to the university or satisfy general education or major course prerequisite requirements. With some exceptions, it usually makes sense to take courses that will count towards general ed or prerequisites, rather than choosing interesting but less useful courses that simply rack up the total count of college units.

Homeschooled & Headed for College

SAP policies communicate the rules about the number of college credits (including community college) a student is allowed to accumulate at a particular university before he or she is no longer eligible for financial aid. Furthermore, some universities with impacted student populations create policies about how long—either in semesters or quarters, or in number of credits accumulated—students are allowed to remain enrolled. For universities with these policies (frequently, crowded state universities), the student is required to graduate or withdraw from the university after a stipulated number of credits have been earned. Since for homeschoolers, these total credits may start to accrue during the high school years, be sure to check into these policies to make sure your student will not be impacted later on.

Note, though, that the nation's most selective universities generally *encourage* high schoolers to take community college courses to enhance their high school education, and they usually do not allow much, if any, transfer credit from these courses. In other words, these students would come in as freshmen with extra college credits, but these college courses, rather than being transferred into the university, would simply be another metric to help applicants succeed in the admissions process.

Strategies for Using Community College Units

With all these considerations, a bit of strategic planning is in order. First of all, if your student has community college credit but does not want to be considered a transfer student—for one of several reasons, such as not wanting to lose eligibility for freshman scholarships—the key strategy is to clarify with the four-year school that the student is a *homeschooler* and took these courses before graduating from high school. Thus, the community college courses were taken as part of the *high school* coursework. With some colleges, usually small private colleges, your student may be able to enjoy the best of both worlds by making notations on an unofficial copy of the community college transcript to identify some of the courses as "for high school credit" and others as "for college credit." The four-year college may possibly agree to let the student transfer the units desired for college credit, up to the maximum allowable to retain freshman eligibility, and this student will then enter college as a freshman with some college credit already accrued.

Some homeschooled students who enter college as freshmen come in with enough college credits that they can shorten their stay, thus graduating one or more years early. Always check with the four-year college early in the game to avoid surprises or disappointments.

If your student has combined the last year or two of high school with the first year or two of college and is looking more and more like a transfer student, it may be advantageous to go ahead and earn a few more units and transfer in as a junior. Depending on university requirements, these courses can focus on subjects needed for transfer requirements, general education, or prerequisites for a major.

Transfer Application Process

Transfer application requirements vary widely and also depend on whether your student is transferring in as a freshman, a sophomore, a junior, or a senior (senior transfers are rare). *Always consult the college website and admissions office for a full list of specifics.* Generally, for freshman or sophomore transfers with fewer than about 60 units of college credit, requirements include official high school and college transcripts, SAT or ACT scores, remediation of any deficiencies from high school courses, letters of recommendation (this time from college professors), and completion of the school's transfer application. While students who intend to transfer as juniors or seniors and who come in with 60 or more units may not need high school transcripts or SAT/ACT scores, they will need to fulfill all the required lower division courses for university transfer. Their transcripts will be evaluated with respect to progress toward their intended major. Do note that selective universities are more likely to look at the high school record and SAT/ACT scores in addition to the college record, so do not assume that your student can skip standardized testing and simply transfer to his or her desired elite university as a junior. Always check the transfer policies ahead of time, as these vary widely from college to college.

Transfer application deadlines are usually later than freshman deadlines. March is a common month for application deadlines, with notification sent to the student in May. Some colleges accept the Common Application; others have their own applications.

Certain colleges are much more transfer-friendly than others. The most selective schools in the nation take very few transfers—perhaps 6 to 10% of the students who apply. Students at these schools tend to stay for all four years, rather than dropping out or transferring out—thus leaving very little room for incoming transfers.

As a general rule, your state university system will have the most streamlined system for transferring in from your local community colleges. Often, these universities actually encourage students to study at the community college for the first two years and then to transfer to the university. Under this plan, students will receive a more personalized general education with smaller classes, and the university will receive the serious students who have proven themselves in the first two years of college. In this scenario, a homeschooler can strategically cut a year or two off the total length of the college education by taking community college courses during the sophomore, junior, and senior years of high school. If these courses are carefully chosen to fulfill the general education or transfer requirements of the university, the student may be able to transfer in as a full-fledged junior while still being only the age of a typical college freshman or sophomore. (But note that if the "transfer as a junior" plans change or do not work out, a freshman applicant with many units will want to be aware of SAP policies as mentioned previously.)

Many community colleges have set up transfer admission agreements with certain universities to provide a paved path for acceptance. Focused advising, priority admissions processing, and early transfer credit evaluation are other advantages of some of these programs. With all transfer plans, be proactive as a parent and as a student to search out requirements early in the game. Understand all the admission requirements for the four-year university, including GPA requirements for college courses, testing requirements, and whether confirmation of a high school diploma will be needed at any step of the process.

If you are intrigued by the "early transfer" plan but are uneasy at the thought of your student being a year or two younger than his peers at college graduation time, consider other attractive options. The student could stay in college long enough to earn *two* bachelor's degrees instead of one, complete a master's degree by the time his or her agemates complete their bachelor's degrees, or take a lighter load as an undergraduate, leaving time to hold down a job and help pay for college expenses.

In conclusion, homeschooled students and their parents should carefully think through these scenarios and do what is best for the student. Regardless of your student's plans for the community college units, it is wise to know the rules about transfer status ahead of time. Ideally, students need to know these policies at least a year or so before application time, since the transfer application process is significantly different from the freshman application process. This is easier said than done and may require talking to several people in each office—both the community college and the four-year university—before the full story becomes clear. But with perseverance and diligence, you and your student can discover how to maximize the high school/community college years in order to make a good start at the university.

TO SUM UP

Whether your student is applying as a freshman or as a transfer student, be aware of all the components of a typical application. With careful thought and planning, your student can maximize the chances of receiving that "Congratulations" email that evokes shrieks of joy.

Chapter 22

Your Life in 650 Words or Less:

The Application Essay

*J*unior year grades are in, and they are not bad at all. SAT, ACT, and AP exams have all been taken—with quite admirable results. College websites have been thoroughly perused, and applications are ready to fill out. Now you and your student are staring at an array of essay prompts and asking yourselves (mentally, at least) a few questions. Will these essays make or break your student's chances at that dream school? Will a less-than-outstanding essay endanger your student's application even at less competitive schools? And what is its purpose, anyway? *What does the admissions department want to read in an application essay?*

Unbelievable as it might seem, the college application essay, often called the personal statement, is your friend. Especially for homeschoolers, the essay fills in the gaps in the mental picture that the admissions committee is creating of the student—gaps that test scores, transcripts, lists of extracurriculars, and even letters of recommendation can't fill. With the essay, students who have identical "statistics" can be clearly differentiated from one another. And while the essay is a fairly important piece of the admissions puzzle, it is by no means a make-or-break element, unless the essay is poorly written or the student is particularly borderline. But most of all, the college application essay allows the admissions staff to get to know the student's "3-D" self—his or her personality, character, goals, dreams, talents, and individual style.

IMPORTANCE OF THE COLLEGE APPLICATION ESSAY

Students facing the task of writing college application essays may initially have trouble gaining momentum, for good reasons. Self-revelation is always difficult; trying to guess what admissions officers want to read only compounds the problem. In the multifaceted admissions process, an excellent essay is a definite benefit. A mediocre essay, however, will not necessarily eliminate a student unless he or she is equally qualified with other students who have submitted better essays. If your student is already an extremely strong candidate, the essay may not make much difference either way—though this depends heavily on the selectivity of the college.

A number of years ago, an admissions director at the University of California, Berkeley, provided some perspective on the use of the personal statement: "As admissions officers, we are most interested in thoughtful, insightful essays that help us learn about the whole human being. The personal statement provides a way for us to see the person behind the grades and test scores. I advise students to step outside themselves and to think carefully about how they've chosen to spend their time, why they made their choices, and what they've learned from their decisions."[1]

Application essays reveal a student's true "self" and communicate depth of insight, creativity, and character. Because the essay also gives the admissions committee a snapshot of the applicant's writing skills, your student will want to work hard to revise the essay before submitting it.

The most selective schools may require several essays and may scrutinize them more closely than the less selective institutions do. Students applying to less selective schools may find that the college places a lower emphasis on the essay. Some colleges may not even require one; others may substitute a short set of questions to be answered in one or two paragraphs each. Thus, not all students will need to obsess about crafting the "perfect" essay for college applications.

Students and parents frequently wonder whether admissions staff actually read all the essays. The answer is, in general, yes. If a college requires an essay, the admissions department will read it. Many colleges have two readers for each application, as described in Chapter 24, "Behind Closed Doors." However, the reading process is quite rapid. At large universities, or at highly selective schools that receive thousands of applications, admissions readers may have up to 600 essays per day to read during the peak of application season. Thus, it is especially important to write an engaging essay that captures your reader's attention right from the start—and then keeps it.

JUST WHAT IS A COLLEGE APPLICATION ESSAY?

The personal statement is unlike any other piece of writing you have ever produced. In short, it is several things:

- A zoomed and focused photograph of an essential characteristic of *you*.
- A narrative with a purpose. You may utilize hints of cause/effect, problem/solution, or before/after structures, but you will not necessarily follow these formats.
- A showcase of your writing skills—so work hard on finding just the right words, phrases, and images to communicate your message. Aim to both show *and* tell.
- A unified piece with a satisfactory feel—somewhat like a memoir or a reflective piece.
- A highly communicative, highly personal piece that fills in the gaps of your application and helps you cover ground not yet covered.
- A revelation of your heart and passions—with supporting evidence from your life experiences. This piece should answer the question "Who are you?" not "What have you done?" and may demonstrate a change in perspective as a result of an experience or incident.

Typical Essay Topics

In the months before college application time, you and your student should gather personal statement prompts from the application websites of prospective colleges. Try to scope out the topics your student will actually be addressing for each school on the application list. If any of the prospective colleges are members of the Common Application, the student will be choosing one of the prompts listed below for the main Common Application prompt. In addition, many colleges require "supplementary essays"—anywhere from one to five additional statements ranging in length from 50 to 500 words. Prompts for these essays will be revealed when the student begins creating a college list within the Common Application; however, you might be able to get a sneak preview by searching the college's website.

For state university systems, essay prompts will vary depending on the university, and some systems will not require essays at all. Browse the university website to get an idea of the requirements.

The following are the topics from the 2019-20 Common Application®:*

- *Some students have a background, identity, interest, or talent that is so meaningful they believe their application would be incomplete without it. If this sounds like you, please share your story.*
- *The lessons we take from obstacles we encounter can be fundamental to later success. Recount a time when you faced a challenge, setback, or failure. How did it affect you, and what did you learn from the experience?*
- *Reflect on a time when you questioned or challenged a belief or idea. What prompted your thinking? What was the outcome?*
- *Describe a problem you've solved or a problem you'd like to solve. It can be an intellectual challenge, a research query, an ethical dilemma—anything that is of personal importance, no matter the scale. Explain its significance to you and what steps you took or could be taken to identify a solution.*
- *Describe an accomplishment, event, or realization that sparked a period of personal growth and a new understanding of yourself or others.*
- *Describe a topic, idea, or concept you find so engaging that it makes you lose all track of time. Why does it captivate you? What or who do you turn to when you want to learn more?*
- *Share an essay on any topic of your choice. It can be one you've already written, one that responds to a different prompt, or one of your own design.*

Essay topics reprinted with permission from The Common Application, Inc. <u>https://www.commonapp.org/</u> [2]

The following prompts have been gathered from the applications of numerous other colleges:

- *What is the most difficult experience you have ever had, and how did you cope with it?*
- *Compose an imaginary letter to your future college roommate. What things would you want to include in such a letter to give him/her a good idea of the kind of person you are?*
- *What have you read that has had a special significance for you? Explain why.*
- *Twenty years after you graduate from _____ you receive national and international recognition for your work. Describe this work and your hopes for its effects on society.*
- *Attach a small photograph of something important to you and explain its significance.*
- *Describe the reasons that influenced you in selecting your intended major field of study.*
- *If you could travel through time and interview a prominent figure in the arts, politics, religion, or science, whom would you choose, and why?*
- *Describe your experience in living in a racially, culturally, or ethnically diverse environment. What do you expect to need to know to live successfully in the multicultural society of the future?*
- *Make up a question, state it clearly, and answer it. Feel free to use your imagination, recognizing that those who read it will not mind being entertained.*
- *Use the space provided to indicate what you consider your best qualities to be, and describe how your college education will be of assistance to you in sharing these qualities and your accomplishments with others.*
- *Describe your homeschooling approach and how and why your family chose homeschooling. How was your learning process organized, what benefits accrued, and what, if any, choices did you have to make to accomplish this type of education?*

As you can see, essay topics can be quite varied. The common denominator is the task of communicating *who* the student is as a person and *what* is important in his or her past, present, and projected future experiences. If a topic from the second list above is intriguing, and if the college offers a "topic of your choice" option, your student could choose one of these topics. Remember that the student's everyday life is a valid essay topic. The student need not write about a major achievement. The college wants to discover the student's personality and priorities as he or she reflects on life's experiences, big or small.

HELPFUL RESOURCES

Since a full-fledged tutorial on writing application essays is beyond the scope of this book, you will want to seek out websites and books focusing specifically on college essays. One outstanding guidebook is *Escape Essay Hell* by Janine Robinson (website https://www.essayhell.com/). Written by a college application coach who has worked with hundreds of students, this step-by-step guide walks students through the process of listing several key traits or character qualities about themselves and then searching for personal anecdotes that clearly illustrate a time when these traits were developed or displayed. The current trend for many of the personal statements your student will write is the "narrative" format: centering the piece around a memorable story or anecdote that exemplifies the trait you are discussing. When it comes to choosing anecdotes, the quirkier and more unexpected, the better. One of my students wrote an excellent essay about what her insatiable desire to collect souvenir mugs says about her; another used the image of a snail retreating into its shell as a metaphor of his tendency to stay within his comfort zone —and then he explained a summer experience that helped him overcome that tendency. Still another student used the title of her choir's Christmas performance, *Magnificat*, as an image of the way her extroverted personality seeks to "magnify" the value of others with whom she comes in contact.

When choosing college essay websites and/or guidebooks, look for resources containing examples of "good" and "bad" essays, with a clear explanation of *why* the essays are good or bad. After reading through ten or twelve superior essays and a few inferior ones, you will have an idea of what colleges are looking for in the personal statement. Janine Robinson, mentioned above, has an excellent collection of engaging college application essays, called *Heavenly Essays*. This book is also well worth obtaining. Her website, https://www.essayhell.com/, features pertinent blog posts and spot-on advice. I highly recommend this website and the two books I've mentioned, as they are the best and most practical resources I've ever found on the "how to" process for college application essays.

GENERAL TIPS FOR ESSAY WRITING

This section is addressed directly to the individual responsible for writing the essays: the student.

The Number One Piece of Advice: Start Early!

To write an essay that accurately reflects who you are, you need to think about your topics several weeks or even months before the deadline. By the end of your junior year, gather the essay prompts from your top few colleges. Begin pondering them, and during the summer, start working on your essays in earnest.

With some prompts, you may be able to gather ideas long before you apply to college. In your homeschool English courses, use some of these prompts to experiment with writing personal essays that could serve as the beginnings of college application essays. Revise them repeatedly for content, style, clarity, interest, and mechanics. A strong writing curriculum in the early high school years will make essay writing come more naturally and will help you write in your own "voice." Of course, your experiences and insights will change and mature during the years of high school, so you will want to write your final essays to reflect the person you have become by the fall of your senior year.

See the tips for a productive brainstorming session later in this chapter. This session should happen during the summer before your senior year. And whatever you do, don't start your essays the night before they are due.

Tips on Topics and Content

Write the Essay about Yourself

No matter what the prompt is, always relate the topic to *yourself*. If you are describing your volunteer project among orphans in Mexico, don't focus on one particular little girl who captured your heart. This might make an excellent blog post, but here and now, the admissions committee wants to meet *you*. Tempting as it might be to use artistic writing to sketch out the fascinating characters or the breathtaking scenery you've encountered along your life's journey, resist the temptation. Instead, tell *why* this encounter was important to you, *what* it did to affect you or your goals, and *how* it impacted you. Colleges want to see how you have demonstrated leadership, initiative, and the ability to think, so make it very clear how you have done just that.

Consider the essay to be an "interview" conducted by the college for the specific purpose of finding out more about you. Subjects are numerous: your interests, extracurriculars, jobs, family traditions, a move or a major change in your life, a time of failure, an awkward incident, the legacy of your grandparents—and, above all, your comments and reflections on how these helped you to grow and to discover your identity.

For instance, one essay that Julie considered writing involved the fact that, soon after her Ukrainian great-grandparents came to the United States, they deliberately removed all traces of their Eastern European language and culture so that they could be truly American. In that era of bias against "foreigners," embracing one's ethnic background was detrimental to success in the new country. In contrast, Julie found herself longing to seek out her roots, her name origin, and anything she could discover about her Ukrainian heritage. Studying Russian and contemplating a Slavic Studies minor were some ways in which she could embrace this heritage in our modern era when ethnicity adds richness and diversity to life.

Remember that you want to showcase your areas of passion. If these passions are aligned with a special program or department for which the university is well-known, and you can make that connection with finesse, so much the better.

Address the Prompt Thoroughly

Be sure to answer the question(s) asked in the essay prompt—*all parts* of the question. If the prompt asks you to describe a book that had an impact on you and to tell why, do not omit the *why*. The more you show that you can follow directions, the stronger you will look as an applicant. Make sure that you fully understand the prompt before plunging into it.

Capture Your Reader's Attention

An effective essay begins with an attention-getting introduction. This might be an intriguing or startling statement, a provocative question, an unforgettable image (whether humorous or dramatic), a sentence that vividly sets a mood or creates an image, a bit of dialogue or action that draws the reader into a scenario, or a thought-provoking quotation. The idea is to draw your reader into your world—the world that describes your experiences, thoughts, and reflections on life. You might try a creative metaphor, or even an extended metaphor that weaves itself throughout the essay. Think like a film director: what do you want to highlight in the scenes you are capturing? What actions, words, and reflections do you want to show in the vignettes of your life that you have chosen?

After you have captured the attention of your reader, do your best not to lose it. Make your examples specific and realistic. Include observations from all or most of the five senses—not in a contrived or obvious way, but smoothly and artfully. Consider using a theme from a thought-provoking quotation that has meant a great deal to you.

As you write, never forget that the admissions staff will be reading hundreds of essays. What can you tell them about yourself that will be memorable and make them want to admit *you*?

Don't Rehash Your Extracurriculars List

Since the most critical guideline for essay writing is to *be yourself*, be sure to enrich your essay with illustrations and examples from your own life and thinking. But do not simply rehash your list of extracurriculars from elsewhere in the application. Use your essay to fill in gaps or to build up a particular activity or experience. For instance, if you want to highlight your participation in an after-school tutoring program, don't describe the program at length or enumerate how many hours per week you tutored. Instead, use the program as a "jumping-off point" to describe your thoughts, actions, and life-changing experiences gained during this activity—particularly through the use of image-rich vignettes or short anecdotes. Without saying it in so many words, find ways to demonstrate your level of leadership and commitment. Ultimately, your essays and the main part of the application should complement each other to communicate everything you want the college to know about you.

After writing your first draft of an essay, read through it critically to assess what it says about your personal characteristics, such as responsibility, intellectual curiosity, initiative, or any of the traits you listed during your brainstorming session. Ask yourself how you can *show*, not simply *tell* the reader that you possess these qualities. Conveying these ideas in a natural, creative fashion rather than in a mechanical or boastful manner is a tricky task, but by reworking and rewording your essay, you can do it.

Avoid Clichés

Though a talented writer can make even an overused topic fresh and interesting, students' approaches are often clichéd. You may think you are being original, but you probably are not; college admissions officers have seen it all. Overused approaches include the following: "I learned about life while playing my sport," "I helped someone, and it opened my eyes to the world," or "As a (*doctor, lawyer, teacher*) I'm going to make the world a better place." Always look for a fresh, unusual twist to your topic. Note that another overused topic is the "missions trip" or the "house-building for the homeless" trip. These are excellent ventures and are undoubtedly life-changing; the problem is that too many students have written about them, and it is difficult to make them fresh and personal. Sports injuries and academic disasters are also commonplace subjects for essays, so if you are considering one of these topics, create a one-of-a-kind approach that will remove your essay from the "cliché" pile.

Some students overplay hardships they have encountered. While these difficulties may be valid, focus on what you are currently accomplishing rather than on why the committee should feel sorry for you. Above all, do not invent or exaggerate hardships and challenges. If you have, in fact, overcome a significant obstacle such as a serious illness, disability, or family tragedy, use it to highlight what you learned and how it shaped your values, goals, and character. Show how you turned your obstacles into opportunities for personal growth.

Don't Be "Superman"

Avoid writing "Superman" or "Renaissance Woman" essays that brag about your achievements in a dozen different categories. Especially avoid writing an essay that laundry-lists your achievements and extracurricular activities. An essay of this type can't help but jump from accomplishment to accomplishment with neither depth nor meaningful connections. The admissions committee wants to see your passion and focus, not your wide array of skills. If you need to mention some achievements that are not covered elsewhere in your application, use a subtle approach and relate them to the main point of the essay.

Don't Butter Up the Admissions Committee

Refrain from using the essay to tell the admissions staff how excellent their university is, how warmly you were welcomed when you visited, or how it's the only school you truly want to attend. They want to hear about *you*, not about their school. You might slip in a sentence or two about a particular academic or extracurricular program that dovetails perfectly with your career plans, but other than that, save your school-specific comments for short supplementary essays that ask you why you want to attend this university. Note that you might not even have the opportunity to personalize the essay anyway, as the main Common Application is intended to be generic.

Don't Preach a Sermon

Even if you are quite sincere, refrain from using your college application essay to present a gospel message or a Christian testimony to the admissions staff. Though you may come up with a beautiful and encouraging piece of writing, this is not the venue for such a piece. That said, you will find that applications to Christian colleges will likely include personal statement prompts asking you to reflect on certain aspects of your faith journey. Also, it is perfectly fine to mention your faith in the context of your life goals, passions, key extracurriculars, and leadership activities—after all, it is part of who you are. Just keep it natural, maintain perspective, and balance these mentions of your faith with the other information you want to communicate to the college.

Strategize for Multiple Essays

If a college requires multiple essays, think about which aspects of your activities, leadership, and goals you can most strategically emphasize with each essay prompt. Highlight characteristics that might not be adequately covered in your list of extracurricular activities, and avoid repetition. In doing so, show vividly but naturally how homeschooling has helped you become a lifelong learner and a team player.

Always examine the full story that your main application, your transcript, your extracurriculars list, your recommendation letters, and your essays will tell about you. Strategically seek to gain as much "real estate" as possible (in the words of a former University of California reader). In other words, if you have interests, passions, or accomplishments that are not yet fully covered in your application, consider using a well-chosen essay prompt to highlight this facet of you. Your goal is to present a 360-degree view of yourself, without redundancy.

Where appropriate, retool and recycle certain essays for other college applications. To meet the needs of each college, you may have to revise them based on space considerations or slight differences in the wording of the essay prompt. *Be sure to use the correct college name if you mention it within your text.*

If you have the chance to complete an optional essay, do so if it will give the committee new information about you. For example, you could use an essay to explain a semester of poor grades. Use this essay to show what you have learned or how you have changed.

Tips on Style

Organize and Clarify

Without being stiff or sounding as though you're writing a research paper, organize your main ideas and construct logical paragraphs. Don't force your reader to stop and reread an unclear paragraph, and don't keep him or her guessing about where your train of thought is traveling. Check to make sure one idea flows smoothly into the next.

Use Variety

Don't forget your style rules from English class. Rather than always using standard subject-verb patterns, use a variety of sentence openers as well as complex sentences with dependent and independent clauses. Active verbs, concrete nouns, and well-chosen adjectives and adverbs will add sparkle to your essay. Be prepared to use a thesaurus as you've never used it before. Since you have limited space, every word counts. Make sure each one is productive, precise, and powerful.

Be Natural

Use a natural, easygoing writing style—not stuffy or academic. Choose words because they say exactly what you mean, not because they sound impressive. On the other hand, avoid being too informal or frivolous. A light tone with occasional humor is fine, but don't set out to write a funny essay unless you know that you can introduce the "real you" among the lines of levity.

Revise Wisely

Plan to go through your essay many times, each with a specific purpose, to mark changes that need to be made. Read through it at least three or four times for *content*, making sure you have said what you wanted to say and have included pertinent details without being flowery or redundant. Read through it again for *organization*, assessing whether your ideas and examples are presented in a clear, logical fashion. Then read through your essay several times for *style* considerations, choosing just the right words and sentence constructions. However, don't lose your momentum by stopping to make changes every few words. Instead, put a check mark or question mark in the margin if you encounter a rough spot, or circle words and phrases you intend to change later. On your final read-through (again, multiple times are essential), you will check *mechanics*: spelling, punctuation, capitalization, and grammar.

Tips on Mechanics and Length

Check and Recheck

In a college application essay, you have no excuse for mechanical errors—not even one tiny mistake. Check your essay repeatedly for spelling, grammar, capitalization, and punctuation mistakes as well as for typos or for problems with spacing and other formatting issues. Besides simply running your spell checker, consider running a grammar checker to flag errors such as run-on sentences, fragments, or lapses in pronoun-antecedent agreement. Another tip: reading the essay slowly from the bottom line up is a useful technique to help you slow down and look for small mistakes. After you have proofread your essay, ask someone else to read it.

Follow Format Instructions Carefully

Follow the format instructions described on the application, whether that means copying your essay into a text box or uploading the file into the application. Make sure your final version of the essay is clean and professional. If you are uploading the essay and can choose your font, use a traditional font rather than a decorative one.

Pay Attention to Length

Most colleges ask for essays of about 250 to 650 words, though the lengths required are highly variable. Some applications require one primary essay and several shorter essays. For the Common Application, the minimum length of the main essay is currently 250 words, and the maximum is 650 words. Never exceed the word limit specified: one implicit "test" in the application process is whether you can follow directions. Generally, however, the text box will not accept excess words.

Once again, every word counts, so seek to make your writing image-rich, not wordy. Since every word must pull its weight and prove its reason for existing, you will ruthlessly cut out the deadwood (repetition, obvious statements, and wordy phrases). And yes, some cuts will be painful, but overall, they will result in a better, more focused essay. For maximum effectiveness, start by writing a somewhat longer essay than the word count allows. After this "overwriting," cut away redundancies and condense your essay until your writing is concise, tight, on-topic, interesting—and within the word limit!.

USING YOUR ESSAY TO HIGHLIGHT YOUR HOMESCHOOLING

Since homeschooled students still represent a minority of college applicants, admissions officers will be interested in how you completed high school in this unusual way. In your main essay, or in one of the supplementary essays, you might decide to explain some aspects of your homeschooling. Rather than relating a play-by-play description, provide a fascinating, focused glimpse of something you did as a homeschooler that you couldn't have done as a traditionally schooled student.

When planning your essay, you can choose to describe how homeschooling has sharpened your thinking, broadened your education, fostered your capacity for independent study, or in some other way developed you into a one-of-a-kind person who will bring something special to the college. Ordinary life events can spark unforgettable essays if you personalize them and reflect insightfully on the event. Always use concrete examples and an anecdote or two to make your experiences come alive to the reader.

You do not necessarily need to describe your homeschooling—and in some cases, it is not the number one feature of your education and extracurriculars. However, many colleges are interested in hearing about your homeschooling. Some essay prompts that fit well with homeschooling experiences include the following:

"Significant Character" Prompt

Some prompts ask you to describe a significant character in fiction, or a creative work that has influenced you. Use this topic to describe the creative approaches you took as you studied this character through in-depth projects or unit studies.

"Diversity" Prompt

Describe how homeschooling is uncommon and innovative, and explain how you will bring diversity of educational background to the college.

"Personal, Local, or National Issue" Prompt

Highlight your involvement in political action if this has been a significant part of your home-schooling or if you have studied these issues in depth in a history, government, or debate class.

"Person of Influence" Prompt

Carefully think through your options. Consider describing your parent as teacher *only if* you believe you could write a stellar, out-of-the-ordinary essay in this way. You would need to write about how your parents expanded your horizons and developed your creativity and love of learning, all from your home setting—not about how wonderful your parents are. Save those precious words for Mother's Day and Father's Day! Since admissions staff may already view homeschoolers as too "cloistered" inside the home, you might prefer to dispel that myth by writing about experiences outside the home. Thus, consider describing a community college instructor, pastor, coach, or mentor who has significantly influenced you.

"Activity, Achievement, or Experience" Prompt

Focus on almost any significant homeschool-related or community-based activity and tell how it enhanced your education. Again, seemingly trivial details can add a fun sparkle to your essay.

"Why Is This College Best for You?" Prompt

Start by briefly describing your academic background and your exceptional experiences as a homeschooler. Then explain how you can uniquely contribute to XYZ University because of your unusual background. Finally, show how the college can provide what you need for the next stage of your education (research opportunities, a broad liberal education, specialized curriculum or academic programs, study abroad opportunities, campus groups, or other college-specific features). Do your homework and scour the college website for particularly interesting courses, special areas of focus within the major, or other opportunities.

"A Risk You Have Taken" Prompt

Homeschooling can certainly be considered a risk. Much responsibility is placed on both the student and the parent to assure that the education happens as it should. Describe how this came about in your life and how taking the risk was worthwhile.

THE ESSAY-WRITING PROCESS, STEP BY STEP

Brainstorming: Your High School Career in a Nutshell

An unforgettable essay always begins with a lively brainstorming session, and this is arguably the most important part of the college essay process. So don't shortchange yourself. Set aside a block of quality time to devote to this venture. Remember that in brainstorming, there are no wrong answers: you want ideas to flow freely. Jot down your extracurricular activities, experiences, reflections on life, goals, interests, observations, significant people in your life, and events or issues that you have pondered deeply. As Janine Robinson of EssayHell.com suggests, you will want to use your key traits, skills, talents, and character qualities as the main focus points for your essays. In her book *Escape Essay Hell*, she presents an exhaustive, multi-page list of traits you can browse through. What is the essence of *you* that you want the admissions committee to know? This is a time for soul-searching. Are you creative? Reflective? Extroverted? Do this exercise alone and then again with parents, siblings, or a close friend. You will want to choose the most important of these reflections and weave them into your essays.

Next, list quirky, unusual, random examples—stories, images, or anecdotes from your own life that portray one or more of your key traits in an unforgettable way. "Fodder" for these anecdotes or images can come from your likes and dislikes, memorable moments (whether embarrassing, humorous, or touching), items that adorn or litter your room, unusual items you collect, your nicknames, problems you've solved, and countless other sources—the more unexpected, the better. One of my students used the metaphor of smoothie-making to show how she loves the "fusion" of unexpected flavors and combinations, not only in the fruit and vegetable drinks she concocts, but also in her willingness to be creative, take risks, and "mix up" her activities and passions in highly unusual ways. Perhaps you have your own business selling homemade baked goods—and at Christmas, you took on too much work and found yourself elbow-deep in gingerbread house fixings. Or you rushed to arrive at an important piano recital immediately after a sports commitment, only to find that your dress shoes were not in your bag of clothing. Maybe you experienced an odd injury that communicates something about you. For instance, as a teenager, I broke my little toe when my brothers and I were competing with each other to try to kick high enough to touch a decoration hanging in the archway—however, our living room furniture was out of place due to a painting project, and my foot connected sharply with a solid walnut end table. Your job or volunteer work can also yield quirky, humorous examples. One student opened with a vivid image of her crouching in a store display window, with wisps of hay in her hair as she "wrestled" a mannequin and several large pumpkins in extremely limited space to design a window display for her part-time job. Keep the imaginative juices flowing as you search out "snapshots" of your life—something that only you will be able to share.

Choosing and Outlining a Prompt

You may have skimmed through the prompts before you brainstormed, but now take some serious time to examine your choices. Remember that you are choosing a prompt purely as a vehicle for describing *you*, so choose one prompt that will best showcase your experiences, ideas, achievements, or thoughts. Next, construct an informal outline sketching out how you might approach the topic. You might try a mind-mapping or "tree branches" approach to show how ideas are related to each other. Because you are competing with other students using the same essay prompts, try to write from a more unusual perspective. What story will you start with? What "problem" was solved? What traits and characteristics of the "essence of you" were displayed? What bits of humor can you add to give the essay a light touch where needed? Sketch out how you will build the basic structure of your essay, keeping in mind that you may change it as needed. One structure that works well is to begin in the middle of an intriguing story, event, or problem and then backtrack to relate how you found yourself in that situation. Describe the character trait that was being displayed (or that needed to change), and show that process taking place. Reflect on what this incident says about you, and finish up with the end of your story. Again, Janine Robinson's book *Escape Essay Hell* has excellent step-by-step guidance for this process, so be sure to check out her advice.

Most of all, keep in mind that even though you are designing a general structure, you should always write from your heart, so that your essay will stand out among the thousands.

Writing a Rough Draft

The third step is to plunge in and write a rough draft. Many students experience writer's block because they are trying to come up with a killer lead or to produce a memorable piece of writing on the first try. If you're having trouble starting at the beginning of your essay, try starting in the middle. Plunge into any idea or thought that seems to be flowing at the moment. You can always come back to the beginning to introduce your subject when you have more momentum and a better idea of where your essay is headed. As you write your draft, keep your reader in mind, striving to make your essay informative and interesting to someone who does not know you. Provide vivid examples so that by the time your reader reaches the end of your essay, he or she will definitely "know" you.

Revising and Polishing

After finishing your first draft, revise it as much as possible, but save copies of previous versions so that if you must cut a well-articulated sentence or profound thought purely for length reasons, you can resurrect it later for other essays. Plan to spend several hours, in several different editing sessions, finding precise words, revising sentence openers, cutting out redundancies, checking the length, and repeatedly asking yourself, "Is this what I *really* mean to say? Am I creating powerful images and communicating my genuine self?" Don't be surprised if you go through ten, twenty, or more revisions before you are satisfied.

Ask other people to read your essay and give you their comments. Specifically, ask them if it *sounds like you*. Put yourself in the place of the admissions staff who will read your essay. What can you say and how can you say it, to make them want to meet you—and thus to admit you?

"Cooling Off"

Don't try to do revise in one or two closely spaced sessions. After writing and initially revising your first draft, set your essay aside to "jell" for a couple of days. When you come back to the task, you'll discover more changes you must make. This is not a sign that you are a poor writer; rather, it is a hallmark of a strong writer to constantly find ways to improve. Continue to revise until you are satisfied that this essay is clear, concrete, concise, and compelling. Above all, don't stop until you're satisfied that it provides an apt introduction to you as a person and as a potential college student.

Adding the Finishing Touches

When you are happy with your essay—or when your deadline arrives, whichever comes first—reserve an hour or so for final touch-ups. Check your flow of ideas, check your word choice, and, one last time, check your grammar, spelling, capitalization, and punctuation. Run a final word count to check the length. Finally, copy and paste it into the text box or upload your file and consider it done.

Persevering...And Preserving for Posterity

Writing the college application essay is one of the toughest parts of the admissions process. Paradoxically, it is also one of the most rewarding. As you search your mind and heart for ways to describe who you are, and as you choose and reflect on the experiences that mean the most to you, you are creating a most fitting wrap-up of your high school years and, in fact, of your entire homeschooling career. At the end of the process you will have several beautifully polished pieces of writing that serve as a portrait of who you are as a high school senior, ready to enter the next phase of your life. Save these essays in a scrapbook, a journal, or another meaningful location. You will want to read them again someday when you have accomplished the goals you are now dreaming about, or when God has replaced those early dreams with some that suit your talents and His purposes even more.

TO SUM UP

Students, enjoy this soul-searching, ultra-creative, once-in-a-lifetime process of creating a snapshot of you as a high school senior.

Parents, as your student tackles the application essay, be there to brainstorm, to encourage, and to make a few comments as you read through rough drafts. By and large, though, let the student handle the whole task, for he or she is definitely ready for it. In fact, time and encouragement may yield several masterpieces!

And get the scrapbook ready. You'll want to preserve the final copies as evidence of the fascinating person your soon-to-be homeschool graduate has become, under your tutelage and by God's grace.

1. University of California Office of Admissions, "Personally Speaking: Just Tell It Like It Is," *California Notes*, October 1998.

2. The Common Application®, Inc., *The Common Application for Undergraduate College Admission: 2019-20 First-Year Application*, 2019. Accessed January 30, 2019. https://www.commonapp.org/.

Chapter 23

The Sealed Envelope:

Letters of Recommendation

While the previous pieces of the admissions puzzle—test scores, transcript, extracurriculars, and essays—have all focused on the student's accomplishments, one more piece of the puzzle deals with what *other people* think of the student. By carefully choosing who should write letters of recommendation, a homeschooler can highlight another facet of his or her personality and can emphasize attributes that have not been revealed elsewhere.

WHY COLLEGES WANT RECOMMENDATIONS

As with the essay, recommendations add a personal touch to what should ideally be a personalized process. All too often, this process disintegrates into a numbers game of GPAs, test scores, and a tally of AP or honors courses. With so many students presenting stellar test scores and similar transcripts, a college may encounter thousands of applicants who fulfill all the academic requirements. Letters of recommendation from people who know the student well can give colleges a glimpse of this applicant as a "three-dimensional" individual by presenting his or her outstanding character traits, love of learning, and motivation. Additionally, the teacher who writes the letter can indicate how the student might fare in the college environment.

TYPICAL REQUIREMENTS

Schools vary as to how many letters they require and who should submit these letters. Most require one or two teacher recommendations, plus one from a counselor or school administrator. The latter is commonly submitted via a standardized format provided by the college (within the Common Application, it is called the School Report/Counselor Letter). The teacher recommendations should be submitted by instructors who taught the student in eleventh or twelfth grade and who are acquainted with the student's accomplishments and abilities. Furthermore, many colleges specify that these letters should come from teachers in two different subject areas—for instance, one from a math or science teacher and one from a humanities teacher (English, social studies, etc.).

Some schools require or allow one more letter. This additional recommendation can be from another person who knows the student well, such as a coach, employer, volunteer supervisor, or pastor.

Certain schools adamantly state that a student may not submit more recommendations than those outlined in the application. Others allow extra submissions but warn that more letters may not raise the chances of admission, especially if they do not add any new information. For homeschooled applicants, some colleges specifically request, or at least allow, additional letters. With so much variation from college to college, it is important to read the application instructions closely and carefully, and to follow up any confusion with a phone call or email to the admissions office. If you find that you are allowed to send extra letters, confirm how and where to submit them, as the Common Application system will handle only the nominal number of letters.

CHOOSING YOUR RECOMMENDERS

Because they don't sit in five or six teachers' classrooms every day for four years, homeschoolers have fewer choices of recommenders than do traditionally schooled students. However, with a little planning, foresight, and creativity, your student can still arrange a set of personalized, well-written recommendation letters by the time college application season arrives. Parents, outside teachers, ISP or PSP administrators, coaches, volunteer supervisors, and other adults can all fill this role in your student's application process.

Parents

Since the parent is the primary homeschool teacher and is the individual who knows the student best, he or she is most qualified to write on behalf of the student. Typically, the arrangement is that the parent writes the counselor letter, while the students' outside instructors write the teacher evaluations. Check with specific colleges regarding guidelines for homeschooled students. Information may be found on the admissions website, but more often, you will need to make a phone call to the admissions office. Specifically, confirm whether the parent should prepare the School Report and Counselor Letter for the Common Application (or should prepare similar documents for non-Common Application schools).

Outside Teachers

Even with the parent writing the counselor letter, the student will still need to select at least one or two others to write letters. The best choices are community college instructors, teachers of homeschool group classes, or instructors in any other day school programs or outside classes the student has taken. To be most effective, these teachers should have taught the student in eleventh or twelfth grade and should be able to comment on academic strengths and personal qualities. A PSP administrator who sees the student only once or twice per year for twenty minutes at a time will not have enough information to comment well on the student. Thus, if you are counting on your PSP administrator to be one of your recommenders, plan ahead. Don't wait until the senior year to start informing your administrator of your student's progress, accomplishments, and goals and to make sure your student has sufficient in-person time with the administrator.

Use a bit of strategy as you plan which recommenders your student will match with which applications. The most appropriate recommenders are those who possess insight into the student's character, academic accomplishments, and leadership traits, are articulate and skilled in writing, and are willing and able to write an honest but favorable appraisal. The strongest recommenders should be asked to write letters for the most selective colleges or for the colleges at the top of the student's list of favorites. For colleges in the Common Application system, the student will invite a number of recommenders to write generic letters that do not mention a college name, and then will have the opportunity to "assign" specific recommenders to specific colleges. For instance, suppose Teachers A, B, and C agree to write letters, and College 1 requires one letter, College 2 requires two letters, and College 3 requires two letters but allows one additional letter. The student could assign Teacher A (who will potentially have the strongest letter) to College 1, Teachers A and B to College 2, and Teachers A, B, and C to College 3. Chapter 20 has an explanation of the Common Application, including how to manage teacher recommendations.

Other Adults as Optional Recommenders

For the often-optional category of recommendation by "someone else who knows you well," homeschoolers generally have a number of people to choose from. Ministry leaders, pastors, employers, coaches, Scout leaders, volunteer supervisors, tutors/academic coaches, and other adults with whom the student has worked in extracurricular activities or community service projects are excellent choices. Anyone who has served in the role of "mentor" during the high school years could write a meaningful letter. Again, make sure that these individuals know the student well and will comment on the characteristics requested by the college.

Some of the most insightful letters can be written by non-teachers, so make use of the opportunity if it presents itself. For example, if a student has completed an internship in a specialized field of study, the mentor or supervisor would be a logical person to describe work habits, passion, strengths, and goals.

As you might imagine, homeschoolers would be wise to begin early—even in ninth grade or so—in thinking about and developing their potential references. Knowing what is coming up, they can plan to take a number of courses outside the home or to develop strong leadership skills under one or more adult mentors. As a student works with an adult who could potentially write a letter, he or she should continue to strengthen this relationship by frequently sharing information about current activities and future goals.

Celebrities and Connections?

Students (but mostly parents) often wonder whether a letter from someone famous or well-connected would be a "winning" recommendation. Perhaps a friend of a friend is a political figure, a celebrity, or a well-known alumnus of the university. Or Aunt Mabel's doctor went to school with someone on the admissions committee.

The most important criterion for an effective letter—vastly more important than the celebrity of the recommender—is how well he or she knows the student. A letter from a high-level figure who writes only generically is far inferior to a warm, detailed, personal letter from someone with whom the student has worked closely. Moreover, this optional letter must be a statement that can provide insights and information that the other letters and components of the application have not yet provided. Choosing a celebrity means forgoing the chance to include a letter packed with personal details and observations, and thus, this choice could be detrimental to the overall content of the application.

All in all, a detailed, insightful personal letter from someone who knows the student well is much more meaningful than an impersonal letter from someone with high profile status who may never have met the student. Admittedly, students sometimes do get accepted to college because of these connections, but by and large, it is better to seek letters from people who truly know the student. Before having a "celebrity" write a letter on your student's behalf, ponder a few questions. Is this celebrity letter worth pursuing? Realistically, will it help your student's case? More importantly, might it hurt his or her case?

ELEMENTS OF A COLLEGE RECOMMENDATION LETTER

Many colleges provide standard recommendation forms on their online applications, asking recommenders to rate the applicant on certain characteristics and to add their own descriptions and thoughts. Other colleges simply want a letter highlighting the student's abilities, character, accomplishments, and goals. Since so much variation exists, see if you can find the recommendation forms online ahead of time. For instance, you can view the Teacher Recommendation form for the Common Application to take a look at the questions that will be asked of the recommender. Previewing this information will get you and your student thinking about which teachers would make the best recommenders, what they might say, and how your student can develop these character qualities if some are currently lacking.

Below are some examples of characteristics on which the recommender might be asked to comment. Because this is a compilation from many applications, not all recommendation forms will ask for all of these characteristics.

- *Academic, extracurricular, and personal strengths and weaknesses*
- *Intellectual promise*
- *Motivation*
- *Maturity*
- *Integrity*
- *Independence*
- *Productive class discussion*
- *Quality of writing*
- *Disciplined work habits*
- *Initiative*
- *Leadership potential*
- *Capacity for growth*
- *Special talents*
- *Enthusiasm*
- *Concern for others*
- *Respect accorded by teachers*
- *Respect accorded by peers*
- *Reaction to setbacks*
- *Intellectual curiosity*
- *Creativity*
- *Sense of humor*
- *Self-confidence*
- *Sense of responsibility*
- *Impact on the community*
- *Adjectives that come to mind to describe the student*
- *Factors that might interfere with academic performance or personal relationships*
- *Approach to learning*
- *Anything else the college should know about the student*

TYPICAL FORMAT FOR RECOMMENDATIONS

Some recommendation forms use a chart or table listing many of these characteristics. First, the recommender rates the student using a ranking scale that ranges from "Below average" to "One of the top few I've ever encountered." Next, the recommender writes additional comments about the student in paragraph form. Other recommendation forms ask the recommender to comment on as many of these characteristics as possible while writing the recommendation letter. Hopefully, your writer will avoid a dry, mechanical "list" approach while still covering many of these qualities and presenting an accurate picture of the student's capabilities.

Typical questions might include the following:

- *How long have you known this student?*
- *In what capacity have you known this student?*
- *In what subjects or courses have you taught the applicant?*
- *What are the first words that come to your mind when describing this student?*
- *How might you distinguish this student's academic performance from that of other capable students?*
- *Please comment on the student's intellectual attitude, curiosity, and enthusiasm for learning.*
- *Please assess the applicant's personal and academic qualities and promise as a college student.*
- *In what ways has the student made an impact in your class, the school, or the community?*
- *Describe this student's ability to communicate effectively and get along with others.*
- *The admissions committee is interested in admitting students who can and will show excellence in the classroom, contribute to the college community, collaborate with professors and peers, challenge themselves, display independence in their academic coursework, and show qualities of leadership, creativity and self-motivation. Please elaborate on these and other characteristics you believe would assist the committee in making a decision in the candidate's best interest.*
- *We would like to know about strong or weak points and whether you feel that this student has worked to the limits of his or her potential. Please give us your impression of what we might have learned in an interview that we could not have learned from the written application. We would be interested in anecdotes about the student.*
- *Are there any factors that might interfere with the candidate's academic performance and/or personal relationships at college?*
- *Is there anything else we should know about this student (e.g., personal circumstances, unusual accomplishments, obstacles overcome)?*
- *Please attach a letter describing the student's academic and personal characteristics as demonstrated in your classroom.*

Almost always, the letter will be submitted electronically to the college without the student ever seeing it. This permits confidentiality and assures the recommender that he or she can be completely honest, even to the extent of including some negative comments. As part of the application process, the student will indicate whether he or she waives FERPA rights (Family Educational Rights and Privacy Act)— in this case, the right to see a copy of recommendation letters once he or she matriculates at the college. It is best to waive these rights, allowing recommenders to write more candidly because the student will not read these remarks. Certain recommenders may voluntarily give your student a copy of the letter if it's a complimentary recommendation. Mom will probably want to add it to the scrapbook.

TIPS FOR REQUESTING LETTERS OF RECOMMENDATION

Besides choosing the ideal persons to write these letters, your student can take action to make this part of the application process go smoothly. The following tips are addressed to the student to help him or her take charge of the recommendation process.

Allow Enough Time for Completion

This is the single most important step in the process. You will not be doing your recommender *or yourself* any favors by requesting a letter only a few days before it is due. Recommenders need time to think about the letter, time to compose the right words, and time to keep up with their personal and professional responsibilities, which take precedence over your need for a letter. Thoughtful, high-quality letters can take as much as three or four hours to write (I am speaking from personal experience). Ideally, you should ask your potential recommenders *several weeks ahead of time* if they would be willing to write letters for you. If they are willing to do it, thank them graciously and ask how much notice they will need before the deadline. Then provide them with preliminary instructions such as a list of the questions to be addressed. Be sure to send or give them any necessary materials (links, email addresses, physical addresses, names) *at least a week or two in advance of the date they name.* For instance, if they require two weeks to work on the letter before the deadline, give them the materials three or four weeks before the deadline. Since computer glitches do occur, you may send a follow-up email a few days later just to make sure they received the materials and are on track to submit the letter by the deadline.

Don't Overburden Any One Recommender

If you will be needing numerous letters that will be sent to a variety of institutions—for example, the Common Application, three other colleges not on the Common Application, and three scholarship programs—communicate well with your recommenders. Choose which recommender(s) will be most strategic, and streamline their work for them by telling them up front about *all possible letters* you will be requesting from them. In this way, they will be prepared to save their files and "recycle" a letter written for one institution, to use it for another. (Remember that for the Common Application, a letter will be written once and then distributed to several colleges, so this counts as only one letter to prepare for you.) If the recommender will be too busy to keep preparing and sending slightly different versions of the same letter, find a second recommender to handle some of the other submissions.

Choose Recommenders Based on the Portrait of You They Can Present

If you have previously applied for another program, internship, or award and have had letters written on your behalf, you may have been fortunate enough to have seen the letters your prior recommenders wrote. From these people, choose those who have a talent for writing winning recommendations. If you have not had this experience, decide what your various teachers and mentors know about you and your goals and accomplishments, and choose accordingly. One might comment on your intellectual curiosity; another might focus on your strong teamwork and leadership abilities; still another might praise your sense of initiative.

Be Organized

Make a list, chart, or calendar of deadlines for recommendations, noting all forms, supplementary information, and electronic submission requirements. Decide which recommenders will write letters for which applications, and then prepare a checkoff system so that you can make sure you've emailed or otherwise delivered the materials to all of your recommenders on time. If you are applying to several colleges, don't let any of these small tasks get lost in the shuffle.

Provide Recommenders with All the Needed Information and Materials

Prepare an email for each recommender that includes a brief description of what you need from him or her and a quick rundown of your deadlines. Attaching a resume of your accomplishments and ambitions is extremely helpful, as it provides a wider view of your experiences. If you had this teacher for several classes, remind him or her of what those classes were and when you took them. If your recommender will submit the letter electronically through the Common Application School Forms, make sure that he or she understands the process and knows how to contact you if technical difficulties arise. For the Common Application and many other university systems, you will provide the recommender's name and email address, and he or she will receive an email with login instructions. You must both "invite" and "assign" recommenders; otherwise, they will not receive the email.

You may think that your teachers will remember your strong performance in class, your intelligent questions, or your helpfulness in assisting others in lab. However, this teacher may have taught hundreds of students, and sometimes the details blur together. You will be better off giving your recommender a brief summary sheet about yourself, your goals, the classes you took, and your academic accomplishments. Include a few bullet points about class projects you completed, assignments you particularly enjoyed, or topics that stand out in your mind. If you completed extra projects such as tutoring, assisting in a lab, or leading a team of volunteers, or if you did anything else out of the ordinary, mention this. Clearly communicate the goals of the recommendation letter(s), including which colleges will be receiving them and what the colleges want to know. If you are asking this recommender to write several letters for you, be sure that the deadlines and instructions are clear for each institution. For example, when writing a teacher evaluation for the Common Application, recommenders should not mention the name of any specific college.

Offer a Reminder

When you request your recommendations, politely ask whether your recommender would like a reminder shortly before the letter is due. This reminder can be important both for you *and* for the recommender, who would certainly be embarrassed to forget your important letter.

Remember Your Manners

Since letters of recommendation are so important and take time and effort to write, thank-you notes are a must. At the very least, write a sincere note of appreciation just after the letters have been submitted. For teachers or other adults who have written multiple letters for you, consider other gestures of thanks, such as homemade baked goods (you can finish up your Life Skills credit at the same time), or another small acknowledgment. One teacher we know at a local high school collects and displays college pennants as "thank-yous" from students who were successfully accepted at these colleges. If appropriate, you could also give a gift card for coffee, books, or anything else you know your recommender likes. If your recommender is a close, longtime friend, you might treat him or her to lunch or coffee one day—as you chat about your exciting college plans. Gifts are by no means essential—but a sincere "thank you" definitely is.

THE SCHOOL REPORT AND COUNSELOR LETTER

Chapter 20 introduced the School Report, a portion of the Common Application traditionally filled out by a guidance counselor. A typical School Report requests information on senior year courses, cumulative GPA, and some School Profile data that does not apply to homeschoolers. Additionally, the form provides space for several paragraphs of evaluation. It asks how long the evaluator has known the applicant, requests the "first words that come to mind" to describe the student, and provides columns for rating the student in academics, extracurricular achievement, personal qualities, and creativity. The evaluator is asked to indicate how strongly he or she recommends the student for college acceptance.

For homeschoolers, the School Report is generally filled out by the parent. The parent provides information on the "school" as well as on the student, uploads a transcript, completes some rating checkboxes, and writes a detailed Counselor Letter highlighting the student's academic and personal characteristics and his or her readiness for college. The Common Application also has a Home School section designed to give colleges insight about your homeschooling methods and the student's accomplishments. In addition to answering basic questions about course titles and grades, use this area of the application as another chance to highlight your student's educational opportunities and accomplishments, using the tips described below. It is also wise to send a detailed list of course descriptions for the entire high school course of study. See Chapter 20 for details.

HOW A PARENT CAN WRITE AN INFORMATIVE, EFFECTIVE LETTER

In all likelihood, you as a parent (whether it's Mom or Dad is up to you) will write at least one letter on behalf of your student—probably the Counselor Letter or, less likely, a teacher recommendation. This is an excellent opportunity to "fill in the gaps" when looking at the application as a whole. Think through the aspects of your student's persona and outstanding qualities, and make sure to communicate them clearly and with strong evidence. You might categorize your comments according to academic, extracurricular, social, and character qualities. Here is where you can explain your student's ability to "dig deeper" academically, to strive to be an effective leader even when it is uncomfortable, to work as a team on group projects, or to display integrity or kindness. Always provide brief examples to support your claims.

While parents are truly the most knowledgeable about the student's academic abilities, they are also the most biased. You and the admissions officer both realize this. How can you write a letter that will be credible to college admissions committees? Though it is a tough task, it is entirely possible to write such a letter. Here are some caveats and tips for objectively *showing*, not *telling*, your student's strengths.

Caveat #1: Don't Make Unsupported Favorable Comments About Your Student

Naturally, you will comment favorably about your student, since you want him or her to be admitted to this college. At the same time, you may be concerned about your "ulterior motive." Realize, though, that this situation is not much different from the scenario of an overzealous guidance counselor or schoolteacher who thinks your student is the greatest, wants him or her to be admitted, and also wishes to gain prestige for the high school by having students admitted to high-ranking colleges. All this is to say that not even traditional teachers and counselors are unbiased when it comes to writing recommendation letters. You can minimize the appearance of bias by deliberately supporting each favorable comment you make.

Tips: As you express what your student has done well, always back up what you say with concrete examples. Instead of simply marking a high score in the "initiative" column, describe a class or a club that the student arranged entirely by himself or herself. Instead of commenting mindlessly on "independence," describe how your student studied public transportation routes to commute to a summer research job thirty miles away, used four different types of conveyances to get there, found alternate routes when buses did not show up, and footed the bill for all the transportation costs. Best of all, quote or paraphrase what other adults who have worked with your student have said about these qualities.

Caveat #2: Don't Comment Too Unfavorably About Your Student

That heading may have prompted a double take. Wouldn't a homeschooling parent report *only* on the positive? But in our quest to be honest and objective, we may inadvertently rate our students more unfavorably than we should. We may tend to use perfection or adult-level maturity as the gold standard for each characteristic we are asked to rate. In contrast, a guidance counselor or teacher compares the student to a population of perfectly normal (but not 100% mature) teenagers. If we fail to keep the student's peer group in mind, we can be unfair in our ratings.

In addition, parents inevitably spot all the student's problem areas that crop up at home, while a guidance counselor or teacher would be shielded from the vast majority of these. For example, does the perpetually messy room mean that your student is disorganized? Do the normal teenage attitudes and the occasional bouts with disrespect mean that he or she should be graded down on maturity or concern for others? Does the habit of leaving assignments to the last minute betray a problem with time management? Remember that classroom teachers never see the late-night efforts; they see only the finished product. As a parent, I have concluded that we need to "grade on the curve" when it comes to rating our homeschooled students.

Tips: Again, draw on what others have told you about your student. Combine this with your own most objective observations and your comparisons of your student with other teens. Spend time jotting down ideas about how your student works and acts when accountable to others, not just to you. This, after all, is what colleges are trying to measure.

Of course, your student will have weaknesses. But colleges are most concerned about those weaknesses that affect a student's ability to survive the college environment academically, socially, and emotionally. If your student has no significant shortcomings, you can justify marking a higher score in the pertinent categories.

Do be forthright as you write your evaluation, acknowledging the difficulty of rating your own student. Then explain your final rationale and describe the criteria you used. Your candor will be appreciated by the admissions committee.

Caveat #3: Don't Write with a "Braggy" Tone

By all means, avoid any trace of a boastful tone in your evaluation. It should not read like the proverbial Christmas newsletter or a letter to Grandma.

Tips: Keep "HUMming" as you write this piece. In other words, remember that your biggest aids are light HUMor, HUMility, and HUManity. Use *humor* as you point out a particularly comical moment that characterized your student pursuing his or her passion. Inject a tone of *humility* by noting honestly that both you and your student sometimes felt unequal to this task of homeschooling. Admit that you and your student have had some difficult moments but have found the overall journey to be rewarding. Since colleges will want your student to fit in with others, make your student sound like a *human being* by dropping brief hints that, although homeschooled, this teenager still likes to hang out with friends, pig out on junk food, and maintain a messy room. Parents can quite realistically comment on creativity, confidence, abilities, achievements, and more, as long as they *show*, and not just *tell*, how wonderful this student is.

Caveat #4: Don't Write with a Stiff, Sterile Tone

The recommendation letter is not a legal document and does not require four-syllable words or an erudite tone. Some warmth is perfectly appropriate. Additionally, don't restate the obvious, rehash the transcript, or recite the extracurriculars. This is your opportunity to focus on aspects of your student not adequately covered elsewhere in the application. Bring out quotes from others, noteworthy incidents, pertinent anecdotes, and anything that will help create a three-dimensional representation of your student.

Tips: Since most colleges request a description of the high school course of study, this is your big chance. Explain your student's intellectual curiosity and thirst for knowledge by giving real-life examples. Many admissions officers still think that the homeschooled student is home all day, *every* day with Mom and has little contact with the outside world. For their benefit, highlight your student's interpersonal skills by describing times of team learning, leadership, problem solving, and situations in which others depended on or looked up to your student for guidance. You might be able to gather and quote from short "testimonials" or mini-recommendations from teens your student has tutored, or from parents of children your student has led in clubs or community service. These concrete examples will breathe life into your letter.

While you don't want to rehash the list of accomplishments recorded elsewhere, you may want to *highlight* one or two activities—for example, because they show your student's leadership in action. Take your time writing these descriptions and read them over several times to make sure the tone is lively, down-to-earth, and informative—not braggy, stiff, or stale.

Caveat #5: Don't Climb onto a Soapbox

Families choose to homeschool for a variety of reasons. Some are faith-based reasons; others stem from poor learning environments in local schools. Your counselor letter, however, is *not* the occasion to address the numerous problems you encountered in your neighborhood schools, nor to preach a full gospel message to the admissions officer. Save the sharing for the appropriate time and place.

Tips: When asked to explain your reasons for homeschooling, express your views in a positive, upbeat way. Focus on how you helped your student learn, instead of on what a negative place the public schools are. If you are explaining the faith-based reasoning for your home education, keep it short, simple, and well-integrated with the rest of your description of *how* your school was conducted and *how* your student learned. If your student is applying to a Christian college, however, you can expand a bit more on the benefits to your student's faith and Christian growth. Above all, remove any traces of a self-righteous or elitist tone. This is certainly not the time to wax eloquent about how homeschooling is the *only* proper educational method for responsible parents.

THE MID YEAR REPORT

By the time your calendar reads January or February, you and your student will be so tired of filling out forms that you'll be ready to take a permanent break from computers. But as the administrator of your home school, you will need to fill out the Common Application's Mid Year Report. Add this to your list of deadlines, and don't forget to submit it at the end of the first semester. The Mid Year Report is a short update of the student's performance during the first half of senior year. Take heart! This form is much simpler than the other recommendation and application forms.

The Mid Year Report includes an updated transcript with first semester senior grades and an updated GPA. Space is provided for additional comments; here, you will enter noteworthy updates about the student's performance, such as a significant increase or decrease in academic performance, or a change in course lineup since the college application was filed. Another official transcript will be required at the end of the school year. And yes, colleges have been known to withdraw offers of admission for students who show dramatic declines in grades or behavior during the senior year, so urge your student to keep up the good work.

If your student's second semester course of study changes at all from what was outlined on the original application, you must note this on the Mid Year Report. Even if your student has already received an early acceptance from his or her first choice college, contact the admissions office and ask if this proposed change would jeopardize his or her admission status. Believe it or not, certain changes would in fact alter this status. Colleges request that the student maintain the same academic rigor during the second semester of the senior year that was proposed on the original application. If the course of study changes or the academic rigor drops, the college reserves the right to rescind the admission offer.

After Julie was accepted at Stanford under an Early Action decision, she found that she needed to make a change in her second semester courses because of a time conflict involving her community college schedule. A phone call to the admissions office gave her guidance on what was and what was not acceptable. She received permission to drop the final semester of her Russian course, but the college wanted her to keep the microbiology course she had originally proposed, or to substitute a science course of similar rigor. In any case, she was glad she had made the phone call.

THE FINAL REPORT

Just as the Mid Year Report provides information about courses completed in the first semester of the senior year, the Final Report summarizes the courses completed in the final semester. Not all colleges use the Common Application, but even those who are not Common Application members will request a final official transcript of courses completed and grades received, as well as a rundown of any notable accomplishments or problems during that term. At this point you will also send one last official community college transcript, if applicable. Since the student has already received college acceptances by the time the Final Report is submitted, this form is largely a formality, and, of course, it will be sent only to the college the student has committed to attending. However, if grades have dropped significantly or serious problems have surfaced, such as involvement in a crime, the college reserves the right to withdraw the offer of admission.

With forms such as the School Report, Mid Year Report, and Final Report, think "outside the box" (literally) at all times. If a question does not relate to homeschoolers, don't try to force-fit an answer. Simply mark that it is not applicable and perhaps add a note of explanation in sentence form.

TO SUM UP

For a homeschooler, the task of gathering recommendations is a team effort among parents, outside teachers, school officials, ministry leaders, and volunteer supervisors. The objective is to bring out key facets of your student's personality and academic promise, while remaining straightforward and full of integrity.

Pay close attention to the value of recommendation letters. They can be one of your student's most strategic tools in the college application process.

Chapter 24

Behind Closed Doors:

The Admissions Process

Contrary to the popular skepticism of a couple of decades ago, "homeschooling" and "college admission" can definitely be mentioned in the same breath. According to the National Home Education Research Institute, approximately 2.3 million students in the U.S. were homeschooled as of 2016 (roughly 3% of the school age population), with homeschooling now growing at an estimated rate of 2 to 8% annually.[1] The increasing numbers of homeschoolers who have succeeded in higher education continue to pave the way for the next wave of homeschoolers to find favor in the admissions process. With their academic accomplishments over the past years, homeschoolers have proven themselves to be a group of independent, motivated, and intellectually curious students—nontraditional, to be sure, but certainly a group that adds to the college's diversity in a refreshing way.

Whether homeschooled or not, any student's challenge in gaining admission to a particular college depends on how many applications a college receives for every spot available in the entering freshman class. While the information in this book comes with no guarantees regarding college acceptance, this chapter should give you a better understanding of the admissions process and of how your student can maximize his or her chances for admission.

A BEHIND-THE-SCENES TOUR OF THE ADMISSIONS PROCESS

Colleges differ in their methods of selecting applicants, but the following pages outline the general admissions process. If you and your student have the opportunity, you may want to read a book revealing more "behind the scenes" glimpses. *Admissions Confidential* by Rachel Toor, *The Gatekeepers* by Jacques Steinberg, and *College Admissions Trade Secrets* by Andrew Allen relate the details of these mysterious procedures. Knowing how this process works can be fascinating, sobering, eye-opening, intimidating, and empowering all at once. From a practical standpoint, this knowledge can suggest how a student might best present himself or herself to stand out among the thousands of applicants.

The statistics can be discouraging, especially for students who have their sights set on the nation's most selective universities. For the class of 2022, Harvard accepted only 1,962 of the 42,749 students who applied (a record low 4.59% acceptance rate).[2] Yale accepted 6.31% of its applicants, and Princeton and Columbia 5.5%.[3] Stanford, claiming the slot of "most selective university" for the class of 2022, had 47,450 applicants for 2,040 spots (4.3%, another record low).[3,4] Thankfully, most college applicants will not have to face these stark statistics. The majority of U.S. colleges and universities have acceptance rates in the 50% to 80% range, and a few approach 100% acceptance.

Some large public university systems operate a more streamlined, less personalized, and more numbers-based admissions process. An "eligibility index" formula may be used to indicate combinations of SAT or ACT scores and GPAs that automatically qualify a student for admission (though additional factors such as personal statements may still be used for final selection or for more selective campuses). Quality and rigor of coursework and, to some extent, the list of extracurriculars, also figure into the equation, but not to the extent that they would at a private college or university. An important application strategy for these institutions is to find out *early in the game* if the homeschool transcript will be accepted. If not, find out whether homeschoolers may use a combination of AP exam scores, SAT Subject Tests, community college courses, and/or approved online courses to augment the homeschool transcript. As with any college, but perhaps more importantly here, the student should strive to be outstanding in extracurriculars, leadership, and distinctive accomplishments.

As you read through the somewhat daunting "weed-out" process described below, remember that this process may not apply to your student if he or she is not applying to a highly selective college. Students aiming for less selective colleges can relax a bit, since their applications will not be scrutinized to such a high degree. Still, the more your student can stand out among the other applicants, the higher the chances of admission.

Step 1: Components of the Application Are Received by the College

As the pieces of the student's application (main application form, personal statements, supplementary essays, official test scores, transcripts, and teacher recommendations) come together, generally all in electronic form, the admissions office generates a file on each student applicant. If any components are missing, the college may notify students by email, or may provide a link to a website for this purpose. Students should understand how to keep apprised of their application status so each and every element is accounted for as the weeks go by.

Step 2: Admissions Officers Read Applications and Code Them with Scores

For many schools, especially those that receive thousands of applications, admissions officers spend only about twenty minutes reading each application. An entire high school career is boiled down to this short moment of time. Admissions staff are swamped from November through December for early applications, and then even more so from January through March for regular applications. Reading applications is their nightly homework, and they spend hours combing through them to assemble the ideal freshman class. Thus, it makes sense for your student to try to make his or her application stand out from the rest of the pile.

For many colleges, especially selective ones, your student's file will be read by two readers. The student's academic record, list of extracurriculars, teacher and counselor recommendations, personal statements, and test scores are each given a score, often on a scale of 1 through 5. As you might imagine, students with scores of 5 across the board make a stronger showing than do students with scores of 1 and 2. Depending on the college, a student can certainly be admitted without a whole battery of 5's beside his or her name. Even at the selective schools, other criteria come into play that may allow admission of a lower-scoring student. These factors may include athletic promise, legacy status (having a parent or other close relative who attended the college), or some specific need of the school. For instance, the star tuba player may be graduating, and the band will not sound the same unless the college admits your student, a talented tuba player.

Colleges that utilize interviews as part of the admissions process also make a note of how the student did on the campus-based or off-campus interview.

Step 3: Application Readers Recommend "Admit," "Deny," or "Defer"

Most of the time, the two readers will agree on the admissions verdict, since standards and guidelines are clearly communicated for acceptance, denial, and deferral to the Regular Decision pool (in the case of Early Decision or Early Action applications). Thus, if both readers agree, chances are that the decision will stand. Applications are sorted according to the decision made. Students who are neither clear "admits" nor clear "denies" go into another batch for reconsideration or committee discussion.

Step 4: Applications Without Clear Decisions Are Reviewed as Openings Remain in the Class

As the freshman class begins to fill up, at least "on paper," admissions officers will check to see how the demographics of the class are rounding out. Colleges want to select their mix of students from diverse geographical, racial, and ethnic backgrounds, as well as balancing gender percentages and various major fields of study. Seeking to assemble a "well-rounded" class, they will make adjustments toward the desired ratios by admitting more or fewer students from certain categories, based on the applications still left to decide on. For instance, if admitted students have been mostly from the East and West coasts, with few from the Midwest, that sharp student from South Dakota—especially if she is of Native American heritage—will gain a spot over that equally sharp student from California.

At this point, university politics can enter the equation. Athletic coaches may come in asking for more swimmers or more baseball pitchers. A coach may even come in with the name of a student he has just met, whom he definitely wants on his women's basketball team this coming year. The band or orchestra director may submit requests. Admissions officers debate the merits of their favorite students, realizing that not all of the "pet" students can be accepted.

For students whose applications end up in the "debatable" pile, having unusual skills or achievements can come in handy, depending on what the admissions officer finds intriguing at the moment. Essays and recommendations can also nudge a student into the acceptance zone. Suppose the admissions officer needs to decide between your student and another student with the same grades, test scores, and general course of study. If your student submitted a creative, sparkling essay and insightful, intriguing letters of recommendation, he or she will probably get the nod over a more ordinary-sounding student.

Step 5: Students Are Notified

Finally, all the applications have been read, and the debatable ones have been discussed. The admissions committee has come to its final conclusions, and all applications are now clearly marked "Accept," "Deny," "Defer to Regular Decision" (in the case of early applications), or "Waitlist." While acceptances and rejections are self-explanatory, a bit of explanation might be in order for deferrals and waitlist candidates.

Deferrals

When that December letter arrives for Early Decision or Early Action applicants, students may find that they were neither accepted nor rejected, but rather *deferred*. When colleges defer applicants, they are saying, in essence, "We're not accepting you right now, but we like you enough not to reject you. We'll defer you and consider you again for Regular Decision." For students, this means another agonizing wait until March or April to hear their fate from this college—which was probably their first choice. In reality, for the most selective colleges, students should not count on acceptances if they were deferred in the fall. Instead, they should begin to prioritize the remaining colleges on their lists, for it is more likely that they will attend one of these.

Waitlists

Waitlists are most common at ultra-selective colleges, though less selective colleges also utilize them. When selective colleges determine who will be offered admission, they always encounter students who were not as strong as the rest of the admits, but who clearly don't deserve to be rejected, either. Such students are added to a waitlist.

Because colleges never know exactly how many of the accepted students will actually matriculate (enroll) at the college, the waitlist is used as a source of promising students in case space opens up in the spring after admitted students make their final college decisions. Though it may seem counterintuitive to the average person, most waitlists are not ranked. In other words, admissions staff can pick and choose from the list in no particular order. Once they know the overall makeup of the class thus far and can discern what "profile" of students would round out the remaining spots in the freshman class. At this point, some students on the list will be contacted and offered a place in the class. The process of accepting students off the waitlist takes place from May onward—and may continue as late as July or August. This makes for extremely changeable plans if the student has a strong desire to attend the college where he or she is waitlisted. Note, however, that at many institutions the practice of waitlisting of students has increased, and thus the chances of being admitted off the waitlist can be quite slim. Advice: Don't hold your breath—use your time and energy to investigate the schools to which you have been admitted.

Notification

After decisions have been made, the admissions office prepares to notify all the applicants. Typically this is done by email or by sending a link to an admissions notification website; it is followed up by mailing letters to students. Accepted students' letters generally contain additional information such as a financial aid notification and a rundown of the next steps (with deadlines) to keep in mind over the coming months. Students who are not admitted receive a kind but firm rejection, usually with a commentary on how difficult the decisions were and how few students were offered admission. The bulk of students who apply using the Regular Decision deadlines will receive responses any time from January to March or April. For schools with Rolling Admissions policies, responses may start coming in within four to six weeks after applying. And of course, those who applied Early Decision or Early Action will hear back in mid-December.

Step 6: Colleges May Contact Admitted Students to Encourage Them to Enroll

The next phase of the process is much more pleasant for the admitted student. Instead of the student working hard to be accepted by the college, the college now works hard to recruit the students that were just admitted. Realizing that the average student applies to and is accepted by several colleges, some institutions work to increase their "yield," or percentage of admitted students who actually enroll. This is done via additional letters or brochures, telephone calls from alumni or admissions officers, emails, and invitations to open houses or admitted student weekends. These weekends, often scheduled in April, can be quite informative for students who are still making up their minds. Students are invited to visit the campus for two or three days, stay in the dorms, and participate in a slate of activities. Visiting classes, meeting current students, attending Q and A sessions, enjoying sporting events or other entertainment, and, in general, getting a feel for the campus are some of the many opportunities offered. Some parent activities are planned as well, although parents must find their own lodging.

Step 7: The Student Officially Notifies One College of His or Her Intent to Enroll

As April draws to a close, the deadline looms for students to make final decisions about where they will spend their next four years. May 1st is the most common date for students to submit enrollment notifications and enrollment deposits to the colleges they have chosen. As a courtesy, students should contact the other colleges where they have been accepted to let them know that they will not be enrolling. For students who have been in an agony of indecision, the time has come to make that final decision and then to be at peace with it. From here on out, the details will all revolve around getting set up for the next school year: finalizing financial aid business, filling out residence hall forms and roommate questionnaires, and thinking about a schedule of classes. The culmination of the high school years now allows the student to breathe a sigh of relief and to enjoy graduation and a summer free of essays, tests, and college applications.

APPLICATION STRATEGIES

Although no one can guarantee your student admission into the college of his or her dreams, the following strategies may enlighten you throughout this process.

Understand What They Are Looking For

The admissions process can seem mysterious and even secretive. Admissions officers gather countless applicants' files, sequester themselves behind closed doors—perhaps surviving on bagels and coffee—only to emerge several weeks later with an official roster of the freshman class. How do they do it? What is the secret? *And just what are they looking for?*

Truthfully, no magic formula exists. The decision to admit or deny is based on a composite picture of all the elements of the application. Primary attention is given to grades in college prep courses, followed by test scores, grades in other courses, class rank, and the counselor recommendation. However, other factors such as extracurriculars and essays can be extremely important in borderline cases and can sway the application one way or another. Examining these elements one by one may help maximize your student's chances of admission.

Academic Record

Your student's course lineup needs to match or exceed the college's stated course requirements for each subject area. The student should pursue challenging courses but still seek to earn high grades. One or two lower grades may not disqualify an applicant, but a steady pattern or a steady decline will. Grades are especially important in the tenth and eleventh grade years, but a student should strive for a respectable track record in ninth grade as well.

Test Scores

Various colleges weigh these scores differently. Guidelines for acceptable test scores will depend on each college's middle 50% test score range as discussed in Chapters 18 and 19. Preparing well for the SAT or ACT exam is crucial if your student is aiming for selective colleges.

Class Rank

Obviously, class rank doesn't apply to homeschoolers, but for traditionally schooled students, many colleges look for applicants who are in the top 25% of their class. While some highly selective schools seek students in the top 10%, less competitive schools will take students in the top 50%.

Counselor Recommendation (Common Application School Report/Counselor Letter)

Again, for homeschoolers, the counselor is Mom or Dad, the PSP leader, or another adult who knows the student well. This report will help round out the description of the student and put his or her abilities, achievements, and personal qualities in perspective alongside those of other applicants.

Extracurricular Activities

The goal is to show "variety with consistency." In other words, while it is good for your student to demonstrate several different interests such as sports, arts, community service, and journalism, he or she should follow up this variety with a consistent, sustained pattern of involvement in these areas. Colleges look for commitment as well as leadership experience.

Essays

An admission-worthy personal statement should be creative and compelling. Above all, it should reveal a student's true personality. As mentioned in Chapter 22, students should spend quality time preparing their essays and be willing to revise multiple times. The effort is well worth it.

Interview, if Applicable

If an interview is offered, even if it is optional, a student should arrange one. Before the interview, make sure your student does his or her "homework" about the features of the college. A well-informed student will be much more appealing to the college than one who asks only simple, obvious questions about the school or does not show much interest in its specific programs or offerings. Some colleges track all contacts a student makes with the school—starting from that first request for information. Phone calls, emails, and campus visits are all opportunities to leave memorable impressions with these colleges. A student who wants to demonstrate strong interest in a college should keep in contact with the admissions office—without overdoing it, of course.

Recommendations

Strong recommendations may put a student's application at the top of the pile. Like the essay, these letters reveal qualities that may not have been communicated adequately through the other parts of the application. Students should choose their recommenders carefully and allow the teacher or other evaluator sufficient time to prepare the letter of recommendation.

Legacy Status

One factor to be aware of is the power of *legacy* status. Students with parents, grandparents, siblings, or other close relatives who graduated from the school have a much higher success rate in admissions, compared to the average student. The power is especially strong if these alumni have contributed healthy sums of money to the college. Though it might seem unfair, this is one of those inevitable facts regarding college admission, since families with multiple alumni tend to be loyal financial supporters of the college. If your student has legacy status, be sure to note that on the application. Usually you will find a question or two that specifically asks about this.

Stand Out from the Crowd

Face it: countless applicants to super-selective colleges present perfect grades, high SAT or ACT scores, and a long list of extracurricular activities ranging from cheerleading to chess club. How can any student, particularly a homeschooler, hope to stand out among this competition?

First, consider the myth of the "bright, well-rounded kid." Often referred to as the BWRK in college admissions circles, this is the kid that every parent wants. He or she is intelligent, has excellent grades and test scores, and is involved in countless extracurricular activities in a wide variety of areas. This student enjoys and pursues sports, music, clubs, volunteer work, debate, science—in short, a little bit of everything. Who could turn down a dream student like this? Ironically, BWRKs are not exactly what all colleges want. The reason? Endearing as they are, BWRK applicants are a dime a dozen, and distinguishing among them can be nearly impossible.

Instead of the proverbial well-rounded student, colleges often seek more "angular" students in their overall efforts to build a well-rounded class. These are still bright students with excellent grades, test scores, and extracurriculars. The difference is that an "angular" student will display *depth and passion* in one or two specific activities and will have pursued these with zeal and commitment, to the greatest degree possible. Instead of participating in ten extracurriculars to a minimal or moderate degree, the angular student participates in fewer total activities, but with much more involvement and depth—especially in one or two areas of passion. This depth will be measured in years of involvement, along with hours per week and weeks per year spent pursuing the interest. Additionally, this passion will be evidenced by awards, leadership positions, initiative, and innovation in taking this interest to the next level—perhaps even achieving national or state recognition in the fields of deepest interest or using the skill in a significant volunteer or paid capacity.

Although this feat sounds challenging, homeschoolers are in an ideal position to make this happen, largely because of their flexibility of schedule. Early in the high school years, encourage your student to choose one or two high priority extracurriculars and then to pursue these to a greater degree. See what happens from there. Whether it be a sport, scientific pursuits, debate, or music, this activity may take your student to places you never dreamed possible. Passion with commitment and initiative is the key.

For example, Julie's interest in science, which was modest during the middle school years, grew exponentially during high school, producing ample evidence of her passion along the way. She organized two summer science clubs, took many community college science courses, tutored in science, participated in a summer research program, and entered a regional science fair and three national science competitions. Although she also had extracurricular activities in music, English, community service, and swimming, her most fervent interests clearly lay in the sciences, and she pursued this passion fully.

Capitalize on the Uniqueness of Homeschooling

Here's the good news. At least currently, homeschooling is still enough of a novelty that a student who meets all the other admissions criteria *and* also happens to be a homeschooler will actually have a slight edge over traditional applicants. Why is this? Homeschoolers work independently, show initiative in customizing their education, and pursue their passions wholeheartedly. Note, of course, that it is not homeschooling alone that is the magic ticket. Students must first be competitive for these seats in the freshman class by achieving strong test scores and GPAs, pursuing rigorous courses of study, and demonstrating leadership and service through an array of extracurriculars.

Undoubtedly, this trend has its exceptions. A few colleges remain skeptical about homeschoolers, or even biased against them. In our interactions, however, admissions officers have been fascinated by the prospect of a homeschooled student who has achieved and completed a strong college prep course. In the future, as homeschooling becomes more prevalent, this intriguing edge will likely disappear, and homeschoolers may be competing on an equal playing field with traditionally schooled applicants—and, of course, with fellow homeschoolers. But for now, homeschoolers can enjoy a golden age, so to speak, during which homeschooling is no longer an anomaly but is still unusual enough to be intriguing. Most colleges are comfortable with homeschooling and are quite welcoming to students with this out-of-the-ordinary educational background.

In order to make homeschooling work in your student's favor, first make sure that you have "all your ducks in a row" for basic admissions criteria. As a parent-student team, translate your homeschool education into the language of "college-ese" as much as possible for the benefit of the admissions staff, who are accustomed to seeing certain course titles and credit designations on the transcript.

From there, look at your homeschooling through the eyes of someone who is seeking to compare it to traditional schooling. As your student writes the application essay and as you prepare a description of your homeschooling through the Common Application School Report and other venues, make sure that the student's initiative and independent learning are highlighted. Provide concrete examples, demonstrating how he or she had to be proactive to seek out rigorous course options and leadership opportunities. Show your student's passions as well as his or her time and effort spent delving into them. Importantly, also show how the student is "people-oriented" and can work with others as part of a team.

Through all this, of course, be honest—don't embellish or exaggerate. But do focus on the pursuits in which your student was self-propelled in the quest for education and leadership. By and large, homeschooled students display fascinating talents and a track record of independent learning. They bring diversity to a college campus by virtue of their unusual educational methods and individual passions. To put it simply, this is the type of student who belongs in college.

Homeschoolers have progressed tremendously since the years when colleges were resistant to, or at least confused about, homeschooling. In the early years, colleges had not developed admissions policies for evaluating homeschooled applications. Today, however, "Home School" is a checkbox choice right alongside "Public School" and "Private School" on college applications, and many colleges post advice on their websites specifically to assist homeschoolers with their applications. Others are increasingly flexible about receiving transcripts, counselor letters, and recommendations from homeschooled students' nontraditional instructors.

Interestingly, some of the most selective and elite colleges have the most open and flexible policies toward homeschooling, because they focus on the whole student and his or her individual uniqueness rather than assigning him or her a number based on GPA or test scores. Some of these colleges do not, in fact, require a high school diploma—a welcome scenario for homeschoolers, though the lack of an accredited high school diploma is not generally a problem for college admissions.

As previously mentioned, formerly homeschooled students who have graduated from college have shown that homeschooling works and that it produces motivated, well-educated high school graduates. These graduates continue to open doors for the homeschoolers that follow in their footsteps.

SPECIAL CONSIDERATIONS

Large Public Universities

Compared to private universities, large state university systems can be much more bureaucratic with respect to official transcripts and, depending on the university, may not even recognize a homeschooler's transcripts unless a significant amount of credit was obtained at the community college or through Advanced Placement exams. High SAT or ACT scores, however, may still get the homeschooled student in the door. As always, knowing admissions policies ahead of time can help a student to strategize and to present his or her application in a clear, understandable way. Thoroughly read the pertinent sections of the university website and clarify any questions early in the game. In addition, ask around to discover what other homeschooling families have done to break through the bureaucracy.

For instance, the University of California system has a preapproval process for high school courses in public and private schools throughout the state, by which these traditional schools submit course syllabi for approval by the university. However, the UC has no mechanism for homeschooled, out of state, or nontraditional students to receive this stamp of approval for their courses. This does not mean that homeschoolers will not be admitted; it just means that they need to present their course records clearly and professionally, making sure to demonstrate the rigor that these studies involved. Homeschooled applicants do their best to clear these course requirements via AP exam scores, SAT Subject Test scores, community college courses, and high-level online courses, as well as by pursuing rigorous homeschool courses. And, in fact, homeschoolers have excellent admission rates to the UC in spite of not having "approved" courses.

Waitlists

If your student is waitlisted at his or her first choice college and has a strong desire to be admitted there, it is important to notify the college in writing to express this interest. Updating the admissions office on any recent achievements, such as a new leadership position or an honor or award, can improve the admissions committee's view of an applicant. Above all, the student should express his or her strong desire to attend this college if accepted and should reiterate why this college is an ideal fit for his or her talents, contributions, and ambitions. This calls for a little more homework: peruse the college website and the department websites to research special programs, intriguing emphases, or courses that are an ideal match for your interests and qualifications.

From a practical standpoint, ferret out the true prospects of being admitted off the waitlist. In other words, how many students are typically admitted, and what factors are used to decide which students will be chosen? Find out whether the waitlist is ranked and if so, where your student is on the list.

Obviously, with the May 1st response deadline, a student who is later accepted off the waitlist at his or her first-choice school will lose the enrollment deposit at the second school. But if that favorite school extends an offer of admission in June, July, or August, and your student is willing to make a quick change in plans, he or she should go for it!

Deferred Admission (Gap Year)

Some students, either at the time of application or sometime later, realize that they are not ready to enroll in college immediately after high school. Reasons might include an opportunity to work or travel, a once-in-a-lifetime volunteer opportunity or missions trip, or personal reasons such as being needed at home because of a family member's illness. These students will want to explore how to defer enrollment after being accepted at a college. Many colleges allow accepted students to wait anywhere from a semester to two years to actually matriculate. In this way, the application process has not been wasted. The student has secured a spot in the freshman class and now has the opportunity to take care of some important life experiences before settling down to studying.

Some colleges will want to know a student's intent to defer at the time of initial application; others may not need this information until after the student has been accepted. Specific forms with explanations of the student's reasons for the deferral may need to be completed, deadlines observed, and perhaps deposits paid. Students will also want to know what procedures to follow when they are ready to enroll. See Chapter 28 for a broader discussion of gap year possibilities.

Note that this term "deferred admission" does not have the same meaning as an applicant being "deferred" from the Early Decision or Early Action round to the Regular Decision round of admissions decisions.

TO SUM UP

In the 21st century college admissions climate, homeschoolers should not expect discrimination, but neither should they expect special treatment. Like any other applicant, homeschoolers must submit timely, professional-looking transcripts, all required test scores, and carefully prepared applications and essays. Homeschooling families should not be too quick to assume discrimination if they are asked to clarify or expand on any of the application materials they have submitted. Most likely, the college simply needs more information in order to assess the applicant side by side with traditionally schooled applicants. By avoiding a defensive attitude and by responding respectfully and professionally, homeschooling families can do future homeschoolers a great favor.

1. Ray, Brian D., Ph.D., "General Facts and Trends," *Research Facts on Homeschooling*, National Home Education Research Institute, January 13, 2018. Accessed August 21, ,2018. https://www.nheri.org/research-facts-on-homeschooling/.
2. Franklin, Delano R. and Samuel W. Zwickel, "Record Low 4.59 Percent of Applicants Accepted to Harvard Class of 2022," *The Harvard Crimson*, March 29, 2018. Accessed August 21, 2018. https://www.thecrimson.com/article/2018/3/29/harvard-regular-admissions-2022/.
3. Top Tier Admissions, "Ivy League Admission Statistics for Class of 2022," Top Tier Admissions, 2018. Accessed August 21, 2018. https://www.toptieradmissions.com/resources/college-admissions-statistics/ivy-league-admission-statistics-for-class-of-2022/.
4. McDermid, Riley, "Class of 2022 Has Stanford's Lowest Admit Rate Ever," *San Francisco Business Times*, April 2, 2018. Accessed August 21, 2018. https://www.bizjournals.com/sanfrancisco/news/2018/04/02/class-of-2022-stanford-admission-rate.html.

Chapter 25

Show Me the Money:

Financial Aid

*F*or the student, the toughest aspect of the college application process is the incessant round of tests, essays, and tasks designed to prove the applicant's worth. But for the parent, the most daunting part —other than suffering vicariously alongside the student—is the prospect of *paying* for four years of expensive and rapidly-inflating costs. This chapter and the next will help you navigate the path to receiving as much financial aid as the student is entitled to receive.

GETTING ACQUAINTED WITH FINANCIAL AID

Before delving into the financial aid process, please realize that this information is extremely changeable. Websites, names of financial aid programs, and eligibility rules may change, and dollar amounts will certainly change from year to year. Always refer to the current websites and official publications to confirm the tips and suggestions in this chapter and to find the most up-to-date information.

Dealing with Sticker Shock

With total annual costs of $70,000 at many private universities and $30,000 at some public universities, even for in-state residents, parents are rightfully shocked at college price tags. However, with financial aid available, and with other creative ways to minimize the cost of an education, you should not initially cross expensive private colleges off your lists. This is particularly true if your student is a high achiever. Many of these schools want to help families afford the educational features they offer, and they have the resources to do so. For the most expensive colleges, a surprisingly large number of students receive aid. The College Board reports that about two-thirds of all full-time students receive some aid in the form of grants and scholarships (the type that does not need to be repaid).[1]

Remember, too, the costs of forgoing an education. A good education will serve your student and his or her future family for the rest of their lives, and it is worth a significant investment. Though estimates differ depending on location, methodology, assumptions, and, unfortunately, gender and race, U.S. Census Bureau statistics estimate that over a person's lifetime, the gap between the earnings of a college graduate and those of a high school graduate is about $900,000, with a master's degree worth an additional $400,000 over a lifetime.[2] Additionally, a college graduate's employment is usually steadier, with greater career opportunities, more options, and a greater chance of working in a job he or she will enjoy.

Finding information on financial aid, of course, is the key. Once a student has selected several colleges that seem to be a good fit academically, the next information a family should look for is the total cost: tuition, room and board, books and supplies, fees, and other expenses such as transportation, health insurance, and personal expenses. You can find this figure on each college's website.

Financial Aid Lingo

You will want to become well-versed in financial aid "lingo" early in the game—by the student's junior year or even earlier—to place yourself in the best position to search for aid. Here are some basic definitions of terms commonly used in discussing financial aid:

Scholarship: Financial aid, usually based on merit, academic achievement, leadership, or talent, that does not have to be repaid.

Grant: Financial aid, usually based on financial need, that is a "gift" and does not have to be repaid. Grants may come from the federal or state government, or from the college itself.

Loan: Financial aid in the form of money the student borrows, to be repaid later with interest (usually after graduation) according to the specific terms of the loan. Some loans are taken out and repaid by the parents, and repayment may start immediately.

Federal Work-Study: A program in which students can earn some of their financial aid by working a few hours per week in jobs on or off campus. Colleges may also offer their own work-study programs.

FAFSA (Free Application for Federal Student Aid): An essential form filled out after October 1 of the senior year. Information from this form is entered into a standard formula to calculate the Expected Family Contribution (EFC).

CSS/Financial Aid PROFILE: A form required by certain private or public colleges and some scholarship organizations to evaluate financial need. This is filed through the College Board website and, unlike the FAFSA, is not free. Applicants are charged a fee for each school to which the PROFILE is submitted.

SAR (Student Aid Report): A report generated after submission of the FAFSA and sent to the family and designated colleges; it summarizes FAFSA information and reports the Expected Family Contribution.

Cost of Attendance: The total cost of tuition, fees, books, supplies, room, board, transportation, and personal expenses the student will likely incur per year. This will be different for every school.

Expected Family Contribution (EFC): The estimated amount the student and/or the family are expected to pay for one year of college from their own financial resources. It is determined according to standard formulas and is based on information provided on the FAFSA from family earnings, assets, savings, family size, and number of children in college. The EFC for a given year will be the same regardless of the cost of the school being considered. In addition to parental contributions, the student will generally be expected to contribute money from summer earnings and/or assets. The EFC will be different each year because it will depend on that year's income and expenses.

Financial Need: The difference between the Cost of Attendance and the Expected Family Contribution. This is the amount to be made up through financial aid packages.

Financial Aid Package: A combination of grants, scholarships, loans, and work-study jobs (from federal, state, and/or institutional sources) offered to students, depending on eligibility. The package is offered by the college, though various government and private sources provide some elements of the funding.

Need-Based Financial Aid: Aid offered to bridge the gap between the Expected Family Contribution and the Cost of Attendance.

LOCATING FINANCIAL AID INFORMATION

Useful Websites

College Board (http://collegeboard.org)

One convenient place for beginning the financial aid search is the College Board website, where students and families can take care of a number of preliminary tasks:
- Understand how financial aid works.
- Search for scholarships.
- Find a step-by-step guide and informative videos regarding applying for financial aid.
- Search for financial information for specific colleges.
- Seek out loan information.
- Understand student loan payback scenarios using a Student Loan Calculator.
- Gain tips on dealing with financial aid offices.
- Calculate college costs, including effects of inflation.
- Estimate how much parents should be saving for college.
- Estimate family contribution by using an EFC calculator (this is a useful preview).
- Compare financial aid awards from multiple colleges side by side.

Fastweb (http://fastweb.com)

Fastweb stands for Financial Aid Search Through the Web and is one of the best-known sites for searching out scholarships and other aid. Students can enter a personalized profile and search for information on local, national, or college-specific scholarships. More than 1.5 million scholarships, grants, and loans totaling over $3 billion are available through this search. The individualized searches eliminate the need to comb through lists of scholarships for which the student is not eligible. After registering on the site, the student will receive ongoing email updates of scholarships that fit his or her profile.

U.S. Department of Education (https://studentaid.ed.gov/)

The U.S. Department of Education website for financial aid will lead you to both federal and non-federal aid (scholarships, grants, loans, work-study).

FAFSA4caster (http://fafsa4caster.ed.gov)

Ideal for high school juniors, this site previews the federal financial aid process, including its official form, the FAFSA. Families can receive early estimates of eligibility by filling out the FAFSA4caster.

FinAid® SmartStudent™ Guide (http://FinAid.org)

The FinAid SmartStudent Guide has financial aid estimators and a wealth of other helpful tips about finding and applying for financial aid. The articles about how to spot scholarship scams are on point; however, some of the other information is a bit behind the times.

Notes on Online Financial Aid Estimators

When using online financial aid estimators that preview the Expected Family Contribution prior to sending in the official FAFSA, realize that these are only estimates. They are not a guarantee of the actual EFC nor of the financial aid a student will receive. However, in most cases the estimated EFC figures should be quite close to the official figures and can be useful tools for families who want a ballpark estimate of what to expect. Having this knowledge before senior year can provide your family with some clues as to what will be the most feasible financial plan as you investigate private and public universities.

Other Sources of Information

College Financial Aid Offices -- Request financial aid information from prospective colleges. Each college may have its own programs in addition to national or state programs.

Financial Aid Nights at Local Schools — Ask a friend whose student attends a nearby public or private high school to alert you to information nights for parents and students, or regularly check the school websites.

Scholarship Handbook — Published annually by the College Board, this book (about $30) lists funding sources for federal, state, and private aid and also provides tips for finding internships and loans.

UNDERSTANDING THE TYPES OF FINANCIAL AID

Federal Government-Based Financial Aid

To be eligible for any federal aid, students must complete the FAFSA (Free Application for Federal Student Aid). It is advisable to complete this form even if the family is not expecting to be eligible for any need-based aid. Family circumstances may change, and filling out the FAFSA creates a "safety net" allowing the family to receive aid if eligible. Moreover, colleges require the FAFSA before they give out any type of institutional aid, even merit aid. FAFSA deadlines come in three shapes and sizes: college deadlines, state deadlines, and federal deadlines, reflecting the three main sources of financial aid. Usually the college deadlines are the earliest, and some aid is distributed on a "first-come, first-served" basis, so be sure to meet the FAFSA deadline required by your colleges. These deadlines will be posted on the college's financial aid web page. You do not want to miss FAFSA deadlines, because this oversight amounts to forgoing what could be a sizable amount of help.

For up-to-date information on government aid, browse through the resources available on the Federal Student Aid site. Go to Student Aid on the Web, at http://studentaid.ed.gov/sa/resources/. You will find a variety of publications, fact sheets, and online tools to help you understand and search for financial aid.

Grants (Do Not Have to Be Repaid)

- **Federal Pell Grants** These grants are given to the neediest undergraduate students, with the amount depending on program funding and on the student's need.
- **Federal Supplemental Educational Opportunity Grants (FSEOG)** FSEOGs are for undergraduate students with exceptional financial need. Students receiving Pell Grants have higher priority for FSEOG grants. Amounts depend on need, funding level, and financial aid policies at the college.
- **TEACH Grants (Teacher Education Assistance for College and Higher Education)** These grants are provided for college students who intend to enter the teaching field, and by accepting the grant, students agree to teach for a specified period of time in a high-need field or in a school serving low-income families. High-need fields depend on the need in a particular state but can include

bilingual education, science, mathematics, special education, and several other fields. For students who accept the grant but do not complete the terms of the agreement, the grant becomes a loan to be paid back with interest.

Loans (Must Be Repaid)

Due to budget cuts at federal and state levels, more aid is shifting toward loans rather than grants. Before signing for significant dollar amounts of loans, count the true costs, since heavy debt can severely limit the student's financial freedom after graduation. You must be willing to accept the responsibility for repayment (including interest charges, fees, and penalties) and thus should discuss whether the loan makes good financial sense. Will your student soon be earning enough money to support himself or herself and also to repay the loan, or would you as parents plan to repay the loan yourselves? Be sure to investigate all other financing options before accepting a loan. Sometimes families inadvertently overlook other options offering free money.

For all of the following loans, refer to the Federal Student Aid website for current loan types, eligibility, repayment policies, and interest rates.

- **William D. Ford Federal Direct Loan Program** includes several types of loans, for which the U.S. Department of Education is the lender. Two of these options (sometimes called Stafford Loans) are the Direct Subsidized Loans and the Direct Unsubsidized Loans. Subsidized loans do not accrue interest until repayment begins (in the meantime, the interest is paid by the government), while unsubsidized loans accrue interest from the initiation date of the loan. For subsidized loans, students must demonstrate financial need, while for unsubsidized loans, students without demonstrated need may apply. Repayment begins after the student graduates, leaves school, or drops below half-time enrollment.
- **Federal Perkins Loans**, available to students demonstrating exceptional need, are low-interest loans for undergraduates. Repayment begins nine months after the student graduates or drops below half-time enrollment and is made directly to the school. Funds depend on financial need and availability of the program at the college you have chosen.
- **Direct PLUS Loans** are variable interest loans made to the parent, not the student (they are also available for graduate students). For these loans, families do not have to demonstrate financial need. You can take out a PLUS loan for any amount up to the difference between the college's COA (cost of attendance) and the financial aid awarded the student. Repayment starts once the money is paid out and is paid to the U.S. Department of Education.

Federal Work-Study

Federal Work-Study provides jobs, either on campus or off campus at a public agency or private nonprofit. The work hours range from just a few hours per week to a maximum of twenty hours per week at minimum wage or higher. To receive these work-study jobs, students must demonstrate financial need. Sometimes the type of work is related to the student's course of study; for instance, a student may work as an assistant in a science lab.

Parents have been known to be concerned about students working during college, thinking that the job will distract from study time and hinder academic progress. In fact, the opposite has been shown to be true. Studies have demonstrated that students who work a modest number of hours per week actually develop greater time management skills and are more focused on their studies. Often they demonstrate better grades and better progress toward a degree than do students who do not work at all. On-campus jobs are ideal, as the working hours can be customized to fit the student's schedule, and the student does not have to spend time and money commuting. However, in the absence of opportunities for on-campus jobs, nearby off-campus jobs can be beneficial too.

State Government-Based Financial Aid

Like the federal government, each state government offers grants, loans, and other awards to students pursuing a college education. These may include awards for four-year colleges, community colleges, transfer arrangements, or occupational programs. Search for your state's information by contacting in-state colleges, by picking up an information packet from a local high school or community college, or by going to the website of the Department of Education for your own state. It is important to find out your state's deadline for the FAFSA, as these vary from state to state (generally March through May, but the earlier the better for some types of aid).

States may have their own application forms in addition to the FAFSA. Check for eligibility requirements, both for the student's state of residence and for the college to be attended.

Your state most likely has an informative website designed to acquaint you with its financial aid programs. Through this site, you may apply online or request additional information.

College or University-Based Financial Aid

In addition to federal or state government-based aid, colleges frequently have funds available for students with financial need or with outstanding academic, artistic, athletic, or leadership promise. These funds may come from alumni scholarship funds or endowments from private donors.

Grants and Loans

For students with demonstrated financial need, the college may offer *grants* (money that does not need to be paid back) or *loans*. The college may also have campus jobs available that are not associated with Federal Work-Study.

Merit Scholarships

One of the most desirable forms of financial aid, especially for students who do not qualify for need-based aid, is the merit scholarship. Varying from college to college, these scholarships are given names such as President's Scholarship or Dean's Scholarship and can provide anything from a few hundred dollars per year to full tuition for four years. Frequently, merit awards are offered at the time of college acceptance and may be based on the student's GPA, test scores, rigor of courses, and extracurricular activities—in short, the qualities that made the student a strong applicant in the first place. Some of these awards are renewable from year to year; others are not. You should be able to find information about merit scholarships on the college financial aid web page. If not, be sure to ask about requirements. Some scholarships are automatically awarded on the basis of high GPA and test scores alone; others have an application process the student must complete, so you'll want to note deadlines.

Academic scholarships, sometimes quite substantial, are often used to "lure" promising students to a particular college. Competition for these merit awards may not be as stiff as competition for private scholarships. Certain awards may be guaranteed to students meeting basic GPA or test score criteria upon admission. Some colleges offer merit scholarships to National Merit Finalists or even to Semifinalists.

Performance-based scholarships in fields such as art, music, debate, drama, journalism, or athletics are also awarded at many colleges. Students are screened and selected by the specific department of interest. Start the process early by contacting the appropriate division to learn about scholarship requirements, application procedures, and deadlines for auditions, interviews, resumes, or portfolios.

Athletic scholarships are the dream of many a talented high school athlete. Statistically, however, the chances of a student receiving a generous scholarship are rather slim. NCAA (National Collegiate Athletic Association) limits the number of available scholarships per sport, and of all students playing high school sports, only about 2% receive NCAA athletic scholarships each year of college.[3] While football and basketball programs give out some full rides, most athletes receive only partial scholarships, and these can be quite small. Students should also count the cost of the large time commitment required for practices, games, and travel, and should ascertain whether they can still succeed in their progress toward their academic degrees.

For better chances of scholarships, athletes should become acquainted with university coaches ahead of time. For instance, if your student will have a game or a competition near the college of interest, he or she should let the coach know. Coaches may also run summer camps, which can be another way to make contacts.

If your student is considering an NCAA college, contact the NCAA for information on college recruiting rules such as those involving GPA, testing, and other requirements. The NCAA website has information, including a downloadable brochure, *The Guide for College-Bound Student Athletes*. The site also answers a few FAQs directly relating to homeschooled students. Be sure to check this site early in the high school years in order to understand and maintain eligibility.

Other College-Based Scholarships

Additional awards may include specialized scholarships—for instance, a family grant if more than one student is attending the college, or grants for descendants of alumni. If you do not see a full list of scholarships on the college website, ask the financial aid office to send you information.

Private Scholarships

Private scholarships, offered through national or local organizations such as clubs, employers, foundations, religious organizations, or corporations, can be good resources for students without demonstrated financial need. Many are merit-based and thus may require test scores, transcripts, essays, projects, or other qualifiers. The application process for these scholarships is completely separate from the process used to award federal, state, and institutional aid. An overview of private scholarships, along with a list of application tips, is covered in detail in the next chapter.

APPLYING FOR GOVERNMENT AND COLLEGE-BASED FINANCIAL AID

The senior year is a busy one, not only with the rush of college applications, but also with the crush of financial aid applications. Families who are counting on getting financial aid should be careful not to miss any steps or deadlines.

Become Familiar with the Process

Prior to the senior year, visit the Federal Student Aid FAFSA4caster at http://fafsa4caster.ed.gov to get a sneak preview of the federal financial aid process. In addition to becoming familiar with the FAFSA form, you can receive an early estimate of your financial aid eligibility.

File Early Applications

If the student is applying Early Decision or Early Action, the college may request its own financial aid application, along with the FAFSA and the CSS/Financial Aid PROFILE (see description below). The college may also request copies of the parents' previous year tax returns or other financial information— be sure to find out exactly what is required and when the deadlines are. Colleges request this financial information so that they can offer a financial aid package at the time of acceptance. If necessary, financial figures will later be verified and updated, and awards may be adjusted up or down if necessary.

Prepare to File the FAFSA

Even before college applications are due, students and parents will want to be on their toes. The FAFSA is available beginning on October 1, and should in fact be submitted as soon as possible after this date. This key form is absolutely required for any student who hopes to receive federal aid, and it is also used to determine eligibility for state aid and college-based aid. While the FAFSA can still be filled out on paper, the online method at http://fafsa.ed.gov is the preferred way to submit your information. You can access your Student Aid Report, describing your Expected Family Contribution, within two weeks after you complete the FAFSA online. The FAFSA may also be filled out via the myStudentAid mobile app.

Before you officially file the FAFSA, both student and parent will need to create their own Federal Student Aid ID, or FSA ID (user name and password), which will allow you to access the FAFSA information you entered and to sign your form electronically. Set up this ID early so that you don't hold up your FAFSA filing (some functions are not available until this step checks out with the Social Security Administration). Never give out your FSA ID to anyone, even to someone who is helping you complete the FAFSA.

Organize Your Paperwork

Information to have on hand when completing the FAFSA includes Social Security numbers, income and asset statements for both parents and student (W-2 forms or earnings statements, tax returns from the previous year, records of untaxed income, bank and investment statements, mortgage and business records), and the names of colleges to which FAFSA results should be sent. You may list up to ten schools to receive the information and can add more schools after your initial submission. When you are finished, print a copy of your completed FAFSA and keep it with your financial aid records. The FAFSA is submitted in the fall, using the previous tax year's information. For instance, for students entering college in 2020, the FAFSA will be completed in the fall of 2019, using 2018 tax return information. Most families will be able to import their tax data directly into the FAFSA form using the IRS Data Retrieval Tool (DRT) but you will still need your W-2 and tax forms handy for other portions of the FAFSA.

Meet Deadlines and Requirements

Always meet financial aid deadlines. While aid may sometimes be awarded even for late applications, students who apply before the deadline will receive priority. Many sources of aid are on a "first-come, first-served" basis. Additionally, to be eligible for federal and state aid, young men must register with the U.S. Selective Service, as required by law, within thirty days of their eighteenth birthday.

Complete the CSS/Financial Aid PROFILE

The College Scholarship Service® form called the CSS/Financial Aid PROFILE is another document that many colleges and scholarship programs use to collect information before awarding private grant and scholarship funds. This profile, filled out online, analyzes family income, assets, number of children in college, and other financially relevant data. Using this information, plus the data gained from the FAFSA, the college financial aid office can determine the parental contribution to college expenses.

Both the FAFSA and the CSS/Financial Aid PROFILE can take several days to fill out, even if you have all your income and asset information on hand. Do not save these tasks for the last minute. In fact, it is wise to set aside two or three weeks to fill these out properly, since you may need to dig up additional pieces of information, and emails or phone calls may have to go back and forth to answer specific questions.

For both the FAFSA and the CSS/Financial Aid PROFILE, the student lists code numbers for the colleges to which the information should be sent. Since some college names are similar, double check the proper code numbers. The codes should be listed on the college's financial aid web page.

Observe Any Additional State Requirements

Take note of extra requirements your state government might have regarding eligibility for state aid. For example, in California, students must complete a GPA verification form. GPA forms may present a problem for homeschoolers, since non-accredited schools may not be eligible for GPA submission. In this case, SAT or ACT scores might be acceptable—check your own state's guidelines, and take note of whether an unofficial copy of the SAT or ACT scores is acceptable in place of an official report.

Submit College-Specific Forms

In addition to the FAFSA and CSS/Financial Aid PROFILE, students may have to fill out financial aid forms originating from the college itself. Gather these ahead of time and submit them promptly to be in the running for financial aid awards. College-specific forms are generally shorter and less complicated than the others; nonetheless, they are important if your student's colleges require them.

Submit Income Tax Forms as Requested

If your student is eligible for financial aid based on the FAFSA and/or CSS/Financial Aid PROFILE information, colleges may request a copy of the parent's tax return and W-2 to verify income. Have these documents ready if they are needed, and observe all deadlines and procedures for submitting them. For instance, documents requested for the CSS/Financial Aid PROFILE are submitted through a service called IDOC which sends a facsimile of these forms electronically to the appropriate colleges.

Receive and Verify Financial Need Analysis

Once the forms have been submitted, the financial information is analyzed and verified. Based on the FAFSA information, the Student Aid Report (SAR) will be submitted to your family. Review the SAR to check for errors, and then promptly provide corrections or additional information so that schools will have updated information to process financial aid. The SAR contains the Expected Family Contribution (EFC) figure, which tells you and your student how much you can expect to pay out of your own funds.

Colleges will receive the EFC figure along with the rest of the student's information, including the CSS/Financial Aid PROFILE and college-specific financial aid forms, if applicable. The financial aid office will calculate the aid package based on the stated financial need, which is the cost of attendance minus the EFC. The cost of attendance, or student budget, includes the total cost of attending the college for one year. Items included are tuition, fees, room and board, books, supplies, transportation, and personal expenses.

Receive Financial Aid Offers from Colleges

Using the financial need figure calculated from the EFC and the cost of attendance at that college, the financial aid office will prepare a "package" of financial aid which will be different for every student. Amounts and components of aid will depend on need, types of aid the student is eligible for (including merit aid), and the funding available from government and college sources.

The first item to go into the package is government grants, both federal and state. After a student has been awarded these grants to his or her limit, the college will provide grants from the institution itself, if available. These may be modest or sizable. Whether from the government or from college sources, grant money will not need to be paid back.

After grants, the student will be awarded Federal Work-Study or college work-study funds for which he or she is eligible. Over the course of the school year, the student will earn these funds by working at a campus job. Most jobs will require just a few hours of work per week.

Finally, to make up any difference remaining in the student's financial need, government or college-based loans will be offered.

The college will communicate the details of the financial aid package to your family in an official document called the award letter, and any government aid the student is entitled to will be paid out through the school. These funds will be applied first to tuition, fees, and room and board. Any funds remaining after these expenses have been paid will be issued to the student to cover other expenses.

Many schools follow a practice called *gapping*, meaning that they do not award aid to meet the full need of their students. Colleges have limited funds available and may offer a financial aid package that is significantly less than the demonstrated need. In this case, you will need to pay not only the EFC but also this "gap" figure from your own resources. To supplement inadequate aid, your student may be able to find a job on campus even if he or she doesn't qualify for the Federal Work-Study Program. Other options include finding private scholarships. See Chapter 26 for tips.

Accept the Offer

After you and your student confer about the aid being offered, you will then either accept or reject the aid and will sign and return a copy of the award letter to the college (or, if the aid was offered via electronic communication, you may sign online). The financial aid offer may be an important factor in making the final decision as to which college to attend, so take your time discussing the ramifications. You are free to accept some parts of the offer (such as grants and scholarships) and reject others (such as loans or Work-Study) if you prefer not to accept them. You would then be responsible for this amount yourselves.

TO SUM UP

By being aware of the sources of grants, loans, and scholarships and by understanding how to apply for them, you will have a good chance of defraying at least some of the tremendous costs of college. As you navigate the complex financial aid process, take heart in the fact that, even with the high cost, a college education is still one of the best investments you can make for your student's future.

1. The College Board, "Financial Aid: FAQs," BigFuture, 2018. Accessed August 21, 2018. https://bigfuture.collegeboard.org/pay-for-college/financial-aid-101/financial-aid-faqs.
2. Longley, Robert, "Lifetime Earnings Soar with Education," *ThoughtCo.*, June 4, 2017. Accessed August 21, 2018. https://www.thoughtco.com/lifetime-earnings-soar-with-education-3321730.
3. National Collegiate Athletics Association, "Scholarships," NCAA.com, 2018. Accessed August 21, 2018. http://www.ncaa.org/student-athletes/future/scholarships.

Chapter 26

More on Financial Aid:

Private Scholarships and Helpful Tips

Seeking out financial aid is no trivial task. The previous chapter described the types of financial aid available and explained how to apply for government and institution-based aid. This chapter delves into private scholarships, which utilize a completely different application process. Additionally, you will find tips you can apply to the entire financial aid process to maximize your student's chances of receiving aid.

APPLYING FOR PRIVATE SCHOLARSHIPS

Students who have not received much federal, state, or institutional aid due to demonstrating little or no financial need may benefit from merit-based private scholarships, offered through clubs, religious and community organizations, employers, and corporations. Here are a few things to know about private scholarships, including some bad news and some good news.

The Bad News About Private Scholarships

Outside Scholarships May Reduce Amounts of Other Aid

Students are required to report to the college financial aid office any outside (private) aid they receive, and colleges are in turn required to reduce the student's financial need figure by this amount. Thus, outside aid can reduce the need-based financial aid students would otherwise receive from government or college sources. However, the good news at most schools is that the outside scholarship may first reduce the amount of "self-help" aid offered (loans or work-study) before reducing the amount of grants or "gift" aid. Other schools will reduce grant aid and self-help aid equally or may even reduce grant aid first. Check your school's policy to confirm this. You may also be able to work out a plan with the donor of the outside scholarship whereby you receive one-fourth of the total award each year, thereby spreading out the overall impact of any reduction in aid. Or you may seek to defer the award to a subsequent year.

Your logical mind may now be prompting you to ask, "Then why go through the trouble of applying for outside scholarships?" The answer is that it depends on your circumstances. Some families are in an income category in which they will show no demonstrated financial need and thus will not be offered any need-based aid at all. Other families will be offered loans as part of their aid package; outside scholarships may reduce the amount of loans they need to borrow (depending on the college's policy on outside scholarships). Additionally, you cannot assume that 100% of your financial need will be met at a particular college. In fact, the term "gapping" refers to a situation where there is a gap between the student's need and the aid offered. In all of these cases, outside scholarships can help bridge this gap.

Applying for Scholarships Can Be Time-Consuming

While completion of the FAFSA and the CSS/Financial Aid PROFILE is primarily a project for the parents, scholarship applications are the student's responsibility. Some applications are quite involved and require goal statements, essays, and lists of extracurricular activities and leadership positions. Certain scholarships even involve lengthy research projects. Letters of recommendation, transcripts, and test scores are also common requirements.

Frequently, parents give their students the "assignment" of locating and applying for scholarships, saying that this is their primary job for the senior year. While this philosophy is reasonable and appropriate to a point—perhaps five or six applications—be sensitive to your student's time commitments and don't expect more than is humanly possible. Especially if the student has a heavy senior year course load, a plethora of scholarship applications on top of schoolwork can make the second semester every bit as grueling as the first semester was with college applications. Sit down with your student and decide which scholarships are the most reasonable to apply for. Prioritize the opportunities: those at the top of the list should be the ones the student is most likely to receive, as well as those with the highest dollar value. In other words, aim to get the most "bang for the buck" (i.e., the most bucks per hour spent applying).

Competition Can Be Stiff

While the level of competition for scholarships can vary, the most lucrative scholarships involve quite a bit of competition. A few examples of these highly competitive nationwide awards are the Coca-Cola Scholars, the Gates Millennium Scholars, and the Dell Scholars® Program. Though your student should not be overly optimistic, if he or she has outstanding accomplishments, go ahead and give these a shot. Scholarships with smaller pools of applicants, such as those sponsored by local community groups, clubs, or employers, offer greater odds for your student than do national competitions.

Many Awards Are Nonrenewable

Some scholarships from private sources (though not all) are offered for one year only and are not renewable. If you want to fund four years of college with private scholarships, the application process will need to continue each year.

The Good News About Private Scholarships

Some Scholarships Are Relatively Easy to Win

In spite of the bad news mentioned above, certain scholarships *do not* have extremely high levels of competition—either because few students know about the awards, or because many of those who hear about them are not eligible or fail to follow through in applying. Diligence in scouting out scholarships early in the game and preparing suitable essays ahead of time can pay off with a collection of small scholarships that can make a dent in the tuition bill. Junior year is not too early to start hunting for likely prospects, though the student will not apply until senior year.

A Little Planning Goes a Long Way

Cleverness and foresight while preparing college applications can help tremendously when applying for scholarships. The carefully prepared resume, the clearly defined goal statement, and the sparkling application essays can be recycled and customized for use during the scholarship application process.

Even Small Scholarships Provide a Psychological Boost

After four years of diligent work, including an arduous senior year spent submitting applications, your student can use a bit of encouragement. Winning even small local awards, often accompanied by a short writeup in the community newspaper, can provide a sense of accomplishment for a job well done. As your student reaps the fruit of years of hard work and discovers that homeschooling helped accomplish these goals, he or she can enjoy these achievements and thank God for the gifts, abilities, and grace that made it all possible.

How to Locate Private Scholarships

During the sophomore and junior years, your student should try some of the searchable databases (such as Fastweb®) mentioned in the previous chapter, and become familiar with the types of scholarships available. Other search sites include College Board's Big Future™ search feature, Niche.com, Scholarships.com, and Zinch.com, but there are others, so read a few reviews. Scholarships can vary based on the scope of eligibility (national, regional, or local) or on qualification method (academics, talent, community service, or essay). Create a profile on the site, with your proposed major, ethnicity, religion, special interests, sports involvement, and other details that might flag a possible scholarship opportunity.

National Scholarships

One major national scholarship is the National Merit Scholarship Program, first mentioned in Chapter 19. Students from each state who receive high scores on the PSAT/NMSQT exam are notified of Semifinalist status during the fall of their senior year. These students fill out scholarship applications, and from this pool, Finalists and then winners are chosen in the spring. These awards can be college-sponsored awards, corporate-sponsored awards, or National Merit $2,500 Scholarships.

Homeschooled students are eligible to compete, provided that they take the PSAT/NMSQT exam during their junior year. If your student is chosen as a Semifinalist, you as the parent may fill out the "school principal" portion of the application, and a teacher or PSP administrator may fill out the teacher/counselor recommendation. The website of the National Merit Scholarship Corporation has full details about eligibility and competition procedures.

Besides those mentioned earlier, other examples of private scholarships include the AXA Achievement[SM] Award, Italian Catholic Federation, Hispanic Scholarship Fund®, Japanese-American Citizens League National Scholarship, and Association for Women in Science. *Many* other scholarship competitions are available; you can search them up through the previously mentioned services.

Scholarship Programs for Gifted or High-Achieving Students

If your student is gifted or high-achieving, be sure to look into a few programs that can provide financial aid during high school and/or college.

The Davidson Fellows Scholarship, sponsored by the Davidson Institute for Talent Development, provides high-achieving students the opportunity to be named Davidson Fellows and receive large scholarships by submitting original work demonstrating significant achievements in science, technology, math, music, literature, and/or philosophy. See http://www.davidsongifted.org/ for more information.

The Jack Kent Cooke Foundation Young Scholars Program works with high-achieving, low-income students throughout the high school years, providing them with individualized educational resources. Students apply as seventh graders, entering eighth grade and, if chosen, receive scholarships to cover high school educational expenses. For students entering college, the Cooke College Scholarship is available to students with financial need and with SAT/ACT scores and GPAs above a specific level. Additionally, a Cooke Undergraduate Transfer Scholarship is available for students transferring from a community college to a university. See https://www.jkcf.org/ for more information.

The QuestBridge® College Prep Scholarship Program identifies high-achieving, low-income high school juniors and assists them in the college application process through summer college programs, campus visits, college admissions counseling, and other helpful programs. Students participating in the National College Match program submit the free application by the end of September and "rank" up to twelve colleges by October of senior year. If selected as Finalists, students are considered for a College Match Scholarship and may be matched to one of the colleges they ranked. If they are not selected or not matched, they can still apply Early Action, Early Decision, or Regular Decision to these colleges. See https://www.questbridge.org/ for more information.

Talent or Performance-Based Scholarships

Some scholarships require the student to "do something." For example, essay-based competitions use student essays as the major criterion for awarding scholarships. Talent-based awards such as those offered through music, art, or theater groups require entries based on student projects, auditions, or achievements in these disciplines. Science-based awards can appeal to young researchers who would like to enter competitions such as the Regeneron Science Talent Search. Local science fairs offering small or large prizes often feed into major regional or national science fairs with larger awards. Over the years, homeschoolers have done well in these competitions.

Some scholarships are based on outstanding community service and volunteer work. Whatever your student's forte is, he or she can probably find a scholarship to match. As your student becomes specialized in a pursuit or passion, encourage him or her to ask teachers, professors, mentors, volunteer coordinators, and others in the special field of interest to recommend appropriate scholarship opportunities.

Local Scholarships

Check your community for scholarships in your own "back yard." Look at local service clubs, women's and men's clubs, religious organizations, and employers. Spring of your student's junior year is a good time to read your community newspaper to see what scholarships local students are winning. Take note of these opportunities for next year. If your student has taken community college courses, find out whether scholarships are available to students moving on to four-year colleges.

Application Tips and Procedures

A scholarship application is a miniature version of the college application. Much of the same information will be requested all over again: activities, leadership, achievements, awards, goals, and often transcripts, test scores, recommendations, and/or essays. The following tips may help streamline the process.

Tips for the Student:

Prepare

- Start early! Give yourself a personal deadline that is a couple of weeks earlier than the official deadline, to allow time to complete and proofread the application, clarify confusing instructions, gather additional documents, and submit the application with time to spare.
- Read scholarship eligibility rules carefully to make sure you may compete. If you think that home-schooling might be a problem, ask for clarification or an exception.
- Keep a well-worded resume on file, listing your extracurricular activities, volunteer and work experience, and leadership experience, with the most important items listed first.
- Prepare a well-articulated paragraph or two about your goals and ambitions to use as a template when you encounter this common question.
- Have an up-to-date official transcript available at all times, whether generated from your home school or from your PSP. You might also want to have an official transcript from the community college (in a sealed envelope) in case you need a transcript at a moment's notice.
- Let the teachers who wrote your college recommendation letters know that you may need to call upon them again for scholarship applications. This way, they can keep your letter on file.

Apply

- Make sure your application is complete, with "Not Applicable" noted where questions do not apply to you as a homeschooler. Include all required forms, attachments, transcripts, and letters.
- If requested, include a compelling, engaging essay that conveys your strong points, achievements and personality. You may be able to recycle college application essays, but check the prompts carefully to make sure that they match. Be sure to address all parts of the question.
- If you have questions as you fill out the application, don't guess. Instead, contact the scholarship organization to clear up your questions.

Finalize

- Keep electronic or printed copies of anything you submit, in case items are lost.
- Though most scholarship applications are submitted electronically, some are still submitted by mail. When mailing important applications, consider obtaining a certificate of mailing to prove that you sent it by the required date. Use the post office tracking number to confirm delivery.
- If the application needs to *arrive by* a certain date rather than simply being *postmarked* by the date, you may have to mail very early or use a guaranteed overnight delivery method and track the item's travels and arrival online. If your item was guaranteed to be delivered the next day and was not, you can submit this proof to the scholarship administrators, and they may have mercy on you. This happened to Julie—and yes, she did get the scholarship!

Cautions

Unfortunately, scammers are rampant in the business of scholarships. Beware of any scholarships with the following circumstances:

- You have to pay to enter the competition, other than small fees to enter a science fair or other event that has bona fide expenses.

- You are "guaranteed" to receive a scholarship.
- You receive a mass mailing letter telling you, "You have been selected for financial aid."
- You are asked for a credit card number or bank account number.
- You are notified that you won a scholarship when you know you didn't enter the contest.

Also beware of identity theft, and be extremely careful about offering personal information such as your name, Social Security number, and date of birth unless you know it's a legitimate competition (even so, in general, avoid sharing your Social Security number). Use all the usual cautions you exercise when working online, such as checking that you are in a secure site and that you are not on an impostor site. Keep your FSA ID secure at all times.

Additionally, do not use scholarship search services for which a fee is required, since a vast amount of information on scholarships is available to the public without charge. The FinAid SmartStudent Guide at http://www.finaid.org/ has useful articles on how to recognize and report scams.

NAVIGATING THE FINANCIAL AID PROCESS

Record Keeping Tips

If you haven't already guessed, the financial aid process generates a tremendous amount of form-filling and document-sending, and *all* of it is important. While good record keeping is always a smart idea during the college application process, you definitely want a paper or electronic trail when you are dealing with financial aid. Create an organized system so that you do not lose track of requirements, miss deadlines, or waste time at the last minute scrambling for critical documents.

For financial aid purposes, you should keep several different types of records:

School Records

School records include homeschool or PSP-generated transcripts, community college transcripts, and SAT or ACT test scores.

Financial Records

Financial records include tax returns from the previous year or two, W-2s with current year income information, bank statements, investment account statements, records of stocks, and records of any money that is in the student's name.

File of Submitted Forms

Since mistakes or miscommunications can bring the financial aid process to a screeching halt until they are resolved, keep electronic copies of all forms you submit as well as of emails that contain important details. Designate an electronic or paper folder to safely store copies of the forms and attachments you have submitted to FAFSA, CSS/Financial Aid PROFILE, colleges, and private scholarship programs.

Phone and Postal Records

Also log phone conversations, recording the name of the person with whom you spoke. For time-sensitive items mailed by U.S. Postal Service, obtain and save a Certificate of Mailing to prove that items were postmarked by the deadlines—or you could even pay extra for Certified Mail® with a return receipt.

Questions to Ask College Financial Aid Offices

During your college visits, stop by the financial aid office. In addition to the information found on their financial aid web pages, most schools have a brochure or booklet describing their policies and explaining how to apply for aid. Here are some questions that should be answered, either in the materials you read or in your personal encounters with the financial aid office.[1] Of course, always read the information first and then ask any remaining unanswered questions.

1. What are the total costs of tuition, room and board, books and supplies, fees, transportation, and miscellaneous expenses for the first year of college?

2. Approximately how much can the tuition and other expenses be expected to rise during the next four years? Can you provide historical data for the past three to five years?

3. What are options for reducing these expenses (less expensive residence halls, meal plans, etc.)?

4. How will the aid package change from year to year?

5. If the family's financial situation changes during the year, requiring more aid, how will these changes be acted upon? Will the Financial Aid office reconsider the aid award?

6. Does the college offer merit scholarships to students without financial need, or does it offer only need-based awards? How would a student apply for these merit awards? Are there applications in addition to the usual FAFSA and/or CSS/Financial Aid PROFILE?

7. Are the admissions policies "need-blind"? In other words, are admissions decisions made without knowledge of the student's financial status? (At schools that *do not* practice need-blind admissions, a student who is marginal for admission but has sufficient financial resources may be accepted over an equally qualified student who would need significant financial aid.)

8. Does applying Early Decision affect (i.e., reduce) the potential financial aid offer? This decision plan is binding, and thus you would not have the opportunity to compare financial aid offers from other colleges.

9. How does the college treat private or outside scholarships in calculating aid awarded by the college?

10. What application forms, financial aid procedures, and deadlines are specific to this college? What are the priority deadlines?

11. When are bills sent, and what are the deadlines and penalties for late payments? Does the college offer monthly tuition payment plans or financing options? What interest rates apply, if any? Can bills be paid by credit card?

12. For grants and loans originating from the college, can a student apply for renewal? What are the academic requirements? What are the repayment terms on loans?

13. How much student loan debt does the average student have after graduating from this college?

14. What out-of-pocket expenses should be expected at the beginning of each term when the student is buying books and starting up classes, labs, and dorm life? What other out-of-pocket expenses might accrue during the year?

15. How is financial aid paid out? Is it credited toward the student's account, or paid directly to the student?

16. How many hours per week does the typical student work in a Federal Work-Study job? What jobs are available? Are the funds paid directly to the student, or are they credited toward the university bill? Are jobs available for students not eligible for Federal Work-Study?

17. Is there a college debit card for the student to use in the bookstore and campus eateries, or for other on-campus services? What banking services are available on or near campus?

(Excerpted and adapted from "20 Things You Need to Know About Financing College," The College Board, ©2017. https://secure-media.collegeboard.org/CollegePlanning/media/pdf/20-things-about-financing-college.pdf. Used with permission.)

Other Helpful Tips for Students and Parents

Be an Early Bird

Since financial aid is awarded on a first-come, first-served basis, watch all deadlines carefully and submit the FAFSA as early as possible after October 1 to maximize opportunities for awards.

Provide Updates

As the year goes on, update the financial aid office if any changes or unusual circumstances have come up since the FAFSA and CSS/Financial Aid PROFILE were filed. These might include the loss of a job, high medical expenses, or a significant drop in income. If appropriate, ask for a reevaluation of your aid. The college may have a special form and process for this, sometimes called a "reconsideration request." Give specific information and show how your situation has changed or is different from what the college originally perceived. Provide supporting documentation to prove your point, and if the college is local, make an appointment and meet in person.

If the initial aid offer seems unexpectedly low, don't hesitate to ask about it. Mistakes do happen, and you want to make sure your student receives everything he or she is entitled to.

Keep the College Apprised of Outside Aid

You will need to report scholarships obtained from other sources, such as private scholarships, even if your student does not receive a penny of federal, state, or institution-based financial aid. This helps the financial aid office prepare to process any outside funds that may come directly to the college.

Reapply Next Year

Remember, too, that students must apply for aid each year of college. This process involves updating the FAFSA and completing any additional forms the college wants.

MINIMIZING THE COSTS OF COLLEGE

While college definitely takes a big bite out of the family finances, you can work to decrease the damage. Some of the following tips will save a little; others will save a more significant amount.

Distance Learning and Online Degrees

One of today's most intriguing concepts for higher education involves online college courses, entire online degrees, or distance learning. In essence, these courses represent ways to "homeschool through college." A student works toward a degree from home, frequently at a discount compared to the cost of traditional colleges. Students who are motivated to take ownership of their learning and their lives can be successful in this nontraditional way of earning a degree.

While it is beyond the scope of this book to gather and review providers for online courses and degrees, you might want to keep several concepts in mind if you shop for these providers. First of all, look for accredited institutions and choose nonprofit rather than for-profit schools. If the program is sponsored by a brick-and-mortar university, that fact will lend additional credibility to your degree. When confirming accreditation, check with the Department of Education to make sure the accrediting agency is actually legitimate as well. Secondly, check the relative rankings of these programs and seek out the best ones.

Find reviews of these courses and programs, try to find someone who has completed the same degree, and ask them how successful they have been in the post-college job market. Statistics such as graduation rates and student employment rates will also be a clue as to the viability of the program. Thirdly, look into transferability of the courses, in case you want to transfer to another university. Also evaluate the help and support services that the program provides students. Finally, assess how well your goals, study habits, and personality would match up with online study. For example, how interactive would courses at this particular institution be? Online study is definitely not for everyone; moreover, not all fields of study lend themselves to this mode of study. Business, education, computer science, graphic design, and communications are a few fields that might have promise; science and engineering, with their high level of hands-on learning, would be less likely candidates.

With a more traditional approach to a college education, families can still cut costs in various ways, by seeking to minimize costs of tuition, room and board, fees, books and supplies, transportation, and personal expenses.

Minimizing Tuition Costs

- Take college courses at a community college, either while in high school, during the summers, or for the first two years of college, before transferring to a four-year college. Be sure to check university policies to confirm individual course transferability and limitations on units transferred in to your four-year college.
- Take Advanced Placement exams or CLEP exams to gain credit in some subjects.
- Investigate distance learning degree programs, using online courses or credit by examination to earn college credit and even college degrees.
- Look into Armed Forces programs such as ROTC to help pay for college. Students serving in the Reserves can also earn money for college or for loan repayment.
- Take a full load of courses, scheduling classes strategically so as not to incur additional semesters.

Minimizing Living Expenses

- Live at home or with a relative or friend if you are close enough to the campus.
- If you live in the residence halls, choose the least expensive room arrangement. Purchase a meal plan with fewer meals and then keep healthy food and snacks on hand as supplements.
- Later in college, consider applying to be a resident assistant in exchange for reduced room and board charges.

Minimizing Costs of Books, Supplies, and Fees

- Find out titles and ISBNs ahead of time and buy the books online. If possible, find used copies.
- Be proactive and organized in order to avoid "penalty" fees such as those for replacement ID cards or room keys, late fees for the library, and rush fees for transcripts or other documents.
- Shop around for lab or art supplies that may be purchased elsewhere at a discount.

Minimizing Personal Expenses

- If your college is far from home, shop "smart" for less expensive airline tickets, travel on off-peak days, or use frequent flyer miles for your trips home.
- Stock up on cosmetics, toiletries, and over-the-counter medications at a discount store or online.

- If possible, avoid having a car on campus. Insurance, gas, maintenance, and repairs can add up.
- Keep entertainment costs (restaurants, movies, and outings) to a minimum and hunt for ways to socialize without spending much money. Look for student discounts on food and entertainment.
- Set a budget for yourself and stick to it. If you find yourself going over budget in one category, cut back in another.

Other Ways to Save or Earn Money Toward Education

- Continue to be alert for scholarships, grants, and other "free" money available to you during your years at college. In particular, check your department for awards you might be eligible for.
- Find a campus job or nearby off-campus job that fits into your schedule.
- Look for strategic summer jobs that will pay well above the minimum wage. Market yourself to employers who will pay you for your *brains* to think and to plan, and not just for your warm body to flip burgers. Fields that might yield more lucrative returns are hospital work, accounting, and technology. Or, start a business such as providing lessons or classes in music, dance, or drama.
- Seek out private tutoring jobs in your areas of proficiency—either for college students or for nearby high school students.
- Find a few good books and websites on money management, and implement the advice they offer —especially strategies for avoiding credit card debt.
- Read up on tax credits and other tax benefits for students or their families. Since these programs change from time to time, check an up-to-date Internal Revenue Service Publication 970, "Tax Benefits for Education," for full details on credits, rules, and eligibility. As of this writing, the American Opportunity Tax Credit can provide tax credits of up to $2,500 per year per student, and the Lifetime Learning Credit can provide up to $2,000, depending on family income and other qualifiers. Other benefits to look into can include deductions for student loan interest and, in certain income situations, even deductions for tuition itself.
- Repay your loans as soon as possible. If extra money becomes available before the loan begins accruing interest, pay it off early. If your loan is accruing interest while you are in school, aim to pay the interest that accrues each month rather than letting it compound.
- Check into AmeriCorps®, a network of service organizations sometimes called the "domestic Peace Corps." Many AmeriCorps members receive a modest living allowance, and at the end of a year of full-time service they are eligible for the AmeriCorps Education Award to be used for educational expenses or to repay student loans.
- If you are going into the fields of teaching or child care, check into the following programs that offer loan debt forgiveness in return for teaching in designated high-need areas or schools:

  Teacher Loan Forgiveness Program (for Direct Subsidized and Unsubsidized Loans and for Subsidized and Unsubsidized Federal Stafford Loans).
  Perkins Loan Teacher Cancellation. Check the U.S. Department of Education Federal Student Aid website for details.
  State-specific teacher incentive programs or student loan forgiveness programs. Check your state's student aid website.
  Teach for America®. Offers incentives such as loan forgiveness, scholarships, and other benefits in return for teaching commitments in designated high-need areas.

Family Saving, Investment, and Tuition Payment Options

Parents, with the guidance of financial advisors or accountants, can look into college savings and investment plans to see which might be advantageous. This is a highly individual decision and will be different for each family's circumstances. Note that impacts on federal income tax, state income tax, and the student's financial aid eligibility should all be carefully considered before using any of these options. One or more of the following options might work for your family:

- *Section 529 College Savings Plans*
- *Coverdell Education Savings Accounts*
- *Tuition payment plans at individual colleges (some are interest-free and allow you to spread out tuition and other expenses throughout the year)*

The College Board website ("Pay for College" section) and the National Association of Student Financial Aid Administrators (http://www.nasfaa.org/) provide discussions of the pros and cons of various savings vehicles, as well as tips to help maximize your student's chances for receiving financial aid. Consider these programs in light of your own circumstances, and always consult your own accountant and financial advisor so that they may be tailored to your own situation. Neither of these organizations, nor any part of this book, has any intention of giving you tax or financial advice. Note also that future changes in the tax code or in the FAFSA methodologies may make some of these tips obsolete.

SPECIAL CONSIDERATIONS FOR HOMESCHOOLERS

Eligibility for Freshman Scholarships

As discussed in Chapter 21 on college application tips and in Chapters 13 and 14 on community college courses, homeschoolers who have taken many community college classes—or sometimes even just one class—may be vulnerable to losing their freshman status when applying to a four-year college. Besides being "forced" into the transfer category when this is not their intent, they may also become ineligible for freshman scholarships which, at some schools, can be lucrative and fairly easy for top students to win. Some of these scholarships are awarded automatically to students with high GPAs or test scores. At some campuses there is also the issue of SAP (Satisfactory Academic Progress). See Chapters 13 and 21.

This is in many ways a "Catch-22" situation. Homeschooled students frequently *need* to take an array of advanced classes (which may include community college courses) to supplement their work at home and to enhance their college applications. Avoiding college classes simply to stay in the running for possible scholarships can be a poor choice unless these awards are particularly lucrative and the student's chances are very high. For many selective colleges, the decision to take fewer community college classes could reduce the chances of admission in the first place.

As mentioned in more detail in Chapters 13 and 21, with some colleges, a student can negotiate the best of both worlds. Talk to the admissions officers about the situation far in advance, and you may discover that for homeschoolers, community college courses do not adversely affect freshman status. If you run into difficulty, you may be able to indicate on an unofficial copy of the community college transcript which courses were taken purely to fulfill high school/home school requirements and which were taken with the hopes of transferring them to the university. If the "college transfer" courses add up to fewer than the maximum units allowed for freshman status, the student might be able to stay in the running for freshman scholarships.

On a positive note, a common policy among colleges is that if community college courses are taken before high school graduation, they will not affect freshman status or count against a maximum number of units allowed. Make it clear to the university that your student is homeschooled and has taken college courses to expand and enhance the homeschool curriculum during the high school years.

GED Test "Requirement" for Federal Aid—and HSLDA's Fix

Years ago, homeschoolers were frequently asked to submit proof of passing the GED Test in order to validate their graduation from high school, since they did not have diplomas recognized by the state or awarded by accredited high schools. This testing was used as a requirement for receiving federal financial aid.

However, the requirement to pass the GED Test did not sit well with homeschoolers. This test carries a stigma of "high school dropout," and many homeschoolers are reluctant to seek this unnecessary credential for fear that their non-traditional high school experience may be misunderstood by colleges.

Because of the work of HSLDA attorneys, legislation was prepared to specify that a student completing high school at home is indeed still eligible for federal financial aid. A 1998 amendment to the Higher Education Act specified that there is no federal requirement that homeschool graduates prove that their diplomas are state-certified; they can self-certify the validity of their diplomas. Unfortunately, ongoing misunderstandings continued among colleges admitting homeschooled students. Subsequently, HSLDA persuaded the U.S. Department of Education to send a clarifying letter to colleges, emphasizing that the GED test or other "ability-to-benefit" tests are not required and that students do not need to receive state certification of homeschool completion in order to receive federal financial aid or to be admitted to institutions receiving federal funds.[2]

Universities have all been assured that they can admit homeschoolers without jeopardizing their eligibility for federal funding. If you are a member of HSLDA and have trouble with financial aid simply because of the high school diploma issue, contact HSLDA for advice.

TO SUM UP

Exploring and applying for financial aid can take quite a bit of time and should be initiated early. Fortunately, even with the plethora of paperwork and multiple agencies to deal with, the process has become more streamlined in recent years. For nearly all financial aid sources, help is available online or by phone. As you plunge into the financial aid process, be proactive and organized so that your student doesn't miss out on the opportunities and benefits.

1. Excerpted and adapted from "20 Things You Need to Know About Financing College," The College Board, 2017. Accessed August 25, 2018. https://secure-media.collegeboard.org/CollegePlanning/media/pdf/20-things-about-financing-college.pdf. Used with permission.
2. Home School Legal Defense Association, "Victory over College Discrimination," Home School Legal Defense Association, June 17, 2002. Accessed August 25, 2018. http://hslda.org/docs/news/hslda/200206170.asp.

Also used as a source of basic information:
U.S. Department of Education, Federal Student Aid Information Center, *Do You Need Money for College? The Guide to Federal Student Aid, 2018-19*, Washington, D.C., 2017). Accessed August 25, 2018. https://studentaid.ed.gov/sa/sites/default/files/2018-19-do-you-need-money.pdf.

SECTION IV

THRIVING, NOT JUST SURVIVING— AND EQUIPPING YOUR STUDENTS FOR THE REAL WORLD

Chapter 27

A Taste of Reality:

Internships and Career Planning

The traditional routine of a student heading straight from high school into college, declaring a major, studying in that subject, and emerging as a graduate to begin a successful career in that same field is occurring less frequently today than it once did. What's more, this pattern does not guarantee that students will actually enjoy their chosen disciplines, for they may have traversed this path without ever gaining any practical experience in those fields. Although some students find part-time jobs in their specialties during college, many others have accumulated only academic knowledge by the time they graduate.

Internships can be an ideal way for students to get a taste of reality. While internships have traditionally been the domain of college students, a motivated homeschooler with a flexible schedule could certainly try to arrange a strategic internship to explore the suitability of a field of interest.

WHAT IS AN INTERNSHIP?

More than just a job, an internship is a time of focused, learning-based experience in a particular field of interest. In contrast to an entry-level hourly job, an internship usually involves gaining higher level skills and perspectives by working directly with a manager or other professional. It focuses on experience—particularly, getting a chance to integrate classroom knowledge with practical, hands-on applications.

Through internships, students can develop professional contacts that may help with future employment or education. Depending on the arrangement, the internship may be paid or unpaid. If the student is paid, the compensation is often in the form of a stipend rather than an hourly wage. Interns usually, though not always, earn less than they would as regular employees.

WHY CONSIDER AN INTERNSHIP?

An Internship Is an Excellent Source of Experience

An internship allows a student to learn about a career field by experiencing a true sampling of its day-to-day operations. Whether this is business, scientific research, teaching, or another field, the high school student can get an idea of what it would be like to work in this field.

An Internship Is Challenging

By definition, an internship is considerably more challenging than the typical part-time job. It may require study and research outside of working hours, further stretching the student's strengths and abilities. The intern may be given one or more projects to organize and develop, with an appropriate amount of oversight but also with his or her own freedom to come up with solutions. These challenges and experiences can breathe life and renewed motivation into the student's academic and extracurricular goals.

An Internship Shows Seriousness of Purpose Without Long-Term Commitment

A student who applies for an existing program or arranges a customized internship is committing to several weeks or months of focused work. Whether the internship takes place during the summer or during the school year, the student must be willing to sacrifice free time and flexibility of schedule to devote significant time to study and work. This commitment rapidly builds maturity. However, the student is not signing up for a full-time job, and if this field turns out not to be a good match, he or she is not committed forever. And how much better it is to make this discovery early on—no one wants to launch into a long educational process, only to later conclude that this field is not what he or she wants after all.

An Internship Can Provide an Edge in College Admissions

Especially at the nation's top colleges, every item on the application that can set a student apart from other applicants is vital, particularly for homeschoolers. An internship is an ideal way to show both an interest and a commitment to that interest. Moreover, the contacts developed through such programs can be excellent sources of recommendation letters. Even for students who do not apply to selective universities, internships often open doors to colleges and special programs. It is to your student's advantage to participate in an internship before applying to college if this opportunity becomes available, for in addition to yielding letters of recommendation, internships will provide material for fascinating application essays.

An Internship Offers a Chance to Try out Multiple Interests with Real-World Involvement

Summer internships provide a bridge between high school and college experiences, helping students firm up their career ideas and fine-tune their goals. Motivated high school students who are good planners might squeeze in two, three, or even more internships during the high school years. These experiences would allow them to examine several related or totally different career fields—and to be that much ahead of the game upon entering college.

An Internship Can Be a Source of Contacts in the Field

For homeschoolers who may not have accumulated many classroom teacher contacts, internships can pay off in terms of professional contacts as well as in experiences gained. Over the course of the internship, the student will meet and work with managers, directors, and other professionals within the organization. All can be involved in a student's future. Whether your student needs letters of recommendation for college or employment, advice on undergraduate or graduate programs in the field, or a future part-time or full-time job, these coworkers and supervisors who have seen the student's work habits in action can likely offer this kind of assistance. An internship is the perfect opportunity for a student to develop responsibility, intellectual curiosity, teamwork, and people skills—characteristics that will be noticed and commended later.

A Paid Internship Will Provide Some Income for the Student

Many internships are unpaid, and even paid internships typically do not pay as much as a student would earn elsewhere. The stipend may not even equal the minimum wage in your area. However, when considering the learning experiences and contacts that the student receives, the money can be considered a bonus. Even if performed on an unpaid basis, a strategic internship in a potential career field can be far more beneficial than a summer of work at the local drugstore.

An Internship Can Serve as a Stepping Stone to Future Employment or Education

Even though the student may not immediately seek a job, the internship experience can open doors in the future, either for this organization or for a similar organization. As the student develops computer skills, laboratory skills, people skills, or business skills, he or she will be more competitive for employment, in comparison to other applicants whose skills are still at entry level. Your student may even receive awards or begin working on publications or patents.

Application to graduate school, too, may be enhanced by such programs. Increasingly, graduate and professional school applicants need to have internships or similar experiences on their resumes.

IDEAS FOR INTERNSHIPS

Ideas for internships are almost limitless. Programs in some fields are already set up for high school students. Others might be created by teamwork and brainstorming between your student and a professional in the field of interest. The following are a few ideas for internship experiences:

Sciences

Students interested in science or engineering may arrange internship experiences in research laboratories, hospitals, biotechnology companies, or companies that make products relevant to their field of interest. Although high school students will not have a great array of skills to offer, they can quickly learn some basic laboratory techniques, while also absorbing some of the theory behind them. As an intern, not simply a lab assistant, your student may be involved in strategic department meetings and project planning.

Business

In the field of business, students may help prepare materials for sales or marketing efforts, assist a real estate or insurance agent, learn about the world of banking, or become acquainted with the basics of finance or accounting. They may assist with retail merchandising in a nonprofit such as a Goodwill thrift store, or learn the basics of advertising or public relations for a small business or a charity.

Arts

Opportunities in the arts include performing, teaching younger students, or organizing events and performances in the fields of music, dance, or drama. For example, a student could teach and coordinate a summer drama program for preteens. Visual arts, such as graphic arts, are another area in which students can learn while helping a professional artist. Interested and talented students may also learn and apply multimedia skills such as sound, video, lighting, and creation of multimedia presentations.

Education, Recreation, and Youth Work

With proper clearance and background checks, high schoolers may be able to arrange an internship or other temporary experience at a preschool or elementary school. This might involve classroom or computer lab work or assisting with after-school or enrichment programs. Tutoring centers might be another opportunity for interested students. Camps, community centers, sports facilities, and recreation centers are other venues for working with children or youth. In these settings, your student might help run a specialized program in the arts, music, science, or sports, or even a full after-school program. Students interested in cooking and nutrition could learn about meal planning for school or day care center lunches. Your church may be a source of internships with youth or children and is always a good place to start. Remember that an internship should go beyond a basic part-time "entry level" job and should include opportunities for leadership, innovation, independent work, responsibility, and shadowing of people in managerial positions.

Politics

Local, state, or national political campaigns welcome volunteer help. Here, hands-on activity is the most effective and most empowering way of learning. A student might take charge of canvassing a neighborhood for voter registration. Other experiences could include helping with publicity for a political candidate or a ballot initiative, organizing community meetings, planning events, doing program research, or helping with data entry and analysis.

As mentioned in Chapter 15, Generation Joshua's Student Project provides an opportunity for students to volunteer in political races such as House and Senate campaigns, thus increasing their skills and knowledge of the political process and opening the possibility of an internship experience later on.

Technology

If you have an avid computer "geek" in your house, put these skills to work by arranging an internship to add to your student's existing knowledge. An internship could enhance skills in programming, troubleshooting, game design, robotics, artificial intelligence, refurbishing or building computers, designing websites or apps, or assisting people with using or setting up their computers. In addition to seeking out opportunities at tech companies, your student might contact a community center and offer to teach basic computer skills to seniors, children, or other "beginners." Tech-skilled students are always in demand, especially among the tech-illiterate.

Local Community Services

Your student might enjoy interning with your city parks department or community center. Opportunities could involve upgrading parks, conducting safety audits, or providing services such as kids' clubs. Community-based education, nutrition, and health programs are other worthwhile options for a student with a heart for community service.

Other Ideas

Other potential opportunities include journalism (newspaper, web, radio, or TV), disaster preparedness or relief, service to disabled people or senior citizens, poverty relief, museums, historical societies—and many, many more.

HOW TO SET UP AN INTERNSHIP

Brainstorm

The first step in planning an internship is to brainstorm as a parent-student team about what the student would like to learn. What field, and what specialty, is most intriguing? What kind of environment would be most suitable: an industrial environment, a research laboratory, a classroom, an outdoor location, or an inner-city setting? Once the ideas start flowing, write them all down regardless of how far-fetched or impossible they might sound. One far-fetched idea combined with another far-fetched idea might just yield the perfect solution.

Brainstorm, too, about the skills and abilities your student has to offer. Have your student ask himself or herself a series of questions. Am I good with people—adults, small children, or teens? Am I skilled with animals? Do I have excellent manual dexterity? Am I familiar with computers and technology? Am I talented in art or music? Am I organized and logical, able to think through a problem from beginning to end? In arranging an internship, your student, as a novice in this specialized field, will want to highlight all current skills and abilities.

Search

After picturing the ideal situation, search online to find existing internships in your local area, or in locations to which your student could travel if accepted. Some colleges and universities, as well as some corporations, offer special programs to high schoolers. Keywords to try are *internship, summer,* and *high school,* paired with more specific words related to your student's interests, such as finance or science, plus a keyword for your geographical area. Existing internships often have competitive entrance requirements and early deadlines, so it is wise to think about them as much as a year ahead of time. This way, your student can do what is necessary to enhance the chances of admission.

One site to check is Fastweb (also mentioned in Chapters 25 and 26), which features internship and part-time job searches as well as scholarship searches. In addition, take a look at http://www.internships.com/student. Although internship programs on both of these sites are most frequently offered for college students, you may be able to find an interesting program open to younger students. Additionally, your searching might create an idea for a program that your student can design independently with a local organization.

If your student takes classes at a community college, he or she can check with instructors or with the career development office to find out if any opportunities are available.

Prepare to Apply

If you find one or more interesting internships, carefully check the application and entrance requirements. Programs designed for high school students may have requirements relating to GPA, high school coursework, teacher recommendations, or even PSAT/NMSQT, SAT, or ACT scores. Searching up this information early allows you to tailor your homeschooling curriculum, community college courses, and outside experiences to help your student be more competitive for the program.

If the program is local, try your best to contact and meet the director of the program. The simplest way is to discover whether the program includes an event that is open to public visitors. The immunology program in which Julie participated held a poster session at the end of the summer. Open to the public, this event featured students presenting their summer research findings via academic posters. For two summers prior to applying (when she was still too young to apply), Julie attended the poster session and introduced herself to the director of the program. By the time she applied, he remembered her and knew of her strong interest in the program. This may have positively influenced her application.

Your student might also try making an appointment with the director to inquire about the program. If a personal meeting is not possible, the student could send an email describing his or her goals and background and asking for more information about the program. These proactive steps may fix your student's name in the director's mind.

Once your student is ready to apply, the next task is to gather all documents needed, prepare them in a professional way, write personal statements, and request any letters of recommendation required. This procedure is excellent practice for college applications. Your student should work hard to present talents, accomplishments, and goals in the best light possible. See the tips for college essays in Chapter 22.

As your student waits for a reply, encourage him or her to think about Plan B, C, and D, in case this first program does not work out.

Self-Design

If the search for ready-made internships does not yield any possibilities, another option is to design one from scratch. This will take a little more doing, but it can be well worth the effort. A self-designed internship experience can be modeled on an existing program, or it might simply begin with a list of goals for an internship setting. As a parent-student team, discuss what your student can offer the organization as well as what skills and concepts he or she would like to develop. Organize these thoughts until your student can articulate them clearly and confidently. Be sure to seek input from friends and acquaintances who currently work in this field and who know what is realistic for a high schooler.

For this venture to work out, the student must be strongly motivated, courageous, and willing to put forth effort in scouting out contacts and responding gracefully to "rejections." Not every student will have the right mix of opportunities and circumstances to make a self-designed internship a reality. However, if your student is determined to find a way to gain experience in a field of passion, do all you can to assist with the process.

Gather Potential Contacts

While convincing an employer to offer an internship (even an unpaid one) might sound like a formidable task, you and your student can break this task down into simpler phases. First, have your student research local opportunities or identify professionals with whom he or she would like to work. For example, to prepare for an internship in veterinary medicine, begin to investigate veterinary clinics, animal shelters, zoos, wildlife preserves, and any other businesses that use veterinarians, even on an occasional basis. Then make a list of people you know who work in similar fields, or at these sites (even in a non-veterinary capacity), or who might know someone you could approach.

Likewise, to seek out a science or research internship, make a list of nearby organizations and universities involved in this field. Utilize the help of friends, acquaintances, and family members who can give you ideas and help you find a receptive contact person within the organization. One student I know was able to organize a research mentorship with a university professor because he had become acquainted with this professor through a math circle he was involved with. Thus, don't overlook club advisors, regular or guest speakers, or anyone you come in contact with in your field of interest. In essence, when seeking formal or informal internships, ask everyone you know. You never know what connections your everyday friends and acquaintances may have.

Prepare a Resume

Simultaneously with the process of locating contacts, your student will need to create an informative, professional-looking resume and a cover letter in preparation for setting up informational interviews. This resume will explain the student's background and might include a list of pertinent courses taken, other experience in the field, activities demonstrating leadership, and a short goal statement. For internships that emphasize academic ability, listing pertinent test scores might be appropriate.

Though telephoning contacts can be an effective way to initiate a dialogue, the resume could also be emailed or mailed with a detailed cover letter. Either way, your student could start by expressing an interest in investigating possible careers. At this point, the concept of an internship arrangement does not need to be spelled out, but the student should simply express strong interest in supplementing his or her study of careers and in talking to someone who could help with this research. Suggesting a time frame for this meeting (twenty to thirty minutes) is much more considerate than assuming that you will have all the time you want.

Detailed advice on how to prepare a resume and a cover letter is beyond the scope of this book, but check out the plethora of job-hunters' resources available online to point you in the right direction and help you organize your information into a concise, professional-looking format.

Interview

If the contact person agrees to an interview, your student should practice some interviewing skills before the meeting. These include speaking clearly, smiling, shaking hands in a confident, friendly manner, and explaining his or her interests and goals. The student might want to prepare supplementary materials to bring along, such as a homeschool portfolio tailored specifically to this field of interest, with a summary of pertinent accomplishments such as research papers, field trips, projects, or classes. Letters of recommendation could also be a possibility. Additionally, work together to prepare a list of questions describing what your student would like to learn about this organization or about the field of work. The Khan Academy website at https://www.khanacademy.org/ has some tips for informational interviews. Also see Chapter 21 for some typical interview questions. Though these are used for college admission, many will be similar to what a student may be asked when contemplating a potential internship.

At this point, unless it seems entirely inappropriate, your student may propose the idea of an internship, either now or at some time in the future. The student should clearly articulate his or her skills, previous knowledge, and learning objectives. If the contact is hesitant to agree to a paid internship, the student could agree to an unpaid arrangement. Note, however, that some arrangements for unpaid or low-paying internships may violate state or federal labor laws, since for-profit employers are required to pay employees at least minimum wage unless the position meets specific requirements. If these laws are applicable to the business with which your student is trying to make an arrangement, the contact person may be reluctant to take on your student, even as a volunteer. Such laws generally do not apply to government agencies or nonprofits, however. Despite restrictions in certain situations, unpaid internships are quite common, and students are usually happy to gain experience in a field of interest.

It is quite likely that the contact person will need some time to consider this proposal or to consult with other decision makers. After setting up a time to be back in touch, your student can gather additional information, credentials, or references the contact may have requested. Regardless of whether this meeting yields the response the student is hoping for, it is essential that he or she write a gracious, sincere thank-you note within a day or two after the interview.

Perform the Task with Excellence

Students who succeed in designing their own internships or being accepted into existing programs have won half the battle. But the other half, making a good impression, is just as important. Student interns are representing high schoolers—specifically, homeschoolers. And, as discussed earlier, they may eventually ask these employers to write letters of recommendation for them. Responsibility, motivation, and hard work will thus be rewarded.

CAREER PLANNING

Another vital aspect of any high schooler's education is preparation for a future career. You might enjoy designing an entire career exploration course, using some or all of the following activities and ideas. Or, you might select only the activities and experiences that would most benefit your student.

As you design a career planning unit, your goals are first to discover your student's skills, aptitudes, and interests, and then to seek out career fields that use these natural inclinations. Once you know what these are, your student will want to try some real-life experiences by participating in job shadowing, internships, or volunteer work.

Assessing Career Interests and Aptitude

Eighth and ninth grades are good years for students to *begin* to think about future career plans. Most likely, students who are this young will change their minds several times before the end of college, but it is helpful to get an idea of their strengths, interests, and skills as well as of their dislikes and weaknesses.

Career guidebooks containing career aptitude tests can be useful and even fun to work through, as long as you remember that they measure only general trends, not hard and fast rules about which career field a student should enter. While some questionnaires focus more on career interests, others focus on aptitudes. Students may be surprised at what some of their strengths and interests are. For a resource specifically designed for homeschoolers, check out the book *Career Exploration: For Homeschool High School Students* by Carol Topp. Including interest and personality assessments, advice on how to research careers, and tips for interviewing and job shadowing, this short but pertinent book can get your student started on the thinking and evaluating process. Also consider *What Color Is Your Parachute? For Teens*, a spinoff of the highly successful book by the same title for adults. This book even has a chapter on do's and don'ts for wise use of social media with respect to the job market.

The *Career Direct® Complete Guidance System* by Crown Financial Ministries is a Christian-based career guidance system that allows individuals to profile their personality, interests, skills, and values, generating approximately thirty pages of individualized reports. Basic, detailed, and customized analyses are available for different prices ($25 to $80 and up). Go to https://careerdirect-ge.org/.

Mapping Your Future® at https://mappingyourfuture.org/ is a site aimed at students, with tips, advice, and questions to consider as they plan their careers and future education. Students can look up various careers or career clusters and investigate job titles, duties, education requirements, and salaries. For career and education planning, the site offers free helpful printable guides for each year of high school to help students start thinking about key factors in their future.

CareerOneStop at https://www.careeronestop.org/, a resource sponsored by the U.S. Department of Labor, offers free assessments, occupation profiles of more than 950 careers, and other tools to help students (or anyone) explore the careers that would be right for them. Descriptions of various careers, as well as career videos showing people at work in hundreds of occupations, can be a great help as your student begins to search for his or her "niche" in the world. Students can also compare career characteristics side by side or browse through lists of "hot" careers.

Career Key™ (https://www.careerkey.org/) is another online career guidance program. Many of the tips and resources are free. Your student can take a Career Key online personality test for about $15 that will assess skills, abilities, values, and interests and will then match the student's personality with some suggested careers.

You can also use more informal ways to ascertain your student's career aptitudes. Talk about careers in your everyday conversations and encourage your student to converse with friends and family members about varied career fields. Seek to help your student identify and enhance current interests and skills in order to take them to the next level. Most importantly, pray for and with your student during this season of seeking and discovering gifts and abilities. This whole process can be a dynamic time of prayer as your student investigates his or her callings and dreams about how he or she might serve future employers, coworkers, and the Lord.

Researching Careers

Once high school students begin to understand their own talents and abilities, they are ready to start researching careers that fit with those abilities. One comprehensive resource is the *Occupational Outlook Handbook*. In the old days, this was a dusty book on the reference shelf of the public library. Now, you can search up career descriptions online at the Bureau of Labor Statistics site at https://www.bls.gov/ooh/. This resource describes job duties, working conditions, training and educational needs, typical earnings, and expected job prospects for a wide range of occupations.

A useful subsection of the Bureau of Labor Statistics website designed especially for students is found at https://www.bls.gov/k12/. In an interesting, interactive way, this site asks students about their interests and then suggests possible careers. From here, students click on these career links to receive more information about the duties, pay, skills, and education needed for each job. Another excellent career research site is O*Net Online at https://www.onetonline.org/. On this site, students can browse careers or career clusters of their choice, or choose categories such as "bright outlook," "green economy," "STEM," and other useful criteria.

Students can also consider taking the ASVAB Career Exploration Program, which includes a widely used and well-respected aptitude test, an interest self-assessment, and various career exploration tools. Several students I know have taken this assessment, which helps young people zero in on the most suitable career areas for their personalities and interests. See https://www.asvabprogram.com/.

Career fairs can be a lively, interesting way for your student to investigate careers. Keep in touch with your local high schools to find out the schedule for these informative events.

Trying Out Careers Through Short Term "Shadowing"

Students with a few career fields in mind can take the fun and fascinating plunge into trying out these job fields. One practical way to do this is by job shadowing—accompanying someone in a particular occupation for a day and taking note of the job duties, working conditions, and job environment. To arrange job shadowing, have your student contact friends and family members in a spectrum of careers and ask their permission to shadow them for a day. Ideas might include an accountant's office, medical or dental office, veterinary clinic, elementary school, research laboratory, small business, or dance studio.

Exploring Careers Through Work and Volunteer Experience

Students who are fortunate enough to find paid part-time jobs in their general field of interest can test the waters to find out if they would indeed like to pursue this career field. The job need not be in the ultimate career field but should at least be in a related area. Even students who work at entry-level positions (for instance, as a receptionist at a veterinary office, when the goal is to become a veterinarian) can gain practical experience and make useful observations as they watch the other professionals at work.

Like internships or paid jobs, volunteer work can be a way to try out career fields. While landing a paid job or a paid internship can be difficult, finding work as a volunteer is much easier. After all, how many organizations can turn down the offer of free labor? Once a student is volunteering and demonstrating responsible work habits, he or she may be surprised at the opportunities that these efforts generate. Volunteer work can be a stepping stone to a paid job, since supervisors can "try before they buy." And at the very least, a student will have gained a few more contacts and references for future jobs, as well as picking up the terminology and practices of this particular field.

A useful place to start searching and brainstorming is Idealist at http://idealist.org, a site that catalogs volunteer organizations. On this site, students can type in a category of interest and a geographical location, and receive a list of nearby volunteer opportunities, with descriptions of hours, duties, and skills needed. A student could sign up to be a counselor for an asthma camp, an administrative assistant for the Arthritis Foundation, a garden volunteer for a program that teaches children to plant and care for school gardens, or a website guru for a small nonprofit organization. This site can streamline your student's search for a fulfilling volunteer position close to home. In addition to publicizing volunteer opportunities, Idealist also posts internship opportunities.

Practicing Resume Writing and Interviewing Skills

Along with the practical experiences of working, interning, volunteering, or shadowing, your student can practice other useful job-hunting skills. In tandem with creating a student resume for college application purposes (Chapter 20) and with practicing college interviewing skills (Chapter 21), encourage your student to sharpen these skills for his or her future job-hunting ventures. Seek out well-written, informative books and websites to explain how to construct a resume that will clearly communicate skills, goals, and past experiences. Then go a step further and discover the elements of a successful job interview. If your student can become familiar with these basic tools of a typical job search, he or she will be ahead of the game in the years to come.

TO SUM UP

Parents of college bound students should understand that hitting the books is not the only way to prepare for the future. Whether formal or informal, career preparation is vital to the student's wise choice of fields of employment. Real-life experiences gained in an internship or in volunteer or paid work can dovetail nicely with academic information. As the student learns to take ownership of tasks entrusted to him or her, these experiences may yield bonuses such as paid employment and validation of a student's character and work ethic—and they can also prevent wasting time and money by pursuing the wrong path.

Chapter 28

More of a Good Thing:

Considering a Gap Year or a Super Senior Year

*T*hough your momentum along the college prep path is going strong, do pause for a moment to gaze at the scenery. And as you do, realize that your student actually has the opportunity to take a side road for a more picturesque and fulfilling journey. More and more students are choosing to pursue a gap year rather than progressing directly from high school into college, and there are many good reasons to consider this side trip.

WHAT IS A GAP YEAR?

A gap year is a year taken "off" from formal schooling, often (but not always) at a milestone point between two phases of education. Moreover, as the American Gap Association describes it, a gap year is an "experiential semester or year *'on,'*"[1] an apt description, because the student actively and deliberately pursues learning and personal growth during this time. Most commonly, this involves a year taken between high school graduation and matriculation at a college or university, but it can also take place between two academic years of college, or perhaps between college and graduate school. For the purposes of this book, we will examine scenarios of a gap year taken at the conclusion of high school, because this option has ramifications for college plans and for some aspects of the application process.

Though fewer than 1% of college students currently choose to take a gap year, the trend has definitely been growing over the past few years.[1] The concept of a gap year has also been popularized by high-profile students including Malia Obama, who deferred her matriculation to Harvard by one year in order to participate in a cross-cultural immersion program in South America, followed by interning at a film and television production company.

WHY TAKE A GAP YEAR?

Gap years are becoming increasingly popular, perhaps because of the breakneck pace of college preparation during high school, or perhaps because we as a society have a heightened enthusiasm for exploring our world, pursuing special interests, and maximizing our potential contributions to the world. Either way, you and your student should give thoughtful and serious consideration to whether a gap year would make sense in your case. Even though a gap year extends the educational timeline, it may end up saving time and money in the long run, as it clarifies the student's goals and career aspirations.

Reasons for taking a gap year fall into several primary categories, with some of them focused on maximizing the student's education and life experiences and others focused on addressing a situation or need in the student's life.

Taking a Gap Year to Maximize Life Experiences

Many families make use of that pivotal time between high school and college by encouraging the student to gain wider life experience in work, service, travel, or other "stretching" activities. Below are a few pursuits the student could explore, any of which would serve to make him or her a more interesting, dynamic, and experienced individual by the time college starts a year later.

Pursuing a passion for ministries or missions. Many students are passionate about serving domestically or globally in ministries and are not sure just when they would fit this service in unless they do it "now."

Serving in the local community. Students with a heart for volunteer work or a desire to sharpen a particular skill set as a volunteer can put full-time effort into community service.

Feeding the travel bug. Dreams of extended travel, or of immersion experiences for language learning, can come true for students who have the time and the means to travel.

Gaining additional nontraditional education. Though you should be cautious about taking college courses during a gap year (see explanation later in this chapter), look into online courses, informal group classes, or many of the same types of course venues the student used throughout high school. Life is short—and many students would love the opportunity to devote a year to "pure" learning without the stress of exams and grades.

Launching a personal project. Is your student a writer? This is the time to draft that novel. Do you have a "Thomas Edison" inventor in the family? He or she can pursue those innovative ideas that have been brewing. Likewise, aspiring composers, artists, and other creators can pour their efforts into original masterpieces while time commitments are still flexible.

Pursuing elite athletics and other competitions. Many student athletes, after years of practice and coaching, have reached a high level in their sport—perhaps even with Olympic potential—and want to take a year to continue competing. With travel, practice, and conditioning taking up so much time in the schedule, it would be difficult to do well both in college and in the sport. This concept also holds true for students in academic or other types of competitions.

Exploring side interests. Some students are still deliberating about a major field of study, while even those who have chosen a major may be nurturing other strong interests. A year of freedom to explore can confirm primary interests and develop secondary ones, perhaps with the ultimate result of merging several passions into a career pathway. And quite honestly, having the time to delve into questions that the student is curious about can be an invaluable and intellect-expanding investment into future learning.

Performing scientific research. Your student may have snagged an excellent opportunity to work side by side with a researcher at the university or in industry—whether close to home, across the country, or abroad. For students who want to explore this type of work, it would be hard to turn down the chance to be immersed in research for a year.

Starting or solidifying a business. Students with an entrepreneurial spirit may have already started a small business during high school, or may have all their ideas lined up and simply need some time to devote to the project. A gap year can provide the uninterrupted time to build a business.

Working in a formal or informal internship. Perhaps your student has been offered the opportunity to work in a paid or unpaid capacity in a field of interest and would like to take a gap year to follow up on this chance before the demands of college set in.

Job shadowing or confirming the proposed career field. Similarly, your student could use the year to line up a succession of job shadowing ventures and to investigate careers in a focused, fruitful way.

"Catching up" on life skills. Though it may not be worthwhile to take an entire year off to practice cooking or auto maintenance (unless this is a particular area of skill and passion), nailing down a few more life skills could constitute one segment of this gap year. I have known students who used the flexible time of the gap year to learn to sew and to obtain a driver's license.

Enjoying family time. Sometimes it's worthwhile just to be together, living life as a family for one last year before everything changes. Particularly in families where elderly relatives are visiting for several months, or where the student can contribute to homeschooling younger siblings, intentionally investing in family time can be rewarding.

Taking advantage of a special opportunity. In addition to the categories mentioned above, occasionally a student will be presented with an opportunity through work, church, the community, or another venue that is just too good to pass up. In this case, taking a gap year would be ideal.

Taking a Gap Year to Address a Need

Other families decide to take a gap year in order to address needs, circumstances, or problems that preclude immediate matriculation at college. The following are some of the more common goals for a "necessary" gap year:

Gaining additional maturity. Especially for students who accelerate through the last couple of years of high school and are accepted into college at a young age, the chance to spend a year at home working, studying, or otherwise gaining maturity will pay off in more social and emotional stability later.

Taking a much-needed break. In our fast-paced 21st century society, a rigorous college prep high school program is no joke. Nearly all students will experience uncomfortable stress here and there during the high school years; many will need to address burnout or even anxiety or depression. A mental health break in the form of a gap year can be an invaluable gift.

Working to raise money for college. From absolute necessity or from a desire to ease the burden on their parents, some students choose to take a year off from their education, find a job, and devote their earnings to the college bill.

Attending to family needs or crises. During the senior year, a family crisis may crop up: a serious illness or death of a parent, sibling, or grandparent; a divorce or separation; serious problems involving a sibling; or another family emergency. In these situations, it simply may not be the right time for the student to go away to college. Instead, he or she may decide to stay home for a year to lend moral and practical support to the family circumstances.

Taking care of a health issue. The student may face a personal health situation that needs treatment and monitoring close to home. Then, when the time is right and his or her condition has improved or stabilized, college will make more sense.

HOW TO ARRANGE A GAP YEAR

Colleges and universities are no strangers to the concept of gap years, and this option is becoming increasingly common. Many colleges embrace the opportunity to welcome students who have extended the high school-to-college interval in order to gain valuable life experiences. Harvard actively encourages gap years—even suggesting the possibility in their acceptance letters. Tufts University offers a "Tufts 1+4 Bridge Year Service Program" that funds students for a year of international or national service. Princeton selects a number of students for a Bridge Year Program involving cultural immersion and community service for nine months in China, India, or a couple of other countries.

Certain other colleges have fellowships or other funding dedicated toward gap year activities, and some institutions might even waive foreign language requirements if the student participates in a language/cultural immersion program during the gap year. Studies have shown that students who take a gap year have higher retention and graduation rates once they are in college. As mentioned above, they are also more focused and more sure of their major and career choices.

As you might imagine, arranging a gap year involves two main considerations: what the student will actually do during the year, and how to work out the details with the college the student will eventually attend. We will first examine the latter, before getting to the creative part about what pursuits to plan during the year.

Application Scenarios

Two main pathways are possible for taking a year off between high school and college:

1) The student goes through the application process during the fall and winter of the senior year as usual, but after being accepted to a college, he or she notifies the college and arranges to defer the admission and matriculate one year later.

Typically, the student will request the deferral after his or her acceptance is received (thus, any time from December for early applications, through April for regular applications) but before the first tuition payments are due. May 1st is the most common deadline for committing to attend a university, but the student does not need to feel compelled to ask for a deferral at this point. He or she can commit to the college, pay the deposit, and then within a few weeks request the deferral. If you and your student have done your homework ahead of time by investigating the college's policies, you will be fairly confident that the deferral will be granted.

In general, federal and state financial aid will not be deferred. Instead, the student will reapply the next year, and if family financial circumstances haven't changed, the aid will likely be similar. Merit scholarships offered by the university or by outside sources require additional inquiries, but hopefully the student can arrange to have these held for a year.

2) The student takes a gap year after high school graduation and during this year, applies to college as a freshman.

In this scenario, the student must keep up with application procedures and deadlines while immersed in gap year activities. Taking any last SAT or ACT exams, gathering teacher recommendations, writing personal statements, and completing applications for Early Action or Regular Decision deadlines will need to be calendared and carefully monitored so as not to miss out on anything important. For homeschoolers, this scenario will be somewhat easier than for traditional students, since the parent will be available for counselor recommendations, and outside instructors in the homeschool community may still be available for teacher recommendations (though community college instructors may be more challenging to track down). Still, this option is inherently more complicated, especially if the student will be traveling during the year. Here are some tips, directed to the student, for enhancing the application:

- During the spring of your senior year, communicate with your high school teachers regarding your upcoming need for recommendations, and then keep them apprised of the deadlines during the fall.
- Consider requesting a recommendation from someone with whom you work or study during the gap year, as this letter can add valuable, timely information on your personal characteristics and work ethic.
- If you are happy with your previous SAT or ACT scores, simply be ready to submit them when you apply. If not, schedule a retake of the exam, carefully arranging to take the test at a site that works for you even if you are traveling.
- Work with your parents to have your high school transcript and list of course descriptions "perfected" and up to date before you embark on your gap year travels so that it will be a simple matter to submit these documents.
- As you write your application essays, use them to the fullest advantage to reflect on your gap year insights and accomplishments.
- Continue to build your resume. Keep a formal or informal journal from wherever you are, to highlight your projects and experiences. Then turn them into interesting, specific resume line items that illuminate your skills and accomplishments. These may include service, volunteer work, paid work, skills, certifications, awards, classes, competitions, and other noteworthy achievements. Likewise, keep track of contact information for your supervisors so that you may request recommendations if needed.
- If you took a gap year as a result of personal, financial, or family needs, be honest with the admissions office. In your essays and statements, portray how you used your time and what you have learned and accomplished during the year or portion of the year before applications are due.

Overall, it is logistically easier to apply to college during your senior year, rather than doing it during your gap year, especially if you will be traveling. As a side note, if parents are "on the fence" about the idea of a gap year, they may be more supportive if you go through the admissions process first and secure college admission, rather than planning to apply during the gap year and perhaps losing educational momentum. However, this is an individual decision, and plans should be made after open, honest family communication—as well as after careful research regarding the policies of your favored colleges.

How to Coordinate with the College Admissions Department When Planning a Gap Year

As you research colleges, find out if the schools you are interested in are open to students deferring admission. While many—perhaps even most—universities are favorable to this choice, some are not, and it's extremely important to check ahead of time. Many state university systems do not offer deferral programs—thus, students should apply just prior to the year they want to attend, *and they should not take any college classes in the interim, so that they will not be viewed as transfer students.*

If you are concerned that your inquiry about deferring college entrance might trigger a rejection (for instance, if the college is intent upon filling the freshman class with "sure bets"), make your inquiries cautiously, tentatively, and hypothetically at first. You want to make sure that you are not dealing with a school that absolutely never allows deferrals. Try to find out most of your information from college websites, or perhaps by asking this general question at a college information session. Then, after you have been accepted, formally ask for the deferral.

See Gap Year Association at http://gapyearassociation.org for a list of college policies toward deferred matriculation, but be sure to contact each college for the most updated and accurate information.

When you contact the university to request a deferral of your entrance, the admissions office may have a separate form or application for you to complete, or may just want a letter in your own words detailing why you want to defer admission and what you plan to accomplish in the intervening year. From here on out, keep in close communication with the college so that you understand any additional steps you need to take to arrange your year "off" and so that you know what they need from you when you are ready to matriculate. Be sure to check on financial aid arrangements as well.

IDEAS FOR FILLING THE YEAR

As mentioned above in the reasons for taking a gap year, students can pursue strategic activities, once-in-a-lifetime experiences, or meaningful family or professional relationships during the twelve months "off" from formal academics. Below are some more thoughts, as well as some hints on how to get started on these pursuits.

First of all, you will want to decide whether you will self-structure your gap year, or will sign up for one of the many available structured programs. For instance, you might seek out programs that offer food and lodging in return for work. *Exercise due diligence in checking out the integrity, safety, and overall reputation of these programs so that you do not encounter any unpleasant surprises.*

Volunteer work or community service. You might continue current favorite activities by diving in full time, seeking additional leadership positions, and taking on increased administrative and project management functions for the organization, now that you are an adult. Or seek out new opportunities. Take time for brainstorming and daydreaming—what would you really like to do, and for whom? Would this be in the local community while living at home, or in a different community or state while living with friends or relatives? Or would this type of service take you overseas so that you could combine service with travel?

Consider becoming involved with AmeriCorps, which offers health care benefits, a small stipend, and a Segal AmeriCorps Education Award to be used later at college (amounts and eligibility depend on the extent of the student's service). AmeriCorps is a network of national service programs that address needs in communities across the nation, and just a few of the projects include mentorship of youth, disaster preparedness, disaster relief, building affordable housing, and maintenance of national parks.

Missions and ministries. Faith-based organizations are always looking for committed, willing people to serve in a variety of capacities, and a student taking a gap year has the freedom to say "Here I am, send me!" and to travel domestically or internationally. If you or your church community support a particular slate of global ministry workers, find out if they have need of a college-age helper or intern to serve for a year. Perhaps this could involve medical work, church planting, children's programs, house-building, community education, or a number of other areas of focus. Check out all considerations: finances, insurance, lodging, health and immunization needs, safety, political volatility of the area, communication, and other such aspects. Time spent serving and becoming more aware of global needs can be an unforgettable and formative experience in your life.

Travel. If you have the opportunity to travel—because your family has the funds, you have secured a job abroad, or you have relatives or friends with whom you can stay—this could be a life-changing opportunity. Look into all the practicalities and, as appropriate, link up with traveling companions to maximize the fun and safety. A year of travel can also mean staying in the U.S. but exploring the grand variety of our fifty states—perhaps working or staying with relatives in order to experience new ways of life. A farm, a ranch, a big city, a small town, or any other new environment will expand your horizons.

Special opportunities in an area of passion. As mentioned above, you may be offered the chance to work, teach, write, lead, volunteer, or otherwise be involved in an area you are passionate about. For instance, you may get a job teaching English overseas. I have known older teens who take a year to travel about the United States teaching debate principles to high schoolers, and others who have a chance to delve deeply into musical training and performance. Sometimes these opportunities come along only rarely, so if you come across something you are extremely excited about, a gap year may provide the perfect chance to seize the opportunity.

Athletics and other competitions. Taking your sport or your specialty to the next level is no trivial matter. Perhaps you have invested many years and many thousands of dollars into sharpening your skills, positioning yourself for elite teams, receiving coaching and teaching, traveling to tournaments and competitions, and in numerous other ways pouring yourself into this activity that you love. If a gap year would allow you to cap off all your work and dedication from your high school years and compete at a national or international level, consider devoting this time period to the pursuit of your goals.

Research. Whether this research involves an organic chemistry lab, an immunology study, a specific physics investigation, or fields such as mathematics or social sciences, linking up with a professor and rolling up your sleeves to do some genuine research can be an eye-opening growth experience. Of course, since you have not yet been to college, you will have limited contributions to offer, but if the opportunity presents itself and the principal investigator is willing to train a high school graduate for certain tasks, this experience can launch years of further investigations. On the flip side, the chance to work in a research environment can let you know that "this is not for me," a conclusion that is also extremely valuable.

Employment. Whether you work at the local coffee shop or find a job related to your eventual career, a year of full-time work can provide valuable funds and invaluable experience. The responsibility of getting up each and every day (or staying late at work each and every night), reporting to supervisors, performing job duties with diligence and intelligence, using the right combination of common sense and company protocol when questions come up, and practicing good interpersonal relationships with co-workers and customers will rapidly build maturity. If the earnings from work are used to defray college expenses, this plan will ease the burden on your parents, or if you get the chance to build up your own savings, this is an excellent scenario as well.

Internships. Internships are not always easy to come by, so if you have snagged one through diligent application procedures or through being in the right place at the right time, spending a year pursuing this internship can pay off well in terms of valuable experience—whether the internship is paid or unpaid. More than just a line item on a resume, this focused work/learning environment can solidify or nullify a potential career choice (saving years of tuition and time), can spark a fresh interest, and can make you more employable for future jobs and internships.

Nontraditional education. If you have an insatiable love of learning, the chance to learn, explore, deepen current interests, and merge or integrate multiple areas of interest (such as literature and philosophy) can be another excellent way to spend this gap year. For ideas to supplement your own brainstorming, go back through Chapters 4 and 5 and peruse all the different ways to take courses, gather knowledge, and feed the love of learning. In particular, you might look at MOOCs and OCWs (see Chapter 5), but other online courses or good "old-fashioned" books will fill the bill too. (However, in order to preserve your freshman status, you should generally plan *not* to take college classes after high school graduation.)

Creative pursuits. Perhaps your creative talents have felt a bit stifled during the intense years of college preparation. Ideas and inspirations for stories to write, sculptures to create, or music to compose may have stacked up in your creative mind, and now is the time to let the creativity flourish to produce some of those masterpieces. A year spent pursuing your artistic or literary goals can result in a satisfying sense of accomplishment. Perhaps the year can be capped off by submitting a book for publication, displaying the year's art at a personalized art exhibit, or performing original musical compositions.

Lessons, coaching, or special study. Talents, gifts, and passions often need a focused time of specialized lessons or coaching. Athletic, musical, theatrical, and even scientific skills can benefit from a dedicated time of sharpening these skills. Whether the gap year involves working with an excellent gymnastics coach, taking lessons from a renowned pianist, attending a specialized theater program, or doing research with an immunologist, the investment of a solid year can make a tremendous difference in your abilities, as well as in your confidence in this area of specialization.

Inventions and innovations. We live in an exciting, ever-changing age of innovation, and the new products and concepts that are constantly being offered to us originate in the minds of creative problem solvers. You may be one of these inventors/tinkerers who simply needs the gift of focused time to produce something original and unique. Consider using this year to think, brainstorm, sketch, engineer, innovate, prototype, test, and start all over again until the concept truly begins to take shape. A study of prior patents and the patenting process would also be a "must."

Entrepreneurship. Rather than inventing a tangible object, your "invention" may be a viable business idea. Taking your current skills and matching them to a need out there in the marketplace, you as a young entrepreneur can pour yourself into this business idea and put together a sensible business plan. Fundamental studies in marketing, taxation, local regulations, and other considerations can also help this idea come to life.

Family time. Whether this takes place in your home or elsewhere in the nation or world, the chance to spend time with immediate or extended family can be an irreplaceable use of time. If grandparents are elderly or have health challenges, you may be a godsend as you spend time with them and help care for them. If they are healthy and active, these twelve months can create lifelong memories. Likewise, if you want to make an extended visit to an out-of-state sibling, aunt or uncle, or other family member, a gap year can provide an opportunity. If you take a gap year simply to stay home and treasure some extra family time, you will probably want to plan a number of other goals to accomplish during the year so that it does not end up being a year to simply "play" and to fall out of the habit of accomplishing goals.

Teaching, coaching, or tutoring. Some students seek out (or are offered) the chance to teach younger students or peers about an area in which they are skilled. Math, writing, debate, science, a language, the arts, sports—the possibilities are endless for a chance to share your expertise and make a difference in the life of another learner. Seek out homeschool groups, church groups, clubs for children and teens, local sports teams, and other venues with possibilities for personal or group coaching.

Humanitarian work and special projects. Consider Habitat for Humanity, the American Red Cross, Big Brothers or Big Sisters, and other worthwhile organizations. A year of committed work with these or other groups could form the backbone of a gap year that "gives back." Brainstorm for favorite humanitarian causes, matching them with skills you already have or skills you want to develop. Some of the same sites you may have examined as a high schooler may spark ideas (in particular, https://www.fastweb.com/ and https://www.idealist.org/). Or take a look at the numerous programs available that offer gap year experiences.

Job shadowing and exploring career interests. You may have done a bit of job shadowing during high school, or perhaps the schedule was just too busy to arrange it. A gap year might be the time to organize a slate of several extended job shadowing experiences, as well as planning a time of research and exploration of career fields. See Chapter 27 for a discussion of how to delve into career research. "Inventory" your relatives and family friends to assess which of them might be amenable to allowing you to shadow them at work, whether for just one day or for a more extended time period, if appropriate.

CAUTIONS AND CONSIDERATIONS

As with everything, you need to be careful about the details of a gap year in order to avoid unpleasant surprises. Here are some of the more common considerations, though there may be others for your situation.

1) Community college courses (or any college courses). Some students enjoy the thought of brushing up on a couple of subjects during the gap year or taking a course purely for fun—maybe a PE course or an art course. Be sure to check with your university to find out whether this is acceptable. In many cases, courses taken after high school graduation can force you into the category of a transfer student rather than a freshman, both for academic purposes and financial aid purposes.

2) Health insurance and finances. Since you may not be working and receiving employer-sponsored health insurance, and since you will not be using the university's health insurance, make sure you are covered by your parents' policy throughout the entire gap year, and that it covers you even if you are out of the country. Also check on banking arrangements for both routine and emergency financial needs.

3) Careful planning. Creative and carefree as a gap year may sound, it can be a complete waste of time if you do not have a plan. Work "hard and smart" ahead of time in researching what you will do, and be sure that you are not simply drifting through the year. June has a habit of turning into September, which quickly becomes January and then April. Without proactive plans, you may end up with very little to show for your year off. On the flip side, don't be overly optimistic and pack your year so full of goals and activities that you become stressed and overcommitted. Seek a balance and keep your goals in mind at all times.

As you plan, check out a couple of helpful resources:
USA Gap Year Fairs http://usagapyearfairs.org is a nationwide circuit of events that bring together reputable gap year programs, organizations, students and parents, and gap year experts. In addition to the fairs, the website highlights gap year programs in various categories: academic, adventure/trips, community service, environmental conservation, internship/work experience, and travel/culture. Helpful articles on the site are another useful resource.

Gap Year Association http://gapyearassociation.org (formerly American Gap Association) is a nonprofit accreditation and standards-setting organization dedicated to encouraging students to take at least a semester of gap time. Its website catalogs gap year opportunities, lists colleges that are favorable to gap years, offers articles and helpful advice, and provides planning guides for families, advice for the gap-to-college transition, and more tips. Some gap year programs have detailed application processes, so plan carefully if these land at the same time as college applications.

4) A team approach. Work closely with parents, teachers/mentors, potential employers or ministry leaders, and the college admissions office to make sure that your gap year plans are a "go" and that any snags are addressed right away. In particular, discuss all financial considerations. How much will it cost for the program, airfare, insurance, and miscellaneous expenses? Who is paying? Also openly discuss the issue of whether your educational momentum will be disturbed or even destroyed by taking a gap year. Come to an agreement about how and when you will resume your formal education.

5) Financial aid. Check and recheck financial aid arrangements to make sure you are not losing out on any financial aid eligibility. Keep up to date with all forms and information that the university financial aid office needs from you, and thoroughly understand the process of getting your academic year (with its tuition bills and financial aid) up and running when you are ready to start school.

As previously mentioned, if you have already been offered admission to a college, along with an offer of financial aid, you will probably not be able to defer federal and state financial aid, but will reapply during your gap year to secure financial aid for the next year. Chances are, your aid will be similar if your family financial circumstances haven't changed. With regard to merit scholarships offered by the university or by outside sources, be sure to check into the deferability of these awards. Explain your situation and request that the scholarship be held for you until you matriculate at the college.

SUPER SENIOR YEAR (FIFTH YEAR SENIOR)

One modification of the gap year process, though it does not include the same type of "gap," is the idea of a Super Senior year. The name sounds upbeat and positive, as well it should, for this plan amounts to an extra year of high school to allow the student to maximize his or her academic strengths, maturity, extracurricular record, or any other attribute that will benefit a rising college student. Many of the reasons for a gap year also apply to the Super Senior year. The difference is that in a gap year the student generally goes through the admissions process, is accepted to college, and then delays matriculation for one year, or applies to college during the gap year after high school graduation, while in a Super Senior year, the student takes that extra time during high school–applying for admission in the fifth year of high school instead of in the fourth.

Reasons for taking a fifth year of high school can include the following:

- *The student needs additional time to enhance one or more areas.* Perhaps a couple of subjects are still weak, or a few academic courses still need to be worked into the course of study. Or perhaps the student got off on the wrong foot during freshman year and the academics are still progressing, with some courses needing to be retaken. As a result, it makes more sense to invest some extra time rather than rushing and cramming the remaining work into the traditional senior year.
- *The student has health needs that have slowed down or interrupted academic progress during high school.* Whether this involves a temporary condition such as recovering from surgery, a serious illness

such as cancer that is now in remission, a chronic illness such as diabetes or lupus, or some other medical situation, taking an extra year can help the student get back on track.

·   *The student has learning challenges and needs a little extra time to finish the high school curriculum.* Learning differences and learning challenges are far more common than most of us realize, and the gift of time often makes the difference between stress and success. A somewhat slower pace can help the student prepare more thoroughly for college.

·   *The student has projects, sports, extracurriculars, or creative ideas that he or she still wants to pursue.* Though this is a less common scenario for extending the high school career, some students do have good reasons for this choice. Perhaps the student is involved in major competitions (such as speech and debate or mathematics) for which he or she is still age-eligible, and has reached a level of excellence that merits continuing with this activity as long as possible and before high school graduation. Or, the student is pursuing creative arts and needs another year to hone his or her talents before the college years begin. Sports, too, can come into play (no pun intended) if the student has the opportunity to sharpen his or her athletic skills and participate in another year of competitions or tournaments.

·   *The student, for various reasons, has not yet completed all the SAT or ACT testing.* Particularly for those with learning differences, college entrance exams are something to work up to, and students may not have started practicing in tenth or eleventh grade as many students do. Adding time to the "clock" and allowing a more reasonable pace can make sense.

·   *The student has a family or personal situation, either during senior year or earlier in the high school career, that has interrupted or impacted the scheduled senior year.* As mentioned in the discussion of a post-high school gap year, a family or personal difficulty may interrupt the flow of high school, necessitating waiting until the following year to apply to college.

·   *The student is positioning himself or herself for admission to a selective college by packing in additional high-level academics and leadership experiences.* Of all the reasons to take a Super Senior year, this one is the least sensible. Some students do it, but this plan can come across as self-serving and artificial: an already elite student is strategically adding to his or her appeal by tacking on an extra year of the excellent accomplishments he or she is already pursuing. These might include additional AP courses, specialized intensive academic programs, internships, leadership roles, or an additional year of the current extracurriculars. Students do this with the belief that they will look even better to colleges; however, the college will see that these activities were spread across five years, not four, and the unfair advantage will be fairly clear. But even worse is the message this strategy sends to the student: getting into an elite college is the only possible "success," and the student has failed if this does not happen. How will the student feel if, after investing an entire year of his or her life as a fifth year senior, the end goal does not come to pass? This plan has the potential for undue stress, low self-esteem, and even resentment of the parents for their "perfect plan."

How Do Colleges View Super Senior Year Applicants?

Note that some public high schools actually have programs for fifth year seniors. Though such programs often cater to students needing to addressing academic or maturity challenges, rather than to candidates for higher-level universities, the existence of Super Senior arrangements is not foreign to colleges. In certain cases, however, you might choose not to highlight the fact that your student took five years to complete high school. For some excellent perspective, read Lee Binz's article "Super Senior Five Year High School" at https://www.homehighschoolhelp.com/blogs/super-senior-five-year-high-school.

Portraying the five-year course of study without advertising the extra year can be done in a couple of ways. One way is to create a subject-by-subject transcript instead of a year-by-year transcript (see Chapter 11 for examples). In this way, grade levels or years are not posted for each group of courses. Instead, all the mathematics courses, all the English courses, and so forth, are listed together without reference to a particular grade level.

Another method is to list only the past four years of courses, leaving off the ninth grade courses as if they were an extension of middle school, or were high school level credits earned in middle school. This would only work if the "tenth through thirteenth" grade courses fulfilled all possible high school graduation and college admission requirements. If not, you could include some of the ninth grade courses in the tenth grade section.

Tips and Cautions

- First and foremost, the student should be on board with the plan to extend the high school path, or it will be very difficult all around. Honest and respectful two-way communication and discussions of pros and cons are essential in order to avoid disappointment and resentment.
- If your student takes any community college classes during the Super Senior year, check ahead of time as to whether these courses will put student in the "transfer boat" if he or she is aiming for freshman status. Typically, if the student has not yet graduated high school, the courses should count for high school and not toward college transfer status.
- Maintain a strong mix of extracurricular and leadership activities during the Super Senior year so that the student stays active, vital, and happy.
- Be extremely cautious and do some deep soul-searching if you are planning a Super Senior year arrangement for an already-strong student, purely to "get him or her into that ultimate dream school." Tinkering with a year of your student's life simply to craft a stellar application for an acceptance that may not even materialize is living dangerously on many levels. Instead, focus on finding schools that would be a perfect fit for your student and that would be more attainable.

TO SUM UP

A gap year gives a student benefits not often found in traditional academics. The student gains real-world experience, including people skills, appreciation of other cultures, and increasing maturity. He or she has the chance to gain perspective on the true meaning of life aside from the parade of studies, degrees, money, and "success." And your student will likely emerge from this year "on" with a sense of confidence, renewed energy, and a readiness to focus on academics and career preparation. The personal growth that occurs during these twelve months is something that the student will make use of for the rest of his or her life. If you are intrigued by the idea of a gap year, do a bit of research and then go for it!

1. Williams, Geoff, "The Gap Year: Good Idea or Bad for Your Teen?" *U.S. News and World Report*, July 22, 2016. Accessed August 25, 2018. https://money.usnews.com/money/personal-finance/articles/2016-07-22/the-gap-year-good-idea-or-bad-for-your-teen.

Chapter 29

You Can Do It!

Survival Tips for Parents

You may be wondering how on earth you can survive the rigors of homeschooling high school for *each* of your children. With all the details to be considered, as well as the sheer bulk of work, is the task really do-able?

The answer is that it is not easy, but it *is* do-able—as well as being worthwhile and rewarding. What could bring more satisfaction than investing your time and energy into a customized education for your students and then seeing them graduate and go on to pursue their dreams? And what could be more rewarding than knowing you've shared a true partnership with your students along the way? Nothing can ever replace the bond that you form with your students as you work together to make their goals a reality, and no one can ever take away the memories that you create during the journey.

Some survival tips are in order, though. Hopefully, these ideas, along with pearls of wisdom you gather from fellow homeschoolers, will help you not only to *survive*, but also to *thrive* during your journey.

SURVIVING ACADEMIC CHALLENGES

Remember That This Is an Individualized Program

Unless your student aspires to attend an extremely selective college (and, in fact, even if he or she does), you actually have a great deal of flexibility in the high school program. Feel free to choose course content that will enhance interests while developing strengths and overcoming weaknesses.

Use Your Summers to Plan Your School Year

If you want a strong college prep program, "winging it" is not a good idea. You need time to select curriculum, to decide how best to use it, and to sketch out a schedule for the year. Setting aside a few weeks during the summer to gather your thoughts and prepare your paperwork will serve you well once the busy school year starts. Then throughout the year, try to predict the ebb and flow of your time commitments, and use the quieter times to gear up for the busier times.

Know When to Call for Help

Understandably, certain courses are more difficult to prepare than others are. And the courses *you're* puzzled about will differ from what other families are concerned about. Use the suggestions from Chapter 5, "Sources for Courses," to help you find outside help and to create a list of ideas to solve your own homeschooling dilemmas.

Be Creative in Motivating Your Student

Some students are born self-motivated and plunge enthusiastically into most learning experiences. Some are motivated only in their favorite subjects. But not all students will dive wholeheartedly into a full lineup of college prep courses and extracurricular activities. Often this reluctance stems not from a lack of interest but from a lack of confidence in their own abilities.

If your student lacks motivation for certain academic subjects or even questions the value of learning them, remind him or her that a young person does not know what the future will hold. Thus, all high schoolers take English, algebra, geometry, science, and history even if these subjects are not their favorites. Being diligent in these subjects helps students keep several options open in order to prepare for attractive possibilities in the future.

For students who have difficulty with motivation, try to gauge when to back off on your "demands" and when to change your approach. Setting up some sort of a reward system is often effective in motivating your student in a particularly difficult subject. Depending on the situation, either a series of small rewards or a pathway toward a larger reward might be appropriate. Rewards might include books for pleasure reading, money, outings or special treats, sports equipment, or "credit" toward a larger item the student would enjoy. As long as the student does not try to manipulate you with these reward systems, you need not feel as though you're "bribing" your student. You are simply offering an incentive for hard work and extra effort, just as employers offer raises and bonuses.

During rough spots in your homeschooling, try to discern whether your student is overwhelmed, overscheduled, overstimulated, or just bored—and then plan for appropriate changes. For a discouraged student, provide frequent, specific encouragement from as many sources as possible. As you try different approaches in your teaching, you will not always know until later whether you made the right decision, but always strive to *know* your student and to listen to God's leading.

Be Active, Curious Learners

Encourage your student's curiosity: new interests can be sparked by following a "rabbit trail" that springs from a session of pure learning for learning's sake. Skipping the day's formal lesson is sometimes the best decision of all. Be alert for unusual learning methods, materials, outings, and activities. As we all know, not every lesson must be completed from a textbook, but we tend to forget this fact as we go about our day-to-day routines. To set a good example, be "teachable" and interested in learning yourself—perhaps by sharing intriguing tidbits you've discovered that relate to what you are learning. Your enthusiasm can be contagious. Likewise, if you appear bored, your student will inevitably "catch" your boredom. The number one tip for motivation is to keep a sense of humor and to have fun together as you learn.

Whenever your student shows a strong interest in something, do your very best to go check it out together—a topic in history, a style of music, a math camp you see advertised, a fascinating series of books, or anything that sparks that love of learning. Of course, you cannot work every intriguing opportunity into your school schedule, but be on the alert for those special circumstances that can increase motivation for learning and perhaps even lead to a lifetime pursuit and passion.

SURVIVING SPIRITUAL CHALLENGES AND ENCOURAGING MATURITY

Though this book is intended for all homeschoolers, regardless of religious background, the survival tips in this section may be of particular help for families whose faith is a key part of their lives and educational philosophies. Because your student is a multifaceted person with a spiritual nature as well as an academic nature, you as a parent will want to make sure that his or her spiritual life is not neglected.

Pray for Your Student

If there is ever a time when prayer is essential, it is during the high school years. Set aside time to pray for your student in key aspects of his or her life: physical, spiritual, academic, social, and emotional. Meeting regularly with other parents is also beneficial because you can share each other's burdens and support each other in the complex undertaking of raising godly children. The power of prayer cannot be underestimated, and this time with God will bring you peace when life seems chaotic.

Encourage Spiritual Maturity

A high schooler may attend church regularly and know hundreds of Bible verses by heart but still not be spiritually mature. At some point, teens need to make their faith their own and integrate it with the other aspects of their lives. The goal is that as they go out into the world, they will live their faith—not to please their parents, but to please the Lord because they are devoted to Him.

This is an area that we as parents can't legislate or control. Teens need to do this independently and by the Lord's leading. We can, however, set a good example and guide them along the path of strengthening their own faith.

Keep open communication with your student about spiritual matters, and keep an open mind, too. Rather than being dogmatic about all issues, recognize the difference between significant spiritual issues and minor variations from believer to believer. In this way, you can help your teen understand what is basic and essential to the faith.

Assess and Encourage Maturity in Other Life Areas

As our students grow older and we contemplate the day they will leave home, we begin watching closely for those elusive signs of maturity. Sometimes we are satisfied; other times, these signs are not appearing quickly enough. How can parents gauge maturity in teens, and more importantly, how can we encourage and develop it? Recommendation forms used with college applications may list a dozen or more desirable character qualities and ask the recommender to rate the student in comparison with his or her peers. These traits are also necessary for life in general—not simply as benchmarks for college admission. Looking at a list of these attributes can help parents pinpoint characteristics that need more work, encouragement, positive role models, or practical experience. *Realize that no student will display all these traits, because even adults don't.* Nor should we set up this list as a formidable hurdle for our teens to leap over before we allow them to live away from home. That, too, would be quite unrealistic, and, in fact, many of these traits are developed out of necessity when a young person is already out on his or her own.

Most of the following characteristics have been gathered from college applications, while others represent character qualities that Christian families may want to nurture in their students. Their arrangement according to the fruit of the Spirit from Galatians 5:22 may help us as we pray for our students.

Maturity Characteristics Prayer List

Fruit of the Spirit: Love

Courtesy
- Showing respect for others: young or old, wealthy or poor, educated or simple.
- Going beyond basic etiquette to meet people's needs and make them feel comfortable.

Willingness to Sacrifice
- Giving up leisure time, money, or free choice of activities for the welfare of someone else.
- Taking the time and effort to pray for the needs of others.

Generosity
- Sharing material blessings willingly, whether by giving gifts or by contributing to people's needs.

Fruit of the Spirit: Joy

- Expressing a positive attitude and enthusiasm.
- Getting through the day without grumbling or complaining.
- Looking on the bright side, seeking help from the Lord, and persevering in the face of difficulty.
- Learning from one's mistakes instead of wallowing in discouragement.
- Displaying enthusiasm for learning, for new situations, and for meeting new people.
- Showing a deep joy rooted in thankfulness to the Lord, regardless of the circumstances.

Fruit of the Spirit: Peace

Acceptance of Oneself
- Refraining from self-criticism or demeaning attitude about appearance or performance.
- Seeking to improve where possible, but accepting the rest.

Confidence and Poise
- Entering unfamiliar or challenging situations with at least an outward portrayal of confidence.
- Drawing upon inner strength to navigate unfamiliar or socially challenging paths.

Reaction to Setbacks Without Excessive Anxiety
- Taking disappointments in stride; changing what can be changed and accepting what cannot.
- Refraining from dwelling on problems and mistakes; avoiding excessive worry and anxiety.

Balance of Realistic vs. Idealistic Views
- Showing practicality in pursuing goals and ideas.
- Injecting a dose of realism into plans and dreams—enough to know that there will be obstacles.
- Making plans for surmounting these obstacles.
- Maintaining enough hope and optimism to pursue something just beyond his or her current reach without giving up too easily.

Fruit of the Spirit: Patience

Ability to Defer Gratification
- Seeing the big picture and postponing small, momentary pleasures to pursue a future goal.
- Exercising patience in interpersonal conflict.

Problem-Solving Skills
- Discovering the root of a problem.
- Approaching a problem with creativity.
- Discerning when to get help and when to tackle the problem alone.

Fruit of the Spirit: Kindness

- Focusing on others; being sympathetic and empathetic.
- Refraining from teasing, gossip, harassment, and malicious behavior.

Fruit of the Spirit: Goodness

- Providing leadership to the peer group in a positive way rather than going along with the crowd.
- Recognizing and following through with doing what is right; appropriately respecting authorities.
- Acting respectfully and responsibly when using other people's property, or when out in public.

Fruit of the Spirit: Faithfulness

Spiritual Maturity
- Possessing a firm foundation in the faith and a desire to keep on growing.
- Showing consistency in spiritual habits of Bible reading, prayer, worship, and sharing God's love.
- Learning to spot cults and false teaching.

Responsibility
- Displaying ownership and "follow through," rather than beginning and abandoning projects.
- Owning up to mistakes even when this admission is uncomfortable, unpopular, or expensive.

Work Ethic
- Conscientiously and dependably finishing a job; giving 100% effort to tasks and assignments.
- Seeing the connection between working hard and achieving goals, but avoiding "workaholism."
- Successfully interspersing work with recreation.

Time Management
- Prioritizing tasks, setting a schedule, and accomplishing the most important tasks each day.
- Turning in assignments or completing jobs on time.

Fruit of the Spirit: Gentleness

- Showing tact and sensitivity by knowing what is and is not appropriate to say or do to others.
- Being empathetic with others (able to sense what they might be feeling) and putting this sensitivity in action by treating them kindly.

Fruit of the Spirit: Self-Control

Goal Setting
- Looking to the future and setting attainable goals, rather than simply living for today.
- Breaking larger goals down into manageable pieces and pursuing the pieces one at a time.

Financial Maturity
- Knowing and applying principles of budgeting, investing, saving, giving, and spending.
- Starting on a path of increasing his or her income while decreasing personal expenses.
- Limiting impulsive purchases, with the goal of being able to save and give.

Impulse Control
- Controlling the temper.
- Resisting temptations such as alcohol, drugs, peer pressure, and sexual activity.
- Respecting and responding to limits.
- Setting self-imposed limits.

Proper Degree of Independence
- Separating appropriately from home and family.
- Taking ownership of goals and of the means to achieve them.

Remember that these are simply goals to aim for. Some people do not achieve progress on this list until they are in their twenties, and most of us have lifelong struggles in many areas. Do not be discouraged if your teen still has many days of immaturity, or if you find yourselves butting heads frequently. As you look at the overall trend, you should be seeing growth and improvement.

Help Your Student Develop Maturity

To encourage maturity, parents need to let the student gradually take ownership of certain responsibilities. In the academic realm, this might include selecting courses, creating deadlines for assignments, or arranging the daily schedule. For extracurriculars, it could involve performing volunteer work or paid employment, or taking ownership of personal finances and time management. Inevitably, your student will make mistakes. Whether they are small ones or big ones, strike a balance between coming to the rescue in these "jams" and letting the student take the consequences for these actions—paying for the lost textbook, working to repair something that was damaged, or suffering the consequences of missing an important deadline.

Surrounding your student with wise, responsible role models is another tactic for encouraging maturity. For instance, if you put your teen in the company of motivated, responsible students, some of the goal-oriented behavior may rub off. Likewise, find adults who can relate well to teens and give encouraging advice, since students tend to emulate people they admire.

SURVIVING TIME MANAGEMENT CHALLENGES

Homeschooling a high schooler will stretch your time management skills to their limits, so it is wise to boost them up before you begin. The first two rules of time management listed below are common ones that you have heard repeatedly. Still, they are the two greatest tools for getting more done in less time.

Before I offer my own tips, I also want to recommend a book I've read three times now: *The Sweet Spot* by Christine Carter. Subtitled "How to Accomplish More by Doing Less," this helpful book addresses the stress and busyness of modern life and gives practical, do-able suggestions for building constructive habits, "taking recess," prioritizing our goals, working efficiently, and much more.

These tips for parental time management are every bit as valid for students. As you, the parent, seek to streamline your life and routines to maximize efficiency and minimize wasted time, pass these concepts on to your student. Seek to model a good example of setting goals, using small pockets of time, addressing the hardest or most important tasks first, and following other key principles.

Learn to Say "No"

You cannot be all things to all people, no matter how much you might want to. Think carefully whenever you are asked to serve on another committee, head up a project, or help in any time-consuming endeavor. Decide ahead of time how much leeway you have in your schedule, and avoid "maxing out." When asked to help with ongoing, open-ended committees or projects, think and pray carefully, and then choose the ones that best match your gifts, talents, personal vision, and schedule. Say "no" to those that are not a good fit for you. Be flexible enough so that you can help with spontaneous needs—preparing a meal for a family dealing with illness, or providing a ride to a field trip for a family with car problems. In order to have this flexibility, you need to make sure your schedule is not already jam-packed. And thus, you sometimes need to say "no."

Prioritize Your Tasks

Another essential principle of time management is prioritizing your tasks. You may be surprised at how magical this technique is. Though it seems like a commonplace piece of advice, when you make a day's or a week's "to-do" list with your overall priorities in mind, and strive to accomplish the most important tasks each day, you will be on your way to meeting long-term goals in several areas of your life.

Prioritizing may mean assigning your most important tasks to the earliest days in the week or the earliest parts of the day so that you will still have time to work on these tasks if the schedule slips a bit. You may also recognize your "high energy, high focus" times of the day or week and slate your most urgent, difficult, or strategic tasks for these times, leaving lighter and quicker tasks for times when you are feeling brain dead. A high-priority task, if left undone one week, needs to stay at the top of your list into the next week so that you will be sure to accomplish it. A side benefit of consciously prioritizing your tasks is that as you see certain low-priority tasks never getting done, you may suddenly realize that you have permission to remove these from your list. You can also see at a glance which tasks can be delegated to someone else, as well as which tasks should logically fall to you.

Another benefit of prioritizing tasks and tackling the toughest or most important ones first is that this pattern sets a good example for your student. By addressing the most important tasks first, you avoid the "last minute" approach and prevent being sidelined by the unexpected.

Learn to Say "Good Enough"

Perfectionism and homeschooling do not mix well. If you have perfectionist tendencies, make a decision about how good is "good enough" for a given task. Obviously, some tasks will need more polish than others. Consider yourself done when you have reached that predetermined level—not when you have achieved perfection.

Communicating to your students the difference between *excellence* and *perfection* is critical. In our fast-paced, high-stress society, we suffer when we confuse the two and fiercely pursue perfection (for the sake of others' opinions of us) instead of excellence (for the joy of a job well done). This suffering can manifest itself in stress, anxiety, depression, fatigue, and loss of motivation.

Make Lists and Master the Art of Organization

Lists are a handy and effective tool for time management. Even for parents who are not already addicted to lists, a good list-making procedure can become habit-forming *and* useful. Lists can keep you from going crazy trying to remember what else you need to do this week. Whether you prefer time-honored paper and pencil lists, weekly or monthly planners, or electronic "To Do" lists such as Google Keep® or another favorite platform, use your lists to their full advantage as sanity-saving tools. My technique is to do a "brain dump" into an electronic "To Do" list , once per season, to capture all the large and small tasks I can think of. These seasons generally break down to early fall (just as the school year starts), the holiday season, early January, early spring, and early summer. Then I categorize the items (work, school, family, miscellaneous administrative, health, spiritual, long term goals, etc.) and sort the tasks by when I plan to attack them. I slate tasks for a particular week, not a specific day, and if the task does not get done, I roll it over to the next week. I keep the list in electronic form for easy revising but often I also print it out.

A list-making parent is usually an organized parent, and organization is a key tool of time management. Suffice it to say that you need to think through each year of school for each student and then think through each course he or she will be studying so that you are prepared for each course. What supplies will you need? What online resources should you or your student look up ahead of time? What ideas do you have for tests and quizzes? If you are giving a lengthy assignment such as a research paper, what written instructions will you give the student ahead of time? If films, musical selections, specific books, field trips to businesses or museums, or other outside resources will be needed, have you made time in your schedule to gather and organize these?

Double Up

One technique that helped me during the high school years was the concept of "doubling up," or trying to do at least two tasks at once. Multitasking is something that all parents do anyway, but homeschoolers need the technique even more. I almost always used waiting time that would otherwise have been unproductive to work on school planning or grading. Whether I was waiting at a swim meet, a doctor's or dentist's office, choir practice, or sports practice, I carried a sturdy bag filled with the pertinent books, papers, and supplies, and I was ready for anything. I found that I could get quite a bit done in time that might otherwise be wasted thumbing through six-month-old magazines.

Multitasking can also take the form of actually *teaching* your children while *doing* another task. Try preparing dinner while discussing questions from the history chapter; exercising while giving a spelling test (I've done that many times), or folding laundry while orally quizzing a student in preparation for a test. Any chore that requires your hands but not much of your mind can be combined with a teaching task that requires only your mind and your voice. Meaningful discussions—whether school-related or not—can also be accomplished while driving to those innumerable destinations.

Search Out Time-Saving Household Tips

Just as you collect ideas for intriguing curricula or worthwhile extracurriculars, start collecting tips to help you manage your household. One that I've recently discovered is iheartorganizing (http://www.i-heartorganizing.com/), with blog posts and excellent photos by Jen Jones. Cleaning, organizing, and making a house an uncluttered, pleasant home are Jen's fortes and she communicates them well. Another, rather whimsical, website devoted to helping homemakers manage the never-ending whirlwind of home tasks is http://flylady.net. With humor, clever ideas, and unforgettable catch-phrases such as the "27-Fling Boogie" method of decluttering, this site will inspire and instruct you as you make homeschooling coexist with real life.

Make Quick Work of Meals and Kitchen Duty

I suspect that only the rarest of homeschooling families sit down to elaborate meals every night. Unless one of your students, or your spouse, adores cooking and can't wait to try the next new recipe, time is simply too short to spend most of it in the kitchen. And yet, a family needs to eat every night. Moreover, studies show that families who sit down to dinner together enjoy benefits that go far beyond the nutritious fare on the table.

To accomplish the feat of placing a meal on the table several nights a week, we all need some shortcuts. Here are a few that may help you:

- *Try once-a-month cooking.* Books such as *Once a Month Cooking* by Mimi Wilson can show you how to cook "marathon-style" once a month, and then freeze all those home-cooked meals to speed up daily meal preparation.
- *Cook double portions and freeze the remainder.* You will always have at least one meal in the freezer.
- *Freeze some of your extra food in single servings* so that a family member who misses dinner or needs to eat early can heat up a portion of lasagna or whatever you have frozen.

- *Prepare the meal in the morning* so that longer cooking times will be completed while you're home, and the food can simply be reheated on those busy evenings.
- *Use healthy "convenience" foods* such as bagged salads, pre-cut vegetables, or other staples.
- *Cook a large quantity of chicken or ground beef at once,* distributing it into freezer bags for later use in casseroles, tacos, or wraps. This way, the cooking time and the mess are taken care of all at once.
- *Plan meals ahead of time.* Aim for at least a week ahead, but you could also plan a cycle of four weeks of menus and shop for the less perishable ingredients ahead of time. This eliminates the day-to-day planning and the last-minute thawing problems.
- *Plan and perfect three or four standard but delicious "company" meals* and keep most of the supplies on hand so that you can have guests without stressing about it.
- *Keep a printed grocery list on the fridge,* organized by food category; circle items as needed.
- *For cleanup, assign each member of the family one after-dinner task* to do each and every night, such as clearing the table, washing or drying dishes, sweeping the floor, or wiping the counters. If your kitchen is large enough, you can enjoy a few minutes of family time while you work.

Learn the Art of Schooling on the Go

If you are in the car more often than not, pack a "car survival kit" to include anything you might need in order to do schoolwork with one student while waiting for a sibling. This kit might include pencils, rulers, sticky notes, tape, glue, notebook paper, books, educational games, snacks, water, paper towels, and anything else you deem essential.

Seize the Moment

In the evenings, as often as you can, schedule regular time to read with your younger children, play board games, bake together, take walks, or do all those things you enjoyed doing before schooling became so busy. It is well worth deferring an hour's worth of grading or lesson planning to spend that time together. The *urgent* tasks will always eventually get done, but you need to focus on the truly *important.*

Be a Unified Family

Regardless of the enthusiasm and gusto you and your high schooler may feel for each year's crop of extracurriculars, don't let these activities take over your family life. Too many mealtimes where family members are missing, or too many weekends away at activities involving just one student, can impinge on a family's togetherness. Schedule, plan, and commit according to reality, not idealism. Try not to over-commit, at least not for extended periods of time. If your family functions best when most members are home most of the time, limit the activities to manageable chunks and to nearby locations. If, however, your family loves to dive in and participate in each other's events, including out-of-town trips, you may be able to handle the more time-consuming or distant activities.

SURVIVING SOCIAL LIFE CHALLENGES

The high school years are a naturally social time in a young person's life, and homeschoolers should not be deprived of the fun and the development opportunities that these years will bring. Social relationships occur in the context of friendships, dating relationships, leadership roles, and interactions with adult authority figures. Although social skills cannot be taught by means of a packaged curriculum, they still need to be addressed with timeliness and wisdom.

The Social Scene for Homeschoolers: FAQs

How can a young person form beneficial friendships?

For years, you've counseled your student about choosing the right friends. Now is the time to reinforce that advice, as your student has more freedom and opportunity to meet people. It's a tricky balancing act to encourage social growth while still watching out for compromising or dangerous situations. Though parents should not veto everything a student wants to do, they must still say "no" occasionally.

Counsel your student on issues such as safe driving, alcohol, drugs, and crimes such as graffiti, vandalism, and shoplifting. Caution him or her, too, to be alert for teens whose language, attitude, or behavior shows signs of rebellion. Any teen should be careful about developing deep, close relationships with people who can drag him or her down into wrong behavior.

Though it may be a cliché, the best way to *have* a friend is to *be* a friend. Your teen may need to seek out others who need a friend rather than waiting to be "sought out." Taking the initiative to talk to a new person at a field trip or social event might be the start of a friendship. Ultimately, people want to be around those who speak kindly, who do not gossip, and who are truly interested in what the other person has to say. By developing these characteristics, your student can expand the network of friends. Not surprisingly, most students find that church youth groups, 4-H clubs, debate teams, choirs, bands, and sports teams offer fun and fellowship, focused around a common interest.

If you belong to a homeschooling support group with lots of teens, your student has a potential outlet for enjoyable social times. Be sure that your group is not simply sponsoring an activity but is actively supervising it so that the students are in a safe, friendly environment. Homeschool co-ops and academies are another source of friendships. Students who are together once or twice a week, perhaps for several school years in a row, can form strong friendships based on common experiences.

How can teens learn to relate well to adults in their lives?

As our students move into adulthood, they will work with a variety of personalities among their employers, teachers, coaches, youth leaders, supervisors, and other leadership figures. Whether in the context of academics, extracurriculars, volunteer work, or employment, these selected adults can help our students gain a measure of independence and can provide some extremely rewarding relationships.

Entering the reality of the working world, even part time, students learn to interact with their employers and supervisors and thus can develop respect, friendliness, teachability, and a willingness to work. As they realize that they are giving up some free time and rights to their schedule in exchange for payment, students learn meaningful lessons. Do be sure, though, that your student's employer is not taking advantage of him or her, whether workload-related or otherwise. This goes for any adult working with your student in any capacity. Keep an open communication and have your student talk to you if any behavior makes him or her uncomfortable.

Relationships with teachers, pastors, coaches, volunteer supervisors, and other key adults can be valuable at college application time, so you will want these mentors to become acquainted with your student and with his or her aspirations. But even more, you will want your student to develop strong relational skills simply because it is the right thing to do. Encourage your student to demonstrate responsible effort and hard work even if the subject matter is difficult. Additionally, remind him or her of the enduring value of a personable attitude, enthusiasm, and initiative.

How are grown-up homeschoolers doing?

If the socialization issue has been nagging at you, or if relatives and friends have been doing the nagging, examine some excellent studies completed by Dr. Brian Ray of the National Home Education Research Institute (NHERI). Details of these studies are available on his website, http://nheri.org. In particular, Dr. Ray performed one study surveying previously homeschooled students who are now adults. This study, commissioned by HSLDA, shows that homeschoolers are definitely not lacking in social skills. On the contrary, they assimilate into the social life of their communities without any difficulties.

Dr. Ray surveyed about 7,300 homeschool graduates, of which more than 5,200 had been homeschooled for more than seven years. His statistics were based on those with at least seven years of homeschooling experience. Among many other positive trends, the study specifically found the following outcomes when comparing former homeschoolers to the general population:

- Homeschool graduates were twice as involved in community service, twice as likely to vote, and far more likely to contribute to or work for a political cause, party, or candidate.[1]
- 95% of the graduates surveyed were glad they had been homeschooled, and 82% planned to homeschool their own children. 59% of them considered themselves "very happy" with their lives, compared to 27.6% of the general population.[2]

Other studies show similar encouraging results. None of the former homeschoolers were unemployed or on welfare.[3] Additionally, 79% of them said that homeschooling helped them to interact with individuals from different levels of society, and 94% said that it prepared them to be independent.[4] Not surprisingly, homeschooling does a good job of meeting key social needs such as personal identity, values and moral development, autonomy, and relationships. Socialization is a multifaceted jewel. We want our students to grow "in wisdom and stature" (academically and physically) but also, very importantly, to grow "in favor with God and man" (spiritually and socially). Having God-pleasing relationships with parents, with other adults in their lives, and with friends of the same or opposite sex is a vital but complex long-term goal. By reinforcing the principles taught from childhood, by setting wise rules and guidelines, by gradually allowing more freedom and responsibility, and by maintaining loving communication with our teens, we can help encourage maturity and healthy social relationships.

SURVIVING STRESS AND ANXIETY CHALLENGES

The Reality of Stress

Clearly, the efforts required to build a strong college application are significant. If parents and students were to use *every* idea or suggestion in this book, impossible levels of stress would build up on the student and the family. Remember that this advice is intended to be customized to your family. Choose what works best for your situation and discard the ideas that are too much for you. Most homeschoolers, with their flexible approach to education, aim to keep the proper perspective on this whole adventure. Still, there will be times when the stress becomes excessive. In some students, it may manifest itself in physical symptoms, or it may lead to anxiety, panic attacks, or depression. This outcome is difficult for any family to witness, and unfortunately, it is all too common today.

Some students naturally tend to place undue stress on themselves, but at the same time, they thoroughly *enjoy* challenging themselves and meeting those challenges. However, if this self-imposed stress builds up in the wake of a heavy load of courses and extracurriculars, a job, and numerous college applications, it can result in significant problems. The work expands while the energy level drops, and with no margin for getting sick or for any down time at all, daily life may feel truly impossible. This is when anxiety may manifest itself in physical symptoms such as nausea, stomach aches, headaches, heart palpitations, shortness of breath, tingling sensations, and dizziness or lightheadedness.

Watching your student manage the effects of stress while continuing to passionately pursue the path that he or she feels called to pursue can be painful. Always think and pray carefully about what is right for your student. You can no longer completely control his or her purposes and pursuits, especially if you recognize that this student is uniquely gifted and aspires to serve God out in the world by pouring extra effort into some challenging areas.

What, then, can you do to help? Stay close and remain vigilant. Propose ways to streamline the schedule. Urge your student to sleep and eat. Take him or her to the doctor or counselor as needed. Pray without ceasing, and demonstrate your unconditional love and encouragement. A particularly stressful year may even end up being your sweetest and most memorable year of all, because of what you've gone through together. You may recognize later that it was "the best of times and the worst of times." Here are some ways to cope—both for students and for parents who find themselves in the throes of stress.

Praying

Pray as a husband/wife team, as student and parent together, and individually on behalf of your student. Let your student know that you are praying for him or her.

Understanding the Situation, Talking About It, and Nurturing Friendships

Physical symptoms caused by stress can be frightening. Understanding the "mind-body" connection can sometimes improve or halt the vicious cycle whereby adrenaline causes symptoms, generating more anxiety, more adrenaline, and more symptoms. The goal is to bring some common sense back to the mind-body connection. And, importantly, by talking to your student you can keep apprised about how he or she is doing and whether it is time to get additional help or to make adjustments in the schedule.

Since stress and anxiety are so common among high schoolers and college students, a student often benefits simply by realizing that he or she is not alone. Moreover, knowing that others care is a tremendous help. Though the days and weeks are busy, encourage your student to spend time with friends—talking, laughing, and enjoying therapeutic "down time."

Setting Healthy Expectations

Communicate clearly that you love and value your student unconditionally—not because of achievements and accomplishments, but because of who he or she is. Your love will not be diminished one bit by perceived "failures." Frequent discussions about the true, multifaceted meaning of success, as opposed to the common definition of "being number one" or "being perfect," are vital in keeping your student grounded in reality. Try to set a good example of resilience—the ability to bounce back from disappointments, discouragements, and defeats, having learned something from the experience. From there, one can renew the resolve to keep striving for excellence rather than for the elusive and impossible perfection. The ability to move confidently among life's pleasant and unpleasant surprises is a key life skill.

Practicing Healthy Eating and Taking Time to Exercise

Eating a balanced diet of fruits, vegetables, grains, and protein is always preferable to eating junk food. Some students, when stressed, lose their appetites. Others eat too much. Either way, you may need to step in and help by making healthy food easily accessible at all times of the day.

Exercise helps in two ways: by releasing stress and preventing anxiety attacks in the first place, and by helping to use up the excess adrenaline that accumulates during an anxiety or panic episode. Research has shown that exercise is clearly beneficial in preventing and treating anxiety and depression. Whether the exercise of choice is walking, running, swimming, sports, or other forms of exercise, your student should practice it on a regular basis.

Removing Stressors and Protecting Sleep and Rest Time

Not surprisingly, teenagers are known for getting too little sleep. Their bodies also seem to be on a different clock compared to younger children and to adults: they love to stay up late, and they have a hard time getting up early. Lack of proper sleep also fuels anxiety symptoms, so do all you can to encourage sufficient rest. Look at your student's lineup of activities and see if you can trim away unnecessary commitments to allow for more rest and uncommitted time. You may have to do painful "major surgery" by eliminating one or two entire courses or extracurriculars.

Scheduling Medical Checkups and Seeking Professional Help

If your student begins to experience physical symptoms, take him or her to the doctor to rule out a medical cause. The doctor can help discern what is causing the symptoms, and if they are indeed anxiety-induced without any other physical disorders, he or she can help you learn to deal with this condition.

If your student's situation is not responding to "home care," seek professional help. While self-help can go a long way, it is not always enough. Seek medical help or counseling as soon as you suspect that your student needs it. As we all know, some students have such serious struggles with anxiety and depression that their lives are in danger, so getting help sooner rather than later is extremely important.

Setting a Good Example

Likewise, if you as a parent are experiencing burnout, use all of the same suggestions listed above. At times, you will feel justifiably exhausted and ready to give up. Take the cue and share tasks with another homeschooling parent, or brainstorm for other ways to reduce your load. Remind yourself *why* you are homeschooling in the first place, and cut out any unnecessary tasks that take too much of your time and energy. Seek to leave the foundation intact—namely, strengthening your relationship with your children and following God together. Think ahead to the big picture of what you want for your student in the future, and rejoice in the progress you have made so far.

TO SUM UP

Some of these tips have been practical; others, more conceptual. Remember that your day-to-day survival kit—in addition to God—is your homeschool support group. Your homeschooling will be enriched as you share concerns with other homeschoolers and receive advice and suggestions. Aim to be supportive in the lives of your homeschooling friends as well!

1. Ray, Brian D., Ph.D., excerpt from *Home Educated and Now Adults: Their Community and Civic Involvement, Views about Homeschooling, and Other Traits,* by Brian D. Ray, Ph.D., 2004, available from http://nheri.org.
2. Ibid.
3. J. Gary Knowles,"Now We Are Adults: Attitudes, Beliefs, and Status of Adults Who Were Home-Educated as Children." Paper presented at the Annual Meeting of the American Educational Research Association, April 3-7,1991, Chicago, IL, cited in "Facts on Homeschooling" by Brian D. Ray, Ph.D., National Home Education Research Institute, February 2003, available from http://nheri.org.
4. Ibid.

Chapter 30

Ready, Set, Go!

Gearing Up for College Life

ONE LAST SUMMER ...

The last morsel of cake from the graduation party has been consumed. The graduation tassel is proudly displayed in your student's room, along with a colorful collection of cards, stuffed animals in caps and gowns, and other graduation debris. Figuratively and literally, the books have been closed forever on high school studies, and some serious "sleeping in" has commenced, unless a summer job has dominated your student's schedule. Unbelievably, you've finished homeschooling this particular student.

And now, you have one last summer together—the last summer of childhood, so to speak. Certainly it is one to be savored and celebrated, after all you've been through. Finally, you will have a relaxing summer. *Or will you?*

Mom and Dad, did you really think you were done with plans and checklists? As your student prepares for college, your list of errands and tasks may grow with each passing week. And, as your student shows increasing independence, the dynamics of your relationship may begin shifting dramatically.

This last summer of childhood is a crossroads you and your student have anticipated with hard work, planning, and prayer. Now, on the brink of this next season, you may be wildly tempted to change your mind and insist that "your baby" stay at home for another year or two. But this summer is also a season of anticipating the new adventure for all of you—albeit with a "to-do" list as long as your student's graduation gown. With foresight and organization, you can make that checklist more manageable, allowing your family to plan some special times together in the weeks ahead.

AN END AND A BEGINNING

The advice in this book could very well conclude when your student is accepted into college. A congratulatory note to families who have achieved this milestone—with some further encouragement to keep up the good work for the next sibling—might wrap up the book quite neatly. However, college preparation doesn't end with that last GPA calculation of the senior year. The surprising amount of preparation that must be compressed into those last two or three months before your student leaves for college makes for an intense time of educating your student on practical issues, common sense, and wisdom. You are laying the final groundwork for independence. Since roles are changing rapidly and emotions are running at full strength, this can be a challenging summer for both parents and students. Don't be surprised if you face a few unexpected confrontations with your normally mild-mannered student, or if you experience some sentimental, tearful times with your typically stoic teen. Growing up is never easy—for students *or* for parents.

ADMINISTRATIVE TASKS

Enrollment Commitment and Deposit

First of all, your student will need to submit a commitment to enroll (usually online) to the college he or she has chosen. The most common deadline is May 1st, and generally the enrollment deposit of a few hundred dollars will be required as well. Soon after receiving this response, the college may send a packet of information or a link to a website detailing a list of tasks to be completed over the summer. (Here's another checklist to post on the fridge.) Compared to the college application marathon you have already been through, none of these tasks will be difficult, but meeting the deadlines is important.

Final Transcript

Your last task in your role as guidance counselor is to submit an official transcript for the final semester as soon as it is available. You will do this through the Final Report for the Common Application, or through another mechanism for colleges not on the Common Application. Request transcripts from community colleges in a timely manner so that they arrive by the deadline the college has set.

Residence Hall Information

Late in the spring or early in the summer, your student will receive residence information: choices of residence halls, room types, and meal plans, as well as the all-important roommate selection questionnaire. Go through this information together, giving input on budgetary constraints as necessary. Many schools offer meal plans providing a combination of residence hall meals and "flexible" meals offering a monetary allowance toward food purchased elsewhere on campus. Students find these flexible dollars useful for times when classes or activities make it inconvenient or impossible to return to the residence halls at mealtimes.

As your student completes the roommate questionnaire, encourage thoughtful and honest answers to questions such as sleeping and waking hours, TV and music preferences, or desire for a quiet or a more "social" room.

Health Questionnaires

Another summer task will be completion of health questionnaires or even a full physical exam. Be prepared to dig up a copy of your student's immunization record and possibly to update some immunizations. Also decide whether you will sign up for the student health insurance or whether your student will be covered under your existing plan. If you opt out of campus health insurance, you will probably have to take specific action to waive it; otherwise, fees will be automatically added onto the university bill.

ACADEMICS

Although academics will not be a heavy emphasis during the summer, a few academic decisions and tasks will find their way onto the to-do list, especially if your student attends an orientation session during the summer instead of just before the fall term.

AP Scores

If your student took Advanced Placement exams, make sure that these test scores have been submitted to the appropriate office so that your student will receive credit according to the university's AP policy. Your student may be able to bypass one or more introductory courses or receive university credit. During the final set of AP exams in May, your student may have designated which college should receive the scores. If not, you will need to go to the College Board website and follow the procedures for submitting scores.

Transfer Requests

Similarly, your student should contact the registrar's office to arrange for transfer credit for courses taken at the community college. Transfer request forms may be available on the college website, and the process will involve requesting an official community college transcript, filling out information about course content, and possibly submitting syllabi or course descriptions. The process is more streamlined for universities in your own state that have an articulation agreement with the community college your student attended; also, universities differ widely on how much transfer credit they will allow. However, it is worthwhile to apply for as much as possible. One exception might be if your student intends to take and transfer other courses later, such as summer community college courses, and the university has limits on transferable units. In this case, the student might forgo some of the transferable work from high school to allow for key courses later. Also, keep any applicable SAP (Satisfactory Academic Progress) in mind. See Chapters 13 and 21 for details.

Summer Reading Assignments and Placement Exams

Believe it or not, your student may have some summer homework. Julie received three books in the mail and was assigned to read them and be prepared to discuss them during orientation week. Of course, this assignment was not graded. Colleges may also require placement exams in mathematics, writing skills, or foreign languages. The results will help place your student into the appropriate course.

Academic Advisement and Registration for Classes

Well before the registration deadline, your student should study the college website for his or her major and understand the requirements and electives necessary for the degree. Examining a chart or grid of the four-year course of study can be extremely helpful in strategizing which courses will be taken during which terms. Some of these decisions depend on freshman requirements or performance on placement exams; others, on major requirements, course availability, preferences, or interests. Academic advising appointments may be offered during orientation week to help with final decisions about courses. Getting the right advice is important so that your student does not inadvertently take the wrong course, wasting time and money.

Managing Workload, Extracurriculars, and "Grade Shock"

As a parent, you will be doling out lots of advice during the summer, and hopefully, your student will be receptive to it. One important consideration is the schedule and workload for the freshman year. Your student will need to be realistic about the time these courses will take and should also allow time for extracurricular and social activities, church attendance, rest, and other responsibilities. Students tend to be overly optimistic about how much they can handle. If they take on too much work and too many activities, they will experience stress and fatigue when reality hits later in the term.

Similarly, take time to review wise time management, emphasizing that maturity often means doing what we *need to do* rather than what we *want to do* at that moment. To allow enough time for studying, your student must set a few reasonable limitations on TV, internet use, social media, video games, music, parties and socials, off-campus outings, phone calls, and just "hanging out." Of course, every student needs time for relaxation and socialization; the goal is to strike a healthy balance between work and play.

"Grade shock" can be quite a blow to a young person who has always performed with excellence and has always been rewarded with A's. Now that your student is surrounded by hundreds of talented students from all over the nation or the world, earning A's will not come so easily. Facing difficult exams, brutal grading curves, and constant uncertainty about what professors want, he or she may struggle to achieve even a B or a C in certain courses. These difficulties inevitably lead to discouragement, and many freshmen begin to question whether they belong at that university. When this initial shock hits, common sense should prevail: the student should make full use of office hours, review sessions, tutoring services, and study groups in order to delve more deeply into the material and address weaknesses.

As parents, try not to add to the stress by arbitrarily demanding stellar grades. Both parent and student should remember that a person's value and worth are not tied to the GPA. Encourage your student to do his or her best, but clearly communicate that although these effects may not always translate into perfect grades, you will still give him or her your support and vote of confidence.

SOCIAL LIFE

Handling Social Pressures

One high-priority warning to pack into this summer's advice relates to drinking and drugs on campus. Even if the campus is "dry," alcohol seems to find its way onto almost every college campus, or at least into off-campus parties. Help your student, who may be rather innocent about such things, learn to identify when alcohol or drugs are in use and to come up with ways to exit these situations safely. Another danger involves riding in vehicles with students who have been drinking, even if the drinking was merely in the context of a dinner out among friends. If your student can be the designated driver, or arranges an Uber® ride or other method of transportation, the safety of the whole group will be improved.

Drugs are another unfortunate reality on many campuses. Now is the time to re-emphasize the devastating consequences of using and becoming addicted to drugs.

Pressure to become involved sexually will also be at an all-time high during the college years. Roommates may think nothing of overnight visitors, and the relationships your student may initiate in those first months will have to be sorted out according to your student's standards. Loneliness, a desire to be liked, or a wish for opposite-sex companionship may also place your otherwise sensible student in tempting or compromising situations. Encourage strong personal convictions and healthy friendships with both sexes.

Dealing with Loneliness and Homesickness

After the excitement of the first weeks of school has worn off, many freshmen experience tremendous loneliness or homesickness. Even if your student has met dozens of people and has a wonderful roommate, he or she may still lack close friends with whom to communicate on a deeper level. With or without homesickness, your student may experience acute longing for "old" friends from the high school years.

Freshman deans' offices can attest to the fact that loneliness is one of the most common difficulties freshmen experience. Friendships take time to develop, and students forget how long it took to forge the strong bonds they have with their high school friends. Continuing to meet people and forging deeper connections with those they already know is key—but is not always easy. Encourage your student to be involved in one or more extracurricular activities and to spend a few extra minutes conversing with other students each day, as a way to make new friends.

PERSONAL HEALTH AND SAFETY

As you prepare to relinquish "your baby" into the nebulous and impersonal care of the university, moments of trepidation may mar the idyllic summer you had planned. You will find yourself following your student around, offering tidbits of advice, only to hear in reply, "Yes, Mom, I know that," or, "You already told me that." One aspect for which you need to think ahead involves your student's personal health.

Campus Health Center

Every college, large or small, has a campus health center. On large campuses, it may provide so many medical services that the student never has to set foot off campus for health care. On small campuses, the health center may have limited hours of operation and be staffed by a nurse and student assistants, with a doctor available only once or twice a week. Regardless of the setup, the health center is generally the first stop when your student has a sore throat, a migraine, a strange rash, a broken toe, or an anxiety attack (of course, in the case of an emergency requiring a 911 call, the student should seek appropriate help). After assessing the situation, the health center staff will tend to your student's needs themselves or will provide an off-campus referral to a doctor or hospital.

When your student first moves in, try to stop in at the campus health center to ask all your parental questions. Find out how the health center operates, how often a doctor is on site, what services are available on campus, and what the costs are. Often, routine services such as treating a strep throat or a sinus infection will be covered by a student health fee paid at the beginning of the year. Depending on the college, services as varied as mental health counseling, immunizations, prescriptions, and physical therapy may be available at a reasonable rate.

If your student is younger than eighteen, find out how health crises will be handled and how you will be informed. If your student is over eighteen, realize that HIPAA privacy regulations restrict the communication of medical information to a person other than the patient—even to a parent—unless the patient has specifically given permission to share this information.

Health Insurance and Medical Records

If your student is already covered by your health insurance, you will most likely use this coverage for any health needs not included in the basic student health fee. If you don't have insurance, or if it is not applicable to the college's geographic area, you may want to sign up for the student health policy offered by the college. In fact, you may actually be required to sign up. Either way, make sure you understand which doctors, hospitals, and other facilities your student may use, as well as what paperwork, copayments, billing procedure, or reimbursements will be applicable. It is better to do this research ahead of time so that you are not scrambling for doctors if your student has a sudden medical need. This is especially important if your student has a chronic health problem and needs to see specialists. You might even check with your own physician for a referral to a good physician in the vicinity of the college. Additionally, if your student has a complicated medical history, it would be wise to obtain a copy of his or her medical records in case they are needed by the college health team. Again, students who are eighteen or older will need to personally request these documents.

Also scope out dentists in the area in case your student needs more than the traditional Christmas-and-summer dental checkups.

Emergency Contact Info

College medical documents will ask you for names, phone numbers, and addresses of people to contact in case of an emergency. Make sure that the names and numbers you list are current and are the most sensible ones to use.

Immunizations

Since the college will request a rundown of your student's vaccination history, this is a logical time to update missing immunizations or arrange for any others that you have been considering. A few immunizations to discuss with your doctor are those for meningococcal disease, Hepatitis A and B, and pertussis (which is on the upswing among young adults because the childhood immunization loses its effectiveness). Tetanus shots should also be up to date so that your student has one less detail to think about in case of injury. You might also encourage your student to receive a flu vaccination. Most likely, one or more flu shot clinics will be offered on campus. If your student plans to travel abroad, the campus health center may offer typhoid, yellow fever, and other recommended vaccines.

PREVENTIVE HEALTH

Healthy Eating

Gaining the "Freshman Fifteen" is preventable if a student can make wise eating choices even when confronted by unlimited food in the dining halls. Keeping a stash of healthy snacks in the room may be a big help for late night hunger attacks. It beats ordering pizza!

Some students do not like the taste of the college's tap water. A water filtration pitcher in the room or a stockpile of bottled water may encourage the student to drink plenty of water.

First Aid Kit and Medicines

Many colleges require that each student bring a first aid kit stocked with bandages, antiseptic, and other common necessities. Even if it's not required, it is a wise thing to have. Additionally, prescription medications the student takes should be refilled before school starts. Make sure your student knows where and how to get refills. Over-the-counter pain relievers, cough drops, allergy tablets, and vitamins may be packed with the first aid kit. Include a fever thermometer for those inevitable illnesses.

Illnesses and Injuries

Students who are on their own for the first time in their lives have the task of diagnosing their own illnesses and injuries and assessing whether they need more than simple care. Remind your student to call you for advice or to check with the student health services if an injury or illness seems unusual.

Because students tend to be optimistic and sleep-deprived, they may not seek care right away. Fortunately, most of their health problems will be minor, but it is always better to be safe than sorry. One common and often severe illness among overworked, closely-packed college students is infectious mononucleosis. A case of "mono" lasts for weeks or months and can range from fairly mild (sore throat, swollen glands, and low energy) to so severe that your student may need to drop his or her classes for that term.

Exercise

Students who want to stay healthy should also seek out options for exercise: a P.E. class, intramural or informal sports participation, running, swimming, biking, or working out at the gym. A regular exercise program will reduce stress and enhance overall health.

Sleep

You will not have much influence over your student's sleep schedule and would probably be appalled to discover what hours he or she is keeping. Providing earplugs for noise reduction, proper blankets to regulate the temperature, and advice to "get a good night's sleep" may be about all you can do from here on out. "Don't let the bedbugs bite" might be another helpful admonition. Apparently these little creatures are on the rise in hotels and college dorms, so you may want to educate your student about how to check for them.

Campus Safety

Especially if the school is in an urban or high-crime area, you will want to caution your student about personal safety. However, all students, regardless of the campus, need to take responsibility for wise behavior. Many colleges provide safety services to escort students to destinations on campus after dark. Confer with the campus police department to get tips about student safety and to learn what to do if an incident occurs.

If your student rides a bike on or off campus, encourage helmet use, proper lights, and regular maintenance of the bicycle for tire and brake function.

ID Card or Driver's License

As parents, we all hope that our students will never be in a serious accident or have an illness that causes them to lose consciousness. But just in case, encourage your student to always carry a driver's license or ID card. Information from this card can be used to notify family members and to access additional information in case of emergency. Your student may prefer to carry a laminated photocopy of the driver's license instead of the real thing when running or working out. If it is lost, it is a simple matter to make another copy of the original.

Online Safety and Security

Make sure your student's computer has appropriate security features and up-to-date antivirus protection, and also that operating system updates are installed as they become available. A cautious approach is wise for phones and other mobile devices as well. Needless to say, passwords should be kept secure and should never be shared. Students should avoid transmitting sensitive data such as passwords, credit card numbers, or bank account numbers over public hotspots. Together, read a few web pages on wireless security tips so that your student knows the appropriate safeguards.

MANAGING BELONGINGS

Keeping track of one's "stuff" is another feature of independent living. Students can no longer cry, "Mom, can you help me find my math book?" or "Dad, can I borrow your house key? I can't find mine." Now your student must manage a multitude of belongings, especially important items such as keys and credit cards. Don't be surprised if a few minor crises occur over these issues, but over time, your student should improve his or her "stuff-handling" skills.

College ID Cards

In addition to a driver's license or ID card, your student may now have a college ID to manage—though many institutions are moving to electronic IDs to eliminate the need for handling plastic cards. If your student does have a physical card, it may also serve as a prepaid spending card for campus offices, stores, and eateries. In the event that the card is lost or stolen, the student should report the loss right away and put a hold on it so that no one can access the funds.

Keys and Room Security

Again, your student may have a card or a smart card instead of an actual key, but in any case, a key is another expensive-to-replace item that the student should keep track of. Moreover, students should make agreements with roommates to always keep the room locked when they are out, so that personal items such as laptops and wallets are not stolen. Sadly, theft is frequent on college campuses, and students need to be vigilant. Car keys, bike lock keys, mailbox keys, and house keys for your own home should also be kept in secure places. Additionally, the student should never let unauthorized persons into the residence hall.

Computer

Laptop computers are handy for taking to class and for studying anywhere on campus, but they are hazardous from a theft standpoint. For this reason, your student must never leave the laptop unattended when out on campus or in the community. Look into buying a security lock to anchor the computer to a desk in the dorm room or in a library. Security programs are also available so that in case of theft, you can log onto a website and determine the location of the computer.

Bicycle

Your student should always lock his or her bike with a heavy U-lock, even when leaving it for only a few minutes. Even so, bikes are relatively easy to steal. For extra security, some students double lock, using both a U-lock and a cable lock. A bike store or biking website can provide tips on smart ways to lock up a bike and to secure the seat and wheels if necessary.

LIFE IN THE RESIDENCE HALLS

Outfitting the Dorm Room

One of the more enjoyable tasks of the summer will be shopping for items to personalize your student's room. Many colleges reveal roommate names and contact information during the summer, allowing students to confer with each other and decide who will bring large items (such as a mini-fridge) and what color scheme will be used for bedding and decorations. If roommates will not meet until move-in day, you may choose neutral colors or wait to shop until after the students have met. If you live far away from the school, buying some items near the campus might be a better plan, anyway. Many colleges partner with linen purchasing services: you place your order for sheets, comforters, and other necessities during the summer, and the items show up on move-in day. Or order them from a local store or online and have them delivered to the campus.

As you make your list, find out what items are prohibited. These often include candles, hot plates, and heaters. Here is a list of the types of items your student may need. Not all will need to be packed and transported; many can be ordered online and shipped to the college, or purchased locally as needed.

Basics

- Clothing, with plenty of hangers (include at least one business casual/"interview" outfit)
- Raincoat or other climate-specific outerwear; umbrella; gloves (even for California)
- Shoes (including dress shoes)
- Robe and slippers if desired
- Over-the-door closet storage rack for shoes or other items
- Bedding, usually twin extra-long (sheets, blankets, comforter, mattress pad, pillows, pillowcases)
- Decorative throw or ultra-soft blanket and decorative pillows to use while studying on the bed
- Towels and wash cloths (including large beach towel, which doubles as a picnic blanket)
- Toiletries
- Small mirror
- Dishware for snacks (one or two mugs, plates, bowls, and utensils—or paper plates and utensils)
- Electric teakettle or pot for heating water, if allowed
- Shower caddy or tote; shower sandals
- Laundry hamper with detachable laundry bag
- Laundry soap, fabric softener sheets
- Small travel iron if no iron and ironing board are available
- Small sewing kit
- First aid kit, medicines, and vitamins
- Desk supplies (pens, pencils, highlighters, tape, stapler, scissors, sticky notes, etc.) and organizer
- Storage bins
- Study lamp
- Graphing calculator or other specialized calculator, if needed
- Laptop computer
- Extension cords, power strips, and/or surge protectors
- Flash drives for file storage
- Books in addition to textbooks
- Expanding file or pocket folder for important papers and documents
- Stationery, stamps, and envelopes
- Mounting material for hanging posters (find out what is allowed)
- Memo board for room door
- Backpack or duffel bag
- Wastebasket if not provided
- Antibacterial cleaning wipes
- Headphones or earbuds (consider noise-canceling headphones)

- Batteries as needed
- All necessary chargers (most commonly forgotten item)
- Sports equipment and apparel as needed

Optional Items

- Clothes drying rack
- Decorator items such as posters, pictures, or small rug
- Camera, if desired
- Speakers for playing music
- Dorm-safe coffee maker
- Compact refrigerator – handy for keeping water, cold drinks, and healthy snacks on hand. Your student's residence hall may also have a refrigerator available for students to store larger items.
- Compact microwave – helpful when the student misses meals or needs snacks. Again, the residence hall will probably have a microwave.
- Small fan if room is not air-conditioned
- Comfort items from home, whatever those may be

College Student Insurance

In case you haven't noticed, outfitting a college student's abode can be quite expensive, especially when considering the cost of the computer and peripherals, phone, books, a bicycle if needed, sports equipment, bedding, and clothing. You can insure your student's belongings in case of theft or damage by fire, flood, or other calamity for a nominal premium and a small deductible. CSI Insurance Agency (College Student Insurance) at https://www.collegestudentinsurance.com/ is one such company we discovered, which will insure the loss or damage of these items. Also check whether your homeowner's insurance will cover these losses or whether your provider offers college student insurance.

Telephones

College students cannot bear to be separated from their phones. Make sure you are both clear about plan details, available minutes, fees, and billing responsibilities. Depending on the location of the school, certain providers will offer better signal coverage. Also talk about procedures to follow if the phone is lost or stolen.

Though most students rely solely on their cell phones, you will also want to investigate a couple of backup plans for communication in case the phone is not working or is lost or stolen.

Laundry

The stereotypical college problem—doing the laundry—may not be an issue for your homeschool graduate who aced Life Skills 101. At any rate, review the costs for the washing machines and dryers as well as basic rules on sorting laundry and selecting the proper water temperature. Machines may be coin-operated or may use a prepaid card system.

Roommate Compatibility

Far above laundry in priority is a harmonious living arrangement with one's roommates. While the residence questionnaires may match students for compatibility in sleep habits and music preferences, more serious issues such as dealing with drinking, drugs, or overnight guests can crop up during the year. Sometimes these personality mismatches are apparent right away; other times, they take several weeks to surface. Either way, the first step should be to try to work things out via clear communication, patience, and goodwill. If the situation cannot be resolved, your student should bring up the issue with the residence hall staff. In extreme cases, a new roommate may be assigned.

Resident Assistants

Every residence hall is staffed with one or more resident assistants. These may include adult residence advisors, student assistants, or others such as social or cultural assistants, academic assistants, and technology assistants. Encourage your student to make use of these resource people. Getting to know older students can be a great help during your student's rough spots, whether these be as simple as computer glitches or as complex as roommate troubles, major loneliness, or depression.

FINANCES

Personal Finances

The start of college may be the first time your student has needed a checking account or ATM card. Summer is an ideal time to get this account up and running. Investigate locations of branches near the college (preferably banks or credit unions with branches in your home town as well) or decide whether the banking will all be done online. If your student has a regular income, look into direct deposit. Likewise, consider automatic bill pay for some of the regular expenses such as a cell phone bill.

Some families start their student with a credit card at this point, to build up a credit history and to have funds available for emergencies or unexpected expenses. Determine whether your student is responsible enough to safeguard the card and not to charge excessive expenses.

If your student does not yet have a credit card or checking account, you may want to provide a supply of cash to be used for books, fees, and other start-up expenses. Or, the college debit card may be loaded with an appropriate amount or tied to an account. Prepaid credit cards or gift cards are other options. Provide reminders on how to keep checks, cards, and cash secure, as well as discussing how much "extra" money the student truly needs.

Paying the University Bill

Your first university bill will arrive sometime during the summer. That sinking feeling when you see the grand total will not go away for at least four years. Check the bill to make sure all the charges are correct, and investigate payment options. The college may offer a payment plan allowing you to spread your payments throughout the year. Most colleges also offer online payment options. Money can be transferred directly from your checking account to the university account just before it is due. Some universities allow credit card payments. If so, understand what extra fees are added for this convenience.

You will likely be able to add money to your student's personal funds online. Usually this account is tied to the student ID card, and the money loaded onto this card can be used at the bookstore, campus eateries, and other campus locations—a convenient way to help your student pay for on-campus needs.

After all your hard work in applying for financial aid, make sure it is properly credited to your student's account. When you receive the university bill, check to see what financial aid has been credited. Sometimes scholarships and grants lag behind the issuing of bills, so you may need to contact the financial aid office to find out when the remaining funds will be credited. Then follow up appropriately.

TRANSPORTATION

Transportation was one of those issues you pondered as your student applied to colleges. Now whether your student will be just a few miles from home or three thousand miles from home, plan how he or she will get around—both to come home and to take care of business off campus.

If your student will be far from home, decide how many trips home you can afford during that first term. If you book air travel early or use frequent flyer miles, you can save money on airfare. Also plan transportation to and from the airport.

For local transportation off campus, investigate bus lines, trains, and shuttles. Will the student use Uber, or rely on rides from other students with cars? Would a bicycle be helpful on campus and in the surrounding community? Browse maps of the area and find the locations of points of interest for your student, or for the rest of your family to explore during visits to the college town. If your student will have a car on campus, investigate parking permits and emergency road service arrangements.

SPIRITUAL LIFE

During the changeable and often stressful college years, a growing faith will be a valuable asset. If you have scoped out local churches, your student will have an idea of which churches to try. Even better, students in campus fellowships can get together to attend church as a group.

In addition to attending weekend worship services, your student may benefit from faith-based organizations on campus. InterVarsity Christian Fellowship and Cru (formerly Campus Crusade for Christ) are two major campus-based Christian organizations helping college students find Christian fellowship and serve their local communities. Bible studies, prayer meetings, socials, retreats, and service projects are some of the activities these groups offer. Becoming involved in these groups can be an excellent way to make friends and receive spiritual support. Keeping ties with the home church through online sermons and attending church during school breaks is also a vital way of staying connected spiritually.

SUMMER DYNAMICS

As the "last summer of childhood" proceeds, you may notice some changing family dynamics. Parents' and student's emotions will be heightened and may clash periodically. Your student may be asking for increased independence, and you may be hesitant to grant it, while realizing that your student will be exercising tremendous independence in just a few short weeks. Small conflicts may mar the serene summer you had anticipated. At the same time, each of you (parents and student) may be processing the emotions of the coming separation in different ways. One parent may be excited about the new adventure and ready to release the baby bird out of the nest. The other parent may be nostalgic about the years of homeschooling and become teary-eyed at the slightest provocation. The student, while perhaps experiencing a mix of all these emotions, may display them by making more independent decisions. He or she may also spend a great deal of time with friends, when parents had hoped to have lots of "together" time.

Understanding this vast array of emotions is half the battle. If conflicts erupt, exercise extra doses of patience and understanding. Try to plan some family time, such as a vacation, day trips, outings, or get-togethers with friends so that this summer will hold plenty of happy memories.

ORIENTATION

Whether offered during the summer or just before the start of classes, orientation is a prime opportunity for your student to get a feel for the campus. Information sessions, intriguing speakers, academic advising sessions, residence hall events, introductions to campus services, and recreational activities all combine to help your student feel at home. Many colleges offer a parent orientation during the first day or two of student orientation. These sessions can help you learn what to expect and how to help your student have a successful transition to college. In addition, a parents' weekend may be scheduled later in the fall. Or, if you don't want to pay for a pricey parent orientation, organize your own personalized orientation by making a list of all the questions you need to have answered (financial aid, banking, health, campus ministry, etc.) and visit campus offices until they are all answered.

MOVE-IN DAY

The summer before college contains the whole gamut of emotions, but move-in day goes one step further, revisiting all these emotions and packing them into a twenty-four hour period. Expect to be extremely busy in the days leading up to move-in day, as you make a few more purchases, gather last-minute items, pack up the huge load of essentials, dole out more advice, and pull yourself together as the goodbyes approach. The prevailing theme of the day will be excitement as you arrive at the residence hall, find the room, meet the roommate, and start on yet another long list of tasks. But as you might imagine, other emotions will soon surface for all of you. You may experience fatigue and burnout after a day of toting and organizing in hot summer temperatures; you may grow dizzy and disoriented with all the new experiences you are trying to assimilate. Most notably, you as parents will feel sadness at this "goodbye" to your student. For the parent, an era is ending. For the student, a season of adventure is beginning.

Survive move-in day with an organized list, a sense of humor, and the confidence that your years together have given your student independence and wisdom to launch into this next phase of life.

CRISES

We never want to think about our students going through crises, but they do crop up from time to time. Crises can range from small (homesickness) to moderate (academic difficulties) to more serious (physical or mental health problems).

The Freshman Dean's office can provide advice, reassurance, and direction to sources of assistance as you help your student. For homesickness, loneliness, and grade shock, the office can give you perspective on this particular crisis and can suggest how best to deal with it. You can also get a sense of whether you should tackle the problem actively or whether your student should work it out on his or her own.

In the case of significant crises such as health problems, disciplinary issues, serious academic problems, or emotional instability, stay in close touch with your student. Work with the college resources as well as with your own resources from church or community. Most colleges have counseling services available for students experiencing depression, anxiety, or major emotional crises. Often these services are available at no additional charge, at least for the first few visits. Friends from home can also be a tremendous help to your student who is going through difficulties. Phone calls, notes, emails, care packages, visits, and prayer can go a long way toward helping your student feel loved and connected.

LETTING GO

After eighteen years of parenting, you will understandably have some difficulty in "letting go" of your teenager. The separation will likely be much easier for the student, who has exciting surroundings and experiences to explore. Still, both parent and student should expect to go through an adjustment.

Homeschooling parents, in particular, need to learn how to be there for the student without "hovering." During those first weeks of college, resist the urge to call or text too frequently or to insist upon many visits home or parental visits to the campus if it is local. The early weeks and months of college are a time when the student is learning how to navigate a whole new system. Simultaneously, the parents and the remaining siblings are adjusting to life and routines at home without the college student. This transition will work best if the student is given some time and space. Let the student take the lead in choosing the ideal amount of contact, as well as the best times of the day or week for long chats.

If you can't resist connecting with your student, assemble a care package of goodies, gift cards for favorite coffee shops or restaurants, a funny card, or other items your student may enjoy. Sharing the contents of the package with residence hall neighbors can help your student meet people and make friends.

... AND STARTING OVER

"Reverse homesickness," the phenomenon in which Mom and Dad miss the student so much that they feel a void in their lives, is to be expected, at least temporarily. After pouring your heart into homeschooling and living with your student 24/7 for eighteen years, you will naturally feel that a part of you is missing. The best way to deal with the void is to *embrace* this next season in your lives. With one less student to homeschool, your time is freed up somewhat, and you may seek out a new ministry, a hobby, or even a job if your homeschooling duties are finished or drastically reduced. Just as you encouraged your student to pursue a passion during high school, you may now have passions you would like to pursue with renewed energy. Focus on your other children's needs, take a class, start a major home project, plan next spring's garden, teach or advise other homeschoolers—or just relax for a few extra hours each day.

While you are done teaching this particular student, your role as trusted advisor, sounding board, and unchanging source of love and encouragement is gathering momentum. Be assured that you *will* adjust to this changing role, just as your student will adjust to college. Best of all, the love, prayers, and wisdom you poured into your season of homeschooling, in spite of the mistakes you made along the way, have not been in vain. Soon you will find your student asking your advice, sharing triumphs and challenges, and perhaps even educating his or her friends about the adventurous homeschooling journey!

Chapter 31

Concluding Thoughts:

Encouragement for the Journey

Looking back on a total of sixteen years of homeschooling, plus ten additional years of teaching and helping other homeschoolers, I know as well as anyone that there are times when you just want to give up. You ask yourself, "Why am I doing this?" You convince yourself that the whole venture was a mistake. You shed tears of frustration or fatigue. You lose your temper at your children and are sure that you would be a better parent if you were not homeschooling. You wonder why you ever thought you could tackle this mammoth task all the way through high school.

And then the next day, the scene suddenly changes. Your growing-like-a-weed teenage son gives you a big hug, for no particular reason. Your daughter comes up to you and spontaneously thanks you for homeschooling her. Your student finally "gets" the complex math concept that has frustrated both of you for a week. You all enjoy a Friday morning of sleeping an extra hour, grateful that you don't have to rush out of the house on this particular morning. A neighbor comments that she enjoys conversing with your children because they have such interesting ideas and are not embarrassed to be caught talking to an older person. You are overcome with affection and love for your children, realizing that your own offspring happen to be some of your favorite companions. You shed tears—this time not from frustration, but from a wistful sadness that this stressful but wonderful season of life will be drawing to a close in just a couple of years. You find yourself almost wishing for the toddler years again, diapers and all. *Almost.*

What is the difference between the two days? Why do we feel as though we're doing an abominable job of homeschooling one day, and an awesome job the next? The answer is that both days are normal, not only in a homeschooling parent's day, but also in any parent's day. However, in homeschooling, the feelings are intensified because we are around our students constantly and because so much responsibility rests on our shoulders. We worry that one little mistake will permanently derail our students' educational success.

What is a parent to do on those dark days when homeschooling seems like a mistake and when teaching a high schooler is the most fearsome task on earth? Here are a few principles to keep in mind.

REMEMBER YOUR REASONS FOR HOMESCHOOLING

When the going gets tough, remind yourself *why* you chose to homeschool in the first place, whether that decision took place twelve years ago or two months ago. Those reasons are still valid. That decision, undoubtedly made by looking at all options and by trusting God to fill in the gaps, still stands until God shows you a different path for a different season. If you need a refresher, here are some of the reasons that may have meant a great deal to you when you began homeschooling.

Communicating Faith and Values

When you began homeschooling, you may have sought to impart significant values that your students might never have heard about in a public school or might never have internalized in a private school, even if it was a Christian school. You wanted them to love God, to know and do what is right, and to stand up for the truth. Even on the darkest days of homeschooling, the light of your faith can still shine if you remember to stop and hug your children and remind them that God loves them, you love them, and you are all seeking God's path together.

Developing Family Closeness

Time together is priceless. Many people never know the privilege of parents and children, brothers and sisters, and perhaps even grandparents and grandchildren bonding with one other. Even when you feel that you may be seeing a bit too much of one other, homeschooling is still a boost to your family relationships.

Teaching According to Learning Styles

At the outset of homeschooling, you acknowledged that no two children learn in the same way. Observing your own student, you realized that he or she might need extra time to grasp math concepts, more hands-on activities to reinforce science lessons, or deliberate auditory input to understand history concepts. You discovered whether your child was a quick but superficial learner or a slow but deep learner. You found out whether you had a thinker, a feeler, a dreamer, a doer, a reader, a writer, a speaker, or a listener. From there, you were determined to help your student learn by customizing the instruction to his or her personal style.

Sometimes roadblocks appear because we gradually slip away from our student's optimum learning style and start teaching according to our *own* style—or according to what seems quickest and easiest at the moment. We revert to "read the textbook and answer twenty questions" instead of using a more interactive, customized approach. Acknowledging your student's optimum learning style and inserting a few activities aimed at that dominant style will minimize frustration for both of you.

On Day One of homeschooling, you were excited to offer your student a smorgasbord of educational options and to choose the most intriguing subjects, the most fascinating topics of study, and the most useful learning activities, outings, books, and online materials. Did some of these ideas get lost in the shuffle? If you and your student are caught in a rut, try to inject some variety into your courses again. You don't have to concoct anything elaborate, but perhaps you could brainstorm to come up with activities that would be simple and fun, but still educational.

Minimizing Peer Pressure

For many parents, the avoidance of negative peer pressure is a major reason for teaching children at home. Parents do not relish the thought of a preteen or teen feeling compelled to be a carbon copy of the peer group in order to fit in. Whether the critical issues are clothing, obscene language, media choices, drinking, drugs, or the boy/girl scene, parents are understandably concerned. They want their students to be strong enough to resist peer pressure and smart enough to realize that they can be themselves. If you are in the homeschooling doldrums, stop to consider whether your students are peer-dependent or whether they are on their way to becoming independent thinkers with strong values. Be thankful for the freedom from the demands of a large, active daily peer group. Even if your students are displaying some peer dependency, realize that these tendencies would only be magnified in a school setting.

Enjoying a Flexible Schedule

One of the perks of homeschooling is the freedom to be flexible about the daily schedule. You don't need to be up early every day to get to school, and your flexibility may allow your high schoolers to have a part-time job during the day, to take a family trip (educational or not) for a few days, or to do schoolwork early in the day or late at night. Though the schedule is much busier and more unpredictable now with a high schooler, it is still under your guidance and control, rather than being dictated by school and sports schedules. With traditional schooling, you might not see your student much at all.

COUNT YOUR BLESSINGS

On those tremendously challenging days of homeschooling, focus on the positive and strategize about the negative. If you are having some struggles with your teen, stop and think of five or ten things you *do* appreciate about your student and your relationship. Pray about the situation. Then brainstorm about what to do about the current problem. Seek advice and wisdom, consult Scripture, and from God's wisdom, together with your storehouse of knowledge about your student's personality, come up with ideas to approach the problem in a fresh way. The key, again, is to count your blessings and realize that the situation could be much worse.

Similarly, continue to be thankful for the privilege of homeschooling. Homeschooling in the twenty-first century is a far cry from homeschooling in the 1980s and 1990s, when curriculum was less plentiful, support groups were few, and college acceptance was more difficult. While not exactly mainstream, homeschooling is now usually listed as an educational choice on college application forms. The fact that it is even acknowledged is worth celebrating. Be thankful that homeschooling is legal in all fifty states and that, by and large, homeschoolers are encountering fewer challenges from school districts.

SAVOR THE TEEN YEARS

To many parents, savoring the teen years seems like a contradiction. "Don't you mean, 'savor the years when your children are little'?" they ask. The teen years have gained a reputation for being something to survive, not to savor. But for a family that has invested fourteen to eighteen years together, the teen years are definitely worth cherishing. Granted, the hormonal fluctuations often play with your teen's mind and behavior. And the continuing growth toward independence produces a tugging at rules and restrictions that were once adequate. Nevertheless, this season can produce some of the happiest and deepest memories your family will ever create.

By now, your teens have formed their personalities, sense of humor, likes, dislikes, strengths, and weaknesses. Some admirable character traits, albeit not fully developed, are emerging. In a new reversal of roles, your teens can come to *your* rescue from time to time, instead of you always solving their problems. They can serve as delightful companions and savvy sounding boards for your own ideas, just as you serve as a sounding board for theirs.

Whatever you do, don't rush your students to grow up. Of course, you want to see more mature behavior as the years unfold, but be sure that it's not at the expense of letting them enjoy their last bit of childhood and letting *you* savor these last years of teenage fun and silliness intermingled with philosophical discussions about life, love, God, the future, and everything in between.

As you know, you can't just *schedule* your quality time with your teenagers or select times that are convenient for you. Chances are, your students will have something going on when you have an available time slot, and vice versa. One job of a parent of teens is to be ready to "drop everything" for those conversation opportunities. Usually this will occur late at night, just as you stop by their rooms to tell them it's time to turn out the lights and go to bed. Conversations will start, and before you know it, an hour will have passed. But these can be some of the sweetest times of parenting you will ever know. It is here you will glimpse some of the fruits of your many years of effort.

By the same token, try to arrange time blocks in your schedule to be available for your students' needs and opportunities. This is not an inconvenience; it is an investment in the life of your teens as well as a concrete way of saying "I love you and care about you." While you can't be at every activity—after all, you have other children, a spouse, and perhaps a job or volunteer work—try not to fill up the whole week with busy work and times away from your kids. Remember that school time doesn't necessarily count as "together time." Arrange some time each week when you will be available for more than just ten minutes in the car as you drop your teens at their next destination. Attend their special events, whether these be sporting events, debate tournaments, or musical performances, and be their cheering squad, especially on days when they may feel that no one appreciates them.

The teen years are a brief season of your parenting and an even shorter season of your whole life. Pouring your heart into your kids for these last few years at home is by no means a foolish decision. Of course, you don't want to "helicopter parent" them or smother them with excessive control and constant advice. Strike a wise balance between your guidance and their emerging independence. They can learn to do more on their own, make their own decisions, and take their own consequences while benefiting from your input and advice. In summary, picture the end of the journey, but savor the current moment!

BATHE YOUR STUDENTS IN PRAYER

If faith plays a central role in your family, the most valuable gift that you can give your teens is to uphold them in prayer for the vital aspects of their lives. Enlist prayer support during these teen years for any difficulties *you* are going through with schooling or with the relationship with your teens. Find some prayer warriors who will be happy to uphold you and your family.

Never underestimate the power of prayer in your students' lives. Especially as they go out into the world and you begin to feel less "in control" as a parent, realize that your most effective way of helping them still works.

DON'T GIVE UP TOO EASILY

If you are tempted to drop the whole idea of homeschooling a high schooler, whether from everyday frustration or as a result of more serious problems, set aside time for some serious thinking before you make any final decisions. Talk to other parents who have been on the brink of giving up homeschooling and who have navigated back to a smoother path. Find out what worked and what didn't work. Take the time to lay out other educational options both within and without homeschooling, and evaluate them as objectively as possible. Try to figure out just where the problems arise and how you might approach the main source of trouble without overhauling your whole schooling plan. Be creative within the homeschooling options, trying outside classes, interesting summer experiences, and other ways of helping your student see himself or herself in a different light. Sometimes getting out of the well-ingrained patterns and habits in the home can have a positive effect on the student's attitude and can bring a fresh perspective to homeschooling.

Having said all this, one vital point remains. *Do not consider yourself a failure if you ultimately decide that your student needs to be in a traditional school, whether public or private.* If, after thinking through the decision, praying, seeking advice, and discussing the issues thoroughly as a couple and as a family, you believe that the best place for your student is in a traditional school, be at peace with your decision. Your greatest priority is to discover where your student needs to be right now for his or her schooling. Rest assured that the foundation of independent learning that you have already provided will be invaluable in the next phase of education. Regardless of whether this education takes place at home or in a traditional school, continue to come alongside your student to help, encourage, and motivate him or her to do the best job possible.

PUT FIRST THINGS FIRST

As a final note of encouragement, remember what your true objectives are for your student. After reading this book, which focuses on helping homeschooled students be more competitive when applying to college, please don't come away from these chapters thinking that the *only* worthwhile goal is that your student is accepted into an elite college—or any college, for that matter. Even though college is important, it is not necessarily the right place for every student. Furthermore, highly competitive colleges are definitely not for all students. Far more important is your student's growth into a young man or woman of godliness, responsibility, and character. Hopefully, along with this growth will come a desire for academic challenge and a motivation to "stretch" and develop a full repertoire of skills, abilities, and gifts. This book is about making the most of those existing abilities so that college admissions committees will understand and appreciate your student's strengths. But the more critical task is for the parent and the student together to build a life of character that will endure beyond the years of college and will accompany your young adult into the realities of life. The student who can maintain a strong faith, use skills and talents wisely, and live with integrity, kindness, and love toward others is truly a success.

May God bless you as you make your homeschooling decisions and as you guide your students through the high school years and into the exciting times that lie ahead.

Thank you for persevering through this lengthy book! I would truly appreciate it if you would take a moment to leave an honest review at Amazon.com. These reviews help tremendously in communicating the book's content and value to other families on the homeschooling path. You may also drop me a note at my website, https://HomeschoolRoadMap.com. Thank you very much, and enjoy the journey!

Appendix

USEFUL WEBSITES AND RECOMMENDED RESOURCES

Please note that we have not personally used all the resources listed here or in the text of the book, so a mention of a resource does not constitute an endorsement or a guarantee that it will work for you. Always do your own investigation of resources to find those that are most suitable for your family.

> ***Visit our website for articles, tips, and resources for homeschooling your college bound student.***
> ***https://HomeschoolRoadMap.com***

GENERAL HOMESCHOOLING RESOURCES

Home School Legal Defense Association (HSLDA)   http://hslda.org
Legal assistance, state by state laws and information, and a variety of valuable tips. HSLDA also serves as a helpful clearinghouse for other homeschool sites. Topics provided on the HSLDA site include college admissions, transcripts, curriculum choice, extracurriculars, distance learning, sports, military, internships, financial aid, parent/teen relationships, and more.

National Home Education Research Institute http://nheri.org
Brian D. Ray, Ph.D., President. This organization produces high-quality research on home-based education, educates the public concerning findings of all research on home education, and serves as a clearinghouse to distribute this research to the public, homeschoolers, researchers, the media, and policy makers.

HELPFUL RESOURCES FOR HOMESCHOOLING A HIGH SCHOOLER

The High School Handbook: Junior and Senior High School at Home by Mary Schofield
Christian Home Educators Press, 7th edition, 2013. Available through CHEA of California, (800)564-CHEA. http://cheaofca.org
Indispensable, down-to-earth guide on setting up a high school course of study for a homeschooling student. Covers credits, course descriptions and documentation, transcript creation, and many more practical topics.

The Well-Trained Mind: A Guide to Classical Education at Home by Susan Wise Bauer and Jessie Wise, W.W. Norton & Co., 4th edition, 2016.
A "road map" of classical education for the homeschooler.

The Well-Educated Mind: A Guide to the Classical Education You Never Had by Susan Wise Bauer, W.W. Norton & Co., updated and expanded edition, 2015.
A guide to classical education and to the art of reading.

Aiming Higher Consultants (Jeannette Webb) https://www.aiminghigherconsultants.com/
An educational consulting firm that seeks to bring out the unique qualities of students to make the most of the high school planning and college application processes in order to "tell their story" to college admissions staff.

PROGRAMS FOR GIFTED AND TALENTED STUDENTS

Duke Talent Identification Program	https://tip.duke.edu/
Northwestern University Center for Talent Development	https://www.ctd.northwestern.edu/
Johns Hopkins University Center for Talented Youth	https://cty.jhu.edu/
Center for Bright Kids Western Academic Talent Search	https://www.centerforbrightkids.org/
Davidson Institute for Talent Development	https://www.davidsongifted.org/
Jack Kent Cooke Foundation Young Scholars Program	https://www.jkcf.org/

SOURCES FOR SCIENCE EQUIPMENT TO USE AT HOME

Everything you need for biology, chemistry, physics, and other branches of lab science – plus lots of fun science gadgets!

Home Science Tools	http://homesciencetools.com
Apologia Educational Ministries	https://www.apologia.com/
Nature's Workshop Plus	http://workshopplus.com
Steve Spangler Science	http://stevespanglerscience.com

WORLDVIEW EDUCATION

A number of books, authors, and curricula are helpful in this area of instruction:

The works of Francis Schaeffer. Writings by Francis Schaeffer lay out the biblical worldview with its foundation in the personal God who has spoken to man in history and who gives a basis for human dignity, morals, thinking, and creativity.

Total Truth: Liberating Christianity from Its Cultural Captivity **by Nancy Pearcey.** Written by a former agnostic who studied under Francis Schaeffer, *Total Truth* tackles the topic of the sacred/secular split in our society and makes the case that Christianity is not just *religious* truth but *total* truth.

Finding Faith **and other works by Brian McClaren.** This book cuts to the most basic issues of faith—often with startling simplicity and severity. From the first questions of "faith in whom or what?" it walks the reader, rationally but never forcefully, through the thought process leading to why, of all belief systems, Christianity makes so much sense.

The works of C.S. Lewis, including *Mere Christianity*. Though some are eight decades old, Lewis' works remain classics of thought and reason, showing that Christianity is not simply a leap of faith, but rather, a message from a loving and reasonable God. Lewis, himself a former atheist, communicates the truths of Christianity so well that other notable believers, including Charles Colson and Francis Collins, converted to Christianity after reading *Mere Christianity*.

The Case for Christ **and other writings by Lee Strobel.** As an atheist, a Yale Law School graduate, and a top investigative reporter for the *Chicago Tribune*, Lee Strobel put his legal skills to work to investigate the evidence for Jesus Christ, coming to the conclusion that Christ's claims were valid and His message was true. Strobel uses his investigative skills to clearly explain Christian truths in his books, *The Case for Christ, The Case for Faith,* and *The Case for a Creator,* among many others.

Works by Josh McDowell. Formerly a skeptic about Christianity, Josh took a hard look at the claims of Jesus Christ during his college years and was shocked to find facts, not fiction. Josh has shared these principles with young and old alike in his many apologetics books, including *More Than a Carpenter, Evidence That Demands a Verdict,* and several other resources.

World Views of the Western World **by David Quine (Cornerstone Curriculum).** This course, a three-year program based upon the thoughts and ideas of Francis Schaeffer, works well in a co-op or class. The curriculum covers literature, composition, Western civilization, world history, humanities, U.S. history, art and music appreciation, political science, economics, U.S. government, philosophy, and theology. Through extensive reading, students emerge with a strong grasp on the origins, development, and influence of Western thinking. To prepare your student for this course, you may use a one-year program called *Starting Points: Where Our Thinking Begins.* http://cornerstonecurriculum.com

Understanding the Times **by David Noebel (Summit Ministries).** Another commonly used and well-respected program, this course helps students to clearly understand the principles of the Christian worldview and then to compare this view with humanistic worldviews. For each of these worldviews, the course analyzes aspects of philosophy, theology, economics, law, psychology, ethics, sociology, politics, history, and biology.

http://summit.org

ACKNOWLEDGMENTS

To my family, thank you for your support and patience during the years when this book originally took shape, as well as during the surprisingly grueling process of producing the second edition. I could never have completed this project without your love and support. Each of you in your own way has provided sensible advice, helpful perspectives, and solid contributions in the writing process as well as in designing the cover, helping with technical issues, and constructing the website.

To my husband, Ron, thank you for your faithful encouragement, for your business ideas and practical advice, and most of all, for your inspiration! Because of you, I resisted the temptation to give up on the project.

To Julie, thank you for being a partner in the writing of "The Book" from the first day the idea ever occurred to us. Thank you for the chapters you drafted early on, for the outlines you created, for your constant stream of suggestions, and for your sensible perspective on what needs to be communicated to homeschooled students and their families.

I am truly grateful to the many families in the homeschooling community who gave of their time, energy, and goodwill to inspire the project, make suggestions, proofread chapters, and encourage me to hurry up and finish so they could read the book! In particular, thank you to Angela Abel, Crissi Allen, Kathy Young, Michelle Burke, and Billie Ngotiaoco for your advice, suggestions, and promotion of the book to homeschooling families. And I greatly appreciate Liz Shimada, Jody Goff, Wendy Huang, Sarah Kuchipudi, Laura Lee, and Esther Beal for proofreading many of the chapters in the second edition.

Most of all, I thank God for giving me the energy, ideas, and perseverance to finish this task.

Index

DENISE BOIKO and her husband, Ron, homeschooled both of their children from kindergarten through high school. With acceptances to multiple colleges, their daughter earned a B.S. and an M.S. in biology at Stanford University before going on to medical school, and their son chose the University of Southern California, earning a B.S. in engineering. Since then, Denise has successfully walked more than 150 homeschooled and traditionally schooled students through the college admissions process, with acceptances to universities such as MIT, Columbia, Cornell, University of Pennsylvania, UCLA, UC Berkeley, Duke, and Rice. As a speaker at homeschool workshops, and in one-on-one sessions, Denise loves to partner with homeschooling parents and lend a hand as they construct customized curricula, create credible transcripts, and craft compelling counselor letters.

Homeschooled & Headed for College was written to help other homeschoolers benefit from the many years of research and personal experience that facilitated the Boiko students' admission to selective universities. This second edition is an updated and expanded version of the original.

With a degree in biology and a lifelong passion for writing, Denise has taught high school biology, composition, and literature since 2006 at a local homeschool academy and at other homeschool class sites. Since she seeks to make these subjects come alive, a classroom visitor might witness a mock-up of the Berlin Wall, an Ides of March party to conclude Shakespeare's *Julius Caesar*, or a lively model of the cell's plasma membrane, composed entirely of teenagers.

In her pockets of spare time, Denise enjoys making friends with neighborhood cats (especially black ones), baking lemon bars and peanut butter-oatmeal-chocolate chip cookies for the holidays, watching old *Monk* crime drama episodes, creating colorful quilts, meeting former students for coffee, and reading dozens of books while running on the treadmill or climbing the never-ending stepmill.

Connect with Denise!
Website: https://HomeschoolRoadMap.com
Email: contact@homeschoolroadmap.com to receive a free tip sheet,
"Top Twenty Tips for Homeschooling the College Bound Student"
Facebook: @HomeschooledAndHeadedForCollege

Please spread the word about Homeschooled & Headed for College.
Reviews on Amazon.com are sincerely appreciated
and will help other homeschoolers launch their individual journeys!

Made in the USA
San Bernardino, CA
21 August 2019